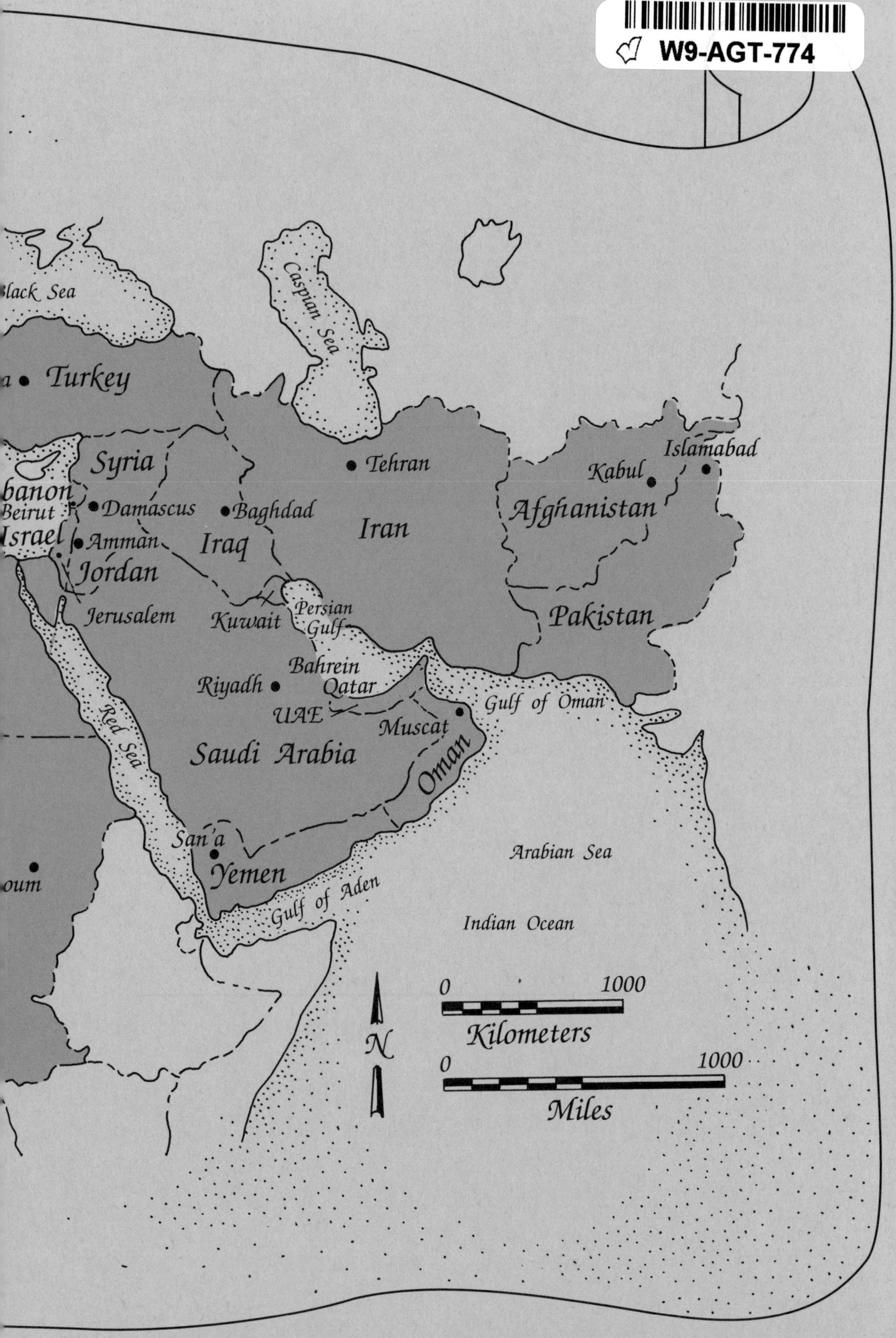
lack Sea
Caspian Sea
a
Turkey
Syria
Tehran
Islamabad
Kabul
banon
Beirut
Damascus
Baghdad
Afghanistan
Iran
Israel
Amman
Iraq
Jordan
Jerusalem
Kuwait
Persian Gulf
Pakistan
Bahrein
Riyadh
Qatar
Gulf of Oman
UAE
Muscat
Red Sea
Saudi Arabia
Oman
San'a
Arabian Sea
Yemen
oum
Gulf of Aden
Indian Ocean
0
1000
Kilometers
N
0
1000
Miles

The Middle East: A Political Dictionary

The Middle East: A Political Dictionary

Lawrence Ziring
Western Michigan University

ABC-CLIO
Santa Barbara, California
Denver, Colorado
Oxford, England

Library of Congress Cataloging-in-Publication Data

Ziring, Lawrence, 1928–
The Middle East : a political dictionary / Lawrence Ziring.
p. cm. — (Clio dictionaries in political science)
Includes index.
1. Middle East—Politics and government—Dictionaries. 2. Middle East—Dictionaries. I. Title. II. Series.
DS61.Z58 1992 956'.003—dc20 92-15379

ISBN 0-87436-612-7 (alk. paper)
ISBN 0-87436-697-6 (pbk: alk. paper)

99 98 97 96 95 94 93 92 10 9 8 7 6 5 4 3 2 1 (hc)
99 98 97 96 95 94 93 92 10 9 8 7 6 5 4 3 2 1 (pbk)

ABC-CLIO, Inc.
130 Cremona Drive, P.O. Box 1911
Santa Barbara, California 93116-1911

This book is printed on acid-free paper ♾.
Manufactured in the United States of America

This book is dedicated to
Mohammad Vardag Khan,
a much remembered teacher,
and to Raye,
who knew him,
and to Sarah and Leigh,
who can find him
in these pages

Contents

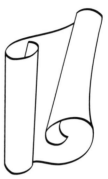

Preface

Since the end of World War II no region of the world has been the subject of more attention and debate, or experienced more conflict, than the Middle East. Nowhere else have different civilizations interacted more dramatically and more persistently. No other global zone is as geopolitically and strategically significant to the major power contenders of the late twentieth century. And no other area is so mired in contradictory and seemingly intractable positions.

The Middle East is a vast area, defined in this volume as all the countries from Morocco on the Atlantic Ocean to Pakistan on the borders of India; from Turkey in the north to the Sudan in the south. Currently, 22 sovereign independent states constitute the region. Almost at its center is the state of Israel, the only non-Muslim entity in this array. Some observers contend that world interest in the Middle East is exaggerated by the Arab-Israeli conflict, and that interest would subside if that conflict were resolved. This volume gives special consideration to the Arab-Israeli conflict, but it also describes and analyzes political dimensions often obscured by that highly publicized controversy.

Like its predecessor, *The Middle East Political Dictionary,* this book identifies the terms, events, characteristics, movements, and institutions that describe the Middle East in the last half of the twentieth century. This is not a small undertaking. I am aware that as an American I am often portraying matters that I can study and attempt to understand, but which I can never truly experience. It is a humbling exercise. Nor can I claim expertise in every facet of Middle East politics. If I am bold in presenting this work, it is because I have painstakingly combed through mountains of data and have tried to inform the uninitiated, or remind the scholar, about events and situations that are of importance to them.

I am mindful that I am working with controversial material. I have endeavored to avoid bias, embellishment, and distortion. If in my efforts at interpretation I sometimes appear one-sided, I hope the reader will remember that informed opinion and learned discourse are what we mean by "truth." If I have erred, it is because of limitations, not intent.

This dictionary is organized so that entries and supplementary information can be located in either of two ways. First, items are arranged alphabetically within chapters. Terms relating to regional arrangements, such as CENTO and the Carter Doctrine, for example, can be found in the chapter titled "Diplomacy." If in doubt as to which chapter to consult for a particular term, or when searching for information on a topic that does not have its own entry, consult the index.

The reader can also use the extensive cross references to explore a topic more fully. The cross references may lead the reader to entries located elsewhere in the same chapter, or to subjects treated in other chapters. Entry numbers have been included in all cross references for the convenience of the reader.

The format of this book offers the reader a variety of useful applications. These include the book's use as a dictionary and reference guide, a study guide, a supplement to textbooks and monographs, and as a social science aid for use in government, business, and journalism.

An important aspect of this book is the analytical or interpretive section following each entry. Located under the heading *Significance,* this section discusses the meaning of each entry and enables the reader to weigh, measure, and evaluate the term presented. Of course, analysis offered in the *Significance* section cannot represent the last word on the subject; its purpose is to provoke deeper insights.

I wish to express special gratitude to my colleague and friend Dr. Jack C. Plano for his assistance and encouragement in preparing this edition. And I am most thankful to my family, who again remained in the background as I made one more foray into the quagmire of Middle East politics. In the end, I hope the reader will find utility in this volume. If the reader finds a bit more, I will know the assignment was one worth assuming.

The Middle East: A Political Dictionary

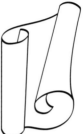

Political Geography and Geopolitics

Aden 1

Aden is a seaport in the Islamic Republic of Yemen. Aden flanks the Bab al-Mendeb and guards the entrance to the Red Sea from the Indian Ocean. Before the merger of North and South Yemen in 1990, Aden was the capital of the People's Democratic Republic of Yemen. Aden is the largest port in the northwestern portion of the Indian Ocean. Occupied by the British, after 1839 Aden became a major naval installation and played a significant role in the Admiralty's dominance of the Indian Ocean. Britain was forced to grant independence to South Yemen in 1967, and thereby denied North Yemen's claim to Aden and the Hadrawmawt, the extended territory along the southwestern end of the Arabian Peninsula. But the struggle to achieve Aden's independence from the British led to the radicalizing of the nationalists there, and the People's Democratic Republic of Yemen assumed a Marxist attitude after the British departed the region. Friendship with the Soviet Union enabled Moscow to utilize Aden as a naval base during the Brezhnev years. A brief civil war in 1986 altered the political picture in South Yemen. It also caused the Soviets to withdraw the bulk of their personnel from Aden, and the port no longer represented an extension of Soviet power. Since the merger of the two Yemens, the Islamic Republic of Yemen has sought a neutral role. ***See also*** CIVIL WAR: SOUTH YEMEN (241)

Significance
Aden is a deep-water port of considerable strategic significance but is no longer accessible to the world's major navies. Yemen's foreign policy, as demonstrated by its opposition to the U.S. action against Iraq's occupation of Kuwait in August 1990, centers on denying non-Arab powers special privileges in the Arabian Peninsula. Yemen's support of Saddam Hussain was consistent with this policy even though the posture seriously undermined its relations with Saudi Arabia.

Amu Darya (Oxus River) 2

The Amu Darya is the river originating in the Pamir Plateau in central Asia. It is approximately 1,550 miles (2,500 kilometers) long and follows a course southwest between Tadjikistan and Afghanistan and then turns northwest between Turkmanistan and Uzbekistan, until it empties into the Aral Sea. The river is only partially navigable and is more important for irrigation than commerce. The Amu Darya has had an important strategic history in the nineteenth and twentieth centuries. The river was established as a line of control between imperial Russian and British interests in the waning decades of the nineteenth century. The Russians swept into central Asia midway through the century, conquering and absorbing the Muslim *khanates* (kingdoms) in the region. The British were concerned that the Russian advance would not end there but would continue until Afghanistan and Iran were brought within the czar's orbit. Sensing a threat to their interests in the Persian Gulf, but especially to their empire in India, the British were determined to check the Russian drive. Such an effort, however, involved establishing Afghanistan as a buffer between the two empires, and the Amu Darya seemed the natural dividing line between the Russian domains and the Afghans. Britain went to war with Afghanistan in 1838–1842 to establish its presence in Afghanistan, and a "Forward Policy" enunciated by Lord Lytton was eventually transformed into holy writ by Lord Curzon (both of them viceroys of India). In addition to troop maneuvers in and near Afghanistan, the British and Russians agreed on the settlement of the border between the czarist state and Afghanistan. Internecine conflict within Afghanistan permitted the Russians to move their central Asian conquests to the Oxus in 1869. The British gave support to Emir Sher Ali, the Afghan king, and the Russians were encouraged to accept the Amu Darya as the northern boundary of Afghanistan in 1873. It was officially affirmed in 1887. The Bolsheviks acknowledged the Amu Darya border in 1920, and the Afghanistan-U.S.S.R. Treaty of 1946 again proclaimed its significance and applied the *Thalweg* (middle channel principle in international law) to the boundary. ***See also*** WARM-WATER PORT POLICY (32); WAKHAN CORRIDOR (31).

Significance

So long as central Asia was divided between numerous rival kingdoms and tribal units, the British displayed little concern for the security of their Indian possession. The elimination of these small sovereignties, by inclusion into the spreading Russian Empire, however, was viewed with considerable apprehension. By 1836 the Russians had almost reached the Amu Darya, and their influence had been established in Iran. Under Russian instigation, a Persian force was dispatched to take Herat, and the local leaders around Kandahar were engaged in a conspiracy, with Persian-Russian assistance, to undermine the Afghan government of Dost Mohammad in Kabul. Russia poised at the Amu Darya was judged by the British to be a direct threat to India. Instead of supporting Dost Mohammad, however, the British also were determined to destroy him. Dost Mohammad was the only Afghan leader capable of welding the heterogeneous Afghan tribes into a unified power strong enough to stem the Russian advance, but the British incorrectly saw Dost Mohammad as serving Russian interests. The result was a costly conflict that prevented Afghanistan from assisting its central Asian brethren in their struggle with the Russians. The British were able to get the Russians to accept the Amu Darya as the northern frontier of Afghanistan, but this did little to guarantee Afghanistan's emergence as a viable political actor in the region. The Amu Darya border lasted through the nineteenth and well into the twentieth century. With the British withdrawal from India in 1947, however, the formidable power that had effected a balance of forces in the region was no longer available. Nor was the United States in a position to fill the vacuum left by the British. The Soviet Union, therefore, quickly gained major influence over the Afghan scene. Between the end of World War II and the 1978 Afghan revolution, which brought a socialist government to power in Kabul, the Soviets worked to establish their preeminence in the country. When the Marxist Kabul regime was confronted by Afghan tribal and Islamic resistance and also suffered from severe internal cleavages and personality conflicts, the Soviets did what their predecessors were constrained from doing. In December 1979 the Russians moved approximately 80,000 troops across the Amu Darya, and they attempted to bring the whole of Afghanistan under their control. The failure of that venture is read in the Soviet withdrawal from Afghanistan in February 1989. With the subsequent dissolution of the U.S.S.R. and the independence of the central Asian republics, the Oxus frontier may prove to be no frontier at all.

Aqaba, Gulf of 3

This important waterway is an arm of the Red Sea that runs along the Sinai to the west and the Saudi Arabian shore to the east. The gulf terminates at a point where Israel and Jordan come together at the southernmost extent of the Negev Desert. The Israeli port of Eilat and the Jordanian port of Aqaba sit across from each other. Eilat is Israel's only outlet to the Red Sea, and considerable maritime traffic, especially oil tankers, use the facilities of the port rather than pass through the Suez Canal to the Mediterranean ports. The port of Aqaba is Jordan's only outlet to the sea. At the entrance of the Gulf of Aqaba (or the Gulf of Eilat) on the southwestern tip of the Sinai is Sharm al-Shaykh, which prior to the 1967 Arab-Israeli War was used by Egypt to block Israeli or Israel-bound vessels from reaching Eilat.

Significance

The Gulf of Aqaba has been a center of conflict in the Middle East. Sharm al-Shaykh commands the entrance to and from the Gulf of Aqaba. The Egyptians fortified this site and attempted to prevent the Israelis from using the Gulf of Aqaba. In the 1956 Arab-Israeli War, Sharm al-Shaykh was occupied by Israeli forces, which then withdrew when a United Nations (UN) peace force was interposed between Egyptian and Israeli forces. The UN force was ordered removed by Gamal Abdul Nasser in 1967. When the UN secretary-general, U Thant, complied with the Egyptian president's demand, the Israelis launched their surprise attack known as the Six-Day War of 1967. The Israeli army again swept through the Sinai and seized Sharm al-Shaykh, as well as the Golan Heights in Syria and the West Bank of the Jordan River. Israel agreed at Camp David in 1978 to withdraw its forces from the Sinai when Egypt signed a peace treaty with Jerusalem. Sharm al-Shaykh and the entire Sinai were returned to Egyptian control on April 25, 1982. By the terms of the treaty Sharm al-Shaykh was demilitarized, and the Gulf of Aqaba opened to innocent passage.

Arc of Crisis (Crescent of Crisis) 4

The Arc of Crisis is a phrase first used by the U.S. government during the presidency of Jimmy Carter and attributed to President Carter's national security advisor, Zbigniew Brzezinski, although it may have been coined by others. The phrase describes a region from the Horn of Africa north through the Sudan and Egypt and east across the Fertile Crescent, the Arabian Peninsula, Iran, Afghanistan, and Pakistan to India. All along the arc can be identified violent conflicts between competing ideological systems and rival states. Moreover, the superpowers were deeply involved here. The United States originally perceived this area as off limits to the Soviet Union. The arc fronts on the Indian Ocean and overlooks the traditional sea lanes essential to the industrial world. Before the 1970s, the Soviet Union was still considered a continental power. Its armed forces were supposedly more concerned with defense of the territorial state and its satellites than with global extension. The construction of a blue-water navy in the 1970s, however, altered this perception. It also displayed Soviet power at many points on the globe. Efforts by the United States to transform the shah's Iran into a formidable military edifice during this period show U.S. preoccupation with Soviet maneuvers in the Indian Ocean. The collapse of the shah's government and the revolution that destroyed the intimate relationship between Washington and Tehran destabilized U.S. policy. The "crisis" that this presented to Washington created "opportunity" for the Soviet Union. The United States, therefore, began to look more seriously toward Egypt, where Anwar el-Sadat was drawing closer to the United States in his effort to neutralize Arab-Israeli antagonism. American difficulties in a variety of Muslim countries, including Pakistan, where the U.S. embassy was attacked and burned by an angry crowd of students, led to the evacuation of U.S. personnel and dependents and the paring down of U.S. representation in several Muslim countries. The Soviet invasion of Afghanistan in December 1979 added to the feeling of crisis. Moreover, the inability to resolve the Palestinian-Israeli dilemma, the spreading of fundamentalist beliefs, and the assassinations of Sadat in October 1981 and Bashir Gemayel in 1982 magnified U.S. concerns. The Iran-Iraq War (1980–1988) dramatized the brittle character of the region. It also tended to confuse the role of the superpowers, who were equally perplexed about the course of their interests. The Iraqi invasion of Kuwait in August 1990 added more complexity to an already hopelessly tangled situation. The decision by the United States to enlist the services of the UN Security Council in repelling Iraqi aggression and Soviet compliance with the UN resolutions placed Washington and Moscow on the same side. The Arc of Crisis remained the most critical area of world concern even after the combined action forced Iraq to abandon its conquest of Kuwait. *See also* WARM-WATER PORT POLICY (32); CARTER DOCTRINE (203); OPERATION DESERT STORM (258).

Significance
The Arc of Crisis involves multidimensional conflicts, some localized, some broad in scope and impact. From the Somali-Ethiopian conflict, to Egyptian-Libyan antagonism, to Arab-Israeli hostility, to the Syrian and Israeli intervention in Lebanon, to the struggle between Iraq and Iran, to the Soviet invasion of Afghanistan, to potential conflict between India and Pakistan, the picture is one of violence and chaos, tragedy, and destruction. That destruction was multiplied several times over by the Persian Gulf War of 1991. The U.S.-led coalition decimated Iraq's war-making capability and destroyed much of the country's infrastructure and industrial capacity. Iraq's weakness seemed to entice the Iranians to seek revenge for Baghdad's earlier aggression. The

Kurds also sought to press their long-held objective of self-determination. Kuwait was liberated but in shambles, and its government faced new pressures for change. So, too, the Gulf War caused new problems for the Saudis and the Gulf shaykhdoms, for the Turks and the Pakistanis, for the Egyptians and the Jordanians. Most confused was the Palestinian question, which was greatly complicated by the PLO's support for Iraq during the war. Although Israel indicated some willingness to pursue a dialogue with the Arab states on the one side and non-PLO Palestinians on the other, there was no indication Jerusalem was prepared to yield land for peace with its Arab neighbors. Even with Syria "willing" to negotiate with Israel, the countries in the Arc of Crisis seemed programmed to intensify their conflicts. The peace conference arranged by the United States and held in Madrid, Spain, in late October 1991 was aimed at avoiding still another bloody Middle East encounter.

Aswan High Nile Dam 5

The Aswan High Nile Dam represents the largest single engineering project in modern Egypt. It was described in terms of national survival and it symbolized the Nasser administration's revolutionary commitment. Originally the United States was to provide the major assistance in constructing the dam. Difficulties over perceptions of the Israeli and Soviet threats to Egypt and the region, however, caused the United States to withdraw its offer. Therefore, the decision to proceed with the project, which was first taken in 1954, could not be implemented until 1959, when the Soviet Union agreed to finance and build the vast structure. The project was completed approximately 15 years later. It cost well in excess of original estimates (some $2 billion), but it promised to increase agricultural yields and to electrify hundreds of Egyptian villages. In time, however, there was grief as well as achievement. Not as much agricultural land as forecast has been reclaimed. Fewer villages were electrified than had been anticipated. More significant, Lake Nasser (an artificial lake caused by the damming of the Nile) was filling up with rich Nile silt at a rapid rate, preventing the nourishment of agricultural lands farther down the river and destroying the fishing industry. Vegetation in Lake Nasser also grew so rapidly that it could not be dredged effectively, so the irrigation channels clogged, creating stagnant water and a breeding ground for a variety of disease-bearing insects and sea urchins. Bilharzia, a debilitating snail-borne disease, has been a perennial hazard; a majority of Egyptians are believed to be affected. Bilharzia is on the ascendancy, and eradication appears to be hopeless. Despite these negative aspects, the Aswan project has facilitated double and triple croppings and the country's agricultural yields have soared. Unfortunately, there is little to show for this success because Egypt's population continues to grow rapidly and the additional production is quickly siphoned off by the greater number of mouths to feed.

Significance

The Aswan High Nile Dam has done what its advocates predicted. It has increased agricultural production, provided water in time of severe drought, electrified village communities, and managed water during flood stages. The dam is also an ecological headache that could develop into a nightmare. Egypt has commissioned renowned ecologists to investigate long-range prospects. There is hope that something can yet be done to head off a major calamity that could threaten Egypt's food supply and environment. The Soviet Union gained some initial political successes by making it possible for Egypt to construct the dam, but in the long run Soviet gains were ephemeral.

Bab al-Mandeb

6

Bab al-Mandeb means "Gate of Tears" in Arabic. It is the narrow strait between the Arabian Peninsula and the African continent that guards the southern entrance to the Red Sea. The Bab al-Mandeb is approximately 20 miles wide and connects with the Gulf of Aden. The strait has two distinct channels on either side of Perim Island, which stands near the Arabian shore. These narrow passageways create swiftly moving currents, hence the name given to the strait. The Bab al-Mandeb is a vital chokepoint in geopolitical terms and an important international waterway for commercial and maritime traffic. Dominating the strait is the port of Aden in the Republic of Yemen. Across the strait on the African side is Djibouti, an independent city-state, formerly under French colonial rule. Yemen claims total sovereignty over the Bab al-Mandeb but is challenged by Saudi Arabia, an important user of the strait. Indeed, relations between Saudi Arabia and Yemen were strained significantly during the Gulf War of 1991. Yemen appeared to side with Iraq during that conflict. As a consequence, the Saudis ordered Yemenis working and domiciled in the kingdom to leave. Several hundred thousand Yemenis were forced out of Saudi Arabia.

Significance

The Bab al-Mandeb, like the Strait of Hormuz, is a vital, internationally recognized waterway. Petroleum destined for Western Europe from the Persian Gulf uses the Bab al-Mandeb in its northward journey. Israeli use of the port of Eilat is dependent on an open Bab al-Mandeb. The Soviet Union earlier had established relations with Somalia and constructed a naval base at Berbera on the Horn of Africa. When Somalia severed relations with the Soviet Union over Moscow's support for Ethiopia, Berbera was denied to them, and the Kremlin shifted its forces to Aden. The United States, attempting to counteract these Soviet tactics, received permission from Somalia to use the Berbera base. At the same time, the Saudis were engaged in building new port facilities on the Red Sea, and they notified Yemen that the Bab al-Mandeb is a recognized international waterway and that any attempt to block passage through it would be considered an unfriendly act.

Dhofar

7

Dhofar is the westernmost territory of the sultanate of Oman. It also has been the site of protracted insurgency against the ruling Al bu Said dynasty. The Dhofar insurgency is linked with an older, more widespread attack upon the monarchy. From the Treaty of Sib (1920) until 1954, Britain aided the sultan of Muscat, while an Ibadhi imamate held forth in the interior of the country. Relative tranquility prevailed after decades of tribal warfare. This tranquility was disturbed in 1955 when British forces assisted the sultan's mercenary army in occupying Nizwa, the capital of Omani interior and the seat of the imamate. The campaign was aimed at consolidating the power of the sultan, preventing Saudi penetration of the region, and opening the country to oil exploration. Prior to World War II, Muscat and Oman were important to British geopolitical interests. After World War II, the importance of this country as an oil reserve loomed large. Given Britain's control of the Aden protectorate in the southwestern corner of the Arabian Peninsula, London was in good position to assist the "friendly" Al bu Said family. Oman, in the immediate aftermath of World War II, had three divisions: (1) the seven emirates that formed the Trucial states and that became the independent United Arab Emirates in 1971; (2) the southeast coastal section of Oman, the original sultanate of Muscat, facing the Gulf of Oman near the mouth of the Persian Gulf; and (3) the Omani interior, seat of the more tradition-bound Ibadhis and the legitimate home of the imamate. Before the twentieth century, the British supported the separation of the coastal area from the interior, sustained their rivalry, and provided the balance between them. The British, in effect, made their presence in Oman indispensable, especially after their European rivals (French and Portuguese) had vacated the region. Infrastructure, communications, and governmental services were largely nonexistent. The reigning monarch, Said ibn Taymur, headed a patriarchal administration that discouraged modernization schemes. Education was nonexistent. Medical facilities were ignored. Social services were denied to a needy public. The sultan's policy of keeping his subjects destitute raised cries against his leadership, and the British had difficulty in justifying their support of his throne. Moreover, development and change had become a central concern of industrial and Third World nations. The population of Muscat and Oman could not be isolated from these activities, and Arab nationalists and Marxists joined forces with Omani dissidents to strike at the power of the sultan. The fusion of the coastal area with the interior had produced the new sultanate of Muscat in Oman. Moreover, the imams of the interior announced their support for the sultan. Both actions, however, added to the already aggravated situation. The acceptance of Al bu Said rule by the imams also drove many Omanis into the arms of the Marxists, who continued their criticism of the regime and its British prop. The Saudis had attempted to fill the political vacuum in the interior in the immediate aftermath of World War II. In 1949, Saudi Arabia renewed a claim to the Buraimi oasis, which was thought to be rich in oil deposits. The sultan of Muscat and the shaykh of Abu Dhabi also claimed the site. The Ibadhi imam sided with the Saudis against Sultan Taymur. At the urging of U.S. oil interests (the Arabian American Oil Company, or ARAMCO), Riyadh occupied the Buraimi oasis in 1952. In 1954, the imam declared the independence of the Ibadhi state and sought membership in the Arab League. The British came to the defense of the sultan of Muscat by leading a force of Trucial Oman Scouts in a successful campaign that forced the Saudis to retreat. The Saudis suspended their claim to Buraimi with the outbreak of civil war in North Yemen and the emergence of Marxist forces in the peninsula. Thus, when the rebellion broke out again in 1963, instead of the Saudis assisting the insurgents, the task was assumed by Nasserist Arab nationalists and Marxists. The British retreat from Aden in 1967 left Muscat and Oman's western border in Marxist hands. Britain's decision to remove its forces east of Suez the following year exposed the Al bu Said dynasty to the most serious threat to its survival. The rebellion had been reignited in the Dhofar district, and the British were no longer in position to crush it. In 1970, fearful of seeing the sultanate destroyed, Qabus ibn Said, Taymur's son, forced his father from the throne and authorized broad-scale reform. Oil was located in commercial quantities in 1967, and the new sultan intended to use the revenue from oil to pay for long-delayed development projects. Qabus had no intention of restoring the imamate, however, and the name of the country was altered to the Sultanate of Oman. Sultan Qabus showed himself to be a more sensitive ruler, and he received credit as a reformer. Nevertheless, he was an authoritarian figure and the leader of a family with many adversaries. The Omani state has always been fractious and fragmented. Efforts by Qabus to politically integrate Oman's primitive and diverse population could not succeed without coercive tactics. And the more forceful the regime, the more intense the hostility for the ruling family. Although Qabus's royal paternalism is more compassionate than that of his tyrannical father, it is nonetheless rigid. The Dhofar rebellion, therefore, did not terminate with Qabus's assumption of power in Oman. In fact, the insurgency intensified and expanded, given the support and sanctuary provided to the rebels by the Marxist South Yemen government. Unable to attract support from brother Arab states, somewhat abandoned by the British, Qabus turned to the shah of Iran and the once-rival Persians for military assistance. The shah dispatched a large force to Oman, and it was given primary responsibility for eliminating the Dhofari problem. By 1975, Iran's troops had turned the tide of battle. The insurgents were forced to retreat across the border into South Yemen, and the sultan was given a new opportunity to bolster his throne through reform programs. Sultan Qabus also sought the assistance of Pakistan, and Oman was permitted to recruit Baluch for service in the Omani army. The United States also began to display broad interest in strengthening the Omani government. When the shah fell from power in 1979, the Ayatollah Khomeini ordered Iranian troops withdrawn from Oman. The U.S. Navy took up positions near the Persian Gulf, and Washington sought and obtained bases from the Omani government. The protracted war between Iraq and Iran forced the Arabian Peninsula shaykhdoms to reexamine their relations. In January 1987, Oman and Yemen resolved their differences over the Dhofar district and exchanged ambassadors. Oman, alone among the Arab states, also maintained good relations with Egypt following the Egyptian-Israeli Peace Treaty. It was therefore instrumental in gathering the other gulf states—Bahrein, Qatar, and the United Arab Emirates—and assisting them in restoring diplomatic ties with Cairo. Thus, Oman was no longer concerned with the loss of its Iran connection and sought security in its peninsula neighbors, Egypt, and, especially, the United States. During the 1991 Gulf War, Oman and Egypt were the only Muslim countries, apart from Turkey, in which the United States conducted routine business. ***See also*** IBADHIS (87); MUSCAT AND OMAN (19); IMAMATE (37).

Significance

The Dhofar insurgency threatened to destroy the Al bu Said dynasty. The Dhofari rebels claimed to be the vanguard of a revolutionary movement that would sweep aside one of Arabdom's longest-surviving dynasties. Despite feverish attempts by Sultan Qabus to modernize his country, Oman is deficient in trained manpower and is heavily dependent on external technicians and labor. Tribalism remains a dominant feature of society, and sociopolitical fragmentation is difficult to address. The country receives considerable revenue from oil production (accounting for approximately 95 percent of the government's annual budget), but the sultanate has not been able to husband its resources or avoid extravagances. And where the government has not been able to win the affection of the disparate population, it has resorted to repressive tactics, including the execution or long-term imprisonment of opponents to the throne. And while British and U.S. companies are busily engaged in constructing housing, schools, and medical facilities, half of the government's budget is spent on military needs, and the remainder benefits a small fraction of the population. The large majority therefore is untouched by reform or development schemes and is subject to recruitment by opposition bands. Moreover, the regime's historic and continuing dependence on foreign powers, most recently the United States, will not close the gap between the sultanate and its subjects. As in the past, the external power is perceived to be an instrument of the throne and the primary support base for the preservation of the Al bu Said dynasty. In spite of the Oman-Yemen Agreement, the opposition still claimed it represented progressive change and was the only hope of the vast majority of Omani people. The Oman government has revealed a realism not generally identified with the Middle East. The Dhofar settlement and improved relations with Yemen were matched by Oman's insistence, along with the United Arab Emirates, to maintain normal relations with Iran during the Iran-Iraq War in the face of Saudi pressure to sever the relationship.

Durand Line

8

The Durand Line is the conventional name for the boundary between Afghanistan and Pakistan, demarcated by Sir Mortimer Durand, a British officer, in 1893. The border, which divides the tribes residing in the region, was never agreed to by them, and it was a matter of considerable controversy from the moment it was formally established. The tribes living in the area are identified as Pathans or Pashtuns or Pakhtuns. The English word commonly in use is Pathan. However, that word does not describe the numerous tribal groups that comprise the Pathan nation. The Ghilzai, Wazir, Mohmand, Afridi, and others were divided between Afghanistan and British India and, after the dissolution of the latter, between Afghanistan and Pakistan. The Pathans have always insisted on their independence, and their tribal loyalties have proved more solidarist than their ties to either Afghanistan or Pakistan. Moreover, the Afghan government anticipated a modification in the frontier separating Afghanistan from the subcontinent at the time of Britain's withdrawal from the region. The creation of Pakistan was not supported by Afghanistan, given Kabul's impression that the plan was to divide India and thus maintain a British puppet government. Moreover, when Pakistan insisted on maintaining the Durand Line intact, Afghanistan felt cheated. Hostility between Afghanistan and Pakistan erupted almost from the moment that Pakistan gained its independence in 1947. Afghanistan claimed it was protecting the Pathans on both sides of the frontier, and on the Pakistani side it called for the creation of a separate state of Pakhtunistan, a homeland for the Pathans. This support for Pathan nationalism caused considerable diplomatic difficulty and frequent military skirmishing between elements of the two armed forces. The Soviet Union gave its support to Afghanistan in the struggle with Pakistan, but the border remained essentially what it was when Sir Mortimer Durand drew it up in the latter part of the nineteenth century. ***See also*** PAKHTUNISTAN (98).

Significance

The Durand Line was a part of the larger British program of establishing defenses for the Indian colony. The Durand Line, along with the demarcation of other Afghan borders in the nineteenth century, transformed the mountain state into a geopolitical buffer between the Russian and British empires. And the new independent state of Pakistan, which guarded the historical gateway to the subcontinent, inherited problems that could not be resolved. Rivalries between Afghanistan and Pakistan and between Pakistan and India brought India and Afghanistan into common endeavor. Despite befriending Afghanistan, India remained ambivalent on the subject of the Durand Line. The Soviet Union, however, sensing another opportunity to win favor in Kabul, early supported a change in the Durand Line, which it described as an "imperialist plot." Afghanistan and the Soviet Union called for an end to colonial occupation and the creation of a Pathan state. Because of threatening neighbors, Pakistan looked to the United States for assistance in maintaining its territorial integrity. Pakistan and the United States entered into a mutual defense treaty in 1954; it was reaffirmed in 1959. Pakistan also joined the Southeast Asia Treaty Organization (SEATO) and the Central Treaty Organization (CENTO). Nevertheless, strains in U.S.-Pakistani relations left Pakistan exposed to its adversaries. The loss of East Pakistan in the internationalized civil war of 1971 appeared to embolden the Afghans. In 1973, Mohammad Daud deposed his cousin, King Zahir Shah, and seized control of the Afghan government. Daud immediately called for the reopening of the Pakhtunistan question and pledged aid to Pathan nationalists. Daud's death in another coup in 1978 signalled one more turn in Afghan-Pakistani relations. The 1978 affair brought Marxists into power in Kabul, and their inability to maintain a stable government precipitated Soviet intervention in force in December 1979. After more than nine years of bloody conflict, the Soviets withdrew their troops from Afghanistan in February 1989. Pakistan's "frontline state" role appeared to diminish, but the guerrilla war against the Soviet-installed Kabul government continued. Thus Pakistan continued to house more than 3 million Afghan refugees and the Durand Line remained a demarcation of tension between the two Muslim states. An agreement entered into by the U.S. and the U.S.S.R. in the summer of 1991 announced their decision to cease sending arms to their respective sides in the Afghan conflict. All arms shipments were halted as of January 1, 1992, and the warring Afghans were encouraged to find a solution that would bring peace to the region.

Eastern Question 9

From the close of the seventeenth century to the first two decades of the twentieth century, the Ottoman Empire was forced to yield territory to the Europeans, particularly to the Hapsburgs of Austria-Hungary and Imperial Russia. During this period of decline, the Ottoman court attempted to adopt European customs and techniques of government, commercial activity, and social behavior to arrest the slide to oblivion. The European powers, however, fought over control of the strategic Turkish waterway linking the Black Sea with the Mediterranean Sea. Russia was especially interested in dominating the Turkish straits, and Great Britain was just as determined to prevent the Russians from achieving their goal. This contest between Russia and Britain for influence over the Ottoman Empire was known as the Eastern Question. The British announced a policy in 1791 that was sustained up to World War I. It specified that Britain would strengthen Ottoman resolve in the face of Russian pressure. In point of fact, the British policy was aimed at propping up a dying Ottoman Empire; if not for this British intervention, the Ottoman Empire would have succumbed before World War I. ***See also*** TURKISH STRAITS (30); TANZIMAT (107).

Significance

The Eastern Question was significant historically because it placed western European power behind an Islamic kingdom and against another Christian monarchy. The weakness of the Ottoman administration enabled Napoleon to move against Egypt (with a view toward opening a route to India). France assisted the Ottoman governor Mohammad Ali in the establishment of an independent Egyptian government, free from Ottoman control. Mohammad Ali, not content with ruling Egypt, launched an attack against the Ottoman sultan and quickly occupied Syria, the Hejaz in the Arabian Peninsula, Yemen, the Sudan, and Crete and even threatened Constantinople (Istanbul), the seat of the Ottoman sultanate. Only the combined armies of Europe prevented him from destroying the Ottoman Empire. Mohammad Ali, therefore, had to content himself with the creation of a dynasty in Egypt, which incidentally did not come to an end until the 1952 coup against King Farouk. The Eastern Question assumed new dimensions with the Greek war of independence and the deterioration of the Ottoman position in the Balkans. The Greeks also placed themselves under British protection, and in the St. Petersburg Protocol of 1826, Britain and Russia agreed to mediate between the Greeks and Turks. Russia used the opportunity to lay claim to Ottoman territories in the Balkans. Moscow argued its right to protect the Christians of the region. In 1828, Russia declared war on the Ottomans, further weakening the regime. In the Treaty of Adrianople in 1829, it was decided that Greece should obtain its complete independence, a matter finally resolved in the London Protocol of 1830. Pressure on the Ottomans continued, however. Mohammad Ali expanded his control at Ottoman expense, and only the Europeans were able to restrain him. The Crimean War of 1854–1856 was fought by the Europeans to prevent further Russian expansion against the Turks, but Moscow remained undaunted. The Armenian Revolutionary Movement of 1890–1897 brought increased Turkish repression, which continued through World War I. It also gave Russia renewed opportunity to meddle in troubled waters. With an insurrection in Albania, the Ottomans were hard-pressed to maintain any control in Europe. Moreover, the Russians encouraged east European rebellion, and on October 30, 1914, Russia again made war on Constantinople. The contemporary significance of the Eastern Question rests on the constancy of the Russian quest to dominate the vital straits. During World War I, the Russians were secretly promised control of the waterway by Great Britain and France when the Ottomans allied with Kaiser Germany. That secret agreement was made null and void when Imperial Russia succumbed to the Bolsheviks. The Soviet Union, however, sustained pressure on the Republic of Turkey (the successor state to the Ottoman Empire after World War I) and continued to press for control of the straits. This pressure intensified after World War II, and the United States assumed the role theretofore played by the British. With the Truman Doctrine of 1947, the United States pledged assistance to Turkey in warding off threats to its sovereignty. In 1952 Turkey became a member of the North Atlantic Treaty Organization (NATO) and was made the linchpin of the alliance in the Mediterranean area. Turkey's NATO role was dramatized by Ankara's quick response to the U.S.-led coalition against Iraq in the Gulf War of 1990–1991. Despite formidable street opposition to the

Turkish government's decision to join the alliance against Baghdad, Turkey proved a staunch ally of the West and anticipated receiving more consideration for its internal as well as international problems. More significant in regard to the Eastern Question, Moscow was inclined to seek a new relationship with Ankara and the Turks, one that emphasized improved diplomatic ties and a multitude of economic and commercial ventures.

Fertile Crescent 10

The Fertile Crescent is a term used to describe an arable tract of land in the Middle East, which in great measure is desert or semi-desert. The Fertile Crescent is a region stretching from the Nile delta northward along the eastern Mediterranean, and from there east and southeastward through the Tigris-Euphrates Valley to the Persian Gulf. Because of harsh conditions throughout the Middle East, the Fertile Crescent has been the object of numerous invaders and warring tribes. Surrounding the Fertile Crescent are the mountains of eastern Turkey and western Iran and the vast desert wastes of the Arabian Peninsula. The Fertile Crescent includes parts of Egypt, Israel, Lebanon, Syria, and Iraq, and in some respects it is another term for the Levant in contemporary usage.

Significance

Some of the more significant population centers of the Middle East are found in the Fertile Crescent. Cities have either developed as ports or as way stations on the great rivers. Civilizations have been spawned and nourished by the waters that made the Fertile Crescent possible. The grandeur of the cities on the Nile and Tigris-Euphrates systems also attracted outsiders whose less hospitable environs drove them to seek greener pastures. The great migrations that have coursed into and through the Middle East brought about the interaction of varieties of people drawn from Eurasia and Africa. By the same token, the power enjoyed by Fertile Crescent inhabitants permitted them to roam among, and often conquer, distant peoples. The spread of ideas and cultures form the Fertile Crescent is a notable historical fact.

Gaza Strip 11

A somewhat rectangular section of territory in southern Israel and north of the Sinai. Originally part of the British Palestine Mandate, the Gaza Strip was occupied by Egypt in the 1948–1949 war with Israel. Israel forced the Egyptians from the territory in the 1967 war and has maintained a military government there ever since. The strip is 25 miles (40 kilometers) long and 5 miles (8 kilometers) wide and borders on the Mediterranean. Approximately 450,000 Arabs reside in the Gaza Strip, the majority in the principal city of Gaza.

Significance

Gaza city sits astride a major highway to Beersheba and Dimona, the latter the gateway to the Negev, the southernmost sector of the Israeli state. With the return of the Sinai to Egyptian sovereignty and administration, the Gaza Strip assumes greater importance as a strategic zone for Israeli security. Considerable discussion has focused on providing the Gaza Strip with autonomy, possibly as a model of what could be expected on the West Bank. The Israeli government, however, is reluctant to tamper with current arrangements, pending a signal from the Arab states that they will entertain a comprehensive peace settlement for the area. The Israelis are reminded that the Gaza Strip was a primary guerrilla (*fedeyeen*) base prior to the 1967 war; numerous terrorist forays originated there. Even though the Israeli-Egyptian peace treaty addresses itself to the matter of self-government for the Gaza Strip, progress has been lacking. Moreover, the *intifada* (uprising) and Palestinian support for Iraq in the Gulf War appear to have retarded efforts for a solution acceptable to both sides. ***See also*** INTIFADA (151)

Gibraltar Strait 12

The Strait of Gibraltar separates Spain from North Africa; at one point they are less than 10 miles (16 kilometers) apart. The strait also connects the Mediterranean Sea with the Atlantic Ocean. The Rock of Gibraltar, which lies astride the northeastern part of the strait on the Spanish side, dominates the waterway. Although Spanish territory lies to the south of the rock, and normally would better command the strait, the absence of a harbor has conferred this role on the Rock of Gibraltar. The rock was seized by Great Britain from Spain in 1704, and the British have maintained a garrison there ever since. The Rock of Gibraltar has no commercial utility, but its important geopolitical position has tended to keep it in British hands. Spain has insisted on the return of the rock, but Britain has consistently rebuffed Madrid's demands.

The southern part of the Strait of Gibraltar falls within Moroccan jurisdiction. In the latter part of the nineteenth and the early years of the twentieth centuries, Germany, France, Spain, and Great Britain sought to extend their control over the waterway. Morocco had come under French tutelage, but the southern shore of the strait was occupied by Spain. The city of Tangier in the territory was internationalized. This arrangement came to an end in 1956 when the French protectorate in Morocco was replaced by an independent Moroccan state. Tangier and the Spanish zone were reabsorbed within the Moroccan state at that time. Unlike the Turkish straits, there never has been any question about the right of all nations to use the strait for passage to and from the Mediterranean. Only during World Wars I and II was passage restricted in the twentieth century.

Significance
Gibraltar received its name from the Arab general Tariq, who led the Arab armies across North Africa and into Spain in the seventh century A.D. In Arabic, the word for mountain is *jebal*, and the Rock of Gibraltar in Arabic is called Jebal Tariq (the Mountain of Tariq). Gibraltar is the anglicized expression of the original Arabic term. Arab Muslim influence on Spain and Spanish interest in northwest Africa flow from the historical interaction of the peoples of the region. The Arabs (Moors) were not expelled from Spain until 1492, and not until they had created a lavish center of Islamic culture in southern Spain. The first Islamic caliphate, the Ummayyad, had its western extension in Spain, and it survived there long after the demise of the Ummayyad dynasty in Damascus. Apart from the continuing geopolitical importance of the Strait of Gibraltar and the Rock of Gibraltar, this region remains a prominent area of contact between Christian Europe and Muslim North Africa. Britain's reluctance to return the Rock of Gibraltar to Spain can be explained more in terms of Britain's Atlantic strategy than of its Middle East policy. Given the decision to withdraw from its east-of-Suez bases in the late 1960s, Britain has tended to place greater stress on retaining its bases in and near the Atlantic Ocean. The Falkland Islands dispute that erupted into hostilities between Britain and Argentina in 1982 is a graphic illustration of this policy.

And Gibraltar is judged to be far more important than the Falklands.

Golan Heights 13

The Golan Heights overlook the Galilee sector of northern Israel. Israel seized the Heights from Syria in the 1967 war and brought an end to the daily shelling of Israeli settlements in the valley below. The 40-mile (64-kilometer) strip of territory between Lebanon and Jordan was annexed by Israel in 1981 despite condemnation from governments all over the world. In addition to fortifying the Golan, Israel has established 31 settlements in the region.

Significance

The Golan Heights are geopolitically important to Israeli security. With a foothold in the heights, the Israelis are in a formidable position from which to strike at Damascus, the Syrian capital, approximately 30 miles (48 kilometers) distant. They also are able to deal more effectively with the Palestine Liberation Organization (PLO), which settled its principal units in southern Lebanon following their expulsion from Jordan in 1970. The principal organization within the PLO, Al-Fatah (led by Yasir Arafat), occupied the barren, rocky area of Lebanon known as the Arkoub, in sight of the Mount Hermon range and next to the Israeli-controlled Golan Heights. The Arkoub area became known as Fatahland because it was an assembly point for Fatah guerrillas intent on raiding inside Israel. In fact, it was the attempt by Fatah to expand its control over southern Lebanon that brought it into conflict with the indigenous Christian and Druze villagers. The latter wanted no part of the contest between Israelis and Fatah guerrillas. More important, they did not want their land transformed into a permanent battleground. Fatah was unsympathetic, however, and its decision to forcibly suppress the local inhabitants eventually brought the Lebanese to accept Israeli assistance. Fatah sought assistance from Syria, and the Arafat Trail was conceived as a supply line from the Syrian border to Fatahland. With the Israelis in the Golan, the Arafat Trail failed to materialize. The Israeli invasion of Lebanon in 1982 virtually eliminated PLO presence in the southernmost region of Lebanon. The Gulf War of 1990–1991, however, placed the Golan Heights in a new light. Syria was a member of the coalition that defeated Iraq, and it raised the question of the return of the Golan Heights in exchange for a possible working relationship with Israel. Jerusalem was guarded in its reaction to the offer, however, and the possibility of its yielding the Golan in return for an agreement with Syria seemed remote. How remote will be determined in future negotiations, especially those begun at the 1991 Madrid conference on a comprehensive Middle East settlement. In return for peace with Israel, Syria insists on the return of the Golan Heights.

Judea and Samaria (The West Bank) 14

Judea and Samaria are the biblical Hebrew names for the territory that has come to be called the West Bank in present times. The West Bank refers to the area lying west of the Jordan River that, along with present-day Israel, the Gaza Strip, and the Kingdom of Jordan, comprised the original British Mandate of Palestine. The West Bank was seized by Transjordan in the 1948–1949 Arab-Israeli War. Its army, the Arab Legion, drove the Jews from Judea and Samaria and East Jerusalem, and they were not permitted to return. After incorporating the region, Transjordan became the Kingdom of Jordan. In the 1967 Arab-Israeli War the Jordanians were forced to withdraw from East Jerusalem and the West Bank, and the region has been occupied by the Israelis ever since. The West Bank is a 3,700-square-mile (5,900-square-kilometer) area bounded on the west by the 1949 armistice line and in the east by the Jordan River. The area is divided into two regions: Judea in the south, with Hebron, the burial place of the Jewish patriarchs Abraham, Isaac, and Jacob, as its principal metropolitan center; and Samaria in the north, with Nablus its main town. The Arab Muslim population of the West Bank is approximately 95 percent of the total of 1.3 million. The area's 60,000 Christians are concentrated in the towns of Bethlehem, the birthplace of Jesus, and Ramallah. The inhabitants of the West Bank are mainly Jordanian nationals, and the status of the area is that of an occupied territory under Israeli military administration. Jewish settlements were especially promoted by the administration of Prime Minister Menachem Begin. More than 25,000 Israelis lived in 78 Jewish villages on the West Bank in 1981. That number increased to approximately 100,000 in 1991. The West Bank is predominantly rural. Nearly 40 percent of its inhabitants are agriculturists who live in the region's 500 villages and towns. There are also 23 Palestine refugee camps on the West Bank with a population of about 125,000. Following the 1967 war, Israel permitted visitations by relatives and friends of the Arabs of the West Bank and also allowed 45,000 Arabs to return to the region under the family reunification program. Moreover, the bridges over the Jordan River generally remained open to commercial traffic, Arab labor from the West Bank was encouraged to work in Israel, and there was regular commerce between the West Bank and Arab countries. However, many of these activities came to an abrupt halt with the eruption of the intifada in the late 1980s. The violence characterized by the intifada caused the Israelis to use repressive tactics, and normal life was made impossible by its protracted nature. The war precipitated by Iraq's invasion of Kuwait also affected the West Bank, where the Palestinian community swore allegiance to Saddam Hussain. Although international pressure sought to convince the Israelis to relinquish their occupation of the West Bank, Jerusalem seemed even more determined to retain some control over the territory. Moreover, Israeli Jews, especially new Soviet emigrants, were expected to settle there. Washington's opposition to Jewish settlements on the West Bank left little doubt the U.S. government wanted the West Bank given to the Palestinians for Palestinian self-rule. Moreover, the Madrid Peace Conference of 1991 addressed this central issue. ***See also*** AUTONOMY (73); REAGAN PROGRAM ON PALESTINE (177); INTIFADA (151); SOVIET JEWS (183).

Significance

The West Bank is the focal point for one of the Middle East's principal dilemmas. The Camp David accords and the subsequent peace treaty between Israel and Egypt place maximum attention on resolving the Palestinian question, the Israelis speaking in terms of administrative autonomy and the Egyptians, other Arab states, and a majority of the world's governments emphasizing self-determination. The Israelis have been willing to provide Palestinian Arabs with control of their political life, such as allowing them to elect their own leaders, but the Israelis do not accept the oft-stated view that the Palestine Liberation Organization is the primary spokesman and representative of the West Bank population. The Israelis fear that a PLO state would be a mortal threat to their country. Despite claims by the Begin government and the orthodox Jewish religious leaders in Israel that Judea and Samaria are, by right and faith, integral components of the Jewish state, the basic reason for sustaining Israeli influence over the West Bank is strategic. The entire central sector of Israel effectively falls within Jordanian artillery range. The Israeli territory immediately to the west of the West Bank houses Israel's principal cities of Jerusalem, Tel Aviv, and Haifa. The majority of Israel's population lives in this zone. Moreover, the width of this zone ranges between 11 and 17 miles (18–28 kilometers). Israel literally has its back to the sea, the Mediterranean Sea. Israelis have always feared that a concerted Arab drive from the West Bank to Tel Aviv, approximately 11 miles away, would effectively cut Israel in two. Furthermore, Arab guerrillas used the West Bank territory to launch terrorist raids into Israel prior to the 1967 war. Since the Israeli occupation of the West Bank, those raids virtually have come to an end. The question of what to do with the West Bank is difficult. The PLO has never indicated that it would accept the West Bank as a final settlement of the Arab-Israeli dispute, even if the Israelis would agree to deal directly with them, which they have not. The Israelis have also insisted that their settlements on the West Bank will not be removed. Some Arab land has been and continues to be seized by the Israelis for new settlements as well as for Israeli military garrisons. The area of Judea and Samaria is about 1.5 million acres (60,000 hectares), of which the Jewish settlements represent 50,000 acres (20,000 hectares). The Arab population of the West Bank remains defiant. Periodic and sustained demonstrations and acts of violence against the Israeli occupation are commonplace. Modern weaponry, particularly rocket-launched projectiles, as demonstrated by the Iraqi Scuds, can strike Israeli cities even with the greater defensive depth provided by Israeli military positions on the West Bank. A solution satisfactory to all parties remains elusive.

Karakoram Highway 15

Described by some observers as the "eighth wonder of the world," the Karakoram Highway connects Pakistan with the People's Republic of China. Constructed amid the Himalayan Mountains, "the Roof of the World," it passes from Abbottabad in the North West Frontier Province of Pakistan through the mountain states of Gilgit and Hunza to the Khunjerab Pass on the Chinese side of the frontier, and from there it links Kashgar and Urumchi in Chinese Sinkiang Province. The highway is approximately 500 miles (800 kilometers) in length. It was started on the Pakistan side in 1959, and after the 1963 border agreement between Islamabad and Beijing, it was decided to transform the road into a two-lane highway following the historic silk route of Marco Polo. The Chinese constructed 24 bridges through the mountainous terrain. Although the highway was formally inaugurated in June 1978, the Khunjerab Pass, 15,000 feet (4,600 meters) above sea level, was not opened until August 1982. ***See also*** WAKHAN CORRIDOR (31).

Significance

The Karakoram Highway links Pakistan and China with an all-weather road and is of particular interest to military tacticians. Although a potential boon to trade and tourism between the two countries, its immediate importance lies in its strategic role. China is brought into near proximity to Pakistan's northwestern frontier through the use of the highway. Chinese military supplies can be moved more rapidly to Pakistani forces. The Soviet Union had registered its concern over the use of the Karakoram Highway, believing the route to be a threat to its central Asian interests. India also protested the building of the highway. It did so again when the Khunjerab Pass was opened. New Delhi argues that the territory through which the highway passes is in dispute and, furthermore, that Pakistan has no legal right to settle the Himalayan border with China without taking India's claim into account. Islamabad rejects India's argument and sees no basis for it in international law. The Chinese also repudiated the Indian protest, declaring that the Chinese section of the highway is not subject to Indian complaint. India's fear involves the ongoing dispute in Kashmir, through which the highway passes. Although India controls the Vale of Kashmir and Jammu, it does not dominate the entire region. Pakistan's intimacy with China and the possibility that Indian positions in Kashmir could be assaulted by combined Pakistani-Chinese forces remain troublesome issues.

Levant 16

Levant is derived from the Italian language, meaning "east" or "orient." The term, however, was identified with the eastern end of the Mediterranean. Countries normally included in the Levant today are Syria, Lebanon, and Israel. In a broader interpretation, the Levant could be considered as extending from Italy to Egypt and Syria. Levantines are persons of Italian and French lineage born in the eastern Mediterranean territories. The term is seldom used by Americans, but it is still prominent among Europeans, who are historically intertwined with the Middle East trading communities.

Significance

The term *Levant* addresses itself to centuries of cultural and commercial contact between the Europeans, especially those with Latin ancestry, and the indigenous Middle East communities. The Mediterranean region long has been considered a cradle of civilizations, and from earliest recorded times, traffic between the Middle East and North Africa and Europe was sustained by merchants determined to sell their wares and obtain goods not available in their own environment. The creation of great metropolitan areas was the outcome of the interaction of these persistent commercial agents. Although religious and political conflict have captured attention, the activities of the merchant communities are key to understanding the course and destiny of the Middle East.

Maghreb 17

The Maghreb is the western region of the Islamic world. The Maghreb usually refers to the North African states of Morocco, Tunisia, Algeria, and Libya. The Maghreb was Islamicized and heavily Arabicized between the seventh and eleventh centuries. Arab armies reached Morocco in the eighth century, but the social transformation of the region was slow and deliberate. By the eleventh century the Arab movement across North Africa gained momentum, and the founding of new settlements brought cultural breakthroughs. The Berber population of North Africa continued to resist the Arab advance, but the political sophistication demonstrated by the Aghlabids and the Fatimids established Islam as the prevailing socioreligious experience. Maraboutism, a mystical form of Sufi Islam, developed in the Maghreb in the thirteenth and fourteenth centuries. The Ottoman Empire extended its loose authority over the region, dividing it into the regencies of Tripolitania, Tunis, and Algiers. Dominated by the Barbarossa brothers, coastal North Africa became known as the Barbary Coast and was renowned for the piracy that preyed on European shipping. The Maghreb remained an unstable region in subsequent centuries. Divisions between Berbers and Arabs, between austere and mystical Islam, produced clashes of interest and unremitting rivalry. The intervention of the Europeans in the Maghreb, especially the French, the Spanish, and, later, the Italians, further complicated the lives of the indigenous population. The formation of the independent states of Morocco, Tunisia, Algeria, and Libya after World War II gave the region a semblance of order and predictability, but it did not lose its volatility.

Significance

The Maghreb is united only in terminology. Morocco differs culturally and historically from Libya, and indeed the two states are serious adversaries. Morocco also has differences with Algeria, while Tunisia remains suspicious of Libya in spite of their efforts at closer cooperation. Libya and Algeria have preached revolution. Tunisia and Morocco speak of tradition, continuity, and order. The formation of a Maghrebian union has been suggested by various leaders, but fundamental differences rule out a true and genuine confederation. The Maghrebian states are also divided in their orientation and association. Although all are members of the Arab League and address themselves to Arab causes, their identification with the African continent is no less important.

Middle East **18**

The Middle East is a definable region, but no specific geographic delimitation will satisfy everyone. The term *Middle East* is a concept derived from the expressions *Near East* and *Far East*. One assumption is that the Middle East is the area between those two extremities, but even this is ambiguous. In speaking of the "East," whether Near, Middle, or Far, we must keep in mind that we are measuring, comparing, or separating a part of the world from the "West," which is essentially the European world and its extended culture in the Western Hemisphere. In discussing the Middle East, therefore, we are talking about a vast region, comprising great varieties of people, not too distant from the Western world. From the thirteenth century, the area to the immediate southeast of Europe was referred to as the Levant, a word coined by the seafaring and commercially minded Italians. The term *Levant* described that region between Egypt and China, and it was not until the nineteenth century that it began to wane as a descriptive term. Today, some persons still speak of the region as the Levant. The use of *Levant*, however, eventually gave way to the term *Near East*. The *Near East* contrasted with the term *Far East* and referred to those lands closer to Europe. The term *Middle East* did not make its appearance in literature until the twentieth century. It came into prominent use during World War I. It was first used by the British to specify their interests in the vicinity of the Persian Gulf. It did not replace, however, the use of the term *Near East*. In fact, there was considerable reluctance to adopt the Middle East as a definable geographic region, and *Near East* remained in vogue through World War I along with terms like *Levant* and *Asia Minor*. During World War II the British established their headquarters in Egypt to carry out operations in the Mediterranean, North Africa, and eastward through Iraq. This headquarters was described as the Middle East Command and the Middle East Supply Center. When the United States began to work closely with the British in the region, they too adopted the term *Middle East*. Soon the entire world was referring to the region by that designation. Nevertheless, there is still controversy as to what the Middle East includes. Some would prefer a narrow delineation bordering on Egypt in the west, Turkey in the north, Oman in the south, and Iran in the east. Others (including the author of this book) include all the land from Morocco on the Atlantic Ocean, across North Africa (including Sudan) to Turkey, Israel, Lebanon, Syria, Iraq, the Arabian Peninsula, Iran, Afghanistan, and Pakistan. This use of the term *Middle East* eliminates the use of the term *Near East*, but it leaves intact the regions of South Asia, i.e., the Indian subcontinent (less Pakistan); Southeast Asia; and the Far East, which today focuses on China, Japan, the Koreas, and Outer Mongolia. The Middle East can also be subdivided into North Africa (including Egypt) and Southwest Asia.

Significance

The use of the term *Middle East* in this volume aims at clarifying the political, cultural, and technological realities of our present world. In each period of history, geographic designations such as Levant or Asia Minor or Near East reflect the concerns of peoples of a particular period. Given the special emphasis on the Islamic zone, the greater interaction between regional states, the growing interdependencies of an economic, technological, and military character, the importance of petroleum, and critical strategic interests, it seems appropriate to cast a wider net than heretofore. Pakistanis, in the days of Zulfikar Ali Bhutto (1971–1977) and following the loss of Bangladesh, considered themselves to be more identified with the Middle East than with South Asia and India. Saudi Arabia has sought Pakistani military assistance to bolster its small armed force, Libya has sought a semblance of political union with Syria, and revolutionary Iran is closely identified with Algeria. More important, the Middle East crisis extends beyond and involves far more than the Arab-Israeli conflict. Interrelationships of both a conflicted and a cooperative character will continue to develop, and it is useful to examine the Middle East as a complex interaction of states and peoples, cultures and ideas, aspirations and purposes.

Muscat and Oman 19

Muscat and Oman is the older description of present-day Oman. In 1862, the British and French governments, which had replaced Portuguese influence in the Persian Gulf region, agreed to respect the independence of the sultan of Muscat. In 1891, however, the British government in India convinced the ruling monarch to enter into a separate treaty of friendship, commerce, and navigation. The sultan and his heirs pledged never to cede or lease territory to any government other than that of Great Britain. France acknowledged British preeminence in the region and bowed out of the picture in 1904. The United States had a treaty of amity and commerce with Muscat that dated back to 1833, but Washington did not maintain representation in the country, and the British were not very concerned about U.S. intentions. With the establishment of British power in the area, the sultan could depend upon assistance in maintaining his realm against outside as well as internal dissidents. Moreover, the British assisted the sultan in pressing his authority into the Ibadhi hinterland. Through the nineteenth century, the Al bu Said dynasty extended its power over the coastal areas and Dhofar, but not into the interior. The interior Ibadhis paid homage to their imamate and were otherwise independent of the sultan. In 1913, the tribal element attacked the sultan and attempted to establish a rival imamate/sultanate. Britain came to the sultan's defense and assisted in crushing the rebellion and in reestablishing the sultan's fiat. By the Treaty of Sib (1920) Britain assisted the sultan in claiming suzerainty over the interior. The reigning monarch of the Al bu Said family, Said ibn Taymur, was the eventual beneficiary of this development. His rule began in 1932. In 1955, Britain helped the sultan's army conquer the interior, destroy the imamate, and merge Muscat with Oman. ***See also*** IBADHIS (87); DHOFAR (7).

Significance
Muscat and Oman became a formal actor in modern international relations through assistance provided by Great Britain. Britain helped sustain the authority of the Al bu Said dynasty, which today continues to lean heavily on outside powers, notably the United States. Britain maintains military advisors in the sultanate and has aided the monarch in recruiting Pakistanis for his armed force. In the 1980s, the United States sought and obtained the use of Omani territory for Washington's Rapid Deployment Force. The British have maintained naval and air installations on the Omani island of Masirah, and these are now used by U.S. forces in the Indian Ocean. The sultan's dependence on U.S. and other foreign support has provoked considerable criticism in the Arab states. Moreover, insurgent groups have attempted to link forces with Ibadhi tribesmen in Dhofar and in more remote areas of the sultanate.

Nile **20**

The Nile River, the world's longest at 4,145 miles (6,671 kilometers), is the lifeblood of Egypt. Approximately 96 percent of its population lives astride the great river, which has one source in Lake Victoria far to the south in Uganda. As the river travels north it is known as the White Nile. Passing through the Sudan, it is joined by the Blue Nile and Atabara River, which emerge out of the highlands of Ethiopia. In June, the Blue Nile and other Ethiopian rivers begin to flood, and the floodstream reaches lower Egypt near Cairo in August. When the flood period is over, the Nile settles to a steady flow that varies little the rest of the year. The Aswan High Dam was built in the 1960s to conserve the Nile water during the floodtide period. Given Egypt's rapidly expanding population, there was great pressure to increase the arable land. The reservoir at Aswan was constructed with the intention of increasing irrigated acreage, controlling seasonal flooding, and ensuring that Egypt's southern neighbors, particularly Sudan and Ethiopia, did not divert the precious water to the detriment of the Egyptian population. ***See also*** ASWAN HIGH DAM (5).

Significance
Egyptian civilization would disappear if the Nile ceased providing its life-giving water. But Egypt does not control the source of the Nile. Indeed, its effort to integrate the Sudan into a political scheme of Egyptian dominance is predicated on the need to control the movement of Nile water. The high dam at Aswan is not the final answer to Egypt's water problem. Although the high dam has increased agricultural yields, other problems have developed from its construction and use. Even greater dilemmas are forecast in the next decade. Moreover, Egypt requires good relations with its southern neighbors, who will continue to control the water flowing northward to the sea. Attempts by Libya to gain influence in the Sudan are perceived as threats to Egypt.

Nineteenth Province (21)

The Nineteenth Province was the designation given to Kuwait following the Iraqi conquest of the kingdom in August 1990. The Nineteenth Province of Iraq (Kuwait) represents Baghdad's claim to the small territory in the northwest corner of the Persian/Arabian Gulf. Surrounded by Iraq on the north and Saudi Arabia on the west and south, Kuwait represents an area of 6,880 square miles (17,280 square kilometers), excluding a region known as the Neutral Zone, to its west. Kuwait is essentially desert, with one principal city, Kuwait City. The Kingdom of Kuwait also holds sway over nine small islands, the principal ones being Bubiyan and Failaka, all deemed important by Iraq in that their control offers Baghdad greater access to the gulf. The Arab population of Kuwait originates from the Nejd region of Saudi Arabia, however, not from Baghdad or even Basrah in southern Iraq. The first tribes that settled in the region were from the Beni Khalid clan that moved to the territory in 1688. This migration was followed by the Utubi tribe, descendants of the Anaizz who are found in central Saudi Arabia. The ruling Sabah family of Kuwait derive from the Utubi and have been known for their commercial pursuits. From the settlement of Kuwait City, a merchant encampment, Kuwait grew under the Sabah clan in the eighteenth century. In 1756 the head of the Sabah family was selected by the other patriarchs in the region to be their emir, or ruler. The Al-Sabah ruled Kuwait from that date forward. Kuwait was in effect a reality before the modern creation of Iraq in the twentieth century. Baghdad's claim to the territory is spurious and is more a reflection of ancient and medieval history than of present realities. Moreover, the ethnic character of the territory diverges from that of the Baghdadis, except in the domicile of hundreds of thousands of non-Kuwaitis who came to live and work in the region because of its expanding prosperity, a consequence of the oil that was found and exploited there. Kuwait's relations with the British began as a result of the transfer of the British East India Company's southern overland mail terminal from Basrah to Kuwait. Basrah had been captured by the Persians during the Ottoman-Persian War of 1776, and Kuwait sought protection from both the Ottomans and the Persians; hence its link to the British. Nevertheless, it was not until 1904 that a British Political Agency was established in Kuwait. In 1914 the British cited the independence of the kingdom, harboring it from Ottoman threat. It was then that the formal act of protection was also extended to Kuwait by the British. Britain determined the formal boundaries of modern Iraq and Kuwait in 1922, protecting the Sabah family from the Saudis at that time. The Neutral Zone was also drawn at that time as a compromise formula between the Sabah and their tribal adversaries. In 1961 Kuwait formally established its independence, again in an agreement with the British, who were in the process of leaving the region. *See also* AL SABAH DYNASTY (67).

Significance

Saddam Hussain's claim to Kuwait as the Nineteenth Province was a simple act of imperialism. Although the British played a key role in the evolution of an independent, sovereign Kuwaiti state, the territory had been under the control of the Sabah family for more than two centuries. Prior to the discovery of oil in 1938, Kuwait had little more than a subsistence economy and local manpower was sufficient to meet the area's requirements. After the development of its oil resources, however, Kuwait experienced the world's highest rate of population growth, about

9.8 percent, the increase a consequence of the arrival of foreign labor. By 1948, Kuwait's population had doubled, and two years later it was triple what it had been before 1938. Kuwait developed a wage scale that was the envy of the Middle East in the 1970s and 1980s. Moreover, its wealth enabled the government to provide free health care, education, and the other amenities identified with a true welfare state. But as a consequence of its great fortune, and also its significant weakness, especially the absence of a protector like the British, Kuwait became a target of opportunity. Instead of the Ottomans and Persians, or even the Saudis, with whom the Sabahs had come to terms, it was the Baathist socialists of Iraq led by Saddam Hussain who coveted Kuwaiti territory and Kuwaiti oil resources. The Nineteenth Province of Iraq was an afterthought to cover and justify the ouster of the Sabah clan and the annexation of the territory by Saddam Hussain.

Northern Tier 22

This term had been used to describe the countries on the southern perimeter of the Soviet Union in the region of southwest Asia. The Northern Tier countries were Turkey, Iran, Afghanistan, and Pakistan. The use of the term can be traced to efforts by the U.S. government to form a Middle East Defense Organization (MEDO) in 1953. President Dwight Eisenhower's secretary of state, John Foster Dulles, was convinced of the necessity of "containing" the Soviet Union within its own borders. The formation of the North Atlantic Treaty Organization (NATO) in April 1949 was one such effort. MEDO was envisaged as connecting with NATO in an effort to extend the anticommunist defense line. MEDO was stillborn when Egypt refused to become a party to the arrangement, and other Arab countries also indicated reluctance. Undaunted, Dulles convinced the Turkish and Iraqi governments to sign a mutual defense agreement. In 1955 these Middle East states formed the Baghdad Pact. Iran and Pakistan, as well as Britain, joined later, and the United States became an active participant, although not a signatory, to the treaty. Afghanistan, however, refused to join and instead condemned the alliance as provocative and fraught with consequences. In 1958, Iraq entered a revolutionary phase and announced its withdrawal from the pact. The Baghdad Pact was renamed the Central Treaty Organization (CENTO), and the Northern Tier was perceived as a fortified buffer zone between the Soviet Union and the Arab Middle East. ***See also*** BAGHDAD PACT (198); CENTRAL TREATY ORGANIZATION (CENTO) (204); RIMLAND (24).

Significance

The Northern Tier defense against the Soviet Union passed through several permutations before its virtual disintegration in 1979. As early as 1955, the Soviet Union "leapfrogged" the Northern Tier and entered into direct relations with Egypt, supplying weapons and advisors and eventually building the Aswan High Dam. Afghanistan's failure to join the arrangement also permitted the Soviet Union to monopolize Afghan attention. Strains in U.S.-Turkish relations over Cyprus and in U.S.-Pakistani relations over India further undermined the Northern Tier. Finally, the collapse of the shah's regime in Iran removed that country from the pact. The Northern Tier is no longer perceived as a forward defense perimeter against possible encroachment in the Middle East. If the Northern Tier policy was supposed to prevent the Soviet Union from spilling over its borders into the Middle East, it did not live up to expectations. Granted, the Northern Tier defense structure was created to contain the Red Army within its own frontiers. Soviet influence in the Middle East, however, with the exception of Afghanistan, spread not by the Red Army but through diplomatic initiatives, as well as military, economic, and technical assistance. The Northern Tier arrangement succumbed to internal domestic forces and contradictions. In fact, the disappearance of the Soviet Union may eventually create a "Southern Tier" of "friendly, cooperative states."

Persian Gulf (23)

Identified as the Arabian Gulf by the Arabs on its western littoral, the Persian Gulf is almost an inland sea covering an area of approximately 90,000 square miles (235,000 square kilometers). It is 180 miles (290 kilometers) across at its widest and only 35 miles (57 kilometers) at its narrowest. The distance from the mouth of the Shatt al-Arab River at the uppermost extension of the gulf to the Strait of Hormuz, where it empties into the Gulf of Oman and the Indian Ocean, is over 500 miles (800 kilometers). The countries bordering the gulf are Iran, Iraq, Kuwait, Saudi Arabia, Qatar, the United Arab Emirates (UAE), and Oman. The island nation of Bahrein lies midway in the gulf close to Saudi Arabia and Qatar. There are numerous other smaller islands in the vital waterway. Some are little more than sandbanks or mudbanks, rising only a foot or two above the water. Even the larger ones in this category are virtually devoid of any vegetation. Established settlements on these islands are very limited, and most are visited by migratory inhabitants during certain seasons. Several islands in the gulf have attained considerable importance, however. The town of Abu Dhabi is built on a triangular-shaped island. Das Island is an important ocean terminal for offshore oil mining. Similar facilities have been built on Halat al Mubarras. Dalma Island is the center for pearl fishing. Sadiyat Island is being used to experiment with controlled environmental agriculture. Um an Nar has archaeological digs of interest to the scholarly community. Perhaps the most famous islands in the gulf are Abu Musa, which is legally a possession of Sharjah (a member of the UAE), and the Greater and Lesser Tumbs (claimed by Ras al Khaimah, also of the UAE). These islands were seized by Iran in 1971, when the UAE was being formed. The islands are strategically placed near the Strait of Hormuz, and the shah of Iran feared that they could fall under the influence of Iran's enemies, particularly Iraq. Although Iran developed an agreement with Sharjah, Ras al Khaimah never countenanced the Iranian occupation of the Tumbs. After the demise of the shah, Ras al Khaimah had reason to believe the dispute would be resolved, but the revolutionary government in Tehran showed no more willingness to evacuate the islands than had the previous Iranian regime. Iran has sovereignty over many other islands in the gulf, closer to its frontier. By far the most important of these is Kharg Island off the coast of Iranian Khuzistan. Kharg is the principal petroleum refining facility and major transit point for the shipment of Iranian oil from the Persian Gulf.

Significance

In the context of current international politics, the Persian (Arabian) Gulf is the most important waterway in the world. It is from the gulf that approximately two-thirds of the world's exportable oil flows into the principal commercial sealanes. If an unfriendly power were to gain control over the Strait of Hormuz, the gulf could be effectively closed, the oil would cease flowing, and other countries besides the littoral states would be affected.

The world economy depends on the steady movement of gulf crude, and chaos would prevail if it became impossible to move it to the consuming nations. Even the war between Iraq and Iran that commenced in 1980 did not cause the gulf to close. Moreover, the United States established a large naval presence near and in the Gulf of Oman shortly after the shah fell from power. Washington was determined to keep the gulf open, and although Iranian and Iraqi oil production fell markedly, the fields of Saudi Arabia, Kuwait, Qatar, and the UAE were still capable of filling market demand. When the United States lost the use of bases in Iran, it quickly attempted to compensate by acquiring base rights in Oman and on the Omani island of Masirah in the Indian Ocean. Keeping the gulf open and the oil flowing from it was a principal concern of the United States and other industrialized nations during the Iran-Iraq War and the Iraq-Kuwait conflict. The reflagging of Kuwaiti vessels by the United States had as its principal objective the uninterrupted flow of petroleum from the gulf during the Iran-Iraq War. It was during this exercise that the U.S. cruiser *Vincennes* accidentally shot down an Iranian passenger airliner, killing all 290 people aboard the aircraft, on July 3, 1988. Shortly after this incident, on July 18, Iran accepted UN Resolution 598 and agreed to a ceasefire. On August 20, 1988, the Iran-Iraq War drew to a close. Iraq's occupation and declared annexation of Kuwait in August 1990 precipitated still another violent encounter involving the United States. Under UN aegis, a U.S.-led coalition first sought to defend Saudi Arabia from further Iraqi aggression and then, several months later, launched a counteroffensive that drove Iraqi forces from Kuwait. Through all these hostilities, the Persian (Arabian) Gulf remained open to international shipping and the oil never ceased flowing through the waterway.

Rimland 24

The "Rimland" is a geopolitical expression developed by U.S. scholar Nicholas Spykman in 1944. Prior to the publication of Spykman's geopolitical thesis, Halford Mackinder, an Englishman, had publicized his "Heartland," in which Eurasia and Africa were conceived as forming a "World Island." Control of the Heartland by a centrally positioned country (e.g., Germany before World Wars I and II), according to Mackinder, would provide it with the opportunity to dominate the World Island. Spykman's Rimland thesis attempts to counter this argument. The Rimland is supposedly formed by those countries on the periphery of the Eurasian landmass, coupled with mastery of the marginal seas that touch their shores. In the post–World War II era, the contest between a landlocked Heartland represented by the Soviet Union and a Rimland heavily influenced by the United States established the dynamics for the Cold War. The Middle East has been perceived as a crucial part of the Rimland. The significant U.S. presence in the Middle East, however, was judged a threat to Soviet security interests, just as the United States perceived Soviet expansionist policies in the Rimland as an attempt to spread its territorial imperium.

Significance

Geopolitical thinking influences the making of foreign policy, for instance, in characterizing the post–World War II rivalry between the United States and the Soviet Union as hegemonial tension in which one superpower seeks to maintain its maritime imperium, while the other is determined to spread its territorial imperium. The Truman, Eisenhower, and Nixon doctrines were all aimed at preventing the spread of international communism, especially the power of the Soviet Union. The Soviet Union successfully breached the Rimland in Southeast Asia and South Asia in the 1960s. It did the same in the Middle East in the 1970s by establishing bases in and near the People's Democratic Republic of Yemen, Iraq, Syria, Libya, and Ethiopia. It occupied Afghanistan in 1979–1980. It identified with and gave formal diplomatic status to the Palestine Liberation Organization. It sought a working relationship with the revolutionary government in Iran, and it maintains a naval presence in the Indian Ocean. The United States, no longer the preeminent force on the Eurasian Rimland, countered Soviet actions by constructing a base on the Indian Ocean island of Diego Garcia. It signed agreements with the governments of Oman, Somalia, and Egypt for the use of their territory as military staging areas. It continues to supply Israel, and it expanded shipments of sophisticated weaponry to Pakistan and Saudi Arabia. The United States also stationed a sizable armada in the Indian Ocean, and its Rapid Deployment Force became operational during the war to liberate Kuwait from Iraqi aggression.

Shatt al-Arab 25

The Shatt al-Arab is the river formed by the junction of the Tigris and Euphrates rivers. In 1847, Iran, then called Persia, and the Ottoman Empire, which included Syria and Iraq, agreed on the common use of the Shatt al-Arab, which empties into the Persian Gulf. The Treaty of Erzerum (1847), however, declared that the entire Shatt al-Arab was an Ottoman possession. Khorramshahr, the major Iranian port on the river, could only be entered through waters controlled by the Ottomans and their subjects, the Iraqis. With the dissolution of the Ottoman Empire and the independence of Iraq in 1932, Iraq, with British encouragement, insisted on its exclusive dominance of the Shatt al-Arab. The Iranians applied to the League of Nations Council in 1935, asking that the border be redrawn at the midstream or navigable channel, the *Thalweg*, in international law. This effort proved fruitless. In 1939, Iraq agreed to a midriver line opposite the loading jetties at the refinery city of Abadan, and the length of the estuary was open to commercial and naval vessels of both countries. Warships of other countries were also permitted passage if the other country agreed. Reza Shah, the founder of the Pahlavi dynasty, did not like the terms of the agreement, and he blamed both the British and the Soviets for the predicament. Reza Shah was forced into exile during World War II because he appeared to favor the German cause and thus angered the British and Soviets. Mohammad Reza, his son, succeeded to the throne. By 1975, Mohammad Reza Shah was judged the most powerful leader in the Middle East. With huge sums of money earned from the sale of petroleum, the shah was in the process of transforming the Iranian armed forces into a modern, sophisticated fighting machine. In 1971, the United States began to supply Iran with the most up-to-date battle equipment, and the Americans, under the Nixon Doctrine, saw Iran as the chief protector of the vital sealanes leading to and from the Persian Gulf. Iran had already intervened in the insurgency in Oman and had helped the Omani sultan retain his crown. Moreover, the shah's forces had seized control of the strategic islands of Abu Musa and the Greater and Lesser Tumbs near the Strait of Hormuz and, therefore, controlled the Persian Gulf. Iran also supplied and encouraged rebellion among Kurdish nationalists in Iraq. In these circumstances Iraq was pressured to negotiate a settlement over the long-disputed Shatt al-Arab. In 1975 Baghdad agreed to enter into a treaty with Tehran that granted Iran sovereignty over that half of the river washing its shore. Khorramshahr was freed from Iraqi influence. In return for this agreement, the Baathist government in Baghdad was given the shah's guarantee that Iran would cease aiding the Kurdish autonomy movement. The agreement provided the Iraqi government with the opportunity to defeat the Kurds, and the Kurdish nationalists were crushed and their forces scattered. The Shatt al-Arab did not become a matter of controversy again until the shah's demise. The disorder that overwhelmed revolutionary Iran led Baghdad to conclude that the time was opportune to recapture the portion of the Shatt al-Arab ceded to Iran and, furthermore, to invade Iranian Khuzistan, which Iraq called Arabistan because of its Arab population. In fact, Khuzistan had been seized in 1925 by Reza Shah, then Iranian minister of war. He had led his armies into the oil-rich province (petroleum had been discovered there in 1908) and established his military headquarters in the city of Awaz. The Iraqis felt justified in using the occasion of Iran's disarray to retake the region for the Arabs. The success of the Iraqi invasion was also expected to give Baghdad dominance over the Persian Gulf, as well as add to the disintegrative process inside Iran. In September 1980, the Iraqis unilaterally abrogated the 1975 treaty, attacked Iran across the Shatt al-Arab, and at first struck deep into Khuzistan. If the Iraqis expected the Iranians to collapse, however, they were greatly mistaken. What was to be a quick war over the Shatt al-Arab and Khuzistan settled into a long, drawn-out war of attrition in which both sides suffered heavy losses. Iran counterattacked in March 1982 and by June had driven the Iraqis across their frontier. Not satisfied with this victory, the Iranians attempted to penetrate Iraq but suffered heavy losses on the desert before the city of Basra. When the war between Iran and Iraq ended in 1988, Iraq maintained the advantage and hence continued to dominate the Shatt al-Arab. It was only after Baghdad's forces occupied Kuwait in August 1990 that Iranian claims were again addressed. Given the buildup of U.S.-led coalition forces in Saudi Arabia following the annexation of Kuwait, Iraq unilaterally agreed to withdraw from Iranian territory it still retained and agreed to the principles guiding the use of the Shatt al-Arab that were found in the 1975 treaty. This "capitulation" was judged an Iraqi tactic, aimed at reducing the threat on its border with Iran. The maneuver also made possible the redeployment of Iraqi troops from the Iranian to the Kuwaiti theater. Following this Iraqi action, Baghdad sought improved relations with Tehran, and during the hostilities of January–February 1991, Saddam Hussain ordered approximately 150 of his best aircraft to fly to Iran, where they were "protected" from allied destruction. At the end of the Gulf War, however, it appeared that Iran had little interest in bolstering, let alone assisting, the Baghdad regime of Saddam Hussain. ***See also*** IRAQ-IRAN WAR (1980–1988) (247); KURDS (89); BAATH MOVEMENT: IRAQ (115); OPERATION DESERT SHIELD (257); OPERATION DESERT STORM (258).

Significance

The use of a river, important to two or more riparian states, is normally settled to the mutual convenience of the parties. In the case of the Shatt al-Arab, other factors, including superpower rivalry, petroleum, and political instability, have made resolution of the problem almost impossible. The issue of political sovereignty over the land of the Persian Gulf littoral is connected to the question of control and use of the waterway leading into and out of the gulf. Moreover, Iran and Iraq have been led by ambitious personalities who have retained power through violence. Their survival as political leaders is often an extension of their capacity to project authority beyond their frontiers. The Shatt al-Arab remains clouded by political controversy.

Sinai Peninsula 26

The Sinai Peninsula is composed of desert and barren mountains. It is located at the north end of the Red Sea and to the extreme northeast of the African continent. It is separated form Africa by the Gulf of Suez, an arm of the Red Sea, and by the Suez Canal. The peninsula is also separated from Saudi Arabia by the Gulf of Aqaba. To the north, the Sinai fronts on the Mediterranean Sea for approximately 140 miles (225 kilometers). The Sinai Mountains range up to 8,550 feet (2,600 meters) above sea level, and the most prominent among them is Jebel Musa, the Mountain of Moses (the biblical Sinai peak where, according to the Old Testament, Moses received the Ten Commandments). Ancient Egyptian and old Christian sites are also located in the Sinai. The Sinai Peninsula has been a principal theater of warfare between modern Egypt and Israel. The mountain passes have been the locations for celebrated armor battles in the 1956, 1967, and 1973 wars between the two countries. In 1967, Israel occupied the entire Sinai Peninsula and constructed settlements and military installations at strategic points. Sinai oilfields also came under Israeli control. The Egyptian-Israeli Peace Treaty in 1979 signalled an end to Israeli occupation, and a phased withdrawal began that was completed in April 1982. All Israeli settlements were removed, and military installations were abandoned. An international peace-monitoring force organized by the United States and some western European countries was called upon to take up positions in various sectors of the peninsula. The Israelis and Egyptians agreed to maintain only defensive forces in the immediate region, and both governments emphasized their determination to maintain the tranquility of the area. ***See also*** SINAI SUPPORT MISSION (224).

Significance
The Sinai is the principal gateway to Israel from Egypt and vice versa. The decision to partially demilitarize the Sinai symbolized Cairo's intention to maintain peaceful relations with Israel. It also separates the Egyptian forces form the armies of the other Arab states. As the most populous Arab state, Egypt was judged the most important in the struggle against Israel. Without Egyptian manpower and cooperation, the Arab states are in a poor position to challenge Israel. Egypt's geopolitical position between Israel and the rejectionist states of Libya and Algeria reduces the capacity of the latter to directly assist their brethren in Syria, Jordan, and Iraq. The Sinai agreement also permits Israel to concentrate its forces on the Lebanese, Syrian, and Jordanian frontiers. Moreover, the stationing of U.S. forces in the Sinai places U.S. troops in closer proximity to the Persian Gulf, and although this contingent is not considered a Rapid Deployment Force by Washington, its presence in the region cannot be discounted.

Suez Canal 27

The Suez Canal is one of four in the world linking two seas in international passage. Canals like Suez are similar to straits. The oldest of these canals, Suez was opened in 1869. The

Suez Canal is of sea-level construction and does not require locks like those used at Panama. It is 101 miles (162 kilometers) long and includes two lakes, Timsah and Great Bitter Lake. The canal is wide enough to permit the passage of large vessels through its deepest channel. But it is too shallow for the massive supertankers that carry much of the petroleum from the Persian Gulf to Europe and the Western Hemisphere. For those ships using the canal, the distance between European ports and India has been reduced by approximately 5,000 miles (8,000 kilometers). The Suez Canal was constructed by the Suez Canal Company, which was originally organized with French financing. The British obtained 44 percent of the company's shares in 1875 when Prime Minister Benjamin Disraeli purchased those allotted to the *khedive* (maximum ruler) of Egypt. At the time, Britain was already the most frequent user of the canal. In 1882 Britain invaded Egypt, and the latter remained a protectorate of the United Kingdom until after World War I. In 1888, nine states met in Constantinople and signed the Suez Canal Convention, which declared the waterway would "always be free and open, in time of war as in time of peace, to every vessel of commerce or of war, without distinction of flag." This declaration was in part necessitated by recognition that the Canal Company had a 99-year lease that would expire in 1968. Britain maintained troops in Egypt, which became a major theater of action during World War II. It was not until 1954 that Britain finally removed its forces from the canal zone. The Suez Canal Company, however, continued to function. In July 1956, the Egyptian government led by President Gamal Abdul Nasser nationalized the canal. Fearful that the 1888 Suez Canal Convention would be discarded and that they would lose their investment, Britain and France marshalled their forces and attacked Egypt, with assistance form Israel. Nasser immobilized the Suez Canal by ordering the sinking of a number of vessels in the navigable channel. When the British and French were pressured by the United States and the Soviet Union to halt their campaign against Egypt, the canal had already been crippled. It took more than a year to clear the waterway, but the Egyptians permitted all vessels except those flying the Israeli flag, or destined for Israel, to use the canal. The Israelis had reached the canal in the 1956 war but had withdrawn under UN supervision and with the expectation that their ships could use the canal. Nasser, however, argued that a state of belligerency existed between Egypt and Israel, and the host country was not obliged to permit the use of the canal to its adversary. In 1967, Nasser threatened a renewal of hostilities, but the Israelis attacked first and again swept to the eastern side of the canal. Once again the canal was blocked by sunken vessels. This time the canal remained closed as the Israelis held to their positions all along the waterway. There matters remained until Anwar el-Sadat assumed the presidency following Nasser's death. In 1973, Sadat ordered his army to cross the canal and assault the Israeli Bar-Lev defense line. Initially successful in dislodging the Israelis from their fortified positions along the canal, the Egyptians could not sustain their offensive. The Israelis counterattacked and drove across the canal into Egypt proper, surrounding the Egyptian Third Army. Under U.S. pressure, the Israelis agreed to release the Third Army, and a ceasefire was entered into by the warring parties. In the years that followed, negotiations between Egypt and Israel began in earnest through the shuttle diplomacy of U.S. Secretary of State Henry Kissinger. The two sides agreed to seriously pursue peaceful avenues and to reconcile their rival claims. These initial steps laid the groundwork for Sadat's dramatic 1977 visit to Jerusalem and eventually to Camp David in the United States, where discussions engineered by President Jimmy Carter aimed at producing a Middle East peace. The Camp David meetings finally resulted in a peace treaty between Israel and Egypt. Israel withdrew its forces from the Suez Canal and by April 1982 had returned the whole of the Sinai to Egyptian authority. Israel was permitted to use the Suez Canal and, more important, Egypt pledged no more war between their two countries. *See also* ARAB-ISRAELI WAR, 1956 (237); ARAB-ISRAELI WAR, 1967 (238); ARAB-ISRAELI WAR, 1973 (239).

Significance
The Suez Canal has been a flashpoint for international conflict as well as a cockpit of international intrigue since its opening in 1869. The canal falls totally within the jurisdiction of Egypt and is operated and maintained by the Egyptian government. The Canal Company has long been consigned to history. The canal remained closed between 1967 and 1975, and it was only when President Sadat requested the United States to help clear the canal of the obstacles strewn along its navigable channel, as well as remove the silt that had built up over the many years of nonuse, that it was again opened for business. By that time, massive seagoing tankers had been constructed to carry the Persian Gulf's petroleum around the Cape of Good Hope to Europe and the Western Hemisphere. The strategic value of the canal was reduced in the eyes of some observers, but it remains an important artery in international commerce. Modern weapons, however, have made the canal more vulnerable, and in time of war it is doubtful that anything significant could be done to protect it against closure. Furthermore, the canal is not a defensive barrier against a determined foe. The Israeli crossing of the canal, like the Egyptian crossing earlier, proved it to be a feeble line of defense. In military terms, the canal was of minor importance. Anwar el-Sadat understood this and thus insisted on transforming the region into one of peaceful economic development. The real value of the canal lay in its capacity to provide Egypt with a major source of revenue needed for raising the country's standard of living. In addition to reopening the canal, Egyptians turned to the task of rebuilding the cities along its bank that had been destroyed in previous conflicts.

Tigris-Euphrates Rivers 28

Both the Tigris and Euphrates rise in Turkey and flow through Syria and Iraq to the Persian Gulf by way of the Shatt al-Arab. The Tigris forms the extreme northwest border between Turkey and Syria. It also passes through the principal Iraqi cities of Mosul, Tikrit, and Baghdad. Measuring 1,150 miles (1,850 kilometers) long, the Tigris unites with the Euphrates to form the Shatt al-Arab. The main segment of the region in Iraq between the Tigris and Euphrates was known in antiquity as Mesopotamia, the land between the two rivers, and was the location for the biblical civilization of Assyria, Babylonia, and Sumer. The banks of the Tigris were noted for the ancient cities of Nineveh, Seleucia, and Ctesiphon. The Euphrates is approximately 1,700 miles (2,700 kilometers) long and after moving through Syria follows a course roughly parallel with the Tigris through Iraq. The Euphrates was perhaps more important to the early civilizations in Mesopotamia because the irrigation projects there largely drew their water from that source. Centuries of neglect, however, have reduced the fertility of the region, and much of the land along its course is either barren waste or dense marshland unsuited for agriculture. *See also* OPERATION DESERT STORM (258).

Significance
Although not as critical to Syria and Iraq as the Nile is to Egypt, the Tigris-Euphrates river system is nonetheless an important complex of waterways vital to agriculture and hence crucial to the well-being of the people in these two countries. Ancient civilizations drew their sustenance from these waters and great edifices of antiquity developed because of this system. Syria and Iraq are equally eager to reharness the Tigris-Euphrates system, to reclaim the neglected and abused land, and to provide opportunity as well as nourishment for their expanding populations. Joint development of the river system is imperative, and efforts, or at least gestures, have been made toward cooperation. On balance, however, the two countries have gone their separate ways; Syria's development schemes, which aim to divert the flow of water and to limit its passage through Iraq, have intensified the rivalry between them. A principal dispute between the two governments focuses on the use of the waterways and their inability to find a formula acceptable to both. The use of the waters of the Tigris-Euphrates also involves Turkey, where the headwaters are controlled and where large hydroelectric and irrigation schemes threaten the downstream riparians. As Iraq quarrels with Syria, so Syria is locked in a dispute with Turkey over the equitable sharing of the water. During the U.S.-led coalition's campaign against Iraq in January–February 1991, almost all the bridges over the Euphrates and Tigris in Iraq were destroyed. In Operation Desert Storm, coalition forces struck deep into southern Iraq and cut the Euphrates River, thus denying Baghdad's ability to service its forces in Kuwait and compelling the Iraqis to accept the terms of peace laid down in the UN resolutions.

Tiran Strait 29

The Strait of Tiran is the narrow waterway connecting the Red Sea with the Gulf of Aqaba. It is between 12 and 20 miles (19–32 kilometers) in width and touches the southern tip of the Sinai Peninsula on the one side and the far northwestern tip of Saudi Arabia on the other. Dominating the Tiran Strait is the Sinai fortress at Sharm al-Shaykh. To the west of Sharm al-Shaykh is the Gubal Strait, which connects the Gulf of Suez with the Red Sea. The Gubal Strait is vital to ships using the Suez Canal, and the Tiran Strait is vital to those using either the Israeli port of Eilat or the Jordanian port of Aqaba. *See also* AQABA, GULF OF (3).

Significance
The Tiran Strait is an important geopolitical chokepoint. Although belonging to the territorial waters of Egypt and Saudi Arabia, it is part of the larger international waterway that connects the Suez Canal with the Red Sea and the Indian Ocean. Israel has fought tenaciously to keep the Tiran Strait open to their shipping, and in 1956 and 1967 it occupied Sharm al-Shaykh to guarantee use of the Gulf of Aqaba. The Egyptian-Israeli Peace Treaty of 1979 spells out the importance of the Tiran Strait to maritime nations, and its use by Israeli vessels is assured.

Turkish Straits 30

A complex extension of waterways between the Black Sea and the Mediterranean Sea. The complex involves the Bosporus Strait leading out from the Black Sea and the Dardanelles

Strait leading in from the Mediterranean. Between the two straits and connecting them is a small intervening sea, the Sea of Marmara. The Turkish Straits are quite narrow. The Dardanelles are 41 miles (63 kilometers) long and only 1 to 4 miles (1.6–6.2 kilometers) wide. The Bosporus is less than 19 miles (30 kilometers) long, and its width varies from approximately 0.3 to 2 miles (0.5–3.2 kilometers). The entire waterway lies within Turkish territorial limits. Nevertheless, because it connects the Black and Mediterranean seas, it is of substantial importance to the Black Sea states and other maritime nations. When the Turks conquered Constantinople in 1453 and destroyed the last remnant of the Byzantine Empire, they gained possession of both sides of the waterway. From that date, and for the next three centuries, only Turkish ships or those sailing in the service of the Ottomans were permitted to use the straits. In 1774, however, the Ottomans were compelled to sign the Treaty of Kutchuk Kainarji with Imperial Russia. The czar's forces had regained control of the north shore of the Black Sea, and with the 1774 treaty Russia also obtained the right to sail through the straits to the Mediterranean. The Ottomans, however, still limited the shipping passing through their territory, and their armed fortresses along the straits made it impossible to ignore Turkish regulations. The growth of European influence coincided with the decline of Ottoman power, and by 1880 the Turks were encouraged to extend navigation rights through the straits to the more prominent commercial powers, notably the British and French. Later in the nineteenth century, all trading nations were granted similar rights of passage. Warships, however, were still not permitted to use the straits. Moreover, in 1841, Britain pressed for and obtained a treaty that specified that no state could use the waterway for noncommercial purposes. This arrangement extended up to the outbreak of World War I, when the Ottoman Empire joined Germany and Austria against Russia, Britain, and France. The British attempted to seize the straits by force and assaulted the Dardanelles at Gallipoli. The British intention was to move supplies to their Russian allies by way of the straits, but their 1915 Gallipoli campaign proved to be a tragic disaster and they were forced to withdraw. In a secret treaty entered into by Britain, France, and Russia, Russia was to gain control of the straits on the termination of the war, but this arrangement was nullified when the czarist system was overthrown and the Bolsheviks seized control in 1917. The defeat of the Ottomans in World War I forced them to accept the terms of the Treaty of Sèvres in 1920, which further opened the waterway to international shipping. That treaty was later modified in the Treaty of Lausanne of 1923. By this time, the Ottoman Empire had been replaced by the Republic of Turkey, and the new Turkish government accepted an international agreement that described the straits as an international waterway open to both merchant and naval vessels. Turkey's continuing sovereignty over the straits was also recognized and the right to maintain fortifications similarly acknowledged. In 1936, the Montreux Convention legalized the arrangements.

Significance

The Turkish Straits remain one of the many significant chokepoints in the extended Middle East. Czarist Russia and its successor, the Soviet Union, both sought outright control, or at least joint administration, of the waterway. The Turks as well as the Europeans thwarted Russian/Soviet plans prior to World War II, and the United States assisted Ankara in denying Moscow this objective during the period of the Cold War. The Truman Doctrine of 1947, in major part, was declared to dramatize U.S. determination to protect Turkey's territorial integrity. Turkey's inclusion in the North Atlantic Treaty Organization in 1952 was further evidence of this resolve. In the 1970s the Soviet Union built a huge fleet, and, like the United States, maintained surface vessels and submarines in the Mediterranean Sea and Indian Ocean, as well as on other great bodies of water throughout the world. The Turkish Straits were thus supremely important to the Soviet Union, given its limited port facilities. Any effort on the part of the Turks and/or their Western allies to seal off the straits would have been considered an immediate threat to the Soviet Union's security. With the passing of the Soviet Union, the straits nevertheless are destined to continue as a vital geopolitical focal point as well as an internationally important commercial water passage.

Wakhan Corridor (31)

The Wakhan Corridor is a thin finger of Afghan territory that separated the former Soviet Union from India and Pakistan in the Pamir region of central Asia. It is approximately 150 miles (240 kilometers) long and 50 miles (80 kilometers) wide. At the far eastern extreme of the Wakhan Corridor, Afghanistan shares a 40-mile border with China. To the north is the Tadjik republic and to the south the northernmost extension of the Indian-Pakistani subcontinent. Given its mountainous terrain, there are few inhabitants in the Wakhan region. The corridor was demarcated for Afghanistan by Britain and Russia in the nineteenth century, the latter intent on pressing its influence south toward India and the former determined to thwart such ambition. This competition between Russia and Britain, known as the Great Game, led the British to draw the frontier between their Indian colony and Afghanistan in 1893. The Wakhan was part of this larger program of boundary delineation. As early as 1873 the Russians and British had agreed that the Wakhan territory from Badakshan to the Pamirs would remain part of Afghanistan, thus physically separating the two empires. This understanding was affirmed in 1887, but Russia continued to send expeditions into the area. In 1891 one such exploratory mission attempted to claim the Wakhan Corridor for the czar. The British were duly provoked, and after Britain indicated its concern, the Russians agreed to participate in a joint boundary commission. The Pamir Convention of 1895–1896 settled the question, and the Wakhan remained under Afghan sovereignty until the Soviet invasion of December 1979. *See also* DURAND LINE (8); AMU DARYA (2).

Significance

The Wakhan Corridor is a geopolitical contrivance. Rivalry between the Russians and British placed this area under Afghan sovereignty. China refused to accept the delimitation, arguing that the Russians and British were pressing their expansion at the expense of the local inhabitants as well as itself. It was not until 1963 that China officially recognized Afghanistan's control over the Wakhan Corridor. The Soviet thrust into Afghanistan in 1979 and the apparent intention to annex the Wakhan territory effectively sealed off the only border between Afghanistan and China. Moreover, control of the Wakhan provided the Soviet Union with a common border with Kashmir. It also presented Pakistan with a new neighbor in its sensitive northwest frontier region. For the Soviet Union, dominance of the Wakhan provided total control of the Pamir mountain range, a significant defense line for the security-conscious state. Although the Soviet Union withdrew its troops from Afghanistan in 1989, and self-destructed in 1991, the fate of the Wakhan Corridor remains to be decided.

Warm-Water Port Policy 32

The Warm-Water Port Policy is attributed to the Soviet Union. Before the Bolshevik Revolution of 1917, Imperial Russia expanded its empire in the direction of the Indian Ocean, as well as toward the Pacific. In the nineteenth century, the Russians invaded central Asia, destroying established Muslim kingdoms and absorbing the region. The Bolsheviks who brought an end to the czarist system, however, had no serious intention of releasing the nationalities from Russian control. With the formal emergence of the Soviet Union in 1924, the marginal territories on the southern periphery of the Russian state were again forcibly brought within the Russian/Soviet fold. The Soviets, like the Russian imperial forces earlier, paused at the Iranian frontier on the one side and Afghanistan and British India on the other. The position of British power in India, and Great Britain's interest in Iran and the Persian Gulf area, perpetuated that border and prevented the Soviets from pressing toward the open sea. During World War I, the British-French Sykes-Picot Treaty of 1916 divided the Ottoman territories in the Arab world between the two countries. In return for Russian services Moscow had been promised control over the Turkish Straits, but the Bolshevik Revolution cancelled that understanding. The Soviets, however, did not give up their quest for total control over the Black Sea and dominance of the Turkish Straits, and for an outlet to the Indian Ocean. Prior to World War II, Hitler, through Foreign Minister Joachim von Ribbentrop, and Joseph Stalin, through Foreign Minister Vyacheslav Molotov, entered into the Nazi-Soviet Pact. The Germans encouraged the Soviets to press their southward expansion in the direction of the Indian Ocean, which they described as Russia's "natural tendency." The Soviets displayed keen interest in the "the area south of Batum and Baku in the general direction of the Persian Gulf," but they were also insistent on being compensated in Poland, the Balkans, Finland, and the Turkish Straits. In the aftermath of World War II, Britain retreated from India and no longer pressed its Forward Policy against Soviet encroachment in Afghanistan. Neither India, the major power in the area, nor the United States, which sought to contain the Soviet Union, were in a position to assume the role vacated by the British. Shortly after the war, the Soviet Union attempted to establish two socialist republics in northwestern Iran and in proximity to the Persian Gulf. The Soviets also applied pressure on Turkey to share control of the straits with Moscow. Because of this, as well as Soviet assistance for the Greek communists in their struggle against the Athens monarchy, President Harry Truman announced a "containment policy," known as the Truman Doctrine. The Soviets were frustrated in Greece and Turkey and compelled to evacuate Iran, and they did not again press their expansion toward the Indian Ocean until December 1979. In the wake of the collapse of the shah's political system in Iran and the widespread anti-Americanism of both the Iranians and the Pakistanis (the U.S. embassy in Islamabad was burned by Pakistani students shortly after another U.S. embassy and its personnel were seized in Tehran), the Soviets invaded Afghanistan and moved their forces within a few hundred miles of the Persian Gulf and the Indian Ocean. *See also* TURKISH STRAITS

(30); AMU DARYA (2); TRUMAN DOCTRINE (229).

Significance
The Soviet Union's interest in warm-water ports was strong because of the landlocked nature of the Soviet state. Although it was spread over one-sixth the land surface of the globe, the Soviet Union did not have adequate access to the seas. As a superpower with major political, military, economic, and ideological interests and commitments across the planet, the Soviet Union's great-power status appeared to demand ready access to the open seas. Moreover, Soviet defenses were to be enhanced by control of Indian Ocean ports. Offensively, the nation would be in a more advantageous position from which to utilize its vast naval arm. Interdicting western supply lines, and denying the industrialized states access to vital raw materials, would have also provided Moscow with considerable leverage in the ever-present international power game. Dominance in the Persian Gulf was expected to bring Iran within the Soviet sphere of influence. Although some scholars argued that the Soviet Union was not seriously concerned with a warm-water port strategy, the Kremlin's invasion of Afghanistan, its efforts to identify with the Iranian Revolution, and its treaties with Iraq, Syria, and the then People's Democratic Republic of Yemen, as well as continuing friendship and support for Libya and India, suggested the Soviets were not averse to positioning their forces on the Indian Ocean permanently. These apprehensions, however, dissipated in the wake of the Mikhail Gorbachev reforms. Internal crises demanded a shift in Soviet foreign policy in the late 1980s. New understandings with the United States, the relinquishing of influence over Central Europe, and the collapse of the communist governments there directed Soviet policy along more accommodative lines. Moscow's support for the UN Security Council resolutions against Iraq's conquest of Kuwait in August 1990 was a singular case in point. Iraq, a long-time client state and major recipient of Soviet military assistance, was abandoned at a most critical moment. Although the Soviets attempted to save Baghdad from greater damage, Moscow seemed more inclined to pursue its policies of normalization with the United States and neighboring states, such as Turkey and Iran. Moreover, given Soviet troop withdrawal from Afghanistan, the fear that existed in the late 1970s and early 1980s of a Soviet drive to the warm sea no longer seemed relevant. The revolutionary changes accelerated by the failed coup against Gorbachev on August 19, 1991, appeared to put an end to an historic chapter of Soviet/Tsarist expansion. Indeeed, it brought an end to the Soviet Union itself.

Zagros and Alburz Mountains 33

The Zagros Mountains enter Iran from Asia Minor (Turkey) and follow a northwest-southeast axis through the center of Iran. The southern face of the mountain chain overlooks the Tigris-Euphrates basin. The Zagros link with the Alburz Mountains in the north to form the Iranian Plateau, which averages between 4,000 and 6,000 feet (1,200–1,800 meters) above sea level. The rivers Karun and Kharkheh flow off the Zagros into the Persian Gulf along with a number of smaller streams. The others drain into a depression formed by the mountain chain, creating the great desert wastelands of the Kavir and the Dasht-i-Lut. The very dry atmosphere on the Iranian Plateau evaporates the slow-moving streams and rivers, and they all but disappear as they reach the extensive salt-deserts. Central Iran, therefore, is a vast arid region that covers approximately two-thirds of the country. The Zagros Mountains prevent moisture from the Persian Gulf from passing into Iran. Only Khuzistan on the gulf littoral is an exception. The Alburz Mountains, along with the Azerbaijan Highlands, create a barrier against rain from the Black Sea. Iran's coastal Caspian provinces of Gilan and Mazanderan, however, on the northern side of the Alburz, receive enormous amounts of rainfall. Coupled with the Afghan Highlands and the deserts of Baluchistan in the east and southeast, which deny Iran the monsoon rains that annually drench India and, to some extent, Pakistan, central Iran is largely a dry, harsh, inhospitable land.

Significance

Apart from the large reserves of petroleum beneath its soil, Iran is a resource-poor country. The absence of sufficient water has forced its inhabitants to contrive methods for artificially irrigating the parched land. The Persian wheel is one ancient device whereby groundwater is drawn from subterranean wells and spilled over the land. Another is the Persian *qanat*, a water channel that is dug and provided with adequate cover to prevent the heat from evaporating its contents before the water reaches the cultivated area. The collapse of a tunnel or the silting of the system is a major dilemma, and constant maintenance is required if the *qanat* is to work successfully. Landlordism in Iran historically is connected to the construction and maintenance of irrigation systems. The mountain chains that give Iran its essentially dry climate have not protected the country from foreign invasion. Mongols descended upon Iran from central Asia, the Ottomans penetrated the country through Azerbaijan, and the Russians have pressed down from the Caspian. The British came to Iran by sea. Nevertheless, Iran maintained its identity through the great age of imperialism and, although heavily influenced by external parties, has perpetuated its own culture and lifestyle.

Islam

2

Caliphate

34

The caliphate, or successorship to the Prophet Mohammad, originated at the time of the Prophet's death. Arab tribal traditions demanded a dominant leader, but the Prophet had not identified his successor; leadership devolved upon his father-in-law, Abu Bakr. Abu Bakr, Umar, Uthman, and Ali are called the first four caliphs, the protectors of the Muslim *umma* (community) and the viceregent of God (Allah) on earth. They are known together as the Rashidun, the pious caliphs. Although Shiite Islam develops from the role played by Ali, the Prophet's son-in-law (Mohammad had no sons and only one surviving daughter, Fatima), those caliphs that succeeded Ali are judged not to have been as virtuous. Indeed, later caliphs are identified by dynasty rather than by their advocacy of faith. The Ummayyad dynasty (661–750 A.D.) was the first of these. Purely Arab, it succumbed to the Abbasids, a Persianized dynasty (750–1258 A.D.), which was finally destroyed by invading Mongol armies led by a son of Genghis Khan. After a period of eclipse, the caliphate came to rest in Egypt with the Fatimids, where it was wrested from their control by the Ottoman Turks in 1517. The sultan of the Ottoman Empire, reigning from Constantinople (Istanbul), also held court as the caliph of Islam until the institution was abolished in 1924 by Mustafa Kemal Ataturk, the Turkish nationalist who also terminated the Ottoman Empire and raised the new republic of Turkey in its place. Although the actions abolishing the caliphate were questioned by the larger Muslim world as well as in Turkey, it was not revived. The sherif of Mecca, the Hashemite patriarch and protector of the holy places in Mecca and Medina, did lay claim to the title "caliph of Islam" on March 3, 1924, but his declaration was recognized only by the Hashemite dynasties in Iraq and Transjordan, dominated by his sons, and in the Hejaz region of the Arabian Peninsula, where Mecca and Medina are located. The sherif of Mecca gave up his claim to the caliphate when the Saudis attacked his forces and conquered the Hejaz region. The defeat of the sherif gave the Saudis dominance over most of the Arabian Peninsula, and the creation of Saudi Arabia as an independent, sovereign state followed. In May 1926, a Caliphate Congress held in Cairo was attended by delegates from 13 Muslim countries; Turkey was not present. Discussion focused on the need to revive the Islamic institution in order to promote Muslim unity. This theme was especially important to the Muslims of India, who saw their political as well as religious and socioeconomic salvation in the melding of the many Muslim communities. The congress broke up, however, without coming to a unified position. Concern about the caliphate has seldom surfaced since that date. In 1973–1974, it was beginning to emerge as an issue, given the power demonstrated by some of the oil-rich Muslim states declaring an oil embargo. King Faisal of Saudi Arabia was closely identified with that embargo, and, as the largest exporter of petroleum, Saudi Arabia played a key role. No Saudi had ever laid claim to the caliphate, but rumors circulated that Faisal was a suitable candidate for the office and that the Muslim world might consider the keeper of the holy places and the ruler of the world's richest Muslim country as the new caliph of Islam. Faisal's assassination in 1975 ended such speculation. It also put the idea of restoring the caliphate into the background.

Significance
The center of the Muslim world is historically identified with the caliphate. The solidarity and purpose of the Muslim *umma,* or community, can only be achieved when there is obedience to a central command. Islam is a universal religion. National political divisions are judged a threat to Muslim unity, and hence they are considered alien contrivances aimed at keeping the Muslims subdued. Orthodox Sunni Islam, however, does not sanction a church hierarchy, and individual Muslims are free to worship without the presence of clerical authority. The caliph, although capable of issuing *fatwas* (religious decrees), would be a temporal figure, not a theologian. The creation of a present-day caliph of Islam, therefore, may require important changes in political structure and national policy. Indeed, the sovereignty of individual governments and of the variety of political systems in the Islamic world would be threatened. An aspect of this concern is illustrated by fears that the theologians who rule revolutionary Iran are intent on spreading their version of the Islamic state to all corners of the Muslim world. This all-embracing Islamic design frightens conventional rulers not only because it is Shiite-inspired, but also because it aims to replace their rule with something quite different. In these circumstances, any attempt to do more than establish a symbolic caliphate would raise a storm of controversy that would weaken rather than strengthen the cause of Muslim unity.

Dar al-Islam 35

Literally the term means "territory or house of Islam." Dar al-Islam represents the Muslim conquest in the first century of the Islamic era, with Muslims pitted against non-Muslims in a ceaseless struggle. On the opposite side from the Dar al-Islam is the Dar al-Harb, or the territory of war. Muslims are required, by the tenets of their faith, to struggle against the Dar al-Harb, to subdue and transform it into the Dar al-Islam. Related to the matter of the Dar al-Harb is the Muslim concept of *jihad,* or holy war. The *jihad* is judged to be the instrument whereby the enemy becomes a "believer," or perishes. At the very least, the conquered must recognize the One God, even if they do not adopt

Islam. The *jihad* therefore imposes a permanent obligation on Muslims to press on until the Dar al-Harb has been liquidated. Communities residing within the Dar al-Islam but that opt to remain non-Muslim are tolerated so long as they submit to Muslim authority. They become *dhimmis,* protected minorities, permitted to worship according to their customs, provided they are monotheistic, but subservient to the Muslim fountainhead. Non-Muslims thus become clients of the Muslim state, the Dar al-Islam. It is important to note that the Dar al-Islam did not emphasize constant fighting with the Dar al-Harb. It reiterated a permanent state of war, a degree of readiness, and a Muslim awareness of obligation to his faith. Thus, when Muslim power reached its outer limits and resistance became substantial, the Muslim community was encouraged to find peaceful settlements. The obligation of *jihad* remained, but in a dormant state, to be revived only in declared emergencies. The condition prevailing between the Dar al-Islam and the Dar al-Harb is known as the Dar al-Sulh, or territory of peace. The leader of the Muslim community, the imam or caliph, could call upon believers to renew the struggle should the occasion warrant and the opportunity present itself. Sunni and Shiite perceptions of the conflict between the Dar al-Islam and the Dar al-Harb differ in that the Sunnis accept the *jihad* as providing direct access to heaven. Shiites, however, believe *jihad* and allegiance to the imam are intertwined. Salvation is possible only when the imam declares a *jihad;* holy war therefore is a primary function of the imamate in Shiite Islam. The imam is the infallible ruler for all Shiites. Only he knows when it is proper to make war, necessary to establish peace, important to obtain external support, from non-Muslims if necessary, and to avoid great risks. ***See also*** JIHAD (41); SHIITE ISLAM (57); SUNNI ISLAM (60); IMAMATE (37).

Significance
The original doctrine of the Dar al-Islam is judged a relic of religious history. Nevertheless, it is important to understand that Muslims are intimately familiar with the origins of their faith. Religious performance remains much as it was centuries ago. Social practices related to religious obligations and principles have also undergone limited change despite the penetration of the Islamic world by non-Muslims. Alien institutions and ideas have not been digested, nor have they always adapted to the Islamic environment. The turbulence that characterizes the Muslim Middle East can, in major part, be attributed to the breakdown or failure of alien borrowings. It has also caused a Muslim reawakening, which, narrowly defined, reasserts the special preserve that is the Dar al-Islam. The Arab-Israeli conflict, although it may not be articulated as a clash between the Dar al-Islam and the Dar al-Harb, is representative of the modernity of this classic construct. The refusal to recognize the existence of the state of Israel by the vast majority of Muslim states predates the call for a Palestine national home. Israel, for Muslims, is an alien body, a contaminant in the world of Islam. Believers are therefore obliged to struggle against this "impure" community. On the other hand, Muslims will argue that Jews residing in the Islamic world as *dhimmis* will be tolerated and are free to pursue their tradition, assured that Muslim authority protects their status. Interestingly, *jihads* have been called against Israel by numerous Sunni Muslim officials, but they cannot demand obligatory action. Nor are they in a position to punish for noncompliance. The Shiite call to *jihad,* however, raised by an identifiable imam, or *mujtahid* intermediary, may have different results. Reference

can be made to the Ayatollah Khomeini, the recognized imam of the Persian Shiites. The ayatollah's call to the faithful to make holy war on the Iraqis, and particularly on the Baathist regime of Saddam Hussain, met with an enthusiastic response. Revolutionary guards, absolutely committed to the idea of war in the name of faith, have given Persian or Iranian martyrdom modern expression. Not satisfied with forcing the Iraqis from Iranian territory, the ayatollah ordered his faithful to cross the Iraqi frontier and to strike at the "nonbelievers" in their native habitat. The call to sacrifice was presented in expansive terms. Shiite Muslims, and Muslims generally, were called upon to join with the Persian forces in a great campaign to cleanse the Dar al-Islam. According to Khomeini's dictum, the destruction of the Iraqi regime was to be prelude to the reconquest of Jerusalem and the assault on Israeli Zionism. It was therefore incumbent on Muslims to accept *jihad* as a key purpose of their religious expression. The ayatollah was provided with numerous occasions to terminate hostilities with the Iraqis. All overtures were turned aside. Political caution was compromised by absolute belief. Shortly before his death the Ayatollah Khomeini, weakened by illness and pressured by his associates, seemed to acknowledge the forces arrayed against him in his struggle with Baghdad. He publicly admitted to "taking poison" in agreeing to a ceasefire with his enemy, and a temporary Dar al-Sulh was arranged in the summer of 1988.

Faqih 36

The *wali faqih* (ruling theologian) is the foremost religious authority in Iran. He serves as both judge and leader of the Shiite community. The *faqih* provides guidance and leadership by issuing legal edicts, adjudicating Islamic law, and generally protecting Islamic institutions. Political legitimacy, like legal legitimacy, resides with the *faqih,* and his capacity to intervene in state affairs is unlimited. ***See also*** MUJTAHID (45).

Significance

The Ayatollah Khomeini assumed the role as Iran's supreme *faqih,* or law dispenser, following the destruction of the Pahlavi dynasty and his own attempt to establish Iran as an Islamic state. The *faqih* is the sole person capable of interpreting the law in Iran, and therefore all power resides within his person. Khomeini's book the *Wilayat-e-Faqih* (*Rule of the Theologian*) sought to establish the legitimacy of the office.

Imamate 37

According to Shiite Islam, a dozen infallible males served as the legitimate rulers of the Muslim community following the death of the Prophet Mohammad. Shiites maintain that Ali, the son-in-law of the Prophet, was the first true imam. Shiites therefore insist that subsequent imams derive from the house of Ali. More than a millennium ago, Mohammad ibn Hasan Al-Askari, the Twelfth Imam, thwarted plans to assassinate him by going into hiding. He was five years old at the time. Four successive agents served the Shiite community in the absence of the Twelfth Imam. Afterward, no other agents were appointed to safeguard the "hidden" imam's interests. The disappearance of the Twelfth Imam marked the end of the imamate, but it did not terminate or eliminate the imam's power. Furthermore, wherever Shiite "divines" established their authority, as in Yemen or Oman, the ruler was always referred to as the imam and his kingdom as the imamate. This extension of the use of the term did not challenge belief in the historic imamate, nor did it subject its adopters to particular criticism. Indeed, the imamate must be observed in its original configuration, which is considered sacrosanct by all devout Shiites, and in its more pragmatic metamorphosis in different historical periods. In the latter, it is interesting to note that both Ayatollah Khomeini, who was a recognized Shiite divine, and King Hassan II of Morocco, who is not a Shiite, have been addressed by the term *imam*. ***See also*** SHIITE ISLAM (57).

Significance
Shiites believe the Imam Mahdi still lives and that he is the only one with the divine right to exercise legitimate power. All other leaders who try to substitute for the Twelfth Imam are perceived as usurpers. In the absence of the Twelfth Imam, however, the Shiite clerics, or *mullahs,* those learned in holy scripture, have claimed the right to act as guides and authorities on the divine law. Despite this claim, the *mullahs* were largely unsuccessful before 1979 in asserting their right to dominate political life in Iran. Because the potential power of the *mullahs* could not be ignored, given continuing adherence to the concept of the imamate by the Shiite population, secular dynasties often made alliances with the *mullahs* or repressed them.

Islam (38)

The word *Islam* is derived from the Arabic root *salima,* which can be interpreted as meaning peace, submission, and obedience. In religious usage Islam means submission to the will of God and obedience to His law. Muslims, believers in Islam, adhere to the understanding that only by submitting to the will of God and by obeying God's law can one achieve true peace and enjoy lasting purity now and in the hereafter. ***See also*** MUSLIM (46).

Significance
Non-Muslims have often referred to Islam as *Mohammadanism*. Muslims both reject and protest such description of their faith. Mohammad is revered as a prophet of God, one of many to whom God revealed himself. Nevertheless, Mohammad is accepted as a mortal human being. He is not worshipped, nor did he create the Islamic religion. Mohammad was commissioned by God to bring His word to the world. He is best viewed as a model of piety and perfection and the leader of the Muslim community (*umma*). The original founder of Islam, however, is God himself. The Islamic religion spread from the Arabian Peninsula in the seventh century A.D., and today its devotees extend around the globe, totaling approximately 900 million.

Islamic Fundamentalism (39)

Throughout the history of the Islamic people emphasis has been given to preserving the Muslim way of life in the face of significant internal and external challenges. Although other religions are similarly motivated, Islamic fundamentalism assumed a specific character when European imperialism established its hold over the Middle East, North Africa, and South and Southeast Asia. Islamic fundamentalism in major part was a reaction to Western intrusions in the Muslim world. Religious movements like the Salafiah movement in Egypt and especially Jamaluddin al-Afghani's Pan-Islamic movement, which cut across ethnic and tribal affiliations, stressed new Muslim vigor as well as an adaptation to modern expression. As with the Aligarh movement in British India, Muslims sought to revitalize Islam, but they also emphasized a selective adaptation to Western political ideas and technical innovations. Movements such as Wahhabism in the Arabian

Peninsula (later dominant in Saudi Arabia), Mahdism in the Sudan, and Sanusism in Libya were more conservative, austere, and localized. Sanusism insisted on a more pristine Islam. More recently, the fundamentalism of the Ayatollah Khomeini in Iran and the Muslim Brotherhood in several Arab countries, particularly Egypt, Syria, and Jordan, have expressed themselves in violent outbursts against all alien borrowings. Current Muslim fundamentalists are first and foremost concerned with the future of Islam in a world heavily influenced by secular thought and behavior. As absolute devotees to the teachings of the Qur'an, they dare not compromise their religious principles. Firm in the belief that the Qur'an contains the only acceptable message, Muslim fundamentalists judge all other views and expressions as corruptions. Moreover, they are convinced that society as well as Islam is in mortal jeopardy. Licentious behavior, social injustice, and moral and ethical decay are perceived as the inevitable consequences of alien borrowings. Muslim fundamentalists are therefore prepared to use extreme methods to "save" their faith and society. ***See also*** SHIITE ISLAM (57); MAHDI (43); SHIITE MARTYRDOM (58); HIZBOLLAH (130); HAMA MASSACRE (245).

Significance

Islamic fundamentalism reflects weakness and political division in the Islamic world. Blame for the instability of Muslim governments, for the deep social malaise gripping the Muslim world, and for the continuing heavy influence of outside parties on Muslim politicoeconomic life has been apportioned to Europeans and Americans aided and abetted by powerful indigenous authorities and ruling families. Moreover, the Palestine question has symbolic importance in that it dramatizes fundamentalist perceptions of Muslim inferiority vis-à-vis other cultural groups. Islamic fundamentalists argue that only the avoidance of foreign, and especially Western, influence will permit Muslim leaders to regain their self-respect and proper position in the larger world. Muslim leaders who continue to request support from non-Muslim powers are often judged corrupt and deviant. The fundamentalists believe it is their duty to eliminate those personalities who show great dependence on non-Muslims. They also believe that it is necessary to put into effect policies that allow Muslims to regain their dignity and self-esteem. In the Western world Muslim fundamentalism is often associated with political terrorism, and the Shiite Hizbollah (Party of God) based in Lebanon was responsible for the holding of American and European hostages. The major Sunni fundamentalist organization, the Ikhwan al-Muslimin, has often been judged a threat to established Arab governments, and the violence directed against that organization was especially pronounced in Syria in 1982, when an estimated 20,000 to 25,000 people were killed by the Syrian army in the town of Hama. ***See also*** HAMA MASSACRE (245).

Islamic State: Iran **40**

Officially proclaimed the Islamic Republic of Iran in 1979, Iran is an Islamic state. Prior to 1979, and for more than 2,000 years, Iran was a monarchy ruled by a shah, or king of kings. The last Iranian dynasty was the Pahlavi (1926–1979). Iran's constitution (1979) provides for a parliament (*majlis*). The *majlis* is an elected body, controlled by a speaker who is a leading member of the Shiite clergy. The head of government is the prime minister. The head of state is the president. Both the president and the prime minister are subordinate to the *wali faqih,* the ruling theologian (a post created by Ayatollah Khomeini). Political legitimacy resides in the *wali faqih,* and his power to intervene in state affairs is unlimited. In the absence of the *faqih,* or spiritual authority of the stature of Khomeini, the government is overseered by a council of spiritual leaders. The *wali faqih* is assisted by the Revolutionary Council, which is made up of Iran's preeminent ayatollahs, who are committed to the objectives of the Iranian Islamic revolution as described by Ayatollah Khomeini. The dominant party in Iran is the Islamic Republican Party (IRP), which controls a majority of seats in the *majlis* and is the primary political organization of the Shiite clergy. Other parties of note are the National Front (a liberal organization identified with Westernized intellectuals opposed to the former shah), the Tudeh (Masses) Party (Iran's communist organization with heavy Soviet influence), and the Kurdish Democratic Party. Political movements such as the Mujahiddin Khalq, which has opposed the *mullah*-dominated state, and the Cherik Fedeyeen al-Khalq are Marxist-type fronts—the former perhaps less secular than the latter. The Shiite clergy also oversees the SAVAMA (the secret police organization) and the *komitehs* (revolutionary committees composed of religious zealots in rural and urban communities and in the factories and universities). The *mullahs* also manage the Pasderan (Revolutionary Guard), a paramilitary organization capable of recruiting vast numbers of Iranians, including the very young (10–14) and the very old (over 65). The formal military establishment consists of approximately 300,000 to 400,000. Its leadership is determined by the Revolutionary Council and approved by the *wali faqih.* The media is surveiled by the *komitehs* and the SAVAMA, as well as by the ministries of state security and interior. Publication or broadcast of any material must be approved by the *komitehs.* Iran has enormous reserves of petroleum. Before the Iran-Iraq War (1980–1988), Iran was second only to Saudi Arabia in the export of oil. Iran, therefore, is a prominent member of the Organization of Petroleum Exporting Countries (OPEC). ***See also*** RUHANIYYAT (54); FAQIH (36); CLERICAL PRACTICES: IRAN (77); POLITICS OF SUCCESSION: IRAN (102).

Significance
The Islamic state that Iran's clergy has imposed upon the country has had the support of a broad segment of Iranian society. At the same time it has demonstrated a degree of rigidity and vindictiveness that has caused former supporters to feel betrayed. Criticism of the government, however, is severely punished, and the larger Iranian polity is silent and aloof. The more ardent followers of the *mullahs* have demonstrated their approval of the regime and its policies. The call to sacrifice, to martyrdom, has been answered by thousands of Iranians who have given themselves totally to the cause of the revolution.

Jihad 41

Holy war. Muslim jurists distinguish between the *jihad* against nonbelievers and the *jihad* against believers who have either violated precepts of the faith or renounced Islamic authority. In a number of Qur'anic injunctions, Muslims are under obligation to fight polytheists and unbelievers, or those who are judged to threaten the Islamic community and way of life.

Significance
Learned Muslim jurists disagree whether *jihad* is a pillar of the Islamic faith. It is often considered separately from the five demonstrations of faith

incumbent on all Muslims: profession of faith (*shahhada*), prayer (*sala*), almsgiving (*zaka*), fasting (*sawm*), and the pilgrimage to Mecca (*haj*). *Jihad* is sometimes referred to as the sixth pillar of Islam and is obligatory on all Muslims. Unlike the other five obligations, however, *jihad* is subject to abuse and exploitation. It is the one obligation that is political rather than personal. Throughout Islamic history *jihads* have been proclaimed by various leaders representing many separate purposes. The Ottoman sultan-caliph declared a *jihad* against the Allied armies in World War I. Muammar Qaddafi's call for a *jihad* against the Saudi dynasty in 1981 is one example of such exploitation of Islamic principle and sentiment. On the other hand, no Muslim ruler called for a *jihad* against the Soviet Union despite its invasion of Afghanistan. *Jihad* today, therefore, must be considered more symbolic than practical.

Kaaba 42

The black meteoric rock housed in the central court of the Great Mosque in Mecca. It is an ancient focal point that has since been adopted by the Islamic world. It appears to have special importance for Sunni orthodox Muslims. There is considerable evidence that Shiite Muslims view Karbala in Iraq as the center of their faith. Karbala is the city in which Hussain, the son of Ali (the Prophet Mohammad's son-in-law), was martyred, around which event Shiites have developed their distinct ritual. The Kaaba was a center for pagan rites in pre-Islamic Arabia and is known to have been a sanctuary for idol worship. Mohammad preached monotheism and the destruction of all idols. Jewish-Arab tribes in and near Mecca were influential in his teaching. Mohammad, it is said, received his initial revelations when he was 40 years old from the angel Gabriel. In calling upon his Arab brethren to adopt the unity of God and to abandon idol worship, he appeared to reject the Kaaba. Mohammad infuriated the oligarchic rulers of Mecca, who used the Kaaba to sustain their preeminence. Nevertheless, dissatisfaction with Mecca's rulers as well as with polytheism brought adherents to Mohammad's fold. The Prophet's organizing capacity, his administrative talents, and his capturing of popular sentiment made him a target for the ruling elite, and he was forced to flee to Medina in 622 A.D. The exodus from Mecca marks the beginning of the Islamic era. More successful with his teaching in Medina, Mohammad eventually returned to conquer Mecca. The Kaaba, however, because of its symbolic importance, was not totally destroyed. The idols surrounding the black stone were crushed, but the stone itself was retained. Ever since then, the end of the journey for the great migration of Muslims to Mecca from all over the world comes when the Kaaba is reached and circumnavigated by the faithful.

Significance

It is incumbent on all able Muslims to visit the Kaaba at least once in their lifetime. The symbolic center of the Islamic faith, the Kaaba each year draws millions of pilgrims who recommit themselves to the tenets and traditions of their religion. The *haj*, or pilgrimage, makes such worshippers *hajis*, a title they bear for the rest of their lives. Moreover, through the *haj*, Muslims are vicariously united each year in a demonstration of spiritual expression.

Mahdi 43

The *mahdi* in Islam is the messiah who returns on the day of judgment to dispense justice and punishment. In Shiite Islam, and among many Dervish or Sufi brotherhoods (*tariqas*),

the *mahdi* will appear after a period of long absence to combat evil and reestablish piety, justice, and righteousness. The *mahdi* is a mystical concept, sometimes made real by Muslim devotees. Such was the case with Mohammad Ahmad al-Mahdi of the Sudan in the last decades of the nineteenth century. Egypt gained control over the Sudan in 1821 and refused to withdraw until driven out by the *mahdi's* forces in 1885. Egyptian rule had been a travesty. Maladministration, corruption, slavery, and brutal occupation finally provoked a revolt that threatened to envelop the entire Egyptian army that was stationed in the country, as well as its dependents. The Sudanese rebels were fired by their absolute belief in the spiritual power of the *mahdi*. Islamic reform was the central purpose of the *mahdi's* creed, and the construction of a *mahdist* state was the ultimate objective. The total dedication of the *mahdi's* followers transformed them into a determined army, prepared to fight on, irrespective of the power arrayed against them. Martyrdom was a small price to pay for the promise of eternal reward. The British occupation of Egypt coincided with this revolt. Sensing a threat to their occupation, Lord Cromer, the British agent and consul-general in Egypt, sent General Charles Gordon to Khartoum, where he was ultimately surrounded by the *mahdi's* army and killed. A relief force sent to rescue Gordon arrived too late and finally retreated in the face of heavy opposition. The British were reluctant to send another expedition into the Sudan, and the *mahdi* established his Islamic *mahdist* state, which upon his death in 1885 was led by his successor, the *khalifa*. The *khalifa* dominated the Sudan for 13 years (1885–1898). In the meantime, Britain consolidated its hold on Egypt, reformed its administration, improved its financial position, and prompted numerous social reforms. In 1896, the order went out from Cairo to retake the Sudan. The *khalifa's* forces were no match for the British-Egyptian army that was assembled to recapture the Sudan. Nevertheless, they fought on for two years, succumbing to greater firepower in 1898 at Omdurman. The Dervish orders were violently suppressed, and the Sudan was again brought under administration from Cairo. This time, however, rule of the Sudan was by condominium; in other words, it was a joint Anglo-Egyptian affair. Lord Cromer described the condominium as a "hybrid" form of government, until then unknown in international law. Supreme military and civil administration was vested in a governor-general appointed by the *khedive* of Egypt on recommendation of the British government. Both the British and Egyptian flags flew over the country. As late as the Anglo-Egyptian Treaty of 1936, the administration of the Sudan was still managed according to the 1899 Condominium. The insistent demand by members of the United Nations in 1947 that the Sudan be permitted the right of self-determination was also ignored. Even after the Egyptian revolution of 1952, Egypt clung to control of the Sudan, but offered "home rule" in 1953. Sudan finally achieved independence in 1956, in circumstances that suggested the resurrection of a form of *mahdism*.
See also ISLAMIC FUNDAMENTALISM (39); SUFISM (59); NILE (20); PROTECTORATE (103).

Significance
Muslims are not the only religious community craving a messiah to make right their tortured lives. Nor do all Muslims display inclinations toward blind fanaticism. Nevertheless, the power generated by the *mahdi* of the Sudan illustrated the power of an individual over a total population. The lesson was not lost on future generations. When human aggregations decide that other avenues are

closed to them, sacrifice of oneself in a "noble" cause is both purposeful and blessed. An illustration of such behavior in the modern Middle East is the costly encounter between Iran and Iraq. Even the passion of the several Arab-Israeli conflicts did not release the amount of religious fervor demonstrated in the modern clash of Arabs and Persians. It is possible to discern the perpetuation of *mahdist* ideas and objectives in the Sudan. The dominant Muslim brotherhoods of the Khatmiyya and the Ansars became the nuclei for the political parties of the Sudan. Between the military regimes (1964–1969), there were two general elections and five governments in the Sudan. The Khatmiyya became the soul of a secular coalition known as the Democratic Unionists. The Ansars, however, joined the Umma Party, a coalition that represented the *mahdist* tradition of Islamic fundamentalism. The clash between these parties, essentially a continuation of Khatmiyya-Ansar rivalry, precipitated the military coup of General Jafar al-Numayri in 1969. Despite his earlier projection as a Nasserist, Numayri could not establish his legitimacy. Moreover, Muammar Qaddafi sought Numayri's demise. Qaddafi's charisma among the Ansars can in part be attributed to his austere, ascetic lifestyle. With the bitterness between the Ansars and the Khatmiyya enflamed, the issue of the Islamic state overwhelmed all other questions related to Sudan's development. On March 16, 1985, Numayri appointed General Abdul Rahman Swar al-Dahab commander-in-chief of the People's Armed Forces and defense minister. On April 6 of that year General Dahab led a coup against his ruler, deposing him and his government. It was notable that Numayri had insulted the Islamic fundamentalists by publicly denouncing the Ikhwan, or Muslim Brotherhood, and by removing several cabinet members who were associated with the organization. Many members of the Muslim Brotherhood served in the army. They were especially angered by Numayri's behavior; hence, Dahab felt compelled to remove Numayri. In May 1988 a new coalition government representing conservative Arab Muslims took power. This government was led by Prime Minister Sadiq al-Mahdi's Umma Party. It also included the National Islamic Front, led by Hassan al-Turabi, the prime minister's brother-in-law. The policies of the government emphasized Islamic fundamentalism and Muslim jurisprudence. In the course of these developments the Sudan drew closer to Qaddafi's Libya, whose forces were permitted to use the Sudan for forays into neighboring Chad. In 1990 Libya reassumed influence in Chad, in major part as a consequence of its growing intimacy with the Sudanese leadership.

Mujahiddin 44

Those who struggle in the name of Islam. The *mujahiddin* are warriors for the Islamic faith in opposition to forces that seek to threaten or destroy their religious belief. The word derives from the term *jihad* (holy war). The *mujahiddin* believe it to be the greatest honor to die in battle defending Islam from nonbelievers. The *mujahid's* reward for his sacrifice is unity with God. ***See also*** SHIITE MARTYRDOM (58); JIHAD (41); RUHANIYYAT (54); QODRAT (52)

Significance

Martyrdom is intertwined with Islamic teaching. No greater martyrdom is possible than that achieved by giving one's life in armed conflict while defending the religious order. The *mujahid* believes he is performing the highest service for God and that he need not fear the consequences. Modern-day *mujahiddin* are found throughout the Islamic world. Most celebrated today are the *mujahiddin* of Afghanistan, who, though hopelessly outclassed by the Soviet army, waged a protracted war against what they judged to be the *infidels* (unbelievers). The *mujahiddin* are less interested in the national state than they are in expressing the Muslim battle cry "*Allah hu Akbar*" (God is great). The Mujahiddin Khalq of revolutionary Iran was a political/paramilitary organization, originally the vanguard of the revolution against the shah of Iran. It was a major domestic enemy of Ayatollah Khomeini's *mullah*-dominated Islamic Republic. Iran's ruling religious leaders did not accept the religious credentials of the Mujahiddin Khalq, which they labeled Marxist and therefore atheist. The ayatollah's Revolutionary Guard, or *pasderan*, however, are supposedly endowed with spiritual powers. The *pasderan* are considered "true" *mujahiddin*. Iranian successes over the invading Iraqis in the spring of 1982 were attributed to the enormous sacrifice demonstrated by the Revolutionary Guard. Iran's heavy losses in attempting to penetrate Iraqi defenses were also borne by these *mujahiddin*. Ayatollah Khomeini always described his enemies as the enemies of Islam. Therefore, those who struggled in the name of the "imam" (Khomeini) also struggled to strengthen and spread the faith.

Mujtahid (45)

Learned teachers in Shiite Islamic law. The role of the *mujtahid* in Iran supplements that of the *faqih*, or supreme law dispenser. *Mujtahids* are permitted to offer opinions and to interpret principles of Islamic law. ***See also*** RUHANIYYAT (54).

Significance

The day-to-day operation of the Iranian Islamic state is managed by the *mujtahids* and the other ranks among the *mullahs*. The *mujtahids* assumed political responsibilities following the destruction of the monarchy, and they occupy seats in or advise members of the Iranian parliament (*majlis*).

Muslim (46)

A Muslim is one who submits to the will of God, who believes that Mohammad is God's messenger, and who accepts the legal principles and obligations of the faith. ***See also*** ISLAM (38); SUNNI ISLAM (60); SHIITE ISLAM (57); UMMA (62).

Significance

Muslims are found in every part of the world. All Muslims believe in the One God, but their practices and expression vary. The two major groups of Muslims are identified by the words *Sunni* and *Shiite*, Sunni Muslims being more numerous. Sunni Muslims and Shiite Muslims also divide into different groups, and strains exist not only between Sunni and Shiite Muslims but within each classification as well. Although Islam preaches community, and Muslims are called upon to practice unity and brotherhood, violent divisions have characterized the Muslim world from its inception to present times.

Muslim Brotherhood (47)

Identified in the Arab world as the Ikhwan al Muslimin, the Muslim Brotherhood had its origins in Egypt in 1930. Its prime mentor was Hasan al-Banna, a schoolteacher and Muslim fundamentalist who insisted on the chaste observance of Islamic doctrine. Al-Banna's doctrine touched a sensitive nerve and attracted religious devotees to his cause. By 1946 the membership of the Muslim

Brotherhood in Egypt was estimated at 2 million. It also acquired a vast treasury from its many followers and published a newspaper that was circulated throughout the Arab states. Extremism soon became a feature of the Muslim Brotherhood, especially as the central leadership was unable to prevent the growth of numerous factions and cells, each with its reputed leader and program. What began as a religious awakening soon transformed itself into a terrorist movement opposed to everything foreign, but notably those things Western and British. As a disruptive force, the Muslim Brotherhood was judged to be more political than religious. In 1947 Prime Minister Nuqrashi Pasha of Egypt registered his fear of the Muslim Brotherhood and ordered it disbanded. The Muslim Brotherhood responded by assassinating Nuqrashi. The prime minister's death resulted in counterterror, and in 1949 the supreme guide of the Muslim Brotherhood, Hasan al-Banna, was also murdered. The Egyptian government headed by King Farouk was deemed responsible for al-Banna's death, and the battle between administration forces and the Brotherhood ensued in earnest. Thousands of Brotherhood members were imprisoned, and others were executed. When Farouk was overthrown by his army in 1952, the revolutionary council under the leadership of Gamal Abdul Nasser endeavored to enlist the support of the Brotherhood. The Brotherhood at first cooperated with the new administration, but it did not alter its violent course. Nasser, like his predecessors, cracked down on the movement, and a relentless struggle commenced between the government and the fundamentalists. The Muslim Brotherhood spread to Syria, Iraq, Jordan, Saudi Arabia, and other Arab countries. When Anwar el-Sadat, Nasser's successor, went to Jerusalem, and eventually agreed to enter into a peace treaty with Israel, the Muslim Brotherhood dedicated itself to his destruction. Just before the opening of the Israeli embassy in Cairo, the Muslim Brotherhood's weekly newspaper *The Call* argued that Muslims would be submerged in anti-Islamic expression and that they would never regain their lost dignity. Sadat's assassination in 1981 was perpetrated by Muslim fundamentalists, though not members of the Muslim Brotherhood. Another modern Arab leader who has felt the pressure of the Brotherhood is Hafez al-Assad of Syria. In 1980, the Syrian government made membership in the Muslim Brotherhood a capital offense. Damascus blamed Jordan for its difficulties with the Brotherhood, and in 1979–1980 Syria threatened to invade Jordan because of its alleged support for Syrian terrorists. In 1982 a major battle was fought in and near Hama between forces of the Syrian army and several thousand allegedly Muslim Brotherhood dissidents. As many as 20,000 were reported killed in that encounter, but no accurate tally was possible. Later that year Syria broke relations with Iraq because the latter, too, was accused of supporting the Brotherhood in its campaign against Damascus. ***See also*** ISLAMIC FUNDAMENTALISM (39); HAMA MASSACRE (245).

Significance

The Muslim Brotherhood's involvement in violent politics has not been matched by a determination to engage in formal political activity, largely because the rigidly organized, authoritarian regimes in the Arab world do not permit competitive political organizations. No Arab, however, can minimize the appeal of the Muslim Brotherhood among average citizens. Furthermore, an expanding body of young Arab intellectuals finds the Muslim Brotherhood preferable to other political organizations opposed to government policies and personalities. The Muslim Brotherhood is without a formal leader or hierarchical organization. Like so many organizations in the Muslim world, it lacks institutional cohesion. The Brotherhood, however, shares a common philosophy and reflects common concerns. The Muslim Brotherhood seeks an Islamic world free of alien influences and powerful enough to sustain its peculiar lifestyle. Although it emphasizes religious expression, it is deeply committed to political action and insists on the re-creation of political institutions according to traditional mores. Unfortunately, it has fragmented into small units that only disrupt government routine; they have not displayed a capacity to effect changes in policy, programs, or administration. The Muslim Brotherhood, however, is an alternative to the radical Left.

Muslim Nationalism 48

Muslim nationalism addresses itself to the unity of Muslims everywhere, but it is more cultural than political and develops from recognition of a common religious core. Muslim nationalism is therefore more psychological and emotive than practical or deliberate. Despite references to cultural and religious unity, Muslims are no more likely to transcend ethnic, regional loyalties than are persons with other religious experiences. Nevertheless, from time to time movements embodying Muslim nationalism have sought to elevate the Islamic community above the extant territorial polities. An example of such a movement is discernible in the program of Iran's Ayatollah Khomeini. Khomeini claimed that his perception went far beyond the borders of Iran and that the Islamic state he envisioned was aimed at drawing together all Muslims.

Significance

Muslim nationalism is full of contradictions. Muslims are no more unified than Christians, Buddhists, or Jews. Reference to Muslim nationalism is more a reaction to previous conditions of servitude and subordination to non-Muslim power than it is a positive call for Islamic political integration. The call to unity, whether made by Jamaluddin al-Afghani, Gamal Abdul Nasser, or the Ayatollah Khomeini, is usually muted by political realities. Indeed, the ayatollah was judged to be a threat, not a savior, among national leaders in the Muslim world.

Muslims in the Former U.S.S.R. 49

The Soviet Union contained one of the world's largest Muslim communities. It was this understanding that lead some observers to conclude that the Soviet invasion of Afghanistan in December 1979 was in part prompted by fear that Muslim resistance to Marxism in Afghanistan could spill over into Soviet central Asia. Others, however, discounted this perception. They argued that the "threat," if it did exist, was perhaps potentially dangerous but of no immediate consequence. Be that as it may, the role of Soviet Muslims was expanding. After the Slavs, the Muslims were the largest ethnic and cultural grouping in the U.S.S.R. In the last census (1989), the Muslims totalled in excess of 50 million, or almost 20 percent of the entire population. By the end of the century the Muslim population was expected to top 70 million. Accordingly, Soviet Muslims were increasingly more numerous in the work force as well as the armed forces. But along with this increase in numerical strength came a heightened sense of identity and a political consciousness that developed into an active form of nationalism. Soviet Muslims were not unaware of their brethren in Muslim countries, especially in the Middle East. Dissatisfaction at home was a serious matter once associations were made with fellow Muslims residing elsewhere in South and Southwest Asia. Moreover, the relatively poor showing by Soviet Muslim troops in Afghanistan suggested deeper difficulties than heretofore recognized. Soviet Muslim troops were Tajik-, Uzbek-, and Turkomen-speaking, similar to the Afghans on the other side of their Oxus River frontier. Although expected to rally their Afghan counterparts behind the Soviet invasion, their presence apparently had the very opposite effect. Nor did Soviet Muslims relish the thought of "punishing" their co-religionists. The withdrawal of these forces, described as reservists and irregulars, and their replacement with frontline Russian troops marked the intensification of the Soviet campaign against Afghan dissidents. Religious activity among the Muslims of Soviet central Asia was difficult to ascertain. Soviet authorities permitted officially registered mosques to function with their prayer leaders and maintenance staffs. These numbered between 400 and 500 and were divided into four *muftiates*, or administrative divisions. The most significant measure of Muslim religious fervor in the Soviet Union, however, was judged only by the number of extra-legal congregations and Sufi brotherhoods. The former had their local *mullahs*, and the latter their saints and paternalistic leaders. The Sufi orders of central Asia were most active in circumstances where controlled religious ceremony did not suit the needs of the population. Sufi Islam was also very difficult to monitor, given its self-contained, simple folk expression. More orthodox Muslim groups, such as the People of the Qur'an called for the strict observance of Islamic ritual. In the wake of the demise of the U.S.S.R., Islamic consciousness and practice is expected to grow within the independant central Asian republics. ***See also*** SUFISM (59).

Significance

Though concentrated in central Asia and the Caucasus, the Muslims of the former U.S.S.R. are a kaleidoscope of nationalities and linguistic groups. Although they are often referred to as a unit, no more unity exists among them than among Muslims within and between other countries. Indeed, the Muslims of the defunct U.S.S.R. are a diverse, fragmented, scattered congeries of minorities. Moreover, before Gorbachev they displayed only marginal religious interests. The collapse of the Soviet Union in the summer of 1991, however, revitalized Muslim tradition in the central Asian republics. Although the Muslim republics first opted for economic union within a reformed, smaller Soviet Union in October 1991, more determined independence movements were also energized. At the extreme end there were calls for a Greater Turkistan, uniting the Muslims of central Asia in a scheme associating it with Muslims elsewhere. With the passing of the U.S.S.R., however, they were content to express themselves along national lines, as each of the former Soviet republics assumed independent, sovereign status.

Pan-Islamism 50

The general call for all Muslims regardless of ethnic, linguistic, or national affiliation to participate in the revival of Islamic political power. In the latter part of the nineteenth century Jamaluddin al-Afghani called for a spiritual rebirth of the Muslim peoples to remove the yoke of European domination. Al-Afghani's aim was to ensure a more independent spiritual, intellectual, and economic as well as political Islamic world by emphasizing Muslim values.

Significance
Pan-Islamism has failed for numerous reasons. The size and diversity of the Islamic world makes common recognition almost impossible. What may be considered essential in one region of the Islamic world may not be so judged in another. Virtually no harmony of outlook exists in the Islamic world, given vast differences in cultural and historical makeup. National frontiers also tend to filter out the more emotional appeals of the pan-Islamicists. Pan-Islamism reached its height during the medieval Islamic empires of the Umayyads and Abbasids. Later efforts to sustain pan-Islamism have been particularly unsuccessful. In the present era, pan-Islamism is more a rallying cry than a purposeful objective.

Pillars of Islamic Belief 51

The five pillars of Islamic belief are also the duties incumbent on all Muslims. Every Muslim must perform them to the extent possible. They are:

1. *Al-shahadah,* or testimony. The pronouncement "There is no God but Allah and Mohammad is His Prophet" is recited by each Muslim without mental reservations. This statement of faith is at the heart of being a Muslim. Of parallel importance and in accordance with the *shahadah* is the solemn belief in a general resurrection, in the final day of judgment, in all the prophets of God, and in the scriptures of God: the Qur'an, the Pentateuch, and the Christian Gospels.
2. *Al-salah,* or prayer, the "backbone" of Islam. Muslims are called to prayer five times each day: at dawn, high noon, afternoon, after sunset, and at night. Muslims pray in any place, alone or with others. When praying it is necessary to face in the direction of Mecca. Muslims must be clean before offering prayers lest their prayers be rendered null.
3. *Al-siyam,* or fasting. Fasting means the complete abstention from food and drink from sunrise to sunset during the month of Ramadan, the ninth month in the Islamic calendar (which consists of 12 lunar months). The Islamic lunar month is either 29 or 30 days, never 31. Fasting is supposed to train the individual Muslim to be patient, wise, and disciplined, as well as to share the feelings of others. Ramadan is traditionally held to be the month in which the Prophet Mohammad received his first revelation and the month in which the Qur'an was revealed to the Prophet.
4. *Al-zakat,* or almsgiving. Each Muslim is required to give a certain percentage of his annual income, either in money or in kind, to the poor and indigent. Some Muslim countries, like Saudi Arabia, have a Department of Zakat within the Ministry of Finance. *Zakat* is properly about 2.5 percent of income. *Zakat* is considered an act of worship, but it is also aimed at bridging differences between rich and poor, thus strengthening the bonds of Muslim society. It also speaks to the Muslim quest for social justice.
5. *Al-haj,* or pilgrimage. This fifth and last pillar of Islam is explicitly stated in the Qur'an. Every financially and physically able Muslim is supposed to make the *haj* to Mecca and Medina at least once in his or her lifetime. The *haj* is considered the culmination of each Muslim's religious duty. Almost a million foreign pilgrims

make the *haj* each year. ***See also*** QUR'AN (53).

Significance
The five pillars of Islamic belief and practice unite all Muslims irrespective of location or sect, ethnic difference or national identity. They represent the source of the tradition and are unchanging in their character and requirements. Taken as a whole, the tradition and its practices are both simple and demanding, easy to understand and perform while insistent on consistency and purpose. Islamic belief is represented in all corners of the planet. Islam is a dynamic religion, with a celebrated past and an expanding future. Its appeal is measured in the numbers of people who are called to its practices in both the so-called developing and the developed worlds.

Qodrat 52

The Persian word for power. Although there is no easily discernible difference in the way Iranians use power, there is general consensus that Iranian theories and precepts about power are deeply rooted in the history and ideology of Shiite Islam, the state religion in Iran. Iranians do not separate the power of the political world from the power of the religious order. In Shiite Islam, God (Allah) is deemed to be the sole source of power, and the use of power is contingent upon God's will. Moreover, God has delegated power to a select number of infallible agents, specifically, the Prophet Mohammad, a dozen *imams* (spiritual leaders), and four specified substitutes for the Twelfth Imam. These divine agents have left an influential legacy of theories and principles pertaining to power that serve as the doctrinal and ideological basis of Shiite Islam. ***See also*** IMAMATE (37); RUHANIYYAT (54); SHIITE ISLAM (57).

Significance
Given the legacy of God's agents in Shiite Islam, all secular leaders and ruling parties in Iran are judged to be illegitimate and guilty of usurpation of authority. The illegitimacy principle has traditionally served to justify acts of defiance and insurrection against temporal rulers in Iran. Furthermore, this principle serves to validate the idea that the only legal government is an Islamic government. The hostility of Shiite Muslims toward secular rule is also linked to popular conceptions about the imams. The majority of Iranian Muslims profess a belief in the divine power of twelve imams. Belief in the imamate as successor to the Prophet Mohammad constitutes a central pillar in the Shiite faith.

Qur'an 53

The Qur'an is the Holy Book for Muslims. All Muslims believe the Qur'an was transmitted from God, Allah, to his messenger, Mohammad, one verse at a time. During Mohammad's lifetime the verses were recited from memory. Approximately 20 years after Mohammad's death they were compiled and formed into a single book. According to Muslim belief the Qur'an is the earthly presentation of God's law and thus stands by itself above all mundane human-inspired activity. The purpose of the Qur'an is singular and direct—to guide the human family along the correct path. A Muslim believes in all the scriptures and revelations of God as set down in the Qur'an. Although Muslims acknowledge the Bibles of the Jews and Christians, "the books of Abraham, Moses, David, and Jesus," they believe the only authentic and complete book of God is the Qur'an. Unlike other Bibles, it is thought, God protected the Qur'an from subsequent tampering or "corruption." Therefore, all other books are to be judged according to the standard that is the Qur'an. Whatever is in agreement with the Qur'an is accepted as divine truth. Whatever differs is either rejected or suspended. The Qur'an enables believers to determine right from wrong, good from evil. The divine law speaks of obligations that light the correct path (*sharia*), and Muslims are enjoined to follow it dutifully throughout their lives. Such behavior ensures the promise of salvation. Irrespective of location or circumstance, there is no permissible deviance from this stated course. The Qur'an represents all-embracing commands that demand total submission.

Significance
The Qur'an is the heart and mind of the Muslim faith. Everything a Muslim does in life reflects upon the passages of the holy book. Originally written in the Arabic language (many insist this is the only true version), the Qur'an gave form and substance to literary Arabic. Because of the Qur'an, an Arabic book or newspaper published anywhere in the world can be understood by all Arabic readers. Another important consideration is the relationship between religion and political power. Given the power of those responsible for protecting the sacred order and the Muslim community, and the definitive nature of the Qur'an and its teachings, political power is merged with religious power. The spiritual and temporal are fused. Moreover, the authoritarian nature of the Quranic commands provides Muslim rulers with almost absolute authority, of which Saudi Arabia is a prominent example. The Qur'an is the Saudi constitution, and the country's rulers insist that their actions are extensions of scripture.

Ruhaniyyat 54

The revered Shiite clergy, or *mullahs*, who claim responsibility for leading the Shiite community pending the anticipated return of the Twelfth Imam. Although Sunni Islam does not prescribe anything akin to a church hierarchy, Shiite Islam, particularly as practiced in Iran, has historically established such an order. The major transformation occurred during the rule of the Safavid dynasty in the sixteenth century. The Safavids declared Shiite Islam to be the official religion, and this act opened the ranks of the religious teachers (*ulema* in orthodox Sunni Islam) to the Persian Shiite *mullahs* and hence minimized the role of the Arab *ulema*. The Shiite Iranian *mullahs* evolved their own identity and insisted upon their autonomy. The Ruhaniyyat of Shiite clerics manages an informal but extensive network of relationships among themselves and throughout the Shiite community. The hierarchy is determined by consensus among the peers and the community at large, and 50 ranks make up the Ruhaniyyat infrastructure. The highest position in the hierarchy is that of the ayatollah or imam. Unlike the Sunni *ulema*, the Shiite clerics receive their economic support directly from the community of believers. Exceptions to this rule have occurred, however, and the Pahlavi dynasty is known to have provided income allowances to specific *mullahs*. ***See also*** MUJTAHID (45).

Significance
The Ruhaniyyat represents the most influential class in Iranian political life. Given the essential independence of the *mullahs*, their integration with the community of believers, and their apparent distance from secular authority, they wield considerable influence. Their potential power was realized in dramatic form in the revolution that overthrew the Pahlavi dynasty in 1979. Moreover, the rule of Ayatollah Khomeini was directly related to his preeminent position in the Ruhaniyyat.

Unlike other *mullahs,* Ayatollah Khomeini had refused to cooperate with the Pahlavi administration, thus enhancing his role as the genuine leader of the Iranian nation.

Salafism 55

Salafism describes the revival of Islamic orthodoxy in the form of Islamic reformism. It is particularly identified with North Africa and the work of late nineteenth- and early twentieth-century Muslim reformers and scholars such as Jamaluddin al-Afghani, Mohammad Abduh, and Rashid Rida. Salafism appeals especially to Muslims in a period of general decay and rootlessness. It represents an attempt to reestablish identity, purpose, and direction. Salafism is considered the major component in Moroccan nationalism. Moroccan society had drifted away from established Islamic ritual. Dervish orders, Sufi brotherhoods, and saint worship had captured the attention of the community, but they had also fractured it and left it exposed to alien manipulation. Indeed, the French occupation and control of Morocco was, in part, traced to the performance of bizarre Islamic ceremonies. The Salafists of Morocco, therefore, directed their attention at removing foreign presence as much as they aimed at reestablishing traditional Islam. Moroccan nationalism was hitched to religious considerations, and the result was a movement that enlisted broad segments of the community. It also gave prominence to the idea of religious legitimacy. The leaders of the nationalist movement did not stress self-determination or independence until 1944 and the founding of the Istiqlal (Independence) Party. The Moroccan king (still called sultan at this time) openly sided with the Istiqlal, and in 1953 the French exiled him. The French crackdown on Moroccan nationalists occurred simultaneously with this act. Repression, however, only drove the nationalists underground, where they organized terrorist associations and finally, in 1955, a liberation army. With the leaders in prison or in exile, less moderate figures assumed control of the movement, and their actions were not tempered by cultural or temperamental constraints. The nationalists used the monarchy as their symbol of unity, and both Salafists and more secular nationalists joined forces to achieve their political freedom. Interestingly, however, the battle cry of the combined nationalist movement was "revolution of the throne and the people." This emphasis on the monarch reflected divisions within Moroccan society, especially the cleavage between the Arab and Berber populations. Many Berbers had found the French useful in balancing off the power of the Arabs. Berbers often cooperated with the colonizers. Moreover, the Berbers sought to maintain their separate status as mountain folk, and they were disinclined to accept the leadership of the urban population and plainsmen. Furthermore, Berbers clung to their unique lifestyle, which ignored Arabic influences. Islam, too, was less rigorously practiced by the Berber community. The Berbers therefore saw the opportunity to establish greater autonomy, and their divisive character disturbed the nationalists. The king represented a rallying ground. The heterogeneous character of Moroccan society gave the king special importance, and this emphasis on kingship also dramatically altered the shape of the nationalist movement. ***See also*** BERBER (74).

Significance

In spite of the Salafist movement, few sophisticated city dwellers in the Moroccan nationalist movement of the 1920s entertained the thought of sustaining the sultanate. Many Moroccans believed the monarchy was responsible for the country's degradation and its humiliation at the hands of the French. They did not have to be reminded that it was the sultan who "signed away Morocco's sovereignty in 1912." The sultanate had become an appendage of French colonial administration, and it was too weak to defend either the country's integrity or Islam. The sultan during this period of the nationalistic movement was Mohammad Ben Yousef. A young, energetic figure, he saw the Salafists and nationalists as his opportunity to reclaim Moroccan identity and dignity. No less important, it provided him with the opportunity to reestablish the throne as a viable and indispensable institution in Morocco's future. The nationalists thus played into the hands of the Moroccan monarch and prepared the foundation for his later monopolization of power. There was little contact between the sultan and the nationalists until the U.S. occupation of North Africa during World War II. The sultan met with President Franklin Roosevelt in Casablanca in January 1943 and expressed his desire to free the country from French colonialism. Buttressed by U.S. promises of support and his undisputed leadership of the nationalist movement, the sultan demanded independence, not a modification of the protectorate. The sultan cast a long shadow over the nationalist movement. Moreover, the sultan minimized the need for a constitutional monarchy, stressing Morocco's greater need of national unity. In the aftermath of the war, the sultan exploited every opportunity to demonstrate solidarity with the Arab League and the future of Islam. He dispensed with the customary homage to the French mission. By 1951, the sultan's association with the new Istiqlal Party was complete, although the French tried to persuade him to break his ties with the organization. Instead, he called for strikes and protest demonstrations, and the French were compelled to exile him. But the sultan had become a national hero, and the population was aroused by his forced removal. The sultan had autocratic mannerisms before this outpouring of adulation, but those authoritarian traits were now tempered and strengthened in the struggle for independence. With the eruption of the Algerian conflict in November 1954, France was hard-pressed to manage a struggle on several fronts simultaneously. Algeria was declared a province of France, and the French army was ordered to hold the possession and protect the several hundred thousand French settlers. Morocco, however, was a protectorate. Paris had never considered retaining it indefinitely. Thus, with a Liberation Army forming in Rif country, and with terrorism on the rise, the French decided to meet some of the Moroccan demands. The decision was taken to return the sultan, now identified as Mohammad V, to Morocco and his throne. Mohammad V called for a government of national union, avoided identifying with a particular organization, and established the monarchy as a separate political force. Morocco achieved its independence in 1956, and with the expansion of the police force and the development of a formal military establishment, both loyal to the king, Morocco's regal political system became a reality. When Hasan al-Alawi (Hasan II) assumed the throne in February 1961, the king already monopolized the patronage system, controlled the bureaucracy, dominated the parties and factions, and made all the key decisions. The Istiqlal Party challenged this monarchial putsch but was defeated in its efforts by 1960. After May 1960, the king assumed the role of prime minister and appointed and controlled all the ministers, directors of state-run corporations, and public banks. In March 1961, hardly a month after assuming the throne, Hasan II not only became prime minister, but minister of defense, minister of agriculture, and minister of interior, too. Although he was soon to turn these ministries over to trusted followers, the monarch had given ample demonstration of his awesome power. Moreover, Hasan II, because he combined secular and spiritual offices (Sharifian Amir al-Muminin), was also the unparalleled religious figure in Morocco. The Salafist revival had done its job, but the results were unintended.

The Satanic Verses 56

A book written by Salman Rushdie and published in 1989. Muslims described the book as a deliberate assault on their religious beliefs and practices. A British citizen, a Muslim born in Bombay, Rushdie was accused of heresy and apostasy and was sentenced to death by Ayatollah Khomeini. Rushdie was forced to go into hiding, and the ayatollah's successors declared they had no intention of lifting the death sentence on Rushdie.

Significance

The Satanic Verses precipitated violent street demonstrations within the Muslim world as well as elsewhere. Although Rushdie apologized for offending members of the Islamic faith, the controversy raised by the publication of his book was protracted. A Japanese translator of the novel, Hitoshi Igarashi, was found slain in Tokyo in July 1991, and although no one claimed responsibility for the act, it was widely held that he had been killed for his association with the Rushdie work. Moreover, in 1989, the Islamic Center in Japan requested that publishers, newspapers, magazines, and broadcast stations not translate or reproduce the novel, saying it contained "filthy remarks" and "ridicules fundamental beliefs of Islam." Between 60,000 and 70,000 copies of the book had been sold in Japan at the time of Igarashi's death.

Shiite Islam 57

Shiite Islam differs from orthodox Sunni Islam in that the former narrows the qualifications of the candidate for the imamate (the equivalent of the Sunni caliphate) and hence the leadership of the Muslim community. This narrowing not only involves the Prophet Mohammad's tribe of Quraysh but also the descendants of the Prophet's son-in-law, Ali, and his daughter, Fatima. Shiites insist that the legitimate right to the Prophet's mantle is through Ali and his descendants. Although there is no record of any such designation, Shiites believe that Ali was designated by the Prophet to succeed him, and after Ali, his descendants in direct line. Thus, Ali is believed to have been endowed with divine authority, with the secret knowledge to interpret the Qur'an. This knowledge Ali is believed to have passed on to his male descendants. Ali, therefore, is perceived by Shiites to be the repository of Islamic truth, and special powers are ascribed to his person. So total is this belief in the divine ordination of Ali that even Mohammad is sometimes considered a lesser messenger of God. According to Shiite tradition, Ali and his descendants were infallible leaders. This devotion to Ali is further highlighted by his martyrdom and that of his son and would-be successor, Husain. But Shiite Islam is not monolithic; sects abound. Differing opinions on the role and nature of the imamate produced numerous factions and splits. Although Shiite Islam is defined as the "partisans of Ali," his followers have proven to be divisive. On one side are the Zaydis, who argue for the election of the imam from among

Ali's descendants. On the other side are the more familiar forms of Shiite Islam known as the Ithna Ashari, or Twelvers, and the Ismailis, or Seveners. What separates the Twelvers and Seveners is controversy over the death of the sixth imam, Jafar al-Sadiq, who died in 765 A.D. The Twelvers argue that Sadiq's son, Musa al-Kazim, succeeded to the imamate. The Seveners differ, giving their support to the elder brother, Ismail. The descendants of Ismail are identified with the Fatimid caliphate in Egypt. The Ismailis of today are found in India, Pakistan, Soviet central Asia, Syria, Iraq, and East Africa. A socioeconomically successful community, the Ismailis are led by their spiritual leader, the Aga Khan, who today is a cosmopolitan, Harvard-educated, international civil servant concerned with the worldwide refugee problem. The Ismailis are also found in different tribal groups, such as the ruling Alawites of Syria ad the commercially successful Khoja community of Pakistan. The Druze of the Middle East are also an offshoot of Ismaili Islam.

The principal form of Shiite Islam, however, is that of the Twelvers. They follow the line of Musa al-Kazim and his descendants until the disappearance of the Twelfth Imam, Mohammad ibn Hasan al-Askari, who is believed to have gone into occultation in 874 A.D. Until the reappearance of the Twelfth Imam, his role is to be filled by *mujtahids* (secular and religious divines), essentially the *mullahs* and ayatollahs. Until the return of the Twelfth Imam as the *mahdi* (messiah), the *mullahs* and ayatollahs serve in his place. Their dominance in the Shiite sect explains the political dualism always latent in Iran, where Shiite Islam has been a state religion since the Safavid dynasty's proclamation in the sixteenth century. In Iran, any temporal political figure is a mere pretender and an illegitimate usurper of authority. This challenge to authority posed by Shiite belief, as well as the insistence to follow a wholly different course from that of the Sunni Muslims, has put the Shiite community under considerable pressure. Persecution and death stalked the Shiites as successive Sunni caliphs sought to destroy their faith. The Shiite response was to practice dissimulation, to hide their beliefs. Other Shiites, however, risked martyrdom in the tradition of Ali and Husain, and in time martyrdom became the core of the Shiite belief system. Shiites are more mystical in the performance of their faith than their Sunni counterparts, and martyrdom aroused deep emotions and passions, which helped sustain the partisans of Ali. Observers have often described Shiite observances as "fanatical" representations of religious expression. Few, however, doubt the depth of Shiite faith. For these reasons Shiite conceptions of law and politics are far more authoritarian. Obedience to the imam is far stronger than the relationship between adherents of Sunni Islam and their temporal rulers. In Shiite Islam, the imam has the final interpretation of legal doctrine. Such is not the case in Sunni Islam. By the same token, although both Sunnis and Shiites never question the Qur'an, the *hadiths* (traditions of the prophet Mohammad) are not accepted unless the imam legitimates them. Also, the Muslim Sunni practice of *ijma*, judgment by consensus of the learned community, is unacceptable to Shiites if the imam has not participated in the decision-making process. *Qiyas*, or reasoning by analogy, is discounted almost totally in Shiite Islam. The result is a far more rigid system of Islamic jurisprudence and procedure than that followed in the larger Sunni world. Even when one accounts for the different schools of Sunni Muslim jurisprudence—particularly the Hanbalite, which is the most austere, as practiced in Saudi

Arabia under Wahhabism—the emphasis given to the infallible imamate in Shiite Islam and its divine sanctification cannot be equalled by anything in Sunni Islam. ***See also*** CALIPHATE (34); FAQIH (36); PATERNALISM (100); MUJTAHID (45); RUHANIYYAT (54); SHIITE MARTYRDOM (58); WAHHABIS (63); DRUZE (81); POLITICS OF SUCCESSION: IRAN (102).

Significance
Shiite Islam is especially strong in Iran, where the vast majority of the population follows the Twelver tradition. Iraq's population is split between Sunni and Shiite Muslims, but the Shiites are deemed to be more numerous. Shiites are also scattered through every Muslim country, but their numbers are a smaller percentage of those populations. Shiites have their own rituals and special occasions; they also share a long and bloody history with their Sunni brethren. As in the past, today controversy swells around these two major communities within Islam. Periodic displays of brutality by one community against the other continue to occur. In other instances, however, toleration and cooperation are also evident, and mutual assistance, if not compatibility, has been demonstrated. The ruling Shiite Alawites of Syria have been opposed by the Muslim Brotherhood because of what the latter deems to be their un-Islamic behavior. Considerable apprehension also exists in Sunni-dominated countries over developments in Iran. The Ayatollah Khomeini's call to Shiite Muslims, as well as Sunni Muslims, to overthrow their leaders and to join in the resurrection of an Islamic state is considered a significant threat. The ayatollah insisted the Iranian revolution was but one phase of an all-embracing Islamic revolution. Moreover, he saw his role as that of a leader for all Muslims. A claimant to divine ordination, Khomeini insisted that his judgment was unerring and must be heeded by Muslims everywhere. Khomeini's popularity, outside Iran, was limited, but there was no misunderstanding his power among Iranians. Indeed, it was Khomeini's order to his followers that they martyr themselves in resisting the Iraqi invasion of Iran in 1980 that ultimately turned the tide of battle. The Iraqis had reason to believe Iran was in disarray, with its military establishment demoralized and its nationalities demanding separation. According to the Iraqis, a strike across the Shatt al-Arab into Khuzistan could hardly be resisted by a country torn by revolution. What Iraq did not judge correctly, however, was the power of Shiite faith and its management by Iran's theologians. Iranians proved they were prepared to sacrifice themselves for their beliefs. Shiite Islam also reveals much about the shah of Iran's lost contest with Ayatollah Khomeini. Khomeini's death in 1989 did not produce the predicted upheaval in Iranian power circles. The smooth transition and the elevation of more politically inspired clerics, such as Rafsanjani, to the highest decision-making positions points to the strength of the Shiite political structure hammered into shape since the overthrow of the Pahlavi shah.

Shiite Martyrdom 58

Martyrdom is at the core of the Shiite belief system. The Prophet Mohammad's son-in-law, Ali, and Ali's son, Husain, met violent deaths, as did the first 11 pious imams around whom Shiite Muslims center their faith. The last, the Twelfth Imam (the official religion in Iran is known as the Ithna Ashari, or Twelver, tradition), is believed to have gone into occultation and to have disappeared in 874 A.D. Until his reappearance, his role is filled by the *mujtahids* (secular and religious divines), essentially the *mullahs* and ayatollahs. The dominance of these spiritual leaders in the Shiite sect explains the political dualism always latent in Iran and the prevailing view that shahs were illegitimate usurpers. ***See also*** IMAMATE (37); RUHANIYYAT (54); SHIITE ISLAM (57).

Significance
The suffering and martyrdom of saintly, quasi-deified personalities dramatizes Iranian Shiism. In an atmosphere of deep melancholy, Iranian Shiites each year celebrate the martyrdom of Husain. To this day Shiite Muslims have not dismissed the Third Imam's demise as a mere atrocity perpetrated by a tyrannical and unjust ruler. Husain's death is emotionally commemorated every year on the tenth day of Muharram in the Islamic calendar. Known as Ashura, the day is a major Shiite holiday, and passion plays depicting the martyrdom are reenacted throughout Iran. Moreover, Iranians have often been called upon to accept martyrdom, in the tradition of Husain, rather than submit to the whims of a despot. And while the secular rulers may succeed in brutalizing many believers, the argument persists that they cannot extinguish the spirit of the Shiite Muslims or deny them their ultimate victory. Imam Husain's martyrdom symbolizes the preeminent power of Islam over secular absolutism. In the same vein, Shiite Muslims have transformed all the victims of secular tyranny into divine martyrs. Iranian Shiite martyrdom therefore has become a major weapon in combatting an unacceptable regime. The Shiites who lost their lives in the struggle to overthrow the shah became instant heroes and provided the fuel to expand the revolution. An even greater display of Shiite martyrdom is evidenced in the Iranian resistance to Iraqi aggression and subsequent efforts by Iran's *mullah*-inspired revolutionary guards to invade Iraqi territory. Tens of thousands of Iranians are believed to have died following the command of their infallible leader, Ayatollah Khomeini. Veneration of these Shiite Muslim dead is a central theme of Iranian religious life, and it reinforces rather than weakens the rule of the religious clergy.

Sufism 59

An early mystical Islamic order. The word is derived from the Arabic *suf,* or coarse wool, from which their monkish garments were made. Appearing sometime during the eighth century A.D., the Sufis were medicants who usually denied themselves creature comforts or other material distractions. Their central concern was seeking personal redemption through merging their entire being, both physical and mental, in God (Allah). The Sufis therefore were critics of the rigid intellectual and legal aspects of the Islamic religion. They sought to avoid sophisticated reasoning and gathered around them the simple folk who could feel their devotions but who were otherwise incapable of articulating them. The Sufis emphasized personal responsibility and accountability. The avoidance of sinful acts was a major concern. Given their popular, flexible performance, the Sufis appealed to a broad spectrum of people and thus were instrumental in the spread of Islam. The Turkic people of central Asia, for example, adopted Islam because the Sufis won their confidence, not because they were conquered by Arab armies. Given the success of Sufism, monastic orders developed, and the institutionalization of the brotherhoods resembled those of both Christianity and Buddhism. The religious life of the Turks and the Muslims of North Africa was more affected by Dervish orders than by the traditional *ulema* (religious scholars). The Naqshbandis, the Mevlevis, the Bektashis of Asia Minor, and the Marabout (Maraboutism) of North Africa are prominent examples of the spiritual power of mystical Islam. Sufi practices on the one hand deviated from strict doctrine and permitted displays of superstition that appeared to undermine convention. On the other hand, they were popular expressions that simple people readily adopted. In this regard, Islam was intertwined with the lifestyles of people who otherwise might have remained beyond the fold. Sufism also permitted the spread of civilization among less sophisticated peoples and elevated them to a higher culture and greater sense of community consciousness. The fact that it gratified the individual psyche was a small price to pay for fidelity to principle and respect for authority. ***See also*** ALAWITE DYNASTY (64).

Significance
Sufism was important in spreading the Islamic faith among peoples who were otherwise reluctant to adopt an alien creed. The Sufis, however, were able to fit Islam to the traditions of the peoples they endeavored to convert. New adherents to Islam did not have to give up their unique values or customs, rituals, or ceremonies. Islam accommodated diversity through the personal intervention of the Sufis. Moreover, people were more inclined to resist a coercive attempt to change their lifestyle. They were less likely to do so if they understood that their basic way of life would be retained and their larger circumstances improved. The Sufis, in other words, made it possible for primitive peoples to accept Islam and also for Islam to accept them without any sacrificing of familiar experiences. Although it is often said that Islam was spread through the use of the sword, the role of the Sufis indicates that mass conversion occurred when people sensed that their future would be enhanced by membership in a larger community.

Sunni Islam 60

Sunni Islam refers to the majority of Muslims who follow the orthodox tradition (as contrasted with the nondoctrinal Shiite practices). Sunni Muslims identify with the *sunna,* a body of legal and moral principles that predates the Islamic era. The *sunna* represented Arabian customary law and, in its earliest expression, was pagan in character. Idolatry and political fragmentation were key features of pre-Islamic Arab society. The tribal chief, or *sayyid,* was selected on the basis of age, experience, and intelligence, and he held office because of the loyalty demonstrated by his supporters. The most important role played by the chief was the adjudication of disputes by referral to tribal custom. In this context, the *sunna,* or primitive law of the tribal folk, reinforced the authority of the personal ruler. Idol worship also was an integral feature of tribal law and tended to legitimate authority. The rise of Islam did not replace the *sunna,* but it did drastically modify it. The Prophet Mohammad was primarily concerned with warning people against idolatry and impressing upon them the oneness of God (Allah). Although there was resistance to Mohammad's plea, the idols were smashed and God's law was declared supreme over idolatrous law. The ancient *sunna,* however, remained as a foundation for the new Islamic way of life. Sunni Muslims identify themselves with a highly developed juridical order that regulates the totality of the believer's activities and thoughts. The *sunna* of the Islamic era has been described as an ideal system because it is derived from a divine source and thus embodies God's will and justice. Thus, only God, in the Sunni tradition, is the source of ultimate authority.

Sovereignty can only belong to God. It is therefore held in trust by men who act according to God's intentions and will. The caliphs of Islam were God's viceregents on earth, required by law to protect the Muslim community (*umma*) but always recognized to be fallible mortals. By the same token, current reference to the Islamic state, as in Pakistan, emphasizes the sovereignty of God and the governors as his mere servants. For Sunni Muslims, Islamic law was the ideal legal system; it was divine, perfect, eternal, and just. Moreover, it applied to all people, everywhere. Sunni Muslims also insist that the divine law takes precedence over society and state; hence, the declarations in Muslim countries that laws that are repugnant to Islam are invalid. In other words, governments that fail to enforce Islamic law are often judged to be beyond the pale and without legitimacy or raison d'être. Even when governments stood in clear violation of it, believers were obliged to observe Islamic law. The Sunni Muslim's understanding of the correct course to follow, irrespective of his circumstances, is assisted by the *shari'a,* or right path. It is incumbent on Sunni Muslims to fulfill their duties according to the *sunna* and the *shari'a* despite existing conditions. The fulfillment of one's obligations, the adoption of the *shari'a* (the right path), is the single most important objective in life. Happiness in this life, or inner satisfaction, as well as salvation, is the reward of all believers. God's law exists independent of human circumstances and was revealed to men through his messenger. The Qur'an represents God's word as revealed to Mohammad, a verse at a time. Indeed, the Qur'an was assembled some two decades after Mohammad's death. Nevertheless, the Qur'an embodies God's law and will. Its teachings, for all Muslims, are judged to have universal value and application. The path established by the Qur'an, however, is often narrow and limited. Believers are informed of what is required (*fard*) and what is forbidden (*haram*). There are also matters that are recommended (*mandub*) and those that are objectionable, but not forbidden (*makruh*). In areas where the law appears to be indifferent, the Sunni Muslim is judged to have wide latitude (*jaiz*). For example: daily prayers are *fard;* adultery is *haram;* extra prayers are *mandub;* eating certain flesh is *makruh* (pork is specifically forbidden and determined to be *haram*). Selling goods, to be distinguished from usury or interest-taking, which is forbidden, is *jaiz.* Thus, the divine law as revealed to the Prophet Mohammad provided a system of all-embracing legal codes and commands, and it has been noted by Islamic scholars that Islamic law has the character of religious obligation and also provides a political sanction of religion. This is what is meant by Islam's being more than a religion, in fact, a total way of life. It also imposes a form of authoritarianism, and some would argue totalitarianism, on all Muslims. In Sunni Islam, however, this submission to authority is self-imposed. There is no church hierarchy or clergy as in Shiite Islam, and each Sunni Muslim may perform the rituals prescribed by God's teachings. ***See also*** ISLAM (38); SHIITE ISLAM (57); CALIPHATE (34); IMAMATE (37); JIHAD (41).

Significance

Sunni Muslims are the dominant sect in modern Islam, composing approximately 80 percent of the total Muslim world. As has been noted above, the division between Sunni and Shiite developed over the successorship to the prophet Mohammad. Since that time, the Islamic sects have never reconciled their positions, and each order has been embellished with dogma and rituals in keeping with the earlier, more local cultures. In a larger sense the Muslim community was the legatee of God's revelations to Mohammad and customs and traditions long in use in the Arabian Peninsula. This blending of experiences also occurred in lands conquered by the Arab armies in their seventh- and eighth-century surge across North Africa to Western Europe, through the Fertile Crescent, skirting Asia Minor (Byzantium) to Iran, central Asia, and India. The Iranians quickly Persianized the Islamic experience, and the Turks, although a bit more resistant, also adapted their traditions to Islam. Similar interactions occurred wherever Islam gained a foothold, e.g., Malaysia, Indonesia, Nigeria, and the Berbers of North Africa. Given its great geographic expansion, the Muslim community (*umma*) was forced to find ways to deal with phenomena originating in the Arabian Peninsula. Syria, Iraq, Egypt, and Iran had been the sites for sophisticated, developed civilizations, and adaptations to the new austere, demanding, and disciplined life-style of Arabian Islam required patience and innovation. The early caliphs of Islam therefore used personal opinion (*ra'y*) to supplement Islamic teachings. The second caliph, Umar, declared that the Qur'an, the *sunna* (largely Arabian customs at this time, but also some traditions of the Prophet), and reason (*ijtihad*) were to be used in addressing the needs of the different populations and cultures. Others, however, contested this view, insisting that the application of reason violated the notion of divine law and permitted man-made legislation. Controversies such as this produced the four major schools of Islamic jurisprudence, which are still in vogue in current Sunni Islam. The Hanafite school (Abu Hanifa, 699–768) is considered the most liberal of these four schools. Hanifa argued that reasoning by analogy (*qiyas*) was a proper source of law when neither the Qur'an nor the *hadith* (traditions of the Prophet) were helpful in answering a question or resolving a problem. Abu Hanifa's logic especially appealed to non-Arabs who wished to sustain their own characteristic methods and culture. Hanafite tradition is found in modern Turkey and Pakistan. The Malikite (Malik ibn Anas, 718–796) is another Sunni Muslim school of Islamic law. The Malikite school is known for its stress on the *hadith*. The activities of the Prophet as well as the local *sunna* were presented in the form of *ijma* (consensus of the learned community), which Malik is believed to have spawned. Learned theologians or religious jurists were made responsible for determining the correct path whenever the Qur'an was not explicit. The Malikites, however, also had their detractors. The opposition argued that *ijma* was a form of man-made law and thus in violation of divine prescription. Nevertheless, Malikite interpretation of Islamic law held special importance for Iraqis, Syrians, Egyptians, and North Africans, and it was incorporated in their rituals. The third school of Islamic jurisprudence is the Shafite (Shafi'i, 768–820). Reputed to be the most systematic of early Muslim legal theorists, Shafi'i was critical of local *ijma* but adopted it when it was possible to have broad community agreement. Shafi'i also rejected that part of the *sunna* that did not deal directly with, or reflect on, Islamic tradition. He emphasized that only the *sunna*, which addressed itself to the utterances of the Prophet, could be followed. Shafi'i also was more inclined to adopt broad community consensus. Analogy was used sparingly, when none of the other sources of legal performance sufficed. Shafite doctrine, however, proved to be weak despite its erudition. The inability to arrive at broad consensus was a key failing, and controversy has followed this school of Islamic jurisprudence to the present day. The Shafite school of Islamic law is prominent in Muslim Indonesia and elsewhere in Southeast Asia. Moreover, Shafi'i scholarship gave rise to the term *madhhab,* meaning school of law, which was applied to the work of Hanifa and Malik as well as to that of Shafi'i. The fourth school of Islamic jurisprudence is the Hanbalite (Ahmad ibn Hanbal, a ninth-century student of Shafi'i). The most rigid and conservative of the Sunni Muslim schools, Hanbal's work was given significance by Taqi-al-Din Ahmad ibn Taymiyah (1263–1328). Taymiyah insisted that only the Qur'an and the *hadith,* or traditions of the Prophet, were acceptable. He condemned any kind of innovation, mystical expression (Sufism), or saint worship. The Hanbalite school as developed by Taymiyah ultimately gave rise to Wahhabism, the Islamic practice that permeates Saudi Arabia. These four schools of Islamic jurisprudence were well established by the eleventh century, and *ijtihad* (discretion or reason) gave way to *taqlid* (imitation), or acceptance of the four schools. The period is known as the *Bab al-Ijtihad,* the closing of the door to reason. Sunni Islam assumed its unchanging character in this period. Subsequent efforts to challenge prevailing doctrine were met with stiff resistance. Often the charge of heresy was directed at those who appeared to modify the precepts of Islamic tradition. In Pakistan, for example, the Ahmediya community (followers of the nineteenth-century religious leader Ghulam Ahmed) were officially designated non-Muslim because of what was judged to be their heretical beliefs. In part, the Ahmediya accept Ghulam Ahmed as a prophet, but for Sunni Muslims, Mohammad is believed to be the "Seal of the Prophets" (Khatm-i-Nubawaat), the last of the prophets. Sunnis and Shiites are also bitter rivals. Attempts to placate the opposed communities in Lebanon led to a distribution of offices in the government so that a Sunni would be prime minister and a Shiite would be the speaker of the assembly. Conflicts also abound between the Shiite leadership (Alawite) in Syria and the majority Sunni population of that country. The reverse has operated in Iraq, where Sunnis have governed a nation that is predominantly Shiite. Shiite-Sunni clashes are not unusual occurrences in Pakistan, although many Shiite factions have achieved status and influence in the predominantly Sunni state. Discussions about Muslim unity must take into account basic divisions within Sunni Islam and between Sunni and Shiite Muslims. Historic cleavages run deep, and calls to the Muslim *umma* to respond with one will to dilemmas afflicting the Islamic world have yet to be answered. What requires emphasis is the rigidity of Islam and Muslim practices, when compared with other religious and religious-cum-philosophical orders. Islam resists any tampering that could dilute its role and purpose; it is not an absorptive religion, and Muslims are cautioned not to deviate from a narrowly conceived path for fear of being metamorphosed beyond recognition. Although efforts have been made to adopt non-Muslim tradition, particularly education and technological know-how, only a small fraction of the Muslim *umma* has been affected. Moreover, in times of extreme tension, Muslims with such alien experience are often judged to be a threat to the larger Islamic society. The repudiation of foreign ideas, methods, and institutions, therefore, also involves the condemnation of so-called modern cosmopolitan Muslim elites.

Two-Nation Theory **61**

The Two-Nation theory was the justification adopted by the Indian Muslim League for demanding the establishment of a Muslim state within the subcontinent. Under the leadership of Mohammad Ali Jinnah, the Muslim League insisted that two major nations existed within British India, the Hindu and the Muslim. The Muslims, the Muslim League leaders argued, were so numerous (approximately 100 million in 1946) that they constituted a force that could not be ignored. In addition, the Muslims publicized their great differences with the Hindus. Religion, dress, diet, customs, and philosophy were at great variance. Associations between Hindus and Muslims were extremely limited. Religious orders and practices were in total opposition. Historically, the Muslims judged themselves the supreme conquerors and rulers of India (as in the Moghul period), only to be displaced by British power in the nineteenth century. Muslims still believed they were superior in every way to the more numerous Hindus. With the anticipated withdrawal of the British in the immediate aftermath of World War II, many Muslims feared that the Hindus would gain political control of the country. The Muslim League in particular was reluctant to submit itself to the whims of the Indian National Congress, led by Mahatma Gandhi and Jawaharlal Nehru. The only recourse seemed to be the creation of a separate state for the Muslims of India. The Two-Nation theory became a persistent theme of Indian Muslim nationalists, and they finally convinced the British government that only the partition of the Asian subcontinent into two independent, sovereign states would suffice. Pakistan, the creation of the Indian Muslim League, was established on August 14, 1947.

Significance
The Two-Nation theory is the heart of the demand for an independent Pakistan. It asserted that the two major religious communities within British India were essentially incompatible and that each ought to be permitted the right of self-determination. Although Pakistan was formed on the basis of religion, it is important to note that tens of millions of Muslims remained domiciled in India and never considered shifting to Pakistan. Nevertheless, approximately 10 million Muslims did move from India to Pakistan, and about the same number of Hindus transferred their allegiance to the new Indian Union. In the 1990s, the Muslim population of India was estimated to be larger than that of Pakistan. Of course, this does not account for the Muslims of Bangladesh, who before 1971 were also considered Pakistanis. Moreover, the creation of Bangladesh, with assistance provided by India, appeared to make a mockery of the Two-Nation theory. The Indians argued that the Two-Nation theory was dead, given the determination of the Muslim Bengalis to break with Pakistan and form their own independent state. What critics of the Two-Nation theory wished to emphasize was the inability of Islam to hold Pakistan together. Bengali nationalism proved to be stronger than the Islamic connection, and the Muslims of East Pakistan were prepared to accept Hindu help in fighting the Muslims of West Pakistan. Despite this development, however, the Two-Nation theory is still considered vital to the people of Pakistan. Given their bitter relations with India—and their fear that India seeks to destroy Pakistan and annex the territory within a greater India, commonly referred to as Akhand Bharat (United India)—the Muslims of Pakistan continue to give significance to the Two-Nation theory.

Umma 62
The Muslim community of believers. Irrespective of nationality, ethnic origin, racial differences, or historical and geographic circumstances,

Muslims everywhere are believed to form a single, unified community. The significance given to the *umma* in Islam can be grasped by the absence of a Muslim "church" hierarchy, especially in orthodox Sunni Islam. Religious responsibilities in Islam are conferred onto the community. All believers can lead prayers, officiate at wedding ceremonies, or ceremonialize the dead. Islam is essentially a legal code that the faithful are duty-bound to observe. Although learned religious figures have formed themselves into a separate category in Sunni Islam, notably the *ulema,* they are not required to perform any special functions, nor do they have powers distinct from those of the larger community. In Sunni Islam, the imam is merely a believer who leads the congregation in prayer. He need not be a member of the *ulema.* Unlike Shiite Islam, no special prerogatives are provided to such individuals. In a larger sense, this emphasis on the *umma* is counterpoised by an emphasis on individual worship, probity, and personal good deeds. Sunni Muslims appear before God (Allah) as individuals, and it is as individuals that they are tested and judged. This relative independence of the individual paradoxically both reinforces and weakens the idea of the Muslim *umma.* ***See also*** SUNNI ISLAM (60); SHIITE ISLAM (57); CALIPHATE (34); JERUSALEM (154).

Significance

The Muslim *umma* (community) can be interpreted as a political manifestation of Islam. The Prophet Mohammad created his own community of believers to ward off the threat from the established power structure of the period. In the *umma* there was strength and promise, and the expansion of the community was quickly perceived as intertwined with the power of the religion. The incredible advance of Islam during the Prophet's lifetime was only a small beginning. In the decades following his death, the Islamic world spread from the Arabian Peninsula throughout the Middle East, across North Africa, and into Europe on the one side, and on the other, it absorbed Persia (Iran) and swept into central Asia and India. The Arab tide ebbed, but the Persians and Turkic people, and later Arab travelers and traders, carried the teachings of the Prophet to Southeast Asia and present-day Indonesia. Although Islam was successful in winning adherents, the notion of a unified Muslim community was never truly achieved. Even during the centuries of the Islamic caliphate, division and rivalry, competition and conflict characterized the Muslim world. Nevertheless, the emphasis on a common bond, a common doctrine and, above all, the oneness of God (Allah) has always drawn Muslims into a psychological and spiritual community. In present times, reference is still made to the unity of the Muslim *umma* and its capacity to overcome adversity. Different Muslim organizations, such as the Muslim Summit and the Muslim Conference, are testimony to this sense of common destiny. It must be noted, however, that lip service rather than action epitomizes Muslim interaction. For example, there was only limited support for the Muslim community in Afghanistan when it was invaded by the Soviet Union in 1979. Pakistan has fought several wars with India, but no Muslim state has ever placed its lot with Pakistan against India in the name of the solidarity of the Muslim *umma.* Despite these obvious shortcomings, the Muslim *umma* cannot be disregarded. Muslim sentiment can be mobilized in the diplomatic arena, and in such activity the concept of the *umma* must be taken seriously. Incidents in East Jerusalem under Israeli occupation, especially those involving Muslim shrines and worshippers, have angered Muslims the world over. Calls for cooperation within the vast *umma* are especially evident in these circumstances. ***See also*** TEMPLE MOUNT INCIDENT (184).

Wahhabis

63

The modern history of Arabia begins with a puritanical movement deriving its name from its eighteenth-century founder, Mohammad Abdul Wahhab. Wahhab traveled through Syria and Iraq and returned to Arabia convinced that Muslims had deviated from the course established for them by their Prophet. Wahhab was influenced by the Hanbali school of jurisprudence, the most austere and demanding of the four dominant schools in orthodox Sunni Islam. Wahhab preached a simple return to faith and absolute obedience to the tenets of the religion. He engaged his son-in-law, Mohammad ibn Saud, a local leader of a central Arabian tribe, to assist him in spreading a doctrine of discipline, sacrifice, and piety. In the ways of the Arabian tribal chieftains, that could only mean doing violence to those who opposed his teaching. Abdul Wahhab's followers were dedicated to his prescription, and they were named Wahhabis by their adversaries. A long and bloody campaign was launched that spread Wahhabism throughout Arabia. The Wahhabis attacked and burned the citadel of Shiite Islam at Kerbela in 1801. They entered Mecca in 1803 and Medina in 1804 and laid waste many of the historic sites. Gathering a sizable army, the Wahhabis invaded Iraq and Syria and moved all the way to the Mediterranean coast. Fearful that they would spread unrest throughout the empire, the Ottoman sultan ordered his best general, Mohammad Ali (later to found his own dynasty in Egypt), to destroy the Wahhabis. Mohammad Ali did not disappoint his sovereign. The Wahhabis were defeated in 1818 and forced to retreat to the Arabian interior. The Wahhabis did not surface again until Abdul Aziz ibn Saud, in the name of Wahhabism, defeated his two rivals, the Rashidis and the Hashemites, in their respective strongholds following World War I. The Rashidis of central Arabia had lost stature with the Ottoman defeat in World War I. The Hashemites, the keepers of the holy cities of Mecca and Medina, did not have sufficient arms or warriors to stave off the Saudi drive. Moreover, the British supported both the Hashemites and the Saudis, and when the latter proved victorious, London acknowledged Saudi authority. The sons of the defeated Hashemite leader, however, were not to be denied. Britain placed one in Syria and the other in a new state carved out of Ottoman Palestine, namely Transjordan. When the French objected to a Hashemite king in Syria, Britain found a place for him in Iraq. The British role in recognizing Saudi control over most of the Arabian Peninsula was reinforced in 1933 when the Arabian American Oil Company was formed. Saudi Arabia was now an active participant in the constellation of Middle East political powers. Wahhabism became the legitimizing force, the nomadic bedouin were carefully woven into a fabric of Islamic brotherhood (*ikhwan*), and intermarriage between Saudis and the progeny of local rulers and headmen created a new dynasty with a destiny that was not to unfold until the post–World War II years.

Significance

Saudi Arabia's political system is intertwined with religious experience. The Saudis do not claim divine powers. They are a temporal authority, charged, as they see it, with sustaining and expanding the world of Islam. They are, however, devoted to Wahhabism, and they insist on the maintenance of a pious order. The al-Shaykh family, allied with the

Saudis, has had primary responsibility for operationalizing the religious experience. Traditionally, they have been called upon to interpret the Qur'an, which is also Saudi Arabia's constitution. The modernization of Saudi Arabia presents Wahhabism with a significant challenge, however. A middle class has emerged and grown, young Saudis have been exposed to foreign study and customs, and the royal guard must coexist with an updated National Guard and a sophisticated military establishment. Saudi Arabia has placed great emphasis on economic and technological development while retaining a traditional political system that continues to rest upon the religious-social order of Wahhabism. The survival of Saudi Arabia, therefore, appears to rest on an aspect of Islamic expression that on the one hand rejects innovation and on the other promotes progress.

Ethnicity and Political Culture

3

Alawite Dynasty **64**

The Alawite dynasty of Morocco claims descent from the Prophet Mohammad's daughter and son-in-law and has prevailed despite numerous adversities for more than 300 years. The Alawites of Morocco are distant relations of the Shiite Alawites of Iran and Syria. The Moroccan Alawite dynasty, however, is Sunni Muslim as a consequence of the complex tribal and ethnic history of Islamic North Africa. The essential transformation is traced to the Muslim Berbers of Mauritania (from which the term *Moor* is derived). They founded the Almoravid dynasty in the eleventh century and unified Morocco after a long period of anarchy. When the Almohad dynasty followed in the twelfth century, Islamic orthodoxy was blended with the political culture of Berber society. By the fourteenth century, however, Morocco was again torn by conflicting ideas and warring tribes. In reaction to ceaseless rivalry and bloodletting, a movement known as Maraboutism emerged. Boosted by the Berbers, it called for the veneration of saints and the establishment of monastic orders. This mystical Islamic revivalism preserved an Islamic way of life in the face of encroaching Spanish and Portuguese power. (The expulsion of the Moors from Spain in 1492 brought the Spaniards to Morocco.) In 1459 a non-Berber dynasty, the Sa'dis, guided by mystical Sufi Maraboutism, gained brief control. Unable to reconcile themselves with the Berber tribes, the Sa'dis were eventually replaced by the Alawites in 1664. The Alawites, although an Arab dynasty, had adopted Berber characteristics. The intermingling of Islamic fundamentalism and mysticism with Berber austerity sustained the dynasty and continues to influence its performance. ***See also*** BERBER (74); SALAFISM (55); SUFISM (59); POLISARIO FRONT (264).

Significance
The Alawite dynasty today is represented by King Hasan II. King Hasan inherited a traditional monarchial institution from his father, Mohammad V, and combines in his person both

temporal and spiritual authority. The king, like the sultans before him, is also referred to as the imam, or religious leader and guide. Alawite authority therefore rests upon an Islamic foundation that caters to the diversity of Moroccan ethnography. Maraboutism, saint worship, monastic orders, and Sufi mysticism are important ingredients legitimizing the rule of the monarch. They are also imperative in maintaining essential unity between the fragmented mountain tribes and the settled population in the cities. The power of the monarch is also demonstrated in the comparative weakness of the political parties and present ideologies. Shiite Alawites are approximately 12 percent of the Syrian population but have dominated the Syrian government and political scene since 1970, the year Hafez al-Assad seized power in a military coup. Assad has emphasized Syrian and Arab nationalism, which tends to conceal his minority status. His secular constitution was pressed on the country in 1973 and was immediately condemned by Sunni Muslims, represented by the Muslim Brotherhood. Riots erupted in Damascus, Aleppo, Homs, and Hama, the demonstrators insisting that "Islam is our constitution." Assad ordered his troops to fire on the protestors, a harbinger of what was to follow. The Alawites argued there was no distinction between their expression of Islam and that of the Sunnis. Assad went further and insinuated he was also a Sunni Muslim. Indeed, the Sunni *ulema* of Syria were "encouraged" to declare that the Alawite sect was an integral part of Islam. Nonetheless, opposition from Sunni Muslims within and outside Syria continued to castigate the Assad regime and its practices. Assad fell back on his family members and his Alawi praetorian guard, the Siraya al-Difai. When violence was directed against his legions, Assad did not hesitate to bloody his opposition. The climactic phase of this encounter was Assad's decision to destroy the town of Hama and its conservative Sunni majority. After armed militants had seized the town's police station and killed approximately 250 Assad supporters, the government ordered its troops to retaliate. In February 1982, the firepower of the Syrian army and air force was unleashed against Hama. Assad's brother Rifaat led the forces that razed the city and killed an estimated 20,000 to 25,000 people. Since that episode the opposition to Alawite rule in Syria has been virtually nil.

Al bu Said Dynasty 65

The Al bu Said dynasty has ruled Oman from 1749 to the present. Identified with the vital port of Muscat, the center of the realm, the Al bu Saids, with British assistance, have spread their authority along the southern coast of the Arabian Peninsula as far as Dhofar and the South Yemen border, and inland to Nizwa, where the dynasty's historical rivals long held sway. Identified with Ibadhi Muslims, the Al bu Said family traditionally has been less theological in outlook than their hinterland subjects. Al bu Said "cosmopolitanism," although narrow by most definitions, has been influenced by its geographic position astride vital international sealanes. Indeed, Al bu Said rule had extended to Zanzibar and the coast of East Africa in the nineteenth century. They were also active in southern Persia and the southern coast of Arabia during this period. European imperialism reduced the Al bu Said empire, but it also reinforced the monarchy against local adversaries. This relationship between the Al bu Saids and external powers has been sustained and is dramatized by their association with the United States today. ***See also***

IBADHIS (87); MUSCAT AND OMAN (19); OMAN WAR, 1957–1959, 1965–1975 (256).

Significance
The Al bu Said dynasty is one of the longest-surviving monarchies in the Middle East. Its authority, however, has been maintained more by foreign assistance than by inherent legitimacy. Alliances with the British in the nineteenth and first half of the twentieth century provided the family with the power to extend and consolidate its rule. When it was again threatened in the aftermath of World War II, the United States, with substantial assistance provided by Iran, prevented the dynasty from being overthrown. Radical forces continue to exploit religious sentiment against the Al bu Saids, who are perceived as decadent, oppressive, and corrupt by a broad segment of Omani society. The Al bu Saids have yet to demonstrate a capacity to satisfy traditional demands, let alone cope with new ideological forces.

Al-Khalifa Dynasty 66

The Al-Khalifa family has ruled the Persian Gulf island of Bahrein since 1783. The island has a much longer history, however; some historians believe that it was a station for the Phoenicians and ancient Sumerians. Bahrein possesses an excellent harbor, and since the days of antiquity, vessels on the gulf have used its port facilities. The recorded history of Bahrein dates from 1507, when the Portuguese occupied the island. They were not driven out until 1602, when Arabs from the Persian side of the gulf pressed a campaign against them. Persia became the preeminent power in Bahrein, but its rule was challenged by Arabian Peninsula Arabs who seized the island in 1783. After a series of tribal wars, the Khalifa family emerged as the dominant force, and they have sustained their authority to the present day. The British played an important role in reinforcing Al-Khalifa authority over Bahrein. In 1820, the shaykh entered into an agreement with the British East India Company that granted the British commercial concessions and the use of port facilities in return for an annual subsidy and protection. The Persian government was angered by the arrangement because of its claim to sovereignty over Bahrein, a claim that it did not give up until 1971. The Persians argued that the British had acknowledged Persia's claim to Bahrein and had reneged on their agreement. In 1927, Persia (then under the leadership of the Pahlavi family) brought the Bahrein claim before the League of Nations. Britain had earlier entered into a treaty with King ibn Saud in which the Saudis agreed not to interfere with the shaykh of Bahrein. The Persians saw this act as confirming Arab sovereignty over the island. Persia, now called Iran, protested again in 1930 and 1934, when the Al-Khalifa ruler granted oil concessions to Western companies. Bahrein became the strategic center for the British in the Persian Gulf. The shaykh also employed British nationals in his government. During World War I, Bahrein was the principal assembly point for the British Expeditionary Force that fought in Mesopotamia. In 1935, it was a key British naval base. During World War II Bahrein came under Italian air attack.

The Al-Khalifa family trace their origin to the same Utubi tribe that gave rise to the Saudis of Arabia and the Sabah of Kuwait. Even before the discovery of petroleum in Bahrein, the island was developed as a fairly modern entrepôt, given its close association with the British and other European commercial nations. The discovery of oil in 1932 led to vast exploitation, and much of its reserves were depleted by the 1980s. The oil industry was nationalized in 1977, but it was too late to practice conservation. Bahrein, therefore, has had to diversify its economy. It has used its wealth to engage in international finance, and banking has become a prominent activity. Saudi oil is refined on Sitra Island, one of more than 30 smaller islands that are also part of the shaykhdom. Aluminum processing is also being developed along with petrochemical industries, especially gas liquefaction. The major port of Manama and the international airport at Muharraq are the most important, economically speaking, in the Persian Gulf. Bahrein obtained its full independence in 1971 and, like Qatar, refused to join the United Arab Emirates. It is a member of the Arab League, and to some extent has replaced Lebanon as the financial capital of the Middle East. Bahrein is therefore more cosmopolitan than any of the other Arabian shaykhdoms. Its current ruler, Shaykh Issa ibn Salman al-Khalifa, possesses almost absolute power. He ordered the drafting of a constitution and called for parliamentary elections in 1973. When the assembly convened, an impasse developed over a security law. The shaykh ordered the body dissolved in 1975. Radical left-wing politicians were arrested, and a substitute political system has yet to surface.

Significance

The Al-Khalifa family have given Bahrein an air of stability. The Khalifas have not stressed Islamic tradition as much as the mainland shaykhs, no doubt due to their long-term association with international merchants. The ruling family does emphasize its Arab character, however, and it verbalizes support for Arab nationalism, especially in the latter's struggle against Israeli Zionism. The Khalifas, however, have been linked to the West for more than a century, and their security may still rest on those ties. The society of Bahrein is a patchwork of cultures and interests. The country is divided between Sunni and Shiite Muslims. More than a third of the population are non-Bahreinis who play an active role in the shaykhdom's economy. This foreign labor force is also a source of friction. Labor unrest and strikes in 1975 brought an end to the brief "democratic" experiment. Future conflict between the Khalifas and the disparate population is predictable. The Khalifas cannot fall back upon kinship ties to the extent that the Saudis or the Al-Thani can. Nor can they claim special religious legitimacy. Association with the West, both past and present, further sullies the Khalifa image. In a period of revolutionary upheaval in the gulf region, the Khalifas, despite their long rule and the commercial achievement of the kingdom, could be in jeopardy. The United States maintained a symbolic Persian Gulf navy (two vessels) at Bahrein from 1949 until 1979, ostensibly at the request of the shah of Iran and with the concurrence of the Bahreini shaykhs. The presence today of significant U.S. forces near the Persian Gulf and the interest of the Saudis in sustaining Khalifa authority, especially in the face of the Iranian fundamentalist revolution, provide some comfort for the ruling Bahrein authority. Moreover, the renewal of the Iranian claim for sovereignty over Bahrein must be taken seriously. In 1991, following the conclusion of Operation Desert Storm, the United States publicized an interest to permanently station U.S. forces on the island. It was obvious the emir had consented and had perhaps even encouraged such a presence. Saudi Arabia also appeared to agree that a U.S. military role in the gulf region was essential and that Bahrein was the best location for a U.S. base. The U.S. attempt to build a gulf alliance, however, was less successful. Egypt showed reluctance in holding its troops in the Gulf region and indeed withdrew the 36,000-man force involved in Operation Desert Storm even earlier than forecast. Syria likewise withdrew its forces because the Saudis and Kuwaitis displayed discomfort with their continued presence. Bahrein's acceptance of American military units on its soil was not matched by the Saudis, who were more inclined to put Desert Storm behind them and to rely on the secret deliberations of the Gulf Cooperation Council. The Saudi government was not only embarrassed by its dependence on the U.S., it also realized its own troops stationed in Kuwait were a growing cause of friction between Saudi Arabia and the smaller kingdom.

Al Sabah Dynasty 67

Kuwait achieved independent statehood in 1961, but the Al Sabah dynasty has dominated the political life of Kuwait since 1756. The monarchy is a traditional hereditary emirate, and succession is made by selection of a shaykh (a recognized tribal leader) from the descendants of the seventh ruler of Kuwait (Shaykh Mubarak al Sabah Al Sabah). The powers of the reigning emir are dictated by the Muslim *shari'a* (correct juridical path), and he is approved by a majority of the delegates in the National Assembly. In the absence of the assembly, confirmation is obtained through the senior members of the royal family. The Al Sabah dynasty rests upon a network of interrelationships that link the royal family, the preeminent tribal leaders, the *ulema* (learned theologians), the military establishment, and the commercial families. The Al Sabah clan has sustained its authority in the modern period because it is the chief recipient of oil revenues. Funds obtained from the exploitation of petroleum are vast, and they have been used by the Al Sabah dynasty to provide retainers for its loyal supporters. Earlier, the rule of the Al Sabah was dependent on its nobility and the capacity to mediate conflict between competing Kuwaiti tribes. Since the 1960s, however, Kuwait has developed more sophisticated political institutions, and new challenges have arisen. Government posts, once monopolized by the Al Sabah family, are now shared with commoners, usually wealthy merchant families like the Al Khalid, Al Ghanim, and Al Salih. A constituent assembly was also organized with the objective of drafting a formal constitution for the country. That constitution was promulgated by the emir in 1962. It declared Kuwait to be a sovereign, independent state within the larger Arab world. The major source of law was the *shari'a*, and Islam was declared the state religion. Freedom of expression was permitted within the confines of the legal system. Kuwait was slated to have an independent judiciary, an elected National Assembly, and a responsible cabinet of ministers. It remained the only Arabian Peninsula state with an established, modern legal system until 1986, when the parliament was dissolved. The conquest of Kuwait by Iraqi forces on August 2, 1990, forced the emir and his family to flee the country. From their residence in Saudi Arabia they waited for the U.S.-led coalition to drive the Iraqis out of Kuwait. In February 1991 Kuwait was liberated by the coalition, and the emir returned to his country three weeks later. He found a ruined country and a desperate population. Changes in governmental structure and rule were forecast, but the initial period was one of martial law as the authorities sought to reestablish the essential infrastructure. In the long term, however, no one doubted the restoration of the parliamentary order. A political system subscribing to democratic practices was forecast, placing in question the character of the Al Sabah family as the preeminent rulers of Kuwait. ***See also*** IRAQ-KUWAIT: WAR AND

CONQUEST (248); OPERATION DESERT SHIELD (257); OPERATION DESERT STORM (258); UN RESOLUTIONS: IRAQ-KUWAIT CONFLICT (230).

Significance

The Al Sabah dynasty of Kuwait was judged by observers to be among the most enlightened of the ruling families on the Arabian Peninsula prior to the Iraqi invasion of 1990. Under the leadership of the Al Sabah clan, Kuwait had developed socioeconomic institutions that aimed at raising the standard of living of the country's inhabitants. Enlightened self-interest also was responsible for the promotion of modernization schemes that brought a heavy influx of labor from surrounding Arab states. Moreover, Kuwait provided domicile for a large number of Palestinian Arabs. The size of this workforce presented problems for the ruling regime, however. The opening of the National Assembly led to the inevitable division of forces, some joining in opposition against the reigning dynasty. One such group was the Arab National Movement (ANM) of Ahmad al Khatib, leftist in orientation and inclined toward more rapid change than the ruling family permitted. This struggle for power in the parliament affected the ministerial cabinet, and Al Sabah members were forced to relinquish their portfolios to influential commoners. Moreover, the demands initiated by the opposition were quickly buttressed by the non-Kuwaiti population, which sought equal status with the Kuwaitis. Kuwait's political opposition recognized that an alliance with these elements would better their chances in their political infighting with the Al Sabah clan. Developments in the larger Arab world, especially the inability to defeat the Israelis in 1967 and 1973, affected Kuwait. By 1975, the Palestinian population in the country was slightly less than 300,000. It had become very vocal and was often hostile toward the regime. The Al Sabah dynasty had been sympathetic to the Palestinians and had even provided them with opportunities for government service. Nevertheless, the dynasty was judged too conservative, too neutral on issues such as the Lebanese Civil War, and too friendly toward the United States. Thus, with the Palestinians gaining greater leverage in the National Assembly, with the ruling family under increasing pressure to yield its traditional power, with terrorist incidents on the increase, and with the Left on the ascendant, the emir dissolved the legislature and restricted all freedoms. The closing of the parliament in 1976 after 14 years of legislative activity was accomplished to save the monarchy. In fact, the Kuwaiti census of 1976 revealed that the indigenous population had become a minority in their own country. Only 47.5 percent of the population of 1,055,000 were Kuwaiti-born. The continuing settlement of Palestinians and their higher birthrate led observers to conclude that they would soon outnumber their Kuwaiti counterparts. The Palestinians also had acquired influential positions in the business community and educational institutions, from which they swayed the nation's youth. Thus, the National Assembly was not reopened until 1980, after new elections were held. By that time, the Al Sabah family had displayed its determination, had restricted the activities of the political opposition, and had regained the loyalty of the disaffected tribal leaders. The Al Sabah clan used the hiatus between assemblies to restore the monarchy's traditional dependence on bedouin democracy (decision by tribal consensus) to offset the influence of the non-Kuwaitis. But after these initial successes, pressure was again brought to bear on the Al Sabah family by the Palestinian community, which in good part had come under the influence of Saddam Hussain in

Iraq and Iranian radicals, who considered Ayatollah Khomeini their patron saint. Both elements targeted the Al Sabah family, and in the unstable political environment generated by their actions the emir ordered the closing of the National Assembly once again. In 1986 all political activity was suspended and strict security measures were adopted. Kuwait's independent style infuriated both its internal and foreign opposition. And when Baghdad found fault with Kuwait's oil policy, tensions increased between the two neighbors. Iraq's subsequent invasion and annexation of Kuwait, and its defiance of the world community as demonstrated in the United Nations Security Council resolutions, led to a violent encounter in Operation Desert Storm in 1991. Iraq was forced to acknowledge the independence of Kuwait and the reinstatement of the emir and the Al Sabah family, but the events of 1990–1991 appeared to have changed the character of the region, and thus the future of the Al Sabah.

Al Saud Dynasty 68

The Saud dynasty developed during the eighteenth century in the Nejd highland of the Arabian interior. Mohammad ibn Saud, the son-in-law and disciple of Mohammad ibn Abdul Wahhab (an austere Muslim theologian and jurist), led his tribal army in a triumphal campaign that conquered a good portion of the Arabian Peninsula. Armed with the doctrine of Wahhabism, and known as Wahhabis, the Saudis spoke the language of Islamic fundamentalism and insisted on a life of simple but strict piety unencumbered by ritual borrowings or embellishment. The death of Mohammad ibn Saud in 1765 did not terminate the Saudi action. His son and successor, Abdul Aziz, pressed the Saudis to more extensive conquests, and, in 1787, Aziz established the hereditary succession of the Saudi house by having his own son confirmed as his successor by Mohammad ibn Abdul Wahhab before a great popular assembly of tribal leaders. In the years that followed, the Saudi Wahhabis continued their advance into Iraq undeterred by the pasha of Baghdad. The Sunni Wahhabis attacked the holiest city of the Shiite Muslims and destroyed the building over the grave of the venerated and martyred Husain, the Prophet Mohammad's grandson and the person Shiites believe should have succeeded to the Islamic caliphate. The Saudis also spread their authority into the Hejaz of the Arabian Peninsula, seizing the Sunni Muslim holy places of Mecca and Medina. The Saudis were more than warriors consumed by faith, however. Their simple administration provided Arabia with a degree of public security never before experienced. Islamic law replaced personal vengeance, and magistrates were authorized to dispense justice. No one was immune from the law as specified in the Qur'an, and justice was swift and effective. Moreover, religious performance was emphasized, and severe punishments were meted out to violators of divine obligations. The bedouin tribesmen who made up the Saudi Wahhabi army received no payment for their services, but were expected to make contributions in the form of taxes to the Saudi prince for the upkeep of his house and personal retinue. But the Ottoman sultan recognized a threat to his own rule and ordered his army to crush the Wahhabis and the house of Saud. The Ottoman forces led by Mohammad Ali, the sultan's commanding general in Egypt, forced the Saudis to give up their gains and retreat into the Arabian interior. They settled in Riyadh, received the loyalty of the powerful Shammar tribe, and proceeded to reconstitute their forces. Wahhabism and the Saudis remained somewhat in the shadows of Arabian history in the latter half of the nineteenth century. During World War I, their association with the British (begun when Britain occupied Aden in 1839) and their total opposition to the Ottomans propelled them back onto the Arabian stage. But after a halting involvement in World War I, the leader of the House of Saud, Abdul Aziz ibn Saud, decided to hold his forces in reserve, as the British Colonial Office in London seemed more inclined toward mobilizing the forces of the sherif of Mecca, the keeper of the holy places in Mecca and Medina and the dominant force in the Hejaz region of Arabia. The sherif of Mecca, given the Ottoman retreat from the peninsula, saw the opportunity for a Muslim renaissance, and he positioned himself to lead the Arabs. In the aftermath of World War I the Ottoman Empire lost its raison d'être, and Turkish nationalists led by Ataturk eventually brought it to an end. The termination of the Ottoman Empire also involved Turkish relinquishment of the Islamic caliphate. When the sherif of Mecca attempted to establish himself as the caliph of Islam, Abdul Aziz ibn Saud had his cause célèbre. By identifying the sherif of Mecca as a heretic and usurper, ibn Saud was able to rally a large and determined following, and in the name of a revived Wahhabism, they assaulted and defeated the sherif and his forces. The Hejaz as well as the Nejd now came under the rule of the House of Saud. By 1926 the Saudis were recognized as the new protectors of Islam's holiest shrines. In 1930 ibn Saud was crowned king of the Nejd and Hejaz, and the modern dynasty was formally established. Saudi Arabia was formally proclaimed in 1932 and assumed a place in the family of nations. Assisted by the British, the new king attempted to consolidate his power and bring the other reigning Arabian monarchs and chieftains under his influence. Family alliances were pursued with the dominant shaykhs, and through intermarriage (Islam sanctions the taking of more than one wife) links were forged to stabilize Saudi authority throughout the peninsula. Ibn Saud proved to be an enlightened monarch, and due to his contacts with his British advisors, he sensed the need to usher the Arabian Peninsula into the twentieth century. He is sometimes credited with introducing the automobile, the telephone, and the radio to Arabia. More important, however, was his decision to grant oil concessions to U.S. oil companies. As a result of the latter activity, the Arabian American Oil Company (ARAMCO) was established in 1933. The revenue derived from the sale of oil provided the Saudi treasury with the funds needed to purchase the loyalty of the shaykhs, and thus maintain the alliances. When ibn Saud died in 1953, he left his heirs a functioning monarchy with strong ties to both Great Britain and the United States. Abdul Aziz's successor, Saud ibn Saud, lacking his father's talents and strength, was neither able to manage the traditional system nor able to cope with the challenges presented by a changing world, and the new commercial class, which was most influenced by these ideas, began to demand changes in the country's total way of life. Political parties were strictly forbidden, but there was no mistaking the assault on authority. The Saudi family thus took matters into their own hands. In a bloodless coup in 1965 they "retired" Saud ibn Saud and placed his brother Faisal on the throne. It was during Faisal's reign (1964–1975) that Saudi Arabia assumed the role of an economic superpower, and the country, no longer a remote hinterland, began to play a major role in Middle East and world affairs. The assassination of Faisal by an estranged member of the extended family was a blow to the Saudis, but their system prevailed. Faisal was succeeded by his brother Khalid, who was quickly recognized to be a figurehead king. Authority rested with the more dynamic members of the family, and especially with Crown Prince Fahd, another brother. Khalid did not interfere with the administration of the country or the fashioning of its policies in the years of his reign (1975–1982). His death in June 1982, therefore, caused little outward concern. Fahd assumed the throne within hours of Khalid's death, and still another brother, Abdullah, the head of the Saudi National Guard, was named crown prince. Although there had been talk of rivalry between Fahd and Abdullah, the juxtaposition of the two Saudi leaders suggested efforts to placate different elements within the family. ***See also*** WAHHABIS (63); ARAMCO (196).

Significance
Saudi Arabia is one of the world's most formidable economic and financial powers. Within its territory is the world's largest reserve of petroleum, and its dominance of the oil export market has been well established. Saudi Arabia is also in the midst of a vast development program that aims to modernize the society, and especially to prepare it for a time in the foreseeable future when oil stores will be depleted. Recent five-year plans authorized expenditures of $250 billion. The 1975–1980 plan cost in excess of $150 billion, not including military expenditures. Saudi Arabia is also an indispensable prop to the world's financial system, and its leaders have invested heavily in industrialized as well as Third World countries. But with all this sophisticated activity, Saudi Arabia sustains a traditional political system, characteristic of the Arabian Peninsula, and thus far has been resistant to the changes that its own leadership has initiated. Saudi Arabia plays a modern and important role in world affairs, but it is the only country named after a family. Moreover, the House of Saud jealously protects its legacy and continues to monopolize authority. In this regard, the Saudis have seldom expressed territorial ambitions. Conflicts with neighboring states are generally over questions of border delineations, e.g., the Buraimi Oasis dispute, rather than serious efforts at expansion and annexation. The Saudis are more interested in consolidation and equilibrium than in conquest and empire. In any event, financial empire-building is a more successful enterprise than political ambition. The Saudis do have problems, however. Radical ideas and movements have penetrated the region and are judged a threat to the security of the realm. Even Saudi youth, many educated abroad, are restless and demand changes in the traditional order. Critics argue that the Saudis are not backward, but corrupt and profligate. The country's wealth, it is argued, is used to bolster the regime and the family, not benefit the nation. Furthermore, many dissidents also assume a posture of Arab nationalism. They claim that the House of Saud does not do enough to promote Arab unity or to combat the Israelis; and they condemn Saudi Arabia's close relationship with the United States. In the face of this opposition, some of it violent, the Saudi family protects its own. Despite differences within the ruling circle, despite filial rivalries, the overriding tendency is to settle family quarrels in absolute privacy and to sustain the system bequeathed to them by their father. Family differences can be traced to the wives of Abdul Aziz ibn Saud. Ibn Saud had 18 wives and numerous concubines. The Saudi family with its collateral branches ranges around 5,000 members. The primary members of the family, however, are

considerably fewer than that number; the maternal line is most important. Saud ibn Saud was the offspring of Wadhba bint Mohammad. Faisal was the offspring of Tarfa bint al-Shaykh Abdullah. Khalid was the second son of Jauhara bint Musaid ibn Jilwa. King Fahd was born to Hassa bint Ahmad Al Sudairi. Crown Prince Abdullah is the only son born to Al Fahda bint Asi al Shuraim. The Sudairi line, from which King Fahd extends, is perhaps the most notable. Along with his six brothers, King Fahd represents the most numerous branch. In addition, his six sons also have high aspirations. King Fahd's brother Naif is minister of the interior and charged with maintaining domestic security; Turki is a former defense minister; Salman is the governor of Riyadh, the Saudi capital; Ahmad is deputy interior minister; Sultan is minister of defense and in charge of expanding and modernizing the armed forces; and the sixth brother, Abdul Rahman, is one of the country's most important businessmen and is directly connected with the influential commercial sector. King Fahd is the oldest member of the Sudairi branch; he has also been its most influential. Well educated, worldly, and cautious but deliberate, King Fahd has ushered in a "new" Saudi Arabia, but not necessarily one that will pacify detractors or remove the pressure on the Al Saud dynasty.

Al-Thani Dynasty 69

The Al-Thani family has ruled Qatar since the latter half of the nineteenth century. Qatar is a shaykhdom on the Persian Gulf side of the Arabian Peninsula. Long under the occupation and/or control of the Persians, Qatar established its Arab identity with the help of the British in the 1860s and entered into formal relations with the British in 1882. The Al-Thani family were among those Arabian shaykhs with whom the British had intimate relations. The Europeans also assisted the Al-Thani in separating themselves from the Bahreini rulers who claimed dominance over the Qatari Peninsula. In 1916, the Al-Thani signed an agreement with Great Britain, similar to British agreements with the other Trucial shaykhs, that granted pearling concessions and other monopolies to the British. Relations with the other Europeans had to receive approval of the British agent. Before the discovery of oil, pearl fishing and nomadic herding provided the only economic activities in the shaykhdom. The port of Doha, the Qatari capital, lost its limited importance to Bahrein. The result was stagnation and a primitive lifestyle. As in the other gulf shaykhdoms, Qatar's security and foreign policy was made the responsibility of the British. The Al-Thani family made Islam the state religion. They are also devotees of Saudi Wahhabism and are traditional in their tastes and performance. Like the Saudis, the Al-Thani have practiced intermarriage with the tribes of the peninsula. After a century of such activity, the family has spread its branches throughout the country and today represents the largest network of filial relationships of all the gulf shaykhdoms. This broad family structure has solidified the monarchy and contributed to the broad stability enjoyed by the larger population. But as much as Qatar enjoys relative tranquility, the Al-Thani family is not without conflict. In 1960, the ruling emir was deposed by his son Ahmed with assistance from the British. In 1972, Ahmed was forcefully removed by his cousin Shaykh Khalifa ibn Hamad Al-Thani. Qatar's ties to Britain were severed in 1971, the same year in which the other Trucial states achieved their independence, and Shaykh Ahmed was considered too profligate to lead Qatar into a developmental phase. Shaykh Khalifa was judged more serious, more trustworthy, and more dynamic. He was also free from the taint of British tutelage. Qatar considered joining the United Arab Emirates, but then declined. Oil was discovered in Qatar in the 1930s, and in 1935 an oil concession was obtained by a British-registered company, Petroleum Development (Qatar) Ltd., a subsidiary of the Iraq Petroleum Company. The first well was drilled in 1937, and larger fields were uncovered in 1940. Development of Qatari petroleum had to wait for the end of World War II, however. The 1960s and 1970s witnessed considerable growth. Just before the oil embargo of 1973, revenues from petroleum totalled slightly less than half a billion dollars annually. Since that time, profits have escalated, and the shaykhdom has accumulated considerable financial holdings in Europe and the United States. Oil royalties are estimated at $2 billion annually. One-fourth of the oil revenue is reserved for the Al-Thani ruler. He in turn distributes this enormous sum among his extended family. The remainder is spent on government services and modernization projects. As with Saudi Arabia, the pace of development has accelerated. Desalination plants have been constructed to provide fresh water from the sea. Power stations, roads, schools, hospitals, and industrial plants, especially petrochemical, have been built, and others are nearing completion or are contemplated.

Significance
The Al-Thani dynasty is another of the more stable regimes of the Persian Gulf. The family shares the Hanbalite Wahhabi tradition with the Saudis. Its only frontier also borders on Saudi Arabia. The Al-Thani, therefore, reflect similar interests with the Saudis. Qatar is an active member of the Arab League and has been prominent, for its size, in promoting Arab causes in the larger world. It has provided substantial financial support in the Arab conflict with Israel and has even dispatched token military contingents to the front with Israel. Qatar is also engaged in modernizing its political-administrative systems without necessarily destabilizing Al-Thani rule. The ruling shaykh is assisted by an advisory council of more than 20 prominent Qataris, many of whom are family members. Constitutional developments describe a distribution of responsibility, but there is no intention to liberalize the system to include a multitude of non-family officials in the decision-making circle. Educational opportunity is expanding, however, and more young Qataris are studying abroad than ever before. As with the other traditional shaykhdoms, the Al-Thani dynasty recognizes that the modernization it promotes affects its monopoly of power.

Arabization 70

Arabization refers to the spreading of Arab ethnicity and culture, particularly in the form of the Arabic language, from the Arabian Peninsula through the Fertile Crescent and out across North Africa. The Arab conquests that commenced in the seventh century either displaced older indigenous civilizations or superimposed Arab civilization over prevailing lifestyles. Pre-Arab Mesopotamian, Egyptian, and Berber civilizations were either eclipsed or modified to permit the adoption of Arab traits and adaptation to Arab societal forms. Arabization did not succeed in Spain despite a 700-year effort. Nor was it successful in Byzantium, in Iran, among the Turks of central Asia, or among the diverse populations of India. Byzantium effectively beat back the Arab invaders, and the Christian empire was eventually bypassed. The Turks also successfully resisted Arab encroachment. And although the Arabs overran Iran and moved into western India, except for pockets of Arab settlements, Arabization was rejected. Indeed, the Arab Moplah community in western India was established by Arab traders, not by a conquering army. Arabization was more successful in the Mediterranean region in the aftermath of the decline of Rome; control of land was fragmented, political order was minimal, and society suffered overall disarray. Although the Arabs found somewhat similar conditions in Iran, where the long-reigning Persian Sasanian Empire was in an advanced stage of decay, Persian culture proved too strong and too developed for Arabization to occur. *See also* ETHNICITY (84).

Significance
Arabization was facilitated by Islamization. Although the Arabs met resistance along their paths of conquest, Islam was broadly accepted. Byzantium of course rejected Islam, as did the Europeans. But the Persians adopted Islam with practically the same fervor as did the people along the southern shore of the Mediterranean Sea. The Turks, however, proved to be difficult converts. Persians, not Arabs, were responsible for the Islamization of the Turkic people. Moreover, Islamization prompted the Turks to leave their central Asian homeland and to begin their migrations to Asia Minor, the Middle East, and ultimately Europe and North Africa. In the course of this movement of central Asians, the Mongol armies of Genghis Khan struck through the Turkic world to Russia and Eastern Europe in 1258. The Turks were further propelled by these Far Eastern invaders, and even larger migrations occurred until Byzantium was finally destroyed in 1453 by the Ottomans. Turkification competed with Arabization, but neither made serious inroads against the other. Even the Ottoman Turkish conquest of much of the Arab world from the sixteenth to the early decades of the twentieth century did not cause one to yield to the other. Arabic vocabulary intermingled with Turkish and Persian, as well as other languages, but this was a consequence of Islam, not Arab power. Religious ritual and dogma were expressed in Arabic. The Qur'an was an Arabic text. Believers were required by the tenets of their faith to respect tradition. Common belief, however, could not overcome the rivalry between Arabization, Turkification, and Persianization. Arabization proved most successful where Arab settlements combined with Islamic tradition. The Arabs established permanent settlements in the Fertile Crescent and North Africa, and, although efforts were made to remove them, they prevailed, assuring expansion of the Arab identity from its original nesting ground in the Arabian Peninsula.

Asabiyya 71

Asabiyya is the descriptive term in Arabic that specifies family, clan, and tribe. *Asabiyya* is distinguished from *qawm* or *watan*, essentially country or fatherland, and *umma*, the all-embracing concept involving the whole Islamic community. *Asabiyya* focuses on the smallest corporate entity in the Arab, and also in the extended Muslim, world. The term *asabiyya* is used more by Arabs than by other Muslims. But all Muslims practice *asabiyya*, whether or not the word is used to express their activity. *Asabiyya* has been interpreted by scholars of Islam as the "spirit of kinship"; it is reflective of the mundane, day-to-day personal relationships between members of the same family, clan, or tribe. In Arab culture, and again generally found among all Muslims, *asabiyya* involves a hierarchical system dominated by a male member of the family, clan, or tribe. The "family" in this sense is a solidaristic organization in which persons, related by ties of blood, form themselves into an effective cooperative union. Given the supremacy of the family, clan, or tribe, each member is obliged to perform the role assigned him or her by the presiding patriarch. Given the tenacity with which families, clans, and tribes cling to their exclusive circumstances, *asabiyya* is a divisive element. Nonetheless, historically Muslims have looked to the family for protection, support, and opportunity. The Western notion of a territorial entity, a nation-state deserving one's highest loyalty, is in some ways neutralized by the prevailing view that the family, not the state, provides the individual with the best means for survival. ***See also*** UMMA (62).

Significance
Asabiyya is the most prominent form of political organization in the Middle East. Although family ties are important throughout the human family, the Muslims of the Middle East have sustained the notion that family, clan, and tribe come before country and extended community. *Asabiyya* is a form of parochialism. It suggests narrow but intense loyalties. It operates on the basis of exclusivity and runs counter to the idea and purpose of nationalism and abstract community. States and governments have always been identified with distant authorities who know little and care less about the conditions of those over whom they rule. Governments are traditionally resisted, and cooperation is seldom voluntary or instinctive. Moreover, governments have usually been formed by powerful families pursuing their particular interests. Nepotism and its concomitant, corruption, are perceived as the evils of government. In challenging government, therefore, the family also opposes rival clans. *Asabiyya* is a cultural expression of desert life. The independence of the bedouin, or desert nomad, is preferred to the more settled routine and the higher, more complex organization of the city dweller. The perpetuation of *asabiyya* in Islamic societies, and especially Arab politics, indicates the power of tradition over modernity. Legitimacy is an elusive commodity in the Muslim world. Leaders and governments live under constant threat; institutional development is limited; and national integration must still be realized. Given these uncertainties and the *anomie*, or feeling of rootlessness, in societies buffeted by alien ideas and challenged by modern technology, *asabiyya* is both an explanation for political divisiveness and a promise of survival in a traumatic age.

Authoritarianism 72

Authoritarianism in Islam places emphasis on the great leader. This fascination with an all-powerful, all-knowing individual is not unique to Muslims, but there is a compelling tendency to seek both survival in this life and salvation in the next through the pronouncements and performance of venerated figures. The Muslim *mahdi,* the savior, is expected to purify society and to bring about the Kingdom of God. The secular expression of the total leader takes many forms, but the adulation conferred on authorities, whether in monarchial or spiritual form, secular or ideological, is marked in Islamic tradition. There is also a mystical quality to this relationship between the leader and the led. The notion that leaders possess *baraka,* or magical protection, is deeply ingrained. Pakistanis continue to revere the name of the country's founder, Mohammad Ali Jinnah. Even before the independence of Pakistan, Jinnah was called by the title Quaid-i-Azam, or Great Leader. He is still referred to as the Quaid (leader) today, long after his death. The Ayatollah Khomeini commanded blind obedience and was celebrated as the imam, an illustrious spiritual and temporal guide. Even his predecessor was not satisfied with the simple title shah, or king. King of kings was the more appropriate designation for the late Pahlavi leader. Gamal Abdul Nasser could have been crowned king had he expressed the desire. There was no mistaking his maximum leadership as the *rais*, or supreme ruler, of Egypt and the most outstanding personality in the Arab world. Islam gives expression to powerful personalities in part because it is so demanding of individual believers. The faithful are called upon to surrender themselves to the teachings of the Prophet and the unity of God and to minimize private indulgences. But Islam has not reduced nepotism. Nor has it mastered kinship rivalries or opportunistic leadership. Despite Islamic emphasis on egalitarianism, the Islamic world is mired in a form of quasi-feudalism in which the property-owning families owe nothing to their peasant subjects. Dependence, not interdependence, characterizes this relationship. It also perpetuates systems of authoritarianism that remain unaltered by change from traditional theological-monarchial orders to nationalistic-administrative orders. ***See also*** ASABIYYA (71).

Significance

Authoritarian leaders bear heavy burdens in an era of expanding communication, large-scale social mobilization, and complex organization. Mystique is difficult, sometimes impossible, to sustain. Efficiency and effective management are measures by which leaders are more likely to be judged. Moreover, success is only possible if leaders are provided with, and are capable of directing, institutional arrangements that focus on the needs of the broader society. In the absence of such apparatus, "great leaders" are exposed to the condemnation of their opponents and to the criticism of those with legitimate grievances and to that of their sometime supporters, many of whom believe they can do a better job. Appeals to conventional patterns of tradition, to Islamic teachings and principles, do not insulate such leaders from abusive assaults on their persons. As much as Muslims pine for "great leaders," they are just as eager to question those who pretend to lay claim to the title. Interestingly, however, the fall of the titans not only produces a time of trouble; it also usually brings forward new authorities with tastes and techniques little different from those who preceded them.

Autonomy 73

Autonomy refers to administrative decision making by and for a particular ethnic, linguistic, religious, or otherwise specific cultural entity. Autonomy is not the same as sovereignty. An autonomous region operates within the confines of a larger political entity that is sovereign and hence preeminent. Autonomous regions, for example, are not empowered to organize their own army, carry on their own foreign policy, or issue their own currency. They have delegated powers that allow them to administer their daily affairs, but they do not possess independent political power. There are several examples involving autonomy questions in the Middle East, but the most prominent focuses on the Palestinians living in the West Bank territory under Israeli occupation. The Camp David Accords and the Egyptian-Israeli Peace Treaty are both concerned with Palestinian autonomy. Negotiations on this subject between Israel and Egypt have been carried on for several years since 1979. Agreement, however, has not been achieved. Resolution of the Palestinian question is believed to be the key to peace in the Middle East, or at least a large body of opinion argues the Arab-Israeli dispute can be managed if the Palestinians are provided with a homeland. Under U.S. guidance, especially during the Jimmy Carter administration, emphasis was on a gradual process that would eventually permit the Palestinian Arabs to govern themselves. Israel accepted the notion of Palestinian autonomy when it signed the treaty with Egypt. Egypt saw this acknowledgment as an opportunity to press for Palestinian self-determination, something the Israelis were not prepared to accept. Nevertheless, representatives from the two nations have met periodically, and each has presented its case with equal forcefulness. While there has been agreement on defining the subject, no progress has been made on the issues. The major hurdle is the matter of security. Israel wants ironclad assurances. Egypt has argued that the transfer of authority will lower the level of hostility that Palestinians direct at Israel, thus providing Israelis with a favorable climate in which to relate to the Arabs, but Israel does not accept the logic of this argument. Specifically, the Egyptians want internal security on the West Bank to be handled by a local council of Palestinians. They want all Israeli settlements dismantled and the settlers withdrawn to Israel. Israel flatly rejects these demands. It insists on maintaining exclusive responsibility for security, and it intends to increase, not eliminate, the settlements. Clearly, the two countries have entirely different interpretations of autonomy. Israel will permit a small administrative council, like a municipal council, with limited authority and no right to legislate or control either internal or external security. Egypt calls for a large council with wide-ranging powers. In effect such a body would be a surrogate for legislative and executive branches of government. The council would manage internal security and would arrange for its own police force and small defense establishment. It would also control its water and land resources. And not only would Israeli settlements be removed, but also Israeli army deployment would be supervised by the council. Both arrangements were considered interim measures in keeping with Camp David, and lasting for a period of five years, after which the question of eventual self-determination would be entertained. The Israeli complaint centered on the Egyptian definition of autonomy, which appeared to grant sovereign status to the Palestinians even prior to the five-year trial period. From the Egyptian point of view, the Israeli proposal renders the autonomy matter meaningless and merely provides a cover for the perpetuation of Israeli rule over the West Bank. This was the impasse when Sadat was assassinated. Little has occurred in the period following his death to break the deadlock. ***See also*** REAGAN PROGRAM ON PALESTINE (177); INTIFADA (151); ARAB-ISRAELI PEACE CONFERENCES (195).

Significance
The Palestinian autonomy talks have raised the level of frustration and conflict rather than holding out the promise for a peaceful settlement of the Arab-Israeli conflict. Ever since the autonomy idea was publicized by Egypt, Israel, and the United States, the West Bank territory has been torn by conflict. Arab demonstrators have been killed by Israeli troops, and Israeli settlers and soldiers have been murdered by Palestinian Arabs. Since the Hebron incidents of 1980, when several Israelis lost their lives, the Israeli military has given little quarter to the Palestinians. Stone-throwing and molotov cocktails have been answered by automatic

weapons. Many Palestinians, especially the very young, have been killed. Curfews have been imposed, and several Arab mayors of West Bank cities have been dismissed by Israeli authorities. Moreover, the unrest could not be confined to the West Bank. The Gaza Strip is also restless, and the mayor of Gaza, heretofore considered a "moderate," was removed in 1982 for his vitriolic attacks on the Israelis, which were especially directed at the Israeli invasion of Lebanon. Earlier, however, the escalation of the fighting on the West Bank influenced the autonomy negotiations between Egyptian and Israeli officials. It was alleged that the PLO had authorized widespread demonstrations to provoke Israeli violence. Such action, it was assumed, would prevent the talks from proceeding. Moreover, observers on the West Bank detected a resurgence of communist activity. The Palestinian Organization of the Jordanian Communist Party, headed by Bashir Barghuti, and the Palestinian Communist Party, affiliated with a group called the Leninist Lodge (a splinter group of the Jordanian Communist Party), were said to be visibly active in provoking West Bank protests and riots. The communists were few in number, but they had aggressively penetrated the professional organizations, the municipalities, trade unions, and welfare associations. The communists also found willing recruits for their demonstrations among the five small colleges on the West Bank. The reappearance of *al-Talia* (*The Vanguard*), edited by Barghuti, gave the communists even greater opportunity to spread their message. Communist propaganda surfaced in East Jerusalem and other cities and towns, given Israeli reluctance to close down the communist presses. Moreover, Israel's multiparty system makes a place for the communists, and censorship is possible only in security affairs. It appeared that the communists on the West Bank, like the PLO and other political groups, were preparing either for the implementation of an autonomy plan or for the failure of such a plan, which would provide them with a chance to gain adherents. The PLO defeat in Lebanon was destined to enliven the autonomy question. The Israelis may have forced the PLO to assume subordinate status, but the communists were eager to assert their prowess. The Palestinian *intifada* on the West Bank and Gaza that erupted in the 1980s and continued into the 1990s was an extension of the earlier uprisings and demonstrations against Israeli occupation. The PLO took command of the *intifada* and publicized the action around the world. During this period the PLO, under the leadership of Yasser Arafat, publicly declared its acceptance of UN resolutions 242 and 338 and thereby seemed to acknowledge Israel's right to exist. Nevertheless, the PLO did not abandon the Palestine National Covenant, which called for the liquidation of Israel, and the Israelis had reason to be skeptical. Although the PLO established a government in exile in 1988 and declared Arafat the president of the Palestinian state, Palestinian support for Saddam Hussain in his annexation of Kuwait and in the subsequent war against the U.S.-led coalition did not augur well for Palestinian autonomy, let alone independence for the West Bank territory and Gaza. The American-orchestrated peace conference in October–November 1991 was aimed at convincing the Israelis that their continuing control of the West Bank territory was not in their long-term interest.

Berber 74

Berbers are people inhabiting regions of North Africa whose language of the same name is identified with the

Afro-Asian linguistic family. These non-Arabic tribes range in color from caucasian to dark brown, revealing their mixed heritage and the historical blending of diverse civilizations. The Berber language is primarily spoken and seldom found in written form. Berber speakers, however, number in excess of 10 million and represent more than 50 percent of the population of North Africa, including the Arabicized Berbers and excluding Egypt. Morocco's population is approximately 45 percent pure Berber, while Algeria's is roughly 30 percent. Tunisia has a minute active Berber population. The Berbers of Morocco are the most important. These break down into three principal groups, each with its own dialect (there are approximately 300 Berber dialects). The Rifs inhabit the mountains in the northeastern section of the country. The Tamazight-speaking Berbers live in the Middle Atlas Mountains and the Central High Atlas Mountains, and a smaller group reside in the vicinity of the Sahara Desert. The Tashilhit-speaking Berbers are found in the High and Anti-Atlas mountains. Many Berbers, because of heavy Arab influence, speak Arabic. The Za'ir Berbers speak only Arabic, and some Arab tribes of the Suss Valley speak only Berber. The Berbers have lived in North Africa from earliest recorded history. References to their activities can be found in Egyptian, Greek, and Roman inscriptions. Prior to the coming of the Islamic era, the Berbers inhabited the vast area between Egypt and the Atlantic Ocean. The Arab invaders who swept across North Africa and passed into Spain by the Strait of Gibraltar forced the Berbers away from the coast and into the mountainous western region. The Atlas Range and the Saharan margins offered protection from the Arabian warriors. The Berbers converted to Islam when Arabdom was firmly implanted in the region, but struggles between Arabs and Berbers were constant in the decades and centuries that followed. The Barbary Coast also derives its name from the Berber, and the Barbary pirates that preyed upon Mediterranean commerce in the eighteenth and nineteenth centuries were a mixed band of Berbers and Arabs. The young United States joined its European counterparts in sending a military force to crush the Barbary pirates. The Spanish and French subsequently imposed their influence on North Africa, and the region lost its independence to European colonialism. In 1926 the Rif Berbers attacked and defeated the Spanish, driving them from Spanish Morocco. Attempts to spread Berber power into French Morocco, however, were beaten back. The French enjoyed the support of some Berber tribes, and in the post–World War II period, with the assistance of these tribes, they forced Mohammad V ibn Yousef into exile. This act of divide and rule backfired and the majority of Arabs and Berbers rallied together in common cause. With help drawn from Berbers in the Atlas Mountains in Algeria, a combined Arab-Berber force opened terrorist attacks against French settlements and challenged French installations. Observing the loss of Berber support, and facing an insurrection of even more violent proportions in Algeria, the French restored Mohammad V to his throne in 1955 and granted Morocco its independence in 1956. This act only whetted the appetite of the Berber-Arab forces in Algeria, who accelerated their campaign. France insisted on treating Algeria as a province fully integrated with the parent country, and the clash between French and Algerian troops was long and bloody. In 1962, however, Paris realized the hopelessness of its cause and granted Algeria its independence. *See also* ALAWITE DYNASTY (64).

Significance

The Berbers are active in Moroccan politics. Largely monarchist, the Mouvement Populaire (MP), the Mouvement Populaire Democratique et Constitutionnel (MPDC), and the Parti de l'Action (PA) all represent rural Berber constituencies. The MP is the most aggressive of the three groups. Formed in 1957, it reflected rural tribal bitterness over the urban-based Arab Istiqlal Party, which sought to dominate the government. The MP's tactics were to avoid the formal government and to lend direct assistance to the king. Mohammad V saw the utility in gaining Berber support, and given his desire to rule rather than reign, the Berbers were a tremendous asset in his overcoming Istiqlal influence. In return for the king's favor, the MP insisted on calling the monarch the imam, or spiritual leader, of all of North Africa. They were anti-French and lent support to their brethren in Algeria, while at the same time demonstrating their anti-communism. Conscious of the trend toward Marxism among Third World youth, the MP was the first Moroccan political organization to call for the establishment of "Islamic socialism" and the closing of the gap between the privileged and the deprived. But as observers have noted, the MP, above all, stood for "unabashed Berberism." The socialism they preached aimed at retaining the tribal collective unit and the institution of the *jemma,* a council of local tribal elders selected annually. Moreover, the MP demanded the development of educational programs that preserved the Berber dialects and promised young Berbers positions in government, the military, and the commercial sector. The other Berber political organizations were splinters from the MP that were personality oriented. These lesser parties attempted alliances with the urban-based, Arab-dominated groups, but they failed to attract large numbers. The Berbers have survived the vicissitudes of the centuries because they have learned the lesson of adaptation. When King Mohammad V died in 1961 and was succeeded by his son Hassan, the Berbers quickly showed Hassan their allegiance. Despite several coup attempts in the years that followed, King Hassan retained his throne and, with Berber support, became the unquestioned ruler of the Moroccan nation. Algeria's sociopolitical life also reveals deep Berber-Arab rivalry. Precolonial Algeria—that is, Algeria under Ottoman rule—never experienced political unity. The tribes and ethnic groups within the country traditionally reserve their loyalty for local leadership. *Siba,* or anarchic resistance to central authority, is common in Algeria. Following Algeria's independence, revolts erupted in the Aures Mountains southeast of Algiers and in the Kabylie. Both regions are predominantly Berber. But the Berbers of Algeria, like the Berbers of Morocco, are a heterogeneous ethnic group. The four major elements are the Kabyles, east of Algiers; the Chaouais in the Aures, east and south of Algiers; the M'zabites in the Ghardia, south of Algiers; and the Taureg, the Saharan nomads. These Berbers, except for sharing some common linguistic characteristics, are essentially different. Political unity therefore is elusive and, except for a feeling of separateness from the more aggressive Arab population, they have great difficulty in settling on a unified program. Moreover, the absence of a monarchial institution in Algeria denies the Berbers the symbolic base upon which to found greater-Berber programs. The result is a greater mix of political activity in Algeria between Berbers and Arabs, but this does not diminish the tension, the envy, or the rivalry between them. The division of elites in Algeria apparently assists the ruling authority in maintaining a brokerage role, and compromises on political and economic issues are often complex and numerous.

Bourguibism 75

Bourguibism is derived from Habib Ali Bourguiba, Tunisian nationalist, hero of the struggle against French colonialism, and Tunisia's first president. Habib Bourguiba has been the Arab world's most durable leader. Tunisia gained its independence from France in 1956, and Bourguiba, the founder of the Neo-Destour Party (New Constitution Party, 1934), assumed the presidency in 1957. He was reelected in 1959, 1964, and 1969. Bourguiba was made president-for-life in 1974. He "retired" in a palace coup in November 1987.

France had been reluctant to transfer power to indigenous Tunisian leaders, and acts of terrorism took a high toll on all sides. In 1955, France granted Tunisia internal autonomy, but Paris retained responsibility for the country's foreign affairs and defense. Bourguiba returned from a long period of exile following this agreement and assumed the presidency of the Neo-Destour with the central policy of achieving full Tunisian independence. In February 1956 the French yielded to Bourguiba's party and agreed to a phased withdrawal of their forces. The Neo-Destour received the loyalty of all the members of the Tunisian constituent assembly, and Bourguiba became prime minister. The next several years represented a period of consolidation in which the opposition was effectively neutralized. An attempt to assassinate Bourguiba was foiled during this campaign. Egypt was accused of aiding anti-Bourguiba factions, but the affair only added to Bourguiba's popularity. Bourguiba let it be known that there was no place for Nasserism in Tunisia, and his followers appeared to agree. In 1959 Bourguiba reorganized Tunisia's political system to fit the presidential model. The president was the supreme authority in all domestic and foreign affairs and was also commander-in-chief of the armed forces. Indeed, Bourguiba was empowered to make all appointments to civil and military posts. In the first presidential elections, in 1959, Bourguiba won unopposed, and his Neo-Destour Party took all 90 seats in the new National Assembly. Tunisia supported Algerian independence, but it was repelled by the extremist doctrines of the Algerian government. Shortly after achieving its freedom, Algeria conspired to have Bourguiba killed. Bourguiba weathered this storm, too. In 1964 he expropriated foreign landholdings and issued a call for "Tunisian socialism." The Neo-Destour also began calling itself the Socialist Neo-Destour Party. So powerful was Bourguiba that he was able to appoint his son foreign minister. Internally, Bourguiba was unassailable, but his moderate policies toward the West incurred the enmity of the more militant Arab states. Bourguiba's statement that the Arab states should recognize Israel in return for the ceding of territory to the Palestinian Arabs was categorically rejected by the conference of Arab heads of state meeting in Casablanca. Bourguiba again accused Egypt of conspiring against his government and of using the Arab League for its own purposes. Nevertheless, Tunisia sent troops to the front line in the 1967 war against Israel. In 1968, however, Bourguiba was again attacked for his "anti-Arab" position. The Tunisian leader, however, lost none of his popularity. When he was elected president-for-life in 1974, even more extensive powers were conferred upon him. Moreover, his party continued to fill all the seats in the National Assembly. Between 1974 and 1976, Bourguiba authorized a political purge, and hundreds of dissidents, primarily Marxist students, were arrested for "plots against the state." Union with Qaddafi's Libya was also proposed, with the Tunisian patriarch becoming the new country's first president. Bourguiba rejected the idea, sensing a plot to reduce his effectiveness and eventually to remove him. Political conditions were more unstable in Tunisia from 1977 to 1987, and given his feebleness, he was removed by his newly appointed prime minister, Zine Al-Abdine Ben Ali. Ben Ali had the backing of most of the leaders in the ruling Destour Socialist Party, as well as that of the Tunisian military establishment. Ben Ali was made the new president of Tunisia shortly thereafter.

Significance

Bourguibism is related to Tunisization. It reflects the unique socioeconomic traditions of the Tunisian people. It also blends with European ideas and institutions. Bourguiba built Tunisia around his own personality. He was essentially an idealist with a practical outlook. He placed emphasis on evolutionary, step-by-step procedures rather than the revolutionary change publicized by virtually all other Arab leaders, save the most conservative. But Bourguibism is not to be equated with programs or philosophies in vogue in the still-prominent monarchies. Bourguiba was rational, not conservative. He was systematic and cautious, incremental and purposive. He rejected the extremes both of political Islam and the radicalism of the secularists. Although sometimes harsh to his opponents, Bourguiba seldom appeared vindictive or vengeful. Bourguiba believed progress could be achieved only through human development. He was therefore the enemy of institutions and customs that were perceived as impediments to the perfectibility of society. Nowhere else in the Arab world had a leader pursued female emancipation as vigorously as Bourguiba of Tunisia. Bourguiba believed the state had the responsibility for elevating the masses, materially as well as ethically. He was therefore dedicated to controlled government. Democracy must wait upon greater political sophistication. In the meantime the government must wield a monopoly of power, not only to persuade and, if necessary, to coerce, but also to ensure national unity. Bourguiba's pragmatic methodology, philosophy, and ethics are referred to as Bourguibism. The major question confronting Tunisians is the survivability of Bourguibism following his passing. Tunisia is now administered by Bourguiba's heirs. Their success suggests the continuation of the centralized state and economic planning. The Socialist Neo-Destour Party has had many years to recruit members across Tunisia's political spectrum. These figures have a stake in sustaining the established order. Bourguiba's charisma is non-transferable. His personality has made the Neo-Destour an institution of incredible power. Can it maintain its unified front in the absence of a revered patriarch? Bourguiba answered the question of his passage by noting that Destourian socialism will endure so long as the government's emphasis remains on the "good of all." Others have noted: "In its etatism, elitism, gradualism, view of man, emphasis on planning, and ultimate goal, Destourian socialism very much resembles Fabian socialism. Whether it actually constitutes an ideology is subject to debate. The important point is that in the case of Tunisia it performs the same function as an ideology."

Citizenship 76

Each country determines how citizenship is to be achieved. In many Middle East countries, persons residing in, or even born in, a particular country are not granted the rights of citizenship. Kuwait is a good example of the overall problem. Kuwaiti law specifies two classes of citizens: first-class citizens are those who can prove that their forefathers lived in Kuwait before 1922; second-class citizens are persons who arrived in Kuwait, or who are descendants of those arriving, after 1922 but before the end of 1945. Anyone arriving after 1945 cannot be considered a citizen. Any person born in Kuwait whose parents, or parent, arrived in the country after 1945 cannot be considered a citizen. Citizens and noncitizens are subject to Kuwaiti law. Noncitizens are provided the same economic opportunities and the same educational opportunities as citizens. The distinction between citizens and noncitizens is found in the political realm. Noncitizens are effectively disenfranchised; they cannot vote. Women are also disenfranchised. Nationality, the right to identify and be identified by a particular country, is also a power conferred upon the state. In Kuwait, only Muslims can carry Kuwaiti nationality. ***See also*** AL SABAH DYNASTY (67).

Significance

The strict rules determining Kuwaiti citizenship have been enacted to protect the Kuwaiti royal family, its political authority, and the integrity of the state. Approximately 60 percent of Kuwait's population is foreign and hence noncitizen. Almost half of this number is Palestinian. The Palestinians, therefore, are roughly equal in number to the Kuwaitis. Moreover, between 15 and 30 percent of Kuwaiti citizens are Shiite, whereas the reigning al Sabah dynasty is Sunni Muslim. Kuwaiti leaders have reason to be apprehensive. On the one side, the Palestinians have been troublesome, many having identified with George Habash's Marxist Popular Front for the Liberation of Palestine (PFLP) and Ahmad al Khatib's radical Kuwait Arab Nationalists. Prior to 1976, the Palestinians had the opportunity to engage in formal political activity, and they influenced the Kuwaiti parliament. The dissolution of the parliament in 1986 was prompted by tensions in the Arab states caused by the Lebanese Civil War, especially regarding the role of the Palestine Liberation Organization. The government feared its own Palestinian population before Kuwait was overrun by Iraq, and it now has more reason to disassociate itself from the refugee community. Palestinian representation in Kuwait's new parliament is a matter of conjecture. Indeed, the future of the Palestinians in Kuwait is bleak following the liberation of Kuwait from Baghdad's control.

Clerical Practices: Iran 77

Islam does not address the question of church hierarchy, but Shiite Islam, particularly as practiced in Iran, runs counter to orthodox doctrine. The Iranian Ruhaniyyat represents a formidable institution of clerics, tied together in ways personal and organizational. The character of the system sets the *mullahs* apart from the lay public and especially from nonclerics with political ambition. Secrecy lies at the heart of the Ruhaniyyat and its operations. The dynamics of Iran's clerical system involve mystery and mysticism, mystique and manipulation. The clerical network is dependent on practices known as *taqiyeh* and *tanfiyeh. Taqiyeh,* sometimes referred to as *ketman,* calls for deception and dissimulation. It harks back to the eighth century, when the sixth imam designed a tactic aimed at protecting Shiites from their enemies among the Sunni Muslims. The practice proved successful and, with time, became an aspect of normal clerical behavior. Pretension, disguise, and mendacity were judged necessary and proper in all matters.

See also RUHANIYYAT (54); QODRAT (52); SHIITE MARTYRDOM (58); ARMS SHIPMENTS TO IRAN: IRAN-CONTRA CONTROVERSY (197).

Significance
Taqiyeh has always been judged lawful by Iranian clerics concerned with their purposes and well-being. The deliberate management of facts and the avoidance of truthful discourse sustain the revolutionary government in Iran in modern circumstances. The Iranian *mullahs* instinctively protect their power by misleading their compatriots, co-religionists, and especially outsiders. Everyone outside their system is perceived as being opposed to it and bent on destroying it. The clerics therefore trust no one and are morally justified in obfuscating and distorting reality. No question of personal or group conscience arises from such behavior. No less significantly, *taqiyeh* allows *mullah* decision makers to avoid responsibility for their actions. This attitude relates to another practice known as *tanfiyeh,* or ignoring events, detaching oneself, or even the entire Ruhaniyyat, from the harsh realities of the mundane world. Options are never weighed in terms of ethical requirements. Expediency becomes the guiding principle in circumstances requiring the use and consequences of power. In effect, the "leader" can do no wrong in such conditions, especially if he is judged spiritually correct. The development of charismatic leadership in Iranian society as well as the emphasis on martyrdom explains the institutionalization of practices such as *taqiyeh* and *tanfiyeh.* With such performance, clerics represent not only piousness but also wisdom. The strength this gives the Ruhaniyyat is demonstrated in the rule of the theologians in Iran today. The *mullahs* address the goal of "divine justice," or *adalat,* and claim that they alone can assist the faithful in realizing such an objective. Hence everything beyond the pale of the Shiite clerics is satanic and evil. As in the days of ancient Persia, the struggle remains one pitting "good" against "evil," and the clerical system rests upon the popular belief that only *it* can manage a struggle against great odds. The failure of Oliver North's secret plan to trade arms for hostages and to use the profit from the sale of the arms to bolster the Nicaraguan Contras can be traced to North's lack of understanding of the dynamics that drive the Iranian clerical system.

Confessionalism 78

Confessionalism is the term used to describe the principle of fixed proportional sectarian representation in Lebanon. Confessionalism has been applied to the entire frame of Lebanese government. From the highest political positions in the land, through the administrative service, the armed forces, parliament, and the judiciary, all positions are assigned according to the proportional size of each religious community as determined by the 1932 census. Maronites, Greek Orthodox, Greek Catholics, Armenian Orthodox, and other smaller Christian sects gave a majority to the combined Christian community. This also meant that Christians would be the major power in the country at large. Sunni and Shiite Muslims along with the Druze community were placed in the position of a permanent minority. Nevertheless, in a country of minorities, with no one of them capable of dominating the others, considerable brokering was necessary. Paternalism, patronage, and family organization were more important than political parties. Instead of institutional development, however, the confessional system produced a panoply of influential patriarchs and notables, each with his own constituency and private militia. Competitive politics was a matter of elite interaction. As a consequence, formal political institutions were weak and unable to meet the tests of a changing environment. *See also* PHALANGES LIBANAISES (138); LEBANESE NATIONAL MOVEMENT (133); LEBANESE CIVIL WAR, 1975–1976 (250).

Significance
The confessional system and the National Pact of 1943 between the Maronite and Sunni leadership removed the flexibility necessary to adjust to changing circumstances. The Christian element in the government refused to hold a new census, which would require the rearranging of seats in parliament as well as of positions throughout the government. Despite all indications in the 1950s and 1960s that the Muslim population was larger than the combined Christian community, the census of 1932 remained in force. Political power was equated with economic privilege, and the wealth of the Christian community stood in stark contrast to the poverty of the Shiite Muslims. It was not surprising, therefore, to see the leader of the Lebanese Shiites, Musa al-Sadr, organize a movement of the "deprived" and join with the forces on the Left, especially the Palestinians, in an effort to destroy the confessional system. A new Lebanese National Covenant was announced by Maronite President Suleiman Faranjiyya on February 14, 1976, in the midst of the Lebanese Civil War. Faranjiyya sought Syrian aid against the combined forces of the PLO and Lebanese leftists, who were systematically crushing Christian resistance. In return for Syrian help, the Christians agreed to a modification of the confessional system. Subsequent events, however, made that reform null and void.

Constitutionalism: Egypt and Pakistan **79**

Constitutional government in the Middle East has been more facade than substance, with the exception of Israel. Constitutions are charters or primary documents reflecting historical experience and projecting future objectives. They describe structural arrangements and supposedly establish limits for authority, thus assuring individual freedom. But constitutions are only as sound as the societies they represent. A weak, divided society cannot overcome its deep-seated problems through constitution making, no matter how eloquent and sophisticated the rendering. Constitutions are influenced by the political environment; they do not constitute that environment. Constitutions, therefore, are mirror images of the world around them, not ideal models to be adopted and operationalized. If the document does not conform to conditions prevailing within the nation, it will not survive. This is the lesson of constitutional experience and it has been demonstrated, if not always learned, in a number of Middle East nations. None of the Muslim countries in the Middle East has emphasized the building of democracy more than Egypt and Pakistan. Both countries have experienced a form of European constitutionalism, and each has experimented with several types. Their difficulties in promoting genuine constitutional systems illustrate the larger problem of transforming Middle Eastern society from its traditional, authoritarian character to a more modern, popular representation of democratic procedure. During the administration of Gamal Abdul Nasser, Egypt was launched on a program of sociopolitical mobilization. The Arab Socialist Union was the principal device employed to integrate the variety of political, cultural, and functional groups in the country. But Egypt was influenced by an elitist body of military personalities that made up the Revolutionary Command Council (RCC), which was dominated by Nasser, its chief architect. The RCC decreed a provisional constitution in 1953. It was replaced by the 1956 constitution, which did little more than confirm Nasser as the fountainhead of Egyptian power. As Nasser and his brother officers continued to search for a political formula that best represented their interests and philosophy, the 1956 constitution was phased out, and an interim constitution was promulgated in 1964. The 1964 document sought to place Egypt in the center of a broader revolution, promoting Arab unity. This objective was asserted despite failure in forming a lasting union with Syria and Yemen. In 1971, the country was presented with still another constitution. The 1971 constitution was promulgated after Nasser's death, and it was eventually shaped to meet the needs of the new president, Anwar el-Sadat. The United Arab Republic was dropped as the official name of the country, and the Arab Republic of Egypt took its place. Sadat had already begun to emphasize Egyptian purpose and objectives, unlike Nasser, whose major emphasis had been on broader "Arab" affairs. Sadat's assumption of the presidency was challenged soon after Nasser's death, however. Although one of the original eleven Free Officers in the 1952 coup against the monarchy, Sadat was not the most influential. But he had been loyal to Nasser and effective in several leadership roles. Because of indecision among the leading personalities, Sadat succeeded to the office without initial resistance. But once the other members of the inner circle realized what they had done, they attempted to oust him. In April 1971 Sadat accused his associates of conspiring against him. Ali Sabri, his vice-president; several ministers; members of the National Assembly and the Arab Socialist Union (ASU); and a number of high-ranking military officers were accused of plotting Sadat's demise. All were found guilty and several, including Sabri, were sentenced to death. Although Sadat commuted their sentences to life imprisonment, he was determined to steer his own course. After signing a 15-year treaty of friendship with the Soviet Union in May 1971, Sadat, claiming non-delivery of promised Soviet weaponry, ordered the Soviets out of Egypt. Disturbances had shaken Egyptian society in 1972 and had threatened the regime; Sadat believed the Soviets were aiding his opposition, and thus they had to go. Riots flared again in 1973, and this time Sadat publicly blamed the Marxists for inciting the unrest. Sadat purged the ASU in 1973, expelling more than 100 journalists from the organization. He also dismissed his prime minister and replaced the secretary-general of the ASU. Sadat held new elections within the ASU in 1973, and purged the organization of its Marxist bias. By September 1973, Sadat had consolidated his power. In October he launched a war against Israel, which, although not totally successful, placed the Israelis on the defensive. Sadat was greeted as a hero of Egypt and the Arab world, and his authority was never again in question. Sadat placed his personal stamp on Egyptian affairs. A de-Nasserization program was promoted, deemphasizing socialist policies. Nationalized enterprises were returned to their owners, the ASU was downgraded and reorganized, and public pledges were made to reinstate a multiparty political system. Husayn al Shafi, another member of the original Free Officers and a ceremonial vice-president, was forced to step aside for Air Vice Marshal Hosni Mubarak, a hero of the 1973 war and a loyal confidant of the president. Mubarak shared Sadat's views as well as his philosophy, and he reinforced the perception that Sadat was the *rais*, Egypt's undisputed president and ruler. In a dramatic display of his power, Sadat journeyed to Jerusalem in 1977 to meet with Israeli leaders. Pledging no more war between their countries, Sadat raised a storm of controversy in the Arab and Muslim worlds. Within Egypt, however, opposition was marginal. In 1978, Sadat kept to his promise and reinstated competitive politics. Only approved parties were permitted to compete, however, and when the politicians strayed from the path established for them, they were quickly silenced. Sadat also inaugurated his own National Democratic Party (NDP), and in 1979 the first competitive election campaign was sanctioned. Sadat's NDP won a one-sided victory and dominated the new People's Assembly. But even a small opposition in the assembly proved more than the president could tolerate. In 1978, Sadat had ordered restrictions placed upon the new Wafd Party. He now moved against the National Progressive Unionist Party of Khalid Moheiddin, a former member of the RCC. Elections were held again in 1980 that virtually wiped out the remaining opposition in the assembly. Sadat's multiparty program had quickly degenerated into a one-party dominant system. Moreover, Sadat, sensing efforts to destroy him, demanded the neutralization of his foes. The leader of the Socialist Labor Party noted that Egypt only had the "shape of a democratic system." Moheiddin argued that vast differences existed between rhetoric and practice. The opposition was especially outraged by Sadat's intimacy with the United States. Indeed, it was strongly held that the Egyptian president's power rested on a U.S. support base. Sadat, for all his authority, could not control the passions of those who opposed his rule and policies. In September 1981, the president ordered the arrest of several thousand dissidents across the political spectrum. Islamic fundamentalists and avowed communists were caught in the police net. So, too, were scores of intellectuals, especially journalists and university professors who had voiced criticism of the regime. Sadat also ordered all Soviet personnel out of the country, and Cairo ruptured relations with Moscow. Sadat claimed that the Soviets were again conspiring with his opposition in an effort to destroy him. Although the system he constructed served him faithfully, Sadat could not control, let alone eliminate, all those who opposed him. In November 1981, while he reviewed a military parade in commemoration of the 1973 war, Anwar el-Sadat was attacked by several Muslim extremists who had concealed themselves within the procession. Although the assailants were apprehended, and later were tried, sentenced, and executed, they had carried out their assassination mission with great precision. Sadat was succeeded by his vice-president Hosni Mubarak, who quickly emphasized the continuation of his mentor's policies. Given what had transpired in the 30 years since the revolution against the monarchy, there was no reason to conclude that Egypt was better prepared for constitutionalism.

Constitutionalism has suffered a similar fate in Pakistan. Despite numerous protestations about democracy, Pakistanis have never experienced genuine freedom. At independence in 1947, the country was governed by the India Independence Act, which was a modification of the Government of India Act of 1935. After nine years of political squabbling, the politicians in the constituent assembly (the first constituent assembly had been dissolved by a dictatorial governor-general) drafted a constitution. It was promulgated in 1956 but never fully implemented. In 1958, the army perpetrated a coup, abrogating the constitution, closing the national and provincial assemblies, and banning all political parties. Martial law was imposed, and it remained in force for 44 months until Mohammad Ayub

Khan, the general responsible for the coup d'état, drafted and promulgated another constitution in 1962. That constitution was scrapped in 1969 when General Yahya Khan swept Ayub from office. The 1956 constitution had focused on a parliamentary system. The 1962 constitution was described as a presidential type. Yahya could not decide between the two but promised to reinstate constitutionalism pending elections. In 1970, under the auspices of a military junta, Pakistan experienced its first national election campaign since achieving independence. The elections, however, proved to be the undoing of the Pakistani state. The country divided along provincial lines, but the East Pakistani Awami League obtained far more seats in the National Assembly than the Pakistan People's Party (PPP) in West Pakistan. The leader of the PPP, Zulfikar Ali Bhutto, refused to permit the leader of the Awami League, Mujibur Rahman, to form the new government. Moreover, the junta did not resolve the matter; the result was the alienation of the East Pakistanis. When the Pakistan army attempted to quell disturbances in East Pakistan, a bloody civil war developed. This conflict was internationalized by India, which sided with the East Pakistanis and quickly turned the tide of battle. The defeat of the Pakistani army prompted India to assist in the dismemberment of Pakistan, and the new state of Bangladesh was created from the former East Pakistan. The military junta in Pakistan was thoroughly discredited, and with the country in a state of near paralysis, authority was transferred from the military to the PPP, and especially to Zulfikar Ali Bhutto. Bhutto attempted to pick up the pieces. He arranged for a new constitution, which was promulgated in 1973. It was a quasi-parliamentary, quasi-executive constitution, but there was no mistaking Bhutto's intention to become Pakistan's maximum ruler. Bhutto avoided elections until 1977, and when they were finally held, his PPP proved victorious. But PPP success was short-lived. The opposition had combined forces, and they now cried foul and fraud. Bhutto was called upon to resign, and violent demonstrations broke out all over the country. Martial law was again imposed, and in July 1977 Bhutto was overthrown in still another military coup. Led by Mohammad Zia-ul-Haq, the military pledged to conduct new elections on several occasions but each time reneged on the promise. Martial law continued in force through 1983 as Zia and his colleagues dismantled the 1973 system. Zia's stated intention was the creation of an Islamic state. Pakistan's new constitutional system, he asserted, would reflect the genius of Muslim people, not the borrowings of alien, especially Western, ideas and techniques. Zia died in the explosion of his military aircraft in August 1988, but his legacy guided his followers along the Islamic path he established for his countrymen. Following the Benazir Bhutto interregnum, the civilian leader of his movement became the country's prime minister. Nawaz Sharif sought to justify the merger of Islam with democracy, although the latter was modified by the emphasis on the former. Nevertheless, constitutionalism appeared to receive more credibility with civilians at the helm of state affairs. ***See also*** ARAB SOCIALIST UNION (114); PROTECTORATE (103); POLITICAL PARTIES: PAKISTAN (140); AUTHORITARIANISM (72).

Significance

Egypt's and Pakistan's experiences with constitutionalism are recounted here because, more than most Muslim countries in the Middle East, they have expressed genuine interest in constructing workable democracies. Other Muslim states have never or seldom established such objectives. Turkey is the only other Muslim country that has seriously entertained constitutionalism. But Turkey, too, found the obstacles to such a goal almost insurmountable. Turkey established a constitutional republic after World War I, but the personality of Kemal Ataturk symbolized authoritarianism, not representative government. When opposition parties were finally countenanced in the 1940s, they proved to be divisive instruments. In the 1950 election, the Turkish Democratic Party replaced the ruling Republican People's Party of Ataturk. Ataturk had died in 1938, and his successors could not assume his charisma. The Democrats promised more liberal programs but in practice proved to be dictatorial. When they were overthrown by a military coup in 1960, Turkey inherited a chaotic constitutional system. The original constitution was replaced and another promulgated. But that, too, could not reduce interparty conflict. By the 1970s the Turkish party system represented little more than political anarchy. Radical behavior and extremism were unleashed on Turkish society. Terrorism took several thousand lives, and successive coalition governments could do nothing to stem the carnage. In 1980, the army stepped into the political arena once again, abrogated the constitution, outlawed political parties, and imposed martial law. In November 1982 the Turkish voters were asked to approve another constitution, drafted to meet the requirements of the military establishment. Few citizens had read the 193 articles of the new constitution, but they overwhelmingly accepted it. Passage meant the automatic election of General Kenan Evren to the presidency. Turkey's chief martial law administrator was thus "legally" provided with sweeping executive authority. He and the military junta that he led were confirmed in power for another seven years, and the country was supposedly returned to a form of quasi-civilian government. Parliamentary elections, however, were not anticipated for another 18 months.

The question arises: Are Muslims culturally and psychologically ill-equipped for competitive politics and its concomitant constitutionalism? There appears to be a clear preference for personal leadership over institutional methods. Limited government is denigrated in favor of absolute power. Arbitrary judgment prevails over procedural due process. The notion of a government of law, restricted by law, is no match for the presence of strong-willed individuals. Leadership prevails so long as countervailing power is weak and ineffectual. In such circumstances, governors are deemed infallible, and subjects must blindly accept their *diktat*. Whether one speaks of the continuing monarchies in the Middle East, such as Saudi Arabia and Jordan; military dictatorships, such as Syria and Libya; or one-party dictatorships, such as Iraq and Iran, there is little interest in promoting constitutionalism. Constitutionalism may well be a luxury that inchoate states can ill afford. But this is also true elsewhere, beyond the Muslim world. It cannot therefore be argued that Islam is in itself an impediment to constitutionalism. It is simply enough to assert that constitutionalism has not fared well in the Middle East.

Democracy 80

Democracy is a form of government in which the sovereign power resides in and is exercised by the entire body of free citizens. Democracy is distinguished from monarchy, aristocracy, or oligarchy by its broad distribution of power and authority, its emphasis on fundamental rights, and its stress on legal-institutional remedies that apply equally to the governors as well as to the governed. According to theory, in a democracy every citizen should participate directly in the business of government, and the legislature should reflect the interests of the total population. Unlimited information and free choice are absolutely essential. Democracies are often described as "representative democracies" with special importance given to constitutions of both the written and unwritten variety. Democracy replaces hereditary and arbitrary systems and allows for maximum predictability and accountability. Popular sovereignty and the power of the electorate to choose its leaders are hallmarks of democratic expression. ***See also*** CONSTITUTIONALISM: EGYPT AND PAKISTAN (79); AUTHORITARIANISM (72); LEGITIMACY (91).

Significance
Democracy is given exceptional lip service in the states of the Middle East, but precious little evidence exists to demonstrate democratic performance. People's democracies such as described in Libya or Algeria are simply terms obscuring highly centralized authoritarian systems. Monarchies, military dictatorships, one-party states, theocracies, or administrative politics better describe prevailing systems within the Middle East. Only in the state of Israel are references to representative democracy taken seriously. Democracy is a form of government requiring deliberate effort. It does not emerge without careful planning and sincere intention. Many Muslim leaders in the Middle East nations have argued that democracy is a form of government requiring a literate, sophisticated, reasonably affluent population. They assert that Western-type democracy is not true to the genius of the people, nor are the people prepared to work its complex institutions. "Guided democracy" or "basic democracy" are terms sometimes employed to convey the need for tutelage, a prior stage before launching a full-blown experiment in democracy.

Druze 81

The Druze are members of a relatively small Muslim sect (more than 300,000) residing in the southern mountainous region of Lebanon, southern Syria, the Golan Heights, and northern Israel. A Shiite Ismaili order, the Druze are followers of the sixth Fatimid caliph, Abu Ali Mansur al-Hakim (985–1021). The Druze believe al-Hakim was an incarnation of God (Allah), and he so described himself in Cairo in 1016 A.D. Al-Hakim's *vizir* (principal advisor) established the ritual and ceremony that is followed by the Druze community today. The religion bears neither's name, however. Historians assert the term *Druze* is derived from Mohammad ibn Ismail al Darazi, a major influence on the Fatimid caliph. The Druze consider Hakim the last in a line of divine incarnations, deputized to call humankind to redemption. Although the sect is an offshoot of Islam, Muslims perceive the Druze as heretic because the former deem the Prophet Mohammad to be the last of God's messengers. Nevertheless, given their warrior character and fierce independent ways, the Druze gained overall acceptance in both heterogeneous Lebanon and Syria. The Druze do not believe in proselytizing, hence their regional existence. They are, however, a close-knit community who cooperate with one another and whose major activity lies in agricultural pursuits. Conflict between the Druze and the Maronite Christians of Lebanon in the nineteenth century precipitated the French incursion into Lebanese affairs in 1860. The death of several thousand Christians gave justification to France to impose its will upon the region despite the area's continuing connection with the Ottoman Empire. With the establishment by the French of a Christian governor-general in 1864, the Druze community went into political eclipse, and the Maronites began their monopoly of the region's political life. Except for Druze-Ottoman conflict over excessive taxation, the Druze were not active again until a contingent of volunteers joined the Hashemites in their struggle against the Turks in World War I. In 1921, the French mandatory power in Syria recognized Druze autonomy in the Jebal Druze. The French refused to honor their agreement, however, precipitating a revolt by the Druze community. In the ensuing clash, Lebanon was separated from Syria and each region sought an independent status. The Druze were deeply involved in both the Lebanese and the Syrian demands for sovereign independence. World War II provided new opportunity to terminate the mandates, and after a succession of French governments, power came to rest in the hands of Charles de Gaulle and his Free French forces. De Gaulle was reluctant to give up France's colonial possessions. Appeals to the United Nations called for the withdrawal of foreign forces from the country, and full sovereignty was finally conferred on the Lebanese and Syrian governments. The Druze had grown in sophistication by the postwar period, and their involvement in the politics of the two countries was assured. Moreover, their stubborn adherence to tribal custom brought them into conflict with the Syrian military dictatorship of Adib Shishakli in 1954. They also were deeply involved in the family and tribal conflict in Lebanon in 1958 and again in the civil war that erupted in 1975. The Druze attempted to shift with the political-military tides in the Lebanese Civil War, but they paid a high price in dead and destroyed property along with the other inhabitants. Blood feuds between rival armed families took their toll, and even the leader of the Druze community, Kemal Jumblatt, could not escape an assassin's attack. After Syria's loss to Israel in the 1967 war, the Druze community on the Golan Heights came under Israeli administration. Before Israel decided to absorb the Golan, there were rumors that Jerusalem contemplated the creation of an independent Druze state. In the aftermath of Israel's invasion into southern Lebanon in June 1982, the idea of establishing a Druze state between southern Lebanon and Syria again surfaced. Numbering approximately 55,000, the Druze of Israel have the status of an autonomous religious community with their own spiritual leadership and religious court system. Druze reside in the Galilee and on Mt. Carmel. Approximately 10,000 live on the Golan Heights. Unlike the Arab Israelis, who are not expected to serve in the Israeli armed forces, the Druze of Israel have been required to do compulsory service since 1957.

Significance

The Druze, like the Kurds, are an independent, devout, warrior people who have long dramatized their uniqueness. Situated in the mountainous region astride three countries, they have played secondary roles in the larger history of the region. In Lebanon, the Druze have attempted to cope with the *zaim* system. The *zaim* system developed around the electoral "list" system developed by the French in which any group of Lebanese could represent themselves. The "lists" tended to follow family lines, with the patriarch of the family usually heading the list and thus expressing the power and purpose of his particular constituency. In effect, the French set out to conscript the local family and tribal leaders. By playing one against the other and increasing the rivalries between the families, the Europeans made a place for themselves at the center of the political process. French administration was the great compromiser, the court of last resort, in quarrels between the various *zaim*. Although the *zaim* were secular as well as religious leaders and tribal headmen, their common denominator was land ownership. Those possessing the larger holdings influenced the greater number of constituents. In time the *zaim* became para-governments, governments within a government. Each *zaim* had its personal bodyguard and militia, and factional strife was a constant among the competing aristocrats. The Druze were fitted into this system, and alliances and counter-alliances sought to balance off would-be and actual foes. Despite an elaborate constitutional system, the *zaim* system directed Lebanese politics, and it remained intact despite, and perhaps because of, the ravages of the civil war. Conflict between Druze and Maronite factions flared anew in the wake of the Israeli invasion and occupation of southern Lebanon. Efforts by Israel's armed forces to interpose themselves between the warring communities were only partially successful. In Syria, the French attempted to enlist the Druze and another Shiite Ismaili offshoot, the Alawite Muslims. It was French intention to sustain the notion that Druze and Alawites were non-Arab, again an attempt at divide and rule. The Arab nationalists, however, were determined to draw the communities into their movement, and their efforts met with considerable success. The Druze, however, insisted on maintaining their individuality, which meant the maintenance of their established leaders and system of administration. The Druze revolt in 1925–1926 shattered the community's ties to the French, and in the Franco-Syrian Treaty of 1936 the Druze areas, until then free of general Syrian administration, were brought under the control of Damascus, although the Druze received special status. The Druze and Alawite minorities were embittered by the forced union with Syria, and another rebellion broke out in 1937 and again in 1939. In the latter struggle the Druze chased all Syrian officials from Jebal Druze, and it was declared independent under French protection. The Alawites acted in similar fashion, providing the French with the justification to divide Syria and the Syrian nationalists. When the Free French forces of Charles de Gaulle assumed power in Syria from the French puppet regime known as Vichy (after the Fall of Paris and the collapse of French resistance in 1940, the Germans permitted the French to operate the remnant of their country from the southern French city of Vichy), Syria was again unified, and the Druze and Alawites were forced to make their peace with Damascus. The establishment of the state of Israel opened a new chapter in Druze relations. Although the Alawites eventually gained control of Damascus through the Baath Party and the leadership of Hafez al-Assad, the Druze, given their insistence on isolation, were less effective in influencing Syrian politics. The opposition to Shishakli in the 1950s was the harbinger of events to come. Druze dissatisfaction with the Alawites gave the Israelis leverage in establishing countervailing power in the region.

Etatism 82

A French word emphasizing the dominance of the state, *etatism* was used by Mustafa Kemal Ataturk, the father of modern Turkey, to describe the country's need to stand on its own feet. The Ottoman Empire, from which Turkey emerged, was victimized by its dependence on external powers. *Etatism* to Ataturk meant state socialism, an independent economy, and self-help. Intertwined with *etatism* was the pursuit of national dignity, national purpose, and national pride. Ataturk was concerned with overcoming the inferiority that permeated Turkish society, the feeling of helplessness brought on by backwardness and subjugation. Institutionally, *etatism* was expressed in the opening of the Ish (Business) Bank in 1924, the Sumer Bank in 1925, and the Eti Bank in 1935. With advice provided by the Soviet Union and Nazi Germany, Turkey's economy became state-controlled. Foreign holdings were purchased by the government and expanded. Private Turkish enterprise required state authorization and was heavily dependent on the state-managed banking system. Agriculture, industry, mining, insurance, and finance were dominated by the state. The *etatist* program was described as an "advanced type of socialism" that had no need for Marxist doctrine. ***See also*** REPUBLICAN PEOPLE'S PARTY (142).

Significance
Although initially a necessary program in mobilizing national resources for state-building programs, *etatism* was not without its pitfalls. Ataturk emphasized self-sufficiency, which in Turkey meant becoming independent from foreign imports. The country was launched on a program that emphasized industrialization at the expense of social needs. Services to the public were ignored, labor was left without the necessary protection, and there was no assistance for those dislocated by the economy or insurance for the rank-and-file. Unions were also forbidden, and wages were maintained at dangerously low levels. Ataturk's program of instilling national pride, therefore, eventually transformed itself into a cruel burden. Popular dissatisfaction with the Republican People's Party (RPP) was muted during Ataturk's lifetime, but after World War II it could not be contained. Criticism was sharpest from the rural peasantry and industrial workers. The disparities in wealth between the government-sponsored industrialists and large merchants and the laboring masses were glaring. *Etatism* was the target of the disenchanted, and they demanded an end to state controls. In 1950, the RPP lost the election to the Democratic Party, which had run on a free-enterprise platform. The Democrats, under the leadership of Adnan Menderes, forgot their promise, however, and state-managed industrialization was pressed to its outer limits. Inflation wreaked havoc in all sectors of society, and Menderes's dictatorial tactics only added to the suffering. In 1960, Menderes was overthrown in an army coup, following widespread rioting. Martial law was imposed, the constitution was abrogated, and Menderes and his associates were first imprisoned, then put on trial and finally executed. The Democratic Party was banned, but when political activity was again sanctioned by the armed forces, the Turkish political party system was in shambles. Unstable coalition governments opened Turkey to widespread acts of terrorism in the 1970s. In 1980, the military again intervened in the country's political life.

Ethnic Atrocities **83**

Following the defeat of Iraqi forces by the U.S.-led coalition in February 1991, and the subsequent uprising and suppression of Shiite and Kurdish minorities in Iraq, the UN Security Council circumvented Article 2 of the UN Charter, which cites the exclusive jurisdiction of a state over its internal affairs, and condemned Iraq's brutal suppression of the Kurds. Baghdad sought to ward off the vote by agreeing earlier to accept a UN fact-finding mission to investigate the conditions of the Kurdish refugees in northern Iraq and the Shiite population in the south. The resolution was sponsored by France, Belgium, Britain, and the United States. The resolution cited a threat to "international peace and security" in the region if these problems were left unattended. It called upon Baghdad to "immediately end the repression" and expressed the hope that "an open dialogue will take place to ensure that the human and political rights of all Iraqi citizens are respected." Iraq was authorized to open all its borders to international humanitarian agencies. ***See also*** IRAQI-KURDISH CONFLICT (246); KURDISH ENCLAVE PROPOSAL (90); KURDS (89).

Significance

The resolution condemning Iraqi repression against its own citizenry was unprecedented in tenor and content. As it stands, it modifies a fundamental characteristic of the UN Charter acknowledging the sacrosanct nature of the nation-state as an independent, sovereign entity. By citing the treatment of a country's own citizens as a threat to international peace and security, the Security Council moved well beyond the question of what represents an internal matter. For human rights proponents, long dedicated to emphasizing the human imperative over the territorial imperative, this resolution was a major victory. With hundreds of thousands of Kurdish refugees descending on Iran and Turkey as a consequence of Saddam Hussain's aggressive policies toward his own people, the message seemed to be, correct your ways or expect international retribution. What that retribution might be, given the intention of the coalition powers to terminate their joint operations and withdraw their forces, was a matter of conjecture. It was clear, however, that the resolution was too late to help the Kurds and Shiite Iraqis already victimized by the Baathist regime in Baghdad. The resolution also left open the question of its application elsewhere, especially in the Palestinian situation, where the *intifada* had been met with a stern Israeli response. The *intifada* was of a lower order of magnitude when compared with the plight of the Iraqi resistance to Saddam Hussain. It seemed that in an effort to clear its collective conscience in not having prevented the slaughter of at least the innocent in Iraq, the Security Council members, and especially the United States, France, and Britain, were on record sanctioning interference in the domestic affairs of other states where human rights violations are egregious or deemed extraordinarily flagrant.

Ethnicity 84

Ethnicity is usually associated with language and culture. In the Middle East this is particularly notable. An Arab is someone who speaks Arabic. Despite racial and historical differences, language draws otherwise disparate peoples into a common feeling of community. Arab states therefore are unusually homogeneous. Exceptions of note are found only in Iraq (the Kurdish community), Algeria and Morocco (the Berber tribes), and the Sudan (Black Africans). Although linguistic minorities are also found in Lebanon, Syria, Kuwait, Tunisia, and the Persian Gulf shaykhdoms, they do not modify the Arab character of these societies. Other Middle East societies are not as homogeneous, however. Pakistan is torn between Punjabi, Pushtu, Sindhi, Baluchi, and Urdu speakers. Afghanistan is divided between Pushtu, Dari Persian, Tajik Persian, Turkic, and other linguistic groups. Iran, despite the preeminence of Persian, is challenged by Turkic-speaking tribes, and Arabic, Baluchi, and other languages are also significant. Turkey, however, is more ethno-linguistically homogeneous than its non-Arab neighbors. Although Kurdish is an important minority language, it does not detract from Turkey's homogeneous appearance and temperament. Israel is a special case in the Middle East. The continuing emphasis on emigration to the Jewish state has brought language-speaking groups that are not familiar with Hebrew. The Russian-speaking emigres are a prominent example. Nevertheless, Israel makes strenuous efforts to instruct the new arrivals in the use of the Hebrew language. Despite the great variety of racial and national types in the country, Hebrew attempts to bridge the distances between them. ***See also*** ASABIYYA (71); ARABIZATION (70).

Significance
The above description of ethnicity deliberately ignores religion. Religion is, of course, the other side of the ethnicity question. Religion, too, draws people into an awareness of community, and certainly Islam and Judaism have increased a consciousness of community. Nevertheless, religion does not appear to hold as strong a position as language in determining ethnicity. Islam has not bridged ethno-linguistic differences in Pakistan. The attempt to establish a lingua franca for all Pakistan was predicated on the need to cement a religious community into a sociopolitical configuration. Efforts at making Urdu the national language of Pakistan continue, but progress is limited. By the same token, linguistic homogeneity is no promise of political unity. Arabs may well be persons who speak Arabic, but this does not mean that all Arabs will act with one voice. Indeed, neither religion nor language prevents fragmentation and societal atomization. Kinship and family associations, tribalisms, and specific ethnocentrism must also be evaluated in determining degrees of cohesiveness. Ethnicity therefore is not another word for unity. Ethnicity refers to identity, and it can be said there is an Arab identity, a Turkish identity, an Israeli identity. By this measure Pakistan and Afghanistan, and possibly Iran, are still in search of their identity.

Green Book *85*

The Green Book contains the thoughts of Muammar Qaddafi, the preeminent ruler of Libya. Qaddafi was an obscure lower echelon officer in the Libyan army when he led the revolution that destroyed the Sanusi monarchy headed by King Idris in September 1969. The Sanusi were derived from a Sufi religious order that had lost its vitality during the Italian occupation of Libya in the 1920s and 1930s. When Italy was defeated in World War II, Libyans regained their freedom. The victorious Allies identified the Grand Sanusi, the leader of the order, as the only political power in the country, and he was installed as king of Libya following the termination of hostilities. It was that Sanusi system that Qaddafi toppled. Qaddafi and his followers showed nothing but contempt for the Sanusi Sufi orders, calling them bastions of corruption and incapable of establishing Libya's independence. Qaddafi spoke of bringing "pure" Islam to Libya and ultimately to Arabdom and Muslims everywhere. He denounced nationalism and its offspring, the nation-state, as a divisive arrangement that separates peoples and regions and propagates selfishness and exclusivity. Qaddafi insisted that the real Islam is a continuous revolution that will benefit all humankind. For this reason Qaddafi urged the translation of the Qur'an (Muslims believe the Qur'an was given to man through the medium of Arabic and that no other language can accurately present its message) into the languages of people everywhere, a position orthodox Muslims judge to be irreverent. Qaddafi, however, has been equally abrasive with other established doctrines. From the outset of his rule he has attempted to separate himself from previously established ideas and practices. Soon after the revolution he publicized what he called the "third international theory." The third theory was Qaddafi's response to capitalism on the one side and communism on the other. Capitalism, according to Qaddafi, emphasized the individual over the collectivity; communism did the opposite. The third theory was developed to avoid the excesses of the former and the limitations of the latter. The third international theory is divided into: (1) political aspects; (2) economic aspects; (3) metaphysical aspects; (4) social aspects; and (5) dialectical aspects. The theory speaks of positive neutralism, nonalignment, and peaceful coexistence abroad. It mentions popular rule through people's committees at home. It cites socialism as the approach to social justice and the leveling of all stations. It emphasizes the connection between religious belief and modern science. The view is expressed that only through religious observances is social morality achieved. Finally, it speaks of the persistent struggle between right and wrong, and ultimately the success of light over darkness through belief in God's will. These views were amplified in Qaddafi's Green Book. The Green Book is in three parts. Part one talks about the problem of democracy and authority resting with the people. Part two addresses economic questions and emphasizes the building of socialism. And part three describes the ideal society, social relationships, obligations, and responsibilities. In a manner of speaking, the Green Book is a small compendium of Qaddafi's ruminations on the subject of popular revolution. For Qaddafi, "the instrument of governing is the prime political problem which faces human communities." The Green Book asserts that it "presents the theoretical solution to the problem of the instrument of governing." The Green Book makes it clear that what is called democracy in current times is really concealed dictatorship. Majority rule means the minority's interests are ignored. Parliaments are called misrepresentations of the people. And political parties are the tools of tyrants. In announcing his popular revolution, Qaddafi called upon his supporters to manage the universities, the directorates of education, printing houses, and cultural centers. Moreover, trade unions, women's unions, and youth groups, as well as individual doctors and nurses, were encouraged to seize the governorates of labor, social affairs, and health services. Later, even Libya's embassies abroad were occupied by bands of young people.

Significance

The Green Book of Muammar Qaddafi bears a striking resemblance to the Red Book of Mao Zedong. Like Mao, Muammar Qaddafi unleased a "cultural revolution," which was supposed to sweep aside all vestiges of the previous Libyan experience. Like Mao, Qaddafi envisaged his revolution spilling over his nation's frontiers into other lands. Like Mao, Qaddafi saw himself in the vanguard of a historical movement that promoted revolutionary change and promised a fundamental metamorphosis in the human condition. Like Mao, Qaddafi attempted to elevate himself above his compatriots. And like Mao, he endeavored to create a cult of personality. Qaddafi has sustained his authority since the 1969 revolution, and his Revolutionary Command Council continues to dominate the decision-making process in the Libyan state. Colonel

Qaddafi's relative success at home, however, has not been matched by achievement abroad. Efforts at integrating Libya and Egypt collapsed when Anwar el-Sadat recognized the threat that Qaddafi posed for his administration and his personal perceptions of the future. Qaddafi's attempt to overthrow the Sudanese government of Jafar al-Numayri, his active support for Idi Amin of Uganda, and his invasion of Chad also weakened his position in the international arena. Moreover, his identification with terrorist organizations from the Philippines to El Salvador has brought him and Libya a threatening reputation in the community of nations. The Green Book has not been dramatically portrayed in the Western world, but the actions of Colonel Qaddafi are given considerable attention. And despite setbacks, the Libyan leader is undaunted in his posture. He continues to see himself as the leader of a worldwide revolution. Assisted by massive oil revenues, he continues to pass his time and spend Libya's money in ways that seem, to him, most likely to bring changes in the existing international power structure.

Hashemite Dynasty *86*

The Hashemites extend from the Bani Hashim clan of the Quraysh tribe of Mecca, the tribe of the Prophet Mohammad. The family had ruled Mecca and the Hejaz section of the Arabian Peninsula from the tenth century to the second decade of the twentieth century. As the protectors of the holy cities of Mecca and Medina, the Hashemite leaders bore the title sherif, an aristocratic rank. It was the Hashemites to whom the British turned for support during World War I, and they responded by providing troops for the war against the Turks. Hashemite ambition was stimulated by the knowledge that the Ottomans would be forced from the Arabian Peninsula and possibly from the Arab world. The sherif of Mecca, observing the opportunity to establish his claim to broader Arab leadership, amassed a large army somewhat in concert with British forces. Moreover, the sherif's religious credentials were sound. His alliance with the Europeans against the Turks nullified the Ottoman sultan-caliph's declaration of a *jihad* (holy war) against Great Britain. Hussain ibn Ali, the sherif of Mecca, called upon his sons to lead his army and, after the war was over, Great Britain rewarded their performance by installing one son, Faisal, in Damascus and the other, Abdullah, in the Transjordanian sector of Palestine. The French forced Faisal to leave Syria in 1920, but the British reestablished his throne in Baghdad. Neither Hashemite was familiar with the region he was called upon to govern. Moreover, the fact that the British were responsible for the sons' political authority did not endear the latter to the surrounding population. Hussain continued to rule in Mecca and the Hejaz. In 1924, he claimed the caliphate after an order abolishing it was made by the leader of the new Turkish Republic. But, except for his sons in Iraq and Transjordan, no other Arab authority recognized the claim. In that same year, Hussain was attacked by an army led by Abdul Aziz ibn Saud and was defeated. Hussain was forced to abdicate in favor of his third son, Ali, but the Saudis defeated Ali in 1925 and incorporated the Hejaz into their realm. The Hashemites lost the seat of their power to ibn Saud, but with the assistance provided by the British their rule over Iraq and Transjordan was preserved. The Hashemites of Iraq were eventually overthrown by disaffected army officers in 1958. The king and his family were murdered, and the dynastic line was terminated. The only remaining Hashemite authority resides in the territory east of the Jordan River. At its creation Transjordan was a desert hinterland with a population made up of bedouin tribesmen numbering several hundred thousand. The state lacked economic resources and was almost completely dependent on a British subsidy and the Arab Legion, organized and officered by the British. The British granted autonomy to Abdullah, but full sovereignty was not conferred until 1946, at which time the country became the Kingdom of Transjordan. The character of Jordan was altered by the Arab-Israeli War of 1948–1949. The Arab Legion seized the West Bank territories and the eastern part of Jerusalem, including the holy shrines. In December 1948, Abdullah was proclaimed king of Palestine by a conference of prominent West Bank Arabs. In 1950, the king annexed the West Bank, and the country was renamed the Kingdom of Jordan. Abdullah and the Hashemites had to contend with a different composition of population. The Palestinian Arabs were more numerous, and many were educated, sophisticated, and industrious. They were also politically conscious and provoked by the plight of tens of thousands of refugees from the region now under Israeli sovereignty. Thus, the relatively tranquil desert kingdom was suddenly transformed into a polyglot land of intrigue and despair. In addition, the Palestinians looked to the authority of the Mufti of Jerusalem and the Husayni family, who had been the overseers of the Muslim holy places in Palestine. Their outspoken anti-British position contrasted with long-term Hashemite dependence on the United Kingdom. King Abdullah was perceived as an instrument of British imperialism. When rumors spread that the king had met with Israel's Golda Meir, the bitterness directed at his throne was even more pronounced. King Abdullah was assassinated in July 1950 by disgruntled Palestinians. His son Talal succeeded to the throne but was deposed in 1952 because of a debilitating mental disorder. Talal's son, Hussain, assumed the throne in 1953, upon his eighteenth birthday. The Hashemite dynasty has clung to a precarious perch in the intervening years. Martial law was imposed over the country in 1957–1963, 1966–1967, and 1970–1973. King Hussain has survived numerous assassination attempts, although his ministers and close associates have not been as fortunate. Although the British presence was removed from Jordan in 1956, the Hashemites failed to win the confidence of the other Arab states. Jordan did not participate in the 1956 war against Israel. It also accepted a U.S. subsidy when the British no longer found it possible to support the monarchy. The pro-Western orientation was thus sustained. After the 1967 war with Israel, in which Jordan lost control of East Jerusalem and the West Bank territory, Palestinian revolutionary activity increased. The Palestine Liberation Organization (PLO) gained popularity and influence throughout the Arab world and established its principal bases and headquarters in Jordan, the state with the longest border with Israel. In short order, the PLO became a state within a state, threatening the survival of the Hashemite dynasty. Increased attention was given to the PLO as it launched guerrilla raids into Israel and then instituted a worldwide campaign of terror with the seizure of passenger aircraft engaged in international travel. Three planes were seized in September 1970 and flown to an airstrip outside Amman. The destruction of those planes several days later precipitated action by the Jordanian army against the PLO. As a consequence of this struggle the PLO was forced to leave the country, finally regrouping in Lebanon. Since that episode King Hussain has attempted to avoid further embarrassment by limiting his ties to the United States (although his wife is an American) and by seeking a rapprochement with Yasir Arafat and the PLO. King Hussain steadfastly refused to join Sadat at Camp David. He was also critical of the Egyptian-Israeli Peace Treaty, and he appeared to support Saddam Hussain in his confrontation with the gulf monarchies. Nevertheless, the Jordanian king was among the first of the Arab leaders to accept the American invitation to a peace conference with Israel. In June 1991 he dismissed the Jordanian cabinet and asked his foreign minister, who also favored a negotiated settlement with Israel, to form a new administration. The move was aimed at bringing Jordan out of diplomatic isolation. The king's purpose was also to neutralize the Islamic fundamentalists. The new prime minister was Taher Masri, who was educated at North Texas State University and on good terms with the Bush administration. He was also the first Palestinian in 20 years to be named prime minister in Jordan. In spite of his family background, and perhaps because of it, King Hussain opposed the Muslim Brotherhood's attempt to turn Jordan into an Islamic theocracy. By selecting Masri to head his government, the Hashemite king hoped to weather still one more storm in his long reign. *See also* HUSAYNIS (150); AL SAUD DYNASTY (68); REAGAN PROGRAM ON PALESTINE (177).

Significance
The Hashemites come closest to representing Islamic legitimacy, given their descent from the Prophet's tribe and their historical aristocratic base. Nevertheless, the dynasty is an anachronism in present Middle East politics. By contrast with their counterparts in the neighboring Arab states of Syria and Iraq, the Hashemites hold to a moderate course. During Nasser's ascendancy in the Arab world, King Hussain was considered an outcast, and efforts were launched to unseat him. Difficulties with the Baathists and the Palestinians compounded the king's troubles. Nevertheless, the dynasty survived. Hussain has displayed a combination of courage and pragmatism that has helped sustain his regime. He has also surrounded himself with loyal bedouin chiefs who observe a traditional desert lifestyle and who are highly suspicious and strongly opposed to the more urbane Palestinians. The Royal Jordanian Army is made up of bedouin recruits who have pledged their lives to the monarch, and Palestinians are noticeably absent. The king did recognize the PLO as the sole legitimate spokesman for the Palestinians in 1974, but he has endeavored to keep their presence in his government to a minimum. Jordan is described as a constitutional monarchy, but the monarch dominates policy making, legislation, the management of the armed forces, and all significant decisions. It is King Hussain's attention to detail, his regular visits with his troops, and his understanding of tribal needs that have preserved his kingdom. But he remains vulnerable. His support for Iraq in its war with Iran and later in its confrontation with the U.S.-led coalition contrasts with neighboring Syria's aid to Iran and the coalition. Syria has threatened the Hashemite king, but Iraq's proximity in the past has caused Damascus to hesitate in assaulting Jordan. Iraq's weakness in the wake of Desert Storm is a serious blow to Jordanian security. Jordan lives in a complex world of interlocking relationships and violent crosscurrents. The last of the Hashemite dynasties looks out on an uncertain future.

Ibadhis 87

The Ibadhis are Shiite Muslims residing in the sultanate of Oman. Ibadhism is an offshoot of the Kharijite movement, which developed in the earliest period of the Islamic era. The Kharijites (seceders) recognized only the first two caliphs and claimed the right to elect the imam or religious leader from the universality of the Muslim population. Other Kharijites rejected all government and insisted on the rule of God through a Council of Elders. The Kharijites were persecuted unmercilessly, and the survivors sought refuge in the southern wastelands of the Arabian Peninsula, where their descendants, the Ibadhis, are found today. Modern Ibadhis live in Oman, which dominates the Masandam Peninsula overlooking the Straight of Hormuz, and the southern region of Arabia from the entrance of the Persian Gulf to the border of Yemen. Omani Ibadhis can be divided into two groups: (1) the more secular, worldly Ibadhis who rule Oman and (2) the more austere hinterland Ibadhis. Ibadhi Muslims have often been compared with Wahhabi fundamentalists, whom they resemble in doctrine. Ibadhism was established in Oman in the ninth century and has had to cope with numerous invaders. In the seventeenth century, the Ibadhis were successful in overcoming Persian influence, but the imamate in the interior could not compete with the sultanate in the coastal area. In 1954, an independent Ibadhi state was proclaimed, but it was crushed by the sultanate's mercenary forces. ***See also*** MUSCAT AND OMAN (19); DHOFAR (7).

Significance
The Ibadhis occupy an important strategic region between India and East Africa and hold a dominant position at the mouth of the Persian Gulf. In the age of discovery, European adventurers considered the southern region of the Arabian Peninsula important for commerce and navigation. The Portuguese invaded the region in 1508 and built a naval station and commercial center at the port of Muscat to supplement their other facility on the eastern shore of the Strait of Hormuz. Muscat became more important when the Portuguese were forced from their Persian possession. The Portuguese were in a period of decline, however, and local Arabs forced them from Muscat in 1650. The success of these Ibadhi Arabs led them to pursue the Portuguese in their East African colonies. As a result of these actions, Mogadishu, Mombasa, and Zanzibar also came under Ibadhi control. The success of the Ibadhis whetted the appetite of the Persians, who again assaulted the region. After a fierce struggle, the Ibadhis beat back the invaders, and a more established Ibadhi dynasty emerged. Identified as the Al bu Said, it has ruled Oman from the middle of the eighteenth century until today. It was during the reign of Said ibn Sultan (1804–1856) that the dynasty reached its highest level of accomplishment. During this period, the capital of the Ibadhis was located in Zanzibar, and the dynasty's influence extended all the way to India. After ibn Sultan's death, however, the kingdom split into two dynasties, one ruling East Africa from Zanzibar and the other governing the Arabian sultanate, from which Oman ultimately emerged.

Jirgah 88

The *jirgah,* or tribal council, is the institution through which the Pathan population of Afghanistan and Pakistan administer tribal codes and customs and dispense justice. As a collective body of senior tribesmen, it is revered and respected. In conditions where blood feuds still predominate, the local *jirgah* plays an important role in moderating interpersonal and intergroup behavior.

Efforts by the Afghan and Pakistan governments to replace the tribal system were unsuccessful. Where government proved sensitive to tribal ways and sought to blend national with parochial systems, greater headway was achieved. Nevertheless, the *jirgah* has persisted as an important institution in all legal and political matters. Given the Pathans' pride of lifestyle and tribe, the only truly legitimate decision-making institution was the tribal *jirgah,* comprised of strong headmen, saintly figures, and wise patriarchs. Afghanistan's 1965 constitution created a representative form of government in that the parliament, or Shura, consisted of a directly elected Wolesi Jirgah (House of the People) and a more or less appointed body called the Meshrano Jirgah (House of Elders). Above these two houses was the Loya Jirgah, or Great Council, made up of members drawn from both houses of the Shura as well as the chairmen of elected provincial *jirgahs.* The Loya Jirgah's functions were more traditional in that it followed older patterns of organization. Historically, the Loya Jirgah was assembled in time of great emergency. Its meetings were always informal in atmosphere, but defined by custom and usage. The 1965 Afghan constitution attempted to institutionalize the Loya Jirgah and bring it to the service of the central Afghan government. Such a Loya Jirgah was supposed to reflect public opinion and counsel government in crisis circumstances.

Pakistan did not experiment with such a system. The tribal *jirgah* was not interfered with, and it continued to administer local questions such as disputes, grievances, and material need. The tribal *jirgah* utilizes a legal system known as pakhtunwali that combines both tribal and personal law. *Pakhtunwali* governs the relations of the tribesmen and of one tribe with another. In theory, the system of tribal law is complete; future law-making is unnecessary. Where doubts arise concerning interpretation, such as intertribal disputes or disputes between individuals within a tribe, affairs are resolved either violently or by the tribal *jirgah.* The *jirgah,* with the assistance of a respected theologian, will prescribe the law. Enforcement of a *jirgah* decree is also handled informally. The tribes are their own police agency. Law enforcement comes in the form of *lashkar,* the tribal use of force. The *lashkar* also has been associated with tribal warfare. *Lashkars,* for example, were ordered by tribal *jirgahs* against the British in the three Anglo-Afghan wars of the nineteenth and twentieth centuries. ***See also*** TRIBALISM (110).

Significance

The *jirgah* is an important tribal institution among the Pathan tribes. The Pathans are characterized by disunity and fragmentation. Tribes jealously protect their native habitat and seldom cooperate in the absence of high emergency. Left to themselves, the tribes focus their attention on day-to-day concerns. Local *jirgahs* address mundane questions that threaten to disrupt conventional ways of life. Local *jirgahs* are highly respected, and decisions taken in these bodies are seldom ignored. Violations of directives are judged antisocial, and violators are subject to heavy penalty. In this manner, the tribes police their individual communities. The *jirgah* represents all the government a tribal Pathan normally requires. In the republican atmosphere of the tribes, tribesmen do as they please so long as tribal codes are not affected. The most celebrated form of tribal *jirgah,* however, is the Loya Jirgah, which brings together the leaders of the many Pathan tribes in one great conference. Such calls are rare. In Afghanistan they have occurred when a king has been deposed or murdered and the new authority seeks the allegiance and support of the tribes. The Loya Jirgah acts as a legitimating institution. More celebrated use of the Loya Jirgah is the Pathan response to aggressive intruders. A Loya Jirgah was assembled to deal with the Soviet invasion of Afghanistan in 1979. Although the tribes resisting the Red Army fought under numerous individual commands, and sometimes only as detached small groups, the Loya Jirgah provided a semblance of unity. Its informal character, ad hoc nature, and lack of central authority, however, prevent the Loya Jirgah from developing greater coherency. Despite the pressures brought to bear on the Pathan population by the war, there is no indication that the Loya Jirgah will be transformed into a more permanent assembly with specific functions. Najibullah succeeded Babrak Karmal in 1986 and like his predecessor served Soviet interests. Najibullah was deemed by the Kremlin a better leader, more capable of covering the Soviet withdrawal, which was completed in February 1989. Najibullah recognized the need to placate the tribal and ethnic diversity of the country. His effort to induce the Loya Jirgah to assume greater responsibility for managing the country was aimed at moderating his rule. But the U.S.-Soviet decision prior to the dissolution of the U.S.S.R. to suspend all military assistance to the belligerents in Afghanistan and the effort to find a political solution left little if any room for Najibullah to maneuver. Najibullah announced his decision to step aside on March 18, 1992, but in April he was forced from office and his government collapsed. The victorious *mujahiddin* entered Kabul but a new government required the cooperation of a majority of the warring factions. The Loya Jirgah held out the possibility that a consensus might be achieved between the rival groups composing the resistance.

Kurds **89**

The Kurds inhabit a region of the Middle East that extends from Kermanshah in Iran to the northeastern section of Iraq and the eastern provinces of Turkey, especially Kars and Ardahan. The Kurdish nation also spills over into the Soviet Union, where Kurds are found in Soviet Armenia. Although a mountain people, many Kurds today are plain-dwellers, residing in towns and cities throughout the region. The Kurds are an ancient folk, divided into many tribal communities and speaking Indo-European dialects of their distinct Kurdish language. They share little in common with the Arabs, Turks, and Persians other than their identification with Islam. Kurds are predominantly Sunni Muslims who have separated themselves from the Shiite state religion of Iran as well as the majority Shiite population of Iraq. More than 4 million Kurds live in Turkey, almost 3 million in Iraq, and another 2 million in Iran. Approximately 450,000 reside in Syria and about 10,000 in the Soviet Union. It is reported that 300,000 Kurds lived in Germany in 1992. The Kurds put up fierce resistance to the invading Seljuk Turks in the eleventh century but were eventually subdued. They were again conquered by the Ottoman Turks, who brought them within their empire in the fourteenth century. The Kurds could not avoid being sandwiched between the warring Turks and Persians, and their dream of an independent state was made impossible by these larger powers. The spread of nationalism in the nineteenth and early twentieth centuries provoked renewed political consciousness among the Kurdish intelligentsia living in the settled areas. They prodded their semi-nomadic countrymen to join in a movement for national independence. The Treaty of Sevres with the Ottomans in 1920 gave the victorious allied forces an opportunity to grant the Kurds their independence. The promise was not kept, however. The Treaty of Lausanne of 1923 nullified the Treaty of Sevres and the Kurds were denied their right of self-determination. The Kurdish Revolt of 1925 was a consequence of this action. Although the revolt was crushed, the Kurdish demand remained, and sporadic conflicts coursed through Turkey, Iran, and Iraq. Suppressed in Turkey and Iran, the Kurdish national movement centered its struggle on Iraq. In 1970, after eight years of conflict, the Kurds were granted autonomy over their region of Iraq and obtained cabinet status in the central government. Kurdish was also declared an official language. Subsequent developments in Iraq that consolidated Baathist power undermined these agreements. The Kurds resumed their fight, this time assisted by the Iranians. Earlier, the Soviet Union had given assistance to the Kurdish national movement. When Iran signed a treaty with Iraq in 1975, Iranian support and sanctuary ceased, and the Kurds were subjected to a ferocious Iraqi offensive that virtually destroyed the movement. The Kurdish national movement reappeared in Iran, however, following the Iranian revolution. The Kurds opposed the Shiite formula that Ayatollah Khomeini imposed on Iran, and battles ensued between Kurdish dissidents and the ayatollah's revolutionary guards. The Kurds also displayed a degree of restlessness in Turkey but were neutralized by the military coup of 1980 and the imposition of martial law. Kurdish self-determination in Iraq remained a quest with a doubtful future until Operation Desert Storm seriously damaged the Iraqi war machine. Kurds in northern Iraq re-energized their movement in February 1991 and immediately launched attacks on Saddam Hussain's forces. ***See also*** IRAQI-KURDISH CONFLICT (246); ETHNIC ATROCITIES (83); KURDISH ENCLAVE PROPOSAL (90).

Significance
The Kurds have had three opportunities in the twentieth century to establish an independent homeland. The first came in the wake of World War I. The Kurdish nationalists requested Woodrow Wilson, the president of the United States and a principal at the Versailles Peace Conference, to accept Kurdistan as its mandate. The U.S. president was opposed to the mandate system, however, and the Kurdish plea was rejected. If the Americans had agreed to assume the administration of the Kurdish mandate, the Kurdish state would have achieved sufficient identity ultimately to achieve independent status. The second opportunity was provided by the Soviet Union, which occupied northwestern Iran in 1945–1946. The Soviets established the state of Mahabad (Kurdistan), and a nationalist leader, Zaki Mohammad, was elected its president on January 22, 1946. Following the Soviet withdrawal, the Iranian army reoccupied the area, and Zaki Mohammad was seized, charged with treason, and put to death. Kurdistan was reabsorbed within greater Iran, and the Kurdish national movement was scattered by the shah's forces. The third opportunity emerged in the winter of 1991 with the defeat of Saddam Hussain's army by the U.S.-led coalition. Kurds in the Mosul-Kirkuk region of Iraq pressed forward with a struggle that they hoped would have U.S. support. The purpose of the Kurdish assault was the unseating of Saddam Hussain, an objective cited by President George Bush during the war. Bush called upon the Iraqi people and military to rid themselves of the Baath leader. The Kurds in the north and the Shiite Iraqis in the southern portion of the country responded to this call, but their uprising was crushed by Baghdad's superior force.

The future of the Kurds, whether in Iraq, Iran, or Turkey, remained desperate.

Kurdish Enclave Proposal 90

In the wake of the Gulf War of 1991, Kurdish resistance forces, prompted by calls to rise up and throw out Saddam Hussain, and sensing that Iraq's army had been weakened and could no longer defend the larger territory of Iraq, rebelled against the Baghdad government. For a brief few days the Kurds successfully commandeered the major cities and towns in Iraqi Kurdistan. But after regrouping its forces, and with the U.S.-led coalition determined not to resume the fighting, Baghdad directed its army to counterattack. The Kurdish resistance could not cope with the greater firepower and substantial numbers of Saddam Hussain's forces. Baghdad regained control of the northern region and routed the Kurdish fighters. Fearing reprisals, the Kurdish population followed their retreating soldiers. Thus began a massive movement of people, estimated to exceed 2 million, or more than two-thirds of the entire Kurdish population of Iraq. Their trek was in two directions, over the mountains to Turkey and eastward to Iran. While the bulk of the refugees fled toward Iran, which opened its borders to those seeking refuge, Turkey was less agreeable to such action, and the Kurds were left to fend for themselves in barren, forbidding terrain, without shelter, food, water, or medicine. Moreover, Saddam's troops, especially his helicopter gunships, were still reported striking at the refugees as they fled. Coalition forces did nothing to prevent Baghdad from victimizing the Kurds in the first weeks of the exodus. International relief efforts were mounted, however, and then the French government announced it could not stand by and watch the decimation of the Kurdish nation. Other European nations added their voices and began to send relief supplies. Prodded by the European community to join the effort, President Bush ordered an air drop of relief supplies. But this emergency reaction did not relieve the plight of the refugees, who by Washington's account were dying at a rate of 1,000 each day. Thus, at a meeting of European Community members on April 8, 1991, Prime Minister John Major of Great Britain proposed that the United Nations create an enclave and a haven for the fleeing Kurds in northern Iraq that would insulate them from further repression. Major said the details should be worked out by the Security Council. He also left open the possibility that a UN peacekeeping force could be sent to the region. The Bush administration initially rejected the scheme, arguing it would embroil the United States in a Vietnam-type conflict. On April 10, however, Bush altered his position. He warned Saddam Hussain that both his fixed-wing aircraft and helicopters would be shot down if they moved north of the 36th parallel, an area that also included the major city of Mosul. Two days later the United States expanded its air drop, but the haphazard character of the program, the absence of a semblance of order on the ground, and the high mountain ranges made servicing the needs of the Kurdish people an impossibility. Hence, on April 16 President Bush announced the establishment of six bases in the northern area of Iraq where U.S. special forces were already on the ground. France and Britain also sent troops to the region to bolster the U.S. effort. Operating out of Turkey, which now allowed the Kurds to move to flat areas, the U.S. and European forces began the construction of temporary airstrips and roads through the region. Bush insisted it was still U.S. policy not to interfere in the domestic politics of Iraq. The establishment of an enclave for the Kurds, he said, was centered on purely humanitarian needs. Eventually the United Nations was to assume the task of administering to the refugees, at least until they could safely return to their homes. The Baghdad government angrily denounced the action, saying it was a violation of Iraq's sovereignty. The Soviet Union and China were reluctant to give their support to the enclave plan, and Baghdad sought to take advantage of the perceived division among the permanent Security Council members. Moreover, the larger portion of Kurdish refugees had moved in the direction of Iran, and the Western allies had not yet decided to assist Iran in administering to the needs of that population. Baghdad appeared to have seized the initiative on that as well as the larger issue when Jalal Talabani, one of the more notable Kurdish leaders, met with Saddam Hussain and on April 14 in a joint communiqué they declared the Iraqi Kurds would be given autonomy. Masoud Barzani, the dominant Kurdish figure and head of the Democratic Party of Kurdistan, announced shortly thereafter his acceptance of the agreement. Nevertheless, the larger Kurdish population refused to take the accords seriously, noting that earlier understandings, such as the autonomy agreement of 1970, had been violated by the same Saddam Hussain, who expressed little interest in the welfare of the Kurdish nation. *See also* ETHNIC ATROCITIES (83).

Significance

The Major enclave plan for the Kurds was a unique approach to the problem insofar as it appeared to contravene that body of international law that makes paramount the sovereignty of individual states. It also seemed to contradict the Charter of the United Nations, which in Article Two addresses the matter of state sovereignty and emphasizes the principle that each state has total and exclusive control over its internal affairs. Baghdad therefore would have to approve such a proposal, which the Saddam Hussain regime said it would never do. Moreover, Baghdad insisted Iraq was being victimized by foreign forces bent on its destruction and that the Kurdish problem had been exaggerated as a means to pursue such a policy. Baghdad rejected the enclave proposal. On April 10, 1991, the United States also announced it opposed the arrangement. The enclave proposal, however, was pressed by the British and French, and the German government also emphasized its concern for the Kurds. Germany launched its own relief campaign, second only to that of the United States. Later, the German foreign minister called for the trial of Saddam Hussain as a war criminal. He also approved the effort made by other European nations to set up the enclave. Under pressure from his allies as well as at home, Bush was compelled to take the matter in hand. Only the United States seemed capable of establishing order from the chaos in northern Iraq. Only the United States could assure Turkey that it would not be burdened by an even larger Kurdish dilemma. The U.S. acceptance of the enclave proposal was confirmed on April 16 when President Bush announced he would send U.S. forces into northern Iraq in an effort to relieve the suffering of the Kurdish refugees along the border with Turkey. The United States, assisted by France, Britain, and Canada, carved out a slice of northern Iraq and compelled the Iraqi military and police contingent to vacate the area, and the long, tedious process of bringing the Kurds down off the desolate mountains began in earnest. The withdrawal of coalition forces, however, exposed the Kurds to both Iraqi and Turkish assault. Iraq moved to reduce if not eliminate the Kurdish zone, and

Turkey, in March 1992, opened an offensive, ostensibly against the Kurdish Workers Party, a separatist political movement in Eastern Anatolia, but also aimed at scattering the Kurdish population on the Turkish-Iraqi border. While Germany openly charged Turkey with the commission of atrocities, the United States maintained its silence.

Legitimacy 91

Political legitimacy refers to the ability of government to effectively manage the affairs of state. Legitimacy is often equated with support and implies that governmental decisions will be obeyed and authority sustained in its capacity to speak for the whole nation. Legitimacy can be described in various ways. Hereditary legitimacy refers to monarchy and the special place reserved for the royal family. Theological legitimacy places importance on religious rites and confers power on spiritual divines. Military legitimacy is recognition of the physical power held by uniformed officers. Administrative legitimacy is equated with efficiency and effectiveness and is usually ascribed to bureaucrats in high political office. Ideological legitimacy is the secular version of theological legitimacy in that rule is effected by leadership charged with sustaining a body of doctrine crucial to the survival of the social system. Electoral legitimacy emphasizes the power of the people and their right to select and control their governors. With the exception of electoral legitimacy, all forms of legitimacy dramatize the power of authority and its dominance over society. It cannot be said, however, that one form of "legitimacy" is more legitimate than another. Legitimacy is a relative term. Moreover, the types of legitimacy described above are seldom mutually exclusive; different forms of legitimacy are likely to interact. The result is a blend of legitimacies that either enhances or detracts from governmental operations. The key to the legitimacy question is the degree of stability enjoyed by government and its capacity to accomplish the objectives of state and society. Middle East governments suffer from a lack of legitimacy. Whether cast in monarchial, theological, military, administrative, ideological, or electoral form, all suffer from lack of genuine popular support. All are faced with irrational behavior, suspicion, and physical abuse. Changes in government are seldom predictable or conducted through institutional devices. Crude displays of power produce changes in leadership, as well as in policy and overall orientation. Each change is justified by reference to popular need even if the public has little voice in the outcome. The succession of one government and the demise of another is also no guarantee that the legitimacy necessary for the purposeful employment of government will evolve. ***See also*** DEMOCRACY (80); CONSTITUTIONALISM: EGYPT AND PAKISTAN (79); AUTHORITARIANISM (72).

Significance

Legitimacy is an ambiguous concept that seeks to describe the "right" of a particular leadership to govern a particular society. Iranian revolutionaries would argue that the shah, despite his long reign, was a usurper of authority and that his rule was illegitimate. Army officers who seize power through coups d'état are also deemed to be illegitimate. In states with conflicting ideologies, even if one succeeds over the other, who can say which one, if either, is legitimate? If monarchs today are perceived to be without legitimacy, and power through coup is also judged illegitimate, how can a military coup that ousts a monarch be legitimate? And why, too, does such "legitimacy" evaporate when the military refuses to yield power to civilian officials? Answers to questions of legitimacy and illegitimacy are inadequate. Nevertheless, it can be noted that the military government of General Zia-ul-Haq in Pakistan was no more appreciated by the rank and file than was the ideologically imposed government of Babrak Karmal in Afghanistan. Although Ayatollah Khomeini received broad public adulation, large segments of Iranian society found his rule unacceptable. The same is true for the monarchies of the Arabian Peninsula, the one-party arrangements in Syria and Iraq, and the dictatorial rule of Muammar Qaddafi. It is enough to suggest that in the modern Middle East, all governments, to a greater or lesser degree, suffer from an absence of legitimacy.

Maronites 92

The Maronites are Arabic-speaking members of the Uniate Church, having communion with the Vatican, but who use Syriac in their liturgy. Lebanon has the largest community of Maronites, estimated to be in excess of 600,000. Other Maronites reside in Israel, Egypt, Syria, Cyprus, and the United States. The Maronite world population is believed to be approximately 1.5 million. The Maronites had their origin in the seventh century when they centered their faith around monothelitism, considered a heretical belief. The doctrine of monothelitism was first promulgated in the seventh century by the Byzantine Emperor Heraclius. Although in conformity with traditional Christian doctrine that Christ had two natures, divine and human, the monothelitists also insisted those natures were manifested in one will and activity. In the twelfth century, the Maronites reestablished their ties with the papacy. Nevertheless, they are ruled autonomously by a religious patriarch known as the patriarch of Antioch, in Lebanon. Although the liturgy follows Roman Catholic lines, it is more Byzantine or Eastern in character. Approximately 200,000 Maronites live in the United States, and a delegate of the patriarch of Antioch oversees the religious needs of this community. American Maronites are sensitive to the needs of Lebanese Maronites. ***See also*** PHALANGES LIBANAISES (138); DRUZE (81); LEBANESE CIVIL WAR, 1975-1976 (250).

Significance

The Maronites have experienced centuries of discrimination, but they have been undeterred in the practice of their faith. Faced with mortal threats, the Maronites have learned to adapt to changing circumstances to preserve their way of life. The French assisted the Maronites when they were attacked by the Druze midway through the nineteenth century. France used the persecution of these Christians as a pretext for imposing its will on Lebanon and Syria. France was also responsible for insulating the Arab Maronites from the shocks of Arab, and particularly Syrian, nationalism. The departure of the Europeans and the emergence of an independent Arab-Muslim world was viewed with apprehension by the Maronite community. They therefore sought separation from Syria and a guarantee of their political preeminence in tiny Lebanon. The Maronites proved to be successful businessmen; they also controlled significant tracts of land, thus dominating the economic life of the region. Supported by European power, they also achieved considerable political influence. World War II, however, saw the end of French dominance in the area. It also brought the crystallization of a number of Arab states, as well as the state of Israel on Lebanon's southern border. Given Arab Muslim intransigence on the matter of an Israeli state, the subsequent conflict between Muslims and Jews disturbed the Maronites. Like the Jews, who insisted on political opportunity to safeguard their way of life and physical well-being, the Maronites voiced similar demands. The best they could expect was a union between Christian and Muslim Arabs with the Christian Maronites maintaining political preeminence. But just as the Muslim Arabs refused to accept a Jewish state in their midst, so, too, they found Christian Maronite dominance in Lebanon unacceptable. The result was sectarian strife through the 1950s and 1960s. The shift of the Palestine Liberation Organization to Lebanon from Jordan in 1970 brought a major explosion. The Lebanese Civil War of the 1970s was aimed at the destruction of the Maronite power base. It also suggested the transformation of Lebanon into a Syrian province and the creation of an extensive military bastion for the Palestine Liberation Organization. The Maronites were sympathetic with the Palestine Arab cause, but they did not want Israel and the Palestinians using Lebanon as a battleground. Moreover, they did not want a power in the region greater than their own. The Maronites found themselves in the middle of a bitter contest that threatened to consume them. They therefore decided that Israel, rather than their Arab brethren, offered their best hope for self-preservation. At first, seeking Israeli assistance in southern Lebanon in the June 1982 Israeli-PLO War, the Maronites joined with the invading Israeli army in pressing for the removal of the PLO from Beirut and the destruction of its war-making capability. The perpetuation of Maronite rule, however, was more a Syrian concern. It was the Syrians who ultimately influenced the course of Lebanese politics in Beirut. Under Syrian tutelage a modified Lebanese government was established that sustained the Maronites in leadership positions, but with considerable power-sharing among the non-Christian communities of Lebanon.

Militarism 93

Militarism refers to the intervention of the armed forces and their officers in the domestic politics of a country. Justification for such involvement is customarily expressed in terms that describe the weakness, indecision, and/or corrupt activities of the civilian leaders, their parties, and bureaucracies. The idea is always raised that members of the armed forces are more patriotic, honest, and effective than their political counterparts, and also that the politicians are responsible for creating unrest but are not capable of controlling it. Politicians are castigated for rousing popular passions, for inciting chaos, and for instigating anarchical situations. Law and order can only be managed by the armed forces, which are constantly called upon to restore tranquility to a disturbed society. It is not surprising, therefore, that the uniformed officers should assume a mandate to rectify inequities or to put society back together after civilian leadership has proved itself bankrupt. There is also a body of opinion that asserts that the military coup is a necessary and expected stage in the political modernization of a society. It is argued that Third World countries require mobilization of human and natural resources. The disciplined use of such resources is possible, at a certain level of development, only by military personnel, who also command a degree of public respect. Military intervention in the political process of Middle East countries is more often the rule than the exception. In the post–World War II era, the armed forces have seized power in Egypt (1952), Iraq (1958), Turkey (1960, 1980), Pakistan (1958, 1969, 1977), Libya (1969), Algeria (1964),

Sudan (1969), and Syria (1949, 1953, 1970). The military has also bolstered the rule of King Hussain in Jordan, King Hassan II in Morocco, and Habib Bourguiba in Tunisia. It was a key factor in both North and South Yemen, and it brought the Marxists to power in Afghanistan. Saudi Arabia has avoided military intervention, possibly because the country ignored the development of a professional armed force until recently. The shaykhdoms along the gulf also deemphasized military establishments or, as in Oman, leaned heavily on foreign mercenaries. And despite Israel's garrison state condition, its civilian armed force, pluralistic political parties, and interest groups have insulated it from ambitious military personalities. To what extent militarism in the Middle East is related to Islamic political culture cannot be satisfactorily assessed. It is important to note the dominant role of the military establishment in Muslim history. It is also notable that Muslim leaders have sought to constrain their officers, to dissuade them from intervening in politics, and to encourage them to pledge their loyalty to the supreme leader, in many instances a quasi-military figure. Still it must be pointed out that Mohammad Ali was a general in the Ottoman army, as was Ataturk a century later. Both employed the armed forces to produce major political and social transformations in Egypt and Turkey, respectively. The prominence of the military role is probably due to its durability when other institutions begin to crumble or have already collapsed. The military institution lives by its own codes and precepts. Its hierarchical structure and its emphasis on discipline and collective obligation sustain it when everything else appears frail and disordered. Given states that are not yet integrated nations, given backwardness and drift, and given an authoritarian tradition, Middle East societies will continue to exaggerate the military role in politics. *See also* AUTHORITARIANISM (72); LEGITIMACY (91).

Significance

Militarism is no panacea in the Middle East. The exceptional importance given to the expansion, modernization, and sophistication of the armed forces contrasts with the limited attention paid to political innovation and development. Defense expenditures drain national treasuries and leave little for social improvement. Even economic development often follows a framework emphasizing military preparedness. Governments are seldom sustained without military assistance, and the more the armed forces are required to assist an unpopular government, the greater the likelihood they will eventually seize power for themselves. Moreover, the Middle East is the last great bastion of absolute monarchy. Kings, sultans, and emirs are considered anachronisms in a fast-changing world. They are judged antiquated, unadaptable to current needs, and squanderers of scarce resources. Ideological movements such as Marxism either enlist support among the armed forces or provoke the military to seize power in order to arrest them. In either case monarchs are in grave jeopardy. Finally, there are the rivalries between existing states and states challenged by insurgents or external forces. Fear of military encounter provokes even greater outlays for military purposes. With a legacy of colonialism immediately behind them, Middle East states will not ignore new threats to their independence from ambitious distant powers. By the same token, Middle East nations are not yet at peace with each other. So long as neighbors seem determined to harm each other, the armed forces will continue to receive maximum attention and resources. Militarism will continue to be a major characteristic of Middle East politics.

Millet System 94

The millet system was formalized within the Ottoman Empire and represented an institutional framework for the preservation and expression of minority culture and tradition. *Millet* is an Arabic word that has been incorporated in Persian and Turkish languages. Translated, millet describes a distinct religious community or "nation." The Ottoman Empire was a congeries of peoples, communities, and nations, Muslim and non-Muslim, Turk and non-Turk. Under the Ottomans, the Islamic tradition of protecting "People of the Book" (*Ahl al-Kitab*) or "scriptuaries," such as Christians, Jews, and Zoroastrians, was provided concrete form. Toleration was an act of faith, but it was also made necessary by the character and structure of the Ottoman state. After the conquest of Constantinople (Istanbul) by the Ottoman sultan in 1453, the conqueror called upon religious leaders to administer the civil and spiritual affairs of the city's minorities. This dispensation developed into a system of local autonomy in civil affairs for non-Muslim sects. The administration and maintenance of holy places, marriage, education, inheritance, and the disposal and ownership of property were all managed by the individual millet. Millet courts were created to resolve controversies between sect members. Millets also selected their own local administrators, although their activities required the sanction of the sultan. The millets were arranged in hierarchical structure; preeminent leaders were also members of the government and thus had a say in broader decision making. With the disappearance of the Ottoman Empire, the millet reverted to its informal character. Minority groups maintained their distinct identities, but they did not receive special political-administrative privileges. National states are recognized agglomerations of humanity, but their central theme is national unity. Sovereignty supposedly rests with the general population. Government exists, at least in theory, to protect the interests of the total citizenry, irrespective of their diversity. To speak in favor of a millet system is tantamount to encouraging divided sovereignty. ***See also*** AUTONOMY (73).

Significance

The millet system was a demonstration of tolerance in a period when minorities lived precarious existences. The development of the Ottoman millet, for example, coincided with the Inquisition in Spain. Substantial segments of Spain's minority population fled the country in an effort to avoid persecution and took up domicile within the Ottoman Empire. This is not to suggest the Ottomans were always compassionate and helpful, but they did tolerate religious-cultural expression, so long as it did not threaten the power of the realm. The Soviet Union absorbed some of the features of the Ottoman millet system. The division of the Soviet state into nationalities and subnationalities, the encouragement given to cultural expression, and the strict controls placed upon minority political behavior bear some resemblance to the Ottoman system. In the present-day Middle East, the situation is clouded by political strife. The Kurds, for example, were denied millet status even by the Ottomans. Today's Kurds, given their desire for political expression, have been suppressed in Iraq and Iran as well as in modern Turkey. Armenians suffered enormous atrocities at the hands of the Turks in the early decades of the twentieth century. In the aftermath of World War I, Greeks living in Turkey had to be exchanged for Turks living in Greece to prevent further communal warfare. Greek-Turkish conflict flared again in the Cyprus dispute in the 1960s and 1970s. Moreover, in the wake of the Palestinian Arab exodus from Israel, Jews long domiciled in the Arab world were forced to flee to the new Jewish state. When the government of Ayatollah Khomeini was established in Iran, the Baha'i community found itself under renewed pressure. Suffice it to say that minority expression in the Middle East today is intertwined with political activity, and the consequence is a more uncertain existence.

Monarchy: Saudi Arabia 95

Saudi Arabia is named after the Saud family. Bolstered by his family's identification with Wahhabism, an austere, puritanical, and demanding Islamic sect, the founder of Saudi Arabia, Abdul Aziz ibn Saud, better known as ibn Saud, defeated his tribal rivals in the years preceding and immediately following World War I. The country achieved independent status in 1926 after ibn Saud's forces defeated those of the Hashemite sherif of Mecca. Britain recognized ibn Saud's authority and also assisted him in consolidating his power. In 1932 the Kingdom of Saudi Arabia was officially proclaimed, and by 1934 tribal rivalry was terminated. Saudi Arabia's government is controlled by the House of Saud, its approximately 5,000 members having intermarried among the regional tribal shaykhs, and they and their progeny monopolize government and commercial activity. Although the political system may be described as a form of patriarchy, maternal lines are significant in the distribution of power and responsibility. Decision making is also a family affair, and consensus is the key to successful operations. It also helps to bridge intrafamily conflict and confine it to family processes, and thus avoid opening wounds in the ruling circle that could be exploited by outside elements. The Qur'an is Saudi Arabia's constitution, and Islamic law is strictly enforced. Tribal laws and customs are also sustained. The Saudi king is "first among equals" within the ruling house. He is both head of state and head of government. Saudi Arabia's kings are: Abdul Aziz ibn Saud (1927–1953); Saud ibn Abdul Aziz al Saud (1953–1964); Faisal ibn Abdul Aziz al Saud (1964–1975); Khalid ibn Abdul Aziz al Saud (1975–1982); and Fahd ibn Abdul Aziz al Saud (1982–). Not all the kings have been effective leaders. Ibn Saud is given very high marks for statesmanship. His successor, Saud, however, proved incompetent and was quietly eased off the throne. King Faisal, by contrast, was both inventive and dynamic. His power was only just becoming evident when he was assassinated by a disgruntled prince in 1975. His successor, Khalid, was a reserved, unworldly figure, but adept at managing the family's inner quarrels. His death in June 1982 brought the younger, more enlightened Fahd to the throne. Expectations in and outside Saudi Arabia focus on a more energetic king, and particularly one eager to provide leadership for a fragmented Arab world. Saudi Arabia's vast oil wealth has enabled it to launch the most impressive development program in the history of any nation. Moreover, its financial activities stretch around the world, and its deposits and investments in foreign banking institutions, industrial corporations, farmland, and tourist sites promise to increase its wealth beyond the country's earnings from the exploitation of petroleum. Modernization has also meant the creation of a sophisticated armed forces, divided between the national guard that protects the royal family and the regular military establishment that is charged with warding off external aggressors. Despite Saudi power and influence in the larger world, legitimacy is still based on the adherence to Islamic doctrine. The longtime alliance with the Al-Shaykh family, the fount of Wahhabism, remains intact despite the forging of new relationships with nouveau riche commercial families. The Saudis have also acknowledged the need to permit trusted commoners to play a role in the government. Although the ministries and significant councils and commercial establishments are managed or influenced by members of the House of Saud, the country's progressive development has generated the need for greater technical know-how. Such needs are being met by Saudi citizens as well as by foreign experts on an expanding basis. It is difficult to see how the emphasis on rapid economic and technological development will not eventually influence changes in the ruling structure. Radical movements have surfaced that seek to enlist the disenchanted while they mobilize their forces for a direct assault on the monarchy. The seizure of the Sacred Mosque in Mecca by a group of religious fanatics in 1979 frightened the ruling family and illustrated the unrest that lies just beneath the surface. The actions of Ayatollah Khomeini were condemned in Saudi Arabia because they also threatened the regime. Leftist organizations, particularly those identified with factions of the Palestine Liberation Organization, have also become worrisome. Saudi Arabia's traditional ties to the United States are viewed by the regime's critics as reinforcing an archaic, autocratic system, and the Saudis are conscious of the need to maintain the loyalty of their armed forces in a period of increasing tension and uncertainty. ***See also*** AL SAUD DYNASTY (68); WAHHABIS (63).

Significance

The Saudi leadership insists that throughout their history the kingdom has pursued policies in support of political modernization and economic stability. In keeping with the tribal customs of the bedouin of the Arabian Peninsula, the Saudis emphasize cooperation, negotiation, and compromise. They also speak of a strong sense of justice that is required by Islamic teaching and precept. Since Saudi Arabia's inception in the 1920s, and particularly following World War II, material and environmental changes have been phenomenal. Nevertheless, Saudi Arabia's political system has not advanced from its original beginnings. Government has grown to assume the responsibilities necessitated by economic development, but the relationship between ruler and ruled, superiors and inferiors, has not changed. Moreover, the incredible changes in the economic life of the nation tend to exaggerate the traditional political system. The power of the royal family is carefully guarded and delegations of responsibility in no way suggest limitations on the authority of the monarch. Saudi Arabia is a current superpower in financial circles the world over. It displays considerable sophistication in dealing with other governments. It remains to be seen if the monarchy can adapt to the changes that it has itself initiated by its vast modernization program. In 1992, King Fahd announced formation of a new consultative council (Majlis al-Shoura) with authority to question the government. Members of the council must be Saudi nationals, well qualified, of good reputation, and not less than 30 years old. The council was the Saudi answer to pressures for democratic reform, but any measure not approved by the council must be referred back to the king. The new council consists of a speaker and 60 members selected by the king, and their rights and duties are identified by royal decree. It was also announced the Prince Abdullah bin Abdul Aziz will continue to act as crown prince, deputy premier, and commander of the national guard. In effect, rule remains confined to the sons and grandsons of the kingdom's founder.

Multinationalism: Lebanon

96

Lebanon was established as a republic in 1926, under French supervision. Full independence was not achieved until 1946. Its constitution of 1926 has been frequently amended, but the salient features have remained stable. Executive power is vested in the president, who is elected for a six-year term and who by convention must be a Christian. The president selects a prime minister who must be a Sunni Muslim. The prime minister and his cabinet, all appointees, are responsible to the Lebanese parliament but need not be members of the body. The parliament consists of the Chamber of Deputies, and members are elected on the basis of universal adult suffrage for four-year terms. Seats in the legislature are apportioned according to the relative importance of each religious sect in the country. The speaker is the dominant officer in the chamber and by convention is supposed to be a Shiite Muslim. Relations between Christians and Muslims in Lebanon have been guided by the unwritten National Pact of 1943. With that pact Christians agreed to divorce themselves from French tutelage, and the Muslims promised to maintain the integrity of Lebanon and discard a plan to make the country an integral part of Syria. Lebanon was also assumed to have a Christian majority despite the influx of tens of thousands of Muslims and the higher birthrate of Muslims over Christians. According to the 1932 census, the Maronite community was established in a preeminent position with 29 percent of the total population. Sunni Muslims were listed at 21 percent, and Shiite Muslims, at 18.5 percent. The other Christian minorities, such as the Greek Orthodox (9.7 percent), tipped the scales in favor of the Christian community by approximately 55 to 45 percent. Reluctance of the Christian Maronites to modify the agreed-upon relationship became a *cause célèbre* as Lebanon began to develop and prosper as a financial outpost in the post–World War II Middle East. Moreover, the Maronites were most interested in protecting their material gains and less inclined to join in the conflict with the new state of Israel. The eventual domicile in Lebanon of Palestinian refugees, and after 1970 the central organization of the Palestine Liberation Organization, destroyed the fragile balance between the contending communities. In 1958, a relatively minor threat that was posed to the existing order was quickly brought under control by the landing of U.S. forces in the country. In 1975, however, internecine conflict could not be avoided, and a brutal campaign of destruction was visited upon the country. The civil war not only involved Lebanese but also brought the PLO into a dominant role. The latter's presence provoked the Syrians to send major forces, and even a token Arab League contingent attempted to police the country. The civil war destroyed the Lebanese armed forces and made a mockery of the Lebanese government. Syria, the PLO, the Maronite Phalange, and the Lebanese Druze divided the country between them. But hostilities continued. Estimates ran as high as 60,000 dead and 300,000 wounded in the civil war, an enormous toll in so small a country. The economy was in shambles, and survival, not progress, was the objective of the inhabitants. The Israeli invasion of June 1982 attempted to destroy the Palestine Liberation Organization, oust Syrian forces from the country, and restore Lebanon as a neutral buffer state in the Arab-Israeli conflict. The Maronites saw their opportunity to regain lost leverage and lent their support to the Israelis much as they had to the French and the Americans. The Israeli invasion swept all the way to Beirut. After weeks of air, sea, and land bombardment, the PLO in West Beirut agreed to a ceasefire (the eleventh) and, according to a plan developed by U.S. mediator Philip Habib, began the withdrawal of its troops from Beirut and their dispersal to other Arab states. During this exodus the Lebanese parliament met to elect a new president. Elias Sarkis's six-year term expired in September 1982. On August 23, 1982, despite Muslim and Druze opposition, Bashir Gemayel, the son of the Phalangist leader Pierre Gemayel and the head of the Phalange Maronite militia, was declared president on the second ballot. Given Lebanon's continuing crisis, some doubt was expressed about Bashir Gemayel's capacity to unite the Lebanese factions, and the forecasts were not hopeful. Most observers appeared to agree that Lebanon's "time of trouble" had not yet ended. The pessimists did not have long to wait. Bashir Gemayel and a number of his aides were killed when a bomb destroyed their East Beirut headquarters on September 14. After a brief period of mourning, Bashir's brother, Amin, was selected to take his place. Amin was installed as president of Lebanon on September 23, 1982, following a vote of the deputies of the legislature. Amin, a less controversial figure than his brother, pledged to begin the healing process between Lebanon's disparate, warring communities. He did not succeed in this effort, and Lebanon was still convulsed by civil war when his term expired in 1988. What followed was a struggle for power that essentially was reduced to a contest between Iraqi-backed elements in the Christian militia and Syrian-backed elements among the Phalange. The war in the gulf initiated by Iraq in 1990 provided Syria with the opportunity to bolster its support for Elias Hrawi, who assumed the Lebanese presidency in 1990. Although another aspirant, General Michel Aoun, had Baghdad's backing and had declared himself to be the troubled country's president, the Syrian army resolved the dilemma when it forced Aoun to seek refuge in the French Embassy and systematically liquidated his loyal militia. Approximately 800 of Aoun's troops were disarmed and promptly executed. The Syrians continued to support a modified confessional system for Lebanon, but the scales were no longer tilted in favor of the Christians. Although they continued to hold on to the presidency, most power had shifted to a half-Christian, half-Muslim cabinet, and parliamentary seats were divided equally between Muslims and Christians. ***See also*** MARONITES (92); PHALANGES LIBANAISES (138); LEBANON CIVIL WAR: THE PROLONGED MIDDLE STAGE (251); LEBANON CIVIL WAR: THE CONCLUDING PHASE (252).

Significance

Lebanon's experiment with multinationalism has produced mixed results. Because it is divided between religious communities that are historically hostile toward one another, the nation's efforts aimed at moderating differences have been painful and only moderately successful. Moreover, internal cleavages have provided foreign governments with opportunities to meddle in the state's affairs. Alien powers have acted as balances between the antagonistic communities, but they have also sought advantages for themselves. The French, Syrians, Israelis, and even the Americans (for a brief period in 1958) have played this role in the twentieth century. Lebanon has been described as a mosaic nation, and political institutions have been assembled to satisfy the fundamental needs of such a society. The civil war of 1975–1976 put these institutions through their most severe test to date.

The Israeli invasion of Lebanon in the aftermath of that war was aimed at preserving those institutions and stabilizing the country's political life. Israeli failure provided Syria with an opportunity to balance the relations between Lebanon's different communities. In 1991 it appeared that effort had at least brought the civil war to an informal end.

Nasserism 97

Nasserism is a modern ideology stressing Arab, and ultimately Muslim, unity. It is derived from the philosophy rather than the work of Gamal Abdul Nasser. Nasser was the first Arab in several centuries to capture the imagination of Muslims everywhere. He became the symbol of Arab vitality and, by all measures, the leading Arab figure in the post–World War II era. Nasserism is more important for its philosophy, because Nasser did not succeed in most of his practical endeavors. Nasser believed it necessary to promote military prowess and through physical struggle to achieve the modern goals of the Arab world. His misadventure in the Yemeni civil war and his humiliating defeats at Israeli hands in 1956 and 1967 made achievement difficult. His failure to sustain the merger between Egypt, Syria, and Yemen and his inability to resolve the Jordanian-Palestinian crisis also tainted his performance. Nevertheless, Nasser is remembered and revered as the spiritual father of current Arab nationalism. His "philosophy of revolution" is required reading for aspiring pan-Arabists. Nasser's philosophy is a pronouncement on hero worship. According to Nasser, the frustrated, restless Arab world required a great leader, a Salah al-Din (a leading Muslim figure during the crusades), to rally the population against foreign intervention and to rid the Middle East of European exploiters. Nasserism addresses itself to a heroic role. Nasser spoke of such a role as "wandering aimlessly about seeking an actor." He questioned why the role should suddenly settle upon himself, but he also seized it with alacrity. Nasser raised the imagery of three concentric circles in the pursuance of Islamic unity. The inner circle is Egypt itself. Egypt is the key to the Arab circle, and the Arab circle is connected to the more extensive Muslim circle. Pan-Arabism and pan-Islamism are thus merged through Nasserism. But above all, Nasserism symbolizes the Arab quest for identity, dignity, and national purpose. The Nasserists who emerged following his death, however, had none of his charisma, compassion, or sense of proportion. In their hands, Nasserism took on an aggressive, bombastic character. Revolution became an end in itself rather than the vehicle for social uplift and political reform. ***See also*** GREEN BOOK (85).

Significance
Nasserism is synonymous with revolutionary doctrine. It suggests radical behavior, whether extreme Left or Right. In its current metamorphosis Nasserism is a negative force, opposed to established authority and seeking its destruction. The primary exponent of Nasserism in the present Arab world is Libya's Muammar Qaddafi. Qaddafi idolized Nasser. As a young man, he believed that Nasser was destined to rehabilitate Arabdom, to strengthen it, and ultimately to unify it. Qaddafi seized power in 1969 with a view toward fulfilling Nasser's dream of Arab unity. But his idol's death shortly thereafter left a considerable vacuum. Qaddafi pressured Sadat to hold to the course developed by Nasser, and the merger of Libya and Egypt became his principal objective. Nasser had emphasized the importance of Egypt in rallying the divided Arab population, and Qaddafi was

no less convinced of it. Sadat's tacit agreement to the merger was followed by rejection and confrontation. Instead of a willing ally, Qaddafi talked of betrayal. Sadat's subsequent campaign to de-Nasserize Egypt inflamed the relationship between the two men and their respective countries. Qaddafi enlisted the support of Sadat's opposition, and Nasserism quickly degenerated into internecine conflict.

Pakhtunistan (98)

Pakhtunistan is the focus of the quest by Pathan nationalists to establish an independent, sovereign Pathan nation. The idea of a free Pakhtunistan was supported by members of the Khudai Khidmatgar (Servants of God), better known as "Red Shirts" because of the garments they wore. The Khudai Khidmatgar was organized by Abdul Ghaffar Khan on the northwest frontier of British India in the 1920s. The original intention of the Red Shirts was to drive the British from the region and the subcontinent as a whole. When the cry of a homeland for the Pathans (also called Pushtuns and Pakhtuns) was raised, the Pakistan idea had yet to be established. The Pathans had resisted British power and were a formidable adversary for British troops stationed on the frontier. The Red Shirts, although Muslim, joined with Mahatma Gandhi and the Indian National Congress in opposing British rule. The Red Shirts also opposed the creation of Pakistan because they believed it would provide the British with a permanent role in the area. Abdul Ghaffar Khan was therefore welcome in India following the British withdrawal. He was also on good terms with the leaders in Afghanistan, who picked up the idea of a free Pathan state and transformed it into Afghan foreign policy. The Pathan population is a congeries of independent, rival tribes that have seldom displayed internal unity, let alone identified with a larger national cause. They are united by a common religion, Islam; a common language, Pushtu; and a common enemy—anyone who seeks to restrict their individual expression. Ghaffar Khan attempted to unite the tribal peoples. The leaders of Afghanistan, especially Mohammad Daud, a member of the ruling Durrani family, also sought to create a united front among them. Generally speaking, however, Afghanistan's call for a Pathan nation implied the Pathans of Pakistan, not those in Afghanistan. Ultimately, the Afghans seemed intent on reuniting the Pathans under their leadership, but with perhaps a more substantial promise of autonomy. Abdul Ghaffar Khan was imprisoned in Pakistan on numerous occasions, and the Red Shirts eventually disintegrated into a series of other organizations. From 1957 until its dissolution in 1975, the National Awami Party (NAP), with Abdul Ghaffar Khan as its most prominent Pathan leader, pressed for a Pathan homeland, or at least greater regional autonomy. The leader of the NAP on the northwest frontier of Pakistan in 1975 was Ghaffar Kahn's son, Wali Khan. He was imprisoned and his party disbanded after the assassination of a Pakistani government official and political confidant of then Prime Minister Zulfikar Ali Bhutto. Wali Khan was released from prison after Bhutto was overthrown in a military coup, only to be placed under house arrest later. Again gaining his release in 1982, Wali Khan was permitted to go to Kabul reputedly to open a dialogue with the Soviet-created Babrak Karmal regime. Ghaffar Khan died in 1989, but he continues to symbolize the Pathan cause. *See also* DURAND LINE (8).

Significance

Pakhtunistan is a passionate concern of people residing on Pakistan's northwest frontier. It is also a dagger pointed at the heart of the Pakistani nation. After the loss of East Pakistan and its recreation as independent Bangladesh, the separation of the northwest frontier from Pakistani control would more than likely produce violent encounters in Baluchistan, and possibly in Sind province as well. Between 1973 and 1976 Baluchistan experienced a large insurgency that was crushed only after the deployment of several Pakistani army divisions. The fragile nature of conditions on the frontier raises concern in Islamabad. The lesson of Bangladesh, a homeland for the Bengalis, cannot be lost on the people of Pakistan. Moreover, they know how quickly the world adjusted to the creation of the new state of Bangladesh. They fear that little external help would be forthcoming if Pakistan were to break into its constituent parts, Pakhtunistan for the Pathans, Baluchistan for the Baluch, Sindu Desh for the Sindhis, and Punjab for the Punjabis. The Pakhtunistan issue therefore is one of the more compelling problems facing Pakistani leadership.

Pan-Turanism 99

Pan-Turanism may be considered another expression of pan-Turkism. Its purpose is the unity of all Turkic peoples, and it surfaced in the wake of the demise of the Ottoman Empire. The Ottoman Empire was equated with the larger Turkic nation, but in reality it comprised the many nationalities and ethnic groups brought under its standard. Non-Turks assumed high positions in the Ottoman administration, and approximately two-thirds of all the grand vizirs (the equivalent of prime minister) were non-Turks. East Europeans, Greeks, and Armenians played conspicuous roles in the army and civil administration, and the regime seldom displayed racist characteristics. Large-scale intermarriage also neutralized narrow feelings and caused considerable homogenization. Pan-Turanism, therefore, was more a reaction to defeat, humiliation, and loss of personal and group pride. In the post–World War I period, it was rejected by Mustafa Kemal Ataturk, but it later found an ally in Nazi Germany. The first important display of pan-Turanism is identified with Enver Pasha, a ranking officer in the Ottoman Court, who preached a doctrine of uniting all Turkic peoples from the Middle East to East Asia in one great confederation. Enver Pasha and his movement died when the Soviets destroyed the central Asian Bashmachi rebels in the 1920s. Pan-Turanism survived, however, and during World War II, the Nazis, who promoted their own brand of "Aryan" racism, encouraged the Turks to revitalize their movement. The Germans sought an ally against the Soviet Union, but the Turkish government had decided to follow a neutral course in the war, and it suppressed the pan-Turanists. Following the overthrow of the Adnan Menderes government in 1960, Turkey's theretofore dominant political parties disintegrated. Smaller, more numerous factions developed, and among them were pan-Turanists, or their equivalent. Identification with Turks residing outside the republic led to proposals for the creation of a greater Turkish republic. This was in clear opposition to Ataturk's philosophy that Turkey eschew all claims to empire and concentrate on building a territorial nation-state. Modern pan-Turanists emphasized race, language, and culture, an orientation that was destined to arouse the Greek, Armenian, and Kurdish minorities in the country. Alparslan Turkesh's Nationalist Action Party became a prominent organization during the terrorists campaign of the 1970s, and attacks on minority communities were often attributed to his agents. Turkesh was one of the more prominent figures seized by the martial law government of Kenan Evren in September 1980. The Turkish government is again on record as deploring all forms of extremism, notably displays of racism. But in the wake of the collapse of the Soviet Union, Pan-Turanism is again a force to be reckoned with. The cultural and historic ties between the Turkic peoples in central Asia and their brethren in Turkey, Iran, Afghanistan, and Pakistan are again emphasized by those with broader intentions, and especially those not confined by the model of the nation-state. ***See also*** TURKEY-GREECE-CYPRUS WAR, 1974 (268).

Significance

Pan-Turanism has never acquired official status in Turkey, nor has the government encouraged racist policies. Nevertheless, periodic clashes between Turks and minority groups occur, and sometimes the loss of life is of a high magnitude. The massacre of Armenians in Turkey during World War I is estimated to have taken more than half a million lives, while a similar number were forced to flee the country. The emergence of the Armenian Liberation Front, a prominent terrorist organization, dramatizes Armenian intention to revenge the deaths of their brothers. Although almost 70 years have passed since that enormous atrocity, the Armenian terrorists have stepped up their campaign of assassination, bombing, and arson.

Turks have also vented their fury on the Greek inhabitants of Asia Minor. In the late stages of World War I, the Greeks joined the Allies in the invasion of the Ottoman heartland. Greece maintained forces in Asia Minor after the Allies withdrew and announced their claim to specific territories. The Greek population of Turkey took the opportunity provided by the Greek expeditionary force to assault the Turks in their midst. Later, when Ataturk led his forces in a successful campaign against the Greek occupation, the Turks took their revenge on the Greeks. The result was terrible carnage, the flight of many Ottoman Greeks to Greece, and long-standing bitterness between the two peoples. This hatred between the communities flared anew with the plight of the Turks living on the island of Cyprus and the subsequent invasion of the island by the Turkish armed forces.

The Kurds of eastern Turkey have also clashed with the majority Turkish population. Kurds opposed Ataturk and his reforms. They also sought an independent homeland. Despite their fierce ways, however, the Turkish army crushed their revolt in 1925. Civil administration was not restored in the Kurdish region until after World War II. But Kurdish nationalism persists irrespective of the efforts to tame and neutralize it. After the 1960 coup, after the 1980 military takeover, and again after Operation Desert Storm in 1991, Kurdish nationalists and extremists were arrested and their movements checked. Successive Turkish governments have emphasized national unity, and it is official policy to avoid demonstrations of racism or exclusivity. Only during World War II, under Nazi influence, did the government institute an oppressive tax program that fell heaviest on the non-Muslim minorities. But even these programs could not be equated with official pan-Turanism. Although the Turks have demonstrated a capacity for communal violence, they reveal far less passion and considerably greater calm in tackling sentimental questions than their Muslim counterparts in other regions of the Middle East. The Turks, by and large, have avoided Islamic extremism. They have neither displayed deep concern for the Arab-Israeli conflict nor identified with the proponents of the Islamic state, whether of the Ayatollah Khomeini variety or that of Zia-ul-Haq. From the official Turkish point of view, neither pan-Turanism nor pan-Islamism is appropriate policy in the last decades of the twentieth century.

Paternalism (100)

In combination with religious notions about power, generations of Arabs, Iranians, and Turks have been conditioned to accept the senior male as the dominant authority figure. Strict discipline and subordination to authority are the norm in the Muslim Middle East. Moreover, rulers never delegate "authority" to their subordinates. The power formula demands plenary power and absolute obedience. ***See also*** AUTHORITARIANISM (72).

Significance

It does not matter who governs or rules in the Middle Eastern countries. Whether it be a king, shaykh, shah, general, bureaucrat, or ayatollah, each ruler maintains his prestige and effectiveness through an expression of political dualism. On the one hand, each will claim legitimacy on the basis of doctrine, either constitutional, mystical, or scriptural. On the other hand, each practices paternalistic authoritarianism and insists on his infallibility, his prerogative to overrule decisions, and his right to use any device to sustain his influence. All rulers therefore control the mass media to some extent and employ arbitrary methods in neutralizing their opposition. Middle Easterners expect their leaders to be repressive; the question they raise is one of degree. They do not seek the elimination of authoritarianism. Dependence on the "great leader" is too ingrained to allow a great deal of expression of individuality. In 1988, Benazir Bhutto became the first women to head a contemporary Muslim state, but her removal in 1990 can be attributed to traditional paternalistic forces in Pakistan and in the Islamic world in general.

Political Integration: Sudan (101)

Sudan achieved its independence from Egypt in 1956 but continues to have difficulty extricating itself from the influence of its northern neighbor. Egypt's destiny is too intertwined with the Sudan to permit the latter to drift into uncertain arrangements. Political instability in the Sudan is therefore a constant source of concern for Cairo, irrespective of the regime in power. Since achieving its independence, the Sudan has had four regimes. A civilian parliamentary system was established from 1956 to 1958. A military coup brought General Ibrahim Abboud to power, and he continued in office until overthrown by a civilian coup, backed by the army, in 1964. Another civilian regime went through several permutations before it was ousted by the armed forces of General Jafar al-Numayri in 1969. Numayri remained in office until he was overthrown in 1985 and replaced by Sadiq al-Mahdi. The Sudan has continued its search for a permanent constitution, but religious and racial differences are enormous obstacles to the development of a coherent political system. Difficulties such as these, in addition to Sudan's economic plight, sustain the military in political power. Nevertheless, it has been no more successful in reducing Sudan's major dilemmas than were the erstwhile politicians. The armed forces neutralized the Anya Nya rebels in the equatorial sector of the country in the 1960s. But they also forced thousands of Black Sudanese, living in the south, to flee to neighboring states. These actions did not endear the Arab-dominated Sudanese government to

Black Africa. The reinstatement of civilian rule in the 1960s was, in part, fostered by an aroused intellectual element that emphasized the unity of the people of the Sudan. A more liberal attitude produced a rapprochement between the different racial communities, but it did not last. Moreover, the Sudanese Communist Party was especially active during this period. Numayri supported and then suppressed the movement when he sensed a threat to his authority. Numayri dissolved the Revolutionary Command Council and established the Sudan Socialist Union (modeled after the Arab Socialist Union in Egypt) as the only legal party in the country. An agreement was signed in Addis Ababa in 1972 ending the struggle with the Anya Nya. Regional autonomy was granted the three southern provinces, and a Regional People's Assembly was created for the southerners. The southerners were also granted a High Executive Council of their own, and the head of this council was made Numayri's vice-president. The agreement also called for the return of the refugees and the integration of the Anya Nya into the Sudanese armed forces. Generally speaking, Numayri moved from ideological to more pragmatic decision making. Denationalization of companies seized by the government was announced in 1973. Sudan looked to the West and offered attractive terms to European investors. Numayri's refusal to permit competitive politics, however, raised a National Front of the opposition parties against him. Coup attempts in 1975 and 1976 were aborted but were nevertheless cause for alarm. The 1976 affair had Libyan backing, but it was ruthlessly crushed, and 100 of its leaders were summarily executed. In 1977, Numayri demonstrated flexibility, and in an understanding with opposition leader Sayyid Sadiq al-Mahdi, he agreed to appoint some of his opponents to government positions and also to permit them to join the Sudan Socialist Union. Ruptures again developed when Numayri angered Sudanese leaders by supporting Sadat's peace initiatives and the Camp David accords between Egypt and Israel. Sadiq and others were also disturbed with Numayri's move to integrate the Sudan's political and economic life with that of Egypt. Under pressure from Saudi Arabia, Numayri veered away from this course in 1979–1980 and began to show greater interest in alliances with Arabian Peninsula states and Iraq. The oil-producing states had considerable capital to offer Sudan that Egypt could not match. In December 1979, Sudan withdrew its ambassador from Cairo, ostensibly because the Israeli ambassador to Egypt was scheduled to make his official arrival. For a brief moment Sudan displayed more friendship with Libya, which only a few years earlier had sought the destruction of the Numayri regime. Relations with Libya took a turn for the worse in mid-1980, however, given Qaddafi's decision to invade neighboring Chad. By 1981, Sudan-Libya relations reached a new low, as Numayri saw Libya's attack on Chad as a prelude for a drive against the Sudan. This development also forced Numayri to reestablish relations with Sadat and Egypt. In March 1981 the Egyptian minister of defense declared that an attack on the Sudan was an attack on Egypt. That same month another attempt was made to overthrow Numayri, but it, too, was crushed. Numayri began a purge of his Sudan Socialist Union, and the size of the Political Bureau, the highest decision-making body in the country, was reduced from 27 to 17, and the number of party secretaries was cut from 15 to 4. New emphasis was given to Islamic law, and the Sudanese administration was overhauled. Sadat's death in 1981 came as a severe blow to Numayri, but the

Egyptian government pledged continuity in its policy toward Sudan. Both governments agreed to support one another in containing Libyan ambitions and warding off Marxist threats. Moreover, Egypt's greater intimacy with Saudi Arabia in 1982 permitted the Sudan to cultivate its relations with the wealthier Arab states without necessarily affecting its relations with Cairo. The Sudan's more fundamentalist posture reignited the civil war in the south of the country, however. Non-Arab, non-Muslim Sudanese again felt the heavy hand of their northern countrymen. A Sudanese People's Liberation Army (SPLA) challenged Khartoum's effort at using religion and culture "to suppress the people." Numayri's ouster in 1985 tended to aggravate the situation. The SPLA developed into a formidable army, capable of taking on the Sudanese force in the south. Khartoum sought allies in its struggle and found them in Libya and Iraq, thus shifting its support away from Egypt. In assaulting the insurgents, the government exploited a difficult food situation in the southern part of the country. Foreign relief organizations, such as World Vision, the Association of Christian Resource Organizations Serving Sudan, the Lutheran World Federation, and the Swedish Free Mission, were expelled from the country. As a consequence, an unstable food situation quickly degenerated into widespread famine. Khartoum prevented the flow of food and medicine to the southern provinces, and by 1991 the situation was so grave that external parties predicted the deaths of 9 million people within the near future. Although some international opinion was focused on the plight of the southern Sudanese and the Khartoum government indicated it had reopened lines of communication to the south for relief shipments, skepticism prevailed. *See also* ADDIS ABABA AGREEMENT (190); MAHDI (43).

Significance
The Sudan's attempt to achieve national integration is a continuing problem. Nation-building efforts have met with only token success, and divisive forces continue to threaten the country's tenuous unity. The Anya Nya movement may have been vanquished, but the conditions that caused its formation were not arrested. Racial conflict remains a substantial issue, and the attitude of the Arab north will have considerable bearing on the future stability of the Sudanese state. Moreover, the religious differences and the religious-secular conflict that burden the government add to the dilemma. The Sudan remains an inchoate state and a troubled nation.

Politics of Succession: Iran **102**

The death of Ayatollah Ruhollah Khomeini on June 3, 1989, deprived Iranians of their most legendary leader in centuries. Prior to his death there was considerable speculation about the chaos his passing would bring to the country. Not a few experts were embarrassed when the succession passed without a serious threat to the stability of the Islamic regime. The Islamic Republic of Iran elected as its president Hojatolislam Hashemi Rafsanjani in July, and the ayatollah's mantle was quickly donned by Ayatollah Ali Khamenei. Although observers envisaged rivalries between these two men, nothing of the kind materialized. Each had served time in the shah's prisons, and both had been tortured by the secret police, the notorious SAVAK. They were proved loyal confidants of Khomeini and each held prominent positions in the revolutionary government. Khamenei had served as president after the ouster of Bani-Sadr, and

Rafsanjani headed the Revolutionary Guards before becoming speaker of the Iranian parliament. Despite their revolutionary zeal, both men were considered moderates (although neither was truly so), and they have joined together in thwarting the ambitions of the more extreme, and potently divisive, fundamentalists. Although Ayatollah Khomeini called for a single successor in a speech just a month before his death, Iran took a different path in the shared power represented by these two men. The emergence of Rafsanjani and Khamenei as the two most powerful men in Iran was confirmed on the one side by a popular referendum of the Iranian people and on the other by the Council of Experts. It is notable that Khomeini's last will and testament did not identify a successor. Between them, Rafsanjani represented the bazaar merchants, while Khamenei came from a long line of Islamic scholars. In their combination they promised the stability that had eluded Iran since the first moments of the revolutionary government.

Significance

The combined power of Rafsanjani and Khamenei can never equal the authority represented by Ayatollah Khomeini. The 270-member Iranian parliament reminded Rafsanjani of this fact when in May 1990 they passed a law that prevented any changes in Khomeini's writings. Radical elements in the assembly were led by Ali Akbar Mohtashemi, a former interior minister, and Ahmad Khomeini, the ayatollah's only surviving son. The latter sought but was denied the succession to his father's mantle. Fear persisted among the radicals that Rafsanjani, a reputed pragmatist, would try to align Iran with the West and especially the United States. Iran's economy in the wake of the war with Iraq was in shambles, and the country was in need of outside assistance, especially technology. But the radicals would have none of this, especially if it meant entering into an association with the "Great Satan." They also criticized Rafsanjani's efforts in seeking the release of Western hostages held by Shiite groups in Iran. While they sought to restrain Rafsanjani, they were cognizant of the need to ally themselves with Khamenei. While factionalism, so much a part of the Iranian scene, threatened to upset the delicate equilibrium, it also, in its peculiar Iranian way, sustained the balance between the country's two most prominent leaders.

Protectorate 103

Protectorates in international politics are states classified as dependent or not fully sovereign. Legal restrictions are imposed on such nations because they are deemed too weak, or too primitive in organization, to be responsible for the full discharge of their obligations under international law. Egypt was occupied by Great Britain in 1882, but it was not until December 1914, after the outbreak of World War I, that the country was officially declared a British protectorate. Britain's invasion of Egypt ostensibly was made to prevent an Egyptian army coup against the reigning monarch. Egypt had been conquered and incorporated into the Ottoman Empire in 1517. It remained a Mediterranean outpost of the Ottoman sultan until the beginning of the nineteenth century. Mohammad Ali, an Albanian general in the sultan's army, was dispatched to Egypt to stop Napoleon's armies and to crush indigenous rebellions against the Sublime Porte (the name given to the ruling sultan's administration in Constantinople). Mohammad Ali remained in Egypt to found a dynasty. His successors were known as *khedives* (later they took the titles sultan and king). The *khedives* were technically subordinate to the Sublime Porte, but in actuality were free to pursue their personal interests. The Ottoman sultan supposedly retained suzerainty over the country, but lacked the power to control events. In these circumstances, Egypt became a playground for a polyglot, alien element. Resentment therefore ran high among Egyptian military and civilian officials, and Colonel Ahmad Arabi organized a revolt aimed at freeing Egypt from foreign domination. Britain, however, not the Ottomans, moved to crush the "Arabi Revolt." Britain's interest in Egypt stemmed from its concern for the Suez Canal, which was opened in 1869. London wanted control of the waterway. Britain also wanted to prevent the French from establishing themselves in North Africa, and it feared that the "loss" of Egypt would further weaken the Sublime Porte and provoke new attacks on Turkish territories by the Russians. Britain defeated Arabi's forces, and in two conventions, 1885 and 1887, it agreed to evacuate its troops when conditions were again tranquil. By 1888, however, Britain indicated that it would remain in Egypt indefinitely. Technically, the sultan still held suzerainty over Egypt, but, in fact, he was powerless to prevent the British from reinforcing their position in the canal zone and throughout the area. The Ottoman sultan was prevented from separating the Sinai Peninsula from Egypt, and the British also blocked the path of Ottoman forces sent to North Africa to defend their Libyan possession from Italian imperialism. France earlier (in the Anglo-French Convention of 1904) had agreed not to interfere with British administration in Egypt, but it was understood that Britain would eventually withdraw its forces. This Anglo-French agreement confirmed and legalized the multilateral convention of 1888, which guaranteed use of the Suez Canal to all countries at all times. The 1888 treaty had been delayed in coming into force by French reluctance to permit Britain to defend the canal. The French now gave Britain their support in return for France's claim to Morocco. While Britain was receiving recognition of its authority in Egypt, London's relations with the Sublime Porte were still unclear. Britain had sent its forces into the Sudan to crush the Mahdi Mohammad Ahmad's revolt (1881–1885). Then when France attempted to annex the White Nile territory in the southern Sudan (the key to Egypt's water supply), Britain judged it essential to reenter the Sudan and to bring it under its administration. The British conquest of the Sudan occurred in 1898. The following year an Anglo-Egyptian Condominium was established over the Sudan. From 1899 until 1924 Britain and Egypt jointly administered the Sudan. The Ottoman government was totally ignored in these actions, although it still held legal claims to the Sudan, as well as to Egypt. The British declaration of December 1914 making Egypt a protectorate had severed the ties of suzerainty held by the Sublime Porte. Britain had also deposed the reigning *khedive* and installed another member of the royal household as sultan, thus confirming the separation. The peace treaties after World War I included clauses that recognized the British protectorate of Egypt. ***See also*** SUEZ CANAL (27).

Significance

The transformation of Egypt into a British protectorate proved to be the final stage in the crystallization of Egyptian nationalism. Resentful of foreign occupation under the Ottomans and embarrassed by their weakness in meeting the British intervention, Egypt's politically conscious public began to demand the right of self-determination. The "Arabi Revolt" proved to be the beginning of an extended period of unrest. But it was not until the aftermath of World War I that the Egyptian nationalists were capable of mounting an effective campaign aimed at regaining Egypt's independence. Zaghlul Pasha, born of peasant stock but provided with educational opportunities by the British and appointed minister of education in 1905, symbolized the new Egypt. Zaghlul was responsible for forming Egypt's first political party, the Wafd, and it was through that organization that Egypt's grievances were publicized to the local inhabitants and the world. Britain strenuously suppressed the nationalist movement, exiling Zaghlul and imprisoning his followers. But the British found their cause hopeless, given the determination of their adversaries. In 1922 Great Britain agreed to terminate the protectorate and to recognize Egypt as an independent, sovereign state. The Egyptian sultan assumed the title of king that same year, and Egypt was given its first genuine constitution in 1923. Nine years of martial law came to an end. Elections were held in 1924, and the Wafd Party captured a majority of seats in the assembly. Zaghlul returned from exile and was named the country's prime minister. The Wafd Party remained in command of the Egyptian government until 1950, just two years before the overthrow of the monarchy and the emergence of Gamal Abdul Nasser. Another treaty between Egypt and Britain in 1936 called for the withdrawal of British forces from Egypt, except those defending the canal zone. Although World War II intervened and Britain maintained a military presence in Egypt throughout the hostilities, Britain's insistence on clinging to the canal zone proved to be more than the post–World War II Egyptian nationalists could tolerate. Indeed, Britain's continuing occupation of the Suez Canal reminded Egyptians of their protectorate status and the fact that full independence had not yet been achieved.

Racism 104

Racism implies that one race is superior to others and therefore has the prerogative to rule over the "inferior" races. Policies and programs have been based on such notions, and governments and societies have justified their behavior according to such declarations. The most celebrated use of the term *racism* in the modern Middle East was during the 30th session of the United Nations General Assembly on November 10, 1975. A resolution placed before the body by members of the Arab League, Cuba, Dahomey, and Guinea accused the Israeli government of abusing the non-Jews in their midst, and equated "racism" with "Zionism." The resolution carried 72 to 35 with 32 abstentions. The action was perhaps the most controversial ever taken by the United Nations. It precipitated numerous articles the world over, either supporting or condemning the vote. According to the drafters of Resolution 3379, the vote aimed at:

- Publicizing Israel's intransigence in dealing with the Palestinian question.
- Isolating Israel in the United Nations and other international forums.
- Pressuring Israel to withdraw from territories occupied during the 1967 war, especially the West Bank and Gaza.
- Criticizing Israel's supporters, especially the United States, for their refusal to recognize the Palestine Liberation Organization as the only legitimate representative of the Palestinian Arabs.
- Demonstrating to Israel and the United States the worldwide

support provided the Palestine Liberation Organization and the Arab League.

In justification of their claim that Zionism is equated with racism, the supporters of the resolution noted Israel's 1950 Law of Return and 1952 Nationality Law, which grant Jews everywhere rights that are denied non-Jews. Jews who wish to emigrate to Israel are usually conferred immediate citizenship; non-Jews are not, and may be denied citizenship altogether. The proponents of the resolution also argued that 90 percent of the inhabited area of Israel falls under regulations of the Jewish National Fund and that non-Jews cannot purchase or rent a house, apartment, or business in these territories. Perhaps the key complaint was a 1952 Knesset action involving the World Zionist Organization and the Jewish Agency. Both organizations were given official recognition and responsibility for immigration, absorption, and settlement projects. In 1954, the Knesset approved legislation integrating the Zionist organization and the Jewish Agency into the Israeli government and established as their primary task the "in-gathering of the exiles," meaning Jewish refugees. This also being the central task of the state of Israel, Jews were judged "more equal" than others, and hence the Israeli state, along with Zionism, was condemned on grounds of prejudice. *See also* ZIONISM (189); CITIZENSHIP (76); PALESTINE LIBERATION ORGANIZATION (137).

Significance
The equation of Zionism with racism by the UN General Assembly demonstrated the success of the Arab campaign to woo supporters to its position in their conflict with Israel. It was also timed to counteract the Egyptian-Israeli agreement disengaging their forces in the Sinai Peninsula following the 1973 war. Henry Kissinger's shuttle diplomacy had produced a breakthrough in Arab-Israeli relations. For the first time representatives of the opposed camps agreed to air their differences and to begin the process of finding a compromise formula. Also, in 1974, Yasir Arafat had been invited to address the UN General Assembly, the first time a leader of a political movement had been extended such an invitation. The Arab nations sought to capitalize on this event, and the resolution describing "Zionist racism" was the device employed. During this same period, numerous African states that had recognized and received technical assistance from Israel severed diplomatic relations with Jerusalem. Furthermore, the Arab oil embargo and OPEC's dramatic increase in petroleum prices gave more weight to the Arab position. The United States condemned the resolution and the vote in favor of it, noting a disservice to the purpose of the United Nations. Moreover, the fact that virtually all the Arab states had denied citizenship status to the Palestinians in their midst, or that approximately 800,000 Jews had been forced to leave their ancestral homes in Arab countries, did not change the final result. The racism issue was a tactic in the war for world public opinion, and in that regard the Arab cause had achieved a victory. Observers generally concluded that Israel was indeed ethnocentric and that its policies catered to Jews. At the same time they noted the actions of other states and societies that benefit themselves and that promote their own causes and protect their special communities. The Zionist-racist question was not a moral issue, merely another aspect of a long, difficult, complex political problem. The Zionism-racism resolution remained on the books of the United Nations over the passing years. In 1991, while addressing the opening session of UN General

Assembly, President George Bush called for the rescinding of the resolution. He urged the UN members to acknowledge the new realities following the termination of the Cold War and the need to address political issues such as those in the Middle East with appropriate diplomacy. On December 16, 1991, the UN General Assembly repealed the resolution equating Zionism with racism by a vote of 111 to 25. China, Egypt, Kuwait, and four other Arab states did not vote. Iran, Syria, and the PLO condemned the decision. Isaeli president Chaim Herzog declared the vote symbolized "a revolution in the world order."

Revolution: Libya 105

Libya declared its independence in December 1951 after a UN resolution in 1949 urged its right of self-determination. Italy had administered Libya as a colony from 1911 until World War II, when the region was liberated by Allied armies. Libya achieved its freedom under the aegis of a constitutional monarchy headed by King Idris I. King Idris was deposed in September 1969 by the Libyan armed forces, led by a young officer, Muammar Qaddafi. The monarchy was abolished as a European contrivance, and the Socialist Libyan Arab Republic was officially proclaimed. Qaddafi was inspired by the philosophy and speeches of Egypt's Gamal Abdul Nasser, and he followed in his idol's footsteps with the creation of a Revolutionary Command Council and publicized Libya's principal objective as the achievement of Arab unity. As Nasser had forced the British to relinquish their base at Suez, Qaddafi closed down British bases at Tobruk and El Adem and the vast U.S. air base near Tripoli in 1970. Nasser's death that year was a severe blow to Qaddafi, who initially looked to Sadat to carry on the dead leader's program. Disillusionment and then hostility toward Sadat in the mid-1970s, however, encouraged Qaddafi to assume Nasser's mantle himself. Qaddafi brought pressure on the foreign oil companies operating in Libya and obtained a significant increase in the share of profits. His lead was assumed by the other oil-producing states, and by 1973, the price of petroleum escalated dramatically. In 1973, Qaddafi also led the field in nationalizing a majority of the assets of the oil companies. British petroleum companies were fully nationalized in 1971, and by 1974 the U.S. oil companies were nationalized completely. Qaddafi also set about revolutionizing the Libyan scene. Popular committees were established to oversee the revolution as political opponents were isolated. Islamic law was emphasized, bureaucracy was purged, and citizens were given the right to bear arms. Qaddafi expressed his philosophy of government and society in his "Green Book," a three-part presentation that condemns Western thought and institutions and calls for the creation of a way of life more in keeping with the genius of the Libyan nation. Mergers between Egypt and Libya and between Tunisia and Libya were stillborn, as their respective governments perceived a threat to themselves in the behavior and policies of the Libyan leader. Frustrated in his efforts to promote Arab unity, and convinced that Sadat, Bourguiba, and other Arab leaders were too dependent on the Americans and Europeans, Qaddafi entertained Soviet assistance. Libya began receiving major shipments of Soviet weaponry in 1975, and deliveries continued through 1982. In the meantime, Qaddafi's name in the Western world became synonymous with international terrorism. Qaddafi believed Israel must be combatted on all fronts, and Libya gave freely to the various factions of the Palestine Liberation Organization. He encouraged terrorists across the planet, offering sanctuary, training, and weapons to armed groups from Latin America to the Philippines. Qaddafi also ordered his forces into Uganda in a futile attempt to save the regime of Idi Amin. His invasion of Chad and the seizure of its northern uranium-rich territory was more cause for concern. Ronald Reagan sought to rein in Muammar Qaddafi. The shooting down of Libyan aircraft by U.S. Navy fighters over the Gulf of Sidra was followed by a U.S. air raid on Qaddafi's headquarters in Tripoli in 1986. The United States said its purpose was to punish Libya for its complicity in a terrorist bombing in West Berlin, but informed opinion believed the target was Qaddafi himself. Although the Libyan leader lost a daughter in the raid, he emerged from the incident with his reputation intact. Qaddafi kept a low profile in the years that followed. Libya's identification with terrorist activities was virtually nil. In late 1990, however, under the cloud created by the Iraqi invasion of Kuwait and the crisis that developed in the gulf region involving the great powers, Libya assisted Chadian rebels in overthrowing the government of Hissene Habre. Libya regained control of the Aouzou strip that it had been forced to yield in 1987 and exerted considerable influence, with an assist from the Sudan, over the newly installed government in the Chadian capital. ***See also*** GREEN BOOK (85); GULF OF SIDRA CONFLICT (243); U.S. RAID ON LIBYA (269).

Significance
Under the rule of Muammar Qaddafi, Libya has gained the reputation as the most revolutionary of the Arab states. Qaddafi's unorthodox and mercurial behavior has caused government leaders in many countries, including the Third World, to judge him as dangerous and threatening. Despite criticism and rebuffs, Qaddafi does not appear ready to "correct" the perception others hold of him. In fact he appears more emboldened to pursue his particular program, convinced that those who oppose him are his enemies. Qaddafi's popularity at home, although somewhat restrained, must be considered strong, and Libya appears destined to pursue the course established by the country's maximum ruler. Qaddafi's modernization of tradition is unique but it is not out of character in Libya, where saints and pragmatists have long interacted.

Shaykhdom **106**

Shaykhdom describes a political entity dominated by the shaykh, or tribal leader. The shaykh in traditional Arab experience is the head of a joint family, the venerable patriarch who is responsible for the stability, protection, and health of the kinship group. Sometimes *sayyid* is substituted for the term *shaykh,* but both terms describe a man recognized as preeminent by the leaders of the individual families constituting the larger union. Shaykhs are selected by these councils because they are perceived to be wise and virtuous. The authority that attaches to the designation is not hereditary, but it is not unusual for the most powerful son to assume the role following his father's death. Nevertheless, the approval of the council is still essential. The shaykh is not considered legitimate until the council members have sworn their loyalty. Support can also be withdrawn in the same fashion, and shaykhs are expected to demonstrate their right to govern the tribe through acts of strength, both physical and intellectual. Wisdom is perhaps the most important attribute, and the charisma surrounding a dominant shaykh is usually a consequence of his intelligent leadership. The shaykh therefore is not endowed with total power. Consensus is an essential aspect of the decision-making process; arbitrary behavior is frowned upon, especially among the more nomadic tribes. The last half of the twentieth century has witnessed modifications in the role and institution of the shaykh and shaykhdom. Contact with the extended world, the establishment of more permanent territorial arrangements, and greater sophistication have reduced the influence of nomadism and have given rise to the corporate unit; the shaykhdom, in some instances, has been transformed into a nation-state. Nowhere is the shaykhdom more apparent than on the Arabian Peninsula, and nowhere are there better examples of shaykhdoms in the process of becoming formal nations. The Saudis illustrate this transition; Kuwait, Bahrein, Qatar, and Oman are additional examples. The United Arab Emirates (UAE) is the latest transformation from remote tribal society to corporate entity with worldwide commercial and financial concerns. Despite the magnitude of change, however, the shaykhdom prevails and provides the foundation for the modern state. The United Arab Emirates (emirate is equated with shaykhdom but suggests a more settled community over which a form of primitive kingdom has been established) was created in December 1971 as a federation of seven "shaykhdoms." Formerly identified by the designation Trucial States, the UAE is about 30,000 square miles (78,000 square kilometers, roughly the size of Austria) and has a population of almost 750,000. Six of the seven emirates lie along the southern shore of the Persian Gulf. They are Abu Dhabi, Dubai, Sharjah, Ajman, Um al Quaiwain, and Ras al Khaimah. The seventh, Fujairah, is situated facing the Gulf of Oman. The shaykhdoms of the Trucial Coast, or Trucial Oman as they were also known, had no specific boundaries, and claims to territory were not always contiguous. Even today, a map of the UAE reveals a patchwork of intermingling territories with most of the shaykhdoms possessing territory in what appears to be another shaykhdom's domain. The legacy and continuing reality of nomadism explains this earlier indifference to fixed boundaries. Moreover, some of the shaykhdoms were parts of others. Fujairah, the most recent of the Trucial States, achieved its "independence" in 1952. The Trucial States were the work of British empire-builders. Treaties with local shaykhs enabled Britain to establish its presence in the region. In return for British assistance and financial payments to the tribal leaders, the Europeans were allowed to establish commercial and naval facilities in strategic zones dominating the Strait of Hormuz. Britain penetrated the region in the eighteenth century, defeating Portuguese, French, and Dutch competition. In the nineteenth century, Britain's India trade was threatened by piracy emanating from the Arabian Peninsula, and a punitive expedition was dispatched from Bombay to neutralize the miscreants. The Wahhabi invasion of the area required a larger British commitment, however, and in 1820 the British eliminated the pirate fleets and their strongholds. Impressed with British power, the shaykh of Dubai called for a truce, hence the term Trucial States, and a treaty was drafted and signed by the tribal leaders and Great Britain. In 1835, a more formal treaty was executed in which the shaykhs agreed not to engage in hostilities during the pearling season. In 1835, a "Treaty of Maritime Peace in Perpetuity" formalized the role of the British in the area, who were solely concerned with free navigation and ready access to port facilities. The British were not concerned with intra- or intertribal affairs, which remained the domain of the shaykhs. Up until 1873, the affairs of the Trucial States were the concern of the East India Company. After that date, the British government in India assumed responsibility for the shaykhdoms' security and diplomacy. When India achieved independence in 1947, this responsibility shifted to the Foreign Office in London, which maintained a political resident on the Persian Gulf island of Bahrein and political agents in Bahrein, Qatar, Dubai, and Abu Dhabi. Although Britain's control over the shaykhdoms' foreign affairs was confirmed by a treaty signed in 1892, it never held sovereignty over the "states." Britain enjoyed extraterritorial privileges giving it jurisdiction over its own and other European nations in the area, and the political agents also performed magistrate functions, but this authority came to an end with the formation of the UAE. Originally, the UAE was to include Bahrein and Qatar, but the desire to remain independent was strong enough to keep them out of the union. The overriding governmental institution in the UAE is the Supreme Council, comprised of the seven ruling shaykhs. It was they who agreed to form the federation, and they continue to sustain it, albeit not without difficulty. Abu Dhabi, the largest and wealthiest of the shaykhdoms, plays a leading role in the deliberations of the Supreme Council, and the smaller states fear the loss of their "independence." Shaykh Zaid ibn Sultan al-Nahayan, the leader of Abu Dhabi, has been president of the federation since its creation. His appointment of Shaykh Rashid al-Maktum of Dubai, the next most powerful shaykhdom in the union, as prime minister raised a storm of controversy. Not all the shaykhdoms are endowed with oil riches, and the distribution of wealth within the federation is a pressing problem. The Supreme Council also appoints the Federal Cabinet, which includes six ministers from Abu Dhabi, four from Dubai, three from Sharjah, two each from Um al Quaiwain and Ajman, and one from Fujairah. A Defense Ministry of the federation was also established, but under the terms of the UAE constitution, individual shaykhdoms maintain their own defense forces. As might be expected, Abu Dhabi has by far the most significant air, sea, and land combination.

Significance

Shaykhdoms continued to influence the political life of the Arabian Peninsula and especially those living in the gulf states. The United Arab Emirates is a case study in sudden modernity. Given the discovery and exploitation of oil in Abu Dhabi, Dubai, and Sharjah, these small shaykhdoms have acquired unbelievable riches. With a population of approximately 250,000, and with oil revenues approximating $10 to $15 billion annually, Abu Dhabi has the highest per capita income in the world. Dubai and Sharjah are not far behind. These remote way stations, heretofore known only for their smuggling and pearl fishing, are now financial heavyweights in international banking circles. While the other shaykhdoms lag behind in their development, the big three oil producers of the UAE are transforming the material life of their small principalities. Modern ports, airfields, industries, and cities have been constructed; others are being built or planned. But in spite of all this economic activity, the political structure is a throwback to the past. The establishment of cabinet ministries and the sophisticated devices by which UAE leaders communicate with one another have not altered their traditional behavior. In fact, tribal consensus, so important in more primitive shaykhdoms, does not have the same influence. The tendency is toward greater centralization of authority, and as the "states" amass more wealth, authority has little desire to share its decision-making power. The more established the shaykhdoms become, the less likely they are to opt for democratic procedures. Another point of increasing interest is the important geopolitical position held by the UAE. With Oman, the UAE stands astride the Strait of Hormuz. Because the UAE was not judged capable of defending their offshore islands in the strait, Iran felt justified in seizing them in 1971. After occupying Abu Musa, Iran agreed to pay Sharjah an annual fee. Ras al Kaimah, however, refused to negotiate for the Tumbs, and Iran took them by force. Iran's revolutionary government made no effort to return the islands to their owners, although Persian troops were withdrawn from Oman, where they had been used to neutralize a leftist insurgency. UAE shaykhdoms still depend on others for their protection. But they have avoided becoming too deeply involved in the perils of the Middle East and remain concerned with the sale of petroleum and traditional affairs.

Tanzimat

107

Tanzimat is the term used to signify the Ottoman Empire's determination to reform its political, economic, and social way of life. By the nineteenth century, the Ottoman Empire had passed into a critical phase and could no longer defend itself against foreign encroachment. Imperial Russia had become its principal foe, and the Ottomans searched for ways to protect their shrinking empire. Assuming that the European way was most suited to the period, the Ottomans attempted to draw experience from their heralded but feared enemies. The Turks experimented with European weapons, drills, and uniforms. The former backbone of the Ottoman military establishment, the Janissary Corps, was attacked and eventually eliminated when they could no longer be trusted to defend the royal household. Their religious order of Bektashi Sufis was also forcibly neutralized. German Prussian officers were called upon to create a more modern armed force, and new recruits were exposed to German, French, Italian, and Swiss methods and traditions. Western literature circulated through the empire. Colleges and medical schools were opened, and newspapers were encouraged to deal in secular subjects. Efforts were also launched to alter the apparel of the Ottomans, and European clothes were encouraged. The first significant reform edict of the period was the "Hatti Sherif of Gulhane" (Noble Rescript of the Sultan's Rose Chamber), which was announced in 1839. As much an appeal to the Europeans as a declaration, it addressed itself to tolerance and safeguarding property and life of all Ottomans, including religious and ethnic minorities. The edict also promised more liberal taxation; non-discriminatory practices in military recruitment; greater justice and equality before the law among all orders and ranks, including the religious divines; and higher salaries for government employees. Efforts to implement the reforms, however, were crushed just two years later when conservative factions forced the liberals from power. Another attempt at reform was made in the mid-1840s, but by 1851 this, too, suffered defeat as the opponents to the program publicized their concern over "Christian innovations." ***See also*** EASTERN QUESTION (9).

Significance

Modern Turkey has its origins in the *tanzimat* reforms of the first half of the nineteenth century. Failure to rapidly transform the Ottoman state and society from a traditional to a forward-looking entity on the one hand exposed the Ottoman Empire to greater dilemmas, while on the other it prepared the leaders of the future, who were imbued with the idea of collective preservation through change and adaptation. The Crimean War (1853–1856), in part, was precipitated by atrocities committed against Ottoman minorities. The Russians hoped to exploit the fear registered by Greek Orthodox Christians within the empire, and they offered them their protection. Neither the British nor the French wanted direct Russian influence in the Ottoman Empire, and along with Ottoman liberals, the sultan was pressured again to give reform a chance. The result was the more successful Hatti-Humayun (Imperial Rescript) of 1856, which led to the Midhat Constitution of 1876. Although they represented guideposts along the way to a more liberal political system, these reforms could not save the Ottoman Empire. The reforms did, however, create the climate and prepare the leadership that, in the aftermath of Ottoman defeat in World War I, created the Turkish Republic.

Terrorism *108*

The word *terror* is derived from the Latin *terrere,* to frighten. Terrorism is the institutionalization of fear, fostered either by authority, to effect its rule, or by elements outside government, who see it as an instrument for obtaining their objectives. Although terror is employed by individuals against other individuals and by groups seeking private gain, political terrorism is considered a function of political movements that see violence as the only, or preferred, method to achieve a desired end. Terrorism in the Middle East has a long history. Assassination of prominent leaders can be traced to biblical times. The Islamic world was ruptured by the martyrdom of Husain, the fourth caliph's son, and Shiites and Sunnis have been archrivals ever since. A spiritual ancestor of today's Middle East terrorists was Hassan ibn Sabah, an eleventh-century Iranian and Shiite Ismaili. A determined evangelist and proselytizer, Sabah secreted himself in a mountain fortress in the Alamut Valley near the Caspian Sea. From there he rallied young followers who were trained to strike at anyone who refused to follow their mentor's version of Islam. Through the selective elimination of his rivals, Sabah extended his power into Syria and spread fear throughout the Islamic world. His agents were dedicated fanatics, conditioned to kill enthusiastically and altruistically. They were also mesmerized by hashish, which supposedly fortified them for their deadly missions. Known as the Hashishim, from which the term *assassin* is derived, these ritualistic murderers wreaked havoc all over the Middle East. Moreover, they continued to ply their trade even after Hassan ibn Sabah's death. The fortress of Alamut finally succumbed to the blows of the Mongol invasion, which ravaged northern Iran in 1256 and destroyed Baghdad in 1258. The Hashishim, however, are frequently referred to as the progenitors of current Middle East terrorism. The Muslim Brotherhood assumed a violent posture shortly after its founding in the 1930s. The *fedeyeen* (Muslim faithful) carried on the struggle against Israeli settlements through the 1950s. The Palestine Liberation Organization (PLO), which commenced operations in the 1960s, is the most notable organized terror movement in the Middle East and the most publicized of the multitude of world terrorist organizations. The purpose of the PLO is the destruction of the Israeli state. Although the organization is divided into numerous factions, some judged extreme and others moderate, PLO leaders are reluctant to accommodate the state of Israel. Nurtured by the perception of divided and duplicitous Arab states, the PLO insists on unrelenting hostility toward the state of Israel. Egypt's separate peace treaty with

Israel received undisguised condemnation, and for the PLO it highlights the difficulty of working with established, self-interested Arab governments. In the context of the means justifying the ends, the PLO and its different factions have taken credit for air highjacking, assassination of political figures, the disruption of the 1972 Olympic Games, and anything else that would give it the notoriety it seeks in keeping its cause alive and exposed to world public opinion. Terrorism stalks every Muslim country. Turkey experienced an unremitting reign of terror in the 1970s, subdued only by the strict imposition of martial law in 1980. Iran's long night of terror did not end with the overthrow of the shah. The official terrorism of the revolutionary government was answered by the opposition Mujahiddin Khalq, which was responsible for the deaths of scores of Iranian officials, including a revolutionary president, a prime minister, and a key ayatollah (religious divine). Anwar el-Sadat was assassinated in 1981 by a small group of determined terrorists, and terrorism and counterterrorism have become a way of life in the Middle East, spawning their own cultural characteristics. Nor is terrorism confined to the Muslim world. Zionist terrorists focused much of their antagonism on the British administration in Palestine. During World War II, the Irgun Zvai Leumi (National Military Organization) and the more extremist Stern Gang attacked British forces, police stations, and administrators. Given the inability to neutralize these terrorists, the British ultimately despaired of resolving the Arab-Jewish question and, in their frustration, decided to leave the question of Palestine's future to the United Nations. In major part, Zionist terrorism was directed at British policy that restricted Jewish emigration to Palestine. Nevertheless, the actions of the underground groups often took their toll of innocent people. In the 1980s, concern with terrorism steadily grew. The transnational nature of political terrorism is especially unsettling. The use of the Japanese Red Army terrorists by the PLO and the belief that a global network unites terrorist organizations in Latin America, Asia, and Europe with groups in the Middle East are especially disconcerting. So is the belief that terrorists are supported by established governments that provide refuge, training facilities, supplies, and encouragement. The inability to counteract terrorism in large measure is a consequence of this support base. ***See also*** MUSLIM BROTHERHOOD (47); PALESTINE LIBERATION ORGANIZATION (137); PALESTINE NATIONAL COVENANT (165); HIZBOLLAH (130).

Significance

Terrorism is an ancient instrument of disruption and change. No part of the world, in any period of history, has escaped the violence of the determined foe of the status quo. Political terrorists represent the whole kaleidoscope of human interaction. Political change involves clashes of opposing ideas and forces, purposes and classes. Reconciling rival moral claims is at the center of the terrorist phenomenon. Terrorists are fanatical in their beliefs, self-righteous in their purpose. They are also at the heart of the change process. Distinctions between terrorists and revolutionary heroes, between savage behavior and legitimate violence, between callous marauders and noble liberators are almost impossible to draw. Terrorism is in the eye of the beholder. On the one side is the victim of violence; on the other side is the beneficiary of violence. Terrorists are true believers. For those who believe with them, or simply sympathize with their cause, force is a necessary means to an acceptable end. For those denied physical or psychological freedom because of a cause, or deprived of life itself, terrorism is a curse on humanity. The Middle East is full of true believers, espousing different causes and determined to ignore mediation. As in the past, so too in the present world—each side insists its purpose is correct, just, and moral. What makes terrorism an exceptional dilemma in this era is not that people are different or that their ideas and objectives have changed. The looming danger in the durability and persistence of terrorism is the technology of violence and the enormous threat its unrestricted use poses not only to the peoples of the Middle East but also to populations everywhere. The engines of destruction have attained optimum levels. The costs of violence are now far in excess of the derived, or anticipated, benefits. Only the ignorant and the blindly passionate can still contemplate the use of force as an instrument of national purpose. Nevertheless, the disaffected and the alienated, the rootless and the humiliated insist on overcoming their deprivation through violent means. In this volatile environment, the possibility that thermonuclear weapons could become the terrorist's new tool is cause for great distress. Terrorism is an extension of primitive behavior. Armed with modern weapons, terrorists become a key challenge.

Tikriti *109*

Someone born in or near Tikrit in Iraq and receiving his or her identity from that location. Tikrit is a town on the Tigris River, approximately 100 miles north of Baghdad and situated on the fringe of historical Kurdistan. Tikrit's importance is highlighted by its location along the Tigris-Euphrates river system, which provides the region with its fertility. As a town within the Fertile Crescent, Tikrit has been an important site in the history of Mesopotamia, and a number of historical and modern Middle East leaders have associated their destiny with being Tikritis.

Significance

Tikrit was the metropolitan site of the Jacobites, or Monophysites, identified with Byzantium. The tenth-century Jacobite translator Yahya ibn-Adi was born in Tikrit. The town is also the celebrated birthplace of Al-Malik al-Nasser al-Sultan Salah al-Din, or Saladin (b. 1138), who substituted Sunni for Shiite Islam in Egypt and made holy war against the Christian Franks. In the Third Crusade (1189–1192), Salah al-Din defeated Richard the Lionhearted, and he is renowned in the history of the Arabs (although Salah al-Din was a Kurd) as the greatest of their warriors and the champion of Sunni Islam. Salah al-Din's sultanate, by conquest, extended from Tikrit on the Tigris to the Nile in Egypt and included the holy city of Jerusalem. The empire crumbled after his death. In the fourteenth century Tamerlane (Timur Lang) brought his Transoxiana army to Tikrit (after capturing Baghdad in 1393), and it was there he is said to have erected a huge pyramid from the skulls of his victims.

In modern history, Tikrit's most renowned son is Saddam Hussain al-Tikrit, who was born there in 1937 to a landless peasant family. At the age of 10 Saddam moved to a Tikriti neighborhood in Baghdad. After failing an entrance examination to the Baghdad Military Academy, Saddam joined with other Tikriti youth in Baghdad who in 1956 sought to overthrow the Hashemite King Faisal II. Unable to achieve this goal, and under threat, Saddam went to Syria, where he joined the Baath Party in 1957. When word reached Saddam in 1958 that King Faisal had been murdered, he helped plot the removal of the new Iraqi strongman, General Abdel Karim Kassem. Failing in this effort too, he moved to Egypt, at

President Gamal Abdul Nasser's invitation, where he developed his organizational skills. Saddam returned to Iraq in 1963 following Kassem's assassination. After Kassem's death, the Iraqi Baath Party, dominated by the Tikritis, became the most prominent organization in the political life of the country, and Saddam Hussain was its secretary-general and chief policy maker. The Tikriti Baathists broke with the Syrian Baath and their power reached new heights when the Tikriti general Ahmad Hassan al-Bakr seized the presidency of Iraq with the help of the Baathist/Tikriti militia. In 1979 Saddam eased al-Bakr from his post and became the country's "father-leader" and "knight of the Arab nation," as well as head of state, chairman of the Revolutionary Command Council, prime minister, and commander of the Iraqi armed forces. As a former member of the Internal Security Force, Saddam built a vast and formidable control apparatus that protected and sustained him in the long war with Iran. The Tikritis, with whom he has always been intimately associated, represent the backbone of Saddam's power and are sworn to his service. Nevertheless, during the war with Iran, Saddam dropped the designation al-Tikrit from his name to portray better the role of leader of the Arab world.

Tribalism **110**

Tribalism is still an important characteristic of some parts of the Middle East. The frontier areas of Pakistan, Afghanistan, and Iran contain some of the world's largest concentrations of tribal folk. The political conflict that challenges these countries can, in major part, be attributed to these oldest of human organizations. While the Iranian revolution of 1978–1979 brought various tribal questions to world attention, such as the Kurds, Azerbaijanis, and Turkomen, perhaps the most notable expression of militant tribalism is found on the frontiers between Afghanistan and Pakistan. The two principal tribal divisions of Baluch and Pathan are found in both countries; the former also spill over into Iran. They are predominantly Sunni Muslim, but some Shiite tribes also inhabit the region. The Baluch inhabit a desolate, dry, mountainous landscape south and southwest of the Hindu Kush Mountains and southward to the Arabian Sea. The largest branch of the Baluch tribes is found in Pakistan. Afghanistan has a smaller number than Iran. Baluch also reside in other parts of Iran and Pakistan. Iranian Baluch are found in more congenial Kerman province, and more Baluch live in Pakistani Punjab and Sind than in Baluchistan. Baluch in both Iran and Pakistan also share their native homeland with other ethnic and tribal groups such as Seistanis in Iran and Pathans, Punjabis, and Brahui in Pakistan. Baluch also work and live in the Persian Gulf shaykhdoms of Abu Dhabi, Dubai, and Oman. Oman has recruited Pakistani Baluch for service in its armed forces. The intermingling with other peoples has diversified the ethnolinguistic character of the Baluch, and variations of lifestyle have resulted. Iranian Baluch have been largely Persianized, and many Afghan Baluch speak a form of Afghan Persian called Dari. Others speak Pushtu, the language of their Pathan neighbors. Moreover, wide differences in custom and tradition exist between the nomadic Baluch of Iran's Sarhad Steppe and the more agricultural tribes of southern Baluchistan. The Brahui (a Dravidian-speaking tribe) live on the Kalat Plateau of Pakistani Baluchistan, thus separating the Suleimani from the Makrani Baluch. Because of centuries of interaction between Brahui and Baluch, however, there is little to distinguish them from one another. Brahui tribes have identified with Baluch nationalism, and some of their leaders have been prominent in the ranks of the Baluch opposition to central Pakistani control. Irrespective of these divisions, variations, and often scattered existence, the Baluch are a recognizable political force. Approximately 75 percent of the Baluch population have Pakistani citizenship. Their total is about 3 million. The Brahuis represent another 800,000. The Baluch of Iran are estimated at between 600,000 and 800,000, whereas the Baluch of Afghanistan are approximately 100,000 and the Brahui Afghans, about 200,000. If a separate Baluchistan state is a conceivable development, it could cover an area from the Strait of Hormuz on the Persian Gulf to the Indus River in the interior of Pakistan, some 700 miles (1,100 kilometers) from west to east, and 400 miles (640 kilometers) from the Arabian Sea coast inland to the Afghan city of Kandahar.

The Pathan tribes are more numerous than those of the Baluch, and historically more active. Almost one-third of Afghanistan and less than one-sixth of Pakistan comprise the land of the Pathans. The region is framed by the Indus River in the east and the deserts of the Iranian-Afghan frontier in the west, the Hindu Kush in the north and the Baluchistan desert to the south; it extends approximately 400 miles (640 kilometers) from the Wakhan Corridor to Quetta (the capital of Pakistani Baluchistan) and approximately 300 miles (480 kilometers) from the Indus south of Kabul to Afghanistan's central interior near Delaram, but including Kandahar. It has long been noted for its remoteness. The Pakistani Pathan region is also one of Pakistan's four provinces; established as the Northwest Frontier Province (NWFP) by the British, it continues to bear that name despite Pathan efforts to change it to Pakhtunistan. The NWFP was divided into 11 districts and 6 tribal agencies in 1972. Four centrally administered tribal areas are also located adjacent to regular districts. The tribal agencies lie adjacent to the Durand Line separating Pakistan from Afghanistan. Among the settled districts are the former princely states of Amb, Chitral, Dir, and Swat. The word *Pathan* is the plural form of *Pushtun* (also Pashtun, Pakhtun, and Pukhtun). The words are interchangeable, although geographic differences do give rise to the usage of one over the other. The language of the Pathan is Pashtu or Pushtu among the Persian-influenced speakers in the southwest and Pakhtu or Pukhtu in the northeast along the Pakistani-Afghan frontier. Moreover, most Pathans, even those residing in Pakistan, describe themselves as Afghans. Indeed, when Pakistan was first conceived in the early 1930s, the northwest border area of British India was known as Afghania by many Muslims. The identification of Pathans as Afghans, however, must be distinguished from those residing in Afghanistan who are also Afghani citizens. The tribal orientation of the frontier Pathans has been exploited by elements bent on undermining, if not destroying, the Pakistani state. The tribal Pathans, after all, have little national consciousness, and they are more inclined to think in terms of narrow tribalism. Pathans have been divided into three groups: (1) western Afghans, Persian-influenced like the Durranis, who ruled Afghanistan from the middle of the eighteenth century until 1973, and their rivals, the Ghilzais; (2) the eastern Afghans of Pakistan living on the Trans-Indus Plain, such as the numerous Yusufzais; and (3) the mountain tribes, the most independent grouping, who give the impression of being more loyal to their personal codes than to national union. Such Pathans are more readily identified as genuine

Pathans, given their self-contained lifestyle. Among them are the Afridi, Wazir, Mohmand, and Mahsud. The highlanders are free-wheeling and semi-nomadic, not given to sedentary existence. They are also poorer than their agricultural counterparts and more associated with brigandage, female kidnapping, and violent interactions. They are more closely identified with their brethren in Pakistan than with those on the Afghani side of the frontier. Nevertheless, it is important to note that the border between Afghanistan and Pakistan often slices the Pathan tribes into two segments. This artificial division, from the Pathan standpoint, is a nuisance. For Pakistan and Afghanistan it has long been a point of contention and sometimes of conflict. The border has been almost impossible to police, and neither the Afghani nor the Pakistani government has ever effectively brought the highland Pathans under their direct control. The Pushtu-speaking population of Pakistan is estimated to be about 12 million, approximately 15 percent of the total population. This figure includes more than 1 million Pathans living and working in the port city and industrial capital of Karachi. Pathans, more so than Baluch, also comprise a sizable component of the Pakistani armed forces. Afghanistan contained about 7 million Pathans prior to the Soviet invasion in 1979. The flight of more than 20 percent of the Afghan population to Pakistan, the majority of them Pathans, however, makes an acceptable estimate almost impossible. *See also* PAKHTUNISTAN (98).

Significance
The tribes of the Iran-Afghanistan-Pakistan triangle are the last heavy concentration of nomadic and semi-nomadic peoples in the modern world. Although the Middle East contains other tribal peoples, such as the Berbers of North Africa and the Kurds of the Fertile Crescent, the Pathan and Baluch tribes are more numerous, and politically more vital. The Baluch stand astride the geopolitically important Persian Gulf and in near proximity to the Strait of Hormuz. The Pathans are the gatekeepers to the subcontinent and the key to the survival of Pakistan. Demands by both the Baluch and Pathan tribes for greater autonomy, and sometimes for independence, have caused problems for the central governments in the countries where they reside. Pathans demonstrated political consciousness earlier than the Baluch. A nationalist movement was launched against the British during their rule in India, but the Pathans lacked the unity to press their objective. The pre-1979 Afghan government picked up the Pathan battle cry for a separate homeland, and since the creation of Pakistan in 1947, it attempted to separate the NWFP from Pakistan proper. This was dramatized by the Pathan/Afghan call for the creation of Pakhtunistan. The Baluch of Pakistan were especially restive in the 1970s. A major insurgency pitting Baluch tribes against the Pakistan army cost several thousand casualties, but was eventually brought under control.

Westernization — 111

Westernization is a code word describing the influence of European culture, institutions, and ideas on the people of the Middle East. Westernization is often used synonymously with modernization. It implies that Middle East civilizations have not kept up with the times and that only a conscious decision to emulate European performance can bring the societies of the Middle East into reasonable balance with their foreign counterparts. It is often assumed that the adoption of foreign ways necessitates discarding, or at least modifying, traditional behavior and institutions. Westernization therefore is viewed as both blessing and curse. On the one side is the desire to "progress" in a material and technological sense. On the other side is the complaint that Westernization means unacceptable innovation, often at the expense of strongly held values and cherished lifestyle. Moreover, Westernization has not touched the vast majority of people residing in the Middle East. In actuality, those imbibing Western manners, ideas, and techniques represent a thin veneer of society. Privileged elites have been affected, often at a cost that permanently separates them from the masses. As a consequence, dissatisfaction with a ruling authority usually involves assaults on foreign values and practices. Westernization has been denounced by dissident elements seeking popular support against entrenched authority. Westernization thus is both a promise of a more dynamic material future and a target of xenophobic nationalism. ***See also*** ISLAMIC FUNDAMENTALISM (39); MILLET SYSTEM (94); TANZIMAT (107).

Significance

Westernization is linked with the growth of European power. European civilization began to flower just when Middle East civilization began to lose its vitality. In this zero-sum relationship, what the Middle East lost, the Europeans gained. Western imperialism commenced with economic penetration, soon followed by political, military, and cultural penetration. Christian missionary activity was most active, especially in the educational field. Schools were opened in the different territories of the Ottoman Empire that were essentially free from government control. Indeed, the Ottoman millet (nationality) system permitted each religious group to practice its faith according to its own tenets. But these Christian schools appealed to Muslims as well as to members of the Christian faith. They were, after all, the only institutions offering what was thought to be a modern education. As such they were a major vehicle for the spread of European ideas. Among these ideas was the notion of the territorial state, which was unknown in the Ottoman world. Ottoman subjects were organized into religious communities, divided into provinces and dependencies. Western concepts of nationalism, therefore, exaggerated the linguistic and broader cultural differences among those comprising the empire. The Ottomans were determined to borrow technologies, institutions, and behavioral traits from their European counterparts, but these borrowings ensured the empire's decay, not its resurrection. The nationalist movements that welled up within the empire were quickly transformed into a revolt against the sultan-caliph. The demise of the Ottoman Empire after World War I did not bring an end to Westernization. In fact, it became even more fashionable as the Middle East states developed into territorial entities that somewhat resembled their European counterparts. But just as Middle East governments and societies sought to emulate the West, and especially to achieve technological competence, there was also resistance to excessive innovation. The popular refrain held that the adaptation was too expensive in cultural terms and tended to guarantee foreign domination.

Young Turks — *112*

Formally known as the Committee for Union and Progress, the Young Turks grew out of a secret organization known as the Society of New Ottomans, which was formed in 1865. The society comprised a group of young army officers who worked in concert with exiled intellectuals in France, Switzerland, and England. The New Ottomans demanded constitutional reforms that would permit Ottoman subjects to compete with their European counterparts. They sought to discredit the sultan without further weakening the Ottoman Empire. Their primary concern was the fashioning of new institutions resembling the European experience. The Midhat Constitution, named after Grand Vizir Midhat Pasha (1822–1884), an ardent reformer under whose administration it was drafted, was promulgated in 1876. It was the first significant accomplishment of the New Ottomans. Although that constitution succumbed to the authoritarianism of Sultan Abdul Hamid, and the New Ottomans were forced to scatter to other countries or return to their underground status, they reappeared with greater effectiveness as the Young Turks. The Young Turk rebellion of 1908 enjoyed army support, and Sultan Abdul Hamid was forcibly deposed. The intention of the Young Turks, mostly exiles in Europe, was to discredit the sultanate and liberalize the country along national lines, but to leave the empire intact. The new sultan's powers were severely restricted by the revolution, and the Committee for Union and Progress assumed control over the Ottoman parliament. Factions within the committee, however, vied for power while the empire suffered repeated rebellions from its Christian subjects. The Young Turks called for liberal, modern Ottomanism, but the European powers were no longer interested in sustaining the "sick man of Europe," as the Ottoman Empire was called in the nineteenth century. In 1911, Italy invaded Tripolitania in North Africa, and Greece seized the island of Crete. In the Balkan Wars of 1912–1913, the Ottoman Empire lost almost all of its Christian-dominant territories in Eastern Europe. Pan-Ottomanism could not be sustained amid the competition between rival nationalist ideologies. The Young Turks promoted their Union and Progress Party, but progress was limited because of the factional squabbling and personality conflicts with which it was burdened. In World War I (1914–1918), except for their defense of the Dardanelles and their victory at Gallipoli, the Ottomans were defeated on almost all fronts. Arab forces joined the British and French in opposing Turkish rule, and the empire lost control over Syria, Iraq, and Arabia. With the surrender of Turkish forces in October 1918, the Society for Union and Progress disintegrated. The Allies moved their forces into the Ottoman capital of Constantinople in violation of the Mudros Armistice and made the sultan virtually a prisoner. The Young Turks were now led by Mustafa Kemal Ataturk, the Turkish military hero in the Gallipoli campaign. Ataturk rallied his beleaguered forces, and the Young Turks established a new Turkish government in distant Ankara. Ataturk declared an end to the Ottoman Empire and proclaimed the new Republic of Turkey. Ataturk abolished the Ottoman sultanate as well as the Islamic caliphate. The Young Turks, under Ataturk's leadership, substituted Turkish nationalism for pan-Islamism and pan-Ottomanism. *See also* TANZIMAT (107); EASTERN QUESTION (9); CAPITULATIONS (202).

Significance
The Young Turks were political reformers who stressed the development of a Turkish nation. The Ottoman Empire had a Turkic core, but it was a polyglot empire comprising a diversity of nationalities and ethnic and religious groups. The central authority was usually obeyed, but unity was ephemeral. As Ottoman power declined and European influence grew, the many nationalities under Ottoman administration broke with Constantinople. Moreover, Ottoman weakness was an invitation to stronger powers, who

capitalized on Turkish frailties. Ottoman efforts at modernization and at adopting European systems and methods also proved unsuccessful. The Young Turks witnessed the disintegration of the empire and they were determined to preserve its Turkish core. Turkish nationalism and a Turkish nation-state were the results of their labors. Ataturk's strong leadership proved to be the difference between failure and success, as the new Republic of Turkey rose from the ashes of Ottoman defeat.

Zaydis 113

The Zaydis of Yemen are Shiite Muslims. They derive their designation from Zayd, the grandson of al-Husain, whom they consider the founder of their sect. Zayd died fighting the Ummayyads in 740 A.D. The Zaydis, unlike other Shiites, do not believe in the hidden imam. Nor do they practice dissimulation *(taqiyah)*. They are, however, opposed to Sufism. The Zaydis are the closest of the Shiite sects to Sunni Islam. The Zaydis inhabit the northern, central, and eastern regions of present-day Yemen. Although they have lived side by side with the Sunni Muslims of the Arabian Peninsula for centuries, conflict has not been avoided. In the Zaydi-dominant sector of the Arabian Peninsula, the largest minority are the Shafii Sunni Muslims. The rivalry between Zaydis and Shafiis is centuries old and carries down to the present day. Indeed, the politics of the region is often determined by this rivalry. In 1633 a Zaydi army forced the Turkish provincial governor to retreat, and a Zaydi imamate was established that lasted until 1871. The Turks began moving back into the region in 1849 and eventually overwhelmed the Zaydis, who did not regain their influence until 1905, when Imam Yahya occupied Sana, the current capital of Yemen. Imam Yahya's autonomy was recognized by the Ottoman court in 1911. Turkish influence in the region came to an end with World War I. Yahya began a long reign that did not end until his murder in 1948. His son Ahmad succeeded him, but Arab nationalism began to seep into the imamate, and with Gamal Abdul Nasser's ascension to power in Egypt, what had been a limited penetration became all pervasive. Ahmad joined Egypt in establishing the United Arab States in 1958, but the experiment failed when Nasser demanded far more than the Zaydis were prepared to grant. Nasser displayed little patience for the primitive imamate, and when Imam Ahmad died in September 1962, Nasser sponsored a coup that overthrew his successor, Imam Mohammad al Badr. Al Badr gathered loyal forces and an eight-year war commenced that involved significant numbers of Egyptians. The Yemeni population was split between the Shafiis, who supported the coup leaders and the Egyptians, on the one hand, and the Zaydis, loyal to their imam, who were assisted by the Saudis, on the other. The nationalists, however, proved successful and the Yemeni Arab Republic replaced the imamate. Although the Shafiis were the technical winners, power in the new government remained in Zaydi hands. In the 1970 Islamic Conference at Jiddah in Saudi Arabia, an agreement was signed between the nationalists and the royalists, who had supported the imamate. A Republican Council was established from the two rival camps, and the Zaydis reimposed their influence, although members of the royal family were excluded. ***See also*** SHIITE ISLAM (57); SUNNI ISLAM (60); IMAMATE (37); SUFISM (59); YEMENI CIVIL WAR, 1962–1972 (271); ADEN (1).

Significance

During the long rule of the imamate, the structure of government in

Yemen was thoroughly tribal. Zaydi tribal leaders supported religious figures, accepted as descendants of the Prophet Mohammad's family. Opposition to the imam from both the Zaydis and the Shafiis was managed by manipulating tribal coalitions. The imam also bought off recalcitrant tribal leaders. The 1962 coup brought an end to this political system, but it did not change the tribal character of Yemeni society. Nor did it quell the bitterness between Zaydi and Shafii. These traditional rivalries are complicated by radical movements, particularly left-wing extremism. Tens of thousands of Yemenis, many Zaydis, shifted their domicile to North Yemen from South Yemen. Settling these refugees was an impossible task for the primitive society, and they simply brought their tribal feuds with them. In addition to this dilemma the government had to contend with mountain tribes that were never loyal to central authority and that continued to operate on the basis of traditional tribalism. Although the merger of North and South Yemen in 1990 forecast a diminution in tribal and sectarian rivalry, that development has yet to materialize.

Political Parties and Movements

4

Arab Socialist Union 114

The Arab Socialist Union (ASU) was Gamal Abdul Nasser's answer to the political party and the political party system in Egypt. A group of young Egyptian army officers, identified as the Free Officers, seized control of the government, sent their king into exile, and abolished the monarchy on the night of July 22–23, 1952. The new government was dominated by a Revolutionary Command Council (RCC), established by the Free Officers, whose average age was only 33. The Free Officers were long on enthusiasm and very nationalistic. Although their long-range plans involved the defeat of Israel and the progressive development of Egyptian society, the most immediate objective was the elimination of British presence in the country. The continued presence of British troops in the Suez Canal zone not only was an affront to national dignity, but it also posed an ever-present threat of counter-revolution. In February 1954, Egypt and Britain agreed on self-determination for the Sudan. Later that year an Anglo-Egyptian agreement called for the withdrawal of British forces, although the canal was to remain under foreign management. Nasser's nationalization of the canal in 1956, however, precipitated a joint British-French attack on Egypt. Israel also used the occasion to strike across the Sinai, and in the process, it destroyed the *fedeyeen* (guerrilla) bases erected there and in the Gaza Strip by Nasser's forces. Nasser survived this attack and was even more determined to challenge the Israelis. In 1955, Nasser had entered into an agreement with the Soviet Union, and Egypt became the first Arab recipient of Soviet weapons. Although he expressed no preference for any ideology other than Arab nationalism, Nasser decided the Soviets represented the only credible source of modern weaponry. After the 1956 war, he was even more convinced that his international leverage rested on obtaining arms from Moscow. The 1956 war also elevated Nasser to the status of a great Arab patriot. His philosophy of revolution spoke of a "role" going in search of a leader. He now made it clear that he intended to assume that role in the Arab world. By 1957 Nasser was perceived as the undisputed leader of all the Arabs, not just the dominant figure in Egypt. In February 1958 Nasser revealed that Egypt and Syria had formed a union of their two countries and that the United Arab Republic (UAR) had been born. Nasser was declared president of the UAR, and Cairo was established as its capital. In March, Yemen, then a monarchy, joined in a separate federation with Egypt, and this arrangement was called the United Arab States. Nasser was now eager to press for broad-scale Arab unity under his leadership. It was also the period in which he stressed Arab socialism, the nationalization of financial institutions, and the commandeering of the print and electronic media. The time also called for the assembly of a political organization, initially identified as the National Union. The National Union was the forerunner of the Arab Socialist Union (ASU). But all was not clear sailing. Syria broke from its federation with Egypt in September 1961; Yemen dissolved its union in December of that year. Nasser, however, went ahead with the program of Arab unity, and Egypt continued under the name of the United Arab Republic. Political parties had been banned in 1953 when the RCC declared its interest in a one-party state. The RCC's National Liberation Rally (NLR) filled the vacuum left by the parties, but the rally was permitted to disappear with the promulgation of the 1956 constitution. The National Union had the political character denied the NLR, but it, too, failed to touch the Egyptian masses. In 1962, Nasser announced a National Charter that provided the framework for the building of a new society. The National Charter emphasized the unity of the working class, and chapter five established the mass party known as the Arab Socialist Union. It had taken the RCC 10 years to find the formula it wished to use in transforming Egyptian society. It was also anticipated that other Arab states would follow Egypt's example. The ASU was authorized to assist peasants and workers, cooperative associations, and labor unions. Authority also was to be transferred to elected local councils. The ASU was made responsible for eliminating capitalism, preventing foreign influence, liquidating landlordism, and generally enhancing social well-being through national planning. Unlike the National Union, the ASU was supposed to be a restricted party, composed of dedicated and disciplined adherents of Arab nationalism. The ASU was also organized hierarchically, with basic units at the village level and running all the way up to the National Congress, the Central Committee, and the Supreme Executive Committee. By 1975, the ASU reportedly had a membership of 8 million, approximately the size of the Egyptian electorate. But even if its actual membership were considerably less than that, it could hardly be described as an elitist party. It is also true, however, that by this date the ASU had lost its influential capacity and provided little more than participatory representation.

Nasser appointed his RCC colleague Ali Sabri to the post of secretary-general of the party in 1965. Differences with Sabri, however, particularly those aroused by Sabri's communist sympathies, caused Nasser to remove him and to assume the post himself in 1967. Overall, the ASU was organized to parallel all levels and agencies of government. The party therefore was indistinguishable from the government, and the Egyptian bureaucracy was heavily politicized. Although considerable effort went into the formation of the ASU, there was no mistaking where real power lay. Egypt, for all of Nasser's reforms, remained a military state, held together by a network of uniformed officers who in turn were loyal to the leadership of a single personality. Nasser's attempt to resign his post following the disastrous Six-Day War in 1967 was thwarted by popular reaction in the streets and agreement among the high military officers. He remained the country's undisputed leader. Thus, when Nasser died in 1970, he left his successor, Anwar el-Sadat, his old colleague in the RCC, with a dual legacy. On the one side was the ASU with its emphasis on Arab socialism, on the other was the looming personality of the great leader, the indispensable and unchallenged ruler. ***See also*** NASSERISM (97).

Significance

The Arab Socialist Union resembled the Communist Party in overall organization and function. But the ASU was the pragmatic version of a Marxist system. The ASU rejected the ideological underpinnings of a communist state. It ignored explanations of class warfare and the dictatorship of the proletariat. It never threatened Islam. Indeed, Nasser was a devout, pious Muslim. He lived austerely and never failed to practice the tenets of his faith. Although the ASU attacked capitalism, it did not obliterate the private sector. The ASU countenanced free enterprise so long as it was judged non-exploitative. The ASU was not a vehicle for transforming Egypt into a Marxist-Leninist state. Nasser's severe treatment of Egyptian communists, even if it meant the elimination of his close colleagues, illustrated his intention to borrow form and action, but to avoid the excesses of dogma. Nasser was equally unyielding with Muslim fundamentalists. The Muslim Brotherhood recognized they could not use Nasser for their own purposes, and they attempted to assassinate him in 1954. The consequences of that act were the relentless pursuit of the religious extremists, their incarceration, and often their execution. When Nasser died in 1970, he had effectively neutralized the political organizations on both extremes. His ASU, however, had yet to develop the institutional strength of a dominant party. Nasser's successor soon learned the ASU was not capable of carrying through the programs he now envisaged. Nor could the organization meet the challenges represented by the turbulent 1970s. Anwar el-Sadat had never been convinced that socialism was the correct path. Moreover, his intuition quickly told him the ASU, without Nasser, if permitted to develop, could rapidly shift toward the communist model. Sadat did not believe this possibility was in Egypt's interest, or his own. He therefore moved to de-emphasize the role of the organization and to stabilize his personal rule. With the 1973 war against Israel, Sadat gained the credibility that until then had evaded him. Nasser's shadow was lifted from his person, and with it went the ASU, too.

Baath Movement: Iraq — 115

The Iraqi Baathist movement developed out of the 1958 revolution, which destroyed the Hashemite monarchy. The Iraqi Baathists were followers of Aflaq and Hourani in Syria. The new Baghdad regime terminated the Arab federation with Jordan (another Hashemite kingdom), announced its withdrawal from the Western-organized Baghdad Pact, and recognized both the Soviet Union and the People's Republic of China. Relations with Nasser's Egypt were good, however, and the Iraqi Baathists, like their counterparts in Syria, called for Iraq's inclusion in the United Arab Republic (UAR). Opposition to such a union forced Karim Kassem to take a neutral position, while divisions among Sunni and

Shiite Muslims as well as among the Kurds proved difficult to manage. Kassem could not satisfy the competing factions, and he resorted to repressive tactics to neutralize his detractors, including those in the Baath. This resulted in a 1963 coup in which Colonel Abdul Salam Mohammad Arif gained control of the government. Arif had Kassem executed and formed a National Council of the Revolutionary Command, weighted in favor of the Baathists. Although not a Baathist, Arif became the recognized authority in the country. Unreconciled, the Baathists used the paramilitary National Guard to offset the colonel's power. Arif retaliated by ordering the Baathists and their military organization disbanded. Arif renamed his ruling body the National Revolutionary Council. He also emphasized a one-party state and assembled the Iraqi Arab Socialist Union. The government implemented socialist programs, and banking, commercial, and industrial activities were nationalized. Arif's death in a helicopter crash in 1966 again gave the Baathists new political opportunities. Arif's brother, General Abdul Rahman, succeeded to the presidency of the council. His reign was short-lived. In 1968, General Ahmad Hassan al-Bakr seized power and asked the Iraqi Baathists to help form his government. Persecution of the regime's enemies followed. The Baathist "takeover" was described as a "Tikrit" seizure of power. Tikrit was al-Bakr's native village; many of his closest associates hailed from the same locality. Saddam Hussain, vice-president of the Revolutionary Command Council and leader of the Iraqi Baathists, was one of this number. With Saddam Hussain playing the role of chief policymaker, the Baathists forged an alliance with the communists and sought to mollify the Iraqi Kurds, who continued to press for greater autonomy. In 1972, Iraq signed a treaty of cooperation and assistance with the Soviet Union, and Soviet technicians began to flood the country. Moreover, Moscow became Iraq's chief supplier of military hardware. Iraq was also one of Israel's more determined foes. Iraq had been instrumental in the organization of the Rejectionist Front, and it refused to entertain any compromise agreement with the state of Israel. Baghdad also nationalized the Iraq Petroleum Company in 1972 and permitted the Soviet Union to draw upon Iraqi oil supplies. The Soviets assisted in the construction of oil pipelines, the development of new oil refineries, and the improvement of Iraqi port facilities on the Persian Gulf. In return for its assistance, the Soviets were granted use of the Iraqi port of Umm Qasr.

In 1980, an ailing al-Bakr stepped aside for the younger Saddam Hussain. A minority party in 1968, the Baathists now dominated the government and the nation. Saddam Hussain was young and ambitious. He was also ruthless in dealing with his real and would-be foes. He ordered the execution of one-time supporters in the army, the party, and government administration. Moreover, Saddam Hussain was a Sunni Muslim ruling a majority Shiite population. After the rise of Ayatollah Khomeini in Iran, the Shiite community in Iraq became suspect. Khomeini had called upon the Iraqi Shiites to join him in revolution and to struggle against the "anti-Islamic" policies of Saddam Hussain and the Baathists. This call to arms was a major reason for Iraq's invasion of Iran in September 1980. After initial Iraqi victories, however, Iran recaptured its lost territory and attempted to penetrate Iraq. Despite heavy losses on both sides the war dragged on until a ceasefire was agreed to in 1988. Saddam Hussain's next adventure was directed against Kuwait, which Iraqi forces occupied in August 1990. The annexation of Kuwait followed shortly thereafter. World reaction, galvanized by the United States, thwarted this exercise in the use of power and Iraq was compelled to leave Kuwait and to renounce all claims to it. The Iraqi Baath Party was placed under considerable pressure by its military defeat. Nevertheless, the Baathists of Iraq remain a vital force. Saddam Hussain's survival, indeed his role as head of the party and government received new definition in the aftermath of Operation Desert Storm. Although having lost its supreme patron, the Soviet Union, the Iraqi Baath remained the sole viable political organization in the country. More tightly intertwined with the army, and more dependent on the Tikriti clan, Saddam Hussain is credited with the formation of a security network surpassing the one leading up to the seizure of Kuwait in August 1990. Burdened by a continuing military embargo and reparation payments to Kuwait, Saddam appears willing to deal in a more cooperative relationship with his neighbors, but he has also excused himself and his party for any economic or political problems resulting from the Gulf War. His central argument, and that of the Baath party: "Iraq has paid a price for a just and noble aim—resisting imperialism, Zionism, and the old system." ***See also*** BAATH MOVEMENT: ORIGIN IN SYRIA (116); IRAQ-KUWAIT: WAR AND CONQUEST (248); OPERATION DESERT SHIELD (257); OPERATION DESERT STORM (258); TIKRITI (109); NINETEENTH PROVINCE (21).

Significance

The Baathist movement is symbolic of the cry for Arab unity and for an Arab reawakening. *Baathism* means rebirth, a renaissance, and it addresses itself to the felt need of Arabs that they can regain their lost stature by joining in collective union. Baathism is therefore equated with pan-Arabism, the amalgamating of all Arab peoples under one political structure. The Baathists believe they can succeed where other Arabs have failed by emphasizing socialism and the centralized state. The original Baathists were heavily influenced by their experience with European imperialism. The Arabs were no match for the Europeans, who exploited the former's inherent divisiveness. The Baathists sought to transcend tribal ties, kinship linkages, and narrow loyalties. In time, however, the founders of the Baathist movement were themselves consumed by the overriding power of Arab political culture. In Syria, power in the 1970s and early 1980s was monopolized by the Alawite Shiites. In Iraq, it was lodged in the Tikrit Sunnis. Religious, ethnic, regional, as well as philosophical and economic differences continue to fracture the Arab community. Baathism pays lip service to Islam. Nevertheless, the emphasis on socialism, Marxism, radicalism, and Syria's and Iraq's association with the Soviet Union did not elevate Islam to a position of preeminence. Rather than Islam, it is the struggle against Israel that provides a semblance of unity. The ruling Baathists are also prone to extreme behavior. Iraq plots the overthrow of the Baathists in Damascus, just as Damascus instigates attacks on Baathists in Baghdad. Doctrine has not bridged these difficulties; it is even less likely to win the support of recalcitrant factions in the two states.

Baath Movement: Origin in Syria — *116*

The Baath movement and the formation of Baath political parties in Syria and later Iraq demonstrates the serious desire of Arabs to escape from centuries of weakness, division, and humiliation. Nevertheless, the Baath has neither promoted unity among Arabs nor reduced hostility between competing Baathist factions. The Baath emerged in Syria in 1953, the result of a fusion between Syria's

Arab Socialists and the Arab Resurrection Party. A leader of the Arab Socialists was Akram Hourani, who earlier had formed the Youth Party. Hourani preached socialism and appealed to the poor, often landless peasantry for support. The Arab Resurrection Party was organized during World War II to promote pan-Arab activity. Its appeal was directed toward Arab students who were devoted to the rebirth of the Arab world through broad-scale unity. The leader of the Resurrection Party was Michel Aflaq, a devoted Marxist who had been trained in France. Aflaq and Hourani appealed to disgruntled intellectuals, middle-class merchants, and labor as well as the Syrian peasantry. Young army officers who, like Hourani, had fought together in the 1948–1949 war against Israel were also brought into the coalition.

Aflaq proved to be the chief ideologue and spirit behind the Baath. The Baathists preached the removal of foreign influence, the nationalization of industry, the distribution of government lands to the cultivators, and the creation of extensive social services. In furthering Arab unity, Aflaq and the Baath called for the pooling of all Arab resources from among the established Arab states. Only in this way was it deemed possible for Arabs to compete effectively with the external world, and especially the Europeans and the Americans, who were envisaged as exploiting Arab divisions for their own purposes. In the late 1950s, Baathist doctrine and policies spread to other Arab countries, and party branches were opened in Iraq, Jordan, and Lebanon. In this same period Syria moved to integrate its political system with that of Egypt, and the United Arab Republic (UAR) was born in 1958. Nasser, however, judged the Baath to be a threat to his program of Arab unity, and in 1959–1960 he ordered the party banned. This was a serious blow to the Baathists, who were instrumental in bringing about the merger with Egypt. In 1961, Nasser increased tension between Cairo and Damascus by calling for the centralization of all commercial and industrial activity. Later that year Syria's regional cabinet was abolished, and a UAR government largely replaced the Syrian government. The Syrian Baathists, sensing the loss of their program and power, rebelled. Elements of the Syrian army took Egyptian army chief Hakim Amer (Nasser's key official in Syria) prisoner and ordered the other Egyptian officers to leave the country. Nasser yielded quickly to the Syrian *putsch,* and the union between Egypt and Syria was dissolved. The Baathists regained power in Damascus, renamed the country the Syrian Arab Republic, and emphasized their intention to encourage pan-Arabism. They proposed a Pan-Arab Federation, complete with a joint executive, legislature, and Arab army. The association, it was stressed, would be voluntary, and each Arab state would maintain its sovereign independence.

In 1963, the military wing of the Baathist movement took control of the country and established a National Revolutionary Command. Splits developed within the Baath, and Aflaq and Hourani found that they no longer controlled the radicals. Nor could they bring together the different Baath factions. In 1964, Syria received a new constitution and became the Syrian Democratic Socialist Republic. Islam, however, was declared the state religion. The dominant body in the new system was the National Revolutionary Council, comprised of both civilian and military leaders of the Baath Party. The army maintained its preeminent position under General Amin Hafiz. Supporting the military establishment against the old-line Baathist politicians was a group of young radicals drawn from both the civilian and military ranks. Within this latter group was a large number of Syrian Shiite Alawis who held important positions in the armed forces. The Syrian Alawites represented a deprived minority, and opportunity for advancement came with service in the army. Military service also gave the Alawis a political role. The new Syrian leadership consolidated its power by condemning Baathist "moderates" like Aflaq, who fled the country. With the purging of traditional Baathist leadership, the radical Baathists signalled their desire to come to terms with the Syrian communists. Their leader, Khalid Bakdash, was invited to return from exile in Moscow, and agreements were entered into with the Soviet Union for military and economic assistance. In 1969 still another constitution was promulgated, making the Baath the only legal party in the country. In 1970, General Hafiz al-Assad, an Alawi, seized power and immediately removed his political opposition. Assad presented another constitution to the nation in 1971 and organized a referendum that approved the document in 1973. With this new constitution Assad consolidated his power. He also drew the fire of the orthodox Sunni Muslims, who found fault with his secularization program. Sensing that Assad was a threat to traditional Islamic practices, Muslim fundamentalists agitated against his rule and received support from Egypt, Jordan, and Saudi Arabia. The attack from the Right drove Assad to coalesce with the Left, and a variety of radical organizations, including the Communist Party, were permitted to function openly. The radical organizations were formed into the National Progressive Front, and all other political activity was banned. The fundamentalist Muslim Brotherhood was forced underground, and a long struggle ensued between Assad's Baathist regime and members of the Brotherhood. Syria's intervention in the Lebanese Civil War increased Assad's influence, but it also placed greater burdens on the Syrian army. In October 1980, Syria signed a 20-year treaty of friendship and cooperation with the Soviet Union, and because of internal and external threats to the Assad regime, Damascus leaned heavily on Moscow's assistance. Moreover, relations between Syria and Iraq were poor, despite the existence of a Baathist government in Baghdad. These strains were further aggravated when Syria supported Iran in its war with Iraq. Syria's Baathists also supported the U.S.-led coalition against the Iraqi Baathists of Saddam Hussain. Damascus denounced Baghdad's invasion and annexation of Kuwait and provided forces for the coalition that swept the Iraqis from Kuwait in February 1991. These actions were extensions of Assad's changing tactics developed since his illness of 1983. Assad had to repair the damage to his authority as a consequence of his feebleness. Factions representing his brothers Rifaat and Jamil were challenged by military and air force intelligence. Friction between and among them produced skirmishes that divided the regime and opened it to attacks from its more conservative adversaries. Assad proposed a solution to the problem in a meeting of the Baath Regional Command, naming Rifaat, Abdal al-Hakim Khaddam, and Zuhair Mashariqah as joint vice-presidents. But even this strategy did not solve the infighting. Thus, Rifaat's militia was disbanded and he finally agreed to self-exile in Paris in 1985. Assad built a new military coalition in the fall of 1985, following a surprising recovery. The original coalition of military officers, Damascene merchants, small farmers, and public sector workers was now replaced by prosperous commercial interests, large landholders, and bankers, with public sector and armed forces representatives in a lesser but nevertheless important role. In 1988 the Syrian Baath launched impressive development schemes, especially in the rural sector. The more capitalist orientation of the Baath government in the late 1980s and early 1990s demonstrated a shift from Syria's dependence on Moscow, which by 1990 was no longer able to service the country's needs. Assad's turn toward the West was received with guarded optimism in Western circles. ***See also*** BAATH MOVEMENT: IRAQ (115).

Significance:
Baathists preached three vague principles: Arab unity, absolute Arab independence, and socialism. They also favored the creation of a one-party state. In Baathist doctrine there was only one Arab state; Syria was its "national" headquarters and Baathist organizations in other Arab nations were judged "regional" extensions of the parent body. Baathists therefore attracted considerable opposition from other Arab leaders. Antagonism between the Syrian Baathists and King Hussain of Jordan, the ruling Saudis of Saudi Arabia, and Tunisia's Habib Bourguiba was especially pronounced. On the other hand, the Baathists tempered their doctrine to accommodate Nasser and the leader of the revolutions in Algeria and North Yemen. Baathism was socialist, but it did not demand the total destruction of private property or free enterprise. To the Syrian Baathists, socialism meant the maximizing of production for broad societal benefit. Capitalism ranged alongside socialist enterprise through the 1960s and continued its course in to the 1990s. Beyond Syria, Baathism spread rapidly among the Palestinian refugees. It influenced the thinking of the professional white-collar class, again comprised in large part of Palestinians who worked for the wealthy shaykhs of Saudi Arabia, Kuwait, Bahrein, and Qatar. Baathism provided these elements with an outlet for their frustrations. Baathists perceived the ruling tribal families as unfairly enriching themselves with unearned wealth, especially from the sale of petroleum. The Baathist slogan was "one Arab nation from the Atlantic Ocean to the Persian Gulf," and the bedouin shaykhs were described as sustaining division to satisfy their personal desires. In the 1960s the Syrian Baathists were excited by the possibility of unifying with Iraq, and eventually they hoped to integrate the entire Fertile Crescent by eliminating the last of the Hashemite monarchs in Jordan. The creation of a Greater Arab State under Syrian Baathism was shattered by the enmity between Hafez al-Assad and Saddam Hussain, the latter seeking to protect the Jordanian monarchy from the former.

Communism: Afghanistan — *117*

Communism in Afghanistan is represented by the People's Democratic Party of Afghanistan (PDPA), which was founded in 1965 by Nur Mohammad Taraki. Marxism-Leninism in Afghanistan can be traced to the Young Afghan movement of the 1930s and the Seventh National Assembly in the 1940s. A splinter group of the Young Afghans, the Wikh-e-Zalmayan (Awakened Youth), organized in 1947, appears to have been Soviet supported. The Marxist-Leninist members of the Awakened Youth group were bitterly anti-Mohammadzai, the family and dynasty that ruled Afghanistan. A hero of these leftists was Mir Ghulam Mohammad Ghubar, the assassin of Nadir Shah, the Durrani-Mohammadzai king of the Afghan state. The work of the radicals was directed by Rahman Mahmudi, publisher of *Watan* (Homeland) and an associate of Ghubar. A young assistant on the newspaper staff was Babrak Karmal. Mahmudi also published the *Nida-i-Khalq* (Voice of the Masses), which, although subsequently banned, was the progenitor of the more successful *Khalq* (Masses). Mahmudi was arrested by Afghan authorities in 1952, suffered severe punishment, and died in 1963. Nur Mohammad Taraki was heavily influenced by Mahmudi. Taking advantage of the new environment created by King Zahir Shah (Nadir's successor), and following the ouster of the king's cousin Mohammad Daud from the government, Taraki formed the PDPA. Many of the leaders of the PDPA were members of the Ghilzai tribe, the largest of Afghanistan's Pathan tribes and arch rivals of the ruling Durrani-Mohammadzais. For a considerable period, therefore, communist activity was a facet of tribal rivalry. Taraki and his cohorts, however, were interested in constructing a chaste Marxist party, eventually capable of governing the country. The PDPA newspaper cited the need to learn from the Bolshevik experience in Russia, and the party's central purpose was described as bringing "the great October Revolution to Afghanistan." In the 1966 elections to the Wolesi Jirgah, the lower house of the Afghan parliament under the new constitution, the PDPA won a number of seats. Babrak Karmal was among the winners, and he and his colleagues in the assembly immediately set out to disrupt its proceedings. Accusing the government of assorted crimes and corruption, Karmal gained the attention of Kabul's attentive public, especially the student body. Aroused by the PDPA rhetoric and the government's forceful reaction, the students rioted, and a number were killed by the police. Although the government responsible for the deaths fell from power, the next one did not fare better. Attempts to establish a competitive party system were fractured by displays of civil disobedience. The more repressive the government actions became, the more intense the conflict between the police and students. The PDPA accepted this course of events as a normal prelude to a genuine revolution. For the noncommunists of Afghanistan, however, the experiment in political democracy was stillborn. The government banned communist newspapers, but the administration's association with the Soviet Union influenced it to allow the publication of *Parcham* (Banner) in 1968, edited by Suleiman Laeq, Mir Akbar Khyber, and Babrak Karmal. The emergence of *Parcham* also underlined the split in the PDPA between the Khalqis of Taraki and the Parchamis of Karmal. Both men were confirmed Marxist-Leninists, but their practical interests differed. The Khalqis emphasized class warfare but placed it in an Afghan context. The Parchamis were more closely identified with the Soviet Union. The Khalqis, by contrast, were more nationalistic. The division between the two organizations was more personality than doctrine, however, and personal feuds aggravated the rivalry until 1977, when the Soviet Union allegedly brought them together. Although the main factions of the PDPA played a role in the political life of the country in the 1960s, progress was tediously slow, and the decision was taken, apparently with Soviet encouragement, to prepare for revolutionary action. That opportunity was maximized in 1973 when Mohammad Daud capitalized on the unrest in the country to depose his cousin, the king, and terminate the monarchy. Daud declared Afghanistan to be a republic, and he became its first president. The PDPA assisted Daud in consolidating his power. The Soviet Union gave its sanction to the takeover, heralding it as a new page in Afghan history. Daud described his program as "New Democracy," but there was no changing the old Afghanistan. In the meantime the various factions of the PDPA exploited the revolutionary environment and were especially successful, with assistance from the Soviet Union, in gaining the support of key field officers in the Afghan army and air force. The military establishment had been overhauled in the 1970s by the Soviet Union and restructured along lines favorable to the Kremlin. Soviet equipment and advisors dominated the Afghan armed forces. Afghan officers underwent training in the Soviet Union and a number of East European countries. The PDPA also infiltrated the government bureaucracy and in a short period had established a government within a government. Daud had come to power through the good offices of the Afghan armed forces; he believed that it remained loyal to his leadership, but he was mistaken. Moreover, the later purging of PDPA members from his government did not neutralize their power. Nor did the dismissal or demotion of officers judged to have PDPA sympathies bolster his position. Daud came to rely on his immediate family members and closest advisors, further removing him from the realities of the Afghan condition. After a number of terrorist acts, Mir Akbar Khyber, a leader of the Parcham faction of the PDPA, was assassinated. Daud was accused of the murder by the PDPA, and although a number of its leaders from both Parcham and Khalq were arrested, others remained at large to conspire against him. Hafizullah Amin, a high official in the Khalq and the central figure in the organization of Marxist-Leninist cadres in the armed forces, managed to alert his followers. In April 1978, Daud and his associates were assaulted in government headquarters by contingents of the armed forces. All were killed and Afghanistan was declared a socialist republic under the leadership of the PDPA. Taraki, Karmal, and Amin assumed key posts in the new government, and the Soviet Union again signified its satisfaction by immediately recognizing the new administration. The PDPA union forged by the Soviets the year before the coup, however, did not last. The Khalqis gained the upper hand and began an unrelenting purge of the Parchamis. Karmal was sent abroad in an ambassadorial capacity but later fled to Moscow when Khalqi assassins threatened his life. The Khalqis launched a major campaign to transform Afghan society. The destruction of "feudal" landholdings, however, struck at the heart of the tribal society. So did the emphasis on secular programs, which denigrated Islamic traditions. The substitution of a new national flag, symbolizing the communist creed, exacerbated an already hostile environment. The tribal population sensed a mortal threat, and it began to fight back. Although Moscow appeared to suggest a slower, more methodical transformation, the Marxist-Leninists of the Khalq saw an opportunity to eliminate tribal encumbrances, and they pursued their program without concern for human cost. As a consequence, the Afghan resistance to the Khalqi government spread and deepened. Moreover, events in Iran that produced the revival of the Islamic State, and developments in Pakistan, which also emphasized a Muslim renaissance, further emboldened the Afghan *mujahiddin.* The Soviet invasion of Afghanistan in December 1979 followed the death of Taraki and the takeover of the government by Hafizullah Amin. Amin was both an embarrassment and a problem for the Kremlin. His death at Soviet hands enabled the Kremlin to place Babrak Karmal at the head of the Afghan government. But *mujahiddin* resistance did not cease. Although the Soviets insisted they were only interested in stabilizing Afghanistan, the *mujahiddin* were convinced that the Soviet aim was to destroy the

Afghan nation and absorb the territory within the Soviet Union. Despite the flight to Pakistan and Iran of more than 20 percent of the Afghan population, resistance to Soviet occupation of the country was protracted. Soviet expectations of a quick victory were dashed by the determination of the Afghan resistance. Aided and abetted by the United States through Pakistani channels, the *mujahiddin* received the weapons necessary to hold the Red Army at bay. The rise of Mikhail Gorbachev to the post of general-secretary of the U.S.S.R.'s Communist Party and government brought a change in policy. Gorbachev revealed a desire to terminate Soviet involvement in the war it had ignited in Afghanistan. Gorbachev eased Babrak Karmal from his position in Kabul and replaced him with the country's security chief, Najibullah, in 1986. With Najibullah in place to resist assaults on the Soviet-installed government, Gorbachev displayed enthusiasm for the UN-mediated ceasefire involving, surprisingly, not the *mujahiddin* or the Soviet Union, but Kabul's PDPA and Pakistan. In April 1988 the UN-managed negotiations bore fruit. An agreement was signed calling for Soviet troops to be withdrawn from Afghanistan. By February 1989, the last regular Soviet soldier had left. Kremlin support for the Kabul government of Najibullah, however, did not change. Although observers forecast the immediate demise of the PDPA government, it remained secure in Kabul. And although the resistance also continued, it diminished in intensity. ***See also*** AFGHAN-U.S.S.R. CONFLICT, 1979–1989 (234); TRIBALISM (110).

Significance

Communism in Afghanistan has never influenced more than a small fraction of the Afghan nation. Nevertheless, Afghanistan's backwardness, its tribal fragmentation, its lack of national consciousness, and its immediate proximity to, as well as dependence on, the Soviet Union magnified the power of the Marxists. The People's Democratic Party of Afghanistan capitalized on the opportunity to form and operate political parties in the 1960s. Its two principal factions, the Khalq and the Parcham, represented the only serious alternatives to the monarchial-tribal politics of traditional Afghanistan. The enlightened urban intelligentsia, and especially the Kabul student population, were attracted to the PDPA. It appeared to hold out the opportunity for reform. It also spoke in terms of transforming Afghanistan into a modern nation, capable of effective relationships with other states in the region. Moreover, tribalism and Islam appeared to reinforce one another. The Marxists therefore attacked tribalism with the full knowledge that they were also assaulting Islam as an impediment to progress. The PDPA was the only political organization in the country capable of obtaining large sums of money. It could also offer other rewards, such as free foreign education and a promise of a professional career. In fact, the Soviet Union promoted the recruitment of young Afghans, and many were sent, at Soviet expense, to live and study in communist states. But for all its leverage with the attentive Afghan public, the PDPA could not resolve its own internal contradictions. Personality conflicts caused the original split in 1967 and caused the same condition after the coup in 1978. This time, however, the PDPA had the reins of power. And it used its authority not only to terrorize the larger nation but also to brutalize members of the party. The repression of the Parchamis by the Khalqis was partially avenged when the Soviets crushed the Khalqi leadership and replaced it with the Parcham of Babrak Karmal. The Parcham showed little interest in a rapprochement, and many Khalqis were arrested and executed. Others fled the country or joined the *mujahiddin* resistance. The Soviets were aware that Afghanistan, was not yet a socialist state. Their actions in Afghanistan and the construction of a Marxist-Leninist system waited on the liquidation of tribalism and its attendant features. In 1991, however, Marxism-Leninism showed itself to be more fragile than tribalism. The repudiation of Marxism-Leninism in the Soviet Union eliminated Moscow as the citadel of communist teaching. The impact on the PDPA of the Soviet retreat from its standing commitments to Kabul could not be minimized. Nevertheless, the PDPA remained the only formidable political organization in Afghanistan. Moreover, conflicts within the *mujahiddin* camp, between Islamic fundamentalists and more secular parties, hinted at an Afghan future in which the PDPA would still play a role in the country's political and administrative life.

Communism: Arabian Peninsula **118**

No communist party was permitted to organize in the Yemen Arab Republic (North Yemen). Marxist organizations, however, did operate through the Yemeni Democratic Party, which had close ties to South Yemen and the Soviet Union. Fearing a radical *putsch* in 1979–1980, the United States, at Saudi urging, rushed military supplies to Sana when a border war flared between the two Yemens. Iraq, however, mediated the dispute, and the hostilities quickly subsided. The Saudis anticipated weaning South Yemen away from its dependence on the Soviet Union through financial transfers, but that venture failed to bear fruit. Rather, North Yemen angered Riyadh, and U.S. assistance ceased as the Marxist People's Democratic Republic of Yemen (PDRY) and North Yemen began to talk about reconciling their differences without Saudi assistance. The two Yemens agreed to a merger in 1990. The Saudi Arabian Communist Party was organized in 1975. Before that date it was called the Saudi National Liberation Front. Although outlawed in Saudi Arabia, the party participates in international communist congresses. It also has ties to the Iraqi Communist Party and the National Front for the Liberation of Bahrein, another communist front organization. It is not clear what, if any, ties the Saudi communists had to the Soviet Union, but they distributed literature condemning Saudi capitalism and the government's links with the United States. No communist parties operate in Kuwait, the United Arab Emirates, or Qatar. Radical Palestinian organizations are active, however; prominent among these are the Popular Front for the Liberation of Palestine (PFLP) and the Popular Democratic Front for the Liberation of Palestine (PDFLP). These organizations have worked in close collaboration with communist organizations in Lebanon, and they are now active in the gulf shaykhdoms since the PLO exodus from Beirut. Oman has been challenged by an insurgency since the 1950s. Identified with the Left in the 1970s, the insurgents received support and sanctuary from South Yemen, with additional aid coming from Cuba and East Germany. The Soviet Union also played a role in the attempt to oust the Sultan Qabus regime. The Popular Front for the Liberation of Oman was formerly called the Popular Front for the Liberation of Oman and the Arabian Gulf (PFLOAG). The PFLOAG has been neutralized in Oman, but it has established itself in the United Arab Emirates, and it also issues challenges to Saudi Arabia. By and large, however, the PFLOAG has been ineffective. The Popular Front for the Liberation of Oman (PFLO) was defeated in 1975 with assistance provided the Omanis by Iran.

Significance
Communist doctrine postulates social unrest as a normal condition. The inevitability of change to the Marxist means violent revolution, and socialist states are duty-bound to accelerate the transformation. Wars of "national liberation" require active support, especially when they are perpetrated by discontented social groups seeking the removal of traditional, conservative regimes. The Arabian Peninsula contains the last of the absolute monarchies, and Marxism-Leninism has long described them as anachronistic and doomed. The ruling families in the Arabian Peninsula, the al Saud, al Sabah, al-Khalifa, al-Thani, and Al bu Said, are therefore determined to confront the Marxist challenge. Gorbachev's support for the Kuwaiti emir in his struggle with Iraq's Saddam Hussain indicated a sharp departure in overall Soviet policy. Indeed, communism in the Arabian Peninsula was less menacing in the early 1990s, given the disintegration of the Soviet Union.

Communism: Arab World (119)

Communism has not made significant inroads in the Arab world, nor are Arab communist parties gaining broad popularity. In the majority of Arab states, communist parties are considered a threat to prevailing authority and have been banned; in others, they operate under close scrutiny. Only in South Yemen was a chaste Marxist-Leninist party in control of a government. With the merger of the two Yemens that is no longer the case. A classification of communist activities in the Arab world takes the following form: (1) established communist parties as in Syria, Iraq, and Lebanon where there are strong nationalist drives; (2) governing parties such as in the former People's Democratic Republic of Yemen (South Yemen); (3) non-Soviet communist parties; and (4) terrorist groups such as those that have flourished in Turkey and Iran and that maintain close attachments to various groups identified with the PLO. Non-Soviet parties may show an affinity for China or some other independent source of communism. Egypt could fit this category. So, too, would leftist organizations in Oman and Somalia. Formerly Maoist in orientation, these groups now concentrate on local social reform and anti-corruption programs. The PFLP and PDFLP are in the fourth category, as would be "Black September" and numerous violent splinter factions. All have some, if not considerable, communist affiliation and were alleged to have obtained support either directly or indirectly from Moscow. It is something of a paradox that as Soviet influence in the Arab states grew, communist parties and organizations in those countries lost favor and support, as, for example, in Egypt, Algeria, Iraq, and Syria. The communists in the Arab states are not so formidable that they can produce successful coups, but they can, as demonstrated in Afghanistan, come to power through front organizations, through subversion, and especially by gaining influence within the armed forces. The Soviet presence in Afghanistan before 1978 appeared to bring Moscow's physical presence to the very doorstep of the Arab countries. It was this possibility that Anwar el-Sadat sought to guard against. It was also this fear that drove the more conservative governments in the Arab world to seek U.S. assistance. In some ways, this also explained Arab "neutrality" in the Israeli attack on the PLO in Lebanon in 1982. The Palestinians were perceived to be a catalyst for communism in the Arab world. Hence, they frightened governments wishing to insulate themselves from radical, aggressive movements. ***See also*** ARAB SOCIALIST UNION (114); BAATH MOVEMENT: IRAQ (115); BAATH MOVEMENT: ORIGIN IN SYRIA (116); PHALANGES LIBANAISES (138); PALESTINE LIBERATION ORGANIZATION (137); TUDEH PARTY (143).

Significance

The communist coup in Afghanistan, the Tudeh Party in Iran, and the Marxist-Leninists in the former South Yemen and in nearby Ethiopia do not add up to monolithic communism. Nevertheless, certain relationships between communist organizations, and between front organizations, require close scrutiny. Communist parties in the Middle East are usually organized around negative questions. They exploit the gap between privileged and underprivileged. There is resentment toward the West, given its imperial legacy in the area and its identification both with autocratic regimes and with Israel. There is also the prevailing tendency to accept authoritarianism, and popular authoritarianism has considerable appeal when compared with traditional authoritarianism. All the same, Arabs are not at ease with communism. It is perceived to be alien in all its features and decidedly non-Arab. In major part, it is judged a threat to Islam and the Muslim way of life. Arabs did not fall under the influence of the Soviet Union. They were not interested in trading one maximum ruler for another, and they cherished their independence, strained though it be. Moreover, the Arabs evolved "Arab socialism" as an alternative to "scientific socialism." In other words, Arabs adopted socialism, but it was socialism without Marx. This may explain why communism in the Middle East had been promoted by ethnic and religious minorities, such as Christians, especially Greek Orthodox, and Kurds. Arab Muslim "socialists" have also proved themselves adept at borrowing and then adapting communist ideas and slogans, as in Muammar Qaddafi's Green Book. This has not prevented Arab governments from rejecting and persecuting communists, however, as did Nasser in Egypt and Saddam Hussain in Iraq. Determined Arab communists, therefore, are left with the options of infiltrating established governmental systems, forming front organizations, gaining leverage in the media, or going underground; but all this must now be accomplished without the presence, let alone the help, of the Soviet Union.

Communism: Egypt — *120*

Communist organizations were first assembled in Egypt in 1919. Communists have operated in the country since that date, but an official pro-Soviet communist party has had difficulty establishing formal operations, and its activities are usually clandestine. Early communist groups were discussion circles, the majority of their members coming from minority communities, including Greeks, Coptic Christians, Italians, and Jews, which were dynamic and expressive in the days of the British Protectorate and prior to the Nasser era. A formal communist party was not attempted until the 1950s. But Nasser's adoption of socialism did not make it easier for the communists to formalize their activities. Socialism for Nasser did not imply class struggle or the heavier ideological baggage of Marxism-Leninism, and the communists were often treated severely. By 1965, the majority of Egypt's identifiable 2,000 communists were incarcerated, and a feeble communist party announced its dissolution. Later the Egyptian communists sought membership in Nasser's Arab Socialist Union (ASU). A few decided to operate subversively, but those communists joining the ASU found it a useful front organization, and the journalists among them, particularly, attempted to propagandize a position that dovetailed communist policies with those of the ASU. The Soviet Union encouraged communist participation in the ASU, and Moscow perceived the organization as a transitional arrangement. Sadat's succession in 1970, however, caused a purge of the ASU. On the one hand, the communists were forced to leave the organization. On the other, Sadat promoted competitive politics, albeit controlled, and the communists again began to reassemble their adherents. But the communist recruitment campaign was unsuccessful, and another strategy was employed. Economic dislocation, spiraling inflation, high unemployment, and dissatisfaction with Sadat's foreign policy, especially his efforts at reconciling differences with the Israelis and his friendship for Americans, had produced considerable unrest. Street demonstrations and riots were forcibly suppressed, frequently with high loss of life. It was this situation that the communists exploited. Assuming the role of Nasserists (Sadat's de-Nasserization program had angered those who revered their dead leader's memory), the communists organized workers' unions and student organizations and used them to agitate against the Egyptian administration. In August 1975, the Egyptian Communist Party was officially reconstituted. Its headquarters, however, was opened in Beirut, Lebanon, side by side with other radical organizations and movements. Egyptian communists continued to work clandestinely inside the country, and some surfaced at each opportunity afforded by the administration. Communists also adopted Khalid Moheiddin's National Progressive Unionist Party (NPUP), and when Sadat sanctioned the holding of elections in 1976, the NPUP drew 200,000 votes. Moheiddin's party had a handful of seats in the assembly, but it was an outspoken, articulate group and a constant embarrassment for the government. Sadat insisted on new elections in 1979, and the National Progressives lost half their clientele and all their seats. Even the Socialist Labor Party could retain only 16 seats, while Sadat's new National Democratic Party captured 315. In September 1980, elections were held for the 210-member Advisory Council that replaced the Central Committee of the ASU. Sadat's party won 140 of these positions, and the remainder were chosen by the Egyptian president. Sadat insisted on maintaining the ban on the Egyptian Communist Party, but an illegal Egyptian Worker's Party was organized and managed by the leftists. Apart from the 25,000 active members claimed by the National Progressives, Communist Party members were believed to total fewer than 3,000, although among this number were accomplished journalists, artists, and lawyers. Hosni Mubarak has shown no more favor for the communists than did his fallen predecessor, but the communists of Egypt have organized a nucleus of dedicated true believers. ***See also*** ARAB SOCIALIST UNION (114).

Significance
Egypt has had the longest experience with communist organizations. When Nasser entered into an arms deal with the Soviet Union in 1955, the communists sensed a new opportunity to spread their doctrine among the country's inhabitants. Nasser, however, was determined to prevent the communists from exploiting and possibly seizing *his* revolution, and despite his dependence on Moscow, he violently suppressed Egyptian communists. Anwar el-Sadat was similarly concerned with communist activity. Moreover, knowledge that the Soviet Union aided the Egyptian communists and indeed conspired

against him and his government caused Sadat to demand the removal of Soviet personnel from advisory roles in the country as early as 1971. Sadat perceived a spreading Soviet threat in the Arab world, and this perception convinced him of the necessity to reestablish intimacy with Washington and to seek peace with Israel. Sadat's dramatic visit to Jerusalem and the subsequent Camp David talks derailed a Soviet policy that sought to give Moscow a prominent role in a projected conference at Geneva. Sadat's action appeared to neutralize this significant Soviet diplomatic thrust. Just weeks before his assassination, Sadat ordered all Soviet personnel to leave Egypt, and he closed the Soviet embassy. Announcing his decision, Sadat noted that Soviet agents were again actively seeking the overthrow of his government. The expulsion of the Soviets coincided with the arrest of several thousand Egyptians deemed to be acting in a manner prejudicial to the health of the nation. Sadat appeared to be concerned that his enemies across the political spectrum were coalescing. A united front of opposition organizations from the fundamentalist Islamic groups to the outlawed communist organizations had become a distinct possibility. Following Sadat's death, the Mubarak government stressed its intention to perpetuate Sadat's policies. Although the government continued to suppress extremist organizations, its relations with Moscow were somewhat improved.

Communism: Iraq **121**

The Iraqi Communist Party, once led by Aziz Mohammad, is even less formidable than its counterpart in Syria. The Iraqi communists also joined in a Progressive National Front, sponsored by Saddam Hussain. The communists of Iraq are traditionally more conspiratorial than their Syrian colleagues. Communist cells have been periodically identified within the armed forces, and the regime purged the entire military establishment in the 1960s, 1970s, and 1980s. In April 1978, there was renewed communist activity in Iraq, in part precipitated by the Marxist overthrow of Mohammad Daud in Afghanistan. Like Saddam Hussain, Daud had long cooperated with the Soviets. His death was attributed to Soviet-directed conspirators within the Afghan armed forces, and the Baathists sensed that the same fate could befall them. Thus, a concerted effort was made to root out communists and their sympathizers from positions within the military establishment. Iraq entered into a treaty relationship with the Soviet Union in 1972, and Baghdad was the recipient of large stores of Soviet weapons. Soviet technicians and advisors operated throughout the country, but Moscow did not intervene on behalf of the Iraqi communists. The Iraqi communists were more influential between 1958 and 1963, during the administration of Karim Kassem. It is alleged that they could have seized power during this period but were restrained from doing so by Moscow because it feared an Arab backlash. When the Baath overthrew Kassem in 1963, the communists were judged a national security threat; thousands were rounded up and executed. Iraqi communists have also been associated with the Kurdish autonomy issue. The Iranian Tudeh, or communist, Party has associated with Iraqi communists, and it could lend support to the Kurds as well as other nationality movements. The Iraqi communists have suffered great losses at the hands of the Iraqi Baath, and they may yet gain their revenge. At the very least they stand to profit from any discrediting of the Baghdad regime. ***See also*** BAATH MOVEMENT: IRAQ (115).

Significance
Saddam Hussain has made gestures toward the Iraqi communists that have permitted them to assume government positions, but sensitive posts remain firmly in Baathist hands. Dissatisfaction in Baghdad over Moscow's ambivalent position in the Iraq-Iran War caused the Baathists to de-emphasize their dependence on Moscow. But that dependence was even more pronounced during and following Baghdad's misadventure in Kuwait in 1990–1991. Iraqi communists are interested in the rearrangement of power in the region; nevertheless, they appear stymied by the continuing turmoil within the country.

Communism: Jordan 122

The Jordanian Communist Party was organized in 1951 as the successor to the Communist League for National Liberation, which had its beginning in the West Bank territory. The party was never legalized and has been a source of concern for Jordanian security forces from its inception. The party is divided into numerous cells and operates underground but has never demonstrated meaningful power. The Palestine Communist Organization in the West Bank has been the spokesman for the Jordanian Communist Party, but there is no formal Palestinian communist party. The Palestine Communist Organization was led by Faiq Warrad, the successor to Fuad Nassar, who was assassinated in 1977. The Palestinian communists engage in active recruitment and propaganda and have direct channels to the Palestine National Council, which is dominated by the PLO. The Palestinian communists also maintain close ties with Gaza and Israeli communist parties. In Israel, the communist parties are legal. Israel, therefore, has been more tolerant of the Palestinian communist organization on the West Bank than have been the Jordanians. The Palestinian communists also support trade organizations and student unions, as well as the Palestinian National Front, which has agitated for Israeli withdrawal from the West Bank and Gaza. As the most dynamic political force on the West Bank, the communists stand to gain if and when the PLO loses its credibility among the Palestinian community.

Significance
King Hussain cannot tolerate the open competition of the Communist Party. The communists are determined to destroy the monarchy and establish Jordan as a socialist republic. Moreover, the bedouin population of Jordan is loyal to the Hashemite monarch and only the Palestinian community provides recruits for the communist cause. The king's decision to unleash his army against the Palestinians in 1970 was prompted by perceptions of a radical takeover in the name of Palestinian liberation. King Hussain's attachment to the West and his reluctance to challenge the Israelis ensure the union between the communists and the Palestinians. This perception also explains Israeli reluctance to support a Palestine state on the West Bank.

Communism: Lebanon 123

The Lebanese Communist Party has been a legal organization and a member of the country's "Leftist Front." As such, the Communist Party fought against the Phalange in Lebanon's 1975–1976 civil war and lost the support of the Maronite Christian community. Between 1976 and 1982, the Lebanese Communist Party actively supported the Palestine Liberation Organization in West Beirut. Israel's invasion of Lebanon in 1982 and Jerusalem's insistence that the PLO leave West Beirut were blows to the Lebanese Left. After the exodus of the PLO, the remaining radical forces were ordered to turn their weapons over to the Lebanese army. The reluctance of the Lebanese Muslims to surrender their arms to the Christian-dominated army was mirrored in the actions of the communists, who fear a revived Lebanon under Phalange control. The general-secretary of the Lebanese Communist Party (CP) was Nicola Shawi, an outspoken supporter of the Soviet Union. Moscow earlier helped the Lebanese communists organize Al-Ansar (the Partisans) within the Palestinian community. The Lebanese CP also supported Naif Hawatmeh's Popular Democratic Front for the Liberation of Palestine; the Organization of Communist Action in Lebanon; the Arab Communist Organization (intimately associated with Iraq); the Labor Socialist Party, which is a front organization for the Popular Front for the Liberation of Palestine of George Habash; and the Communist Labor Organization, affiliated with Hawatmeh's group and financed by Cuba. The Lebanese Civil War and the subsequent division of Lebanon, and especially Beirut, between Syrian, Palestinian, and Phalange elements, virtually destroyed the political base of the Lebanese Communist Party and transformed it into a paramilitary force, much like the other groups it is allied with. The likelihood of its reestablishing its political bona fides is problematical. The Lebanese Communist Party, however, continues as a coordinating agency for leftist factions and organizations. *See also* LEBANESE NATIONAL MOVEMENT (133).

Significance
The Lebanese Communist Party had been the principal representative for communist causes and programs in the Arab and Muslim world. As a legal organization it was permitted to propagandize the positions of clandestine leftist parties throughout the Middle East. The Lebanese Civil War, however, divided the nation into bitterly opposed camps, and the communists were forced to take sides with the other organizations in the country. Thus, the communists contributed to the destruction of the very political system that guaranteed their security. The Israeli occupation of a large sector of Lebanon and the forced removal of the PLO from southern Lebanon and West Beirut provided the Phalange with a new opportunity to rebuild its shattered political edifice. With assistance provided by the international peacekeeping force of Americans, French, and Italians, the new Phalange government of Amin Gemayel was dedicated to the resurrection of Lebanon. Gemayel failed, however, and his retirement in 1988 precipitated a new scramble for power that was not "resolved" until Syria physically crushed the opposition to a Damascus-installed government. That government proved unsympathetic to communist and communist-front organizations.

Communism: North Africa (The Maghreb) 124

Communist parties developed in French North Africa during the colonial period. The Italians who occupied Libya prevented communist party development. The Algerian Communist Party fought alongside the National Liberation Front (FLN) in the war against France. In 1964, it dissolved itself, and its leadership was absorbed within the FLN. When Ahmad Ben Bella was ousted by Houari Boumedienne and the army, the communists reestablished their organization. Since then the party has been known as the Socialist Vanguard Party. However, it is illegal, and its leaders have been either imprisoned, forced into exile, or driven underground. The death of Boumedienne permitted Algeria's leaders to release Ben Bella from captivity, but there was no indication of a shift in political orientation that would permit the communists to participate in the government, let alone influence its policies. Tunisia's communist party was more active in the days of French rule. Since its banning in 1965, it has become a virtual nonentity. Morocco has had a strong communist movement, but the party was banned in 1969. The communists then organized the Party of Liberation and Socialism, but it has worked with, not challenged, the government in power. The leader of the party was Ali Yata, the former general-secretary of the Moroccan Communist Party. This party has presented a meek challenge to Morocco's pro-West orientation. The Moroccan communists appear content to register a small voice in the Moroccan parliament. Significantly, the Party of Liberation and Socialism has supported Morocco's claim to the former Spanish Sahara and is vocally opposed to the Polisario Front. ***See also*** NATIONAL LIBERATION FRONT (136); GREEN BOOK (85).

Significance

Although Marxist parties have been strictly outlawed in Libya, it is in that country that communism represents a major threat. Libya is a revolutionary country, predicated to the export of revolution throughout North Africa, the Middle East, and beyond. Described in the West as the leading exponent and purveyor of transnational terrorism, the Libyan government has provided sanctuary, training, money, and supplies to terrorist organizations in Europe, Asia, Africa, and Latin America. Libya was also heavily dependent on the Soviet Union for its military hardware. Muammar Qaddafi purchased far more weaponry from Moscow than could be absorbed by the Libyan armed forces. Although divorced from Marxist philosophy, Qaddafi's Green Book is judged a transitional statement on the subject of radical revolution, and Libya's communists are prepared to practice patience. Libya's multiple attacks against the leaders of Egypt, Sudan, Tunisia, and Morocco, as well as the country's armed adventures in Uganda and Chad, must be seen as part of a larger program aimed at engineering a new region more in keeping with Qaddafi's somewhat romantic vision. If successful, the change could also benefit the heretofore isolated leftists in the area.

Communism: Sudan — 125

In the 1960s, the Sudanese Communist Party was one of the largest communist parties in the Arab world and the best organized. Its membership comprised the professional, intellectual, and managerial elite of the country. Given mass appeal, it seemed to be a valid representative of the Sudanese Arab population. The Sudanese Communist Party supported Jafar al-Numayri in his rise to power in 1969. It also helped form the government with Numayri at its head. By 1971, however, the communists had second thoughts about Numayri. The death of Nasser in 1970 and the rise of Sadat to the presidency of Egypt directly affected the Sudanese communist movement. Sadat did not trust the communists, and he convinced Numayri to free himself from their influence. In retaliation the Sudanese communists plotted Numayri's demise. With help provided by the Egyptian army, the coup was crushed. Numerous communists were rounded up, and many were executed. The party was outlawed and forced underground as the government launched an intensive campaign to destroy its effectiveness. In 1976, the communists attempted still another coup, this time assisted by Libya, where several communist leaders had taken refuge. The Egyptian army again offered its assistance, the coup was prevented, and its perpetrators were summarily punished. Although there have been other communist-inspired attempts, they have all failed. When Numayri was finally removed, the communists were not among the conspirators. Moreover, the demise of Marxism-Leninism in the Soviet Union suggested a fading role for Sudan's radicals.

Significance
Sudan's geopolitical significance explains the intensity of the communist drive in the Arab world's most primitive state. Sudan is the key to Egyptian survival. It is also vital to the security of Saudi Arabia. The communization of the Sudan would have posed a mortal danger to both countries, particularly to their political elites. Libya and the Soviet Union put considerable resources into the violent transformation of the Sudan before 1985. The increasing cost of failure, however, convinced Gorbachev that a more open, moderate policy, engaging the prevailing governments in cooperative endeavors, was a far better course of action. The passing of the U.S.S.R may have sealed the fate of the Sudanese communists.

Communism: Syria 126

The Syrian Communist Party was founded during the French mandate prior to World War II. For a time it operated as a wing of the French Communist Party. Its leader was Khalid Bakdash, a member of the minority Kurdish community. Bakdash spent many years in exile in Moscow and was a revered member of the Soviet-supported, worldwide communist movement. The emergence of the Baath Party to prominence in Syria in 1963 did not augur well for the communists. The socialist Baathists refused to tolerate communist activity, given their similar programs and common origins. The communists faced an unrelenting purge. But in February 1966, the more extreme Left wing of the Baath gained control of the administration and instituted a policy of reconciliation with the communists. Some communists were permitted to enter the government on a personal basis. When Hafez al-Assad took power in November 1970, more communists were permitted to join the government, two of them assuming ministerial portfolios. During this period Assad and the Syrian Baath organized the National Progressive Front, an umbrella arrangement for all the leftist parties and factions in the country. The front was controlled by the Baath, but it also provided the Syrian Communist Party with its long-sought legitimacy. Communist Party affiliation in the Syrian government was enhanced by the 20-year treaty of friendship and cooperation entered into by Moscow and Damascus in October 1980. Although the Syrian communists were believed to number less than 15,000, the presence of the Soviet Union in the country magnified their influence. At the same time, the Baath was determined to maintain its monopoly. Any hint that the communists might challenge the regime could ignite sharp retaliation. ***See also*** BAATH MOVEMENT: ORIGIN IN SYRIA (116).

Significance
The Syrian Baath Party appeals to the same groups as the communists and speaks a similar language. The communists therefore have been hard put to establish an independent position. Their power aspirations are dependent on Baathist failure and their own capacity to exploit popular

dissatisfaction with the Assad government. The situation in Syria in the 1980s in some ways was similar to that in Egypt in the 1950s. Damascus, like Cairo, and Assad, like Nasser, realized that intimacy with Moscow often brought in its wake support for personalities and groups that could challenge the established government. Nasser did not hesitate to crush the Egyptian communists despite his association with Moscow. Assad also dealt ruthlessly with indigenous communists who threatened his regime. Following the 1982 Israeli incursion into Lebanon, the Kremlin ordered the resupply of the Syrian armed forces. More sophisticated weaponry was made available to Damascus, and the number of Soviet advisors in the country increased appreciably. None of these activities, however, provided the Syrian communists with political leverage in decision-making circles in Damascus.

Communism: Yemeni Socialist Party 127

The only truly successful communist party in the Arab world, the Yemeni Socialist Party was created in October 1978. It was a classic Soviet-styled organization. It had its politburo, central committee, mass affiliates like the people's militia, youth and women's organizations, and workers cooperatives. The communists of the former South Yemen achieved power on the day that country gained its independence from Great Britain in 1967. At that time the organization was called the National Liberation Front, and then simply the National Front. In 1975 the National Front was joined by the pro-Soviet Democratic People's Union Party and the Baathist Popular Vanguard Party. It was then called the National Front Unified Political Organizations. The creation of the Yemeni Socialist Party illustrated the full integration of the several parties and the creation of a one-party state. The radicalization of South Yemen politics occurred during the struggle for independence and stems from the violent nature of the clash between Yemeni and British forces over the disposition of the strategic port of Aden. When South Yemen gained its independence, it immediately turned toward communist China and then to the Soviet Union. When the Chinese withdrew their support, the Soviets were provided a clear field. The Soviets infiltrated all agencies of government, equipped and trained the Yemeni armed forces, brought Cuban and East German advisors and technicians into the country, opened schools and hospitals, trained party cadres in a School of Socialist Sciences, and established a formidable base at Aden and another on the offshore island of Socotra. South Yemen played an important role in assisting Ethiopia to combat Somalia, despite significant Arab support for the latter. It has also permitted terrorists and guerrilla forces to use its territory for training purposes.

Significance

South Yemen ceased to exist upon its formal merger with North Yemen in 1990. Communist rule is no longer apparent in unified Yemen, and the U.S.S.R. has ceased to exist. The Yemeni armed forces are no longer controlled by Russian officers, East Germany is no more, and Cuba has terminated its role in the region. Heretofore the most doctrinaire communist state in the Arab world, Yemen is now the least affected by communist movements.

Communist Organizations: Turkey 128

The first communist organization in Turkey appeared in 1918–1920. By 1920 a Turkish Communist Party was founded. In 1923 Kemal Ataturk banned the advocacy of communist doctrine; the Turkish Communist Party has led an underground existence ever since. The party was pro-Soviet and formerly had its headquarters in East Germany, where it beamed radio broadcasts to the Turkish Republic. The party secretary-general, J. Billen, resided in East Germany. This operation was terminated when East Germany was united with West Germany in 1990.

Significance

The Turkish Communist Party has been unsuccessful in enlisting the support of Turkish dissidents. Its association with the Soviet Union, a traditional and historical foe of the Turkish nation, drove would-be sympathizers into other leftist organizations. The non-Moscow-oriented Turkish Workers and Peasants Party of Dagu Perincek, the Turkish Workers Party of Behice Boran, and Mehmet Ali Aybar's Socialist Reform Party are radical socialist, but avoid communist labels. Other smaller radical organizations also attract recruits, especially from among the Turkish student population. The actions of the latter suggest some alignment with the Turkish Communist Party. Frustrated by developments inside the Soviet Union, Turkish communists resorted to terrorist activities inside Turkey and networked with fundamentalists and other radical groups violently opposed to Ankara's pro-Western posture.

Destourian Socialist Party **129**

The Tunisian nationalists organized their first political party in 1920, the Destour (Constitution) Party; it was dominated by French-educated members of the middle class. Habib Bourguiba led a disgruntled group of younger members out of the party and formed the Neo-Destour Party in 1934; it was the Neo-Destour Party that succeeded in gaining Tunisia's independence from the French in March 1956. The political strategy of the Neo-Destour was centralization of administrative power and modernization. The party publicized a form of socialism, but in practice the approach was pragmatic and flexible. In 1959, the new Tunisian constitution brought the reorganization of the Neo-Destour. The Neo-Destour assumed responsibility for neutralizing the spiritual leaders. Islam was to be updated and conservative traditions sidelined. To reduce the power of the spiritual elite, all lands controlled by religious institutions (identified as *habus* in Tunisia and *waqf* in the larger Muslim world) were transferred to the state. Bourguiba, as head of state, accused the clerics of impeding change, and he insisted Islam could flourish only if it became more progressive. Bourguiba and the Neo-Destour took advantage of the failure of the Muslim clerics to assist the nationalist movement. The president had popular support for his actions, and he emphasized a plan to fight poverty and underdevelopment, but first the country had to overcome religious obstacles. Bourguiba did not want to be identified as anti-Islam. He emphasized that Islam accentuated the positive, the need to fight public immorality, to practice moderation, and to generate obedience to authority. A conspiracy to assassinate Bourguiba was revealed in 1962. After the dissidents were quelled, all opposition political parties were banned, and only the Neo-Destour was declared a legal party. In 1963 the Neo-Destour was modified again so as to fuse its organization with that of the government. Destourian socialism became the watchword for the country, and the party was renamed the Destourian Socialist Party. Given the effective elimination of political parties, the only serious opposition against the Destour and its leader, Habib Bourguiba, came from the labor unions. After several years of strikes and general unrest, a true confrontation developed between the unions and the party government in 1978. Riots were answered by police repression, and during "Black Thursday" several hundred demonstrators lost their lives. A state of emergency was imposed. The government justified its actions by noting that the riots had degenerated into outright rebellion against the state. Even though he had been declared president-for-life in 1975, Bourguiba was forced to recognize the seriousness of the opposition to his dictatorial, one-party rule. Nevertheless, he overcame those immediate difficulties by promising to review his government's policies and to permit broader recruitment into government service and by opening a genuine forum for the airing of grievances. The Destourian Socialist Party continues as the only legal party in Tunisia, although Habib Bourguiba, frail and ailing, was forced to give up his leadership of the organization in 1987. *See also* BOURGUIBISM (75).

Significance
The Destourian Socialist Party was intertwined with the personality of Habib Bourguiba, but its future without him is no longer in question. Bourguiba's role in Tunisia resembles that played by Ataturk in Turkey in the 1920s and 1930s. Like Ataturk, Bourguiba saw a need to overcome Islamic impediments to modernization. But also like Ataturk, his conception of modernization reflected a European rather than a Muslim tradition. Ataturk's opponents were ineffective in his lifetime, but they quickly exploited subterranean sentiment that suggested the reforms had gone too far too fast. In the aftermath of Bourguiba's reign, an alliance has developed between the sophisticated opposition and the fundamentalist elite. The Destour survives, but multiparty politics is a reality.

Hizbollah 130

Hizbollah is an Iranian-supported radical Shiite group based in Lebanon and often associated with terrorist activities. Hizbollah (Party of God) is largely led by Shiite clerics, the preeminent figure among them being Mohammad Husayn Fadlallah. Fadlallah identifies the Shiite concept of martyrdom as expressed in *ashura*, the roots of Shiite Islam in the seventh century, as the most compelling force for present members of the faith. He has written: "*Ashura* endows us with a sense of purpose and knowledge of how to meet challenges . . . to build a new man . . . for we know that Allah helps only those who help themselves." This faith strengthens Shiite followers of Hizbollah in their resolve to change the pattern of power relationships in the Middle East. Hizbollah emphasizes the need for armed struggle against the infidel and as such followed the commands of the Ayatollah Khomeini, whom Fadlallah venerated as the Na'ib al-Imam (Vicar of the Hidden Imam) and Qaid al-Umma (Leader of the Muslim Community). Khomeini's death has reinforced this belief and converted it into unshakeable faith. The members of Hizbollah, like other Shiite radicals, are prone to reject nationalism in favor of an overarching and all-encompassing Islamic world.

Significance
Hizbollah is a fundamentalist Shiite organization that is best known for its opposition to the more "moderate" but also more powerful Amal organization of Lebanon. The Amal of Nabi Berri has been more closely associated with Syria and the Alawites that dominate Damascus. Conflict between the two Shiite orders has been relentless, with Hizbollah arguing that Amal is the handmaiden of secularism and can never represent the Islamic community. Hizbollah is first and foremost an ideological

organization, and it has demonstrated its determination not only by seizing Western hostages, but also by making intermittent war on Amal. The stand-down of warring Lebanese factions in 1990, following the Syrian army's destruction of the forces of Michel Aoun, produced a tentative peace between Hizbollah and Amal. But there was no peace between Hizbollah and Israel. In February 1992 Israeli helicopter gunships targeted Hizbollah leader Shaykh Abbas Musawi, killing him and members of his party. The assault triggered an intense rocket and artillery exchange between Hizbollah and Israeli gunners and heightened terrorist operations in and outside Israel.

Hostage Takers 131

The principal groups identified with hostage taking in the Middle East are: (1) Islamic Holy War, a Shiite group that originally demanded the release of 17 comrades jailed in Kuwait for bombing the U.S. and French embassies in December 1983. Two of the 17 were released after serving five-year prison sentences. The remainder were freed by Iraq after its occupation of Kuwait in 1990. The group continued to insist upon the release of Shiite hostages held by Israel before they freed the last of their captives. The group had seized Terry Waite, the Anglican Church envoy, and Terry Anderson of the Associated Press, the longest-held hostage, who was abducted on March 16, 1985. Both men were released in 1991. (2) Revolutionary Justice Organization, the group that seized Americans working in the American University in Beirut. (3) Organization of the Oppressed on Earth, believed to be responsible for the kidnapping and execution of Lieutenant Colonel William R. Higgins, a U.S. marine serving with the UN truce observer force in Lebanon. He is believed to have been hanged on July 31, 1989. (4) Organization for the Defense of Prisoner Rights, an unknown group believed responsible for shelling UN offices in Beirut. (5) Islamic Holy War for the Liberation of Palestine, the group that seized Americans working in Beirut University College and demanded that Israel release all Arab prisoners. (6) Cells of Armed Struggle, a little-known organization that held an aged British airman who they claimed had been a spy for Israel. (7) Revolutionary Organization of Socialist Muslims, believed to be a cover for the Abu Nidal organization and the group that claims to have killed the British journalist Alec Collett on April 23, 1986.

Significance
Hostage taking represents a form of psychological warfare and has provided small groups of revolutionaries with the necessary leverage to move more powerful governments. Although the U.S. government has refrained from negotiating directly with hostage takers and has refused to pay ransom of any kind, other governments, such as Germany, Italy, and France, did engage in such efforts. More important, hostage taking is aimed at capturing world attention, influencing world opinion, and creating an ambiance which is deemed beneficial to the hostage takers. The taking of hostages also focused attention on Israel's holding of Arab prisoners for alleged political and/or violent acts. Israel's seizure of the religious cleric Shaykh Obeid was perpetrated in an effort to gain the release of Israeli prisoners believed held in Lebanon or Syria. Hostage takers have long had their patrons as well, and Iran's revolutionary government is believed to have ties with a number of the more prominent hostage taking groups in Lebanon. Negotiations centering on gaining the release of the hostages between the UN secretary-general and leaders of

the Iranian government underlined this reality.

Kurdish Political Parties 132

The Kurdish population is split between Turkey (approximately 4 million), Iraq (approximately 3.5 million), and Iran (approximately 2 million). The most prominent Kurdish political party in Turkey is the separatist Kurdish Workers Party. Emphasizing Kurdish independence since 1984, the party calls for carving a state from Turkey's eastern and southeastern regions. Ankara has moved aggressively against the Kurdish Workers Party and almost 6,000 deaths have been directly attributed to the movement's violent behavior and the government's aggressive response. The principal political organizations in Iraq and Iran are the Kurdish Democratic Party led by Massoud Barzani, the Patriotic Union of Kurdistan led by Jalal Talabani, and the smaller organizations of the Kurdish Democratic Party, the People's Party of Kurdistan, and the Kurdish Socialist Party. The Kurdish parties of Iraq and Iran have periodically sought autonomy within their respective nations, but difficulties with either Tehran or Baghdad have often caused violent clashes between Iraqi and Iranian Kurds and their more powerful but also alien rulers. Mustafa Barzani, the father of Masoud Barzani, was the longtime leader of the Kurdish autonomy movement, but his efforts on behalf of the Kurdish community were unsuccessful. Although agreements have been entered into, such as the 1974 proposals between the Kurds and Baghdad, the latter did not honor its promises to the minority community. Although official statistics are unavailable, observers believe tens of thousands of Kurds have perished since the emergence of Saddam Hussain as Iraq's absolute ruler.

See also KURDS (89); KURDISH ENCLAVE PROPOSAL (90); HALABJA ATROCITY (244).

Significance
Kurdish political parties are perceived as militant organizations, determined to disrupt the larger societies around them. The Kurds have long sought to represent their interests, and the formation of the political party was a twentieth-century manifestation of Kurdish national aspirations. Nevertheless, the Kurdish Worker's Party is not representative of the larger community of Kurds living within Turkey, and the Turkish government is determined to isolate and destroy them even if it means penetrating their sanctuaries in Iraq to do so. Ankara's offensive against the dissident Kurds in March 1992 was brutally effective, but it threatened to impair seriously Turkish-German relations. Germany's reaction in defence of the Kurds was deemed to be prompted by the large Kurdish minority within the country, heretofore identified as Turks. Nevertheless, the Turks refused to yield to the demands of the Kurdish Workers Party. The parties in Iran, especially during the life of Mustafa Barzani, also challenged the shah's regime in Iran. They later sought to gain advantages from the revolutionary government of Ayatollah Khomeini but were again denied. Siding with Iran during the Iran-Iraq War, the Kurds exposed themselves to more danger and their political organizations were unable to protect them. Indeed, the Kurds were not only exploited by the Turks, Arabs, and Iranians, but by the United States as well. The U.S. CIA assisted Mustafa Barzani in his earlier struggle against Iraq because Washington believed Barzani's party would prove a bulwark against Soviet dominance in the region. The Kurds paid a high price for their dependence, especially after being abandoned by every

country that at one time promised to befriend them. The Iraqi Baath destruction of Kurdish cities and villages because of their alleged support for Iran as well as the Kurdish tragedy in the wake of Operation Desert Storm are cases in point.

Lebanese National Movement (Al-Haraka al-Wataniyya) 133

The Lebanese National Movement, a loose association of political organizations and armed militias in opposition to the Christian Maronite Phalange, or *Kata'ib*, was organized in 1969 but did not become active until 1973–1974. Its member organizations are:

- Progressive Socialist Party (Druze)
- Baath Socialist Party (Syria), Lebanese Branch
- Baath Socialist Party (Iraq), Lebanese Branch
- Lebanese Communist Party
- Communist Action Organization
- October 24 Movement (Tripoli—Harakat Arba-wa-ishrin Tishrin)
- Syrian Social Nationalist Party
- Movement of the Deprived (Shiite Muslim-Harakat Al-Mahrumin)
- Independent Nasserist Movement (Murabitun or Harakat al-Nasiriyyin al-Mustaqillin)
- Popular Nasserist Organization (Al-Tanzim al-Shabi al-Nasiri)
- Nasserist Organization–Union of Popular Labor Forces (Al-Tanzim al-Nasiri–Ittahad Qiwa al-Shab al-Amil)
- Nasserist Organization–Corrective Movement (Al-Tanzim al-Nasiri–al-Haraka al-Tashihiyya)
- Arab Socialist Union (Al-Ittihad al-Ishtiraki al-Arabi)

Lebanon's sociopolitical fabric began to unravel in the aftermath of the 1973 war when Henry Kissinger applied his diplomatic expertise to the Arab-Israeli dilemma. Egyptian officials met with their Israeli counterparts, and a process was set in motion that ultimately produced the Egyptian-Israeli Peace Treaty of 1979. In 1973–1974, however, the Lebanese-based Palestine Liberation Organization interpreted these initial efforts as a direct threat to the Palestine liberation movement. Even before the October war, in May 1973, Palestinian organizations clashed with the Lebanese army in an attempt to reinforce their position in the country. Following the 1973 war, the Palestinians reached out for allies against the Phalange-dominated Lebanese army and government. The Lebanese government appeared ready to join other Arab states in seeking a comprehensive peace with Israel. The Palestinians concluded that "peace" could only be achieved at their expense. The radical groups that comprised the Lebanese National Movement opposed Israel, but they also had their independent reasons for opposing the Maronite Phalange, and a coalition between the PLO and the National Movement was almost instantaneous. By the mid-1970s Lebanon was the only country in which the PLO could freely operate politically and militarily. Moreover, as a recognized armed organization, the PLO had the capacity to assist the arming of radical Lebanese groups, and also helped them form their own militias. Apart from the Iraqi and Syrian branches of the Baath Party, the radicals included the Lebanese Communist Party and other communist organizations, the Syrian Social Nationalist Party (emphasizing Lebanon's integration with Syria), and Sunni regional organizations in Beirut, Tripoli, and Sidon. Prominent among the Sunni regional organizations were the October 24 Movement, which emerged from a 1969 clash between the Lebanese army and Sunni radicals in Tripoli, and the Independent Nasserist Movement, or Murabitun, of Beirut, a leftist force intimately associated with the PLO. The National Movement had as its chief spokesman the leader of the Lebanese Druze community. The Druze Progressive Socialist Party, however, remained outside the Palestinian umbrella. Although the Druze agreed to cooperate with the Palestinians, they let it be known that what they wanted was a Lebanon that enhanced their interests. As a large minority with territorial and historical roots in the area, the Druze practiced a form of independence beyond the reach of the other radicals. Nevertheless, the National Movement under Druze leadership agreed to coordinate political action and issues with those of the Palestinians. It was at this point that the lines between the groups became blurred, and later it was virtually impossible to distinguish between Palestinian and Lebanese domestic issues. This merger of forces also reduced the effectiveness of traditional Sunni leaders in Beirut and Tripoli. The National Movement drew additional support from the Shiite Lebanese who were guided by the imam Musa al-Sadr. The imam preached rebellion and called upon the faithful to arm themselves. Training camps were organized in Baalbek and in the Bekaa Valley, and militias were mobilized for the front against the Israelis in southern Lebanon. The imam also used the occasion to attack the Maronite Phalange government. He pledged a struggle against the government that could only end when the Shiites and all "oppressed" groups in Lebanon were free. The imam's organization was called the Movement of the Deprived (Haraka al-Mahrumin), and it accused the Phalange of promoting corruption, monopoly capital, and social strains between Lebanon's many communities. The imam's attacks on the Lebanese government complemented the efforts of the Palestinians and gave greater power to the National Movement. Musa al-Sadr disappeared on a visit to Libya in 1979. His followers accused Muammar Qaddafi of having him killed. When the Lebanese Civil War erupted in earnest in 1975, the National Movement joined with the PLO to destroy the Maronite Phalange. On the eve of victory, however, the Syrian army entered the struggle, beat back the PLO-Lebanese radical drive, and sustained the Maronites in their dominant enclaves. Eventually a Syrian-PLO truce and alliance was arrived at that was maintained until the Israelis invaded Lebanon in June 1982. The National Movement came apart, but several of its more prominent organizations continued in important roles. ***See also*** MARONITES (92); DRUZE (81); PHALANGES LIBANAISES (138); LEBANESE CIVIL WAR, 1975–1976 (250); CAIRO AGREEMENT, 1969 (200); ISRAELI-PLO WAR, 1982 (249).

Significance

The National Movement–PLO coalition protracted and also intensified the violence in the Lebanese Civil War. The variety of groups, organizations, and factions in the field compounded the problem of finding a solution. Each had its own objectives, and coordination among several parties did not counteract the crosscurrents of mutual hostility and local vengeance. The National Movement was leftist in philosophy and policy. If there were ties that bound the components together, it was hatred for Israel and the Maronite Phalange. But this did not always mean that Israel was the first target. By and large, the principal object of the National Movement's wrath was the Phalange. When the Christian Maronites received the "protection" of the Syrian army, the quest of the National Movement was frustrated and retarded. Syria wanted the PLO brought under its control but had less interest in the other organizations. It was not inclined to work with the Druze leadership, it was suspicious of the Nasserists, and it did not agree with the Lebanese-Iraqi Baath or the communist organizations. By the same token, groups within the PLO and the National Movement were opposed to the Alawite Shiite regime in Damascus, and cooperation was often painful between them. The Israeli siege of Beirut in the summer of 1982 and the forced removal of the PLO army revived individual groups within the National Movement. The election of Bashir Gemayel as president-elect of Lebanon in August 1982 raised old fears about Lebanese politics. Gemayel welcomed the Israeli invasion and exploited the action to reestablish Phalange power in Beirut and the surrounding area. Gemayel allegedly agreed to sign a peace treaty with Israel. The Israeli-Phalange partnership provoked the October 24 Movement in Tripoli, which seized control of the city shortly after the election. It also caused the Murabitun, or Independent Nasserist Movement, to surface. Murabitun was the organization most identified with the PLO. Before the PLO pullout from Beirut, PLO equipment and neighborhoods were transferred to the Murabitun. It is also alleged that members of the PLO secretly blended themselves into the Nasserist organization. It was virtually impossible to distinguish between an individual member of the PLO and the Murabitun. Moreover, attacks on the homes of Lebanese Muslim officials who voted for Gemayel were perpetrated by the Murabitun. Gemayel's death in an explosion that wrecked his headquarters on September 14, 1982, was also rumored to be the work of the Murabitun and PLO holdouts. Yasir Arafat, speaking in Rome shortly after the assassination, blamed Gemayel's murder on the Israelis, who, he argued, wanted a pretext to invade West Beirut. The Israeli assault on West Beirut that immediately followed the event was aimed at neutralizing the Murabitun. The Lebanese National Movement appeared to come apart in the months following the PLO exodus from West Beirut. Fighting between Druze and Maronites intensified. More significantly, savage battles were fought in the north Lebanon city of Tripoli between Sunni Muslim and pro-Syrian Shiite Muslim units. Outside the Israeli zone of occupation, the Lebanese government of Amin Gemayel urged Damascus to help end the hostilities. Damascus answered this call, and in the nine years that followed, Syria strengthened its hand in Lebanon. In 1990 Damascus arranged a new constitutional structure for Lebanon, which it began to enforce in January 1991.

Motherland Party 134

The Motherland Party of Turkey was founded and led by Turgut Ozal following the military coup of 1980. When the Turkish generals agreed to transfer power back to civilian hands, Ozal organized his party to compete with those political organizations that the military allowed to engage in the elections of 1983. Second place in the election went to another new organization, the Social Democratic Populist Party. The more established Justice Party and Republican People's Party were banned from this election, and their leaders were forced to run under other banners, unfamiliar and suspect to the voting public. Indeed, the Motherland Party received one of the largest parliamentary majorities in Turkish electoral history, and Ozal was named Turkey's new prime minister as a consequence of that election. The Motherland Party represented the conservative business community, which encouraged Ozal's emphasis on free enterprise. But Ozal was also a devout believer who had already made his pilgrimage to Mecca. In the latter instance his party also identified with religious issues both at home and abroad. Indeed, in his initial years in office, Ozal reached out to Saudi Arabia and other Arab states, describing Turkey as a bridge between Europe and the Middle East. Trained as an engineer, Ozal was familiar with public works and had experience in the State Planning Organization. He later served as a chief economic advisor to President Suleyman Demirel and, when the military took power in 1980, remained on to assist in overcoming Turkey's international debt problems. As a driving force within the military-led regime of General Kenan Evren, Ozal sought the overhauling of the Turkish economic system. His somewhat revolutionary reforms, however, convinced Evren that he should be replaced with a less demanding economic advisor. Thus, in 1982, somewhat frustrated by the power in Ankara and anticipating a return to civilian government, Turgut Ozal organized the Motherland Party to represent his views for a future, more progressive Turkish state. The Motherland Party was successful in winning the November 1987 election as well, gaining 36 percent of the vote, but 65 percent of the seats in the national assembly. This time the older parties were permitted to compete, and the Motherland Party was hard-pressed to secure the government under its command. The Motherland Party formed the government, but with less than the 300 seats needed to override a presidential veto. Thus, when the military stepped aside, Ozal made himself a candidate for the presidency. In 1989 Ozal assumed the presidency of the Turkish state. Some months earlier, on June 18, 1988, he had been shot and wounded by a would-be assassin. The attack was allegedly mounted by the radical right-wing National Action Party. Others believed it was inspired by Kurdish separatists. Regardless, the incident served to make Ozal and his Motherland Party the person and organization of choice, despite continuing difficulties. Riding the crest of a popular wave, Ozal was a candidate for the Turkish presidency, and in 1989 he won the presidential elections. His party, however, was made the target of renewed criticism, and the economic dislocation caused by the war in the gulf was grist for the opposition mill. The contenders hammered away at the Motherland Party's overt nepotism, its mishandling of the Kurdish problem, and its alleged corrupt practices. In the parliamentary elections held in October 1991, the Motherland Party was defeated by Suleyman Demirel's True Path Party, which drew the support of the peasantry and small shopkeepers. The Motherland Party also had to contend with the Social Democratic-Populists of Erdal Inonu, whose party received the third largest number of votes, and Necmettin Erbakan's Islamic Welfare Party. The election results addressed the need for a coalition government and hinted at still another period of political instability. Turgut Ozal, however, remained the nation's president, an office he was slated to hold until new elections in 1996.

Significance

The Motherland Party represented a new opportunity at prosperous, civilian, democratic government, and it was overwhelmingly approved by the Turkish nation in its initial years. But the ensuing years did not relieve Turkey's poor economic condition. Moreover, Turkey was rejected by the European Community (EC) and Ankara's hope of tying itself to an integrated European economic structure remained unrealized. The European members of the EC described Turkey as non-European and nondemocratic. Turkey had come under particular scrutiny for its alleged human rights violations, and the EC indicated it could not be a party to such activity. Under Ozal's Motherland Party, therefore, Ankara looked to the Middle East, and especially to the richer oil-producing Arab states. Turkey's older alignments with Pakistan and Iran were not deemed helpful in lifting the country from its economic doldrums. Ankara's interest in Saudi Arabia, as well as its continuation in NATO, drew Turkey to support the U.S.-led coalition that forced Iraq to yield its conquest of Kuwait in 1990–1991. Ozal and the Motherland Party were quick to respond to the U.S. request for assistance, despite Turkey's trade with Baghdad. Moreover, the Motherland Party government exposed itself to heavy criticism for siding with the United States. Numerous acts of terror were committed against Westerners and their installations in Turkey during the Gulf War. Nevertheless, Ozal held to his commitment to the alliance, and he anticipated some reward for his country when the hostilities subsided. The Motherland Party weathered the immediate aftermath of Operations Desert Shield and Desert Storm. But the administration in Ankara was faced with the catastrophic consequences of the war in the desperate effort of many Iraqi Kurds to find refuge in Turkey. The bridge between Europe and the Middle East that Turkey represented was also more than Ozal and the Motherland Party bargained for. The October 1991 election dramatized the challenges confronting the Motherland Party. Suleyman Demirel's victory returned a personality who had already served the Turkish republic six times as prime minister. Moreover, Demirel had been forced to relinquish his office twice by military command. As in the past, Demirel's victory was only partial in that his party received less than 30 percent of the popular vote. Alliances between the True Path Party and the Motherland Party could not be ruled out, especially with Turgut Ozal presiding in the president's office.

National Front **135**

The Iranian revolution of 1905–1906 forced the drafting of Iran's first constitution. Conceived and managed by secular nationalists like Sayyid Hassan Taqizadeh and Ali Akbar Dehkhuda, the revolution was essentially a liberal intellectual effort aimed at raising representative political systems above the overbearing influence of the monarchy and the Shiite clergy. The nationalists enlisted "enlightened" members of the spiritual fraternity in their efforts to limit the power of the Qajar shah. They also formed a Democratic Party that represented their organizational interests up to World War I. The creation of the Iranian Majlis, or parliament, however, did not mean a simple transfer of authority to civilian rulers. Both the monarchy and external powers, especially imperial Russia, conspired against it. The later collapse of the Qajar dynasty and the Bolshevik Revolution appeared to offer new opportunities for the Iranian nationalists, but their work was exploited by Reza Khan, an officer in the Persian Cossack Brigade, who seized the vacated throne and established his own Pahlavi dynasty. The nationalists were violently repressed by the new shah, and the Democratic Party gave way to a number of smaller associations. It was these smaller political organizations that were regrouped under the leadership of Mohammad Mossadegh in the wake of World War II. Mossadegh's political organization was known as the National Front, and it gained notoriety and popular legitimacy from its demand that Iran's petroleum industry, then under British control, be nationalized. The early post–World War II Iranian Majlis also took advantage of a semi-paralyzed monarchy headed by Reza Shah's young son, Mohammad. The Majlis insisted upon nationalization, and under Mossadegh's leadership the

Anglo-Iranian Oil Company was seized on March 15, 1951. This set in train a number of forces, one of which sought the total destruction of the monarchy. The National Front gained control of the government during this period, and Mossadegh became the country's prime minister. But as in the past, external powers intervened, and after the shah was forced to flee the country in 1953, foreign agents, reputedly members of the U.S. Central Intelligence Agency (CIA), assisted the monarchists in overthrowing the National Front government, and the shah was restored to the throne. The National Front, it was argued, had come under the influence of the communist Tudeh Party, and Mossadegh was little more than a symbol. Real power was in radical hands. Mossadegh was therefore arrested and prevented from ever again engaging in politics. His popularity, however, was so deep and broad that government efforts in silencing him only added to his stature. In this way the pre–World War I Iranian revolution was merged with the post–World War II revolution. In each instance, popular dissatisfaction centered on an unacceptable monarchy bolstered by foreign powers interested solely in promoting their special interests. Iranian nationalism was thus transformed from an institutional effort concerned with providing the population with liberal values based upon fundamental human freedoms (the ideas of Taqizadeh as well as Mossadegh) to a passionate, shrill, desperate call to avoid all alien influence and to re-create Iran in the form of a model Islamic state or model Marxist state. The secular nationalists had endeavored to limit the influence of the *mullahs,* Iran's religious clerics, but developments in the post–World War II years ensured their ultimate preeminence. The shah, of course, endeavored to block future threats to his throne. Toward this end he ordered the creation of two parties, the Melliyun, or Nationalist Party, and the Mardum, or People's Party. The Melliyun was earmarked as the government party and the Mardum as the loyal opposition. The shah's scheme was put into operation by his supporters, but the larger population rejected the contrivance, and after a series of unacceptable elections the parties were eventually disbanded. A few years before his demise the shah attempted once again to create a political party. It was called the National Resurgence Party, and the shah publicly declared that those Iranians who refused to join his party were either members of the outlawed Tudeh or some other illegal organization. Needless to say, members of the National Front refused to join the shah's organization. Under pain of imprisonment, torture, and sometimes death at the hands of the secret police, the SAVAK, the members of the National Front continued to call for constitutional reforms. Before the shah was forced to leave the country for the last time in 1979, members of the National Front were called upon to help form a new government. Their reluctance to accept the offer was due to their fear of being used. The shah had not abdicated his throne, and the National Front leaders sensed a plot to return the shah to power much as had been done in 1953 when Mossadegh was overthrown. The National Front was a congeries of organizations, groups, and personalities. A maximum leader did not exist. Mossadegh had died some years before, and no one could fill the position he had created. Division and indecision within the organization therefore not only proved the undoing of the National Front as a viable organization, but it also left the field to the *mullahs,* who quickly seized control of the new revolution. Mehdi Bazargan, the first prime minister of the *mullah*-dominated revolutionary government, was a member of the National Front.

His ignominious dismissal in November 1979, in the wake of the U.S. embassy hostage drama, seemed to write an end to the influence of the National Front. It also confirmed the termination of an experiment in liberal constitutionalism. *See also* TUDEH PARTY (143).

Significance
The National Front was Iran's answer to liberal constitutionalism. The shah's failure to promote its activities not only cost the monarch his throne, but it also left Iran at the mercy of fundamentalist clerics whose narrow vision was destined to plunge modern Iran into a new "time of trouble." On the other hand, the failure of the United States to understand the role of the National Front in Iranian political life in 1951–1953 also prepared the ground for Iranian extremists of assorted colors and philosophies. The Islamic-Marxists of Ali Shariati (today identified with the Mujahiddin Khalq), the Tudeh Party, and the *mullahs* all vie for power. Little opportunity exists for the "enlightened," liberal intelligentsia to reassert itself. Many leaders of the National Front either have lost their lives, have been irreparably damaged, or have sought exile abroad. The assassination of Shahpur Bakhtiar in Paris on August 8, 1991, illustrates the fate of Iran's westernized leaders. Iran's last prime minister before the Islamic revolution of 1979, he was stabbed to death by executioners who apparently were acting under the orders of a religious court order of May 1979. In exile, Bakhtiar had organized and led the National Resistance Movement. National Front "thinking" is associated with Western ideas about politics and government, and the Iranian temperament has been conditioned to reject anything that resembles either European or U.S. performance. Whether this is a permanent or temporary phenomenon appears immaterial, given the determination to destroy all bridges to the West. Furthermore, the radicals are not inactive. The elimination of a "Western" voice in the National Front and the bitter contest between the *mullahs* and the Mujahiddin Khalq suggest the weakening of forces that thus far have prevented parties like the Tudeh from establishing their preeminence.

National Liberation Front (FLN) 136

The National Liberation Front was the principal organization in Algeria's war of independence against the French, and it remains the primary institution around which Algeria's governments are formed and its policies are developed. The FLN has its origins in the Movement for the Triumph of Democratic Liberties (1946) and its offshoot, the Secret Organization, which collected the resources, prepared the revolutionary cells, and plotted the insurrection against French colonial rule. In 1954, several members of the Secret Organization created the Revolutionary Council for Unity and Action which made the final preparations for the armed attack on the French. When hostilities began in 1955, the revolutionary council assumed the name National Liberation Front; its backbone was the National Liberation Army. All factional elements, from middle-class members of the bourgeoisie to religious patriarchs, fused their organizations with the FLN by 1956. In 1958, the FLN established a government-in-exile, which operated from recently independent Tunisia. The success of the FLN can be judged from the Evian agreements, by which France recognized Algeria's independence in 1962. Ahmad Ben Bella, a civilian leader, and Houari Boumedienne, the commander-in-chief of the Algerian army, formed the FLN's Political Bureau in 1962, and it was declared the chief executive organ of the party. A clash ensued between the Political Bureau and radical members of the multiparty provisional government, which was won by the Political Bureau. The provisional government's power was then transferred to a constituent assembly. With authority at last consolidated, the Algerian republic was proclaimed on September 25, 1962. Ben Bella became the country's first prime minister, with Ferhat Abbas as its ceremonial president. The FLN government banned the Algerian Communist Party and the Party of the Socialist Revolution, and Algeria was converted into a one-party state. Ben Bella pressed for an authoritarian constitution in the face of Berber opposition (revolts had to be suppressed in 1963 and 1964); his more liberal president was compelled to resign. Ben Bella assumed the presidency in 1963. His dictatorial tendencies, however, provoked considerable unrest, and the army under Houari Boumedienne deposed and arrested him in 1965. Boumedienne proved to be a superior political organizer. He gave prominent attention to the FLN, established a Council of the Revolution, and pledged to remedy the abuses of personal power. Boumedienne crushed an uprising in 1967 and purged the opposition within the FLN and army. An assassination attempt was thwarted in 1968, and hundreds of dissidents were arrested. By 1971, Boumedienne's only opposition came from alienated university students. The death of Ahmed Medeghri, and the removal, isolation, or exiling of other leaders, left Boumedienne the only dominant figure in the FLN government. In 1976, the FLN published a National Charter that committed Algeria irreversibly to socialism, although it was a form of socialism free from Marxist doctrine. Islam was recognized as the state religion. The charter also became the nucleus for a new constitution that provided the FLN with a central role in selecting candidates for the national assembly. By 1977 the FLN had been transformed into a mass umbrella organization, overseeing the acdtivities of labor unions, peasants' organizations, and veterans', women's, and youth groups. FLN officials were also placed in key assignments alongside local administration. Boumedienne succumbed to illness in 1978 at the height of his power. The FLN dissolved the Council of the Revolution and substituted a broader Central Committee. Given the fluid situation, the Central Committee chose Chadli Bendjedid, the commander of the Oran military district, to succeed to the presidency. Bendjedid had also been a member of the general staff of the National Liberation Army and the Council of the Revolution. Algeria's first real prime minister was also selected, and the FLN was modified to suit the needs of the new leadership. The Political Bureau was reduced to the role of an advisory body, and all mass organizations were required to assume full dues-paying responsibilities within the FLN. The FLN faced its most formidable domestic challenge in the mid-1980s. Algerian youth rioted repeatedly, demanding improvements in the country's living conditions. Government waste, high prices for necessities, gross unemployment, and a critical lack of housing were their principal complaints. A state of emergency had to be imposed in Algiers, and eventually elsewhere in the country. The unrest finally led President Bendjedid to authorize the formation of a new government. A referendum was held on November 3, 1988, wherein the voters approved constitutional changes shifting more power to the prime minister and the parliamentary assembly and shifting that same power away from the FLN. The once relatively powerless People's National Assembly now received new prominence. As a consequence of these changes, parties were organized in increasing number. The FLN split and was faced with defections. By 1991 approximately 40 political parties were operating inside Algeria. The FLN was no longer the monopoly power in the country, and Algeria appeared to be on the road toward some form of democratic government. The positive nature of this change was seriously undermined, however, when Islamic fundamentalists urged their followers to ignore the elections slated for June 1991 and instead mount a campaign of civil disobedience. As a consequence of this call, riots rocked Algiers causing 60 deaths and leading to nearly 5,000 arrests. President Bendjedid replaced his prime minister, calling on Sid Ahmed Ghozali to form a new government. The army arrested the two principal leaders of the Islamic Salvation Front, Abassi Madani and Ali Belhadj, the latter having called for the forceful overthrow of the Algerian government. The decision taken by the fundamentalists to bypass the parliament and the constitutional system was keyed to the country's 30 percent unemployment rate and its debt burden of $26 billion, which consumed much of the country's revenue from oil and natural gas exports. More significantly, the assault was directed against the National Liberation Front (FLN), which had governed Algeria for 29 years and whose authority had melted away with the growth and spread of the multiparty system. The Islamic Front parties won 188 of 430 seats in the December 1991 parliamentary election, forcing a run-off election in January 1992. The FLN, however, under army influence canceled the elections, fearing a sweep by the fundamentalists. President Bendjedid resigned on January 11 and a spokesperson for the government noted that the Algerian constitution forbids parties founded on religious grounds. Attempts to ban the Islamic Salvation Front further divided the FLN government. *See also* EVIAN AGREEMENTS (209).

Significance

The Algerian National Liberation Front (FLN) sustains only a modicum of its revolutionary fervor. Nevertheless, it has made the successful transition from political movement to political party. Drawing upon its wartime experience, and being the only organization representative of the army, the FLN perpetuates the notion of protracted revolution. The FLN still seeks to represent a wide spectrum of interests. It has been restructured to accommodate diversity and to emphasize depoliticization. Buttressed by the armed forces, which since the early years of Boumedienne's rule have severely restricted leftist activists, the FLN has sustained policies that are aimed at satisfying several publics at the same time. Relations with France, for example, have achieved a degree of amiability. Generally, Algeria appears inclined toward developing economic programs that encourage the growth of a mixed economy. In point of fact, the FLN seeks to be all things to all political, ideological, economic, and ethnic groups in the country. As a secular organization, the FLN sought to introduce democracy in Algeria. It was that experiment that appeared to be under greatest threat in the 1990s.

Palestine Liberation Organization (PLO) 137

The Palestine Liberation Organization was formed in 1964 to act as the umbrella movement for eight guerrilla groups opposed to any negotiated settlement with Israel. Al-Fatah, the principal guerrilla group, assumed leadership of the PLO in 1969 and has retained it in subsequent years. The PLO technically is governed by a 15-member Executive Committee dominated by Al-Fatah and its leading personality, Yasir Arafat. Though it is currently and officially headquartered in Tunisia, the PLO had offices in Beirut that were more significant until their August 1982 expulsion. At the conference of Arab leaders in Rabat, Morocco, in 1974, the PLO was declared the only legitimate representative of the Palestinian people, and that designation has never been withdrawn. In October 1974 the UN General Assembly voted 105 to 4, with 20 abstentions, to recognize the PLO officially. On November 13, 1974, Yasir Arafat addressed the General Assembly of the United Nations by invitation. The PLO maintains observer status at UN headquarters in New York and became a full member of the Arab League in 1976. Moreover, the PLO has been officially recognized by many governments and unofficially by others. Even the Vatican conferred a degree of legitimacy on the PLO in September 1982. The Soviet Union bestowed full diplomatic status on Yasir Arafat and the PLO in November 1981. The PLO Executive Committee is elected by the Palestine Liberation Council, the PLO's legislative arm. Its 15 members are drawn from the principal organizations (6) and independents (9). Linked to the Executive Committee is the Palestine National Council, a several-hundred-member "parliament-in-exile." Seats are obtained on the Palestine National Council by selection of the Executive Committee. Members serve three-year terms. Nominations are presented by Al-Fatah (one-third); other guerrilla groups (one-third); and independents (one-third), who are mainly supporters of Yasir Arafat. The Palestine National Council meets periodically in different Arab countries. The military arm of the PLO is the Palestine Liberation Army, estimated to range between 20,000 and 30,000. Segments of the Palestine Liberation Army are now found in Tunisia, Syria, Libya, Jordan, Iraq, Yemen, Sudan, Algeria, and Lebanon. Yasir Arafat is commander-in-chief of the Liberation Army. The PLO also has a Palestine Armed Struggle Command that acts as a police or security agency, which is controlled by Al-Fatah. A 55-member Palestine Central Council operates out of Damascus. It is selected by the Palestine National Council to carry on its tasks when the National Council is not in session. The principal Palestine Arab guerrilla organizations are:

1. Al-Fatah, with approximately 18,000 members. Al-Fatah conducted military operations under the name Al-Asifah in Lebanon.
2. As-Saiqa, approximately 5,000 members, organized and controlled by Syria. As-Saiqa has been sponsored by the Syrian Baathist Party from its inception. Its guiding spirit was Zuheir Mohsen, an Arafat rival who was murdered in France.
3. Popular Democratic Front for the Liberation of Palestine (PDFLP), approximately 3,000 members. PDFLP was organized by a Jordanian, Naif Hawatmeh, and supports Marxist ideology.
4. Popular Front for the Liberation of Palestine–General Command is made up of approximately 1,000 pro-Syrian activists.
5. Popular Front for the Liberation of Palestine (PFLP) is a force of 2,000 to 3,000 armed insurgents led by a Lebanese Christian and Marxist-Leninist, Dr. George Habash.
6. The Arab Liberation Front identifies with Iraq, and has several hundred to slightly more than 1,000 men under arms.
7. The Palestine Liberation Front, also supported by Iraq has a few hundred followers.
8. The Palestine Popular Front, a small personalized organization

led by Dr. Samir Ghosheh, comprises only a few hundred followers.

Al-Fatah, As-Saiqa, the Popular Democratic Front for the Liberation of Palestine, the Popular Front–General Command, and the Arab Liberation Front are represented on the PLO's Executive Committee. In addition to these organizations under the PLO umbrella, numerous other small groups and factions, such as Black September, operate through affiliation with the PLO. In December 1987, Palestinians on the West Bank and Gaza began a concerted uprising that quickly became known as the *intifada.* The PLO was quick to embrace and gain control of the movement, believing the world would focus attention on the Palestinian cause and point up the heavy-handed tactics employed by the Israelis to contain the *intifada.* The United States was especially responsive in the early stages of the *intifada.* Secretary of State George Schultz made a number of visits to the area hoping to win support for a U.S. "peace" plan. King Hussain of Jordan complicated efforts, however, when in July 1988 he announced that Jordan would no longer assume responsibility for West Bank schools and hospitals or for workers' salaries in the region. The king went on record arguing that the PLO was the responsible party in the West Bank. Although the United States was committed to the security of Israel, it heavily criticized the Israeli government for the killing of stone-throwers, the incarceration of thousands, and the deportation of Palestinian leaders. Shortly thereafter, the PLO announced in November 1988 the establishment of an independent Palestinian state and declared Yasir Arafat its president. Arafat's statements appeared to extend PLO recognition to the state of Israel, although that recognition remained ambiguous. Although Arafat was denied a visa to visit the United States in 1988, by 1989 the United States was engaged in informal talks with members of the PLO through its ambassador in Tunisia. Those talks broke off when Arafat was linked with an abortive terrorist raid on Israel, something he had said he would not sanction. PLO fortunes rose and fell very quickly in 1990–1991 when the organization gave its support to Iraq in the latter's invasion and annexation of Kuwait. Anticipating the spread of Iraqi power throughout the Arabian Peninsula, the PLO gambled that destiny was on its side. Moreover, it anticipated a new war with Israel that would gain the territory required for the creation of a Palestinian entity. The Kuwaiti crisis instead split the Arab world and turned many of the Arab states, theretofore supporters, against the PLO. The principal source of revenue enjoyed by the PLO was lost in the aftermath of Operation Desert Storm, and the PLO's future, as well as that of Yasir Arafat, appeared to hang in the balance. ***See*** Chapter 5: "Israelis and Palestinians." ***See also*** LEBANESE CIVIL WAR, 1975–1976 (250); CAIRO AGREEMENT, 1969 (200); ISRAELI-PLO WAR, 1982 (249); PLO EXODUS FROM BEIRUT (174); INTIFADA (151).

Significance
The Palestine Liberation Organization was created in the belief that Palestinian Arab claims could be better projected by an identifiable and unified Palestinian front. Between 1948 and 1964, the Palestinians were more inclined to defer to the established Arab states. Many Palestine refugees were organized into armed bands of *fedeyeen* (warriors of Islam) by Arab governments, especially in Egypt under the leadership of Gamal Abdul Nasser. Growing frustration with these governments, however, prompted greater independence. In the 1950s, Palestinian students at Stuttgart University in

West Germany organized Al-Fatah (Conquest). It was soon led by Yasir Arafat, one of those students and a cousin of the last *mufti* of Jerusalem. Arafat fled Jerusalem with his family after the eruption of hostilities between the new state of Israel and the armies of the Arab League in 1948. In the 1950s Al-Fatah supported the Algerian Liberation Movement in its war against the French. Following Algeria's independence, Al-Fatah established a training base there. With assistance from Egypt, Arafat's forces began terrorist strikes inside Israel and soon established their preeminence among the Palestinian organizations. In May 1964, East Jerusalem, then under Jordanian control, was the site for the first Palestinian National Congress. This congress gave birth to the PLO, but it was not until the 1967 war with Israel that the organization received special recognition. Amidst humiliation, defeat, and loss of territory, Yasir Arafat's Al-Fatah held off a determined Israeli force at the Jordanian village of Karameh, and in so doing legitimated the organization and raised its leader to new heights in the Arab world. The Palestinian National Covenant was drafted and proclaimed the following year under PLO aegis. Armed struggle, not diplomacy, became the PLO's central theme. Total victory was its objective. The growing strength of the PLO was used to arouse the Palestinians in Jordan to greater efforts, not only against Israel, but also against the Hashemite monarchy of King Hussain. Facing retaliatory blows by Israeli forces for PLO forays against Jewish settlements, and especially embarrassed by the PLO's use of Jordanian airfields as sanctuaries for terrorist skyjackings, King Hussain ordered his Arab Legion to constrain the Palestinians. The consequence of this order was a bloody encounter between the Palestinians and Royal Jordanian forces. Despite Syrian movements in behalf of the PLO, Arafat's organization was badly mauled in the encounter. Estimates of casualties ran between several hundred to more than several thousand dead. No less significant, the PLO was compelled to shift its main operations to Syria and Lebanon. The appearance of the PLO in Lebanon tipped a delicate balance between Christian Phalange and indigenous Muslim elements. Moreover, with the PLO insistent on using Lebanon as its principal base of operations against Israel, Lebanese society was brought under Israeli guns. The dispute between Christians and Muslims and between conservatives and radicals in Lebanon had deep roots. In 1958, the U.S. government had ordered troops onto Lebanese soil to stabilize a shaky political system. The activities of the PLO reactivated and intensified old controversies. The result was a breakdown of law and order, paralysis in the Lebanese government, division in its armed forces—and ultimately a full-blown civil war that commenced in 1975. Given Palestinian assistance to the Lebanese opposition, the ruling Christian Phalange faced almost certain defeat. Syria, however, sent its armed forces into the country and attacked the PLO in its principal bases. The Syrian intervention turned the tide of battle, and the Phalange was able to regroup and sustain its position in East Beirut. The PLO lost several thousand men in the clash. No less important, it was made dependent on the Syrian government. Syria occupied a good portion of Lebanon and offered the PLO assistance in its struggle against Israel. The PLO's principal bases were located in southern Lebanon, in proximity to Israel, and Syria became its primary support base. The joint Syrian-PLO pressure on Israel's northern border precipitated Israeli counterblows. Moreover, Lebanese living in the southern region sought Israeli help in warding off PLO attacks on their villages. The PLO maintained an army of approximately 10,000 men in southern Lebanon. In 1978 Israel raided the region to neutralize the PLO threat, but hostilities continued. In 1981, an understanding was arrived at between Israel and its major antagonists, especially Syria. It specified that Syria would restrain the PLO and prevent future attacks on Israel; Israel promised to respect the frontier between Lebanon and the Jewish state. In 1982, however, after several terrorist attacks against Israel and Israelis abroad, Israel again retaliated. Air raids were made against PLO bases and camps, and Beirut was bombed. In June, Israel moved an invasion force into Lebanon, destroyed PLO bases in the south, and surrounded Beirut. After weeks of heavy shelling and bombing, the PLO agreed to move their forces and headquarters from Beirut, and they were scattered to a number of Arab countries.

Despite PLO determination to destroy Israel, the PLO has never achieved its cherished goal of unity. The differences that separate Arab governments still separate factions within the PLO. Yasir Arafat has sustained his leadership of the PLO through control of Al-Fatah, but he is not above criticism. Rebel organizations within the organization openly seek Arafat's removal from the PLO; so, too, have leaders of Arab governments. Anwar el-Sadat became a foe of the PLO and Yasir Arafat, as a result of the Egyptian president's peace overtures to Israel. Conflicts between the PLO and Jordan as well as Syria are parts of the record. Muammar Qaddafi, Libya's dominant personality, violently opposed to Sadat, also criticized Arafat's diplomatic approach to the Arab-Israeli question. Qaddafi supported an armed uprising against Arafat's leadership in 1983. Arafat weathered that storm with the help of the Israelis, who provided him with safe passage from the scene of the siege that took the lives of many under his command. The declaration of a Palestinian state in 1988 with Arafat at its head was a strong indication that he had not yet lost his grip on Palestinian affairs. It also pointed to the absence of successful substitutes to replace Arafat as the leader of the organization. The assassination of Salah Khalaf, second in command to Yasir Arafat in the PLO, in Tunis on January 16, 1991, illustrated the continuing difficulties of the loose congeries. The PLO's security chief also died on that occasion. It was believed both men had been killed because they did not support Arafat's decision to stand with Saddam Hussain in the latter's confrontation with the U.S.-led coalition. A clue to the killing of Arafat's aides was the murder of Rafiq Shafiq Qiblawi, known as Abu Ziad, a deputy speaker of the Palestine National Council and an important officer in the PLO. He had publicly condemned Saddam Hussain for his invasion of Kuwait, and his death on January 29, 1991, was judged connected to Saddam Hussain's agents. It is notable that he had been expelled from Iraq and was killed in Kuwait. These developments, connected with the general opprobrium in which the Palestinians were held in liberated Kuwait and victorious Saudi Arabia, raised new questions about the PLO's capacity to enter into a meaningful dialogue with the Israelis. Indeed, the Israelis, in the wake of Iraq's defeat by the coalition, insisted that negotiations would have to be conducted at two levels, one with the established Arab states and the other with Palestinians unconnected to the PLO. Palestinian spokesmen at the Madrid peace conference, according to Arafat, no matter how they were selected, and irrespective of the pressures, represented the PLO—and the PLO remained the sole representative of the Palestinian people.

Phalanges Libanaises (Kata'ib) 138

The Lebanese Phalange was organized in November 1936 as a Christian youth club. The Phalange was a reaction to concerted moves by Syrian nationalists and Lebanese Muslims to unify their respective activities. The Phalange was the Christian Lebanese answer to the Muslim plan, which, if successful, would have allowed Syria to reabsorb Lebanon. The Christian Lebanese opposed such a design, insisting on the independence and territorial integrity of Lebanon. The Phalangists were essentially Christian Maronites. The Greek Orthodox Christians did not join the party, and, in fact, one of their leaders, Antun Sa'ada, had founded the Syrian National Party in 1932. The National Party supported the move for union with Syria. The Phalange was modelled after the paramilitary organizations that operated in Italy in the 1930s under the fascist leadership of Benito Mussolini. It was led in those early years by Pierre Gemayel, a young Maronite pharmacist who continued to play a leading role in the party in the decades following World War II. The Lebanese Muslims attempted to balance the power of the Phalange by forming their own paramilitary organization, the Najjada, or Muslim Scouts. Thus the political lines were drawn according to sectarian interests, and partisan activity was heightened. The French also played a role in the formation of the Phalange. The Franco-Syrian Treaty of 1936 precipitated another treaty with Lebanon, making each independent and sovereign, but allied with France. Paris insisted on maintaining military bases in both countries, and the Syrian and Lebanese armies were to be organized under French guidance. The treaties established France as the primary power in Syria and Lebanon, and their governments were brought firmly under French influence. The French-controlled Lebanese legislature approved the terms of the treaty, but the Muslim population of Lebanon was unreconciled, sensing permanent separation from Syria and the perpetuation of Christian Maronite power. Anti-Christian rioting caused numerous casualties. It also convinced the Maronites of the necessity of forming the Phalange. The Phalange was deemed to be the answer to Muslim power in the streets of Lebanon, and a youthful force of Christian Maronites was drawn from the dominant *zaim*, the paternalistic leaders of the landed gentry, tribal, and religious groups. In the face of these private paramilitary organizations, the Lebanese army was never a fully integrated, nationally committed force. The French pressed the unwritten National Pact (*al-mithaq al watani*) on the Lebanese political associations in 1943. The pact represented a compromise between the country's religious communities, in which the president of the nation would always be a Maronite Christian, the prime minister would be a Sunni Muslim, and the speaker of the assembly would be a Shiite Muslim. A numerical formula was also devised placing the Christians in a majority position. Representation in the Chamber of Deputies was fixed at six Christians to every five non-Christians. Although the Muslim community adopted the formula, its displeasure was obvious and remained a source of conflict. Moreover, Lebanese politics could not fully develop given the continuation of the *zaim* (plural *zuama*) system of clannish, self-contained leaders. Although the Phalange developed into a political party, its rival *zuama* emphasized their private objectives more than the organization's larger purpose. If unity was achieved, it was only because of the threat posed to Christian preeminence by the various Muslim groups and sects. The collapse of French administration in

Lebanon during World War II placed the British in a pivotal role in the country. The British pressured the French to give up all their mandatory claims to the region and to provide Lebanon with full independence. In 1944, both the United States and the Soviet Union recognized Lebanese sovereignty; in 1945 Lebanon was offered charter membership in the United Nations. By 1946, Lebanon was fully independent, the French were eased out of all important administrative offices, and both British and French armies were withdrawn from the country. Lebanon had already extracted from the Arab states their recognition of Lebanese sovereignty and independence. Independent Lebanon was characterized by religious, ethnic, and tribal diversity organized around clannish systems with relatively ineffective political party organization. Under the National Pact, however, the Phalange emerged as the most influential body in the immediate post–World War II years. Lebanon was an Arab state, but practiced neutrality in most conflicts seizing the Arab nations. It maintained distance from the Arab-Israeli dispute, while at the same time providing moral support for the Arab cause. Lebanon also insisted on its neutrality during the period of the Cold War, but favored the West. Generally speaking, Lebanese society settled to the task of constructing a modern state with a strong financial and commercial substructure. In the years that followed, it quickly developed a reputation as a cosmopolitan state more inclined toward international business than international politics. The only threat to Lebanon in the 1950s and 1960s was from Syria. The Greater Syria notion involved Lebanon's absorption, but the Phalange was determined to maintain the territorial integrity of the Lebanese state and the political influence of the Christian community. The 1956 Suez War, however, had severe consequences for Lebanon. Phalange President Camille Chamoun's decision to defy the Arab League call to all Arab states to sever ties with Britain and France created even larger divisions within Lebanese society. Lebanese Muslims admired Gamal Abdul Nasser, and their sympathies were with his leadership, not with their own president. Furthermore, Chamoun leaned more decidedly toward the West when he publicly accepted President Dwight D. Eisenhower's policy of preventing the penetration of the Middle East by international communism, the Eisenhower Doctrine. Chamoun's actions embittered his foes and threatened the National Pact and the system built upon it. Thus, when Chamoun attempted to extend his term of office, the criticism levelled against his regime developed into a full-blown rebellion. The coup that overthrew the pro-Western Hashemite dynasty in Iraq in July 1958 had repercussions in Lebanon. Fearing that the Lebanese government was also in jeopardy, and that the Soviet Union was gaining influence in the region, President Eisenhower landed a sizable U.S. military contingent on the beaches at Beirut, and an embryonic civil war was neutralized. The Muslims of Lebanon did not forgive the Phalange president for inviting the U.S. forces to intervene. Although Chamoun was compelled to relinquish the presidency, the National Pact political system was sustained. Lebanon, however, continued to seethe with discontent. At the same time, rivalry between Christian *zuama* undermined the Phalange. By 1970 these weaknesses were in greater evidence. King Hussain's army had chased the Palestine Liberation Organization (PLO) from Jordan, and a new base was established in Lebanon. Supported by Muslim Lebanese, Druze, and Greek Orthodox Christians, the PLO proved the catalyst for a major upheaval. The

Phalange Maronites did not want the PLO using Lebanon as a base for attacks on Israeli villages, but the government was unable to prevent the guerrillas from establishing themselves in strongholds throughout the country. PLO headquarters was situated in the Muslim sector of Beirut, while mainline PLO units forced the inhabitants from southern Lebanon. The attempt to create a *Fatahland* in the south, with direct supply routes to Syria, did not suit the Maronite community. Clashes between Lebanese authority and the PLO proved to be the spark that ignited the Lebanese Civil War in 1975.

The civil war raged between the various communities and virtually destroyed the Lebanese army, which was led principally by Phalange Christians. The Greek Orthodox Christians, however, remained steadfast in their support for the Muslims against the Maronites. Maronite forces were no match for the combined armies of Lebanese Muslims and the PLO, and their ranks were soon decimated. It was at this juncture that Syria decided to enter the struggle, but instead of assisting the Muslims against the Phalange, they moved to the defense of the Christians and took a heavy toll on the PLO. The Syrian intervention brought much of the country under Syrian administration. No effort was made to annex Lebanon; indeed, Damascus approved a Christian Maronite, Elias Sarkis, to be the new president of Lebanon. Syria confined the Phalange to particular enclaves near Beirut and on the outskirts, but it did not totally subdue them. In time, the PLO came under Syrian influence, and a shaky balance was maintained between Muslim Lebanese and PLO forces and those of the Phalange. Sporadic fighting, however, continued into the 1980s between the various communities and between various rivals within each camp. Lebanon suffered more than 60,000 dead in the civil war. Its commercial life was a shambles, and its cities, especially Beirut, lay in ruin. Moreover, the government of Elias Sarkis was merely symbolic. Real power resided in the Syrian forces, the PLO, and the Phalange Maronites. Neither the PLO nor Syria showed any interest in stabilizing Lebanese society, maximum attention being given to the struggle against Israel. Israel, however, had linked forces with Major Saad Haddad and his Christian troops in southern Lebanon. Their cooperative effort sought to keep the PLO at a distance from the Israeli frontier. Skirmishes between opposing forces were commonplace, and the PLO, through Syria, began a significant military preparedness program that caused a crisis in the summer of 1981. An Israeli air raid on Beirut in July 1981 was directed at PLO emplacements and command centers, but because the installations were located in crowded refugee centers, approximately 300 civilians died in the attack. At this point the Syrians began fortifying the Bekaa Valley near Beirut with ground-to-air missiles. The Israelis demanded their removal, but the Syrians rejected the demand. A U.S. emissary, Philip Habib, negotiated a temporary settlement that involved promises on all sides to restrain their forces. However, violations occurred. PLO terrorism could not be restrained, and Israeli retaliation was swift. The wounding of the Israeli ambassador to Great Britain by a PLO splinter group unleashed the fury of the Israeli armed forces. In June 1982, major Israeli forces swept across the Lebanese frontier and moved north, capturing PLO strongholds and destroying its forces. Syrian efforts to blunt the Israeli drive were futile as Israel quickly gained mastery of the skies and eliminated the missile installations in the Bekaa Valley. Israel's forces surrounded Beirut and eventually linked up with the Phalange Christians, who now sensed the opportunity to reestablish their lost prestige. The removal of mainline PLO forces from West Beirut in August 1982 gave the Phalange an opportunity to consolidate its power. Phalange leader Bashir Gemayel was declared president-elect, but before he could assume office a bomb was detonated in his headquarters, and he died with a number of his aides. Next, the Israeli army entered West Beirut in violation of the understanding that had obtained the PLO withdrawal. The Israelis argued that their presence in West Beirut was necessary to prevent sectarian strife in the wake of Gemayel's death. They also used the opportunity to defeat Lebanese Muslim contingents still based in West Beirut and supportive of the PLO. Because Lebanese Muslims were believed to be harboring PLO fighters, elements of the Phalange militia supporting the Israeli drive were permitted to enter the Palestinian refugee camps in West Beirut, ostensibly to identify and eliminate PLO units.

On September 18, 1982, the world was horrified to learn that the Phalangists had arbitrarily seized men, women, and children and, in a fit of vengeance, had executed hundreds of defenseless inhabitants of the camps. The atrocity raised a storm of condemnation all over the world. Moreover, the possibility that the Phalange could restore Lebanon's equilibrium now appeared more distant than ever. The passing of the Phalange's great leaders, Pierre Gemayel and Camille Chamoun, left the party in the hands of lesser figures long nurtured by the civil war. These were men who knew little about compromise. Nor did they have the authority to demand the obedience of large followings. Lebanon's mosaic society was shattered in the 1970s. Where previously there was relative stability, now there was only chaos and disorder. Palestinian-Shiite wars, such as the one that took 2,500 lives in 1985, continued to flare. Syrian-backed Amal units exchanged rounds with Iranian-supported Hizbollah contingents. Palestinians also fought one another, as in the 1988 conflict in Ain Hilwe and again in Shatila and Burj al-Baranjeh. Through it all the Phalange could do nothing to restore law and order. It could not even put its own house in order. Michel Aoun had himself proclaimed president of Lebanon and the successor to Amin Gemayel, but this act was challenged by Syria, which had assumed major responsibility for policing Lebanon in the wake of the 1982 Israeli incursion. Ultimately, it was Syria's writ that carried. Elias Hrawi, selected by Damascus and approved by the Phalange and other established parties among the Sunni and Shiite Muslims, assumed the presidency in 1990 following modifications in the Lebanese government. In 1991 Syrian forces destroyed Aoun's militia, and the issue, for the moment, was resolved. The warring militias agreed to withdraw from Beirut so the new government would have a chance to consolidate its gains and administer to the nation's needs. But it was obvious the Phalange was no longer a driving force in Lebanese politics and possibly would never be again. ***See also*** MARONITES (92); LEBANESE CIVIL WAR, 1975–1976 (250); ISRAELI-PLO WAR, 1982 (249); WEST BEIRUT MASSACRE (187); LEBANON CIVIL WAR: THE PROLONGED MIDDLE STAGE, 1983–1991 (251); LEBANON CIVIL WAR: THE CONCLUDING PHASE (252).

Significance

The Lebanese Phalange has always required outside support to maintain its supremacy. The French were instrumental in providing the Lebanese Maronites with political power. They also developed the system whereby the Maronites were to have permanent control over the country.

In return for this support the Christian Arabs of Lebanon were more interested in Western pursuits, and particularly in commercial and financial rewards, than in joining the struggle against Israel and Zionism. Dissatisfaction with the Maronites and the Phalange, however, had deep roots, and the rivalry between the major actors was always tense and bitter. The intervention of the United States in Lebanese affairs in 1958 quieted the situation for several more years. But the establishment of principal PLO operations in Lebanon in the 1970s was bound to upset a precarious equilibrium. With the Phalange facing imminent destruction, the Syrians entered the fray, surprisingly to counter the power of the PLO and assorted Muslim factions. Again the Phalange was preserved, but in a significantly weakened state. The Israeli invasion of Lebanon in 1982, therefore, was aimed at resurrecting the Phalange and the Maronite community. Its principal aim was the destruction of the PLO, but it also sought the removal of Syrian forces, the reconstitution of Lebanon under terms of the National Pact of 1943, and the modification as well as reiteration of Lebanon's nationhood in the Lebanese National Covenant of 1976. A stabilized Lebanon, neutral and progressive, was not only the aim of the Israelis, but it was also the objective of the Phalange Maronites. The difficulty of achieving a stable Lebanon was tragically illustrated by the assassination of Bashir Gemayel, son of Pierre Gemayel and president-elect of Lebanon. His death on September 14, 1982, was attributed to his close association with Israel and the belief that he intended to sign a peace treaty with the Israelis. The atrocities inflicted on Palestinian refugees in retaliation for Gemayel's murder as well as other acts of violence guaranteed continuing hostility between Lebanese communities, the PLO, and external forces. The Phalange demonstrated little capacity to heal Lebanon's deep wounds. Nevertheless, the Lebanese government went about the business of selecting still another president. On September 21, 1982, Amin Gemayel, older brother of the slain Bashir Gemayel, was made Lebanon's new president. But the civil war raged on throughout his tenure. In the succession that followed, the Phalange ceased to be even a semblance of its former self. France was also no longer a vital actor in the Lebanese scene. Although Syria had not annexed Lebanon, and indeed might not do so given world reaction to Iraq's attempt to annex Kuwait, Lebanon was firmly in Syrian hands. In effect, Syria substituted for both the Phalange and France, as it sought to bring peace to a region that had known so little of it in 20 years. Moreover, if Syria really desired peace in Lebanon, it could do no less than promote tranquility in the general area, namely, with Israel.

Political Parties: Israel *139*

The principal political parties of Israel were organized before the creation of the state in 1948. The numerous political groupings reflect the variety of demographic and functional as well as cultural and philosophical differences among the Zionist community. The multiparty system also provided Palestine Jewry, and later the state of Israel, with its pluralistic character. The Jews of Palestine are politically fragmented. No political organization prior to the creation of Israel, or following its establishment, has ever commanded a majority of the popular vote. The system of proportional representation wherein even a very small organization is capable of acquiring a seat or two in the Israeli Knesset (parliament) reinforces this political divisiveness. Moreover, politics is often bitter, and always controversial. Differing philosophies, ideologies, and party programs produce heated exchanges in the Knesset, the media, and throughout society. Coalition governments, those comprising a number of organizations, are tenuous arrangements, and the environment in which they operate is often superheated by invective and criticism. Nevertheless, Israel has had a largely stable political party history. From the creation of the state in 1948 until 1977, one party, the Mapai, was preeminent. From 1977 to 1992, Herut played a similar role. Neither Mapai nor Herut commanded absolute majorities, but their authority at the head of Israel's coalition governments had never been questioned. The following describes Israel's political parties.

The Mapai (Labor) was established in 1930. Its subsidiary groups in the labor coalition were the Ahdut Ha'avoda–Poalei Zion (1944) and the Rafi–Israel Labor List (1968). In the Knesset, Mapai has been aligned with Mapam, which has always been more to the left and radical. Although Mapai is a socialist party, Mapam (United Worker's Party) is extremist and sometimes identified with Israel's communist organizations. Mapai derived from the Histadrut (General Confederation of Labor), the preeminent labor association, organized in 1920 and still a dominant force in Israeli politics. Ahdut Avoda (Labor Unity) was formed from the amalgamation of Poale Zion (Zion Workers) and lesser groups. Ahdut Avoda, with an assist from Hapoel Hatzir, created Histadrut before fusing their organizations to form Mapai. Mapai's power, therefore, derived from the unification of the Labor movement and the influence it exerted through the Histadrut. Histadrut not only controlled the labor unions, but also was the dominant force throughout the Zionist economy. In addition, Histadrut published a major newspaper, dominated the arts and theater, and provided for the community's health services. Because of Histadrut's multidimensional operations, its alliance with Mapai made the latter the dominant political force prior to and following the independence of the state. Through the charismatic leadership of David Ben-Gurion, Mapai also had leadership roles inside the World Zionist Organization, the Jewish Agency, the National Council, and Haganah.

Likud (Union) defeated the Mapai-Labor Coalition in the 1977 election and dominated Israeli politics until June 1992. The five-party coalition was constructed from: (1) Herut (Freedom), organized in 1925 as the Union of Zionist Revisionists; (2) the Israel Liberal Party, successor to the General Zionists, organized in 1931 (in 1965 Herut and the Liberal Party organized the Gahal—Gush Herut Liberalim); (3) the La'am (Toward the People), comprising three factions, the Free Centre Party, the State List, and the Greater Land of Israel Movement; (4) Shlomzion (General "Arik" Sharon's party); and (5) Ahdut (Unity), an offshoot of the Independent Liberal Party. Likud was formed in 1973 with the specific goal of retaining the territorial gains acquired in the 1967 war. Although Likud drew support from Labor dissidents, its philosophy has been conservative, capitalist, and more religious than Mapai or the Labor coalition. Agudat Israel, founded in 1912, is the country's leading religious party with its headquarters in Jerusalem. The parent organization of the religious parties is the Misrachi (Spiritual Centre), formed in 1902 as one of the first Zionist political factions. Misrachi insisted that Zionism was a form of religious expression and that Jews could only realize their religious ideals in a state governed by Jewish precepts. In 1922, Hapoel Hamizrachi (Mizrachi Worker) was formed to accommodate the new secular socialism that influenced the pioneer community. In 1956 the two dominant religious parties formed the National Religious Party. Another religious party, Poelei Agudat Israel (Orthodox Labor), was organized in 1923. Together with the other religious parties, Poelei Agudat Israel emphasizes the supremacy of the Torah (Sacred Scripture). Generally speaking, the religious parties believe the Torah is all the constitution Israel requires.

Among Israel's numerous other parties and factions is the Democratic Movement for Change (DMC), founded in 1976. Formed from the Shinui (Change), a protest movement organized in the wake of the 1973 war, and the Democratic Movement, representing intellectuals alienated from both Mapai-Labor and Likud, the DMC also attracted previously nonpolitical elements who desired electoral reform and a more stable political party system. Philosophically, however, the DMC is closer to Mapai-Labor than to the Likud.

Other currently active Israeli parties include the Democratic Front for Peace and Equality, founded in 1977 and dominated by Rakah (Reshima Communist Hadasha). This communist organization is supported by the Israel Black Panthers, organized by dissident Jews who have immigrated to Israel from Arab countries, especially Yemen, and independent Arab organizations. Shelli is another socialist party organized in 1977. The Independent Liberal Party is a successor to the Progressive Party; the Citizens Rights Movement was organized in 1973, and the Flatto-Sharon one-man party was assembled in 1977. *See also* INTIFADA (151).

Significance
Israeli political parties are an assortment of ideological and personalistic organizations that are in constant flux. There are, however, four discernible political divisions: (1) labor/socialist; (2) conservative/ secular; (3) religious; and (4) reform/liberal. All the major groupings are Zionist, although gradations and emphases vary. Labor dominated the political scene from independence to 1977 and continues to represent the principal opposition. Since their surprising victory in 1977, the conservatives have clung to power in the Knesset. They also have been assisted by the religious parties and other splinter groups that insist on a more decisive program than that offered by Labor. The Labor bloc began losing votes to the Conservatives in the mid-1960s, and their decline was accelerated by the 1973 war, which caught the government unprepared. Prime Minister Golda Meir, Defense Minister Moshe Dayan, and Foreign Minister Abba Eban, all luminaries in the party, were forced from office. In 1974, a former chief of staff of the Israeli defense forces, Yitzhak Rabin, was called to form a new government. Labor was forced to ally itself with Rafi and Ahdut Avoda, but its attempts to placate philosophically different parties and its inability to prevent fractures within its own ranks identified the party as inept and weak. Indecision on important defense and economic issues further lost popularity for the organization. Held responsible for one of the highest inflation rates in the world, and with taxation at oppressive levels, the party was scandalized by accusations that ministers had misused public funds. Finally, reports that the prime minister and his wife had established undeclared bank accounts in the United States toppled the government and did great damage to the party. The discrediting of its leadership and the apparent disarray within the Labor Party caused numerous defections, leading to the creation of the Democratic Movement for Change (DMC). In the 1977 election the DMC drew away the votes needed to prevent the conservative Likud from

gaining power. The success of the Likud, therefore, was not its publicized platform, but rather a consequence of Labor's decline. Likud, however, came to power with the stated policy of reconstructing a strong, viable state capable of addressing both domestic and international issues. Although slated for defeat in the Knesset, Likud managed to retain power. Its continuance at the helm of Israeli affairs was linked to an international posture that emphasized control of the West Bank and Gaza Strip territories, the annexation of the Golan Heights, the peace treaty with Egypt, and the complete withdrawal from the Sinai. Moreover, the 1982 invasion of Lebanon, which was aimed at neutralizing, if not destroying, the military capability of the Palestine Liberation Organization, also rallied the coalition. The Likud suffered a major scare if not a setback in the 1984 elections. Neither Likud nor Labor could form a government. After protracted efforts it was finally decided to form a national unity government with the unique arrangement that the leader of Labor, Shimon Peres, would serve as Israel's prime minister for the first two years of the term, and Yitzhak Shamir would fill the post in the last two years. The two men also shared the position of foreign minister during this period, but in reverse order. Labor's opportunity came with significant rifts in the ranks of Likud. It was less significant that 26 parties competed in the 1984 elections. Despite the awkward arrangement, the national unity government held, and in 1986 Peres stepped aside for his rival Shamir. Peres had been pressured to dissolve the government and hold new elections, but he resisted, insisting he had made a deal in good faith. Peres nonetheless had a difficult tenure given his efforts at finding a solution for the Palestinian question. Accusing Peres of softheadedness, Likud continued to undermine his and Labor's support within the changing Israeli population, now far more representative of Oriental Jewry. The Palestinian *intifada* therefore played a major role in the 1988 elections. Although Peres sought to present a new Labor Party free from the overwhelmingly Ashkenazic party of the past, attention was more riveted on Peres's peace plan, which promised to return the Occupied Territories to Jordan in the context of an international peace conference. But the intifada had begun and Jordan had indicated it no longer wished to play a role in the West Bank, thus leaving Peres exposed and his party embarrassed. Still the November 1988 polls revealed a virtual tie between Labor and Likud. But the religious parties threw in their lot with the conservatives, and this time Shamir was able to establish a government without Labor's cooperation. In March 1992, foreign minister David Levi announced his resignation, accusing Shamir and his close associates of maligning Sephardic Jews. Although Levi was eventually pressured by Shamir to remain in the cabinet, his accusations provided Labor with the ammunition it needed in the June 1992 elections. The elections, won handily by Labor, ended Likud's 15-year domination of the Israeli government and promised significant changes in foreign policy and the approach to the Palestinian question.

Political Parties: Pakistan 140

Pakistan entered a new era with the death of General-President Mohammad Zia-ul-Haq in August 1988. The country was politically energized more than it had been since the first parliamentary phase (1947–1958) was terminated by a declaration of martial law. Political parties were difficult to represent after that event and the country learned to manage without them. The Zulfikar Ali Bhutto interregnum (1971–1977) returned a modicum of civilian-political life to Pakistan, but Bhutto's paternalistic/authoritarian character colored his time in office and the political parties were never seriously engaged in reflecting popular aspirations. Moreover, Pakistan experienced few national elections. The first was not held until 1970 and it precipitated a civil war and the loss of East Pakistan, now Bangladesh. The second election was experienced in 1977, and it raised a storm of protest that ultimately swept Bhutto from office and presaged his death on the gallows in 1979. Bhutto's successor, General Zia-ul-Haq, took the reins of government under martial law (lifted only in 1985) and ruled Pakistan with an iron hand. Zia called for partyless politics and conducted an election in 1985, Pakistan's third such national experience, on that basis. Zia's regulated and controlled political experience left the politicians and their organizations more or less on the sidelines. But his death, caused by an unexplained explosion aboard his military aircraft, provided Pakistan with new opportunities for political expression. In the fourth national election in November 1988, Benazir Bhutto and her Pakistan People's Party (PPP) won sufficient seats in the National Assembly to install her as prime minister of a civilian-dominated government. There was much discussion of Pakistan's return to democracy. The elections had been conducted along party lines, and the results revealed the divisions that Prime Minister Benazir Bhutto would have to bridge to run a successful administration. She failed to accomplish that task. Her party failed to carry Pakistan's most populous and influential province, the Punjab, where the Islami Jamhoori Ittehad (IJI) held forth. In her native province of Sind she had to content herself with still another opposition party, the Mohajir Qaumi Movement (MQM), which dominated the politics of the country's commercial capital, Karachi. Benazir's weaknesses were evident and in August 1990, less than two years into her term, she and her government were dismissed by President Ghulam Ishaq Khan, who called for new elections. The next round of elections was conducted in October 1990 and the results revealed some changes, but also a crystallization of the political forces. Nine parties, not including independents, won seats in the National Assembly. The IJI, however, proved the big winner, in effect becoming the first national party since the Muslim League lost its credibility in the mid-1950s. The IJI was led by Mian Nawaz Sharif, a Punjabi and a former supporter of the late General Zia. The IJI secured 105 seats in the parliament. It also was able to establish governments in all the four provinces of Pakistan. The PPP pursued the election under the coalition banner of the People's Democratic Alliance (PDA), but even this tactic won only 45 seats in the legislature. The MQM, the next-biggest winner, confined to Karachi and the southern region of Sind Province, obtained 15 seats; independents won 13 seats; and 20 seats were shared by the 6 other contesting parties.

Significance

The Pakistani political parties are only now beginning to evolve. The PPP is not the same party that was organized by Zulfikar Ali Bhutto in the 1960s, and with which he gained power in 1971. The PPP then was an ideologically driven party, verbalizing socialism but practicing features of fascism. The PPP today is a splinter of the older organization, held together by the wife and daughter of the martyred Bhutto. The victimization of Bhutto and his family members was sufficient to propel Benazir into the prime minister's office, but it could not sustain the party or her government. The IJI of Nawaz

Sharif enlists some of the more conservative elements in Pakistani society, but it also appeals to those with feelings of disenfranchisement. It organized the many voters who had not been touched by the PPP, or indeed had been ignored by that organization. The IJI also appealed to the MQM and other smaller political organizations, assuring them that consensus politics was possible in Pakistan and that their voices would be registered in policy planning and implementation. The MQM is a case in point. The party represents the refugees who arrived from India following the partition of the subcontinent in 1947. More significantly, it represents the children of those earlier settlers, who sense that they are still judged refugees by the indigenous community despite their loyalty and contribution to the growth of Pakistan. The IJI, Punjabi-based, proved more sympathetic to MQM complaints than the Sind-based PPP. The political future of Pakistan is intertwined with the success of an expanding coalition of political organizations dedicated to constructing a community of diverse social and economic elements. Pakistan is a more politically conscious, more vital, more introspective society today, but the test of its civilian/political institutions is just beginning.

Radical Movements: Saudi Arabia 141

The occupation of the Kaaba Mosque in Mecca in 1979 by a group of religious extremists was a bizarre and totally unexpected occurrence on the Saudi Arabian scene. Before this event, only two forms of opposition were believed to exist in the country. The one form involved opposition from within the House of Saud. The extended family admitted to a number of rivalries, but no matter how intense, all have thus far been resolved within the family structure or muted. The other form of opposition exists outside the royal household. It has been radical and, generally speaking, seeks the destruction of the reigning power. These opposition groups have operated in Saudi Arabia since the 1940s, but they increased their activity in the 1950s and today represent a formidable force. Dissident operations have surfaced in Riyadh and Jidda, in the oil-producing region in the northeastern sector, and in a territorial zone bordering North Yemen. Radical supporters are usually found among families in Hejaz and Najd, long antagonists of the Saudi family. From time to time opposition members have had the support of elements in the armed forces and even the National Guard, which has the mission of protecting the royal family. No less significant is the support obtained from oilfield workers, both Saudis and foreigners. In the latter group are Egyptians, Palestinians, and Yemenis. The principal opposition groups have been identified as:

- The Arab Peninsula Peoples Union
- The Popular Front for the Liberation of the Arabian Peninsula
- The Revolutionary Najd Party
- The Popular Democratic Front in Saudi Arabia
- The Saudi Arabian National Liberation Front

None of these groups, however, has been either consistent or very successful. All seek to destroy what they describe as an autocratic, illegal, corrupt regime. They seek to replace it with a "people's republic" in which the "patriotic forces" are fully represented. They also call for the equal distribution of oil wealth among the population at large. The groups claim to be anti-imperialist and are therefore opposed to Saudi Arabia's ties to the West, especially the United States. They insist that they represent Arab nationalism and that there is no alternative to the use of violence against entrenched authority. All the radical groups identify with the Palestine Liberation Organization, but particularly with the Popular Front for the Liberation of Palestine and the Popular Democratic Front for the Liberation of Palestine, two of the more extremist groups within the PLO. During Egyptian involvement in the Yemen war in the 1960s, Saudi Arabia was threatened by so-called revolutionary and progressive forces sponsored by Gamal Abdul Nasser. Nasser is alleged to have ordered the assassination of Saudi leaders, and several abortive coups were traced to Egyptian involvement. The most serious occurred in 1969 when members of the Saudi air force and officials of several ministries, including PETROMIN (responsible for petroleum production), were implicated and arrested. After Nasser's death, relations between Saudi Arabia and Egypt improved. South Yemen, however, began beaming anti-Saudi broadcasts into the kingdom and throughout the Arab world, and Libya actively supported guerrilla movements. Iraq also organized the Committee for the Defense of the Rights of the Saudi People. This group was an offshoot of the Saudi National Liberation Front, and it was believed to have contacts in Western Europe, notably in France, Italy, and Germany. In 1980 Iraq withdrew its support from this group, but it continued to operate with Libyan support. *See also* WAHHABIS (63); AL SAUD DYNASTY (68); ISLAMIC FUNDAMENTALISM (39).

Significance

Saudi Arabia is a major actor in international affairs. The economics of numerous countries depend on the stability of the desert kingdom. But Saudi Arabia is also a traditional Arabian construct in an age of rapid change and violent ideological and political clashes. Although none of the many radical opposition groups has achieved much success, their continued existence, spread, and persistence are a constant reminder of the fragility of the Saudi system. The force that emerged in Mecca with the dramatic seizure of the Kaaba Mosque strikes at the heart of the Saudi experience. This new form of opposition emerged against a backdrop of anti-Westernism. Its criticism of the Saudi government is in terms of religion, in part revitalized by the declarations and actions of Ayatollah Khomeini and his religious followers. Although the Saudis remain very conservative in their Islamic performance, the rapid process of modernization that has overtaken Saudi Arabia presents formidable problems for the regime. Foreign ideas and lifestyles do not blend with a society nurtured on religious norms and values. Too rapid modernization, as was noted in the Iranian revolution, can have a negative effect on the established order. It certainly endangers the administration. The Saudi leaders, therefore, seek to sustain their ties to a religious establishment that provides them with their legitimacy. The doctrine of Wahhabism has been sustained and re-emphasized, but Saudi performance is not always in harmony with declarations. The sophistication of the Saudi leadership and their supporters, their worldly outlook and programs, has moved them some distance from their austere creed. The fundamentalists who seized the Kaaba were reacting in the most dramatic fashion to the apparent hypocrisy practiced by the ruling house. Although the dissidents were eventually overwhelmed and executed for desecrating the holy site, the concern lingers that their cause has considerable popular support. Some observers believe that the danger to the Saudi system is greater from such popular fundamentalism than from radical, alien ideas and doctrines.

This also explains why the authorities accused the attackers of deviating from the precepts of Islam and may explain why Islamic law was cited in punishing them. Moreover, the Saudi government obtained a *fatwa* (a religious decree) from the country's theologians, authorizing it to use force in retaking the mosque. The destruction of sacred property in recapturing the holy site brought more criticism of the regime. But no less important in this event was the capacity for violence in the heart of Mecca by a group of poorly trained dissidents. Their ability to move arms into the city and to hold the mosque against a much larger Saudi force demonstrated a tenacity of purpose. It also has brought into question Saudi Arabia's security system.

Republican People's Party 142

The collapse of the Ottoman Empire during World War I prompted Turkish nationalists to find a nation-state solution for their confused and demoralized people. The formation of the Republican People's Party (RPP) was Mustafa Kemal Ataturk's response to the need for political organization. The father of the modern Turkish state founded the People's Party in 1923, and Ataturk was proclaimed its leader. Although other parties were tolerated so long as they did not jeopardize the security of the state, the People's Party controlled the government and policymaking, and through World War II the country remained a one-party dominant state. The principles of the party were publicized by Ataturk in 1931 as: (1) republican; (2) nationalist; (3) populist; (4) *etatist;* (5) secular; and (6) revolutionary. The principles implied an outright rejection of empire as well as all aspects of pan-Turanism, pan-Ottomanism, and pan-Islamism. Territorial nationalism was stressed. Maximum attention was placed on reconstructing a Turkish nation, essentially along European lines. According to Ataturk and the leaders of the People's Party, the primary objective was the modernization of the country, the streamlining of the administration, and the social transformation of the Turkish population. As leader of both the nation and the party, Ataturk was given authority to institute numerous reforms that described the Turkish conception of revolution. In 1932 the party opened the *Halkevis*, or People's Houses, all over the country. These politically managed cultural centers became the primary vehicle of organizational support. It was also from these local centers that party recruits were drawn for service in the vast government bureaucracy. The party was the major voice in the proclaiming of the Turkish Republic on October 29, 1923. In 1924, Ataturk, supported by the People's Party, abolished the Islamic caliphate and reorganized the country's religious administration. *Sharia,* or religious courts, were abolished, and Western-type courts took their place. Despite defections in the organization over these reforms, Ataturk's views prevailed, and the People's Party weathered challenges from the splinter organizations developed by the alienated leaders. On November 10, 1924, the People's Party was formally declared the Republican People's Party (RPP). Ataturk assumed dictatorial powers in 1925 following the Kurdish revolt and decreed a reduction in the number of Muslim "clergy." Religious orders were also suppressed. Religiously significant tombs were closed. The wearing of the fez was forbidden by law, and Western-type headgear was enacted into law. Women were discouraged from using the veil. In 1926 the RPP adopted the Gregorian calendar. A new civil code was adopted based upon the Swiss experience; the new criminal code followed an Italian design. The new commercial code was modelled after that found in Italy and Germany. Civil marriage was made compulsory. In the 1927 elections Ataturk was empowered to name all RPP candidates, and later that year he was unanimously elected president for a four-year term. In 1928 Turkey dropped Islam as a state religion, and the country was declared a secular state. In November 1928 Ataturk took the dramatic step of introducing the Latin alphabet. The Arabic script was discarded, and all Turks under 40 were required to pass an examination in the new alphabet or attend school to learn it. In 1930 women were granted the right to vote in municipal elections. By the time of his death in November 1938 Ataturk had revolutionized Turkish society and had set the nation on a path aimed at making it a full and equal member in the European state system. His successors, however, were challenged by a legacy they could not adequately manage. Ataturk's passing permitted various personalities and factions to surface, and although the RPP was initially successful in neutralizing their activities, the party could not sustain discipline in the wake of World War II. In January 1946 defectors from the RPP formed the Democratic Party (DP) and threatened the People's Party monopoly. Later that year a new electoral law provided for direct secret ballot, and in subsequent elections the Democrats won 61 of the 465 seats in the National Assembly. The Democratic Party used the opportunity provided by its place in the legislature to champion liberal causes. Its "Freedom Charter" of 1947 called for an end to arbitrary judgments, for elections supervised by the judiciary, and for the separation of party leadership from the presidency. Other parties were also sanctioned, and the National Party commenced operation in 1948. Both parties took advantage of the growing unpopularity of the RPP, and in the national elections of May 1950 the RPP suffered an ignominious defeat at the hands of the Democrats, who won 367 of 487 seats. Turkey showed the world that it had the capacity to hold a democratic election, but the country's political difficulties had only begun. The Democratic Party governed Turkey for the next decade, finally succumbing to a military coup in May 1960 that brought an end to Turkey's first republic. The coup also shattered the notion that free political debate would automatically lead to a smoothly operating democratic political process. The democratic Party had defeated the RPP because it promised the population more freedom as well as more prosperity. The DP, however, proved to be authoritarian, corrupt, and administratively inept. The student riots that precipitated the military takeover in 1960 focused on the suspension of political freedom, the imprisonment of ranking politicians, and the chaotic economy. The military judged itself the guardian of Turkey's independence and integrity, and it was determined to steer a new course for the nation. Under its leadership a new constitution was promulgated in 1961. The Democratic Party was dissolved, but the RPP could not make a full recovery. Coalition governments became the order of the day. The Justice Party was formed to take the place of the defunct Democratic Party, and power tended to shift back and forth between Justice and the RPP as the army continued to hold the balance between them. In the 1970s Turkey entered a period of exceptional instability, and the political institutions proved unable to meet society's needs. Moreover, terrorism coursed through the country, causing several thousand casualties each year. Extremism on both the Right and Left disrupted the routine of the universities, provoked the nationalities, and further dislocated an already hard-pressed economy. The RPP developed a more radical program during this period to enlist support from politicized students, intellectuals, and urban workers. The Justice Party also sought to ingratiate itself with a variety of socioeconomic groups, but the result was only further chaos. Governments were formed only to be shattered by increasing factionalism, such as the National Salvation Party, the Nationalist Action Party, and the Turkish Worker's Party, among others. In September 1980, the Turkish army again intervened and declared martial law. The political parties were banned and their leaders taken into custody. The military establishment believed it had no other choice if Turkey was to be saved from self-destruction. In 1982, the military authorities issued a new draft constitution that included a constitutional role for the armed forces. Political parties would eventually be permitted to operate, but no party would be allowed to organize or stand candidates for election if it was judged anti-state. The RPP could not survive the martial law period. It splintered into several smaller parties, each reflecting the philosophy of a different leader. Bulent Ecevit's attempt to steer the party along radical socialist lines failed to attract popular support, and the creation of a Social Democratic-Populist Party under Erdal Inonu, the son of one of the founders of the RPP, eliminated the RPP as a major contender. *See also* ETATISM (82); MOTHERLAND PARTY (134).

Significance

The Republican People's Party was the work of Mustafa Kemal Ataturk. When he died in 1938, the party could never reclaim the authority or the stature of the Ataturk years. The RPP therefore is associated with Kemalism, and it was the Turkish leader's performance that attracted emulators in other countries, e.g., Iran. Ataturk was in the vanguard of early Third World leaders seeking revolutionary change in their domestic conditions and sensing that traditional impediments prevented meaningful programs from reaching fruition. But Ataturk also belonged to another age. The post–World War I period was far different from the post–World War II period. After World War I it seemed plausible to copy the European nations. European imperialism was still potent, and power and prestige seemed to rest on specific institutional grounds that necessitated a departure from customary values and practices. After World War II, however, those same European nations that Ataturk admired had lost their vaunted preeminence, and power passed to the Americans on the one side and the Soviets on the other. Moreover, the new nations in the Third World were insistent on taking a course different from their former European overseers. Nasserism emphasized exploiting more indigenous properties, although it was less tradition-bound than Khomeiniism; both ideologies promised less in the way of emulation than Kemalism. Indeed, they both made a more concerted effort to dramatize the genius of a particular people and to reinvigorate their more narrowly defined historical legacies.

The spread of Marxism in the Third World was another response to Kemalism. To those members of developing countries who saw little future in the re-creation of traditional life, Marxism appeared to promise a current means of achieving stature, development, and influence. Although Marxist political parties survived the changes in the Soviet Union and they continued to press their views on the public, Turkish citizens were little impressed. The Turkish voters opted for Turgut Ozal's Motherland Party, Suleyman Demirel's True Path Party, and Erdal Inonu's Social Democratic-Populist Party. In the 1991 elections Demirel won a narrow victory, forcing the Motherland party prime minister to tender his resignation. The Motherland Party and Social Democratic-Populist Party were runner-ups in the results, with several Islamic fundamentalist and radical parties gathering the remaining votes. What was left of Bulent Ecevit's RPP, now the Democratic Left Party, garnered only 7 seats in the 450-member parliament.

Tudeh Party (143)

The Tudeh Party is Iran's communist party. *Tudeh* (masses) traces its origin to 1904, when the Persian Social Democratic Party was formed, and to the Iranian Justice Party, organized in 1917. The Tudeh leader in 1982 was Nur-ul-din Kianuri. The Tudeh in its present form was established by German-educated Marxist intellectuals in 1941. Within months it was the largest and best-organized political group in Iran. The Soviet Union gave it active support and resources during World War II, and the party was used by Moscow in its abortive attempt to create two socialist republics in northwestern Iran (Mahabad, or Kurdistan, and Azerbaijan) in 1945–1946. The Tudeh was banned in 1949 after an assassination attempt against the shah. It returned to play an active role in Iranian politics during the Mohammad Mossadegh period (1951–1953). It used the heightened nationalism caused by the nationalization of the Anglo-Iranian Oil Company and the subsequent attack on the monarchy to infiltrate the government and the country's armed forces. The shah's temporary exile in 1953 was in part attributed to the actions of the Tudeh, which sought to exploit the revolutionary situation. The counter-coup that forced Mossadegh from power and permitted the shah to return to Iran also provided the monarch with the opportunity to suppress the Tudeh. Between 1953 and 1957, Tudeh leaders and rank-and-file were hounded by the shah's security forces, notably the new secret police agency, SAVAK. Many Tudeh leaders were apprehended and executed. Others fled the country. Low-echelon communists repudiated the Tudeh and pledged loyalty to the shah. But the exiled party leaders were provided haven in the Soviet Union and East European countries. Some settled in the West, especially France and Germany. A major headquarters erected in East Germany generated propaganda opposed to the shah. "Radio Iran Courier" beamed broadcasts to Iran from East Germany, and party recruiters moved freely through the many Iranian student communities located in the West. The students harbored deep grievances against the shah, and the Tudeh found them willing accomplices even if they did not sympathize with or join the party. Indeed, the Tudeh was content to see the organization of other radical movements, especially as this allowed it to keep a low profile, to consolidate its organizational structure, and to avoid broad attacks on its personnel. When the revolution swept the shah from power in 1979, both the Soviets and the Tudeh recognized the singular role played by Ayatollah Khomeini. The Kremlin, which had sustained the Tudeh through difficult years, had a claim on its leadership. It therefore removed Iraj Eskandari from his secretary post and replaced him with Nur-ul-din Kianuri, the son of a well-known religious leader, Ayatollah Fazlollah Nuri, who was martyred in 1907. Kianuri was judged the man best suited to remove Tudeh's anti-Islamic image and thus better able to deal with Khomeini. While still in exile in 1979, Kianuri called for support for Khomeini: "The Tudeh Party approves Ayatollah Khomeini's initiative to set up an Islamic Revolutionary Council. The Ayatollah's program coincides with that of the Tudeh Party." The Khomeini victory in February 1979 enabled the Tudeh leaders to return to Iran after years of exile. The shah's ban on the party was not lifted, but its existence was tolerated by the Khomeini regime. Tudeh opened offices in Tehran and published a daily newspaper, *Mardom,* with a circulation of approximately 25,000. The party was also permitted to propagandize openly and to distribute additional literature, including weeklies, pamphlets, and cassette recordings of Kianuri's speeches. The spreading influence of the Tudeh, however, worried the Khomeini government, and in 1983 it ordered the arrest of the party's leaders and the closing of its headquarters and newspapers. Later, the government officially dissolved the organization, claiming it had become an instrument of Soviet foreign policy.

Significance

The Tudeh harbors ambitions of eventually ruling Iran. It has been the only "true" political party in Iran and the only one with a consistent record in this century. It contains dedicated and disciplined members, many of whom have planned and plotted for decades the takeover of the government. The question arises: Why did Ayatollah Khomeini, avowedly anti-communist and violently opposed to other Iranian leftists, especially the *mujahiddin,* tolerate the Tudeh? Answers are speculative but nonetheless useful. The Islamic revolutionaries feared the Soviet Union. In August 1979, the Revolutionary Guards invaded Tudeh offices, destroyed property and records, and disrupted the publication of the party newspaper. The Soviet Union responded by fomenting disorder among Iranian minority groups, such as the Kurds and Azerbaijanis. Moscow also condemned the excesses of the revolution in its own press. By September 1979, Khomeini was ready to order the restoration of Tudeh privileges. The Soviets showed interest in Iran's defense against the Iraqi invasion of 1980. Soviet supplies were made available to Iranian forces, especially the Revolutionary Guards, and Soviet economic and technical assistance was accepted by the Khomeini regime. Moreover, the Soviets were permitted to establish electronic monitoring bases in Iranian Baluchistan. All of these activities enhanced Tudeh's role, as did the realization that Iran housed more than a score of communist and Marxist-Leninist organizations. Recognition of Tudeh, to the extent that it was tolerated, provided the government with the opportunity to isolate and, if necessary, crack down on the other groups. In the 1980 parliamentary elections, however, Kianuri suggested the formation of a broad front involving the *mujahiddin* and the *fedeyeen* Khalq. Although both rejected the offer, the *mullah*-dominated government had reason to be concerned. The leftist groups were essentially paramilitary organizations, and the Tudeh was suited to adapt to the Islamic revolution, much like Marxists in Latin America, who had allied themselves with Catholic priests. Kianuri, the ideologist, also defined Khomeini's revolution in dialectical terms that were acceptable to Marxists. He had noted that Khomeini discharged the Mehdi Bazargan government because it was liberal-bourgeois. Khomeini, according to Kianuri, favored "change in the political and economic life of the country to the advantage of the working masses." When Khomeini denounced the Soviet invasion of Afghanistan, Kianuri and the Tudeh remained silent. The Tudeh Party has been an organization-in-waiting. It had little support in the new Iranian parliament. But it was well organized and experienced, and it had the Soviet Union as its primary support base. Had the

Islamic state begun to disintegrate and Soviet influence in Iran increased, the Tudeh would have been in position to make its presence felt. Just the opposite happened, however. The *mullahs* have increased their influence and control over Iranian society, and the Soviet Union has ceased to exist. In the absence of its chief patron, the Tudeh party of Iran may never again mount a serious challenge to any present or future Iranian government. The broad-scale assault on the party and the arrest, imprisonment, and torture of its leaders, including its entire Central Committee, was the *mullahs'* response to what is now a less serious threat to the Islamic revolution.

Israelis and Palestinians

5

Arab Legion 144

The Arab Legion was organized in 1930 from a small desert patrol of tribal bedouins. With British tutelage, the Arab Legion became a mechanized fighting force by the end of World War II. The principal organizer and initial commander of the sophisticated legion was an Englishman, Lieutenant General Glubb Pasha, long an officer in the British Colonial Service. The main units of the Arab Legion were financed by Great Britain. When the force became the professional army of Jordan, Britain's 1948 treaty with that country perpetuated the financial subsidy. The Arab Legion is an all-volunteer force and is to be distinguished from the National Guard, which conscripts all able-bodied males. In time of war the Arab Legion and National Guard have similar status. The Arab Legion was a major component of the Arab armies that assaulted Israel in 1948. Unlike the other Arab armies, however, the legion successfully retained control over the West Bank of the Jordan River and East Jerusalem, though with Iraqi assistance. Jordan maintained control of these territories by virtue of the armistice agreement signed in Rhodes on April 3, 1949. The Arab Legion was totally Arabicized in 1956, and General Glubb returned to Great Britain. The financial subsidy that maintained the Arab Legion was continued by the United States, which also assumed responsibility for protecting the Hashemite monarchy. Jordan did not join in the 1956 war against Israel. It did participate in the 1967 war, however, and the Arab Legion was defeated and forced to give up the gains achieved in the 1948–1949 encounter. Israel remains in occupation of the West Bank, and East Jerusalem has been unified with West Jerusalem by Israeli authorities. The Arab Legion was also constrained from becoming embroiled in the 1973 war with Israel. In fact, given the "open bridges" policy promoted by Israel, movement between Jordan and the West Bank and the West Bank and Israel was sustained even during the 1973 war. During the Gulf War of 1990–1991, however, movement was curtailed and the West Bank was placed under curfew. Jordan also used the occasion of the war to warn Israel that any violation of its frontier would face retaliation.

Significance

The Arab Legion was considered a crack force under British command. It has not fared as well since the indigenization policy went into effect. In the aftermath of the Arab Legion's successful campaign in the 1948–1949 war, however, Jordan was faced with the monumental task of administering to the Palestine Arab refugee community. This community had no special attachment to Emir Abdullah, the Hashemite ruler of Jordan; their ties were closer to the followers of the ex-*mufti* of Jerusalem, Haj Amin al-Husayni, Abdullah's traditional adversary. Abdullah at one time harbored dreams of ruling over Greater Syria, an area encompassing Syria, Lebanon, British Palestine, and Jordan. The *mufti* had similar designs and visualized ruling a united Arab world. Although these dreams were dashed by World War II and its immediate aftermath, rivalry between the Husaynis and Hashemites continued. Jordan's annexation of the West Bank, therefore, raised anew these old hostilities. Furthermore, Egypt and Saudi Arabia during this period also opposed the Hashemites. Egypt and Saudi Arabia acted negatively to Abdullah's seizure of the West Bank, leaving little doubt that they preferred a Husayni administration in the territory. On July 20, 1951, King Abdullah entered the al-Aqsa Mosque in Jerusalem, the holiest site in orthodox Islam after Mecca and Medina, and as he knelt to pray, he was shot and killed by a Palestinian Arab. The trial of the conspirators revealed a plot hatched in Egypt with the help of a disaffected Arab Legion officer. Of the five found guilty of assassinating King Abdullah, one was Musa al-Husayni, a resident of Jerusalem and a relative of the ex-*mufti*. All the others were also Palestinians, belonging to a small terrorist organization, trained and sponsored by the Husaynis during the Arab Revolt in British Palestine in 1937–1939. Jordanian authority moved against the Husaynis and their terrorist organizations, the Arab Legion playing a primary role in their suppression. Although the West Bank was thus brought firmly within the Jordanian orbit, the 1967 war shifted the region to Israeli control. Thousands of Palestinians on the West Bank also shifted their domicile to the East Bank, and once again they became a great burden on the kingdom. The emergence of the Palestine Liberation Organization, and its use of Jordanian territory from which to strike at Israel, reinvigorated the long dispute between the Hashemites and the Palestinians, and indeed the Husaynis as well. The violent clash between Jordan's Arab Legion and the Palestine Liberation Organization in 1970 was a continuation of this enmity. Although the PLO was forced to establish operations in Syria and Lebanon after this Jordanian conflict, changing conditions in the Middle East suspended hostilities between the two camps. Suspicions on both sides, however, run deep. The Arab Legion, therefore, has been more an instrument of monarchial protection and domestic peace than a force destined for offensive strategies. Moreover, in spite of the events of 1970, the Palestinian community within Jordan increased in size and political importance. The liberalizing of the political process in the kingdom brought Palestinians into the parliamentary institution, thus further increasing their voice. Jordanian Palestinians stood solidly with Iraq during the Gulf War in 1990–1991, and the Hashemite king found it necessary to reflect the sentiments of his bitter subjects. Although the Arab Legion maintained law and order during the period, its role had grown more complicated.

Arab Lobby 145

The Arab Lobby in the United States seeks to influence U.S. governmental behavior. Because the Israel Lobby has a longer history and its work has been boosted by an attentive American Jewish community, the Arab Lobby has devoted considerable effort to neutralizing the effectiveness of the Israel Lobby. The energy crisis focused special attention on the Arab world. A new generation of Arab leaders, espousing modernization and technological change, speak an idiom closer to that of U.S. society. Moreover, real and potential Arab power vis-à-vis Israel is not lost on Americans, especially those with commercial and financial ties to the Muslim Middle East. The impact on U.S. public opinion of Americans with interests in the Arab nations is beginning to register. Helping this process along is the National Association of Arab Americans (NAAA). NAAA has been organized along lines similar to the American Israel Public Affairs Committee (AIPAC). Like AIPAC it emphasizes U.S. national interests and how they are protected and advanced by association with the Arab states. NAAA, organized in 1972, took 10 years to establish itself. It now claims to represent about 2 million Arab-Americans, but until the 1982 war in Lebanon it did not arouse much support from that community. Since that time it has received offers of assistance, and many Arab-Americans and other U.S. citizens have volunteered their services. This was especially true during the 1990–1991 Gulf War. Demonstrations in Washington and other U.S. cities have focused on protecting the Arab-American community while demanding even-handedness in U.S. policy toward Israel and the Palestinians. NAAA publishes the *Middle East Business Survey*, a sophisticated publication that carries advertisements primarily from the Arab states and U.S. corporations doing business in the Arab world. The PLO also publicizes its cause in the pages of the journal. NAAA's apparent dependence on Arab governments has been highlighted by its critics, who seek to portray the organization as a foreign endeavor. Moreover, Arab-Americans have generally opposed U.S. policy in the Middle East. On the other hand, there is considerable division of opinion among American Arabs on the tactics used by the PLO. The most significant challenge to Arab-American resolve to date was Washington's decision to deny Iraq's claim to Kuwait, and indeed to engage Iraqi forces in Operation Desert Storm. NAAA was hard-pressed to take a stand. On the one side, it found fault with the U.S. government, believing a diplomatic settlement was possible. On the other, U.S. forces had been committed to the conflict and the Arab-American community was called upon to display their support for the troops. NAAA sought a middle course, arguing that Israel, too, should be required to follow the letter of UN resolutions and that pressure should be applied in the form of sanctions that would deny Israel U.S. aid. ***See also*** ISRAEL LOBBY (153).

Significance

The Arab Lobby is destined to achieve greater success in the months and years to come. Washington has long considered an "even-handed" policy to be in the best interests of the United States. The U.S. government believes that Israel is no longer in danger of being annihilated. It has been recognized by the largest Arab state, Egypt; other Arab states, described as moderates by the U.S. Department of State, appear willing to follow that lead, providing Israel makes specific concessions. The

United States is therefore inclined to pressure Israel to return Arab territory seized in the 1967 war. U.S. officials also want to see a resolution of the Palestinian question, and they will press for a self-governing Palestine. Furthermore, the Arab Middle East is threatened by direct and indirect aggression, and U.S. authorities are in agreement that arms must be made available to the Arab states, no matter how loudly Israel and the Israel Lobby complain. Because of this change, as well as the American desire to protect the petroleum resources of the region, the NAAA has an easier task in dealing with the Israel Lobby. NAAA can devote maximum attention toward consolidating its constituency and sustaining momentum in favor of the Arab position. The Arab Lobby has every intention of classifying representatives and senators according to their voting records. In time, the "Arab vote" may become as important as the "Jewish vote" in U.S. political life.

Ashkenazic Jews 146

Ashkenazic Jews are those identified with the establishment of the Zionist Movement and the creation of the independent Israeli state. *Ashkenazim* is a Hebrew word meaning German, and more broadly, European, especially East and Central European, Jews. Many Ashkenazic Jews are descendants of the Roman-enforced Diaspora. ***See also*** SEPHARDIC JEWS (181); YISHUV (188); ZIONISM (189).

Significance

The Ashkenazic Jews were the founders of the Labor movement in Israel, the early settlers of the kibbutz, and those who engineered and conceived the Jewish return to the Holy Land. The original majority Jewish population of Israel, they have been surpassed in numbers by the Sephardic and Oriental Jews. Tensions between Ashkenazic and Sephardic Jews surfaced in March 1992 when David Levi, the Likud Party foreign minister, resigned his position because of the difficulties with the Ashkenazim-dominated inner government. Levi (who ultimately did not resign his position) accused the leaders of Likud with discrimination against the Sephardic—and especially North African—Jews.

Balfour Declaration 147

The Balfour Declaration was a pledge by the British government to provide for a Jewish homeland in Palestine. The declaration was presented in the form of a letter from the British foreign minister, Lord Balfour, to an eminent English Jewish leader, Lord Rothschild, on November 2, 1917. With this letter Great Britain publicly declared its support for Zionist objectives that emphasized the resettlement of European Jewry in the Holy Land, from which their ancestors had been forcibly removed centuries before. The letter stated: "His Majesty's Government view with favour the establishment in Palestine of a national home for the Jewish people, and will use their best endeavours to facilitate the achievement of this object, it being clearly understood that nothing shall be done which may prejudice the civil and religious rights of existing non-Jewish communities in Palestine, or the rights and political status enjoyed by Jews in any other country." The promise to establish a Jewish national home in Palestine was greeted with jubilation in Zionist circles. Among the Arabs, however, there was seething discontent. During World War I, the British had also made promises to the Arabs. The British Indian government sided with Emir ibn Saud, and entered into a treaty with him in 1915, promising the Saudis protection and an annual subsidy if they declared their independence from Ottoman influence. Although not considered an ally, ibn Saud led his forces against the powerful Rashidi tribe, which had sided with the Ottomans. The defeat of the Rashidis prepared the way for ibn Saud's ultimate conquest of most of the Arabian Peninsula in the 1920s. The British also made pledges of support to specific Arab leaders in Qatar and Kuwait, and both were promised independence following the Ottoman surrender. An important correspondence was also carried on between Sir Henry McMahon, the British high commissioner in Egypt, and Sherif Hussain of Mecca, the Hashemite family leader and the chief protector of the Muslim holy places in the Hejaz region of Arabia. The Hussain-McMahon correspondence described British intention and Arab Hashemite desire to reinvigorate the Arab world and, more important, to bring the Arab world under the unified rulership of the Hashemites. Such promises were not only contradictory but also in conflict with secret agreements entered into by Britain, France, Italy, Greece, and Imperial Russia. Perhaps the most significant of these secret agreements was the Sykes-Picot Treaty, which divided the spoils of the Ottoman Empire among Britain, France, and Russia (Russia's involvement was negated by the Bolshevik Revolution of 1917). The promises made to local rival interests, and the intention of the Europeans to sustain their power in the Middle East, set the scene for a long period of turbulence and uncertainty. See also ZIONISM (189); HUSAYNIS (150); WAHHABIS (63).

Significance
The Balfour Declaration and the promises made to Arab leaders described a new political environment in the post–World War I Middle East. They also created a pattern of relationships that were more conflicting than cooperative. The Europeans were prompted to make promises to the Zionists and Arabs to obtain their support for the war effort. There was also some indication that English Protestantism empathized with, or at least was sympathetic to, the Jewish desire for a national home. On the Arab side, there were also positive intentions. Arab scholars and numerous English statesmen were sincere in their concern to help raise the Arabs from the depths of humiliation and to free them from the tyranny of Turkish Ottoman rule. But the Europeans, particularly the British, were also working at cross-purposes. Just as the British in India supported ibn Saud, the British in London were giving assistance to his rival, Sherif Hussain. By the same token, the British were in a poor position to placate both the Husaynis of Palestine and their leader, the *mufti* of Jerusalem, and the Zionists. The *mufti* of Jerusalem also harbored great ambitions. He, too, saw the opportunity to establish his rule over the reemerging Arab world. The pledge to the Jews, therefore, as well as the offer to the sherif of Mecca, threatened that objective. The undercurrents of intrigue, Great-Power interest, and personal rivalry were destined to make the Balfour Declaration an explosive issue for decades to come.

Ethiopian Jews 148

Ethiopian Jews, known as Falashas, are said to be the descendants of migrants who arrived in Ethiopia around 300 B.C. Another view holds they were originally Ethiopians who were converted to Judaism by traders at a much later date. The Ethiopian Jews follow the Talmudic tradition, though with a different emphasis from other Jews. They do not speak Hebrew and use a non-Semitic language. They are also culturally and physically indistinguishable from other Ethiopians, although they live separately from the general Ethiopian population. The term *Falasha* means "dispossessed" in Amharic.

Significance

The Israeli and Ethiopian governments entered into a diplomatic agreement in 1990 that allowed for the transfer of the remaining Ethiopian Jews, said to be around 17,000, to Israel. Some observers believe the arrangement was a "Jews for guns" deal, entered into because the Addis Ababa government desperately needed arms to fend off attacks from the Eritrean Front and other parties. An earlier agreement with the Ethiopian and Sudanese governments had produced Operation Moses, wherein Ethiopian Jews were flown from desolate refugee camps in the Sudan to Israeli settlements. The Arab states undermined that agreement because they saw the influx of Jews as further evidence the Israelis would retain the West Bank territories; Operation Moses was halted in 1985. The 1990 agreement was completed in secrecy and the processing of Ethiopian Jews was also done quietly. Ethiopia drifted from its Marxist moorings in 1991, and refocused its attention on historical links with Israel, which according to mythology brought King Solomon and the queen of Sheba together. It is believed she bore Solomon's son, who later founded the Ethiopian dynasty. Israel also saw Ethiopia as strategically placed and a useful political ally. But the defeat of the Mengistu Haile Mariam forces in June 1991 by the Eritrean People's Liberation Front and the Tigrean-dominated Ethiopian People's Revolutionary Democratic Front raises the possibility that the new Ethiopian government will be supportive of Arab objectives vis-à-vis Israel. Libya and Iraq were supportive of the Eritreans, and Israel's fear that Arab influence in the Horn of Africa and the Red Sea will threaten the Israeli port of Eilat is taken very seriously in Jerusalem. Israel's effort to trade weapons for the Ethiopian Falashas, therefore, had both geopolitical as well as humanitarian objectives. Before the fall of the Mengistu regime Israel was able to realize one segment of its program. It airlifted the vast majority of Falashas to safe haven in the Israeli state.

Gush Emunim 149

Gush Emunim are fundamentalist, often militant Jews of Israel who have moved into the West Bank territory (Judea and Samaria) with the intention of establishing permanent residence there as an act of faith. Gush Emunim are imbued with the sole objective of gaining possession of the land that they believe God promised the Jews. Gush Emunim settlers are permitted to bear arms by the Israeli government. They supplement the Israeli defense forces in the West Bank insofar as they defend their own settlements. Believing that God gave the Jews this particular land, they argue that the Arab inhabitants uprooted by the settlement policy should find domicile in Arab lands. Many Gush Emunim are relatively new immigrants who left their countries of origin because of their strong religious convictions. Gush Emunim can be contrasted with another ultrareligious Jewish sect known as the Neturei Karta, a violently anti-Zionist group residing essentially in Jerusalem. They are the self-styled Guardians of the City (Jerusalem), and they oppose the creation of the Israeli state on grounds that it is contrary to biblical teachings and God's law. The Neturei Karta are sometimes found in league with Israel's Arab antagonists, and some even have been identified with the policies of the Palestine Liberation Organization. The Neturei Karta believe that only God, not humans, can establish the state of Israel. ***See also*** JUDEA AND SAMARIA (THE WEST BANK) (14); AUTONOMY (73); ZIONISM (189); REAGAN PROGRAM ON PALESTINE (177).

Significance
Israelis who oppose the extensive West Bank settlement program also criticize the Gush Emunim as religious zealots. They understand that the Israeli government sees the settlements as an advance defense perimeter, but they question the value of the settlements to Israeli security. Defending the small settlements in a sea of Arabs involves spreading Israel's defense forces extremely thin. A larger Israeli force would be needed in time of war to protect a relatively small number of settlers. Moreover, the money required for the settlements diverts funds from other projects and also causes even steeper inflationary spirals and added taxation. It is estimated that Israel spends in excess of $100 million each year on the settlements. The conservative government in Jerusalem, however, has no intention of reducing its commitments to the Gush Emunim in the West Bank. Unlike in the Sinai, where settlements were destroyed and the settlers withdrawn, sometimes forcibly, the Israeli government is pressing ahead with plans to settle more than 100,000 Israeli citizens in the West Bank. The settlement of Soviet Jews is a case in point. It is this development that brings Arab and outside observers to conclude that Israel has no intention of giving up the West Bank. Annexation, although a possibility, is not an immediate prospect. Palestinian Arab autonomy on the West Bank, from the Israeli point of view, must focus on the peaceful coexistence of Muslim and Jewish communities. The Gush Emunim reject the establishment of an independent Palestine Arab state on the West Bank, and even prefer the expulsion of the Arabs from the territory. Since the eruption of the Palestinian *intifada* in December 1987, incidents of violence between Arabs and Jews on the West Bank have increased. Given the inability of the Israeli army to guarantee protection, the settlers have resorted to self-defense measures, and a mini–civil war rages in the territories.

Husaynis **150**

The most important Arab clan or family in Palestine. The Husaynis were the wealthiest and most powerful Arab family in Palestine during the Ottoman and British periods. Since the time of its incorporation in the latter part of the nineteenth century until World War II, Jerusalem was administered largely by the Husayni clan. The important role held by Al Haj Mohammad Amin al-Husayni between 1920 and 1944 gained him the title of *mufti* of Jerusalem. As *mufti*, Amin al-Husayni was the chief protector and administrator of the Muslim holy places. Given this position, he was also named permanent president of the Supreme Muslim Council in Palestine. ***See also*** NASHASHIBIS (162); ARAB LEGION (144); PALESTINIANS (171).

Significance
The Husaynis were in key positions from which to represent Muslim causes, especially Arab unity. Moreover, the struggle against Zionist settlements, and later the Balfour Declaration announcing Great Britain's intention to establish a Jewish state in Palestine, became the central preoccupation of the Husayni clan. By championing the Arab and Muslim causes against Zionism and European imperialism, the Husaynis were able to defeat their Palestinian Arab rivals, who were dependent on the British. The Husaynis also attracted Arab youth to their banners. Given

their religious appeal, the Husaynis developed the Palestine Arab Party and issued the National Pact, which integrated other Arab organizations and parties with their movement. They also organized Al-Futuwah, a young military body that had its branches in Syria and Iraq. The Husaynis excited Arab passion, and this sentiment and energy were directed against the Jewish settlers of Palestine. The *mufti* of Jerusalem sympathized with Nazi Germany in World War II. He passed some time in Berlin to voice his opposition to the British and Allied war effort. He also had visions of leading the Arab world, stemming from his belief that Britain would be defeated by the German army. Although repudiated by the European community, Amin al-Husayni signalled Arab opposition to Western actions in the Arab world. Moreover, his progeny have carried forward the struggle with which he was so intimately identified. Yasir Arafat, the leader of the Palestine Liberation Organization (PLO), is a member of the Husayni clan, a cousin of the *mufti*, a primary figure in the pan-Arab movement, and a determined advocate of anti-Israel policies.

Intifada 151

The Palestinian uprising in the West Bank and Gaza Strip that began in December 1987. The *intifada* has been described as a spontaneous outburst of frustration on the part of the Palestinians under Israeli occupation. The Palestine Liberation Organization saw the utility in the action and organized the resources necessary to sustain it. The *intifada* is now judged a full-blown activity of the PLO and a growing source of difficulty for the Israelis. Official Israeli action aimed at controlling the *intifada* has produced what observers in and outside Israel describe as an excessive use of force. The protracted character of the uprising has also prompted retaliation by Palestinians against Israelis, both military and civilian. In turn, Israelis have ignored official restrictions, have armed themselves, and have turned their weapons on the Arabs. By 1991 more than 800 Palestinians had died at Israeli hands. Almost 300 had been killed by other Arabs who judged them to be Israeli collaborators or sympathizers. More than 50 Israelis have also perished as a consequence of the uprising. Injured and wounded Palestinians total more than 50,000, while combined Israeli military and civilian wounded are more than 3,000. In addition, approximately 10,000 Palestinians have been incarcerated and more than 60 deported, usually to Lebanon. The Israeli security forces have demolished or sealed more than 500 Palestinian homes as punishment for the sustained mayhem. The cost to the Israeli government in the first three years of the uprising is placed at more than $600 million. ***See also*** TEMPLE MOUNT INCIDENT (184).

Significance

The *intifada* has internalized the Israeli-Arab conflict on a scale that all the formal wars could not. Israel has found it necessary to maintain a war footing that taxes its resources. More important, the use of violence to quell what are essentially civilian demonstrations, often composed of young children, has torn at the soul of the Jewish state. There is constant debate within Israel surrounding the *intifada,* and opinion is divided on the subject of retaining the administered territories. While the settler community on the West Bank and the Jewish fundamentalist organizations are determined to hold on to the territories, other Israelis believe the country must yield them if Israel is to be true to itself. The inability to prevent the *intifada* from reaching into Israel proper was illustrated by the stone-throwing incident on the Temple Mount in Jerusalem in the fall of 1990. Jewish worshippers at the Wailing Wall were assaulted by Palestinians, who soon thereafter were targeted by Israeli security police. Nineteen Palestinians died. The incident produced a storm of criticism around the world, all of it directed at the Israeli use of lethal force at the holy site. The UN Security Council was called to debate the matter, and it eventually ruled unanimously that Israel was in violation of the norms of international behavior and that a special commission should be dispatched to Jerusalem to investigate the incident. Israel called the UN action one-sided. It also criticized the United States for voting to condemn Israel. But Israel refused to comply with the UN order and insisted it would manage its own security. It also said it would investigate the matter and issue a public report. When that report was made public, the Israelis acknowledged that the incident had been precipitated by the accidental explosion of a security guard's tear gas canister. The affair nonetheless demonstrated the deep-seated fears and bitterness in the two communities.

Israel Defense Forces (IDF) 152

The Israel Defense Forces (IDF) were established on May 26, 1948, by the provisional government of Israel. It is essentially a citizen army with a largely professional air force and navy. The army was originally assembled along the lines developed in Switzerland, but it is also influenced by British, U.S., French, and Russian military features. The IDF is a direct consequence of the semi-legal military establishment created in the mandate period. The IDF was assembled from (1) the Haganah, formed in 1921, the largest of the pre-independence military formations; (2) the Palmach, Haganah's special forces or commando unit; (3) the Irgun Zvai Leumi (National Military Organization), essentially a terrorist organization, formed in 1938; and (4) the Lehi or Lohamei Herut Israel (organized in 1940), a small dissident band of a few hundred men. In building the IDF the Israeli government also drew men from the Jewish Brigade of the British Army as well as other contingents that had fought with the Allied armies in World War II. In the initial phase of organization, the Israeli government disbanded the independent paramilitary associations, and after the assassination of UN mediator Count Folke Bernadotte, the depoliticization of the armed forces began in earnest. The IDF is divided into three main components: (1) a regular army of officers and noncommissioned officers; (2) national servicemen and women—all citizens from their eighteenth birthday (men serve for three years and unmarried women for two years); and (3) a reserve of all able-bodied men and women up to the age of 55 (male) and 34 (female). The Israeli Air Force, Navy, Infantry, Armor and Tank Corps, Communications and Supply, Ordnance, Medical and Women's Corps, Intelligence, Engineering, and Civil Defense are all under a single, integrated command structure. Ground commands, however, are divided into three regional operations: Northern, Central, and Southern. These commands are supplied according to estimated need. Corps commanders hold the rank of brigadier. Regional commanders are major generals. The chief of the general staff is the only officer with a rank of lieutenant general. The chief of staff answers to the minister of defense and the prime minister's cabinet and is appointed to a three-year term, which can be extended by the cabinet on recommendation from the defense minister and the prime minister. Efforts have been made to rotate high-ranking officers, and early retirement has become a tradition in the IDF. Many of Israel's highest-ranking officers, however, have obtained positions either within the Knesset or in the executive branch upon leaving the service. Every effort is made to sustain the IDF as a civilian organization and a citizen responsibility. All reserves are on short notice in time of emergency, and each citizen knows in advance where to assemble and which unit he or she will serve with when the call comes to mobilize. The IDF, therefore, can, if necessary, field between 250,000 and 350,000 men and a larger number of women.

Significance

The IDF is not only the shield of the Israeli nation, it is also the glue that unites an otherwise politically divisive and argumentative population. Formed in the midst of the first Arab-Israeli War (1948–1949), the IDF quickly made veterans of inexperienced civilians. What was essentially a ragtag assembly of defiant quasi-military organizations has been shaped into one of the world's most efficient fighting machines. The 1956 Suez War, the 1967 Six-Day War, and the 1973 October, or Yom Kippur or Ramadan, War proved the mettle of the Israeli military forces. Despite numerical superiority overall, the Arab states have been ineffective in challenging Israeli military prowess. Moreover, armed heavily by the United States as well as capable of developing and manufacturing their own weapons systems, the Israelis are skilled in the deployment and utilization of the most sophisticated arms. This success on the battlefield finally brought Anwar el-Sadat to conclude that a continuation of the hostilities with Israel was a futile exercise. Sadat's trip to Jerusalem and the subsequent Camp David accords, and the Egyptian-Israeli peace treaty that followed from that meeting, emphasized no more war between these old foes. The Israelis have always understood that their future rests with the maintenance of a balance of power in the region, a balance that, if not in Israel's favor in an absolute sense, is at least sufficient to deflect Arab desire to overwhelm the Israeli state. Israel's national security program, however, is costly. The country spends a greater percentage of its revenue on military preparedness than most other countries. As a direct result of these expenditures, Israel's economy is in a state of constant strain, and its inflation rate is among the highest in the world. So, too, are its taxing policies. Nevertheless, the country recognizes that it has no alternative but to increase its expenditures for the IDF.

Israel Lobby 153

The Israel Lobby refers to the interest or pressure group of U.S. citizens who seek to influence U.S. governmental decisions in behalf of the Israeli state. The lobby is the principal work of the American Israel Public Affairs Committee (AIPAC), which was formed from the American Zionist Council in 1954. AIPAC maintains headquarters in Washington and has an annual budget in excess of $1 million. AIPAC's raison d'être is the promotion of good U.S.-Israeli relations that impinge directly on Israel's security. AIPAC is therefore as interested in countering U.S.-Arab relationships as it is in making more intimate the U.S.-Israeli connection. As a U.S. organization, however, AIPAC must be careful not to give the appearance of working in behalf of a foreign power. AIPAC's approach, therefore, emphasizes U.S. national interest and how it is enhanced by promoting Israel's well-being. AIPAC does not make broad solicitations from U.S. society. Its contributors are said to be around 10,000, but they are believed to be prominent representatives of the

U.S. Jewish and non-Jewish communities. Contributions to AIPAC are not tax deductible. AIPAC is not a political action group; it does not endorse candidates. Its work must be pursued irrespective of which party controls the administration; much of its operations is directed at the U.S. Congress. Another important organization identified with the Israel Lobby is the Conference of Presidents of Major American Jewish Organizations. This group is concerned with the problems of world Jewry and is not exclusively focused on Israeli issues. The conference also acts as a coordinating board and a screening committee wherein controversial matters are discussed and differences of opinion are reconciled before a public stand is taken. This helps minimize differences and inter-organizational squabbling. Other organizations that are represented in the conference but also possess influence of their own are the American Jewish Committee, the American Jewish Congress, B'nai B'rith, and the Union of American Hebrew Congregations. These organizations are as interested in national affairs as they are in Israel. Some would say they have even greater interest in U.S. civil rights questions and voting rights. Finally, there are the Zionist groups such as the Zionist Organization of America, the Zionist Labor Alliance, and the U.S. Jewish women's organization, Hadassah. The Zionist Organization of America is a branch of the World Zionist Organization, which is headquartered in Israel. As such, it must file regular reports with the U.S. Department of Justice revealing its expenditures. These organizations, however, would be paralyzed without the support they receive from the U.S. Jewish community, approximately 6 million people, and Americans of other persuasions who are sympathetic to Israel and highly protective of its interests.

Significance
The Israel Lobby is one of the best-organized interest groups in Washington. Much of its success has been attributed to the "Jewish vote," which candidates for public office, especially the presidency, believe that they must pursue. It is a matter of conjecture as to whether the "Jewish vote" is as significant a factor as it has been made out to be by journalists, and particularly by critics of the Israel Lobby. Although the "vote" cannot be discounted as a factor, this position ignores the superior organization of the lobby, its sophisticated approach, its astute management, and its persistent attitude. Interest groups are perfectly legal methods for influencing legislation and governmental decision making, and the Israel Lobby has done its work to near perfection. Israel is also important to U.S. interests in the Middle East because it represents a formidable power, relatively speaking, in a critical area of the world. Israel's military achievement in the 1967 war proved to be a turning point in U.S. Defense Department calculations in the Middle East. Although sometimes an embarrassment, and sometimes a thorn in the side of U.S. policymakers, Israel's strong democratic posture is considered an important counterweight to the region's authoritarianism. But if the Israel Lobby had dramatized a beleaguered state, and had succeeded in portraying Israel as the moral choice in the contest with its Arab neighbors, events of the last 15 years have tended to make that task far more difficult. Israel's military victories have altered its image as the underdog. Although Israel is numerically outnumbered, its demonstrations of military prowess have cast the Arabs in the role of mismatched competitor. Israel's punishing raids in retaliation for acts of terror committed against it also are often judged as overreactions. Popular

enthusiasm is sometimes lacking even if concern for Israel's safety remains high. Observers have noted that while the Begin and Shamir administrations have made it more difficult for the PLO to strike at Israeli settlements, they have also made it enormously difficult for the Israel Lobby to sustain its impressive record, given growing sentiment in the United States for a solution to the Palestinian question that would grant the West Bank population self-determination.

Jerusalem 154

Jerusalem was supposed to be declared an international city, under permanent trusteeship by the United Nations, according to the 1947 UN resolution that called for the partition of the British Palestine Mandate into Jewish and Arab states. The established Arab states, however, rejected the UN resolution and attacked Israel on the day of its declared independence—their collective, stated objective was the destruction of the Jewish state. Israel survived the 1948–1949 war and extended its sovereignty over areas originally designated for the Arab Palestine state. In fact, there was no Arab Palestine state. Jordan's army, with assistance from Iraq, had been successful in preventing the Israelis from seizing the whole of the British mandate (Egypt had also occupied a sector known as the Gaza Strip). As a consequence of the war, Jordan annexed the territory coming under its occupation, including East Jerusalem (Old Jerusalem with its significant religious sites). The Israelis occupied and incorporated West Jerusalem (the modern sector) within greater Israel. A fortified line separated one part of the city from the other, until the 1967 war gave the Israelis the opportunity to force the Jordanians from East Jerusalem. Israel also seized the territory that had become known as the West Bank (called Judea and Samaria by the Jews). Although Israel referred to the West Bank as the Administered Territories, and others referred to it as the Occupied Territories, the Israelis joined the two parts of Jerusalem, bringing the entire city under Israeli sovereignty. The formal annexation of East Jerusalem by Israel, however, did not come until the Israeli Knesset approved the act by legislation in July 1980. Muslim reaction to the annexation was one of widespread anger. Jerusalem was a sensitive issue that provoked Muslims everywhere. Sadat had entered into a peace treaty with Israel in 1979; he was now implored to reconsider his decision and to join with the Arab states in their common struggle. Although visibly unhappy, Sadat nevertheless refused to back away from a treaty commitment. Iraq and Saudi Arabia, however, jointly condemned "the Zionist entity's decision to annex Jerusalem and make it its eternal capital." The Saudis urged the nations that recognized Israel to remove their embassies from Jerusalem. Moreover, it threatened to sever all political and economic relations with countries recognizing the Israeli annexation. King Hussain of Jordan described the situation as an "act of aggression" against Arabs and Muslims. Crown Prince Fahd of Saudi Arabia echoed this statement and went a step further by calling for a new Arab *jihad* (holy war) against Israel. Syria was the first Arab state to issue an ultimatum to those countries with embassies in Jerusalem. The Netherlands and 11 Latin American countries were given one month to leave the city or face a break in relations with Damascus. Saudi Arabia was obliged to increase this pressure, and Holland and Venezuela were among the first to close down their offices. Jerusalem was a passionate issue. Sunni and Shiite Muslims consider Jerusalem the second holiest site in the Islamic world. Irrespective of claims made by Jews that it is *the* holiest place in Judaism, the Muslims have long claimed dominance over the citadel. So intense is Muslim sentiment that Bangladesh, Guinea, Lebanon, Indonesia, Jordan, Morocco, Pakistan, Saudi Arabia, Senegal, Sudan, Syria, and Iran sent delegations to the Casablanca conference. Yasir Arafat represented the PLO. The conference called upon all Muslim states to boycott any country that recognizes Jerusalem as the capital of Israel or announces that it will station its embassy there. All nonaligned states were urged to sever whatever diplomatic relations they still maintained with Israel; most had no relations or had severed them earlier. The nonaligned were pressured to impose economic sanctions on Israel. The conference also called upon the Vatican and other Christian states to take "positive" steps to force Israel to reverse its policy. The European states, including the Soviet Union, were urged to prevent the emigration of Jews to Israel. The conference also agreed to promote a campaign to enlist U.S. university students in an effort to influence the U.S. government to change its policy toward Israel. Arab communities residing in the United States and Western Europe were urged to form pressure groups to publicize the Arab position on Jerusalem. Arab efforts were joined with those of Christian clerics in Jerusalem, who were outraged when Jewish settlers insisted on occupying a building in the Christian sector of the city. The Israeli government of Yitzhak Shamir had secretly funded the settlers, the first to settle in the Christian quarter in decades. Mostly rabbinical students and their families, the Jews had moved into the 72-room St. Johns Hospice within yards of the Church of the Holy Sepulcher, the traditional site of the tomb of Jesus. Hundreds of clergymen and Arab Christian and Muslim residents staged a march on April 12, 1990, to protest the action. Their appeal was somewhat answered by the Israeli courts, but not until the U.S. government and U.S. Jewish groups also protested the action. Hardly a month later, the U.S. Congress passed a resolution recognizing Jerusalem as the Israeli capital. It also declared its support for Jewish emigration to Israel from the Soviet Union and for the financing of select settlements in the Occupied Territory. ***See also*** JUDEA AND SAMARIA (THE WEST BANK) (14); TEMPLE MOUNT INCIDENT (184).

Significance

Jerusalem is one of the great symbolic issues in the Arab-Israeli conflict. Muslims everywhere are opposed to Jerusalem being declared the Israeli capital. Religious sentiment is heightened by the Israeli action, and it gives the dispute a peculiarly religious character. In part the Muslims claim that their shrines are desecrated by the Israeli action. Moreover, they argue that the Israeli intention is to convert the city into a wholly Jewish entity. The Israelis are said to have attacked Islam itself. On the Israeli side there is a totally different presentation. Jerusalem, they insist, is the city of the Jews, the focal point for Judaism and the only possible capital of Israel. It is also noted that during the Jordanian occupation of East Jerusalem, Jews were not permitted to worship at their holy sites. The Wailing Wall was off-limits to Jews and was not maintained by the Jordanian authority. Under Israeli sovereignty, Muslims and Christians are free to worship at their shrines. The Israelis assert that they are in a better position to provide equal access. The Muslim world, of course, does not accept the Israeli presentation. They note the attempt to burn a Muslim shrine by an Australian and the killing of several Muslim worshippers by a deranged American-Israeli soldier. The fact that both acts were condemned by Israel and attributed to unstable minds did not appease the Muslims. Israel is nonetheless determined to retain the city in both its parts. Moreover, it seeks to protect Jerusalem from Arab attack by commandeering Arab lands and transferring them to Israeli settlers. The establishment of Israeli settlements in the West Bank territory is also aimed at providing Jerusalem with a defense in depth. Return of the West Bank to Jordanian sovereignty, or the creation of a Palestine state on the West Bank, would place Jerusalem in a precarious position. Nor would Arabs be content with a West Bank state that did not, at the very least, also involve the transfer of East Jerusalem to Arab control. It is reasonable to suggest, therefore, that Israel not only will ignore Muslim and international complaints on its action in Jerusalem, but also will attempt to maintain a permanent presence in the West Bank (Judea and Samaria). The 1981 annexation of the Golan Heights of Syria by Israel illustrates that the Israelis are as much concerned with security as they are with biblical claims. Indeed, religious arguments buttress national security policy, not the reverse.

Jewish Agency 155

The Jewish Agency was organized in 1929. In the World Zionist Status Law of 1952 it was formally recognized by the government of Israel as the "authorized agency which will continue to operate in the State of Israel for the development and settlement of the country, the absorption of immigrants from the Diaspora, and the coordination of activities in Israel of Jewish institutions and organizations active in those fields." In 1971 the agency was reconstituted to include the Zionist Organization and all Jewish fund-raising bodies. Prior to the creation of the state of Israel, the agency was the principal representative of the Zionist movement and the settlement of Jews in Palestine. The original claim to an independent Israel was the work of the agency. The Jewish Agency currently works in conjunction with the Israeli government and is considered an organ of that government. Its primary concern is with immigration, settlements, education, social welfare, health, and rural development. Since Israel's independence in 1948 the agency has brought approximately 2 million Jews to Israel and is responsible for the erecting of more than 500 villages. The agency is financed by voluntary gifts collected by the United Jewish Appeal in the United States and the Keren Hayesod in approximately 70 other countries. The agency is estimated to have collected almost $6 billion since 1948, approximately one-third of that sum coming from contributions in the United States. Prior to the creation of the United Jewish Appeal, contributions were solicited under the name of the Palestine National Fund and the Jewish National Fund. The Jewish National Fund today manages land development. The fund has reclaimed more than 200,000 acres (80,000 hectares) of desert land, planted more than 100 million trees, and built 1,800 miles (2,900 kilometers) of roads in frontier and mountain regions. *See also* YISHUV (188).

Significance

The Jewish Agency was the creation of Zionist President Chaim Weizmann. Weizmann sensed the need to create outside support, both Jewish and non-Jewish, for the building of a Jewish home in Palestine. The agency thus became a principal institution in the governing of the Yishuv (the Jewish community in Palestine). It not only raised funds, but also dealt with foreign governments, the mandatory authority in Palestine, and the League of Nations. The Arabs, however, refused to have anything to do with the organization, fearing that any such action would legitimize the agency's role. By the same token, when the Arabs of Palestine were encouraged to create their own "agency," they quickly rejected the proposal. Along with the National Council (Vaad Leumi) established in 1920 through British mandatory authority, and chosen by the Elected Assembly of Jewish representatives in Palestine, the Jewish Agency laid the groundwork for the political institutions of the new state of Israel. The National Council and the Jewish Agency together secretly sponsored and built the Haganah (Defense Force) despite British attempts to prevent such activities. By the mid-1930s the Haganah had approximately 10,000 men under arms. During World War II, elements of the Haganah and other Jewish recruits served with the British army in defense of the Middle East. By this time the British were prepared to see the development of such a force, and a British general assisted in their training. The Jewish Defense Force increased to 25,000 during World War II, and by 1948, the year of Israel's independence, it could place 45,000 men in the field. The Jewish Agency was also notable in the purchase of land prior to the establishment of the Israeli state. The Jewish settlers lacked the financial capacity to purchase property, and the agency managed this task for them. As a result, Israel emerged into independence without large landholders and with a system of communal farms (kibbutzim) wherein the cultivators owned, worked, and shared the produce of the land equally. The pioneer spirit that this program established in Israel can also be traced to the work of the Jewish Agency. It was this contribution and the administrative effectiveness of the agency that allowed its perpetuation in the Israeli state.

Jews in the Occupied Territories (156)

According to U.S. State Department statistics, in 1991 there were 12,000 Jews in the Golan Heights, 90,000 in the West Bank, 120,000 in East Jerusalem, and 3,000 in the Gaza Strip. ***See also*** ARAB-ISRAELI PEACE CONFERENCES (195).

Significance

Israel annexed the Golan Heights after seizing the territory from Syria during the 1967 war. It has vowed not to yield the heights because of its strategic value. The West Bank territory has witnessed increased Jewish settlements since 1982, and Israel is not likely to remove those settlements as it did in the Sinai following the peace treaty with Egypt. Unlike the Sinai, which Israel does not claim, the West Bank is also considered Judea and Samaria, the biblical lands of the Jews. East Jerusalem was unified with West Jerusalem and established as the capital of Israel. Israel has enabled Muslims and Christians to visit the holy sites in the city, but it will not yield the city to the Arabs who excluded them in the period leading up to the 1967 war. The Gaza settlements are well established but they may be the only sites Israel would be prepared to yield. The Jewish settlements in the occupied territories therefore are not perceived by the Israeli government as bargaining chips in their negotiations with the Arabs. Moreover, although autonomy has been offered the Palestinians on the West Bank, because of the extensive Jewish settlements, it would be difficult for Israel to agree to a sovereign independent Palestinian state there.

Kibbutz (157)

The kibbutz is a village where property is owned in common. It is the most celebrated Israeli practice of voluntary socialism. There are approximately 250 kibbutzim in Israel, with a combined membership numbering 105,000 (3 percent of the population). Members are not paid, but all their needs are satisfied by the commune. Dining, child-rearing, and household chores are all done collectively. Education, minor medical needs, and recreation are all managed internally by the members of the kibbutz. Married couples usually occupy a small apartment of two rooms. Different age groups pass their days in environments and institutions established for their training and expression. Teenagers from a small commune, however, can be expected to attend school in another kibbutz or go to a central institution established to meet the needs of several kibbutzim. Parents and their children spend evenings, the sabbath, and holidays together, and there is virtually no loss of family identity. Weekly meetings are conducted for the purpose of resolving conflict, solving problems, and making decisions. The kibbutz members also determine who should lead them and who should be admitted to new membership. Each kibbutz usually has a secretary, a treasurer, and a person in charge of production. Terms run for two years. Numerous committees address the different needs of the community, e.g., school boards and cultural interests. The first kibbutzim were established in the beginning of the twentieth century and were conceived as frontier pioneer settlements. Exclusively agricultural, they brought Jews who had long been domiciled in cities back to the earth. The kibbutz in most respects was the nucleus out of which Israel sprang in 1948. Present kibbutzim, however, are not only frontier settlements, but also important manufacturing sites, producing finished lumber, furniture, electronic devices, plastics, and precision tools. Farming is also a highly sophisticated operation, utilizing mechanized equipment and emphasizing high yields. *See also* MOSHAV (160).

Significance

The kibbutz should be distinguished from such settlements as the Gush Emunim, which are to be found on the West Bank. The kibbutzniks, as the settlers are sometimes referred to, were originally and are today representative of Israeli youth. They are not necessarily religious in their performance, and many are more secular than spiritual in outlook. The kibbutzniks believe fervently in the Israeli state and are traditional Zionists who believe that Israel provides them with the opportunity to build a life free of persecution and rich in personal development. Kibbutz members historically have recognized the need to defend their settlements from antagonistic Arab forces, and the communal farms provided the manpower for the early Israeli army. Today the kibbutzniks can be found in the Nahal, the Israel Defense Force branch that includes work on settlements as part of the commitment to military service incumbent on all Israeli youth. Many of the more recent kibbutzim were organized as Nahal settlements. The current kibbutz system is highly systematized, with numerous interlocking consortia pooling their resources. They also sponsor teacher-training colleges and publishing houses. The kibbutzim are often identified with Israel's political parties, depending upon the community's ideological temperament; thus, the kibbutzim can wield considerable influence in the Israeli Knesset, often in excess of their numbers. Moreover, because of its tradition the kibbutzniks can be found in the Knesset, the high offices of the Histadrut (the labor organization), and the Israeli armed forces, especially the paratroops, naval commandos, and air force. In the 1967 war, one of every four Israeli casualties was a kibbutznik.

King-Crane Commission

158

The Ottoman defeat in World War I left the Arab region of the empire in British and French hands. At the peace conference in January 1919 it was decided to separate the Arab territories from Ottoman control and bring them under the new mandate system. Britain and France quarrelled over the boundaries between the respective mandates, and Woodrow Wilson, the U.S. president, sent H. C. King and C. H. Crane to the area to ascertain the interest of the people living in the region. The King-Crane Commission returned to make its report to the president, but its contents were not disclosed until December 1922. Although calling for a mandate in Iraq and Syria, the commission believed that both territories should be treated as a single unit. They also recommended that the Syrian mandate be assumed by the United States, and Iraq by Great Britain. The controversial parts of the report focused on the French and the Jewish Zionists. The French, the commission argued, should be denied a mandate in the region. By the time the report was made public, however, the French had already established themselves in Syria. The other controversial issue surrounded the Zionist claim to a homeland under the Balfour Declaration. The King-Crane Commission questioned the propriety of creating a Jewish homeland in the face of Arab opposition and growing hostility. The mandates for Syria/Lebanon (French) and Palestine and Iraq (Great Britain) were approved by the Council of the League of Nations in July 1922, and they became effective in September 1923. Despite its disillusionment with the outcome, the United States concurred with the arrangements in 1924.

Significance

The King-Crane Commission is representative of early U.S. government attitudes toward the changing Middle East, especially the relationship between Jews and Arabs. In the case of Palestine, the mandatory power had full authority to administer the territory. Moreover, the British were required to honor the Balfour Declaration and thus provide political, economic, and administrative conditions that would secure a Jewish national home without prejudice to the rights of the Arab population. Transjordan had earlier been added to the mandated territory, but it was excluded from the area of Jewish settlement. In 1922, Transjordan became a semi-autonomous principality under the Hashemite Arabian leader Emir Abdullah, a son of the sherif of Mecca and an ally of the British against the Turks in World War I. Transjordan received its independence in March 1946 as the Hashemite Kingdom of Jordan. The creation of the state of Israel in 1948 and Jordan's subsequent absorption of the West Bank territory as well as the emir's efforts to reconcile differences with the Israelis led to his assassination in 1951. His grandson succeeded to the throne and began a long reign that continued into the 1990s.

Knesset

159

The Knesset is the Israeli parliament. It is a unicameral assembly composed of 120 members, representing between 9 and 25 parties. The first Knesset also served as the constituent assembly, and it was responsible for drafting the Israeli constitution. The functions of the parliament are similar to those of the earlier Provisional State Council. The vast majority, more than 90 percent, of the members in the first Knesset were born outside Israel. In the several decades that have followed, more Israeli-born members have been added, but the non-Israeli-born still comprise a sizable portion of the body. Arabs and women are also elected members of the Knesset.

Israel was established as a republic and was guided initially by the "transitional law" or "small constitution." Israel has a president, the symbolic head of state, but his functions are ceremonial and his powers limited. The chief of government is the prime minister, who must command a majority in the Knesset. Loss of a majority forces a new election and can produce a new prime minister with an entirely different administration. The second Knesset in 1951 established the practice of members serving four-year terms. Elections are carried out on a national basis, and the ballot is secret and open to all male and female citizens who have attained their eighteenth birthday. Special elections are required after a vote of no-confidence in the prevailing government or can be called by the government. Members of the Knesset do not represent specific constituencies. They therefore lean heavily on their respective parties. Their actions, as a result, are motivated more by party requirements than constituency needs. Given the many parties vying for votes, no political party has been able to muster a majority. Coalitions of parties are the normal condition in the Israeli Knesset. It also means a changeable political situation. Party discipline thus becomes an important factor in stabilizing administrations. ***See also*** POLITICAL PARTIES: ISRAEL (139).

Significance

The Israeli Knesset is the heart of the democratic process. Despite the many parties competing for popular support, the Mapai, or Labor Party, managed to control sufficient votes to form the Israeli government from 1949 to 1977. Dissatisfaction with the Labor coalition, however, caused it to disintegrate. In the 1977 election campaign, the more conservative Likud bloc, led by Menachem Begin, won a plurality of seats and was able to form a new coalition government. The Likud government came into office with the promise to establish new Israeli settlements on the West Bank and Golan Heights, as well as in the Sinai. The dramatic visit to Jerusalem by Anwar el-Sadat, however, eventually caused the Likud to back away from its Sinai settlement scheme and to make a full withdrawal of forces. The Golan Heights, however, were annexed by Israel in 1981, and more Israeli settlements were constructed on the West Bank, despite Arab and worldwide protests. In all of these undertakings, the Israeli Knesset gave its approval, notwithstanding opposition from the Labor bloc and smaller parties. Generally speaking, the Knesset is a reflection of prevailing Israeli sentiment on most issues of national concern, and it remains a fundamental institution in voicing sometimes explosive differences of opinion.

Moshav 160

The *moshav* is a cooperative village involving a number of small landholders who are both individually and collectively motivated. In the *moshav* each family has its own home. The children, unlike those in a kibbutz, live with their parents, and the family prepares and consumes its own meals. *Moshav* farmers tend their own fields and maintain their own finances. The *moshav* village provides a central station where heavy farm machinery is maintained and made available to local farmers. The *moshav* is also a cooperative in the purchase of seed and other farm needs and in the marketing of the produce of the individual farms. Some *moshavim* are engaged in industrial pursuits that are also operated on a cooperative basis. The *moshav*, like the kibbutz, is a concern of the Jewish Agency's Settlement Department. *Moshavim* today total approximately 400, considerably more than the kibbutzim. The population of the *moshavim* is approximately 140,000. ***See also*** KIBBUTZ (157).

Significance
The *moshavim* were developed prior to Israel's independence to meet the needs of those without the capital to purchase their own land and who were disinclined to join the communal lifestyle associated with the kibbutz. It was also an opportunity for older citizens to live a rural life and to contribute to Israel's agricultural as well as small-scale industrial needs. The popularity of the *moshav* grew after the creation of the state of Israel. The refugees from the Holocaust sought a more private existence than that offered by the kibbutz. They were also more conservative and less at ease with socialist planning and programs. The cooperative idea met their needs for capital formation without diminishing their individuality. Most important, the family unit could be sustained. The oriental Jews from North Africa, especially from the Maghreb (western region), Morocco, and Tunisia, also were more accustomed to living within the family, and the kibbutz was not a satisfactory vehicle for their requirements. The *moshav,* however, suited their tastes, and it also assisted in their integration into Israeli society. Government policy has been to settle particular ethnic groups in their own settlements. Second-generation *moshav* members, however, find that they have much in common and the creation of larger cultural units is now underway. The *moshav* has been examined by specialists from African, Asian, and Latin American countries, and Israelis have gone abroad to demonstrate the utility of the institution in countries concerned with rural development. At the same time Israel has developed a program that allows individuals from other countries to live and work in the *moshav* and to gain experience for later application in their own communities.

Mossad **161**

Mossad is the political extension of the Israeli intelligence community, Jerusalem's equivalent of the Central Intelligence Agency (CIA). Mossad is a highly secret organization concerned with both overt and covert operations and generally responsible for high-risk, active (rather than passive) missions connected with and related to Israeli security. Mossad has been implicated in events ranging from assassination to the destruction of the Iraqi Osirak nuclear reactor in 1981. Similarly, the Entebbe raid in Uganda, which gained the release of Israelis held hostage, was carried to a successful conclusion by the operations of Mossad. ***See also*** OSIRAK (259); TERRORISM (108); PALESTINE LIBERATION FRONT (PLF) (163).

Significance
Every country has its political intelligence operations, and although the CIA and the KGB have received maximum publicity, no intelligence organization is judged more professional, more efficient, and more successful than the Israeli Mossad. Although the Mossad has aged and, with time, become something more resembling a standard bureaucracy, it still retains something of its original, innovative, and individualistic character. The major task of the Mossad is counterterrorism, and the Mossad is a feared and efficient apparatus in combatting those of Israel's enemies who have declared perpetual war against the Jewish state.

Nashashibis **162**

A dominant Arab clan or family in pre–World War I Palestine. The Nashashibis were members of the landed gentry and had amassed great wealth in the nineteenth century under Ottoman rule. Long-time competitors of the dominant Husayni clan, they found themselves on the losing side when they sought to work with the British administration in managing the Palestine mandate. The Nashashibis also attempted alliances with the Hashemites, and they developed close relations with Emir Abdullah of Transjordan in an unsuccessful effort to offset the power of the Husaynis. ***See also*** HUSAYNIS (150); PALESTINIANS (171).

Significance
The clash between the Nashashibis and the Husaynis established patterns of power relationships among the Palestinians into the post–World War II years. The Nashashibis formed a nationalist opposition, but they could not acquire the post of *mufti* of Jerusalem or gain a dominant position on the Supreme Muslim Council. Given their frustration, the contest between the Nashashibis and the Husaynis degenerated into a classic struggle pitting one power structure against the other. Sides were drawn along patronage lines, with the smaller landlords and merchants joining one against the other. Eventually, the National Movement organized by the Palestine Arab Congress came under control of the Husaynis.

Palestine Liberation Front (PLF) 163

The Palestine Liberation Front is one of the smallest but most active groups under the umbrella of the PLO. The PLF is led by Mahmoud Zeidan, known to the world as Abu Abbas. Abu Abbas has been a member of the PLO Executive Committee, the PLO's most elite decision-making body. He also participates in the meetings of the Palestine National Council, the PLO equivalent of a parliament. Other Palestinian groups, especially those supported by Syria and Libya, have generally drifted from the PLO banner. They are Ahmed Jibril's Popular Front for the Liberation of Palestine–General Command and Abu Nidal, which operates a clandestine organization under considerable secrecy. Abu Abbas, however, best represents the growing trend toward go-it-alone operations. A former deputy to Ahmed Jibril, he broke away in April 1977 and established his own independent PLF. Based in Iraq for several years, the PLF adopted the policy of the "rejectionist states" in the Arab world. The PLF has also witnessed divisions within its ranks and has split into three smaller factions. One faction, led by the late Tala'at Yacoub, is still backed by Iraq. A second faction, led by Abdel Fatah Ghanem, has Syrian support. The third faction of the PLF is managed by Abu Abbas. It was originally based in Tunisia, near the central headquarters of the PLO. ***See also*** ACHILLE LAURO INCIDENT (233); PALESTINE LIBERATION ORGANIZATION (PLO) (137).

Significance
The PLF illustrates the difficulty of dealing effectively and meaningfully with the PLO. Although the PLO was declared the sole spokesman of the Palestinian people in their quest for an independent state, the PLO has never expressed itself with one voice, even in respect to its perceptions of Israel. Yasir Arafat's attempt in 1988–1989 to speak for the PLO, which he officially heads, on the organization's willingness to recognize the state of Israel was not well received. In May 1990, a PLF-organized raid by sea on an Israeli beach resort was thwarted by security forces. The episode was not immediately condemned by Arafat, who had given assurances the PLO would avoid terror tactics in pursuit of a Palestinian homeland. Arafat's diplomatic initiative had earlier produced direct talks between

the United States and PLO representatives. Washington, however, decided it would discontinue the exercise given what it judged a breach of good faith on the part of the PLO. Arafat claimed he had no knowledge of the raid and did not sanction it, but he also refused to condemn it. It was not the first time the PLF had upset an Arafat plan. The PLF's most well-known action was the hijacking of the *Achille Lauro*, an Italian cruise liner, in October 1985. In the course of that episode, the forces of Abu Abbas murdered an elderly, wheelchair-bound American named Leon Klinghoffer. The old man was killed as a demonstration of PLF resolve, and his body was dropped into the sea. The *Achille Lauro* was eventually released to Egyptian authority and the Cairo government allowed the terrorists to fly out of the country. The plane, however, was intercepted by U.S. fighter aircraft and forced to land in Sicily. Abu Abbas was seized with the others, but the Italian authorities freed him, despite his having been indicted for murder by U.S. authorities. Arafat, it is alleged, did not know about the plan to seize the *Achille Lauro* until it had been commandeered. He nonetheless acted as a mediator with the hijackers and also set the terms for their release.

Palestine National Council 164

The Palestine National Council is a surrogate for a Palestinian parliament-in-exile. Its purpose is to develop broad lines of policy for the Palestinian National Movement. It also acts as a forum for political expression on issues directly related to the Palestinians. The council sustains and publicizes the Palestinian quest for self-determination. It meets irregularly, but at least once each year. Membership is drawn from all walks of life. Palestinians living abroad as well as those domiciled in the Middle East can be members. Efforts have been made to identify articulate or important persons in the arts and sciences as well as in the worlds of business, labor, women's groups, and government. Members also represent a variety of ideological positions and religious experiences. The council symbolically as well as institutionally attempts to bind the Palestinians into a coherent community, irrespective of their location or circumstance. Members therefore are perceived as speaking and acting in behalf of the extended community of Palestinians, not in their individual capacities. Nevertheless, debate and differing opinions are encouraged on matters of consequence. The one area where differences have not surfaced is in the purpose of the Palestinian movement and the achievement of an independent, sovereign Palestine Arab state. The Palestine National Council was organized by the Palestine Liberation Organization in May 1964 when approximately 400 prominent Palestinians met in East Jerusalem, then under Jordanian sovereignty. Thereafter the National Council comprised 180 to 295 members. Members are nominated by a committee of the preceding council after consultations with other Palestinian organizations and prominent Palestinian individuals. Council members serve two-year terms, which are renewable. The council convenes on orders from the Executive Committee. One-fourth of its membership can also call a meeting. During ordinary sessions the council considers reports of the Executive Committee (chaired by Yasir Arafat since its creation) concerning the activities of the Palestine Liberation Committee and its organs. It also examines the Palestine National Fund and the PLO budget. Two-thirds of its membership form a quorum, and decisions are taken by simple majority. In 1973, the National Council created the Central Council, with members drawn from the parent body. The Central Council is responsible for overseeing the execution of National Council decisions. The president of the National Council is also president of the Central Council. ***See also*** PALESTINE LIBERATION ORGANIZATION (PLO) (137).

Significance
The Palestine National Council was the PLO's answer to the need for a Palestine government-in-exile. The PLO was the only fully organized, significantly funded, and diplomatically recognized Palestinian organization. Its elaborate organizational structure reinforced its credentials as the sole representative of the Palestinians, and the Palestine National Council was the organization's response to those who insisted that it was merely a terrorist organization. The emphasis given to broad representation helps to portray the PLO as a legitimate political organization, responsible for its actions and fully capable of governing a future Palestinian state. There is no equivalent body among the Palestinians, and assuming the establishment of a future Palestine state, the National Council will more than likely become the constituent assembly, responsible for drafting the new entity's official constitution.

Palestine National Covenant 165

The Palestine National Covenant (Al-Mithaq Al-Watani Al-Filastini) was issued in 1968 by the Palestine Liberation Organization (PLO). It is considered the most authoritative statement of policy regarding PLO perceptions of the Arab-Israeli crisis. The covenant's 33 articles describe the nature of the Palestine state and its struggle with Israeli Zionism. Article 1 speaks of Palestine as the "homeland of the Arab people" and says that it is "an integral part of the great Arab homeland, and the people of Palestine [are] part of the Arab nation." The covenant lays claim to the entire territory that was the British Mandate of Palestine. It announces that upon "liberation" of the homeland, the Palestinians will exercise self-determination according to their own will (Article 3). Palestinians are described as Arab citizens "who were living permanently in Palestine until 1947, whether they were expelled from there or remained" (Article 5). Moreover, the covenant insists that anyone born of a Palestinian Arab father after 1947, within the territory or outside it, is considered a Palestinian. By contrast, only Jews "living permanently in Palestine until the beginning of the Zionist invasion will be considered Palestinians" (Article 6). The covenant goes on to say that the current phase is one of national (*watani*) struggle for the liberation of Palestine (Article 8). Armed struggle is judged to be strategic, not tactical (Article 9). Guerrilla actions therefore are a necessary device in the conflict. Also given significance is the necessity to achieve Arab unity. Arab unity and the liberation of Palestine, according to the covenant, are inextricably interrelated; "one paves the way for realization of the other" (Article 13). Article 15 specifies that the liberation of Palestine requires the mobilization of all human, material, and spiritual capabilities. In the last instance, the covenant notes that tranquility can come to the Holy Land only when the Palestine state replaces the Israeli state. In this regard, the PLO calls upon other "spiritual forces" throughout the world to assist Palestinians in their endeavor (Article 16). In Article 19, the covenant declares the establishment of the state of Israel in 1947 "null and void." The PLO argues that the Jews have no claim to the Holy Land, that they are "citizens of the States to which they belong," where, it is assumed, they should return (Article 20). In Article 21 the PLO "rejects every solution that is a substitute for complete liberation." In Article 22, Zionism is described as a "political movement organically related to world imperialism and hostile to all movements of liberation and progress in the world." Zionism is also condemned as "racist" and "fanatical," "aggressive," "expansionist" and "colonialist," and "Fascist" and "Nazi" in its means (Article 22). In Article 26, the PLO declares its right to represent the Palestine revolution and the Palestinian people. It notes its desire to work closely with other Arab states and declares that it "will not interfere in the internal affairs of any Arab state" (Article 27). Attached to the covenant is the Fundamental Law of the Palestine Liberation Organization, describing the structure and institutions of the PLO. The covenant can be amended only when two-thirds of all the members of the National Council of the PLO so decide. ***See also*** PALESTINE LIBERATION ORGANIZATION (PLO) (137).

Significance
The Palestine National Covenant details the purpose, justification, and intention of the PLO. It is explicit in promoting violent action against the Israelis and Zionism. It implies that coexistence with the state of Israel is impossible and that the struggle must be sustained until victory has been achieved. The covenant does not address itself to other possible solutions of the Palestinian-Israeli problem. It is usually assumed that such solutions exist and that the covenant merely states the extreme objective of the PLO. The Israelis, however, do not accept this interpretation. The 1968 covenant has never been altered, let alone repudiated, and Israelis take the covenant at face value. Israel, therefore, has refused to consider plans for resolving the conflict. The overture made by Saudi Arabia in 1981, calling upon Israel to return to its pre-1967 borders and to permit the creation of a Palestinian state on the West Bank of the Jordan, was quickly rejected by Jerusalem. Moreover, the Israelis argue that the PLO is not the representative for the Palestine Arabs. They insist that it is a renegade organization, bent on spreading terror, not peace. The Israelis are cognizant of PLO leverage in diplomatic circles, and the organization's official recognition by the Muslim world as well as by communists and much of the Third World is cause for considerable concern. Votes against Israel's position in the United Nations, as on the UN General Assembly resolution equating Zionism with racism, and in other international forums place the Israelis on the defensive. The repeal of the UN racism-Zionism resolution in December 1991 brought a positive response from the Israelis, but their satisfaction was tempered by the knowledge that the National Covenant had not been repudiated by the PLO and that many Arab and Muslim states condemned the General Assembly's decision. Also, pressure from West European countries, especially the European Community, to compel Jerusalem to withdraw its military force from the West Bank and Gaza weighs heavily on Israeli leaders. Nevertheless, Israel has continued to resist all efforts in behalf of the Palestinians, which they interpret as giving carte blanche to the PLO. The Israelis have attempted to enlist Palestine Arabs on the West Bank in a program that would give the inhabitants greater autonomy and control over their daily affairs. Many Arab leaders on the West Bank who have collaborated with the Israelis in this work, however, have been made the target of PLO death squads. Other would-be participants either have been deterred from joining with the Israelis or were effectively intimidated. In the overall circumstances, the Israelis feel that they have no recourse other than to use violence against violence; consequently, the

PLO feels vindicated in pursuing its relentless program. The problem, according to many observers, is insoluble, but the peace conference that opened in Madrid in October 1991 and was followed by other meetings in Washington and Moscow in 1992 at least brought some of the principal belligerents together. Although the PLO was not officially a party at the conferences the Palestinian delegation emphasized its association with the organization, and Israel participated in the deliberations.

Palestine National Fund 166

The Palestine National Fund was organized in 1964 to facilitate revenue collection as well as the disbursement of funds among the various branches and organs of the Palestine Liberation Organization. The fund is staffed by specialists in finance, commerce, and economics, and it provides advice to the Executive Committee as well as manages the PLO's financial requirements. Its responsibility involves the drafting of plans focusing on the educational, social, and cultural needs of Palestinians wherever they live in the world, including those under Israeli occupation. The National Fund obtains funds from "successful" or permanent Palestinians, but its major assets are made available by Arab states. The oil-producing countries, especially Saudi Arabia and Kuwait, have been very generous in making funds available for the PLO. Accurate figures are unavailable, but observers estimate at least $8 billion has been made available to the PLO since its inception. Arms purchases are usually made through established Arab states and trans-shipped to the PLO. The PLO, however, has acquired direct access to arms from governments and international arms merchants. The latter are often contacted by the Palestine National Fund. Solicitation of financial contributions is not confined to the Arab world. Other Muslim states, notably Iran and Pakistan, have provided funds to the PLO. Non-Muslim governments sympathetic to the PLO have also provided needed money or credit. The conferring of official diplomatic status on the PLO by the Soviet Union in November 1981 also conveyed a promise of credit for the acquisition of Soviet weapons. The loss of its Soviet patron was a significant blow to the organization. The Palestine National Fund also aids and cooperates with the Palestine Red Crescent Society, which provides medical and social services to needy Palestinians. The Red Crescent has opened 30 hospitals and 100 clinics to treat war casualties as well as residents of the refugee camps. It also assists in the training of health inspectors and offers courses in basic health education, prenatal care, and child-rearing. Nursing schools and polytechnic institutes have also been promoted through the joint endeavor of the National Fund and the Red Crescent.

Significance

The Palestine National Fund raises and helps allocate the monies required to meet the overall needs of the PLO. In addition to military expenditures, the PLO must service its large, scattered population. Service to the Palestinians is usually funnelled through the PLO rather than dispensed directly by the host country to the refugee camps. In other situations, where Palestinians work in other states as professionals or laborers, their needs are usually the responsibility of the country where they are employed. The PLO therefore is more active among the residents of the refugee camps, where their concern for education, health care, and military recruitment is centered. The success of the National Fund is difficult to evaluate, given the extreme poverty of the refugees in the camps and the PLO's need to fund its military and organizational needs.

Palestine National Salvation Front (PNSF) 167

The Palestine National Salvation Front is the Syrian-sponsored organization opposed to the Yasir Arafat–dominated PLO. It is comprised of the Fatah Uprising, Saiqa, and the Popular Front for the Liberation of Palestine–General Command (PFLP–GC). In 1983, these factions attempted to destroy Arafat's forces, but after a sustained and costly struggle, Arafat was allowed to retreat from his positions in northern Lebanon, with cover provided by an unusual combination of foreign powers, namely the Soviet Union, France, and Israel. Syria had intended to replace the PLO with another group of its own making. Although this plan was thwarted, Damascus continued to provide sanctuary for members of the PNSF. The factions under Syrian influence have been known for their dramatic acts of international terrorism more than for political maneuvering. The PFLP–GC, for example, is led by Ahmed Jibril, and it is his organization that was originally believed responsible for downing Pan Am 103 over Lockerbie, Scotland, in 1988. PNSF tactics appeared to change in the wake of the Gulf War, however, and in April 1991 a statement from the organization called for reconciliation between the PLO and itself. In May 1991 a four-man PLO delegation met in Damascus with officials from the Palestine National Salvation Front. Khaled Fahoum, a PNSF leader and Farouk Kaddoumi, chief of the PLO's political department were counselled by Syrian President Hafez al-Assad, the host of the conference. At the conclusion of the meeting the PLO factions acknowledged the good offices provided by the Syrian president and announced their intention to "bury the past" and work together with Syria in pursuing Palestinian objectives. *See also* PALESTINE LIBERATION ORGANIZATION (PLO) (137); PALESTINE LIBERATION FRONT (PLF) (163).

Significance
The Gulf War has confused relationships between all the parties in the Middle East, and so, too, the Palestine National Salvation Front. The weakening of the PLO, and especially of Yasir Arafat, due in major part to PLO support for Saddam Hussain in the conflict, gave Hafez al-Assad political leverage not heretofore available to him. The PNSF attempt to bridge the rift between itself and the PLO must be seen as a tactic aimed at gaining greater influence for itself and Hafez al-Assad. Following the gulf war, the United States and Israel were in a stronger position to press a Palestine solution favorable to themselves. Given the Palestinian need for a "new" spokesman in Washington, and possibly in Israel as well, Assad seemed a likely candidate; hence, the need to woo the PLO as well as the Palestinian people. Thus, Syria convinced the Fatah Uprising, under the leadership of Colonel Said Musa, better known as Abu Musa, to evacuate his forces from the Beirut area. At the same time the PNSF was making peace overtures to the PLO, Abu Musa relocated his heavy artillery in the eastern Bekaa Valley, under Syrian control. In place of the Palestinian force in Beirut, Syria now had 12,000 of its own troops ranged alongside the Lebanese army of 16,000. Damascus not only consolidated its hold over most of Lebanon, but also maneuvered itself into a position from where it could become the principal spokesman for the Palestinian organizations and people. The May 1991 meeting convened by President Hafez al-Assad to unify the different and often violently opposed PLO factions followed Syria's new role as the dominant Arab state in Middle East

affairs. Yasir Arafat's subsequent journey to Damascus and his meeting with Assad supposedly ended the hostility between the two leaders. Overall, these developments pointed to the resurrection of the PLO in the wake of the Gulf War. It also disentangled the PLO from its Iraqi association and identified the organization with Syria, a principal in the winning coalition that included Egypt and Saudi Arabia.

Palestine Recognition 168

The Palestine Liberation Organization has been accorded diplomatic status as the sole legitimate representative of the Palestinian people by 115 countries (1988). These include many African states, all Muslim countries, and a large segment of the nonaligned world, where it is a member of a coordinating bureau. In addition, Spain, Malta, Yugoslavia, the Soviet Union, and Greece have recognized the PLO. The PLO also has been granted special status in other West and East European countries and Japan. The UN General Assembly consistently votes in favor of the PLO on issues related to Israel. The dramatic vote equating Zionism with racism in 1975, repealed in 1991, was the work of the PLO. In August 1982, in the midst of the Israeli invasion of Lebanon, the United Nations voted to condemn the Israeli action. Only the United States voted with Israel, although 20 nations abstained. Despite this outpouring of support for the PLO, the organization refused to accept UN Resolutions 242 and 338 until 1988, when Yasir Arafat chose a more diplomatic course in pursuit of PLO objectives. In July 1980, a UN emergency session on the Palestine question approved a resolution calling for the right of Palestinians to return to "their homes" in Israel and to establish their independent sovereign state. The action undermined the UN's capacity to deal with the situation. Nevertheless, the diplomatic and political leverage acquired by the PLO and the diminishing support for Israel in world forums was considered a positive sign of PLO success. Yasir Arafat's audience with the pope in Rome on September 15, 1982, was dramatic evidence of the PLO's recognized status. A low point in PLO activity was struck during 1990–1991 when the organization opposed the UN action against Iraq, but it was difficult to find any Israeli gain in this episode. *See also* REAGAN PROGRAM ON PALESTINE (177); RESOLUTION 242 (178); RESOLUTION 338 (179).

Significance

Global recognition for the PLO is a persistent source of pressure on Washington as well as Jerusalem. In the summer of 1982 the United States displayed willingness to relate to the PLO, especially after the organization permitted U.S. negotiator Philip Habib to arrange the PLO withdrawal from Beirut. PLO acceptance of U.S. Marines in the international peace force, with French and Italian units, and the decision not to press for Soviet presence also gained the attention of U.S. leadership. The United States was convinced that it was the only country capable of arranging a comprehensive settlement. Moreover, the Reagan administration, and especially Secretary of State George Shultz, repeatedly publicized the need to resolve the Palestinian question. President Reagan's plan for a Palestine entity on the West Bank and Gaza Strip in September 1982 was a telltale sign of changing official U.S. attitudes. On September 17, 1982, the United States voted with other UN Security Council members to condemn the Israeli occupation of West Beirut and to call for their immediate withdrawal. It was the first time the United States had taken such action. The Bush administration continued the Reagan policies, but with the passing of the Cold War, it took a different approach to Israel; indeed Washington made a more concerted effort to pressure Israel into yielding on the West Bank settlement issue, and more so, to agreeing to trade "land for peace" with the Arab states.

Palestinian Executive Committee 169

The Palestinian Executive Committee is the executive branch of the Palestinian "government-in-exile." It is the equivalent of a Palestinian cabinet. Its membership is assembled from leaders of the several organizations of the PLO, who are officially selected by the Palestine National Council and whose resolutions they are called upon to implement. It claims to represent the same cross-section of groups found in the National Council. The Executive Committee, unlike the National Council, is in permanent session and operates on a daily schedule. Its members therefore work on a full-time basis. The Executive Committee is constitutionally responsible to the National Council and performs the following functions: (1) it represents the Palestinian people wherever they may be; (2) it supervises the various bodies of the PLO in the areas of information, education, defense, culture, and foreign affairs; (3) it has primary responsibility for safeguarding the interests of Palestinians in the West Bank and Gaza territories (not sanctioned by Israel and rejected by Israeli authorities, who prefer to encourage the development of independent Palestinian self-governing bodies in areas under its occupation); (4) it issues directives, drafts programs, and decides how the PLO is to be organized and managed; and (5) it prepares the PLO budget and makes reports on all activities directly to the Palestine National Council. Yasir Arafat has been chairman of the Executive Committee since its creation. In 1988, Yasir Arafat, speaking for the new Palestine government-in-exile, declared the PLO's acceptance of UN Resolutions 242 and 338, thus arguing that the Palestinians had recognized Israel's right to exist. Following this announcement, the U.S. ambassador in Tunisia was authorized by Washington to meet with PLO officials to identify common ground for a Palestinian-Israeli peace settlement. Although Washington insisted it had not formally recognized the PLO, observers thought otherwise. Later, as a consequence of a PLO-associated terrorist raid against Israel, Washington broke off the talks. ***See also*** PALESTINE NATIONAL COUNCIL (164); PALESTINE LIBERATION ORGANIZATION (PLO) (137).

Significance

The Palestinian Executive Committee is the nerve center for the Palestine Liberation Organization. It groups together the leaders of the many factions that make up the PLO, and it acts as a government for the Palestine people. Since the Rabat, Morocco, summit meeting in 1974, King Hussain of Jordan has recognized the Executive Committee's right to represent Palestinians; the king's claim to represent the Palestinians was renounced. This act paved the way for Yasir Arafat's visit to the United Nations, where he was the first representative of a political movement without a country ever permitted to address the General Assembly. Earlier the PLO had been granted observer status at the UN, which permitted it to participate in the deliberations of the UN on all Palestine questions. Recognition of the PLO as the sole legitimate representative of the Palestinian people was thereby extended by a majority of nations in the UN (in excess of 115). Acting on a lead presented by the Palestinian Executive Committee, the General Assembly passed a resolution reaffirming "the inalienable rights of the Palestinian people" including their "right of self determination, . . . national independence and sovereignty." The Palestinian Executive Committee bears primary responsibility for realizing this goal, and over the last 20 years its leadership has been remarkably stable.

Palestinian Refugees **170**

The Palestinian refugees can be described as the entire body of Palestinians who vacated land and homes now in or controlled by the state of Israel, and their offspring. Another view of the Palestinian refugee confines the designation to those persons continuing to reside in "refugee camps." The latter are found in Jordan, the West Bank territory, Lebanon, and Syria. The former are scattered throughout the Arab world, and sizable minorities are also domiciled in Europe and the United States. Palestinians who are employed in a variety of countries may or may not be citizens of those countries, but they are no longer classified as refugees by the UN Relief and Works Agency, which has attempted to maintain a count of the "unabsorbed" Palestinian refugee community. The Palestinians who fled their homes in the new state of Israel in 1948–1949 moved into the West Bank and Jordan proper. In 1950, Jordan, then known as Transjordan, annexed the West Bank; all the Palestinian refugees were made citizens of the Kingdom of Jordan. They were permitted to compete for work on equal terms with other Jordanian citizens. They were also granted the right to vote in local elections. According to the *Statistical Yearbook* (1951), published by the Jordan Ministry of Economics, and the *Statistical Bulletin for Jordan* (1951), compiled by the UN Relief and Works Agency for Palestine Refugees, approximately 972,000 Palestinians resided in Jordan. Of these, 400,000 lived on the West Bank as residents, 100,000 lived in Jordan proper, and 472,000 were classified as camp refugees by the United Nations. Earlier the United Nations had indicated a figure of 538,000 refugees. It can be assumed that another 100,000 to 200,000 Palestinians made their exodus to Syria and Lebanon during this period. If all these figures are combined, the overall number of refugees totalled approximately 1.3 million. Camp refugees, however, would range between 600,000 and 750,000. Given the high birthrate of the Palestinian Arabs, more than 1 million Palestinians today live in Jordan, approximately half of these in refugee camps. Israel and Israeli-occupied territory contain the largest number of Palestinians, approximately 1.8 million (including 531,000 Israeli Arabs). The refugee population in Israel may be less than 10 percent given their domicile in established villages and towns. Nevertheless, the Arab description of their condition would classify as refugees all West Bank and Gaza Strip residents, approximately 1.3 million. The major refugee camps as perceived by international agencies are found in Jordan, Lebanon, and Syria. Their figures indicate that more than 1 million Palestinians are officially classified as having refugee status. ***See also*** UNITED NATIONS RELIEF AND WORKS AGENCY FOR PALESTINE REFUGEES (UNRWAPR) (185); PALESTINIANS (171).

Significance

The Palestine refugee question is heavily burdened by political issues. For purposes of international relief and assistance, the refugee is someone who is unable to look after his or her own needs or who does not receive adequate assistance from other sources, particularly the country where he or she sought refuge. Judged by these standards the Palestinian refugees describe a huge population, but only a lesser segment of the total Palestinian Arab population. Palestinians, however, consider themselves to be refugees whether they reside in camps or not, whether they are successful professionals, businessmen, or skilled laborers. Given a consciousness of nationality, the continuing stress on reclaiming land now in Israel, the reluctance of Arab states other than Jordan to confer citizenship, and the lingering hope that Israel will finally be defeated by Arab armies, Palestinian statelessness has become a worldwide issue. Statelessness is often equated with the term *refugee;* therefore, all Palestinians are refugees. Even the conferring of citizenship on Palestinians residing in Jordan and the occupied West Bank has not changed this interpretation. Nor have the achievements of Palestinians in the Middle East and elsewhere removed that designation. The Palestine refugee community is not the largest in the world. The Afghan refugees and the Somali refugees are more numerous and in comparatively more desperate circumstances. Their despair, however, has not received the attention gained by the Palestinians. Nor is consideration given to the Jews who fled or were driven from the Arab states. According to Israeli statistics approximately 800,000 "Oriental" Jews have been resettled in Israel. These immigrants are no longer considered refugees although problems of assimilation have been complex. The Israelis have long argued for the absorption of the Palestinian Arabs in the Arab lands where they now reside. Unlike the Oriental Jews, who have virtually no inclination to return to the land of their birth or ancestry, however, the Palestinians continue to express the opinion that they will return. Discussion on the creation of an independent Arab Palestinian state on the West Bank and Gaza may deal with the question of statelessness, but it does not effectively resolve the refugee dilemma.

Palestinians 171

The word *Palestine* was adopted by the Romans and refers to the biblical land of the Philistines. It was seldom used to describe the region following the Arab conquest in the seventh century. Great Britain revived the term when it established its mandate over the territory, having seized it from the Turks after World War I. All the people residing in the territory were considered to be Palestinians by the British, including Jews and Christians as well as Arabs. Among the various communities, the Arabs were least satisfied with the designation, preferring to be known as Arabs and members of the larger Arab nation of which "Palestine" was an integral part. At the end of World War I approximately 650,000 Arabs lived in Palestine, compared with approximately 60,000 Jews, after another 20,000 Jews had been forced to flee or were deported by the ruling Ottoman Turks. The Ottomans had been severe governors of the region, and there was little economic product until the early years of the twentieth century. Palestine had been a ravaged and neglected hinterland, satisfying only to the nomadic desert bedouin. But the development of more productive agricultural practices, albeit through absentee landlordism, in the early part of the twentieth century began to revive the territory. The sale of land to the Zionist Agency for distribution to Jewish East European settlers also gave the area new economic promise. As a consequence, Arabs from the surrounding area, especially Syrians and Egyptians, moved into the region in search of economic opportunity. Palestinian Arab society was based on agricultural activity. The land, however, was dominated by feudal-type land-owning families. Prominent among these were the Husayni, Abdul Hadi, Tajji, Shawwa, Ghesiani, Khudra, and Fahoum. Combined, these families controlled more than 4 million acres (1.6 million hectares) of land, or approximately half the cultivated land. Although smaller landholders controlled the remainder, the majority of the Arab population were peasant sharecroppers, totally dependent on their respective landlords. The Zionists purchased land for the exclusive use of the Jewish settlements, and the Jewish settlers had little to do with the Arab population that surrounded them. Despite tensions between the Jewish and Arab inhabitants, the former persisted. Moreover, during the British occupation of the Palestine mandate, not only did the Jewish community grow, but the commerce of the region also improved because of the administration's policy promoting commerce. The growth of trade in Palestine benefitted Arab families like the Nashashibi and the Khalidi, who left the land for the urban communities and who generally effected close relationships with the British. The movement of impoverished rural Arabs to the cities also added to the influence of the Nashashibi. Moreover, growing antagonism toward the Jewish settlers, who were blamed by the rural Arabs for their economic plight, was exploited by the Palestinian leaders. The Palestinian Arab leaders did not feel threatened until Zionist land acquisition spread and gave the Jewish settlers political leverage. Sensing a threat to their holdings, the Husaynis led the other landlords in condemning both British rule and Zionist activity. The Nashashibi and the other commercial families were less outspoken, but they, too, attempted to rally the aroused Arab masses in the cities. Although both the rural- and urban-based leadership exploited Arab sentiment and fear, nothing was done to alter the tribal and feudal relations that existed between the leaders and their supporters. As a consequence of this relative inaction—Arab riots against the Zionist community aroused passion and hatred on all sides but did nothing to advance political consciousness or the development of political institutions—nothing was done to instill national identity among the Arabs of Palestine. It was only after the creation of the state of Israel in 1948 that such consciousness began to emerge. Indeed, neither the 1948–1949 war against Israel nor the 1956 Suez War provided the Arabs with their distinct Palestinian identity. Arabs fled their lands and homes in great numbers in 1948. Some observers believe that they could return when Israel had been liquidated. Others insist that the exodus came at the urging of the invading Arab armies, the assumption being that the Arabs fled after the Israeli attack on the village of Deir Yassin, where 240 people were massacred. Fearing more such attacks, this argument goes, the Palestinian Arabs were compelled to take flight. Whatever the explanation for the large Arab Palestinian refugee community, Israel refused to permit the return of persons it judged hostile. It also wanted the land to resettle new immigrants. Those Arab Palestinians who remained in place, however, were absorbed within the Zionist state and made Israeli citizens. If there was a consciousness of Palestinian identity in this period, it should have been manifested in opposition to the annexation of the West Bank and East Jerusalem by Jordan. But even this development did not provoke the Palestinian Arabs to think in terms of a separate Palestine state. It was only with the publication of the Palestine National Covenant by the PLO following the 1967 war that Palestinian nationalism surfaced in a tangible and formidable way. The National Covenant denied the existence of Israel, and Palestinian consciousness developed in tandem with the notion that the children of the displaced Palestinians would return to the land and homes of their forebears. Israel's greater prowess in the military area, however, eventually brought Egypt to accept the Jewish state's existence. Although other Arab states were reluctant to follow Egypt's course, they demonstrated a willingness to acknowledge the state if certain conditions were met. Only the PLO and the rejectionist states, Iraq, Libya, Algeria, and South Yemen, refused to acknowledge the fact of a Jewish state in the Middle East. The Israeli attack on the PLO in Lebanon in 1982 was in part aimed at getting the PLO to recognize the realities of Israeli existence and power. It was also a signal to the Palestinians under Israeli administration in the West Bank and Gaza that their desire for political recognition could only be satisfied through political negotiation and compromise. There is little indication, however, that the Israelis did more than arouse Palestinian nationalism to a new pitch of intensity with the removal of the PLO from Beirut. Indeed, the Palestinian *intifada* that began in December 1987 gives ample credence to the growth of Palestinian political consciousness and national identity. According to PLO statistics, the Palestinians are scattered in states and territories. ***See also*** INTIFADA (151).

Significance
The Palestinian Arabs have received worldwide attention in the last 30 years. Their desire for a homeland has been dramatized in numerous ways. The United Nations has devoted more Assembly time to the Palestinian question than all other questions combined. International and transnational terrorism has been intimately associated with the Palestine Liberation Organization. Although other "terrorist" organizations predate it, the PLO has become a model as well as the inspiration for other violent political movements. Despite its identification with terrorism, the PLO has established a legitimate presence in the world community. Governments have recognized its purpose, and people in different parts of the world support its cause. Nations that earlier recognized Israel and accepted its aid and technical assistance have severed or modified their ties. Whether the break in diplomatic relations is caused by an appreciation of the Palestinian case or by pressure from influential, oil-producing Arab states, the fact remains that Israel was becoming more isolated. This development speaks to the most important aspect of the Palestinian question. The question of Palestine has symbolic as well as practical importance in the Arab world. Symbolically, the struggle for an Arab Palestine is related to the Arab quest for unity. Arabs generally perceive Israel as the last vestige of Western colonialism in the Middle East. They argue that Israel's placement prevents the unification of the Fertile Crescent Arabs with the Arabian Peninsula Arabs and the North African Arabs. As a ploy of the Western industrialized nations, Israel is said to be a current illustration of the "divide-and-rule" policy. Moreover, the Arabs see Israel as the opening wedge of a more concerted campaign to spread European ideas and institutions throughout the region. On the practical side, Israel's expansionist and settlement policies are given as evidence for the complaint that the Zionist state is not content to live within frontiers originally arrived at. Israel's initial expansion in the 1948–1949 war and again as a result of the 1967 war are supposedly proof of Israeli purposes. Annexation of East Jerusalem and the Syrian Golan Heights, as well as reluctance to give up the occupied Gaza Strip or West Bank territory, is ample

evidence. Israel's role in Lebanon in the 1982 war with the PLO is also described as an attempt to bring Lebanon under Jerusalem's control and neutralize Syria. Israel's response to these allegations, accusations, and condemnations has been serious and bitter. Jerusalem has offered the Palestinians a form of autonomy under Israeli supervision, but self-determination for the Palestinians has been rejected as inappropriate and a threat to Israel's security. Moreover, because the Palestinians are internationally recognized only through the operations of the Palestine Liberation Organization, and because Israel absolutely refuses to deal with the PLO, the impasse is virtually unbreakable. Israel will not recognize the PLO as the sole spokesman for the Palestinians; the PLO remains divided and ambiguous on Israel's right to exist. Neither actor, therefore, is willing to come to grips with the realities of their joint predicament. Compromise appears to have been ruled out. An all-or-nothing attitude is projected by both sides. The concerned world, including the United States, wishes to see a solution, and the establishment of a self-governing Arab Palestinian state is thought to be essential. The PLO has succeeded in establishing the principle that a separate Palestine Arab state must be created. Where, when, and how that state is formed may prove to be more tedious, but there can be little doubt now that the Palestinian Arabs are a national entity in the making and that the Palestinian Arab nation has achieved a sophisticated level of cultural and political exclusiveness. Assisted by some oil-producing Muslim nations, buttressed by conservative Arab and non-Arab Muslim states that seek a more tranquil environment in which to promote their modernization programs, and reinforced by revolutionary governments and radical political movements, the Palestinians appear destined to realize their goal. The key problem is not whether there should be an Arab Palestine, but how mutual fear and hatred and the clashing interests of Israelis and Palestinians can be overcome.

Parliamentary State: Israel **172**

The Republic of Israel was established in 1948 as a secular, parliamentary entity. Elections to the parliament (Knesset), a unicameral body, are held every four years, and members are elected by universal adult suffrage on a nationwide system of proportional representation. There are no constituencies, and the electoral system encourages a multiplicity of political parties, and hence the subsequent formation of coalition governments. The prime minister and cabinet are drawn from the leading party and coalition in the Knesset. The prime minister is the head of government. The prime minister can be removed and a new government formed prior to a regular four-year election if the administration loses its majority in the Knesset. The head of state is the president, elected by the Knesset for a five-year term. He or she operates in a more or less ceremonial capacity, but is empowered to sign all laws and appoint diplomatic and national officials. Israel's presidents have been Chaim Weizmann (1948–1952); Yitzhak Ben-Zvi (1952–1963); Zalman Shazar (1963–1973); Ephraim Katzir (1973–1978); Yitzhak Navon (1978–1983); and Chaim Herzog (1983–). Israel's prime ministers have been David Ben-Gurion (1948–1954); Moshe Sharatt (1954–1955); David Ben-Gurion (1955–1962); Levi Eshkol (1962–1968); Golda Meir (1968–1974); Yitzhak Rabin (1974–1977); Menachem Begin (1977–1983); Yitzhak Shamir (1983–1984); Shimon Peres (1984–1986); and Yitzhak Shamir (1986–1992).

Israel does not have a written constitution. As in the United Kingdom, the parliament prefers the evolution of a constitution through the incorporation of specific laws, such as the Law of Return (1950), the Election Law (1951), Equal Rights for Women (1951), the Nationality Law (1952), the Judges Law (1953), the Basic Law (1958), the Courts Law (1969), and the Contracts (Remedies for Breach) Law (1970). Israel's many communities are represented in the Knesset, and although debate is often passionate, the parliament is expressive of the country's diverse citizenry. Apart from the continuing Arab-Israeli conflict, a primary problem facing the Zionist state is Israel's ever-expanding Arab population. Arab-Israelis are 20 percent of the total population, and their birthrate is considerably higher than that of the Jewish community. Moreover, approximately 1.5 million Arabs live in the occupied West Bank and Gaza. Any attempt to absorb those territories would bring the Arab component almost abreast with the Jewish population. Ten percent of Israel's electorate is already composed of Arab-Israelis. No less significant, the Arab birthrate is two-and-a-half times that of the Jews, which is increasing at less than 1.5 percent annually. Also, emigration of Jews to the United States and other industrialized countries drains away vital citizens. A study released in 1981 revealed that from 1969 to 1979, 510,000 people had left Israel, while only 384,000 had settled in the country. Even without the Arabs of the Occupied Territories, Israeli-Arabs would be more than 25 percent of the total population by the year 2000, if it were not for the volume of Soviet Jews arriving in the country. Israel, therefore, is undergoing important demographic changes that must influence the character of its overall performance. Greater emphasis on the Oriental Jews, especially those originating in Arab countries, means catering to somewhat different values and interests. Not only is Israel in a stage of transformation, but European Zionism is also destined to undergo metamorphosis. ***See also*** POLITICAL PARTIES: ISRAEL (139); KNESSET (159).

Significance
Israel is the only state in the Middle East governed according to democratic principles and motivated by liberal ideas. Offices are conditional grants of authority, leadership is fallible and accountable to the nation, and the population is provided with opportunity to register dissatisfaction with its leadership without penalty. Moreover, Israel's heavy dependence on its armed forces and the enormous expenditure on weapons do not appear to threaten political institutions. There has never been a hint of a military takeover, and the armed forces are broadly civilianized, including their professional core. Israel is not without problems that appear to undermine the political process, however. The integration of the many nationalities, the clash between European and Oriental Jews, and the dilemma of fully integrating the Israeli Arabs, as well as the Arabs in the Occupied Territories, continue to burden the nation and weigh heavily on the democratic system. In 1989–1990, Soviet Jews began entering the country in large numbers. Projections indicate as many as 250,000 will arrive in Israel by 1995. Providing for this number is a monumental problem, but their arrival promises to maintain a relative balance in favor of the Jewish population of Israel.

Peel Commission *173*

Formally known as the Royal Commission of Enquiry, and led by Earl Peel, an important figure in the administration of British India, the

Peel Commission was empowered by Parliament to study Arab-Zionist relations in the wake of the 1936 Arab revolt. From the beginning of their administration of the Palestine Mandate, the British found themselves caught between Zionist insistence that the Balfour Declaration be honored in all its parts and Arab resistance to increased Jewish immigration to Palestine. Great Britain assumed its role in Palestine with a view toward strengthening its strategic position in the Middle East vis-à-vis its rivals, especially France and, to a lesser extent, Russia, Germany, and Italy. It is doubtful that the British were seriously interested in promoting either Zionist or Arab nationalist aims. And they were certainly ill-equipped to mediate differences between the Semitic antagonists. Nevertheless, the British were trapped in a situation primarily of their own making. There was little cooperation between the communities. Only in the marketing of citrus fruits was there genuine interaction, and as a consequence, Arabs and Jews placed considerable distance between one another. Moreover, the Arabs displayed little sympathy for Jews fleeing persecution in Nazi Germany. The many German Jews who worked their way to Palestine were considered a threat to the Arab way of life, and their growing numbers only added to the fear that Zionists would eventually overwhelm them. The Arabs, therefore, found common cause with Hitler. Hitler's anti-Jewish program suggested an Arab ally in the struggle with Zionism. Paradoxically, the Nazi persecution of European Jewry also made the Zionist quest more desperate and hence accelerated the shift of population from Europe to Palestine. In the first four years of Hitler's rule in Germany (1933–1937), the Jewish population of Palestine increased almost twofold, but the Arabs did not make the connection. Instead of condemning the Nazi policy of religious persecution, Palestine Arab leaders, like the *mufti* of Jerusalem, appeared to justify the German program. The British came to dread their assignment in Palestine. Their administration attempted to improve the economic infrastructure of the region, and they were not reluctant to promote development. But the major portion of British time, energy, and resources were consumed in policing the Zionist and Arab communities and maintaining law and order in a superheated environment. Numerous investigations were carried out by sincere and dedicated people after the riots of 1921. These commissions reported that hostilities between Arabs and Jews had commenced with the end of World War I. There was only minor conflict when the Zionists first began settling in the Holy Land. The Balfour Declaration, however, collided with the emergence of Arab nationalism, and the Palestinian Arabs sensed that they, unlike their brethren in the Arabian Peninsula, Mesopotamia, or Egypt, could not satisfy their aspirations for political independence. Although the British were perceived as the culprits, the Palestinian Arabs targeted the Jewish population of Palestine. Arabs attacked Jews in their settlements and at religious sites. In 1929, Jews were assaulted at the Wailing Wall in Jerusalem, and efforts were made to restrict their use of facilities near Muslim religious places. The prevailing view held that the Jews were growing too numerous. The only way the Arabs could be mollified, therefore, was to limit Jewish immigration. The Mandate Commission of the League of Nations insisted on such a limitation, and the British dispatched Sir John Hope-Simpson to the region to make still another report. The Hope-Simpson Report of 1930 strongly urged a sharp curtailment in the Zionist program, fearing that too much arable land was coming under Jewish control. The

1930 Passfield White Paper reiterated this position and argued for the distribution of new land to the Arabs, not to the Zionists. The Zionist Organization, however, was not docile. It decried the reports that placed impediments in the way of Jewish settlements, and the British prime minister was pressured to modify the White Paper restrictions. The Arabs spoke of betrayal in the wake of this action, and the gulf between the communities and their European administrators widened. The British, however, continued to send their emissaries to the area in the vain hope that a formula might yet be found to break the impasse. The League of Nations did likewise, but each committee did little more than reiterate what earlier bodies had already discerned. The Zionists and Arabs were irreconcilable foes, and no measure of mediation could alter the situation. The Peel Commission of 1936, therefore, went to Palestine with a realistic appraisal of conditions. They quickly concluded that binationalism was no answer to the problem. The binational Arab-Jewish state had been promoted by non-Zionist Jews, and some important members of the Jewish community in Palestine sought to encourage it. The Peel Commission, however, reflected on the European character of the Palestine Jews and the Oriental character of the Arabs. In its judgment, the two were not compatible. For this and other reasons, the Peel Commission took the first step toward the partition of the British mandate into two separate states, one for the Arabs and the other for the Jews. The Arab state as conceived by the commission was many times larger than the Jewish state. Moreover, the Jewish state was divided into a number of small fragments, which caused observers to question its viability. Thus, the Zionist Congress of 1937 rejected the proposal, insisted on the maintenance of the mandate, and called for increased Jewish immigration. The Arabs also rejected the partition plan and demanded a freeze on Jewish immigration. In the end, the Peel Commission, despite its noble intentions, merely increased the fury of the Arab population and frustrated the Zionists. Despite the intensification of Arab riots, London dispatched the Palestine Partition Commission to the area in 1938. But this body merely rescinded the proposal of its predecessor. Partition was declared impossible in the face of violent Arab opposition. The commission recommended a meeting of all the parties to draft a mutually acceptable program. This conference, however, was never held. In 1939 London issued another White Paper that reflected its total frustration. Jews would be permitted to enter Palestine for a five-year period, and once their numbers were one-third of the total, such immigration would cease. Land sales to Jews would be greatly limited, and the Arabs would have a larger voice in any future Zionist activity in Palestine. ***See also*** ZIONISM (189); YISHUV (188); HUSAYNIS (150); BALFOUR DECLARATION (147); PALESTINE NATIONAL COVENANT (165).

Significance
The Peel Commission was the culmination of numerous British efforts aimed at reconciling the rival moral claims of Jews and Arabs. Its inevitable conclusion, that only partition of Palestine between Jew and Arab, the Solomonian decision, would give each community the objective it sought, could not conceal the Arab view that the Jews were not entitled to a national home in Palestine. The Arabs had only begun to reassert themselves after centuries of eclipse and subordination to alien powers. The British decision to establish a Jewish state in their midst was judged a form of European imperialism. According to the Arabs such a state would be used to divide and

thus rule the Arab world, and they were violently opposed to the program. The Peel Commission further revealed how deeply divided the communities were. It emphasized the almost total absence of communication between Arabs and Jews, the different idioms spoken, and the disparate cultures and traditions represented. Neither the Peel Commission nor any of the others, however, examined the political rivalry in the Arab world and how this affected the Zionist question. Nor did the commission seriously attempt to absolutely favor one side against the other. Each commission sought some form of compromise in circumstances where compromise was unthinkable or simply was not psychologically or culturally defined. The Arabs believed they had the capacity to prevent the Jews from creating an independent state in their midst, and they refused to accept anything that would prevent them from realizing their objective of a unified Arab Middle East. The Jews, on the other hand, faced with the savagery of the Nazi regime, saw no other recourse but to move as many of their brethren to Palestine as resources and conditions allowed. During World War II, the Jewish Agency and Zionist organizations used all means, including illegal ones, to transport as many European Jews as possible to Palestine. Moreover, Zionist terrorist organizations such as the Irgun Zvai Leumi and the Stern Gang struck directly at the British administration in Palestine, because it was perceived as limiting the immigration of Jews who, fleeing from Hitler's death camps, had no other place to go. The Peel Commission proved to be the last real opportunity for Arabs and Jews to arrive at a modus vivendi. In the wake of the commission's recommendations, however, events assumed an importance greater than any of the principals could have imagined. The result was to be a relentless campaign in which violence obscured all calls to reason.

PLO Exodus from Beirut *174*

In accordance with arrangements negotiated by the U.S. diplomat Philip Habib, the Palestine Liberation Organization withdrew its headquarters and troops from West Beirut during the last 10 days of August 1982. Included in the evacuation (the Israelis called it an "expulsion") were mainline units from Al-Fatah; the Popular Front for the Liberation of Palestine (PFLP); the Popular Front for the Liberation of Palestine–General Command, As-Saiqa (the Syrian-officered contingent); the Arab Liberation Front; the Popular Democratic Front for the Liberation of Palestine (PDFLP); and the Popular Struggle Front. Regular Syrian army units also withdrew from Beirut during this period. ***See also*** PALESTINE LIBERATION ORGANIZATION (PLO) (137); ISRAELI-PLO WAR, 1982 (249); WEST BEIRUT MASSACRE (187).

Significance

The slight discrepancy in the total count between Lebanese and Israeli authorities (Lebanese count: 14,656; Israeli count: 14,614) was ignored, since it was the virtual termination of PLO presence in Beirut. Both the Israelis and the PLO publicized a great victory for their cause. The Israelis insisted that the PLO had been dealt a devastating blow from which they could not recover. The PLO praised the staying power of its fighters in the face of a vastly superior army. Indeed, the PLO reveled in the thought that its forces had held off the Israelis longer than any other Arab army. Behind the oratory and rhetoric, however, were a number of realities, some old, some new. The Israelis eliminated the PLO threat to their northern settlements. West Beirut had been freed from the PLO grasp, and its headquarters, leadership, and forces fell back to Syria, other Arab states, and non-Arab countries sympathetic with their cause. A good portion of the PLO army was either scattered in a number of locations, some of them distant from Israel, or held as prisoners-of-war. The Israelis nonetheless paid a high price for their military success. In excess of 400 Israelis had been killed. Many hundreds more had been wounded. Guerrillas continued to operate in southern Lebanon against Israeli occupation forces, although in very limited force. West Beirut was free of the PLO, but it was still the home of the Murabitun. These Muslim Lebanese leftists violently opposed the Phalange government, and some observers believe they were responsible for the assassination of president-elect Bashir Gemayel. Gemayel's death provoked the Israeli army to occupy West Beirut to neutralize the dissident factions, but it also became more entangled in Lebanon's historical domestic cleavages. Moreover, Syrian and PLO forces remained in Lebanon's Bekaa Valley. Northern Lebanon, especially the major city of Tripoli, became an outpost of the remaining PLO and their Lebanese Muslim supporters. The major portion of the PLO army was encamped in Syria, in proximity to Israel, and other contingents could be expected to join them at an opportune moment. Although increased terrorist activity was a distinct possibility, given sympathy for the PLO position in Europe and elsewhere, its leadership appeared more likely to use the political leverage gained from the Lebanese campaign to expand its diplomatic efforts. Yasir Arafat's audience with the pope in Rome in September 1982 was one dramatic indication of this policy. Moreover, President Ronald Reagan's call for a self-governing Palestinian entity, controlled by Jordan, indicated that the U.S. government was also preparing the way for face-to-face negotiations with the PLO. The PLO exodus from West Beirut therefore was not the end of the organization.

PLO in Southern Lebanon 175

In the winter of 1991 there were an estimated 6,000 PLO guerrillas loyal to Yasir Arafat in the southern Lebanese port of Sidon. Sidon, approximately 25 miles south of Beirut, was virtually outside the control of the Lebanese government established by Syria in Beirut in 1990–1991. Sidon was also the port used by the PLO to bring weapons into the country. The total number of Palestinians in Lebanon is approximately 372,000, the figure supplied by the UN relief agency responsible for Palestinian refugees. About half of the Palestinians live in 12 refugee districts in the south, north, and eastern parts of the country. In addition there are some 5,000 PLO guerrillas in the Bekaa region of eastern Lebanon and the northern part of Tripoli, areas under Syrian control. ***See also*** PALESTINE LIBERATION ORGANIZATION (PLO) (137); LEBANON CIVIL WAR: THE CONCLUDING PHASE (252).

Significance

Future Lebanese stability depends on the disposition of the PLO. In the past, Lebanese troops were no match for the Palestinians, who could mobilize a far larger force. Moreover, PLO headquarters in Tunisia had issued a critical rebuff to the Lebanese leaders, who have sought to corral their armed militia in Lebanon. Heavy fighting ensued in June 1991 as a Lebanese force, supported by Syrian units, engaged PLO guerrillas on four fronts in southern Lebanon. By July 2 the PLO was forced to flee to refugee districts in Ain Hilwe and Meih Meih. Sidon, however, fell under Lebanese control, and the guerrilla bases in Ain al Dilb, Jensnaya, Kafr Jarra, Al Krayeh, and Ain Elmir were all neutralized. The PLO called the assault a "massacre of the Palestinian people" and urged a ceasefire. Yasir Arafat declared Lebanese sovereignty could be reconciled with the PLO cause. Israel acknowledged the reoccupation of the region by Lebanese forces, but it insisted on sustaining its security zone, a narrow strip of land along the width of the border. It also pledged to continue its alliance with the 3,000-man South Lebanon Army, a local militia financed and trained by Israel. The Israeli government reiterated its concern that Lebanon's southern frontier was still used by PLO terrorist organizations engaged in hit-and-run tactics against the Israeli state. Israel also insisted that its forces remain in place so long as Syria deployed 40,000 troops in Lebanon.

Rabbinical Council **176**

The Israeli Rabbinical Council is the supreme authority in the religious life of the country. The council consists of one Ashkenazic rabbi and one Sephardic chief rabbi who preside jointly over the body. Its members are also drawn from each of these two denominations. Israeli politics has been dominated by Ashkenazim, who are European Jews or those Israeli-born members of the government who identify with a European heritage. The greater influx of the Sephardic, or Oriental Jews, their higher birthrate, and their greater tendency to remain in Israel have established them as the larger population, however. The Sephardim tend to be more scrupulous in their religious practices, and their demands are often reflected in the work of the Rabbinical Council. The council is divided into departments for kashrut (dietary supervision), regulating religious scribes, sanctioning marriage registrars, validating rabbinical ordination, interpreting biblical precepts, and reconciling conflicts in religious law. The chief rabbis also preside over a Supreme Rabbinical Court that stands at the apex of a pyramidal religious court system. The Supreme Rabbinical Court will hear appeals from judgments rendered in district rabbinical courts. Moreover, every local authority in Israel is required by law to appoint a religious council. The budget for the local religious courts is obtained by local authority and contributions from the Ministry of Religious Affairs. The rabbinical staff of the local councils consists of approximately 400 persons. The overall religious needs of the population of Israel are managed by the Ministry of Religious Affairs, which is a cabinet-level organ. The ministry supervises the upkeep of the holy shrines, supports theological seminaries, and subsidizes the construction of synagogues. It also audits the accounts of the religious councils. The Ministry of Religious Affairs also is responsible for protecting and sustaining Muslim and Christian religious institutions. Representatives from these and other religious orders are officials of the ministry. Nevertheless, Israel is a Jewish state. The Jewish sabbath (Friday sundown to Saturday sundown) and various calendar holy days are official days of rest. No business is conducted during these commemorations. Non-Jews pursue their own days of rest (Muslim: Friday; Christian: Sunday), and the observances of these communities are likewise safeguarded. The Israeli Declaration of Independence guarantees freedom of religion to every citizen. All religions are declared equal before the secular law of the state. All holy places are deemed to be inviolate. The Jewish population of Israel is in excess of 3 million. The non-Jewish population, not including the Occupied Territories, is approximately 730,000. ***See also*** TEMPLE MOUNT INCIDENT (184).

Significance
The Rabbinical Council and the Ministry of Religious Affairs is in keeping with the Middle Eastern orientation toward religion. Judaism is as significant to Israelis as Islam is to Arabs, Turks, Persians, and Pakistanis. Approximately one-third of the Israeli Jewish population practice their religion with intensity. The majority, however, are either casual in their worship or follow a wholly secular lifestyle. Like some Arab countries, Israel, too, has its religious zealots. Involved in the portion that follows a disciplined religious program is a nucleus of very orthodox believers. Some among this smaller group oppose the state of Israel on religious grounds. Others insist that the state should represent biblical teachings and forecasts. Among this element are those who stress the incorporation of lands that are technically the property of non-Jews. The ultra-religious insist upon the establishment of Jewish settlements in lands occupied by Israel since the 1967 war. The West Bank—Judea and Samaria to the Israelis—has been populated by approximately 25,000 Israeli settlers, but the government intention is to create a far more formidable Jewish community in that region. Estimates run as high as 1 million Jews one day residing in Judea-Samaria. The conservative Likud government of Menachem Begin not only spoke of Jewish rights to the West Bank territory, it also spoke of Israel's strategic needs. In this instance, the more intensely religious elements are prepared to settle the Occupied Territories, and their religious purpose dovetails with the country's security needs. The melding of politics and religion, national security and faith, explains the strength of the convictions of those pressing for Israeli supremacy over their Arab neighbors. The clash between Muslim and Jewish communities is thus intensified. The Israeli government insists that it stands for the freedom of all religions, and it pledges protection to all the holy places coming within its jurisdiction. But incidents such as the 1982 assault by a deranged Israeli soldier on Muslim worshippers at the principal mosque in Jerusalem enflamed the entire Muslim world. The Temple Mount incident, in which a number of Muslims were killed in 1990, was deemed so serious that it was brought before the UN Security Council. Although the conflict between Israelis and Arabs, and to some extent Muslims generally, has been couched in politico-military terms, the underlying religious character of the struggle cannot be ignored. Moreover, in a period of heightened religious activity, and with politicized religions on the ascendancy, this condition does not lend itself to the reconciliation of rival moral claims.

Reagan Program on Palestine — 177

On the eve of the final stage of the PLO pullout from West Beirut, President Ronald Reagan spoke to the American people and the world on the subject of Palestine. He noted that he was "determined to seize that moment" (September 1, 1982) to put forward his administration's plan for the settlement of the Palestinian question. Reagan called upon the Israelis to cease all new settlements in the West Bank, to grant full autonomy to the Palestinians residing there, and to permit the Jordanians to reassume the overall administration of the territory. The U.S. president also reopened the question of Jerusalem. Although he indicated a desire to keep the city united, he emphasized the need to negotiate its future status. President Reagan discounted the creation of a fully independent Palestinian state in the West Bank and Gaza, but he also reiterated his government's opposition to any Israeli plan to annex the territories. The president emphasized his support for the Camp David accords and pledged to guarantee Israel's security. But he also noted the impossibility of promoting peace in the region if the aspirations and concerns of the Arabs were not taken into account. Calling his proposal the "new realism," Reagan urged the Israelis to respect Palestinian claims to self-government; he also asked for reciprocity from the Palestinians in respect of Israel's sovereign independence. The Arab states were encouraged to accept the reality of Israeli presence in the Middle East. Given the timing of the speech and the political and diplomatic leverage gained by the Palestinians during the Israeli siege of Beirut, Reagan's presentations tended to buttress the Arab position. In Israel, where the proposal had been received earlier in the form of a letter to Prime Minister Begin, there was angry rebuke. The government rejected the plan in all its parts, describing it as a threat to the existence of the Israeli nation. The Arab world responded differently to the proposal. At a summit meeting in Morocco during the second week of September, the Arab heads of state agreed to a communiqué accepting certain features of the Reagan plan. The Arabs called for guaranteeing Israel's security through the aegis of the United Nations, but they did not specifically call for the recognition of Israeli independence. Moreover, the heads of state demanded the establishment of an independent Palestine Arab state on the West Bank and Gaza, a matter at variance with President Reagan's call for Palestinian autonomy under Jordanian supervision. Yasir Arafat attended the session as chief spokesman for the PLO, which continued to receive official Arab support as the only organization representing the Palestinians. Israel was thus even more determined to hold on to the Occupied Territories. Prime Minister Begin used the occasion of a Knesset debate to declare that Judea and Samaria (the West Bank) would remain within the jurisdiction of Israel. Begin's statement appeared to confirm Israeli intentions to annex the West Bank. Furthermore, the Israeli government announced a plan to expand Jewish settlements on the West Bank, despite President Reagan's call for a freeze on such activity. *See also* ISRAELI-PLO WAR, 1982 (249); PLO EXODUS FROM BEIRUT (174).

Significance

The Reagan proposal on Palestine was meant to be the opening gun in a new campaign by Washington to develop an "even-handed" policy in the Middle East. Secretary of State George Shultz had just assumed the foreign policy post with the stated intention of pushing the Palestinian question toward a solution, with or without Israeli encouragement. The massive Israeli onslaught in Lebanon had caused a shift in U.S. public opinion away from all-out support of the Jewish state. Along with Europeans, Americans now demanded a solution of the Palestine question. The Reagan administration had an opportunity to capitalize on popular sentiment at home as much as it hoped to recapture the support of its estranged allies in the Arab world. The central purpose of the Reagan speech was not to state the only solution to the problem, but to emphasize Washington's determination to force the arch rivals to negotiate a settlement, and in particular, to pressure the Israelis, if not their government, to take a less belligerent approach to the Palestine question. Indeed, there was some evidence that President Reagan was talking over the head of the Israeli government to the Israeli public and also to the Labor Party opposition. Although President Reagan did not threaten to withdraw future aid to Israel, mounting evidence indicated such a possibility. Washington was gambling that in the democratic state of Israel the Israeli voter would have the final say. If Israel expected to continue its close relationship with the United States, the Israelis might well consider the need to replace the Begin government with one more amenable to a compromise settlement with the Palestinian Arabs. A poll taken in Israel in mid-September revealed that Israelis were equally divided between those who wished to follow the policy of the Begin government and those who were prepared to yield the West Bank and Gaza under certain guarantees. The Reagan administration concluded that the time was ripe for diplomacy, but the outright rejection of the plan by the PLO in 1983 indicated how difficult that task would be.

Resolution 242 *178*

Resolution 242 was adopted unanimously by the UN Security Council on November 22, 1967, following the Six-Day Middle East War of 1967. The resolution notes the inadmissibility of acquiring territory by war and "the need to work for a just and lasting peace in which every State in the area can live in security." To achieve this goal, the resolution calls upon Israel to remove its forces from territory occupied in the Six-Day War. It calls upon all the belligerents, indeed all the Arab states, to end their state of belligerency and respect the sovereignty and territorial integrity and political independence of every state in the region. The salient clause affirms "their right to live in peace within secure and recognized boundaries free from threats or acts of force." Navigation through international waterways is also provided, as is the settlement of the refugee question. The secretary-general of the United Nations is also called upon to dispatch an emissary to the area to promote agreement and peaceful settlement among the parties.

Significance

UN Resolution 242 is the most publicized framework for bringing about Arab-Israeli tranquility. It is cited in most situations where interaction between the parties is encouraged. Israel and most Arab states have at one time or another supported 242. Iraq, Libya, Algeria, and Yemen, the rejectionist states, have persistently ignored it. Although 242 received approval from Israel and some of its immediate neighbors, it has never been honored because of the difficulty in promoting simultaneity. Israel has always claimed that it cannot implement its part of the resolution because there is little inclination on the part of most Arabs to comply with the arrangement. Resolution 242 does not spell out Israel's right to exist, nor does it specify Israel by name when guaranteeing the right of all countries in the area to live in peace. The only particular reference to Israel is that section calling for its withdrawal from occupied land. Israel says that it is prepared to negotiate under the terms of 242, but it anticipates action being taken by its adversaries before it would agree to vacate territory acquired in the 1967 war. Resolution 242 is mentioned in the Camp David agreement of 1978, and the subsequent peace treaty with Egypt did produce Israeli withdrawal from the Sinai, occupied in the 1967 war. In the absence of any indication that the other Arab states are prepared to follow Egypt's lead, Israel feels justified in consolidating its hold on the remaining territory. The annexation of the Golan Heights reveals that Jerusalem does not expect its relations with Damascus ever to equal those with Cairo. In absorbing the Golan and in maintaining occupation on the West Bank and Gaza, the Israelis note that 242 somewhat ambiguously permits states "to live in peace within secure and recognized boundaries free from threats of acts of force." Yasir Arafat, speaking for the Palestine Liberation Organization in 1988, said his organization accepted Resolution 242. Nevertheless, continuing attacks on Israeli targets by PLO units caused the Israelis to question the sincerity of the declaration and to harden their stand on the West Bank territories.

Resolution 338 — 179

UN Security Council Resolution 338 was adopted October 21–22, 1973, in connection with the 1973 Arab-Israeli War. The resolution calls upon all parties in the 1973 war to cease firing and terminate all military activity. It then calls upon the belligerents to implement Resolution 242, which was adopted by the Security Council in the aftermath of the 1967 war. Resolution 338 states that negotiations for a "just and durable" peace in the Middle East should commence concurrently with the ceasefire. ***See also*** RESOLUTION 242 (178).

Significance

Resolution 338, like Resolution 242, was prompted by hostilities between Israel and its Arab neighbors. Both resolutions reaffirm the notion of a negotiated settlement between the parties, imply the inability to resolve difficult issues on the battleground, and address themselves to eliminating the underlying conflict in the wars between the parties. Israel and Egypt as well as Syria and Jordan approved Resolution 338. The PLO also claims it accepted 338. The states opposing 242, however, also rejected 338. Resolution 338 is linked with 242 and in fact reinforces the validity of 242. It is important to note, however, that the parties to the 1973 war accepted the ceasefire terms of 338. In the months that followed, after the shuttle diplomacy of Henry Kissinger, Israel and Egypt, and Israel and Syria agreed to the creation of a UN presence between their forces.

Semites — 180

The largest general language group in the Middle East are the Semites. The two living Semitic languages are Arabic and Hebrew. There are also Chaldean and Syriac speakers, but Chaldean and Syriac are primarily limited to religious observances and are not considered current vernacular languages. What is known about the early Semitic languages is often traced to Akkadian records and associated with the Assyrians and Babylonians of antiquity. The only link with an existing survivor of these languages is with those who use Syriac in their rituals. Aramaic, which before the Islamic era was spoken in parts of the Holy Land and in present-day Iraq, is also related to the Semitic languages. Aramaic usually employs the Syriac script. The majority of the Aramaic-speaking population were Christians who converted to Islam and eventually adopted Arabic. The Nestorians of Iraq and the Maronites of Lebanon are descendants of these early Christians. So, too, are the Greek Orthodox and Jacobites who use Syriac in their religious ceremonies. Arabic and Hebrew are traced to the language of the Phoenicians, a Semitic people who traveled between the European continent, the Middle East, and North Africa. Arabic was largely confined to the Arabian Peninsula prior to the Islamic era, which commenced in the seventh century A.D. The Arab conquests changed the character of the conquered peoples, especially those who accepted Islam. Indeed, the Arabic language, with its many spoken dialects, was established throughout the Middle East and North Africa as a result of these conquests. Other languages such as Persian, Turkish, and Urdu were also influenced by the Arabians. Although the term *Arab* does not designate a peculiar nationality, e.g., there are vast differences between Libyans and Syrians, the Arabic language is a binding force and indeed may be more significant to the notion of Arab unity than Islam because there are many non-Muslim Arabs.

Hebrew should not be confused with Yiddish. The latter is an East European-cum-German dialect that includes numerous Hebrew loanwords. Hebrew and Arabic are derived from the same source and use essentially the same grammar, vocabulary, and sentence structure. Jews are difficult to designate. Not all Jews identify with, let alone speak, Hebrew. Language therefore is not judged to be as important to the notion of Jewish unity as religion.

Significance
It is often noted that Jews and Arabs are historical brothers. Their common Semitic origin is often cited both for their inability to reconcile rival claims and for their inherent capacity to find a solution for their joint problems. From time to time, efforts have been made to bridge differences between Arabs and Jews. In the aftermath of World War I, in some quarters, there was talk about promoting cooperation between the two communities. In the wake of World War II and the Arab-Israeli dispute there again surfaced discussion about resolving the crisis through "binational" development. Emphasis has been given to the common source of Jewish and Arab traditions. Despite these efforts and rationalizations, however, the two peoples are largely disposed toward separate, independent political-social lives. There has never been a plan for a greater Semitic state, and it is doubtful that one could ever arise given the many non-Semitic peoples who today consider themselves to be Muslim on the one side and Jewish on the other.

Sephardic Jews 181

Sepharad is the Hebrew word for Spain; Sephardim or Sephardic Jews were located in Spain until the Spanish Inquisition led to their brutalization and finally their expulsion from Spain in 1492. This Diaspora scattered the Jewish Spanish community to areas over the Mediterranean region, with a large number finding refuge in the Ottoman Empire, the precursor of modern Turkey. ***See also*** ASHKENAZIC JEWS (146).

Significance
Jews not deemed to be Ashkenazim are generally referred to as Sephardic or Oriental Jews. Originally, Sephardic Jews traced their origin to Spain, but in contemporary times any Jew, whether coming from Ethiopia, Yemen, or India, is described as a Sephardic Jew. The majority population of Israel in the 1990s is therefore composed of Sephardic and Oriental Jews. This body of Israeli Jewry is more identified with the conservative political organizations, and they are major supporters of West Bank settlements and the government's hardline policy toward the Arab states as well as the Palestinians.

Sons of Palestinian Martyrs Workshop Association (SAMED) 182

The Sons of the Palestinian Martyrs Workshop Association was established in 1970 to train and employ the children of Palestinians who perished in the struggle against Israel. The death of the family breadwinner was cause for great hardship among his survivors, and SAMED was charged with preparing his progeny to assume responsibility for the family. SAMED is divided into three branches. One emphasizes industrial skills. Youngsters are trained in the manufacture of furniture, clothing, textiles, and plastics. The second emphasizes the folk art and handicrafts of the Palestinian people. The third trains cinematographers and offers instruction in the making of documentary films. SAMED does not have its own agricultural program, given the unavailability of land. Arab states are reluctant to yield or sell land to the Palestinians. Nor are the Palestinians encouraged to seek such property. Land that had been seized, as in southern Lebanon prior to the Israeli invasion of 1982, was used for military purposes, and agricultural development was ignored. Nevertheless, SAMED has arranged to send some of its trainees to other countries, especially Africa, where opportunities to learn farming techniques are provided. According to a Palestinian source the number of Palestinians attending universities in 1981 was about 60,000. No mention is made of Palestinians undergoing training in the communist states. The ratio of university students to the Palestinian population is approximately 15 per 1,000. This is equal to that of Lebanon and higher than that of any other country in the Islamic Middle East.

Significance
SAMED is a limited operation in the circumstances in which the Palestinians find themselves. The development of industrial and intellectual skills is really a function of the need for labor in the Arab nations, especially in the Arabian Peninsula states. The urban character of the Palestinian has focused attention on education. Palestinians are impressively intellectual when compared with their brethren of the gulf shaykhdoms. Their sophisticated talents are generally well received, and so long as they abstain from political activity their rewards are quite substantial. SAMED addresses the needs of the more deprived element, and it aims to mobilize some of the labor in the refugee camps. SAMED can also serve as a recruitment agency for the expansion of the Palestinian Liberation Army.

Soviet Jews 183

The Gorbachev reforms in the former Soviet Union had a direct and monumental impact on Israel and all the Arab states. That impact is best described in the lifting of Soviet emigration restrictions heretofore imposed on Soviet Jewry. As a consequence of its open-door policy to all Jews, and especially Soviet Jews, Israel is faced with the challenge of absorbing the new immigrants into Israeli society. Although the influx of Soviet Jews holds great promise for Israel's future, the rapid expansion of the population threatens to overwhelm the country's available resources. During 1990, a climactic year in Soviet emigration, over 200,000 immigrants arrived in Israel, including 185,000 Soviet Jews. This figure represented more than 5 percent of Israel's total population and was the highest influx of immigrants since 1949. Moreover, nearly 1.2 million Jews in the republics of the former Soviet Union are currently holding Israeli invitations to immigrate, thus satisfying the first requirement to leave. Israel anticipates receiving the bulk of these immigrants by 1995. Their absorption is roughly equivalent to the resettling of the entire population of France in the United States. Many of the Soviet Jews are academics, engineers, architects, technicians, schoolteachers, and other professionals. This high professional level of the immigrants will require the rapid expansion of Israel's scientific, technical, and medical sectors and services. The problem for Israel is the speed with which the new immigrants can be accommodated and satisfied. If the problem proves too difficult to solve, the likelihood of the Soviet Jews seeking entry to other countries will increase. See also YISHUV (188); ZIONISM (189).

Significance
There are several important effects of the emigration of Soviet Jewry to Israel. Israel sees the positive dimension as not only assisting a people in need, but also as helping to offset the trend toward an Arab majority within the Israeli state by the end of the decade. The talent that the Soviet Jews add to the Israeli pool can also be a boon to Israeli society in the years ahead. The Arabs, however, view the influx of Soviet Jews with considerable apprehension. They believe Israel's burgeoning population will cause the Jewish state to demand more land and that acquisition of territory can only come at the expense of the neighboring Arab states, especially the Palestinians. The possibility of negotiating the freeing of the West Bank for a Palestinian state seems less likely given pressures on the Israeli government to find places for Soviet Jewish settlements. The United States has called upon Israel not to settle the Soviet Jews on the West Bank and has threatened to cut assistance if such a policy is pursued. Israel has countered U.S. government criticism by noting that less than 1 percent of all Soviet immigrants are settling in the West Bank or Gaza. The Israeli authorities state there is more than enough room within Israel itself to accommodate virtually all the Jews in the world. Of the top 50 towns receiving Soviet Jews, only one, Ariel, is located on the West Bank, and by early 1991 it had received 279 immigrants. By contrast Haifa received 17,762, Tel Aviv 14,307, and Jerusalem 8,070 in the same period. This still left a vast element for resettlement,however, and Arab fears concerning the influx of Soviet Jews to Israel were not arrested.

Temple Mount Incident 184

The Temple Mount in Jerusalem is the second-holiest site in the Islamic world. It houses the Dome of the Rock, a building enclosing the large stone from which it is believed Mohammad ascended to heaven. It is also the site of the Al-Aqsa Mosque. Below the Mount and on the western wall is the holiest site in Judaism, the Wailing Wall, the remnant of Solomon's Temple that was destroyed by the Romans and obliterated by subsequent conquerors of Jerusalem who were determined to erase any trace of Jewish association with the location. The Wailing Wall was uncovered and opened to worshippers after Israel's conquest of Jerusalem in the 1967 war. The Temple Mount, although under Israeli jurisdiction, is administered by the Arab keepers of the holy site. On October 7, 1990, Arab youths provoked by the accidental firing of a tear gas cannister, began hurling stones from the Mount at the Jewish worshippers below. It is said the stone-throwing was both an extension of the Palestinian *intifada* and a reaction to a rumor that orthodox, fundamentalist Jews were going to occupy the Mount in order to place a cornerstone for a new Jewish temple. The rain of stones from above brought an immediate response from the Israeli security forces in the area. They opened fire on the demonstrators, and when the shooting ceased, 19 Palestinians were dead and an estimated 150 others had been wounded. The death toll was the largest in a single day since the *intifada* began in December 1987. ***See also*** INTIFADA (151).

Significance
The Temple Mount incident came as the UN Security Council made serious efforts to force Iraq to yield its

conquest of Kuwait. Some observers argued that Saddam Hussain had engineered the incident to distract attention from himself, but also to demonstrate the linkage between the Palestinian question and all other issues in the Middle East. Indeed, after the UN Security Council took up the issue of the Temple Mount incident and the United States voted with the majority to condemn the Israeli use of violence at the holy site (it was said because Washington feared losing the Arab portion of the international coalition against Saddam Hussain and Iraq), the Israeli government declared that the victor in the exercise was Saddam Hussain. The question of who initiated the action was lost in the debate as the Security Council members moved to censure Israel. Little notice was given to the Israeli government's denial of a permit for Jewish fundamentalists who wished to parade their cause near or on the Mount or to the fact that the Wailing Wall had more than the usual daily worshippers because it was the Jewish holiday of Sukhot. Nor were the Security Council members concerned with the Israeli complaint that the Palestinian demonstrators had attacked and burned a police station, that policemen had been stoned, and that the personnel on duty were not trained or experienced in riot control and hence thought they were in mortal danger. These issues were considered of lesser consequence by the Security Council members, who echoed world public opinion when they condemned the excessive use of force by Israelis against Palestinians under their administration. Later, an Israeli investigation of the incident revealed that the rioting had actually been precipitated by an errant tear gas cannister dropped by an Israeli security guard at the Mount. Assuming they were under attack, the Arabs congregated on the Mount struck back with the rock throwing incident. The revelation provided evidence needed in tracing the true cause of the tragedy, but no amount of explanation could argue away the hatred between Arabs and Jews.

United Nations Relief and Works Agency for Palestine Refugees (UNRWAPR) 185

The United Nations Relief and Works Agency for Palestine Refugees was set up in May 1950 to care for the Palestine refugees. Homeless Arabs numbering between three-quarters of a million and slightly more than 1 million sought refuge in the West Bank territory and in Jordan proper following the termination of the Arab-Israeli War of 1948–1949. It became UNRWAPR's responsibility to feed and shelter this enormous population. It was anticipated that the activities of UNRWAPR would be temporary and that eventually the Palestinian Arabs would be resettled in other Arab countries, including Jordan. In 1952 UNRWAPR received its first large budget; $250 million was allocated for a three-year program of relief and reintegration. This sum of money represented $78.9 million from the UN membership. The additional funds were obtained from voluntary sources, especially from the United States. Despite the availability of this substantial sum of money, few settlement schemes were implemented. UNRWAPR's mandate permitted dispensing relief to refugees, but the agency could not prepare general schemes because the Arab governments did not want the refugees receiving benefits unavailable to their own citizenry. More important, however, Arab governments resisted any scheme that implied "the tacit admission of the existence of Israel." UNRWAPR continued to provide for the Palestinian refugees on a more or less permanent basis. Valid statistics were impossible to determine. Efforts were made to conceal deaths in the camps, and births were reported with astounding regularity. The larger the numbers, the greater UNRWAPR assistance. Although the UN assisted Palestinians to leave the camps and others left of their own accord, hundreds of thousands remained the continuing responsibility of UNRWAPR officials. *See also* PALESTINIAN REFUGEES (170).

Significance
The United Nations was immediately responsible for the partition of the British Palestine Mandate. It therefore assumed responsibility for sustaining the refugees produced by the failure of the partition scheme. Few members of the United Nations perceived that the need to provide for the Palestinian refugees would continue decades after the departure of the British. UNRWAPR was a humanitarian gesture. The United Nations recognized that the sudden influx of refugees into Jordan could not be managed by that state alone. UNRWAPR therefore was established to supplement the work of the Jordanian government and to assist the Arab states in resettling the refugees in new homes. There was sufficient indication that continuing Arab hostility toward Israel, and Israel's problems in settling more than 2 million new Jewish immigrants, precluded the possibility of the Palestinians' returning to the land and homes they fled in 1948–1949. Given the nature of the impasse, UNRWAPR's humanitarian effort was used to perpetuate the Palestinian Arab claim to land that is now an integral part of the state of Israel. UNRWAPR remained on duty through the passing decades, providing for the minimum needs of the refugees. Through UNRWAPR the United Nations was continually sensitized to the plight of the Palestinian refugees. Criticism was directed more at the Israelis for refusing to permit the return of the Palestinian Arabs than it was at the Arab states for failing to absorb the vast number of camp refugees.

Weizmann-Faisal Accord (1919) — 186

The Weizmann-Faisal Accord was the result of conversations between Chaim Weizmann, a British citizen and a leader of the Zionist Movement, and Emir Faisal, eldest son of the sherif of Mecca and head of the Hashemite family. Weizmann was a chemistry professor at Manchester University who during World War I had been instrumental in the development of explosives for use in artillery shells. It was this work that brought Weizmann into intimate relationship with Britain's wartime leaders. It is believed that Lord Balfour's letter to Lord Rothschild concerning a Jewish national home was prompted by Weizmann's discussions with members of the British Foreign Office. Emir Faisal led an army of Arab troops in support of British efforts to dislodge the Turks from the Middle East during World War I. In return for this service, Faisal was established as king of Syria. Although he was forced from the Syrian throne later, the British attempted to make amends by installing Faisal as king of Iraq. Weizmann was to become the first president of Israel after World War II. The deliberations of the two leaders took place at Aqaba in Palestine and again in London in 1918. Weizmann had joined the Zionist community (Yishuv) in Palestine by this date, and his task was to explain to the Arab king the purpose and prospects of Zionism in the Middle East. Weizmann called for cooperation between Arab and Jew. He described the similar nature of their concerns and their mutual desire for self-government and development. Weizmann's explanation was received with graciousness by King

Faisal, and on January 3, 1919, the two men announced their accord. King Faisal, as chief Arab delegate at the Paris Peace Conference, and therefore a voice for the Arab cause, publicly accepted the Balfour Declaration and gave his approval to the continuation of Jewish immigration to Palestine. In his acceptance, however, the king noted he would not be bound "by a single word of the present Agreement" if Arab rights were in any way jeopardized. In return for King Faisal's gesture of cooperation, Weizmann pledged support in the economic development of the region and promised to work closely with Arab leaders. ***See also*** BALFOUR DECLARATION (147); YISHUV (188); ZIONISM (189).

Significance

The Weizmann-Faisal Accord of 1919 was testimony to the fact that Jews and Arab Muslims could live in reasonable harmony. More important, however, the deliberations raised a storm of controversy, especially in the Arab world. Although he was a leading spokesman for the Arab position, it was obvious from the criticism levelled at King Faisal that he could not speak for Arabs generally. Syrians were disturbed by the action of their new king, and they protested the thought that Palestine would be separated from Syrian administration and that a Jewish enclave would emerge in the midst of the Arabs. Moreover, the Zionist contention that the League of Nations should transform Palestine into a Jewish commonwealth was not appreciated among the Arabs of Palestine or their brethren in other Arab lands. The French and British momentarily resolved the controversy by dividing the area among themselves. Syria and Lebanon came under French authority, and in 1921, Britain divided the remaining portion of former Greater Syria, creating Transjordan from western Palestine with Emir Abdullah, the brother of Faisal, at its head. Transjordan was also declared off limits to Zionist settlement. What remained of Palestine was taken under direct British administration, and the long but futile task of reconciling Arab and Jew began in earnest.

West Beirut Massacre 187

On September 17–18, 1982, elements of the Christian Phalange militia were allowed to enter the Palestinian refugee camps in West Beirut by departing Israeli forces that had occupied the city. The mission of the militia was the destruction of PLO resistance. Although the great bulk of the PLO army had been removed from West Beirut by August 31, approximately 2,000 were still believed to be in the city. This was the first opportunity for the Phalangists to penetrate West Beirut since the civil war of 1975–1976. It also came within two days of the funeral of Bashir Gemayel, the Phalange leader and Lebanon's president-elect, who had been assassinated on September 14. There were old scores to settle between the returning Maronites and the now relatively defenseless Palestinians. Once inside the camps the militia herded men into different sectors of the camps, where they were summarily executed. In the mayhem that ensued, women and children were also murdered. According to Israeli sources, when they realized what was occurring inside the camps they moved to stop the killing, but not before an estimated 300 to 1,400 camp inhabitants had been put to death. News of the atrocity spread quickly. Stories and pictures appeared almost instantaneously. Television displayed the magnitude of the bloodletting to a watching world. Anger and revulsion described the reaction among officials in the United States and Europe. Yasir Arafat placed responsibility on Israel, but he also condemned the Americans, French, and Italians for withdrawing their peacekeeping troops. All governments, however, focused their ire on the Israeli government and accused the Begin administration of permitting the atrocity. ***See also*** PHALANGES LIBANAISES (138); ISRAELI-PLO WAR, 1982 (249).

Significance
The West Beirut massacre was seen as a turning point in U.S.-Israeli relations. President Reagan and Prime Minister Begin had exchanged angry notes several times during the Israeli invasion of Lebanon. Divergent positions on numerous questions, especially those involving Israeli military operations in the July–August siege of Beirut and the future of the West Bank territory and its Palestinian inhabitants, threatened to undo a relationship that had been forged with the creation of the Jewish state. Israel's dependence on the United States was acknowledged in Israel and elsewhere. Nevertheless, the criticism levelled against the Begin government and its acrimonious and defiant reaction had caused serious rifts to open. Rumors circulated that advisors close to the president had counselled a sharp rebuke of the Israeli government, a dramatic paring down of U.S. commitment, and a more visible pro-Arab posture. The Beirut massacre provided these associates with the leverage required to modify established U.S. policy toward Israel. Israel, already isolated in the larger international arena, now had to watch its credibility diminish further. Although not directly responsible for the slaughter of the refugees, the Israeli government could not avoid its accountability. Observers expressed the opinion that only the emergence of a new, more pliable government in Israel could correct the country's negative image.

Yishuv 188

The Jewish settler community that moved to Palestine with the onset of the Zionist movement in the late nineteenth and early twentieth centuries. Prior to World War II, the Yishuv comprised more than three-fourths Ashkenazic Jews from north, central, and eastern Europe. The Sephardim Jews, largely from the Mediterranean countries, were less than one-tenth of the population. Jews from Persia (Iran), central Asia, Iraq, Kurdistan, and Yemen filled the remaining category. The Ashkenazic and Sephardic Jews were locked in controversy over ritual and ceremony. Moreover, ethnic, nationality, and social differences produced even more divisiveness. Indeed, the Jews migrating to Palestine from other Middle East countries shared more in common with the Arab population than with the European Jews. With the creation of the state of Israel an even greater influx of Oriental Jews intensified the difficulties of living together. ***See also*** ASHKENAZIC JEWS (146); SEPHARDIC JEWS (181).

Significance
The Jews are renowned as an argumentative people. This tendency toward bitter rivalry has been illustrated prominently as a result of the open-door policy, which permits Jews from any part of the world to obtain Israeli citizenship. The joining together of Jews with distinctly different lifestyles has not been simple. The Israeli government and economy have been dominated by European Jews, the Ashkenazim, but the migration to Israel and higher birthrate of the Sephardim, or Oriental Jews, promises to alter the power structure. This fact, coupled with the out-migration of largely Ashkenazic Jews, has brought the groups into close balance. Despite bitter rivalries between the communities, however,

sufficient unity is sustained in the face of the ever-present Arab threat to Israel's security.

Zionism

189

The Zionist movement grew out of the labors of Theodor Herzl, a nineteenth-century Hungarian Jew and a journalist for an influential newspaper in Vienna. Herzl covered the trial of Captain Alfred Dreyfus, a French Jew who was wrongfully accused of passing secrets to the Germans. He was tried, found guilty, and sentenced to imprisonment at the infamous penal colony on Devil's Island. The Dreyfus case provoked considerable anti-Semitism, and Herzl was moved to publish a book that called for the granting of a homeland for Jews that would be a refuge from the injustices perpetuated on them in other societies. *Der Judenstaat* (*The Jewish State*) was not the only book with such a message, but Herzl's writings, more than any other publication, influenced European Jewry, especially Jews in Eastern Europe. Herzl concluded that no matter how patriotic they were, Jews could not escape prejudice, discrimination, and persecution. This theme prompted some of his Jewish readers, particularly in Poland and Russia, to assemble an organization for the purpose of furthering the idea. Under Herzl's leadership, the first world Zionist Congress was convened in Basle, Switzerland, in 1897. Two hundred delegates from all corners of the world attended. Their sole aim was the creation of a movement for the return to Zion (the name of a hill in Jerusalem on which King David's palace is believed to have been erected). The use of the term *Zion* had been adopted in 1882 by a group of European Jews who called themselves "Lovers of Zion." Notably, there was a variety of expressions concerned with Zionism. The Basle congress, however, created the Zionist Organization and drafted a program that read, "The aim of Zionism is to create for the Jewish people a home in Palestine secured by public law." In time a worldwide organization was developed that, despite inner controversies, never lost sight of the need to fulfill the dream of Theodor Herzl. By the outbreak of World War I, the Zionist movement had established its bona fides. Future Israeli leaders like David Ben-Gurion and Yitzhak Ben-Zvi had already managed to settle in the sparsely populated, neglected, resource-poor land. Land was usually purchased from absentee Arab landlords with money raised through philanthropic overtures in the Western world, despite Ottoman restrictions. Jews who remained in the Turkish-administered territory eventually developed small agricultural enterprises, though many decided not to stay.

The Jewish settlements in Palestine are divided into phases called *aliyah* (ascension to Zion). The first *aliyah*, 1882–1903, involved approximately 25,000 Jews. The second *aliyah*, 1905–1914, brought approximately 40,000. The immigrants of the second *aliyah* were the most important in establishing the pattern of relationships, the institutional structure, and the ideological basis for the Jewish state. They also founded the first kibbutz (frontier community settlement). The kibbutz provided the Jewish settlers with the pioneering spirit, the martial experience, and the sense of sacrifice and cooperation that became the hallmark of the later Israeli state. Many of Israel's leaders were members of the kibbutzim, and the Israeli armed forces were transformed into an efficient fighting machine through the endeavor and dedication of the frontier settlers.

The third *aliyah* followed in the wake of World War I. During the war, the Jewish population of Palestine declined, largely as a result of

Ottoman policy and forced removal. The defeat of the Ottoman Empire and the wartime Balfour Declaration of November 2, 1917, wherein the British government announced its intention to support the Zionist dream of a Jewish homeland in Palestine, created a new atmosphere for immigration to the holy land. Moreover, Palestine had been transformed into a British mandate, and between 1919 and 1923 another 35,000 Jews settled in the region. The fourth *aliyah,* 1924–1931, added still another 82,000 to these ranks. The fifth *aliyah,* 1932–1938, provoked by the persecution of Jews in Hitler's Germany, turned the trickle into a sea, and 217,000 Jews, mostly Europeans, took up residence in Palestine. By 1938 the Jewish population of Palestine had grown to 413,000.

The Arabs, who in the pre–World War I period appeared to tolerate the new settlers, became extremely hostile in the aftermath of that conflict. The Arabs had also been promised freedom and independence by the British, a promise that they argued was only minimally observed. The idea of a Jewish homeland in their midst when they had not yet attained their own goals came as a crushing blow. The Arab rebellion in Palestine began in earnest in 1920–1921, the main point of attack being directed at Zionism, both its representatives and its supporters. The British attempted to steer a course between the Arab and Jewish communities, but growing world tension forced them to issue a number of White Papers. The Peel Commission White Paper of 1936 questioned the expansion of Jewish settlements. A May 1939 White Paper called for drastic restrictions on Jewish immigration and the curtailment of land purchases; this White Paper policy remained in force through World War II. The policy not only embittered relations between Great Britain and the Zionists, but it also appeared to deny refuge to displaced persons trying to escape Nazi death camps. Zionist strategy sought to smuggle as many refugees into Palestine as conditions allowed. In the meantime, more extreme elements of the Yishuv, the Irgun Zvai Leumi and the Stern Gang, engaged in acts of terror against British installations and personnel. The larger body of armed Jewry, the Haganah, however, accepted British military training, and more than 25,000 Jews served in the British Middle East army. The White Papers, Arab hostility, and, above all, the Holocaust unleashed by Nazi Germany against the Jews strengthened the resolve of the Zionists, and the cause of Zionism was transformed into a fundamental issue of survival.

By 1945, 564,000 Jews were living in Palestine. The sixth *aliyah,* 1946–1948, brought another 61,000 to the holy land as what remained of European Jewry (6 million had perished in the Holocaust) sought to find new homes and new countries. The decision by Great Britain in 1946 to pass the Palestine problem to the United Nations, and the UN action in partitioning the mandate between Arabs and Jews, led to the declaration of an independent Israel in May 1948. Massive emigration of Jews from the Arab countries followed, swelling the Jewish community to almost 1.5 million by 1951.

The creation of the state of Israel did not close the book on Zionism. The new state was attacked on the very day of its independence by the combined armies of the Arab world. The latter's inability to defeat the Israelis and destroy the infant state in that war, and subsequent encounters in 1956, 1967, 1973, and 1982, has given new significance and new dimensions to Zionism. Constantly facing a mortal threat, Zionism remains the central ideology and the most influential force in the Israeli nation as well as for many Jews in the Diaspora. ***See also*** PEEL COMMISSION (173);

BALFOUR DECLARATION (147); KIBBUTZ (157); JUDEA AND SAMARIA (THE WEST BANK) (14).

Significance
Zionism is a form of European nationalism and is true to the spirit of classic nineteenth-century nationalism. The demands for self-determination by European Jews, for an independent homeland, and for a place in the community of nations are no different from demands made by other peoples across the planet who sense that true fulfillment can be achieved only through the establishment of an independent, sovereign state reflecting their traditions, customs, and values. What makes Zionism somewhat more dramatic is the selection of the land of ancient Palestine to satisfy the Zionist quest. On the one side, Palestine, although long neglected and used primarily as a battleground for warring armies, is the focal point for the world's three transcendental religions, Judaism, Christianity, and Islam. On the other side, there is the Arab claim to the same territory that is based upon long-term occupation, as well as religious importance. The Arabs emphasize their indigenous status, whereas the Jews are viewed as interlopers and, by many, as instruments of Western imperialism. Indeed, the Arab reawakening, that is, Arab nationalism, developed at roughly the same time as Zionism. After centuries of subjugation at the hands of the Turks, the Arabs saw an opportunity to retrieve their lost status by assisting the British and French against the Ottomans in World War I. In return for this support the Arabs were promised independence, and some among them envisaged a unified Arab world, or at least a confederation of Arab peoples. The promises made to both the Arabs and the Jews as well as their individual nationalistic fervor placed them on a collision course. The Arabs argued that they could never achieve their objectives if the Jewish state were allowed to sink its roots in the region. Many Arabs insisted that Zionism would not be content with the Jewish state described in the UN partition resolution. They cite the validity of this perception given Israel's altered geography after the 1948–1949 war and again after the 1967 conflict. Israel's merger of East and West Jerusalem and its annexation of Syria's Golan Heights in 1981 confirmed Arab fears that the Zionists intend to absorb both the Gaza Strip and the West Bank territory, under Israeli occupation since 1967. The Israelis, on the other hand, despite a separate peace treaty with Egypt that returned the Sinai Peninsula to Cairo's control in April 1982, fear that the Arabs will strike at them whenever conditions are appropriate. The annexation of the Golan Heights, the refusal to give up the West Bank territory, and their continuing role in Lebanon are said to be strategic in nature. Zionism and Arab nationalism, therefore, are facets of self-fulfilling prophecies that encourage rather than diminish belligerency in the region.

Diplomacy

6

Addis Ababa Agreement **190**

The Addis Ababa Agreement of March 1972 was supposed to bring to an end a long and bloody civil war between the Arab population of northern Sudan and the Black African Sudanese in the south. The Addis Ababa Agreement would have granted self-rule to the southern provinces, but economic deprivation and continued feelings of racial and religious discrimination persisted. In addition, discrepancies appeared in the 1956 map used to demarcate the south from the north. Thus, when the Khartoum government moved to reorganize the northern provinces in 1980, the southern sector lost a portion of its territory. The southern Sudanese claimed that this was a violation of the Addis Ababa Agreement. Furthermore, the government announced the discovery of oil in the southern region. Sudan's refining and processing capacity, however, was located in the north. The southern Sudanese leaders were convinced that the Arab north would reap the benefits of the discovery and leave the south in its depressed state. The northerners also pursued an aggressive Islamization policy, which the southerners were determined to resist. *See also* MAHDI (43).

Significance

The Black African Sudanese were especially supportive of the Addis Ababa Agreement. But when the government reorganized the regions at the expense of the Black population, the southerners insisted that they had been betrayed. Subsequent strains between the Arab Muslims and Black Christians and animists caused renewed fighting between north and south, and the accords were abandoned by both sides. The southern Sudanese People's Liberation Army (SPLA)) managed to extend its control over the countryside, but the government still held the urban centers. With neither side prepared to yield, the war continued unabated. Khartoum cut supply lines to the south, and with drought conditions wreaking havoc on the food supply, the entire southern Sudanese population was threatened with starvation. Moreover, relief efforts mounted by outside international agencies were prevented from assisting the stricken areas. Given government tactics, observers believed that southern Sudan faced catastrophe unless a new, more successful agreement could be arranged than that made in 1972 in Addis Ababa.

Anglo-Iranian Oil Company 191

Oil was discovered in Iranian Khuzistan in 1908 by William Knox D'Arcy, an Australian of English birth. D'Arcy had acquired a 60-year concession from the Iranian government in 1901. The concession covered all of Iran, except for five Caspian provinces that the Russians insisted came within their sphere of influence. The discovery of oil led D'Arcy to found the Anglo-Persian Oil Company (APOC), later to be redesignated the Anglo-Iranian Oil Company (AIOC). D'Arcy was supported in his venture by the British Admiralty, which was interested in using oil rather than coal to fuel its vessels, and the Burmah Oil Company, a wholly British-owned company. In 1914 the British government acquired an interest in the company, which was to increase to 55.9 percent in subsequent years. This heavy foreign involvement in Iranian economic and commercial life reflected the historical political interests of the great powers in Iranian affairs. Moreover, oil eventually mixed with nationalism to produce a violent explosion that not only rocked Iran, but much of the world as well. After World War II, the world demand for oil increased appreciably. Iran was already among the chief exporters of raw petroleum, but the profits from the exploitation of the resource remained in foreign hands. In 1948 negotiations with AIOC attempted to ease some of the Iranian dissatisfaction with the foreign oil concession. The British agreed to pay Iran a higher royalty for its oil in 1949, but the Iranian parliament, the Majlis, rejected the offer. The opposition to the agreement was led by Mohammad Mossadegh, an Iranian nationalist and a leader of the National Front, and Ayatollah Kashani and the Fadayani Islam. Kashani represented the Shiite clergy, and they were joined by Islamic fundamentalists who argued that Iran's plight was solely the result of British exploitation. Moreover, the presence of the Europeans had prevented Iran from promoting its Islamic way of life. The National Front, comprised of middle-class elements, emphasized essentially the same theme, although it was less inclined to sing the praises of the Islamic state. The combined opposition demanded the abolition of the oil concession and the nationalization of Iran's oil industry. Those who stood in the way of the demand, such as Prime Minister Ali Razmara, were murdered by terrorist groups. The prevailing atmosphere of violence hastened the passage of the nationalization order in the Majlis, and it was approved in April 1951. The following month Mossadegh became prime minister. Great Britain's attempt to get a legal opinion through the International Court of Justice failed when Iran argued that the court did not have jurisdiction in the matter. Appeals to the Security Council of the United Nations were also fruitless. The AIOC was therefore called upon to close down operations and evacuate its personnel.

Significance

The Anglo-Iranian Oil Company controversy was the first time a Middle East oil-producing country attempted to gain control over its own resources. The struggle for control, however, had far-flung consequences. Within Iran, it aroused passionate nationalistic expression. By 1953, it had caused the shah to flee into exile, only to return to the country after a U.S.-engineered countercoup. Foreign influence in Iran had passed from the British to the Americans. U.S. oil companies were a major component of the international consortium that exploited Iranian oil reserves. The United States had replaced Great Britain as the bête noire in Iranian domestic life. In fact, even when the shah was no longer a factor (he died in Egypt in 1980), the United States was still judged Iran's primary enemy. What had begun as a commercial affair involving a foreign-owned oil company quickly escalated into a political and ideological confrontation of enormous complexity, with great consequences for Iran, the Middle East, and the rest of the world.

Anglo-Russian Agreement, 1907 — 192

The Anglo-Russian Agreement of 1907 divided Iran, then called Persia, into British and Russian spheres of influence. The Persian Qajar dynasty was unable to protect the country's territorial integrity, because of its corruption, profligacy, and maladministration. In the last half of the nineteenth century, Persia had been inundated by foreign concession-seekers. The Qajar shah borrowed heavily from governments and entrepreneurial adventurers, which forced him into debt and into granting wider economic privileges. At the same time, the monarch became more heavy-handed with his own population, and continuing repression finally produced a major revolution in 1905–1906. From that disturbance emerged Iran's first constitution, but this did not end the government's problems. Great Britain and Imperial Russia were equally interested in seizing the country's resources. On August 31, 1907, they reconciled their differences by dividing the hapless country between them. In their treaty it was specified that neither was entitled to obtain concessions in the sphere allocated to the other. As could be expected, the agreement was a blow to Iran's attentive public, which already had been aroused to a new sense of nationalism following the revolution. The Persians were indifferent to the underlying reason for the Anglo-Russian agreement; the fact that Britain and Russia sought to limit their rivalry in the face of a growing German threat could never be appreciated in Iran. The Persians saw the imperial giants as destroying their nationhood and way of life, and they were determined to fight back. Russia, however, enlisted the deposed Mohammad Ali Shah in an effort to destroy the Iranian constitution. Using the Persian Cossack Brigade, which had been formed with Russian help in 1883 and which was still commanded by Russians, the czar's forces occupied Tabriz. In 1911, the Russians presented an ultimatum to the Persian government demanding the removal of an American financial advisor, W. M. Shuster, who, as the country's treasurer-general, had attempted to restore Iran to a position of solvency. The Russian pressure produced a coup that terminated the new National Assembly and forced Shuster to leave the country. From that point, Russian power was on the ascendancy in Iran. It did not begin to diminish until World War I, when the czarist regime itself was toppled, and Iran became a major battleground for Turkish, Russian, and British armies.

Significance

The Anglo-Russian Agreement of 1907 symbolized the plight of twentieth-century Iran. Although roused by democratic movements in the Western world, Iran was faced with foreign penetration, indebtedness, weakness, and humiliation. Attempts to solve domestic problems were compounded by foreign aggressiveness. Iranian governments became the handmaidens of distant powers, and the Persian people were victimized by forces beyond their control. These developments brought an end to the Qajar dynasty in the post–World War I period. The Qajars, however, were succeeded by the Pahlavis, and for many Persians the theme was unchanged. Foreign governments and commercial agents still sought opportunities at the expense of the indigenous population, and despite the strength and determination demonstrated by Reza Khan, the founder of the Pahlavi dynasty, and his successor and son Mohammad Reza, neither could resist foreign encroachment. Neither therefore could quell the turbulence that coursed through Iranian society. In the end, Reza Khan was ignominiously forced into exile by the British and Russians. Mohammad Reza suffered a similar fate, but his flight from Iran was caused by the Iranian people. The U.S. connection with Mohammad Reza, however, was a salient feature in his demise. Indeed, Iranian nationalism sought to deny the United States' influence over Iran.

Arab League 193

The League of Arab States, or Arab League, was formed in 1944 as the first successful expression of pan-Arabism in this century. The Arab League Pact was formally signed in 1945. The original members of the league were Egypt, Iraq, Syria, Lebanon, Transjordan (later Jordan), Saudi Arabia, and Yemen (North). Current members of the Arab League are Algeria, Bahrein, Djibouti, Egypt, Iraq, Jordan, Kuwait, Lebanon, Libya, Mauritania, Morocco, Oman, Palestine Liberation Organization (PLO), Qatar, Saudi Arabia, Somalia, Sudan, Syria, Tunisia, United Arab Emirates, and Yemen. Egypt was expelled in 1979 after Anwar el-Sadat signed a separate peace treaty with Israel. It was readmitted in 1989. The League Charter calls for the collective protection of the sovereign independence of all member-states. It also emphasizes cooperation with other international organizations, and special attention has been given Afro-Asian activities. The Arab League works closely with member-states of the United Nations, and it has won acceptance of Arabic as an official language of that international body and a number of its specialized agencies. The supreme organ of the Arab League is the council, consisting of representatives of the member-states and the PLO. The daily work of the league is managed by the secretariat under the leadership of a secretary-general. The secretariat has departments of political, economic, legal, cultural, and social and labor affairs, as well as departments concerned with petroleum, finance, health, information, communications, protocol, and Palestine. The Economic Council organized in 1950 is comprised of the ministers of economic affairs or their representatives. The Council of Arab Economic Unity was created in 1964 by the Economic Council. Its aims are the removal of internal tariffs, the establishment of common external tariffs, the promotion of labor mobility and capital between the members, and the adoption of common economic policies. Specialized agencies of the Arab League include the Arab Educational, Cultural, and Scientific Organization; the Arab States Broadcasting Union; the Arab Labor Organization; the Civil Aviation Council of Arab States; the Arab Cities Organization; the Joint Defense Council; the International Arab Organization for Social Defense; the Arab Postal Union; the Arab Development Bank (or Financial Institute); and the Arab Common Market. The Arab League's most celebrated activity has been its opposition to the state of Israel. The creation of the Boycott of Israel Office, which blacklisted foreign firms doing business with or in Israel, was one such recognized activity. In 1948 the Arab League declared war on Israel, but the organization could not coordinate the actions of the several Arab armies engaged in the conflict. Disagreement in different Arab capitals over the conduct of the war and policy toward the displaced Palestinians led to increased tension between the member-states that could not be relieved by the league. The Arab defeat in the 1948–1949 war almost destroyed the organization. The league also supported Syria in its conflict with the Hashemites of Jordan and Iraq in the early 1950s. It vehemently opposed Sadat's peace initiative toward Israel in 1977, and it denounced the peace treaty between Egypt and Israel in 1979. League headquarters was closed in Egypt as a consequence of this dispute. It was moved to Tunis in 1979, and again returned to Cairo in 1990 following Egypt's return to the Arab fold.

Significance
The Arab League cannot be judged by its performance. It is more a promise than a successful enterprise. Achievement must be measured in symbols and spirit, not purpose and accomplishment. Indeed the Arab League has failed to promote the unity that is supposedly its raison d'être. As such, it is more a mirror image of divisions within the Arab world. During the Nasser era, hostility erupted between the Egyptian president and the leaders of Saudi Arabia and Jordan. War over North Yemen in the 1960s pitted Saudis against Egyptians, and the Arab League was hard put to speak of Arab unity. Similarly, wars between Arabs and Israelis in 1956, 1967, 1973, and 1982 failed to produce the united front that the league endeavored to publicize. The Arab League has not moderated differences between rival Arab states, nor could it prevent Iraq from invading Iran in 1980. Following the expulsion of the PLO from Beirut by the Israelis in August 1982, the Arab League called a summit meeting of Arab heads of state. A majority attended the meeting in Morocco in early September, and some observers commented that this was the first serious demonstration of Arab unity since the 1967 war with Israel. Iraq's invasion of Kuwait in 1990, and the subsequent war against Baghdad, further divided league members. Following Iraq's defeat, the first major assembly of Arab states was held in Cairo in March 1991, but this meeting did little to heal the wounds caused by the many crises.

Arab Summit **194**
The periodic meeting of Arab heads of state. All the Arab states, including the Palestine Liberation Organization, have representation on the body. The Arab Summit meets irregularly and has been primarily concerned with the development of diplomatic initiatives against Israel. ***See also*** ARAB LEAGUE (193).

Significance
The Arab Summit provides a forum for Arab world leaders. It usually convenes under the aegis of the Arab League. Its deliberations are usually brief, and considerable attention is given to ceremony and ritual. Substantive questions are more likely to be dealt with by the Foreign Ministers' Conference. In recent years efforts have been made to expand the work of the Arab Foreign Ministers to include non-Arab Muslim states in their organization. Both the Arab organization and the expanded Muslim organization tend to concentrate attention on the Palestinian issue. In the wake of the PLO defeat in Lebanon in 1982, the Arab Summit meeting in Morocco and the Islamic Foreign

Ministers assembled in the African state of Niger together called for the refurbishing of PLO military capability. PLO leaders heaped criticism on those Arab and Muslim states that offered little more than verbal support. Although both the Arab Summit and the Foreign Ministers' Conference therefore were concerned with reestablishing their credibility, the 1990–1991 crisis and war in the gulf underlined the weakness of the organizations and their essentially separate agendas.

Arab-Israeli Peace Conferences **195**

Arab reluctance to acknowledge the legal existence of Israel was modified by Anwar el-Sadat's visit to Jerusalem and the subsequent Egyptian-Israeli Peace Treaty of 1979. Although other Arab nations refused to follow the course set by the Egyptians, efforts at bringing the parties to a more general peace conference persisted. Following Operation Desert Storm in 1991, U.S. Secretary of State James Baker engaged in a series of intense negotiations with the more important parties in the ongoing conflict. Following the end of hostilities in February 1991, Baker made eight extensive visits to the Middle East in which he urged, cajoled, and pressured the principals to meet at a conference table. The United States was supported in this diplomatic tour de force by the Soviet Union, and the two nations agreed to be co-convenors of the conference. After considerable bargaining, Baker's efforts were crowned with success on October 18, 1991, when all the parties agreed to a conference that was slated for October 30, 1991, in Madrid, Spain. Major obstacles to the conference had been Israeli insistence that the PLO not be officially represented, that the Palestinian delegation be combined with Jordan, and that no members of the PLO be included. The Israelis also rejected inclusion of East Jerusalem residents in the Palestinian delegation. Syria demanded that the territories seized by Israel be part of the negotiations. It was especially insistent that the Golan Heights be returned to its sovereignty. Damascus, however, was just as vehement in refusing to be involved in regional issues that were aimed at focusing on joint ventures with Israel in matters of water use, arms control, etc. The Saudis hesitated in joining the conference because they did not want to confer legal recognition on Israel. The Palestinians proved to be the most difficult party in that Israel denied the PLO a role at the Madrid conference. In the end, the Palestinians agreed to attend but they refused to allow Israel to see the list of their representatives until their delegation had been assembled. Preliminary to the Madrid meeting, Moscow restored full diplomatic relations with Israel. The Soviet action had been forecast for some time, and it came as no surprise in the wake of other developments within the Soviet Union. The essential purpose of the peace conference was to bring peace between Israel and its neighbors and to work out the final disposition of the Israeli-occupied West Bank and Gaza Strip, home to 1.5 million Palestinian Arabs and a far smaller but growing number of Israeli settlers.

The conference was designed to have three stages. The first was ceremonial, including speeches by Presidents George Bush and Mikhail Gorbachev, as well as representatives of the European Community, the United Nations, and the foreign ministers of the six attending Middle East participants. The countries from the Middle East agreeing to attend were: Israel, Egypt, Jordan, Lebanon, Syria, and Saudi Arabia. After three days of speechmaking the second stage scheduled one-on-one sessions between Israel and Syria, Israel and the Jordanian-Palestinian delegations, and Israel and Lebanon. The question of "land for peace" was the central issue to these negotiations. The third stage of the conference was to provide the participants with opportunities to discuss access to water and regional arms limitations. Although Saudi Arabia and Egypt agreed to this latter session, Syria refused to break its self-imposed boycott. ***See also*** CAMP DAVID SUMMIT (201); EGYPTIAN-ISRAELI TREATY OF PEACE, 1979 (207); LEBANESE-ISRAELI AGREEMENT, 1983 (213); PLO EXODUS FROM BEIRUT (174); WEIZMANN-FAISAL ACCORD (1919) (186).

Significance
The Arab-Israeli Peace Conference brought together nations long hostile to one another. Each came to the conference with its own agenda, the substance of which proved to be controversial to other parties in the negotiations. The presence at the opening session of President George Bush and President Mikhail Gorbachev gave unique character to the meetings, but that alone could not dissipate the years of bloody encounter between Arabs and Israelis or their suspicions of the other's true intentions. Confidence-building was therefore an essential prerequisite, but in order to achieve that goal, material advantages had to be sacrificed. Thus the difficulties to be overcome were enormous.

Moreover, the deep-seated nature of the Arab-Israeli problem was mirrored in earlier efforts at finding a workable compromise. During 1947 to 1951 Israel's leaders and King Abdullah of Jordan engaged in secret talks. The sessions were not fruitful and when news of the meetings was leaked Abdullah was assassinated. The agreements signed on the island of Rhodes in 1949 between Israel, Egypt, Jordan, Lebanon, and Syria brought about a ceasefire in the first Arab-Israeli War. The agreements also arranged armistice lines but did not prevent new, more violent disruptions of the region's tranquility in subsequent years. In 1973 a UN-sponsored Geneva Conference was convened following the Yom Kippur War. Syria refused to attend, and after Israel, Egypt, and Jordan made opening statements the meeting was adjourned and never resumed. In 1974 Secretary of State Henry Kissinger engaged in "shuttle diplomacy," ultimately succeeding in obtaining agreements on the disengagement of Israeli, Egyptian, and Syrian forces. Israel agreed to withdraw from deeper penetrations of the Golan Heights and from parts of the Sinai where buffer zones were created. In 1977 Anwar el-Sadat visited Jerusalem and called for peace with Israel. The Camp David talks followed in 1978, and in March 1979 Israel and Egypt agreed to a formal peace treaty and to mutual recognition and full diplomatic relations. Israel also agreed to return the Sinai to Egypt, a promise fulfilled in 1982. Anwar el-Sadat, however, was assassinated by unreconciled opponents and his death was generally greeted with delight in the larger Arab world. In 1981 American diplomatic efforts were successful in working out a temporary ceasefire on the Lebanese-Israeli frontier. PLO fighters were supposed to cease their firing into Israeli territory, but repeated violations as well as the assault on an Israeli diplomat in London precipitated the Israeli invasion of Lebanon in 1982, Israeli movements into Beirut, and the decision by the PLO to evacuate its forces from that city. The subsequent Israeli withdrawal to the southern region of Lebanon exposed the latter to Syrian military influence, and Damascus eventually gained control over Lebanese affairs. In 1983 Israeli and Lebanese officials agreed to a peace instrument somewhat along the lines entered into by Egypt in 1979, but it quickly fell apart when Syria refused to support it. Finally, the secret 1985–1986 talks between Jordan's King Hussain and Israeli officials over a joint Jordanian-Palestinian delegation to a peace conference broke down under repeated assaults on Israel by the PLO and Israeli counterstrikes. The results of Desert Storm and George Bush's call for a new world order propelled the Baker effort. The leverage provided the United States by the attack on Iraq and the freeing of Kuwait made it possible for Baker to arrange still another, more comprehensive Middle East peace conference. But all the parties to the conflict, as well as the convenors, noted the difficulty in arriving at an overall solution for the complicated issues burdening Israelis, their Arab neighbors, and the Palestinians. The peace conference nevertheless was judged an important step along a difficult road. It represented the first formal acceptance by the major Arab states of Israel's right to exist. It also exaggerated Israel's need to acknowledge the claim of the Palestinians to an independent homeland.

ARAMCO (Arabian American Oil Company) 196

ARAMCO was created by way of a concession granted to Standard Oil of California and Texaco (the Texas Oil Company) in 1933. The concession was somewhat modified in 1939, giving ARAMCO sole rights of exploration and exploitation of petroleum reserves in Saudi Arabia. The original companies were joined by two other U.S. firms, Standard Oil of New Jersey (Exxon) and Socony-Vacuum (Mobil) in 1946. Mobil received a 10 percent share; the other three companies received equal 30 percent shares. ARAMCO was encouraged, assisted, and sanctioned by King Abdul Aziz ibn Saud, who needed the royalties from oil to consolidate his kingdom. Ibn Saud also demanded the expansion of oil production, irrespective of pricing and marketing arrangements established by the major oil companies. Oil proved to be so plentiful in Saudi Arabia, and so much easier to produce than expected, that fear of a price war forced Exxon to seek admission to ARAMCO. Exxon's company, Standard Oil of New Jersey, was not at first welcome by the other companies. Standard Oil of California (SOCAL) was seeking to capitalize on its Saudi holding by investing profits earned from that source in the Blue Line Area (those oil-rich lands east of Suez). SOCAL and Texaco eventually yielded to Exxon's request, however, and as King ibn Saud had insisted, ARAMCO oil was made available on a worldwide basis through the more extensive marketing networks of Exxon and Mobil. The companies avoided the rivalries involved in open competition. Exxon and Mobil also came to dominate ARAMCO management. In 1950, ARAMCO concluded an agreement with the Saudi government providing for a 50-50 division of the net profits, an arrangement theretofore unheard of in the Middle East. In 1952, ARAMCO's headquarters were transferred from the United States to Dahran in Saudi Arabia, thus giving the organization a more localized character. In addition, ARAMCO hired a large number of Middle Easterners to supplement its U.S. technical staff. Besides Saudi Arabians, the company hired Palestinians, Yemenis, Sudanese, Egyptians, Pakistanis, and Indians. The companies always feared losing their concession, and they understood that maintaining good relations with the monarchy was a sine qua non for maintaining operations in the country. ARAMCO maintained its business posture in the aftermath of World War II. The U.S. government also held to a policy of friendship and support for the House of Saud that was symbolized in the wartime meeting of President Franklin Roosevelt and King ibn Saud. The aftermath of war, however, brought a number of complications that ARAMCO could not ignore. The Arab-Israeli conflict put U.S.-Saudi friendship to a severe test. Washington sought to assist the Israelis without destroying its ties to the Arab world, especially those to Saudi Arabia. The death of ibn Saud placed the monarchy in the hands of his sons, who, like their father, understood the importance of the relationship between Saudi Arabia and the United States. Nevertheless, the intensity of the Arab cause against Israel was a constant threat to Saudi-U.S. relations, and ARAMCO could not avoid the politicization of the Middle East oil industry. The creation of the Organization of Petroleum Exporting Countries (OPEC) and the Organization of Arab Petroleum Exporting Countries (OAPEC) were the result of both economic and political demands. And in each instance, Saudi Arabia, because it was first among the oil-exporting nations, played a leading role. The 1973 oil embargo was prompted by, and made effective by, Saudi Arabia. In the 1970s it was apparent that ARAMCO was totally dependent on Saudi authority. The U.S. oil companies continued to market Saudi petroleum, but the manner of that exploitation and the pricing structure had become the responsibility of the Riyadh government and the oil-producing states. Despite these changes, ARAMCO profits continued their upward spiral. ***See also*** ORGANIZATION OF PETROLEUM EXPORTING COUNTRIES (OPEC) (217); RED LINE AGREEMENT (220); AL SAUD DYNASTY (68); PETROMIN (219).

Significance
ARAMCO manages the largest oil reserves in the modern world. ARAMCO and PETROMIN, the Saudi ministry concerned with the exploitation of petroleum, work in intimate association. The two organizations are inextricably intertwined, and from the standpoint of both the Saudi and U.S. governments, their continuing interaction is a vital necessity. Mutual self-interest has sustained the relationship through several difficult decades. Since the oil embargo of 1973, it is no longer possible to separate economic activity from political interest. Oil has been and will continue to be a political weapon, and no country is in a better position to use that weapon than Saudi Arabia. A serious reduction in Saudi oil exports has enormous consequences for the industrialized world. Moreover, despite conservation and the development of alternative fuel sources, the West's absolute dependence on petroleum exports from Saudi Arabia remains unchanged. ARAMCO therefore will do whatever it can to satisfy Saudi demands and will continue to influence U.S. foreign policy in the Middle East. And the U.S. government will tolerate such influence, because of Washington's desire to placate Riyadh. U.S. military posturing in the Middle East and Persian Gulf region centers on protecting the ARAMCO oil fields, as was demonstrated by Operation Desert Shield and Desert Storm in 1990–1991. There is virtual consensus that the Saudis cannot defend their installations without U.S. assistance. The U.S. Rapid Deployment Force strategy was put to the test in shielding Saudi Arabia from Iraqi aggressive intentions. Although Saudi Arabia was reluctant to provide Washington with bases, U.S. military units and military advisory teams have long used Saudi airfields and port facilities, and they are more likely to do so in the future. It is clear that Saudi Arabia is as dependent on U.S. assistance and friendship as the United States is on Saudi cooperation and amity. In these circumstances, ARAMCO is destined to remain a key component in the relationship between the two countries.

Arms Shipments to Iran: Iran-Contra Controversy 197

In November 1987, information leaked by Iran and published in a Lebanese newspaper revealed that the Reagan administration had secretly sold weapons to Iran for use in its war with Iraq. In a later acknowledgement by Washington, it was said the arms were supposed to be a gesture of goodwill to Iran and that Tehran might reciprocate by assisting in gaining the release of Americans held hostage by pro-Iranian terrorist organizations operating in Lebanon. After further investigation, however, the operation proved to be far more complex. The plan was said to have been supported by the president over the opposition of both his secretary of state and his secretary of defense. When faced with public scrutiny, Reagan insisted the arms were not a "swap" for hostages, but that it was hoped Tehran might be inclined to seek their release. It had been long-stated policy on the part of the United States that it would not negotiate with terrorists for hostages; Washington was on record opposing paying ransom. The sale of weapons to Iran seemed to contradict that policy. Under pressure, the president announced no further transactions would be entered into with Iran. The actions of the president shocked the government, especially the Congress, which had not been consulted. Indeed, the entire operation had been conducted from the "basement" of the White House, with Reagan's national security advisor, Admiral John Poindexter, and a staff member and marine officer, Oliver North, as the major actors.

Significance

The sale of weapons to Iran, done clandestinely through private contractors, was also a scheme to use the profits of the sale to purchase weapons for the Contra forces opposed to the Sandinista government in Nicaragua. Reagan insisted he knew nothing of the Contra arrangement, and the Tower Commission, which was assembled to investigate the matter, agreed. In the end, however, U.S.-Iranian relations were not improved, the American hostages were not released, and Iran did not obtain the means to defeat Iraq. The Contras were not successful against the Sandinistas, and the president of the United States had been implicated in a near-impeachable offense.

Baghdad Pact 198

The Baghdad Pact was a treaty of alliance entered into by Iraq and Turkey in 1955. Iran, Pakistan, and Britain joined the pact in the months that followed. The United States, although not a signatory to the pact, participated in all its activities. The Baghdad Pact was a substitute organization for a Middle East Defense Organization (MEDO). MEDO was boosted by the United States in an effort to link Middle East defense with the North Atlantic Treaty Organization (NATO), organized in 1949. Both organizations would have as their central purpose the containment of international, and especially Soviet, communism. MEDO, however, failed to materialize because Egypt's new revolutionary leadership was less interested in containing communism than it was in destroying Israel. Gamal Abdul Nasser saw no purpose in antagonizing Moscow, nor did he fear communist subversion in Egypt. Moreover, when MEDO was suggested by the United States, Nasser was busy impressing upon the British the idea that it was time for them to withdraw their forces from the Suez Canal zone. Nasser was determined to remove the last vestiges of European imperialism, and MEDO would have provided the British and the Americans with further opportunity to use Egypt as a base for their narrow interests. MEDO, after all, could not be used against Israel. The Baghdad Pact became the alternative response for Middle East defense against communist encroachment. Britain's treaty with Iraq, which provided the British with bases in the country, was due to expire, and difficulties were anticipated in extending the leases. Iraq's government was favorably disposed toward the West, but the country's armed forces and large segments of the sophisticated public were no longer interested in serving European interests. Iraq's involvement in the 1948–1949 Arab-Israeli War had increased the leverage of its young army officers and civil servants. Their tolerance of the Hashemite monarchy and government of Nuri as-Said was limited, and the regime sensed the need to practice caution. Turkey had already joined NATO and was a steadfast member of the Western bloc. The U.S. government believed it best to organize an alliance that appeared to emanate from among the Middle East states themselves. Thus, Turkey was requested to join with Iraq. The two Muslim countries pledged to defend one another, and they called upon other Middle East states to join them in common endeavor. Some observers compared the pact with the pre–World War II Saadabad alliance of 1937, which was inspired from among the Middle East states. But there was no obscuring the outside "encouragement" where the Baghdad Pact was concerned. Iran and Pakistan along with Britain quickly added their names to the alliance. The United States decided to avoid formal commitment when it became clear that Egypt, Jordan, and Syria were openly hostile. President Dwight Eisenhower and his secretary of state, John Foster Dulles, concluded that it would be futile to further antagonize the Arab states. But the die had already been cast. Egypt and Afghanistan were especially angered by the Baghdad Pact. Egypt saw the necessity of accepting Soviet offers of assistance, and in 1955 it became the first Arab state to receive shipments of Soviet arms. Afghanistan considered Pakistan its mortal enemy, and with Pakistan receiving military assistance from the United States, Kabul turned even more emphatically toward its other neighbor, the Soviet Union. An agreement was signed in 1956 modifying an earlier understanding, and Afghanistan also became the recipient of Soviet-manufactured weapons. The Baghdad Pact had a shaky start and an inauspicious end. In 1958, the Nuri as-Said government was overthrown in a military coup. Nuri, the king, and the royal family were murdered; the monarchy was abolished. The coup leaders declared an end to their participation in the Baghdad Pact, and the organization lost its only Arab member. To salvage what they could from this turn of events, the other member states and the United States agreed that the Baghdad Pact should be renamed the Central Treaty Organization (CENTO). ***See also*** CENTRAL TREATY ORGANIZATION (CENTO) (204); SAADABAD PACT (222).

Significance

The Baghdad Pact was a poor substitute for the proposed Middle East Defense Organization. The difficulties experienced in its three years of formal operation also reveal the essential indifference of the Arab states to communist threats. The post–World War II Arab states were unlike those before that great encounter. Traditional monarchies were still the fashion, but a new generation, with revolutionary ideas and a high degree of nationalism, had begun to assert itself. There was no returning to the status quo ante. Moreover, Arab nationalism was exaggerated by sustained European dominance in the area, and particularly by the establishment of the state of Israel. Israel, according to its Arab antagonists, was a Western contrivance, a vestige of European imperialism in the Middle East, and a mechanism for the permanent division of the Arab peoples. Because of the hatred for Zionism and the legacy of European imperialism, even the United States could not woo Nasser. U.S. threats to limit and even withdraw assistance did not intimidate the Egyptian leader. Moscow, which earlier had voiced support for Israel, soon realized the new opportunities available in the Arab world. Soviet offers of assistance to Egypt clearly were aimed at widening the wedge caused by the breakdown in Egyptian-U.S. relations. The U.S.S.R. not only provided Egypt with weapons, but also agreed to supply advisors and technicians. Later it also agreed to build the High Dam at Aswan, a project the United States had at first agreed to construct and then reluctantly cancelled. The Baghdad Pact was supposed to be a bulwark against Soviet penetration of the Middle East. The Kremlin, however, showed that it could leapfrog the alliance. Although Moscow's relations with Egypt would prove difficult and often strained, the Baghdad Pact gave the Soviets their initial opportunity to exploit differences among the Arabs, a role they continued to play. The Baghdad Pact can also be considered the precipitate for the destruction of the Hashemite monarchy in Iraq. It also caused considerable dislocation in Turkey, Iran, and Pakistan, although these developments did not mature until later. The Baghdad Pact was an afterthought, not a coherent organization. Nor did its members share a harmony of interests. It did not prevent the spread of Soviet influence and power throughout the Middle East, and because it caused internal difficulties for the regimes associated with it, it may also have stirred the troubled waters, from which the Kremlin was quick to draw its rewards.

Bush Initiative on Arms Limitation — 199

In May 1991, President George Bush announced his government's intention to curtail the flow of arms to the Middle East. "Nowhere are the dangers of weapons proliferation more urgent than in the Middle East," said Bush. In stating his concern the president made no reference to the $34 billion in actual or proposed sales to the region by the United States in 1991–1992. Nonetheless, Bush called upon the permanent members of the UN Security Council to consider the necessity of modifying their individual arms agreements to the states of the area. China was the only country to offer resistance to the plan, an unsurprising reaction given Washington's decision to deny Beijing computer and satellite technology because it was engaged in providing Pakistan with long-range missiles. The Bush initiative did not involve a complete arms ban because of weapons imbalances in the region. China, Britain, France, the Soviet Union, and the United States accounted for between 80 and 90 percent of the arms sales to the Middle East. The issue was debated at the London Economic Summit of the seven industrialized states in July 1991 and gained enthusiastic approval. In October the Security Council's permanent members also agreed to a reduction in arms deliveries. Bush also called upon the world's nations to destroy all poison gas stockpiles and announced the United States would not use chemical weapons "for any reason," including retaliation, and would destroy all poison gas stocks as soon as a treaty was approved. Nuclear proliferation was deemed a more difficult strategic problem and despite reductions in U.S. and Soviet nuclear arsenals, the emergence of new nuclear powers was a constant dilemma. This concern was emphasized when the United States cut off all assistance to Pakistan in October 1990 because it could not be certified that Islamabad was not constructing nuclear weapons. The UN Security Council became responsible for making a determined effort to prevent Iraq from producing nuclear weapons. In October 1991 the Security Council insisted it had the right to sustain its investigation of Iraqi weapons sites and to destroy all weapons of mass destruction located there. Reports that Israel had expanded its own nuclear arsenal and had transferred nuclear weapons technology to South Africa raised a storm of criticism in the Arab states. Claiming the United States followed a double standard, the Arab states insisted their chemical weapons were an essential balance against Israel's nuclear potential.

Significance

The Bush initiative involved the following: (1) a freeze on the purchase, building, and testing of surface-to-surface missiles; (2) a ban on the production or purchase of weapons-grade uranium and the placement of all nuclear facilities under international safeguards; (3) a call for all countries in the Middle East to accept a global treaty banning chemical weapons; (4) a proposal to strengthen the 1972 treaty banning biological weapons; and (5) a call on the world's five major arms suppliers, the United States, Britain, France, the Soviet Union, and China, to develop guidelines for restraining sales of conventional weapons to the Middle East. The initiative failed, however, to impose harsh restrictions on conventional weapons, which made up the bulk of the Middle East arsenal. Critics noted the initiative was "harshest on weapons that don't exist or can't be used, and easiest on weapons that either exist or have been used." Instead of a ban on surface-to-surface missiles, the initiative called for a freeze. Instead of calling for a nuclear-free zone in the Middle East, which even Israel has indicated it might support, the Bush plan merely suggested a freeze on stockpiling materials that can be used in nuclear weapons and a ban on future acquisitions. Shortly after the initiative was announced, the U.S. Defense Department said it would continue to store weapons in Israel. The pre-positioning agreement with Israel was not affected by the Bush proposal. The American Defense Secretary also announced the United States would give Israel ten used F-15 fighter aircraft and would continue supplying three-quarters of the funding for a U.S.-Israeli antiballistic missile project. The defense secretary said this program did not conflict with the spirit of the Bush initiative. The United States also revealed it had developed a program to store large quantities of military equipment in the Arab gulf states. A $365 million arms sale to Saudi Arabia was not blocked in the U.S. Congress, and the agreement allowed for the transfer of laser-guided smart bomb equipment, 2,000 high-explosive aerial bombs, 2,100 cluster bombs, and 770 Sparrow radar-guided air-to-air missiles in 1991–1992. The need to curtail the flow of arms was challenged by the need to merchandise weapons. In addition to the five major powers, North Korea, Argentina, Sweden, and Brazil, along with Middle East countries like Israel itself, were heavily involved in the arms trade.

Cairo Agreement, 1969 **200**

The Cairo Agreement of 1969 sanctioned PLO activity in southern Lebanon so long as the Palestinians respected Lebanese sovereignty. It also gave the PLO administrative power over the refugee camps in Lebanon. Thus, when King Hussain ordered his army to force the PLO from Jordan in 1970, the Palestinians were already prepared to use Lebanon as their principal base of operations against Israel. The Lebanese were unreconciled to this arrangement. Their forces had clashed with elements of the PLO in December 1968, and several months later violence spread, engulfing most of Lebanon's principal cities. Moreover, repeated guerrilla attacks from Lebanon on Israel caused the Israelis to retaliate, and Jerusalem placed chief responsibility for policing the border on the Lebanese government. The Cairo Agreement therefore was not agreeable to the Lebanese, but they lacked the ability to counteract it. The Lebanese Army launched a major campaign against the Palestinians in 1973, but by this time the PLO had drawn support from the Muslim and Druze communities, which wanted to see the undoing of Phalange Maronite supremacy in the country. *See also* LEBANESE CIVIL WAR, 1975–1976 (250).

Significance

The Cairo Agreement of 1969 established the PLO as a state within a state. It gave the Palestinians the opportunity to coalesce with forces opposed to the Maronite-dominated government, and it polarized Lebanon into two bitterly opposed armed camps. The arming of the leftists, the Lebanese Shiite and Sunni Muslims, and the Druze community was facilitated by PLO infrastructure. Indeed, it is suggested that the Lebanese Civil War would have erupted two years earlier had it not been for the Arab-Israeli war of October 1973. Another aspect of the Cairo Agreement is that it nullified the effect of the expulsion of PLO forces from Jordan. Instead of crushing the Palestinian movement, the expulsion made the PLO more determined to expand and strengthen its organization. It was in a better position to develop a network of worldwide communications and establish its bona fides. The Lebanese Civil War can be seen as a stage in the consolidation of PLO authority in Lebanon. Indeed, if Syria had not interfered, Lebanon would have been reformed in accordance with PLO demands, somewhat tempered by the needs of the Shiite and Druze communities.

Camp David Summit 201

The Camp David summit was promoted and organized by President Jimmy Carter in September 1978. Camp David, a retreat in the Maryland mountains for the president of the United States, was the site chosen to bring together President Anwar el-Sadat of Egypt and Prime Minister Menachem Begin of Israel. The Camp David summit was prompted by President Sadat's dramatic visit to Israel in 1977 and the demonstrated capacity of Egyptian and Israeli leaders to discuss their mutual problems. President Carter sensed the need to provide neutral ground for more serious negotiations. He also understood that only the United States wielded significant influence in both Egypt and Israel. Timing was judged important, and while reasonable goodwill existed between the parties, President Carter hoped to press for a basic settlement that would be the beginning for a more comprehensive peace in the Middle East. President Carter, more so than Sadat and Begin, believed an Israeli-Egyptian agreement would encourage other Arab states to resolve their differences with Jerusalem at the conference table. The parties assembled on September 5, with President Carter commuting between Washington and Camp David. After almost two weeks of secret negotiations (the media was kept at a distance), and after strenuous efforts on the part of the U.S. president, the parties arrived at what was called "A Framework for Peace in the Middle East." The agreed basis for a peaceful settlement, according to the "Framework," was UN Security Council Resolution 242 and Resolution 338. Egypt and Israel recognized each other's sovereignty and vowed to respect the territorial integrity and political independence of each state in the area. The "Framework" speaks specifically about the West Bank and Gaza Strip and Egyptian-Israeli relations. Egypt, Israel, Jordan, and representatives of the Palestinians were to cooperate in promoting self-government on the West Bank and Gaza. A self-governing authority was to be established on the West Bank and Israeli military and civilian administration eventually withdrawn. Egypt, Israel, and Jordan were to agree on the modalities for establishing a self-governing authority in both the West Bank and Gaza. A strong local police force was envisaged, with the Israelis redeploying their own police and military. Israeli and Jordanian forces were to participate in joint patrols and in staffing control posts to assure security. As soon as self-government could be established, a five-year transition period would be scheduled to begin. By the third year there was to be a clear idea of West Bank administration, and Jordan and Israel would enter into a peace treaty. The Palestinians were to be represented in all negotiations and their "legitimate rights" respected. Egypt and Israel were also slated to work together in developing a plan for the "just and permanent implementation of the resolution of the refugee problem." In the same agreement, Israel and Egypt pledged to reconcile all their future differences at the conference table. The "Framework" is also described as providing the basis for negotiations between Israel and other Arab states. This document then implied recognition, the abolition of all boycotts, and a guarantee of due process of law. The "Framework" set the scene for the drafting and execution of the Egyptian-Israeli Peace Treaty. ***See also*** EGYPTIAN-ISRAELI TREATY OF PEACE, 1979 (207).

Significance

The Camp David summit brought the United States into intimate partnership with Israel and Egypt in promoting Arab-Israeli peace through diplomacy. The United States acknowledged the importance of Egypt in building a security network in the region, and military as well as economic assistance to Cairo began in earnest after Camp David. Moreover, the United States saw the opportunity to obtain Egyptian permission for the use of military installations. In the months that followed the Camp David summit, the shah of Iran was toppled from his throne, and the United States lost a valuable ally. Egypt, therefore, became prominent in U.S. military strategy, and the U.S. embassy in Cairo was expanded to one of the largest in the world. Camp David, in other words, drew Sadat and Carter into a warm embrace. The Israelis saw their own influence in Washington decline somewhat, but the gains they had achieved by establishing a "no more war" policy with Egypt more than compensated. Although the "Framework" adopted at Camp David was supposed to provide for a comprehensive peace, the other Arab states were outspoken in their rejection of the agreement. Jordan, crucial to the success of the plan, was approached and pressured to accept the terms laid out at Camp David. But King Hussain, fearing for his position, declined all overtures. The Arab states generally verbalized their displeasure and accused Sadat of splitting the Arab world and becoming a tool of the United States. The Soviet Union had had intentions of arranging a peace conference on the Middle East at Geneva. Before Sadat's surprise visit to Jerusalem, President Carter had conferred with Soviet Foreign Minister Andrei Gromyko. Their public statement at the conclusion of their talks suggested that the United States had accepted Soviet participation and that Washington would also promote the Geneva conference. Observers believe that Sadat went to Jerusalem because he did not want the Soviets to play so important a role in resolving this Middle East crisis. Camp David, therefore, effectively removed the Soviets from any participation in the negotiations.

Capitulations 202

The capitulations were legal privileges and taxation exemptions obtained by the European powers in the Middle East from the sixteenth to the twentieth centuries. The first capitulations were granted by the Ottoman sultan to the French in 1535. The agreement between Suleiman the Magnificent and Francis I permitted free access to Ottoman markets by French merchants in return for a quasi-alliance. The capitulations (1) permitted the French to avoid Ottoman taxes, (2) gave them immunity from Ottoman law, (3) guaranteed the sanctity of their business establishments and homes, and (4) generally afforded special rights of extra-territoriality. No less important, non-Muslim Ottoman subjects in the employ of Frenchmen could also be accorded the same rights and immunities. Other European states recognized the advantages to be gained from such a treaty; Austria received similar opportunities in 1567, and Britain followed in 1592. Through the operation of the capitulations the European powers began to assume protective custody over the sultan's Christian subjects. Thus, as the Ottomans began to decline in power and authority, the agreements were used to justify European intervention in the affairs of the Middle East. France, for example, claimed the right to defend the interests of the Lebanese Catholics. France also used the capitulations to land its troops in North Africa and to promote French settlements in Algeria. The British exploited their opportunities in Egypt and spread their commercial strategic interests to Iran and the Persian Gulf shaykhdoms. The capitulations became the cutting edge of European imperialism, and they spread beyond the Middle East as far as China. The capitulations were withdrawn in the aftermath of World Wars I and II. The Middle East states as well as other Third World nations, however, continued to complain about heavy-handed European and U.S. economic activity in their respective countries. The current term used to describe this activity is *neo-colonialism*.

Significance

The capitulations were granted at a time when the Ottomans were at the height of their power. Muslims are prohibited from engaging in usurious activity, and during Ottoman rule non-Muslims were employed to promote commerce and trade between the Ottomans and other nations. The treaty with France therefore was supposed to be of mutual benefit to the Turks and French. In the beginning, the number of European merchants in the Ottoman Empire was small, and they did not pose a threat to the regime. Moreover, the promise of European military support was perceived as reinforcing Turkish interests. The capitulations became a problem only when the empire began to decline and the Europeans took advantage of Constantinople's weaknesses. In time, the capitulations were a burden the Ottomans could not manage. They crippled the sultan's authority and made it possible for rebellious elements to break with the empire. In the last stages of the Ottoman Empire, the capitulations symbolized the vast power of the Europeans as well as the humiliation suffered by the Muslim world. "Neo-colonialism" today is a common complaint of Third World nations, who argue that their economic life is controlled by distant powers and multinational corporations. According to their argument, national dignity and socioeconomic progress are made more difficult by the wealthy industrial nations. Self-determination, they insist, can only be realized when greater equality exists between rich and poor nations and each nation can reap the benefits from its own resources. In recent years, the development of what has been called North-South Dialogue has addressed the imbalance between the "have" countries and the "have nots." The influence that the rich nations exert through their control of international economic mechanisms, such as the International Bank for Reconstruction and Development (World Bank) and the International Monetary Fund, has been challenged by the Third World, but the dilemma persists, and the industrial states show no indication of yielding.

Carter Doctrine 203

The Carter Doctrine was precipitated by the collapse of the shah of Iran's regime and the Soviet invasion of Afghanistan, both occurring in 1979. The abolition of the Iranian monarchy by the revolutionary government also brought the termination of Iranian-U.S. relations. Washington had placed enormous confidence in the shah and his armed forces to defend the Persian Gulf and its precious petroleum reserves. That confidence evaporated with the change in governments, and the United States sensed the necessity of intruding with its own forces into the region. U.S. naval forces from the Pacific and Mediterranean fleets were dispatched to the Indian Ocean in proximity to the Strait of Hormuz. The United States also began assembling a Rapid Deployment Force for ready assignment in the area if the occasion warranted. The Soviet invasion of Afghanistan in December 1979 was believed to be related to the instability in Iran in the wake of the revolution. Soviet forces in Afghanistan were strategically positioned only a few hundred miles from the entrance to the Persian Gulf. Moreover, Soviet presence in Afghanistan extended the Iranian-Soviet border to almost 2,000 miles (3,200 kilometers), making the communist superpower Iran's most immediate neighbor. Observing the mounting threat to Western security interests, President Carter publicly declared the United States' intention to resist a possible Soviet move against the oil fields of the Persian Gulf. In his State of the Union address on January 23, 1980, Carter noted, "An attempt by any outside force to gain control of the Persian Gulf region will be regarded as an assault on the vital interests of the United States of America, and such an assault will be repelled by any means necessary, including military force." Ayatollah Khomeini and his legions had dramatized U.S. weakness in the region. The seizure of the U.S. embassy and its staff had given new urgency to the situation. The Soviet invasion of neighboring Afghanistan followed within weeks of the embassy takeover, and observers believed Moscow's action was timed to coincide with that incident because so much American attention was diverted to the hostage situation. Carter therefore went on record warning the Soviets that their actions would not pass unnoticed. The Afghanistan operation was described as the most dramatic Soviet maneuver since World War II, and Carter said it posed a serious threat to peace. Fear that Iran was on the Soviet list, and that Iran could not defend itself, revived the notion of the American policeman, even if the Iranians wanted nothing of U.S. protection. Although U.S. government officials claimed the president was only re-emphasizing established policy, the declaration involved new foreign and national security policies. To prove its determination, the U.S. administration obtained the use of military installations in Oman, Somalia, Egypt, and Kenya. Efforts to convince the Saudis that U.S. forces should also be located in their country were not successful. But U.S. military personnel were already in Saudi Arabia in large numbers as technicians and trainers. They were bolstered by U.S.-flown AWACS early warning aircraft. The U.S. also agreed to sell Riyadh its own AWACS aircraft as well as the most sophisticated fighter-bombers in the U.S. Air Force. The Reagan administration perpetuated the Carter Doctrine and stepped up the deployment of U.S. forces in the Middle East. It also increased the transfer of weapons to allied and associated states. The action taken by the United States against Iraq in 1990–1991 was done, although not clearly stated, in accordance with the Carter Doctrine. *See also* TRUMAN DOCTRINE (229); EISENHOWER DOCTRINE (208); NIXON DOCTRINE (215); OPERATION DESERT SHIELD (257); OPERATION DESERT STORM (258).

Significance
The Carter Doctrine appeared to merge the Truman, Eisenhower, and Nixon Doctrines: With it the United States again identified the prime threat to the West as coming from the Soviet Union. And although the Soviets were recognized to have greater military prowess than the United States, the Americans placed the world on notice that the Persian Gulf was of such vital concern that they might be inclined to use tactical nuclear weapons in its defense. The threat of nuclear confrontation in the region was clearly meant to deter potential Soviet aggression. The Iraqi invasion of Iran and the threat that this posed to the Persian Gulf did not activate the Carter Doctrine. The United States was still negotiating the release of the hostages, and there was little support for Iran in the United States. Iraq, although somewhat tied to the Soviet Union through a 1972 treaty, was not perceived as acting in behalf of the Soviets. The conflict, from the Washington perspective, was localized and limited by the continuing antagonism of two old enemies. The Soviets avoided choosing sides in the Iraq-Iran War. Moreover, the Persian Gulf remained open to international shipping. Oil continued to move from the gulf states to outer markets. The United States, therefore, had no reason to become embroiled in the conflict. Nevertheless, the United States maintained forces near the Persian Gulf. The Carter Doctrine was dramatically tested when Iraq invaded Kuwait and threatened Saudi Arabia. The United States sent more than half a million men and women to the gulf region, and in operation Desert Storm, that force, with assistance from France, Britain, Saudi Arabia, Egypt, Syria, and other countries quickly defeated the Iraqi armed forces and forced them to give up their gains in Kuwait. The success of the campaign against Baghdad was made possible by Soviet support for the U.S.-led coalition and their agreeing to the UN Security Council resolutions that sanctioned the use of force in repelling Iraq's aggression. The Soviets, however, did not send forces to the region.

Central Treaty Organization (CENTO) **204**

The Central Treaty Organization (CENTO) was the successor to the Baghdad Pact. In 1958, the Iraqi monarchy was overthrown and abolished. Iraq withdrew from the Baghdad Pact. The rest of the alliance, however, remained intact, necessitating a change in nomenclature. The name "Central Treaty Organization" was considered appropriate insofar as it seemed to follow the concept of the North Atlantic Treaty Organization. It also became apparent that a Middle East Defense Organization, centered on the Arab countries, was impossible and that a substitute arrangement on a more or less permanent basis was already available. The creation of CENTO attempted to formalize the alliance between Turkey, Iran, Pakistan, Britain, and, although unofficially, the United States. CENTO thus was conceived as a link in the chain of alliances between NATO and the Southeast Asia Treatly Organization (SEATO), assembled in 1954. CENTO was intended to organize the "Northern Tier" of states, two of which shared a border with the Soviet Union (Turkey and Iran), while another was a near-neighbor (Pakistan). With Britain directly and the United States indirectly involved in the alliance, these strategically placed states were seemingly assured of adequate military supplies as well as protection. A strong Northern Tier was also viewed from Washington as providing a significant buffer vis-à-vis Soviet aggressive intentions toward the Arab Middle East. The United States played the role of a full member of the alliance, participating in many of its committees and subcommittees. It was especially active in military planning, and through bilateral agreements as well as formal arrangements (such as Turkey's membership in NATO and Pakistan's membership in SEATO), Washington was able to transfer or sell large stores of weapons systems to the area states. Moreover, Turkey, Iran, and Pakistan all provided the United States with operational military bases. U.S. air and naval forces made use of extensive Turkish facilities. Iran and Pakistan provided the United States with advanced communications bases from which to surveil the Soviet Union. The CENTO secretariat, housed in Ankara, Turkey, pleaded with the United States to become a signatory state and thus an official member of the alliance. Washington, however, avoided the pressure, sensing that its interests were better served by relationships already in place. The fact that the United States repeatedly refused to become a regular member-state hurt the alliance's morale. It also made suspect U.S. pledges of support in time of emergency. CENTO was different from NATO in that even its member-states did not commit themselves to support one another in moments of crisis. NATO commitments stressed the notion that "an attack on one was an attack on all." There was no such understanding in CENTO. Thus, when member-states found themselves in jeopardy, as in the Indo-Pakistani wars of 1965 and 1971, CENTO stood by, virtually helpless. Although Iran and Turkey made gestures of support for Pakistan and promised to ship arms, Britain did not become involved, and the United States went further by imposing an embargo on arms to Pakistan in 1965. That embargo was still operative when the 1971 conflict erupted. The knowledge that the embargo had also been imposed on India did little to salve Pakistani sentiment or to overcome the belief that they had been betrayed. In a similar vein, Turkey and Greece collided over Cyprus in the 1960s and 1970s. The United States at first threatened to interpose its naval forces between Turkey and Cyprus to prevent a Turkish invasion. By 1974, however, Washington could not prevent Turkish intervention. American congressional and public opinion on these issues was opposed to both Pakistan and Turkey, and relations between Washington and Ankara and between Washington and Islamabad were severely strained. CENTO had internal problems that it could not resolve. Although created to meet a perceived threat of international communism, it could not manage local questions. These contradictions were to prove CENTO's ultimate undoing. When Zulfikar Ali Bhutto assumed power in Islamabad in December 1971, following the loss of the war to India and the creation of Bangladesh from former East Pakistan, he declared Pakistan's formal withdrawal from membership in SEATO. Pakistan, however, remained in CENTO, essentially because Iran, its chief benefactor, had no intention of abandoning the alliance. When the shah of Iran fell from power in 1979, the revolutionary government took the country out of the alliance. Pakistan, under the leadership of Mohammad Zia-ul-Haq (Bhutto had been overthrown by a military coup and was later executed), understood that the alliance was meaningless without Iran. Zia, therefore, announced Pakistan's intention to withdraw. Turkey also had reason to be angered by U.S. actions. It, too, was denied U.S. weapons, despite being described as the "linchpin" of NATO. Washington was distressed by Turkey's invasion of Cyprus, and the embargo on weapons was supposed to pressure the Turks to withdraw. Ankara steadfastly refused to pull its forces out and instead announced the closing of a number of bases used by the U.S. armed forces. Washington reconsidered the deteriorating relations with Ankara when the shah of Iran was forced to flee his country. Arms were again made available to Turkey, but it was too late to save CENTO. Observing Iran's withdrawal and Pakistan's decision to sever its ties, Turkey declared CENTO defunct in 1980. ***See also*** BAGHDAD PACT (198); EISENHOWER DOCTRINE (208); TRUMAN DOCTRINE (229); RIMLAND (24).

Significance
The Central Treaty Organization was more form than substance. Sometimes referred to as "cartographic containment," it appeared impressive on a world map, but it never achieved tangible proportions. Although the United States signed three separate executive agreements with Turkey, Iran, and Pakistan in 1959, pledging U.S. support in the event of communist aggression or subversion, Washington did nothing to assist these countries so long as the Soviet Union was not directly involved. In the Indo-Pakistani War of 1971, India received indirect assistance from the Soviet Union (New Delhi and Moscow had signed a treaty of friendship and cooperation in July 1971), but Washington did not see the conflict as involving communist actions. Pakistan suffered a humiliating and demoralizing defeat, and little confidence remained concerning U.S. pledges of aid. The Soviet invasion of Afghanistan in December 1979 brought a mild rebuke from Washington, and despite the heavy rhetoric, little military assistance was made available to the Afghani resistance by the Carter administration. The Pakistanis also saw the United States abandon the shah, after earlier declarations had established Iran as the principal bulwark against Soviet encroachment in the Middle East. Moreover, Washington had failed to support the Turks in their efforts at preventing Cyprus from being united (*enosis*) with Greece and at insulating the minority Turkish population on the island from Greek attack. There was little reason for Pakistanis or Turks to believe the United States could be counted upon in time of crisis. There was also the general feeling that CENTO was a useless organization. It was also an impediment to Pakistan's diplomacy. Pakistan had denied itself the opportunity to join the nonaligned movement. Its Western

ties had also caused it to strain relations with other Third World countries, especially the Arab states. Withdrawal from CENTO therefore made it possible for Islamabad to pursue a more independent policy. The country moved ahead with its intention, although it was officially denied, to construct a nuclear device. It also sought to identify itself more closely with the Arab states. Revolutionary Iran decried CENTO as an imperialist plot to subvert the Middle East. But its war with Iraq, and its insistence on spreading the seeds of revolution throughout the Muslim world, did not give it the opportunity to capitalize on its anti-U.S. policy. Turkey remained a member of NATO and, after the declaration of martial law in 1980, drew somewhat closer to the United States. Turkey, and even Pakistan, were made the recipients of new U.S. weapons during the years of the Reagan administration, but there was no effort to revive CENTO.

Cooperative Council of the Gulf States (205)

Organized in Abu Dhabi on May 25, 1981, through the efforts of Saudi Arabia, the Cooperative Council of the Gulf States, or Gulf Cooperative Council, links Kuwait, Bahrein, Qatar, the United Arab Emirates, and Oman in a political, military, and economic arrangement aimed at protecting their interests in the Persian Gulf region. The member-states seek the improvement of commercial and technical relationships and have pledged to exchange information and generally promote the well-being of the larger council. The new organization has a Supreme Council composed of the leaders of the six member-states that meets twice annually to establish policy. The presidency of the Supreme Council rotates in alphabetical order by country. A unit of the Supreme Council was given direct responsibility for reconciling differences among the members. In addition, a Foreign Minister's Council acts as the executive arm, and it is scheduled to meet every second month. Finally, a secretariat-general was established in Riyadh by the Supreme Council to ensure the implementation of the organization's decisions. Kuwait's Abdullah Bishara became its first secretary-general. Two deputy secretaries-general were selected for economic and political affairs. In September 1981, the military chiefs of staff of the council states met to discuss regional security questions. The council's Conciliation Commission is charged with resolving potential disputes among members. The council is not a vehicle for merging the sovereignties into one unified state; rather, it is concerned with issues of common concern and cooperation. Political integration is not its chief purpose. In this regard, the council reiterated its contention that the new organization would strengthen the Arab cause against Israel. It could not, however, ward off Iraqi aggression against Kuwait, and in the wake of the Gulf War of 1990–1991 it was apparent the security of the area would have to involve other Arab countries, i.e., Egypt and Syria, but also a long-term U.S. presence. The creation of a joint security command post, involving the United States, on the island of Bahrein, was aimed at institutionalizing the new arrangement.

Significance

The Cooperative Council of Gulf States encourages economic, financial, and cultural interaction, but it is particularly concerned with the security of its members. It therefore emphasizes the need to improve transportation and communication as well as assist in the educational development of the area's youth. It is intended to promote military cooperation. The six member-states concur in the view that the demise of the Soviet Union eliminated a major threat to the region's security. The Israeli problem, however, receives maximum attention. Central to its purpose is the need to convince the United States that Israel is a liability and that Washington's support for the Jewish state destabilizes the region. On the other hand, it remains to be seen if Washington can influence the gulf states to resolve their differences with Israel, to end their state of belligerency, and to recognize the Jewish state in return for a workable settlement of the Palestinian question.

Diplomacy: Gulf Crisis 206

The Iraqi invasion of Kuwait on August 2, 1990, instantaneously became the "Gulf crisis," and it set in train diplomatic maneuvering unprecedented in its intensity in modern times. After the UN Security Council passed the twelfth in a series of related resolutions, this one authorizing the use of force if Iraq had not withdrawn its forces from Kuwait by January 15, 1991, diplomacy took on even greater urgency. The use-of-force resolution was approved by the Security Council on November 29, 1990. On November 30, President Bush invited Iraqi Foreign Minister Tariq Aziz to Washington and offered to send Secretary of State James Baker to Baghdad between December 15 and January 15. Later, President Bush said the Baker visit to Baghdad must be held on January 3, 1991. Saddam Hussain insisted on meeting Baker on January 12, a date President Bush found unacceptable. Iraq also said it would agree to a dialogue with the United States only if the talks also included the Israeli-Palestinian issue. The Bush administration announced it would not accept "linkage" and repeated its call for Iraq to withdraw unconditionally from Kuwait. On December 6, 1990, Saddam Hussain declared he would release all the foreign hostages in Iraq. Iraq rejected the U.S. dates for the meetings and Washington did the same with the January 12 date announced by the Iraqis. On December 12 the U.S. cancelled its invitation to Tariq Aziz to visit Washington if the Iraqis refused to budge on the January 12 date for the Baker visit to Baghdad. On January 3, however, President Bush invited Tariq Aziz to meet with Secretary Baker in Geneva on January 9, and the Iraqis accepted this invitation. Bush said the Baker-Aziz meeting would focus only on the question of withdrawal from Kuwait. Saddam Hussain continued to insist on the linkage of the gulf problem with that of the Palestinians; Washington was equally adamant that no linkage existed between the two issues. On December 5 President Bush declared that unconditional withdrawal was the only way for Baghdad to avoid "terrible consequences." On January 9 Tariq Aziz met with James Baker, and after six and one-half hours of deliberations both parties announced they had not moved from their original positions and that the talks had failed to produce the necessary momentum for a peaceful solution. Tariq Aziz also refused to take back to Baghdad the letter that President Bush had given Baker for transmittal to Saddam Hussain. The Iraqis argued the letter was diplomatically impolite, as it repeated U.S. intentions to unleash a violent war on Iraq if it did not heed the terms of the UN resolutions on its aggression against Kuwait. On January 12 the UN secretary-general went to Baghdad to meet with Saddam Hussain in a last effort to pressure Saddam to withdraw his forces from Kuwait. Javier Perez de Cuellar met with Saddam Hussain on January 12, but his mission also failed to produce the action required to prevent the use-of-force resolution from going into effect on January 15. *See also*

UN RESOLUTIONS: IRAQ-KUWAIT CONFLICT (230); OPERATION DESERT SHIELD (257); NINETEENTH PROVINCE (21).

Significance
Washington, unlike many of its European allies, France and Germany prominent among them, steadfastly refused to accept the Palestinian linkage proposal put forth by Saddam Hussain soon after his conquest of Kuwait. President Bush argued that Saddam Hussain had raised the issue to gain the favor of the Arab and Muslim world, to divide the international coalition arrayed against him, and to make it very difficult for Saudi Arabia and the other gulf states to represent the cause of the Arab and Muslim peoples. Saddam Hussain's threat to attack Israel if attacked by the international force made it difficult for President Bush to sustain the fragile coalition. Bush's November 1990 visit to Damascus and Baker's visit in January 1991 were aimed at keeping Hafez al-Assad within the alliance should Saddam Hussain seek to strike Israel. Assad was likewise pressured by Saddam Hussain to join with his "Arab brothers" against the "infidel" menace to the Arab states. Although Washington acknowledged the connection between the Palestinian issue and the Gulf crisis, it refused to make Saddam Hussain the "link" between them lest this provide the Iraqi leader with bona fides that he could use against the Arab governments supporting the UN resolutions. For its part, Baghdad showed no inclination to leave Kuwait, having annexed and declared it its nineteenth province. In the last analysis, negotiations, despite a last-minute effort by French president François Mitterrand, failed to yield the desired results. On January 10–12 the U.S. Congress debated whether it should support or reject President Bush's stated position. On January 12, the House of Representatives voted 250–183 to support the president. The Senate did likewise, although the margin of success was smaller, 52 in favor and 47 opposed.

Egyptian-Israeli Treaty of Peace, 1979 — 207

With the "Framework" assembled at Camp David in 1978, and with President Jimmy Carter as a constant source of pressure, Egyptian and Israeli leaders commenced negotiations aimed at arriving at a peace treaty between their two countries. The talks moved to a critical stage in February 1979 with Prime Minister Menachem Begin asserting that the Carter administration leaned toward Egypt's position. With U.S. support, President Anwar el-Sadat declared that he would refrain from granting the Israelis concessions until Jerusalem signalled its willingness to proceed with Palestine autonomy. Israel, however, refused to center deliberations on the Palestinians while Egypt's relations with Israel remained ambiguous. In March, Egypt met one demand of the Israelis and announced that it would sell Israel 2.5 million tons of oil each year from its Sinai fields. Israel displayed its good intentions by declaring a phased but total withdrawal from the Sinai and the dismantling of all Jewish settlements on the peninsula. These developments pointed to a peace treaty between Egypt and Israel, although the more difficult issues involving the Palestinians would be left for continuing negotiations. On March 26, 1979, Egypt and Israel brought an end to more than 30 years of belligerency and terminated their state of war. The peace treaty was signed in a White House ceremony with approximately 1,600 guests and dignitaries in attendance. President Carter applauded the efforts of Begin and Sadat, describing their behavior as courageous and visionary. Sadat and Begin, however, used the occasion to heap praise upon the U.S. president, who, they said, had performed a "miracle." The peace treaty called for the opening of full diplomatic relations, the promotion of trade, and the right to freely travel between the two countries. After the Israeli withdrawal from the Sinai, U.S. and West European forces were called upon to play observer roles. Egypt and Israel agreed to pull back their forces and reduce their offensive capabilities. Israel was also promised full use of the Suez Canal as well as the right to navigate the Strait of Tiran and the Gulf of Aqaba. Egypt also agreed that "in the event of a conflict between the obligations of the Parties under the present Treaty and any of their other obligations, the obligations under this Treaty will be binding and implemented." With this understanding Egypt pledged not to assist other Arab states should they launch an attack against the Israeli state at a later date. The signatories also agreed that when disputes arose between them they would resort to negotiations and, if those proved inadequate, to arbitration. The annexes to the treaty spell out in detail (1) the withdrawal from the Sinai, (2) the future placement of military forces, (3) the role of the United Nations, and (4) the creation of an early warning system, monitored by U.S. forces. Additional annexes address themselves to economic, cultural, and good neighborly relations. They are also concerned with transportation, telecommunications, and human rights. The United States added further assurances to Israel immediately following the signing ceremony, when Secretary of State Cyrus Vance and Israeli Foreign Minister Moshe Dayan signed a memorandum of agreement, pledging U.S. assistance for Israel in the event of hostilities. The United States promised to protect sealanes to and from Israeli ports, block any United Nations action "adversely" affecting the treaty, and provide Israel with the necessary military and economic aid to maintain its status in the region. The United States also guaranteed adequate supplies of oil to Israel for the next 15 years. ***See also*** CAMP DAVID SUMMIT (201); SINAI SUPPORT MISSION (224).

Significance

While the Egyptian-Israeli Peace Treaty did not produce the desired comprehensive peace in the region, it brought to a close an adversarial relationship that had begun in 1948 and had spanned four bloody and costly encounters. Egypt's official withdrawal from the confrontation with Israel was a severe blow to the other Arab states and Muslims generally. Bitterness runs deep between Arabs and Israelis, and the Egyptian action was seen as a sellout to the Americans and their Zionist friends. President Sadat became the target for Arab displeasure. Egypt was expelled from the Arab League and denied a presence in other Arab organizations. Financial and economic assistance to Egypt from Arab countries were cancelled. Diplomatic relations were severed. Only the Sudan, Oman, and Somalia, with a continuing dependence on Egypt, refused to join in the condemnation. Egypt's isolation in the Arab world and the general dismay registered in the extended Muslim world, however, did not outwardly disturb the Egyptian leader. Sadat perceived a greater threat to the Muslim nations in the inroads made by the Soviet Union. To Sadat, Israel was a constant reminder of Arab humiliation; the Soviet penetration of the Middle East, however, was a threat to the survival of the Islamic way of life and the independence of the area's people. The Soviet invasion of Afghanistan and the concerted drive to crush the Afghan nation were ample evidence of long-range Soviet intentions in the

Middle East. Sadat, therefore, was prepared to end Egypt's confrontation with Israel, join the United States in collective self-defense arrangements, and emphasize the revitalization of Egypt's socioeconomic life. Sadat could not avoid his detractors inside or beyond the borders of Egypt. Internally, Sadat attempted to consolidate his authority by isolating his enemies, especially among Egypt's outspoken fundamentalists. Political repression, however, did not endear Sadat to his many Egyptian publics, and soaring inflation and widespread economic dislocation made management of Egypt a tedious affair. In September 1981, Sadat ordered all Soviets to leave Egypt, declaring that Moscow was in league with dissidents who were conspiring to destroy his administration. Sadat had hundreds imprisoned during this period, the majority judged steadfast opponents. Muslim fundamentalists and Coptic Christians were singled out, but journalists, politicians, and other professional members of Egyptian society were also incarcerated. Tension ran high in Cairo when Sadat went to review his armed forces in commemoration of the 1973 war with Israel. Then, while he sat reviewing his crack troops, Anwar el-Sadat was assaulted and shot dead by a small band of Islamic fundamentalists hidden within the parade. Sadat's death on October 6, 1981, was the most significant consequence of the Egyptian-Israeli Peace Treaty. There was jubilation in the extended Arab world when news spread of Sadat's passing. In Israel, a heavy gloom descended over the nation. Speculation was rife concerning Hosni Mubarak's capacity to honor the agreements and understandings entered into by his predecessor. For the record, Mubarak insisted that Egypt would keep all its promises. It was also apparent, however, that the largest Arab nation would endeavor to mend relations with its alienated brethren.

Eisenhower Doctrine *208*

The Eisenhower Doctrine is the description given to a joint resolution of the U.S. Congress (H J Res 117) entitled "Joint Resolution to Promote Peace and Stability in the Middle East," passed on January 5, 1957. The doctrine appeared to be a corollary to the Truman Doctrine, as it specified that the United States would assist, through the use of its armed forces if necessary, any country or group of countries threatened by "international communism." Although specific mention is made of the Middle East, the limits of U.S. commitment are never described. It was believed, however, that the Congress intended to include all the countries between Libya and Pakistan and between Turkey and the Sudan. The resolution was prompted by the 1956 Suez War, in which Britain and France attacked Egypt. Britain and France along with the United States had entered into a Tripartite Agreement in 1950, pledging to defend the countries of the area from acts of aggression. The British-French invasion of Egypt shattered the Tripartite Agreement. In 1955, the Baghdad Pact had been signed between Iraq and Turkey at the urging of the United States and Great Britain. That pact was supposed to secure the Middle East against communist encroachment, both foreign and domestic, but the 1956 Suez War also undermined the Baghdad Pact. Israel joined the Europeans in striking at Egypt and as a consequence had seized control of the Sinai Peninsula. Although the Israelis later withdrew in favor of a UN force, the combination of European-Israeli forces ruptured Western relations in the Arab world. It also brought Arab governments, until then favorable to the West, under heavy fire. No Arab government was more exposed by the 1956 war than the Iraqi government of Nuri as-Said. In July 1958, the Said government was overthrown in a military coup. Nuri as-Said was murdered, along with the Hashemite King Faisal II, the cousin of King Hussain of Jordan, and his entire family. The monarchy was abolished, and Iraq declared its withdrawal from the Baghdad Pact. Reflecting developments in Washington, the joint resolution, now in the form of the Eisenhower Doctrine, was invoked to send U.S. Marines ashore at Beirut, the capital of Lebanon. The U.S. government had concluded that communists were behind the coup in Iraq. They also feared that the Jordanian king would be targeted. Moreover, Lebanon was besieged by communal strife. The Christian Phalange president had raised a storm of controversy, and Phalangists and Lebanese Muslims and Druze (perceived as leftist in Washington) had commenced large-scale assaults on one another. Civil war appeared to be imminent. Moscow had stated its support for the rebellion in Iraq and for the anti-Phalange forces in Lebanon. The Soviets had also called for King Hussain's overthrow. President Eisenhower therefore felt justified in sending U.S. troops to Lebanon, especially as the Lebanese president had requested assistance. The troops remained in Lebanon several months. Upon their withdrawal the Lebanese political situation was stabilized, but not resolved. Jordan was offered increased assistance by the United States. And Iraq began a course of international policy that distanced it from the West and brought it into intimate contact with the Soviet Union. Although the Eisenhower Doctrine was not used again in the Middle East, events did bring to mind the need to salvage the Baghdad Pact, and it was renamed the Central Treaty Organization (CENTO). *See also* BAGHDAD PACT (198); TRIPARTITE AGREEMENT OF 1950 (228); TRUMAN DOCTRINE (229); CENTRAL TREATY ORGANIZATION (CENTO) (204).

Significance
The Eisenhower Doctrine somewhat followed the tradition established by the Monroe Doctrine of 1823. In more modern form, it was an extension of the Truman Doctrine. U.S. presidential doctrines are symbolic, sometimes dramatic, representations of policy concerned with U.S. national interest and especially national security. Just as President Theodore Roosevelt's foreign policy was directed at the establishment of U.S. power in the Western Hemisphere, and thus is judged a corollary to the Monroe Doctrine, the Truman Doctrine placed U.S. national security interests in a global setting, and the Eisenhower Doctrine identified the Middle East as an area of vital concern to the United States. Congressional resolutions that provide the basis for policies carry more weight when identified as presidential doctrine. They also appear to generate greater legitimacy when so identified. But because the doctrines are perceived by other states as ethnocentric and self-serving, they do little to address the needs of the regions to which they are applied. Latin Americans have rebelled against both the Monroe Doctrine and the Roosevelt Corollary. Similarly, Arabs reacted with hostility to the Truman and Eisenhower Doctrines. The last two were perceived as instruments of imperialist policy. The Eisenhower Doctrine, for example, did not concern itself with Israel, the primary enemy of the Arabs. Moreover, the emphasis on combatting international communism, or the attempt to reduce Soviet influence in the Middle East, was seen as a ploy to sustain Western control. Popular Arab sentiment was whipped to a passion by policies such as the Eisenhower Doctrine. And

although the United States envisaged its power and resources as protecting the region from foreign threat, in point of fact the Americans were seen as propping up unpopular, antiquated regimes. In so doing the United States not only was seen to be thwarting progressive development in the Middle East, but also was accused of contributing to the divisiveness between the nations and peoples of the area.

Evian Agreements (209)

The Evian Agreements marked the termination of the Algerian struggle for independence against French colonialism. The eight-year revolutionary war ended in March 1962, following several days of negotiation in Evian, France, between the Paris government and the provisional government of the Algerian Republic. The Evian Agreements provided for a ceasefire and fashioned the legal instruments for the formal transference of power to Algerian leaders. An Algerian-French authority, the provisional executive, was given responsibility for organizing elections for the National Assembly. Rivalry between the two dominant figures in the Algerian revolution, however, caused a momentary delay in conducting the elections. Ahmad Ben Bella, the revolution's ideologue, and Colonel Houari Boumedienne, the military commander, differed on the question of political power. Ben Bella was initially successful and formed the first Algerian government. Algeria was declared to be a one-party state managed by the National Liberation Front (Front de Liberation Nationale, or FLN). Moreover, the military establishment was deemed an arm of the party with little political responsibility. Ben Bella wanted to consolidate his power and establish the principle of civilian supremacy. The FLN also assumed the right to appoint all high civil as well as military officials, and Ben Bella became commander-in-chief of Algeria's armed forces. There was no effective legal check on Ben Bella's authority, and he was elected to a five-year term as Algeria's first president in 1963. No candidates were permitted to compete for the office. Ben Bella's power, however, was short-lived. The army was disturbed by the inordinate authority accumulated by Ben Bella, and Boumedienne led a coup against him in June 1965. The civilian branch of the FLN was seriously undermined when the party's Political Bureau was disbanded. The new National Assembly was also eliminated, and Boumedienne proceeded to build his own power base. Ten years passed before the original constitution was replaced by one more satisfactory to the army. The new constitution was promulgated in November 1976. Algeria was described as a republic with Islam as the state religion. The constitution also called for a form of socialism, and competitive party politics was rejected.

Significance

The Evian Agreements ushering in Algeria's sovereign independence appeared to herald a democratic experience. But the long years of bloody encounter that led up to the French withdrawal had taken their toll of the moderate liberals. The revolution belonged to those who proved to be determined activists and skilled in military tactics. Both Ben Bella and Boumedienne represented secularism rather that theological thought. Each supported a form of socialism compatible with Islam and Algeria's quest for modernization. Algerian socialism, therefore, was identified as Islamic socialism. The phrase suggested a form of state control that is not unique in Islamic tradition, but the approach was more pragmatic than ritualistic or dogmatic. Algeria's foreign minister in 1972 emphasized that Algeria was neither communist or Baathist or Nasserist. Frantz Fanon, the poet-philosopher of the Algerian revolution and a prime exponent of nationalism in the Third World, expressed the view that the violence of the Algerian independence movement was a necessary stage in changing the political consciousness of the Algerian people. Under Boumedienne the FLN continued to serve as a vehicle for the mass organization of peasants, women, youth, factory workers, and veterans. The central purpose of Algerian policy was economic development. Democratic expression as suggested in the Evian Agreements had to wait upon more settled times.

Gorbachev Peace Initiative (210)

The Gorbachev peace initiative was launched on February 18, 1991, in a last-minute effort to prevent the coalition forces led by the United States from totally destroying Iraq's war-making capability in and near Kuwait. The initiative called upon Iraq to accept Resolution 660, which called for the withdrawal of Iraqi forces from Kuwait, but it sought to make null and void the other resolutions, especially those that called for a rescinding of the annexation order, the reinstatement of the emir and his government, the reparations due Kuwait for the destruction visited upon the country, and a variety of other requirements. It also called for the immediate lifting of sanctions once Iraq withdrew its forces. In the area of the withdrawal, the Gorbachev initiative insisted on an immediate ceasefire and provided the Iraqis with three weeks to pull their forces from Kuwait. ***See also*** UN RESOLUTIONS: IRAQ-KUWAIT CONFLICT (230).

Significance

The Gorbachev peace initiative was perceived by the coalition as preserving Saddam Hussein as a loyal client of Moscow; retaining Iraq as a strategic ally; holding Iraq as a principal arms purchaser of Soviet weapons and as Moscow's key player in Middle East affairs; and enabling the Soviet Union to represent itself as a loyal ally of Iraq, a supporter of UN Security Council resolutions, and a concerned friend of Arab and Muslim nations. Gorbachev was also seen reaching for greater international prestige as well as placating the more ardent members of his communist government. Although the United States publicly thanked Gorbachev for his effort, President Bush dismissed it out of hand, as he had an earlier Iraqi announcement that it would accept Resolution 660 but only with a variety of conditions. The Gorbachev initiative was ambiguous in that it called for unconditional withdrawal of Iraqi forces from Kuwait while it also attached conditions to such a retreat. President Bush refused to give Saddam Hussein any opportunity to claim victory. Washington sensed Gorbachev was looking for a way to allow Saddam Hussein to save his Republican Guard, the backbone of his Baath regime. The Republican Guard was caught in a flanking movement and the campaign to kill it had just been launched. Operation Desert Storm necessitated the destruction of this elite force, hence President Bush's rejection of the proposal. Bush reiterated the coalition's determination to hold Iraq to the 12 UN Security Council resolutions without conditions.

Islamic Conference (211)

The periodic meeting of heads of government from the countries of the Islamic world. Representatives from the Palestine Liberation Organization are also recognized by the body. The Arab-Israeli conflict remains the only item on the Islamic Conference agenda that unites the participants. The Islamic Conference meets irregularly. ***See also*** ARAB SUMMIT (194); ARAB LEAGUE (193).

Significance

The Islamic Conference lends an aura of worldwide solidarity to Muslims. Conference documents such as the "Jerusalem Document" reject UN Security Resolution 242; declare Jerusalem the capital of an independent Palestinian state; call for a *jihad,* or holy war, against Israel; and appeal to the nations of the world to forbid the immigration of Jews to Israel. The "Jerusalem Document" also calls for efforts to bring pressure upon the Israelis to withdraw from the territories occupied in the 1967 Arab-Israeli War. The Islamic Conference attempted to mediate the dispute between Iraq and Iran and to obtain a ceasefire, but their efforts proved to be in vain. The conference established an Umma Peace Committee with its headquarters in Saudi Arabia. It continued to press Baghdad and Tehran to find a way out of their bitter conflict. Given Syrian and Libyan support for Iran, and Jordanian and Saudi Arabian support for Iraq in the conflict, all attempts at mediation were frustrated. The Islamic Conference failed again in its inability to find a diplomatic solution to the Iraqi-Kuwaiti crisis of 1990. The conference's weakness was an invitation to non-Muslim actors to maintain a high profile in the Islamic world.

KHAD 212

The KHAD was the Afghan equivalent of the Soviet Union's KGB, or secret police. The KHAD was organized in the aftermath of the revolution that overthrew Mohammad Daud in 1978 but was not focused until the Soviet invasion of the country in December 1979. The life of the KHAD revolved around one individual, Najibullah, from the Ahmedzai Pathan tribe in the eastern province of Paktia. Najibullah joined the People's Democratic Party of Afghanistan (PDPA) in 1965 at the age of 17. He was originally a medical student at Kabul University (1965–1976), but he was more consumed by politics than his studies and acted as a recruiter for the PDPA, leading the campus Marxist movement. After the Saur Revolution (Marxist revolution) of March 1978 he joined the new government, but because he was affiliated with the more radical Soviet Parcham branch of the party, he was sent to Iran as Afghanistan's ambassador. Najibullah returned to Afghanistan with the Soviet invasion forces to take charge of the Afghan secret police. In this regard, he worked closely with KGB operatives, and indeed had received his training at their hands. His major objective as head of the KHAD was winning the support of the tribal Pathans in the eastern provinces. It was Najibullah who organized clandestine operations, especially those inside Pakistan. He organized a network of agents who lived and moved among the refugee population inside Pakistan. Their periodic acts of terror were aimed at intimidating Pakistanis. Inside Afghanistan, Najibullah recruited willing cadres who were able to infiltrate the tribal orders in different locations throughout the country. Through bribes and clever divide-and-rule policies he was able to erect a balanced system of control that made the KHAD the best-organized and strongest arm of the Afghan government. In 1986, when the Soviets needed a successor to Babrak Karmal, they went unhesitatingly to Najibullah. With Najibullah's demise and the collapse of his government in April 1992, the KHAD would either be driven underground or cease to exist. Given the uncertainties in Afghanistan following the defeat of the Marxists, the KHAD seemed to be deprived of a future. ***See also*** COMMUNISM: AFGHANISTAN (117).

Significance

The KHAD was the Kabul government's most sophisticated and developed arm; in fact, it was the government of Afghanistan. The PDPA was never an effective organization. It split into Parcham and Khalq factions almost at birth, and the rift between the two elements was never successfully bridged. Initial Soviet efforts to move their policies through the PDPA were cast aside when it became obvious that Afghan politicians were only interested in purging one another. The KHAD operated on an entirely different plane from that of the PDPA. It had the discipline, personnel, resources, and determination to press declared goals. There was no room in KHAD for dissenters or questioners.

Lebanese-Israeli Agreement, 1983 — 213

On May 17, 1983, Israel and Lebanon (with a pivotal role played by the United States) entered into an agreement to terminate their state of war; to respect each other's sovereignty, independence, territorial integrity, and right to live in peace within secure and recognized borders; to seek the withdrawal of all foreign forces, i.e., Israeli, Syrian, and members of the Palestine Liberation Army; and to insist that Lebanon never again become a base for hostile actions against Israel. The agreement specifies that measures be taken to prevent the use of Lebanese soil for attacks on Israel by enemy forces.

Significance

The Lebanese-Israeli Agreement followed in the wake of the Israeli-Egyptian Treaty of Peace formalized in 1979. With this agreement Israel obtained official recognition from another Arab state and, as with Egypt, a shared frontier. Lebanon also sought to regain its independence through this act of diplomacy. If the Beirut government could get Syria and the PLO to accept the terms of the agreement, particularly those focusing on the withdrawal of all external forces, the Lebanese Civil War would be officially terminated, and Lebanon could address the problems of reconciliation between its communities, as well as those of reconstruction. In the summer of 1982, Israel launched what it called Operation Peace for Galilee with the objective of restoring Lebanon's independence. However, the cease fire left Israeli, Syrian, and PLO forces in Lebanon, and the Beirut government exerted control over only a small area of the country. The Lebanese-Israeli Agreement, prompted by the United States, was directed at avoiding a renewal of hostilities. It sought to gain through diplomacy what had not been achieved on the battlefield. Syria and the PLO rejected the agreement, which they described as a "sellout" of the Arab as well as the Palestinian people. The diplomatic effort was doomed to failure, and Israel did not obtain a formal peace treaty with Lebanon. As a consequence, Israel supports predominantly Christian units along Israel's northern border. With the help of this force, it seeks to prevent PLO units also based in southern Lebanon from penetrating Israel proper.

Madrid Peace Conference — 214

The peace conference between Israel, the government of Jordan, which included a separate Palestinian delegation, Syria, Egypt, and Lebanon that convened in Madrid, Spain, on October 30, 1991. The conference was arranged by the United States with the Soviet Union as a cosponsor. The face-to-face meetings between Israeli and Arab officials were made possible by the strenuous diplomatic efforts of James Baker, U.S. secretary of state. The conference was opened officially by President George Bush and President Mikhail Gorbachev. The Madrid conference lasted four days. During this period each of the principals presented an opening statement that generally described its objectives and concerns. Generally acrimonious responses to the opening statements, especially between Israel and Syria, did not augur well for the future of the peace talks. With the first phase completed, the second stage, the one-on-one negotiations between Israel and the different Arab states, were stymied by the inability to agree on a site for the deliberations. The Arab states insisted on remaining in Madrid. Israel demanded that the talks be held in the Middle East. Although initial one-on-one talks were conducted in Madrid, the participants left Spain on November 3 without having selected a location for their continuation. (To break the impasse, the U.S. government offered Washington as the site for substantive meetings, and the parties were constrained to accept the arrangement.) Moreover, Israel insisted that the third stage of the talks, which Syria refused to acknowledge while Israel still held Arab territory, be made part of the overall settlement. The third stage was described as involving regional issues, such as cooperation in the use of water, protecting the environment, and arms control. *See also* ARAB-ISRAELI PEACE CONFERENCES (195).

Significance
No one expected a quick settlement to the Arab-Israeli conflict, let alone the question of Palestinian independence. The Madrid Peace Conference was perceived by the convenors as a first step in confidence-building measures that in time, and with concessions on all sides, would produce the comprehensive peace so much discussed in years passed. The PLO was not officially represented at the peace conference but the Palestinian delegation left no doubt it was in consultation with PLO leaders. Moreover, the head of the Palestinian delegation met with Yasir Arafat before the conferees dispersed. The Palestinians agreed to join the Jordanian delegation at the table, and had also declared they were prepared to accept autonomy rather than seek full self-determination in order to arrive at a settlement. Israeli officials, however, were unimpressed with the Palestinian performance, and months—possibly years—of hard bargaining appeared to lie ahead. Moreover, Israel declared it would not yield the Golan Heights to Syria, and Damascus insisted there could be no movement on a peaceful solution so long as that territory remained under Israeli control. By the same token Israel was not prepared to move its forces from South Lebanon, or to lift its controls on the West Bank and Gaza territories. However, the Labor Coalition's victory over Likud in the June 1992 Israeli election held some promise that the impasse could be broken.

Nixon Doctrine **215**

The Nixon Doctrine, initially referred to as the "Guam Doctrine," was an announcement by President Richard M. Nixon in July 1969 that the United States expected smaller countries threatened by foreign or foreign-assisted aggression to play a greater role in their own defense. This doctrine was stated more fully in the president's 1970 annual foreign policy message to the Congress, and it was reiterated in his 1971 report to the legislative branch of government. The Nixon Doctrine was prompted by several factors and conditions. First, the United States had paid a heavy price in the Indochina War. Opposition to that war in the United States had reached sizable proportions, and

President Nixon was on record that he would work to reduce U.S. commitments, to withdraw U.S. forces, and to find a peaceful solution. The country seemed to demand a general reduction in the U.S. military presence abroad, as well as to display great reluctance to engage in future Vietnam-type conflicts. Second, the British had announced in 1968 their "East of Suez Policy." This meant that British military power, long in place east of Suez (involving the Middle East and South and Southeast Asia), would be withdrawn. British interests were to be more narrowly defined in terms of Europe, the Mediterranean, and the North Atlantic, thus requiring a much smaller military establishment. Countries heretofore dependent on British protection would be required to find other means for their defense. And third, the world environment had undergone significant change. The Soviet Union was a recognized superpower with global as well as continental interests and with offensive as well as defensive strategies. And the less-developed nations, commonly referred to as the Third World, had achieved a degree of independence that made them less susceptible to major-power pressures. Moreover, the Third World was characterized by political instability, intense regional rivalries, and competing ideologies. No single power was capable of domination, nor could it remedy the many complicated situations. Nevertheless, the Soviet Union was perceived as exploiting these inconsistencies and rivalries. The question remained, then, of what to do about communist aggressive intentions and actions when Britain no longer acted as a deterrent and the United States was intent on reducing, if not eliminating, its role as world policemen. The answer supposedly was the Nixon Doctrine. In 1971 Nixon noted: "The postwar order in international relations—the configuration of power that emerged from the Second World War—is gone. With it are gone the conditions which have determined the assumptions and practices of United States foreign policy since 1945." The statement clarified U.S. perceptions about the world and the American role in it. The Truman Doctrine—containing international communism, denying Soviet and Chinese communist activity in the Third World, building Western-type politico-economic systems in the less-developed states, and, above all, defending countries threatened by communist subversion and/or aggression—was no longer feasible. The Nixon Doctrine was not a substitute for the Truman Doctrine. The United States reiterated its commitments to friendly governments, but it also set a more realistic course, modifying policy to suit U.S. capabilities and needs. The Truman Doctrine, it was suggested, had been too idealistic, had stretched U.S. capacities too far to be able to respond effectively. Despite great sacrifice, it did not achieve its intended objective. With the Nixon Doctrine the United States sought to avoid a trend toward neo-isolationism. U.S. allies and client states were encouraged to assume greater responsibility for their individual and collective defense. The United States would provide the means, but each nation would be expected to utilize its own personnel in defending particular interests. The Nixon Doctrine therefore did not liquidate U.S. foreign policy commitments.

The United States established a more realistic defense perimeter, considered vital to U.S. national security, but capable of self-sustained defense. Even before the termination of the war in Indochina, the United States indicated that Southeast Asia would no longer be considered a region vital to U.S. national interest. The Middle East was another story. The Middle East, with the world's largest reserves of petroleum, was inextricably tied to U.S. security, and the Persian Gulf was the focal point for U.S. concern. It was for this reason that the United States turned to Iran, not only to assist in buttressing the Persian Gulf region against Soviet-cum-Marxist threats, but also to demonstrate the effectiveness of the Nixon Doctrine. With the shah as a loyal U.S. supporter, Iran was perceived the "bastion of stability" in a turbulent, volatile, ever-chaotic area. Iran was to be transformed into a formidable military power. Its control would extend over the Persian Gulf and the immediate Indian Ocean littoral. Iran seized the islands of Abu Musa and the Greater and Lesser Tumbs in the Strait of Hormuz in 1971, fearing that they could come under the control of its regional adversary, Iraq. The shah also pledged support for Arabian states on the opposite side of the gulf should they be challenged by alien-sponsored insurgencies. Iran expanded friendly relations with Pakistan, which in the aftermath of the Indo-Pakistani War of 1971 needed external assistance. The Nixon Doctrine pledged the transfer of sophisticated weapons to allied countries, and in 1971–1972 a major program was developed to modernize and equip the Iranian armed forces. U.S. private sector investment in Iran in the period between 1971 and the fall of the shah in 1979 was relatively small. The major emphasis was on military expansion. The United States sold Iran, in equipment and training and in installations and communications, approximately $20 billion worth of military wherewithal in a period of six years. Hundreds of jet fighter-bombers and helicopters, scores of transport aircraft and tankers, and significant numbers of armored personnel carriers, tanks, artillery, and rocket launchers inundated the Iranian army and air force. The navy received destroyers and frigates, torpedo boats, coastal patrol craft, and submarines. Britain made available hovercraft vessels and hundreds of tanks. France and West Germany also made smaller sales. Even the Soviet Union provided military trucks and other items. No country in the Third World, save India (China is not considered a Third World nation) obtained more weapons. It is doubtful that even India had superior arms. The Nixon Doctrine survived Watergate, and the Ford and Carter administrations continued the policy. On January 1, 1978, President Jimmy Carter visited Iran. The U.S. president toasted the shah and Iran, implying that the policy to transform Iran into a bulwark of Western power in the Persian Gulf region had been successful. Moreover, Iran, said Carter, had brought stability to an otherwise unsettled and unpredictable region. In the months that followed, however, the shah and his administration came under severe pressure. Opposition to the monarchy developed into a widespread popular rebellion, and in the winter of 1979, the shah was forced to flee his country, never to return. Iran's revolutionaries denounced the U.S. connection, and U.S. aid was terminated. The U.S. embassy and its personnel were later seized and held hostage for more than a year, shattering the last vestige of the Iranian-U.S. relationship. The United States did nothing to prevent the shah's demise. Nor could the shah, with all Iran's military prowess, neutralize his opposition. Given Iran's collapse as a U.S. outpost on the Persian Gulf and Indian Ocean, the Middle East appeared more explosive than previously. The Nixon Doctrine could no more control events than the earlier Truman Doctrine.

Significance

The Nixon Doctrine was conceived by Henry Kissinger, Nixon's national security advisor and later secretary of state. Kissinger convinced Nixon that the difficulty with the Truman Doctrine (U.S. containment of the Soviet Union) was its less-than-realistic character. The United States was overcommitted, stretched too thin, and too sensitive to problems that were not directly related to U.S. national interest. The Indochina War was the United States' greatest mistake, and the policy framework created by the Truman Doctrine was responsible. Kissinger argued the necessity of choice, of identifying regions and countries of importance, especially those that could be counted upon to respond effectively to serious challenge. Although the logic appeared sound, operationalizing the shift to the Nixon Doctrine was an entirely different matter. The relationship between national and international events was not fully explored. Iran was the classic example. No country received more attention in executing the Nixon Doctrine. No country was more receptive. At least no government appeared more willing to play the role outlined by Washington. But the Americans did not examine adequately the nature of Iranian society, nor did they take seriously the opposition to the shah. It could also be said that the shah assumed greater capacity to rule than he ultimately displayed. The shah believed, especially after his counterrevolution of 1953, that he had built an unassailable governmental and military structure. With his U.S. allies he could beat back any future assault on his administration or person. The shah was flushed by feelings of achievement. Iran, in the eyes of the shah, was on the threshold of a new and greater destiny, and the view was intoxicating. The Americans were also convinced that the shah had his domestic enemies under control, and they were impressed with Iran's role in neutralizing communist subversion in Oman in 1975. The Nixon Doctrine appeared sound, and the United States gave it expression in Israel, and later in Egypt. The miscalculations concerning the shah's internal opposition only became apparent to the U.S. government when Iran was consumed by crisis and the monarch was encouraged to go abroad and leave his government in caretaker hands. Shahpur Bakhtiar had been an outspoken critic of the shah, but the Americans trusted him to sustain U.S.-Iranian relations. The forced removal of Bakhtiar, however, and the emergence of the Ayatollah Khomeini regime finally drove home the realization that Iran's foreign policy was hitched to its domestic situation. The Nixon Doctrine, insofar as Iran was concerned, was bankrupt. It should be noted, however, that although Iran's transformation into a formidable garrison state may not have saved the shah, it did save Iran from Iraq's aggressive forces in 1982. The successful Iranian defense against a well-equipped foe is testimony to the courage and sacrifice of Iranian troops; it is also an important sidelight on the shah's military expansion program within the framework of the Nixon Doctrine.

Nuclear Proliferation **216**

The uncontrolled spread of nuclear weapons to countries large and small, rich and poor. The Non-Proliferation Treaty (NPT) of 1968 was drafted with the intention of avoiding the possibility that every independent state would one day seek and acquire nuclear weapons. Originally described as the Nth country problem, the spread of nuclear weapons capability beyond that of the United States, the U.S.S.R., China, Britain, and France was perceived more threatening to world security. A number of countries refused to sign the NPT, because they believed their sovereign status permitted them to defend their territories from real or potential enemies. India, for example, refused to sign the treaty because China, a major adversary, had achieved nuclear weapons capability. In 1974 India detonated a nuclear device, but claimed it had no intention of building or stockpiling such weapons. Nevertheless, India's action disturbed Pakistan, and it too refused to sign the NPT. Although denying it was engaged in producing nuclear weapons, Pakistan was widely believed on the threshold of joining the nuclear weapons club. Iraq had made serious efforts to acquire nuclear weapons. Its nuclear reactor at Osirak was destroyed by Israeli fighter-bombers in 1981. Following the conclusion of Operation Desert Storm in 1991, UN inspectors located several installations near Baghdad and scattered throughout the country that allegedly were near to providing Iraq with nuclear weapons. Israel constructed a nuclear facility at Dimona in the Negev Desert in the late 1950's and it has long been judged a nuclear weapons power. Although there have been efforts to create nuclear free zones, none has yet materialized. ***See also*** OSIRAK (259); BUSH INITIATIVE ON ARMS LIMITATION (199).

Significance
Nuclear weapons proliferation is found beyond the Middle East. North Korea, Sweden, Brazil, and Argentina are some of the countries believed to be nuclear powers or near-nuclear powers. Libya has also sought to acquire nuclear weapons through purchase or through a sharing arrangement. South Africa is another country rumored to possess nuclear capability. Iran is allegedly involved in developing nuclear arms. The Maghreb (North Africa) to Pakistan and India is judged the most volatile of the world's regions. In the absence of a natural balance of power, given rulers of questionable legitimacy, subject to varying degrees of explosive religious fundamentalism and/or nationalism, the Middle East raises worldwide concern. Moreover, the Middle East is the source of many of the world's most significant arsenals. Such arsenals include not only nuclear, but also biological and chemical weapons. The countries of the area also possess and are increasing their holdings in high-performance ballistic missiles. Israel has the most advanced missile force of any country in the Middle East, holding the Jericho-II, whose range covers all targets in Syria, Egypt, Lebanon, Iraq, Jordan, and Kuwait, plus portions of Saudi Arabia, Iran, and Libya. Israel also possesses cruise missiles. Syria deploys the Scud-B to cover targets in northern Israel and may possess the Chinese M-9 to cover targets deep in Israel. Iraq, even after the 1991 war, retains significant numbers of Scud missiles. Egypt, Iran, Libya, and Saudi Arabia have ballistic missile forces with ranges over 200 miles. Pakistan has the King Hawk under development with a range of 180 miles and has purchased the intermediate range Chinese C-11. India, Pakistan's principal rival, possesses the Prithvi with a range of 180 miles, and the Agni with a range of 1,500 miles. The Agni has been designed to carry nuclear warheads. India is also engaged in producing an intercontinental ballistic missile.

Organization of Petroleum Exporting Countries (OPEC) 217

Organized in September of 1960 by Iraq, Saudi Arabia, Iran, Kuwait, and Venezuela, OPEC today also includes Qatar, Libya, Indonesia, Algeria, Nigeria, Ecuador, Gabon, and the United Arab Emirates (Abu Dhabi, Dubai, and Sharjah). Prompted by an inability to manage their petroleum resources on an individual basis, OPEC sought to present the foreign oil companies with a unified front. Although somewhat successful in preventing further cuts by the oil companies in posted prices, from which their taxes were calculated, in the early 1960s OPEC could neither restore prices to earlier levels nor agree on an arrangement to restrict the production of its members. OPEC continued its efforts to acquire higher revenues through the 1960s, and in 1968 it issued a declaration of principles insisting that the right to control oil production and prices rested with the producing countries. That year also brought the creation of the Organization of Arab Petroleum Exporting Countries (OAPEC). It was the revolution in Libya in 1969, however, that provided OPEC with new strength and increasing leverage against the oil companies. Libya under Muammar Qaddafi initiated action to restrict production and increase the revenue earned from the exploitation of petroleum. In February 1971 Abu Dhabi, Iran, Iraq, Kuwait, Qatar, and Saudi Arabia met in Tehran with members of the foreign oil companies. Using Libya as their example, they pressed for greater rewards, and the companies eventually yielded to their demands. Still another agreement was entered into in April 1971 by Libya and Iraq that brought even more handsome dividends. In December 1971, however, President Nixon devalued the dollar, and the gains achieved by the oil-producing countries were virtually wiped out. OPEC thereupon insisted on further increases, which were again granted by the companies. In June 1973 another price adjustment was won by the organization. Moreover, future posted prices were to follow a formula reflecting fluctuations in the dollar's value.

In addition to these victories, the oil-producing countries began to nationalize many of their foreign holdings. Algeria seized the French operations, and Libya nationalized British Petroleum's interests in 1971. Iraq followed suit in 1972, and Iran, which had taken possession of its fields in 1951, effected total control in 1973. Saudi Arabia, Kuwait, Qatar, and the United Arab Emirates sought a more moderate course, but by the mid-1970s they, too, had gained control over their installations. Management, however, continued under company control. ***See also*** ARAMCO (196); RED LINE AGREEMENT (220).

Significance
The surprise Egyptian assault on Israel in October 1973 emboldened OPEC to insist on higher prices for their petroleum. A demand for $6 a barrel (an increase of $3) was countered by the companies with a much smaller rise. When agreement between OPEC and the oil companies proved impossible, negotiations broke down. OPEC called a meeting in Kuwait on October 16, 1973, and the Arab members insisted on tying the sale of petroleum to the degree of support the consuming nations were prepared to give the Arabs in their war against Israel. In addition to raising prices without the consent of the companies, the Arab members called for a 5 percent reduction in production each month until Israel was forced to return the territories seized in the 1967 war and to respect the rights of the Palestinians. Saudi Arabia quickly increased the pressure by cutting oil production by 10 percent and terminating all shipments to the United States. The United States was called upon to cease supplying Israel with military supplies, but Washington decided against yielding, and in fact increased its arms transfers to Israel. Libya imposed an embargo on the United States, and Saudi Arabia reduced production by 25 percent and completely shut down exports to the United States. These maneuvers played havoc with the world oil market. Fear of vast shortages forced prices to unprecedented levels, with premium oil rising to $20 a barrel. The oil companies were no match for

the governments involved, and the fourfold increase in petroleum undermined economies across the globe. A worldwide recession resulted in 1974–1975, but OPEC still was not content with its gains. Oil was judged a potent political weapon as well as a means toward fulfilling the financial dreams of the producing countries. Although the oil embargo was directed at the United States and the Netherlands, the hardest-hit countries were the industrialized states of Western Europe and Japan, and they generally registered their intention to support the Arab cause against Israel. Nevertheless, Arab political objectives were not realized. OPEC was primarily concerned with economic advantage. OAPEC was divided, and despite verbal displays of unity against a common foe, the member-states could not agree on a uniform policy or measures, especially with reference to their relations with the United States. With the lifting of the oil embargo, Saudi Arabian–U.S. relations were restored to their prior status. Moreover, the civil war in Lebanon, the collapse of the shah's administration in 1979, the revolution in Iran, and the Iraqi attack on Iran in September 1980 seriously damaged OPEC and OAPEC. At the same time, the shortfall in oil supply brought on by the Iraq-Iran War forced oil prices to astronomical heights, with best-quality petroleum selling for well in excess of $40 a barrel.

Despite such high prices, OPEC and OAPEC were less and less able to act as effective organizations. Saudi Arabia refused to follow the dictates of the other members, and its superior production, further exaggerated by the loss of Iraqi and Iranian crude, placed it in a pivotal situation. Furthermore, given the high cost of petroleum, conservation efforts in the industrialized states and belt-tightening elsewhere reduced dramatically the worldwide demand for oil. In 1981–1982 an oil glut came about, forcing a slight reduction in the posted price. Efforts by OPEC were now aimed at cutting production, and Saudi Arabia, after first delaying its decision, began to cut back sales to stabilize prices. There was little indication, however, that OPEC and OAPEC were coherent organizations capable of acting as unified bodies for specific goals. The absence of an integrated approach led to each OPEC nation's seeking its own advantages, a problem that Iraq found especially troublesome. Baghdad's long war with Iran had drained the country's treasury and Iraq was said to have owed its creditors approximately $80 billion when the conflict finally ended in 1988. The low price of oil could not return the needed revenues to Iraqi coffers, especially as Saddam Hussain was involved in rebuilding, expanding, and modernizing his armed forces. Iraq also was determined to build nonconventional weapons, and these developments required even more significant resources, which were impossible to attain without a sharp increase in the price of world oil supplies. When Baghdad accused Kuwait of putting more oil on the market than OPEC quotas authorized, Saddam Hussain threatened to punish his small neighbor. He also had similar concerns about the other gulf oil producers; indeed, at least 12 OPEC members were pumping more oil for the open market, and they, too, were urged to cut back their production. OPEC, however, was relatively uninvolved as an organization in this dispute. Iraq's negotiations with Kuwait in the summer of 1990 were bilateral in nature, and just when it appeared Kuwait was prepared to yield to Baghdad's demands, Saddam Hussain ordered his forces to cross the frontier. Within 24 hours Kuwait had fallen to the Iraqi army, the Kuwaiti government was forced to flee to Saudi Arabia, and the small country was subsequently annexed by Iraq. The United States was aroused by the Iraqi maneuver. Fearing an attack on Saudi Arabia, and possibly Baghdad's seizure of the Saudi oilfields approximately 200 miles south of Kuwait, Washington rushed forces to the region, and Operation Desert Shield sought to protect the Saudis from the fate that had befallen Kuwait. Although OPEC played a minor role throughout this period, oil continued to flow from the gulf in an uninterrupted stream. After initially high prices, by the time Operation Desert Shield had escalated into Operation Desert Storm, those higher prices had been reduced to about the level existing before the Iraqi invasion of Kuwait.

Peace Conference: White Papers on Palestine 218

The British-administered Palestine Mandate was beset with internal difficulties at its outset. Arab revolts against Zionist settlements began in earnest immediately following the end of World War I, but gathered intensity in 1921. Britain's response to the violence was a series of White Papers aimed at placating the Arab community led by Haj Amin al-Husayni, the *mufti* of Jerusalem and the president of the Supreme Muslim Council. Therefore the Passfield White Paper of 1930 limited Zionist immigration to Palestine only to those who could be economically absorbed. On the other hand the paper reserved government regions for landless Arabs. British Prime Minister Ramsey MacDonald, under Zionist pressure, altered the intent of the White Paper to permit the continuation of Jewish immigration but he also made himself an easy target for his Arab critics who referred to the White Paper as a "Black Paper." After the 1936 Arab Revolt the Peel Commission was sent to the region and an Arab Higher Committee, led by the *mufti*, agreed to meet with the Commission. At the conclusion of their talks, however, dissatisfaction had increased. In a final prewar White Paper, Britain pledged self-government to Palestine within ten years. The British also called for a peace conference bringing Jews and Arabs together with their colonial overlords. The principals met in St. James Palace, London, in 1939, to address the terms of the White Paper, which permitted Jewish immigration for a five-year period, but restricted Zionist settlements to a small area of the mandate. Further Zionist immigration was left to a decision of the Arab Higher Committee. Jamal al-Husayni, a relation of the *mufti*, led the Arab delegation at the 1939 "peace conference." Chaim Weizmann, the leader of the Zionist Movement, led the Jewish representatives at the conference. Weizmann accused Britain of retreating from its stated position and of betraying the Jewish people. Although the Arab delegation sensed a small victory, the *mufti* insisted on independence without delay, and both sides continued their agitations, demonstrations, and violent activities. World War II interrupted this exchange of views, and because a foundation for compromise had not been established, both the British and United Nations plans for the transfer of power to the inhabitants of Palestine failed to bear fruit. Thus, when Israel made its unilateral declaration of independence in May 1948, the Arab armies launched an attack aimed at destroying the new state. Arms rather than diplomacy was the chosen method of discourse. ***See also*** PEEL COMMISSION (173); REAGAN PROGRAM ON PALESTINE (177); ARAB-ISRAELI PEACE CONFERENCES (195).

Significance

The St. James Palace Peace Conference of 1939 did not lessen but intensified the tension between the Arab and Jewish communities of Palestine. Although the Arabs sustained their assault on the Zionist settlers, Jewish demonstrators destroyed British government offices, attacked British personnel, and looted shops. During World War II Britain issued still another White Paper preventing Jews fleeing Hitler-occupied Europe from reaching safe haven in Palestine. This added grist for the mills of those groups that were determined to press for a Jewish homeland. Several Zionist terrorist organizations were spawned in the circumstances. The violence demonstrated by both sides prior to the conference assumed new dimensions in subsequent years, especially after the failure of the United Nations to produce a settlement satisfactory to all the sides. Although parallels between the St. James conference and the Madrid Peace Conference of 1991 are acknowledged, especially the fact that still another relative of the *mufti*, Faisal al-Husayni (a nephew of Jamal al-Husayni), was a principal in the latter, the U.S.-Soviet sponsored session was deemed to have a better chance of succeeding because the United States was determined to win a diplomatic victory and Israel feared the loss of U.S. aid. Moreover, like the British White Papers earlier, repeated U.S. demands on Israel not to spread its West Bank settlements were reminiscent of the futility of British efforts at restricting Israeli settlements to specific areas. Finally, violence on the West Bank continued and promises of an escalating *intifada* were made by PLO groups and their supporters. The armed assault on Israeli settlers in the West Bank territory three days before the scheduled opening of the conference in Madrid was deliberately aimed at sabotaging the conference even before it convened.

Petromin 219

Petromin is Saudi Arabia's state petroleum company. It was founded in 1962 to develop the country's natural resources sector and to harness it to the service of overall national development. Petromin seeks to maximize advantages from the exploitation of the nation's oil, gas, and minerals. It is concerned with a range of hydrocarbon products, including petroleum, liquid gas, and asphalt. It is also concerned with the marketing of these products. Within its range of activity are refining, the building and maintenance of pipelines and storage facilities, and power generation. During 1975–1980 Petromin was governed by its own five-year plan. In 1988 Petromin formed Petrolube, a company jointly owned with Mobil Oil. Petrolube is responsible for the production and marketing of the kingdom's lube oil blending plants in Jeddah, Jubail, and Riyadh. Also in 1988, the government formed the Saudi Arabian Oil Company (Saudi Aramco) to manage the assets of ARAMCO. In 1989–1990, the kingdom established the Saudi Arabian Marketing and Refining Company (SAMARIC), which is responsible for refining and marketing all domestic production. SAMARIC holds a 50 percent share in two joint-venture export refineries, at Yanbu (with Mobil) and at Jubail (with Shell). But SAMARIC takes responsibility for the marketing of the kingdom's oil products both at home and abroad. In 1988, Saudi Arabia purchased a 50 percent share in Texaco's petrol refining and retail business in 23 eastern and southern states of the United States, and thus moved dramatically into "downstream" operations. It is intended that PETROMIN will become a state holding company. ***See also*** ARAMCO (196); ORGANIZATION OF PETROLEUM EXPORTING COUNTRIES (OPEC) (217).

Significance

Saudi Arabia has come a long way since its total dependence on U.S. oil companies. It now manages the largest petroleum operations in the world, and while still in close cooperation with U.S. corporations, its independent performance has become the envy of countries over the world. Saudi Arabia's oil reserves remain the world's largest. The country also is chiefly responsible for the amount of oil available on the world market at any particular time. U.S. assistance to Saudi Arabia in Operation Desert Shield merely underlined the strategic importance of the kingdom to the United States and other industrial countries. The long-term interests of Riyadh and Washington are easy to define, and despite periodic points of friction, it is clear the relationship is based upon perceptions of mutual advantage.

Red Line Agreement 220

The Red Line Agreement had its genesis in a restrictive policy established by European oil companies to deny their competition, especially the U.S. oil companies, exploration concessions in the Middle East. In 1901, an Australian, William D'Arcy, received a 60-year concession (covering five-sixths of Iran) enabling him to explore for oil. The Anglo-Persian Oil Company was the direct outcome of this concession. In 1904, the Ottoman sultan transferred vast tracts of territory from the Ministry of Mines to the Civil List. The major, and almost sole, benefactor of this transfer was C. S. Gulbenkian, an Armenian businessman who earlier had made a report to the sultan on the prospects for exploiting Mesopotamian oil. The German Deutsche Bank displayed interest in these ventures and had also obtained a concession from the Ottoman court to build a railway from Berlin to Baghdad. A broad tract of land on either side of the railway, included in the agreement, was believed to contain petroleum. The German defeat in World War I, however, transferred Germany's interests to the French, but the immediate beneficiaries were the Gulbenkian and D'Arcy interests. The Iraq Petroleum Company (IPC), formerly the Turkish Petroleum Company, was organized in 1914. IPC combined British-European interests, and their intention was to use the new company to consolidate their holdings and avoid competition. In an agreement entered into by the British-Dutch groups in 1914, the dominant oil prospectors agreed on a self-denying clause that they "would not be interested, directly or indirectly, in the production or manufacture of crude oil in the Ottoman Empire" except through the Turkish Petroleum Company, soon to be the Iraq Petroleum Company. This was the beginning of the so-called Red Line Agreement. The overall intention was to keep the U.S. companies out of the region. The U.S. companies, assisted by their government, insisted on an "open-door" policy, but not until July 31, 1928, after considerable pressure, were Exxon and Mobil granted a combined 23.75 percent share in IPC. Similar shares were distributed between British Petroleum, Shell, and Compagnie Française Petrole. The remaining 5 percent interest went to Gulbenkian. Competition between the companies, however, was nullified by the "self-denying" clause. Moreover, the Red Line Agreement was given official status in 1928 when a red line was drawn around most of the territory of the former Ottoman Empire (Turkey, Iraq, and the Arabian Peninsula). Within that vast area, oil exploitation could only occur under the auspices of the Iraq Petroleum Company. The formal Red Line Agreement, therefore, was a prime example of restrictive combinations attempting to control an enormous portion of the world's oil supply. *See also* ARAMCO (196).

Significance

The Red Line Agreement was drawn by the large oil companies to deny oil concessions to their competition. The essential objective of the drafters of this understanding was worldwide control of petroleum resources. The ultimate consequence of this effort was the emergence of extremely powerful corporations, managing huge financial fortunes and capable of great politico-economic influence. The scramble for oil concessions was intensified, not eased, by the "agreement." It proved inadequate in denying opportunities to non-members of IPC, who did acquire holdings within the region defined by the red line. An independent company, the British Development Company, obtained a concession in the Mosul area of Iraq. Standard Oil of California found oil on the island of Bahrein and later in Saudi Arabia. British Petroleum, Shell, and Exxon sought to alter the red-line area to deny these concessions to Standard Oil of California. But Shell and Exxon found it impossible to deny Standard its operations in Saudi Arabia. Moreover, the extensive find in the Arabian Peninsula threatened the companies' pricing structure. The IPC companies decided to yield to Standard, and the result was the formation of Caltex, a joint company involving Standard and Texaco. Caltex was superseded by the creation of ARAMCO, dominated by Standard of California and Texaco. By the end of World War II, U.S. companies had gained a dominant share of Middle East oil reserves, and the European companies were generally at the mercy of the giant U.S. corporations. The oil monopoly was somewhat eroded by numerous independent companies that entered the field after World War II, but overall control of oil marketing, even after nationalization of foreign operations, remained the preserve of Exxon, Mobil, Standard Oil of California, Texaco, Gulf, British Petroleum, and Shell.

Regional Cooperation for Development (RCD) 221

The Regional Cooperation for Development was proposed by the president of Pakistan, Ayub Khan. It was established in July 1964 and included Turkey and Iran as well as Pakistan. RCD's objective, according to Ayub Khan, was economic cooperation and cultural exchange between like-minded area states. RCD was conceived as an Asian Common Market, wherein nations would share experiences, promote trade, assist in joint enterprises, and generally enhance the well-being of their respective citizenry. Cooperation, not competition, was the key to the organization's program. RCD organized numerous committees for agriculture, industry, banking, and shipping. Nevertheless, it never measured up to the intentions of its creators. From the outset, Iran was less than inspired. Turkey's economic interests were oriented more toward Western Europe. Little trade moved between the RCD countries, and Pakistan, of the three, had the least to offer. Moreover, other states were invited to join the RCD, but they politely ignored the offer. The three member-states were all identified with the Central Treaty Organization, and RCD was perceived as an extension of CENTO. Indeed, some observers concluded that the United States had prompted Pakistan to form RCD and that Turkey and Iran merely fulfilled an expectation without giving the organization the necessary support. Most states ignored the existence of RCD, and RCD members did not give the organization the attention it needed to make its mark. Nevertheless, RCD survives. Cultural interaction and regional economic planning continue.

Significance
The Regional Cooperation for Development has never achieved the status described by those who conceived it. But it has played a role in reinforcing relations between Pakistan, Iran, and Turkey. Moreover, it is not a threat to any state or group of states. The associations established through RCD have helped officials in all three countries better understand one another, although the overall impact is still negligible. The importance of RCD is not found in its record, but in the idea it represents. RCD was an indigenous product. Its organization and survival is a tribute to the amicable relations between the three Muslim states, and it may yet provide a model for more significant interplay between Muslim countries.

Saadabad Pact 222

The Saadabad Pact of 1937 was signed by Iran, Iraq, Afghanistan, and Turkey in July 1937. Initiated by Iran's Reza Shah, Saadabad was the first alliance entered into by Middle East states without European participation. Reza Shah was especially interested in promoting regional self-reliance in an age of European domination. His principal target was Great Britain, the dominant power in the Persian Gulf area and the most impressive imperial power in the Middle East at the time. The signatories pledged themselves to respect each other's borders, to consult together in time of international conflict, to avoid aggressive postures toward one another, and to honor the sovereign and exclusive rights of each within its own domains. The pact was established for a trial five-year period and made renewable after that period. A permanent council was assembled and authorized to meet at least once each year. Although intended to reduce European influence, the Saadabad Pact was a relic before it could be put into force. The outbreak of hostilities in Europe in 1939 posed a threat to European interests in the Middle East, and Britain was especially active in protecting and expanding its commitments in the region. When the Soviet Union entered World War II in 1941, it, too, became anxious about its border with the Middle East states. Because Reza Shah openly courted Germany, London and Moscow combined forces to remove him from the Iranian throne, force him into exile, and place his son at the head of the kingdom. Turkey and Afghanistan remained neutral during most of World War II, but Iran and Iraq were declared belligerents because of the role played there by Great Britain. Once the war had ended, new forces were at play in the Middle East, and Saadabad was never resurrected. ***See also*** COOPERATIVE COUNCIL OF THE GULF STATES (205).

Significance
Through the Saadabad Pact, Reza Shah attempted to place some distance between himself and the European powers, but he failed in his efforts. He also attempted to establish his bona fides as the lawful and legitimate authority in Iran. His agreement with Saudi Arabia and the marriage of his son to the sister of the king of Egypt were calculated to stabilize his regime and validate his dynasty. Events, however, conspired against him and his dream of royalty. The European powers were not impressed by his regal posturing, and they not only humiliated him but seriously undermined his dynasty by forcibly removing him from the country. His son never could gain the popular respect necessary to effectively manage the kingdom. In 1953 a popular uprising forced the young shah to flee the country, only to return with the help of the United States. Although he then entered a period of extended rule, he was

generally perceived as a usurper and unfit to govern. In 1979 he again took flight from the country, this time never to return. With his departure the "Pahlavi dynasty" came to an abrupt end. Earlier the shah had indicated his interest in reopening a modified "Saadabad" alliance of Middle East states, but he was rebuffed because of his dependence on the United States and because he was not a trusted figure. An indigenous Middle East alliance had to wait until May 1981, when Saudi Arabia assembled the Gulf Cooperation, or Cooperative Council of Gulf States. Saudi Arabia, Kuwait, Bahrein, Qatar, the United Arab Emirates, and Oman called for political, military, and economic cooperation. The council appeared to have a greater chance of succeeding than its long-defunct Saadabad counterpart, but it, too, could not manage the Gulf War of 1990–1991 without Western and especially U.S. assistance.

Sanctions 223

An instrument of pressure applied by a state or states against another. Sanctions are an intermediary step, short of openly aggressive action. During the Gulf War sanctions were imposed on Iraq by the United States, the Soviet Union, Great Britain, and France prior to the UN call for global restrictions. On August 3, 1990, the day following Iraq's invasion of Kuwait, the United States froze Iraqi assets as well as Kuwaiti assets (the latter to protect them from Iraqi acquisition); halted most imports from Iraq, including oil; and banned U.S. travel to Iraq. The Soviet Union said it was suspending all arms deliveries. Britain froze assets and also froze Kuwaiti assets, including the 10 percent Kuwaiti interest in British Petroleum and Midland Bank. France froze Iraqi assets and Kuwaiti assets. Arms shipments to Iraq had already been suspended because of payment arrears. ***See also*** UN RESOLUTIONS: IRAQ-KUWAIT CONFLICT (230).

Significance
Sanctions have never been totally successful in and of themselves in forcing an aggressive state to yield what it has achieved aggressively. At best, sanctions, if complied with by the world community, stand to weaken the target state. Sanctions, however, are more likely to wither with the passage of time, and the state against which they are applied stands little chance of being completely contained. In the case of the UN-imposed sanctions against Iraq, opinion was divided on the question of whether they would force Iraq to yield Kuwait and, if so, how long that might take. Those arguing that sanctions were more symbolic than practical against a determined aggressor pointed to the porous character of the political geography and international traders who insist on pursuing their independent objectives.

Sinai Support Mission 224

The Sinai Support Mission is a team of U.S. military personnel and civilians stationed in the Sinai Peninsula to oversee the peace treaty between Egypt and Israel. The mission has a history that predates the 1979 treaty. In 1956, the Sinai was temporarily occupied by Israel, France, and Great Britain. They withdrew under international pressure and were replaced by a UN force. The latter was withdrawn at the request of President Nasser, precipitating the 1967 Six-Day War, which saw the Israelis regain control of the peninsula. Israeli defenses on the east bank of the Suez Canal were breached by Egyptian forces in the 1973 war, but Israel continued to dominate the Sinai. In the aftermath of the 1973 war, the Egyptian and Israeli governments entered into their first face-to-face discussions, and with the assistance provided by Henry Kissinger, an interim accord was reached calling for limited disengagement. This Sinai I agreement was completed in January 1974. Secretary of State Kissinger then moved feverishly to produce a second Sinai agreement, aimed at attaining a more far-reaching armistice. Despite the intransigence on both sides, a breakthrough was achieved in the negotiations on March 29, 1975. President Sadat announced the reopening of the Suez Canal to international traffic and agreed to a three-month extension for the United Nations Emergency Force (UNEF) that had interposed itself between the belligerents in the Sinai. Israeli and Egyptian forces accepted the demilitarized buffer zone controlled by UNEF, and the former pulled back beyond the Giddi and Mitla passes, the strategic passageways through the Sinai. The United States was encouraged to police both the Israeli and Egyptian surveillance systems near the passes. Moreover, Israel, remembering the UN withdrawal from the Sinai in 1967, requested the United States to establish its own tactical early warning system at the Giddi and Mitla passes; Egypt concurred. Sinai II was agreed upon, and an adjunct U.S. proposal was appended to the document clarifying the U.S. role. Two hundred American civilians were identified to staff the listening posts in the Sinai desert, and after considerable congressional debate the U.S. House of Representatives and Senate approved the measure on October 8, 1975. President Ford signed it into law on October 13, 1975. By the time the Egyptian-Israeli Peace Treaty had been approved in 1979, the United States had established a sophisticated presence in the peninsula. Under the terms of the peace treaty, Israel agreed to withdraw from the entire Sinai, and at the termination of the state of war, the United States anticipated dismantling its installations. Talks between the Israelis, Egyptians, and Americans in Washington, in September 1979, however, provided the United States with a new mandate in the area. Under the terms of the peace treaty, the Sinai was maintained as a buffer zone. The United Nations Emergency Force was disbanded with the fulfillment of the Sinai II agreement. In the absence of a UN force, the United States was called upon to oversee a significantly larger area. This mission was supposed to remain until April 1982, when the final Israeli withdrawal occurred. Prior to that date, however, the Israelis called for a continued and even larger presence of U.S. forces. The Egyptians also gave their approval to this suggestion, but then insisted that troops from the European Common Market countries should also be stationed in the region. After some hesitation in Jerusalem this plan was finally accepted. In addition to the civilians, regular military personnel from the United States and Western Europe took up positions in the Sinai in February and March 1982. ***See also*** SINAI PENINSULA (26); EGYPTIAN-ISRAELI TREATY OF PEACE, 1979 (207); COOPERATIVE COUNCIL OF THE GULF STATES (205).

Significance

The U.S. Sinai Support Mission is the insurance that the Israelis demanded in protecting their interests in the Sinai region. The presence of U.S. forces also brings Israelis and Egyptians into close proximity. With the loss of U.S. bases in Iran, the United States saw Egypt as an important Western base in the Middle East. The stationing of U.S. surveillance systems in the Sinai not only enabled the Americans to monitor the Israeli-Egyptian Peace Treaty, it also gave the United States important observation posts over the Arabian Peninsula, the Red Sea, and the immediate

Indian Ocean littoral. Moreover, the stationing of U.S. military personnel in the Sinai, following joint military exercises with the Egyptian armed forces, permits greater coordination between Cairo and Washington. Some observers viewed the U.S. presence in the Sinai as the initial program in a plan to place a U.S. Rapid Deployment Force in the vicinity of the Persian Gulf. Although this observation was denied in Washington and Cairo, the appearance of several thousand battle-equipped servicemen in the Sinai could not be concealed. Saudi Arabia rejected all U.S. overtures for base rights, but Riyadh was not averse to the U.S. presence in the nearby Sinai. Following the war against Iraq in January–February 1991, Saudi Arabia began to reassess its military defenses. Although Riyadh was headquarters for Operation Desert Shield and Operation Desert Storm, and one American and one Saudi general shared command of the coalition forces during the campaign, the Saudis were still reluctant to allow a continuing presence of U.S. ground forces in the country. Plans were made for joint exercises, for prepositioning war materiel, for continued use of Saudi military airfields by the U.S. Air Force, and for military transfers of state-of-the-art U.S. weaponry. Agreement also was reached to position U.S. naval forces off the Saudi coast on the island nation of Bahrein. Under Saudi pressure, however, the army the U.S. assembled in the Saudi desert to counter Iraqi aggression was rapidly disbanded.

Syria-Lebanon Security Pact — 225

The Syrian and Lebanese governments entered into an agreement on September 1, 1991, ensuring their coordination in all military and security matters. The pact involved the full exchange of intelligence information as well as the extradition of fugitives. The Lebanese Interior Minister said the most important feature of the agreement involved fighting drug traffickers in both countries. Nevertheless, the treaty allowed either country to ask the other for military assistance if its security or stability were threatened. The site for the signing ceremony was the town of Shtaura, 28 miles east of Beirut. The treaty was later approved by a council comprised of President Elias Hrawi and President Hafez al-Assad.

Significance
Lebanon had sought to play a neutral role in Arab affairs but the long civil war had transformed the country. Moreover, the dominant role played by Syria in Lebanon was formalized in 1990–1991 and the Lebanese state was fixed to Damascus's worldview. In a way the security treaty tied Lebanon to Syria, much as it was in premandate days. Although the Lebanese government, with Syrian cooperation, was now able to constrain the PLO and the Muslim Brotherhood, as well as the Maronite, Druze, and Shiite organizations, it could not avoid conflicts that involved Syria, notably any future conflict with Israel.

Syria-Libya Merger — 226

On March 3, 1980, Damascus and Tripoli simultaneously announced the merger of their two countries. The declaration followed negotiations between Muammar Qaddafi and Hafez al-Assad and was approved by their respective assemblies. The merger called for the creation of a single state, entirely sovereign, emphasizing political, military, and cultural unity. The Syrian-Libyan union was described as the harbinger of a unified Arab socialist society, and its principal concern was the promotion of revolutionary action. It was also described as a bulwark for the "steadfastness and confrontation" fronts in opposition to Israel and the Camp David accords. Apart from its attack on Zionism and U.S. imperialism, the merger represented one feature of the worldwide liberation struggle and its alliance with "socialist" forces. The unitary state proposed by the declaration was supposed to establish a national congress as well as a single executive authority, and the leaders of both countries were to meet to establish the procedure for implementing the plan. Although never formally repudiated, the Syrian-Libyan merger did not bear the promised fruit, and it was to remain a declaration of intention, not a program for tangible action.

Significance

The merger between Syria and Libya was encouraged by Muammar Qaddafi, who over the years has attempted to link his country with other Arab states, e.g., Egypt and Tunisia. These efforts were likewise unsuccessful. Qaddafi made this gesture toward Syria in a speech marking the eleventh anniversary of his revolution. Assad was apparently informed in advance and acknowledged the "noble" effort toward achieving Arab unity. But Assad no more entertained sharing power, let alone stepping aside, than Qaddafi. Qaddafi's action was perceived as a cover for his foreign relations failures. He had aggravated relations with Malta, caused a rupture in communications with Tunisia, continued to sow antagonism in Egypt and the Sudan, and angered African states by his forceful action in Chad as well as his support for Idi Amin in Uganda. In the extended world, Qaddafi had gained a reputation for supporting international terrorists from Latin America to Southeast Asia. As a result of these misadventures Libya found itself more and more isolated. Qaddafi found in Syria a country with somewhat similar experiences. Syria had been condemned for its intervention in Lebanon in behalf of the Christian Phalange. Although it later sought to make amends with the Palestine Liberation Organization, its actions had proved to be a severe setback for the Palestinian cause. Relations with Iraq and Jordan had deteriorated further, and both countries were accused of supporting elements of the Muslim Brotherhood in their campaign to destroy the Assad administration. Moreover, the anti-Egyptian Front that had been prompted by Syria, Libya, and Algeria lost its impetus when Algeria became bogged down in a struggle with Morocco over the former Spanish Sahara. Another former supporter, South Yemen, since the change in leadership from Abdul Fattah Ismail to Ali Nasser Mohammad, had lessened its rhetoric on revolution and displayed interest in cooperating with Iraq and Saudi Arabia. Syria and Libya, therefore, found they shared common concerns and interests, and the joint declaration was little more than a resolution, with no binding effect. Although both countries had become the chief recipients of Soviet arms in the Middle East, and Russians, Cubans, and North Koreans assisted their armed forces, Syria rejected Qaddafi's suggestion that Syria begin a war of attrition with Israel along the Golan Heights and in South Lebanon. The two nations could mobilize a combined force of 350,000 men, equipped with almost 5,000 tanks and more than 600 aircraft, but Syria would pay the higher price in such an encounter. Moreover, setbacks would more than likely provide Assad's enemies with the opportunity to unseat him. Indeed, Assad could not avoid the thought that Qaddafi wanted him removed so that he would have greater opportunity to galvanize the other Arab states in the struggle against Israel. Qaddafi always assumed that he was Nasser's successor and that his role lay in providing leadership for a divided Arab world. Sadat had rejected Qaddafi's suggestion for merger on almost the same grounds as Assad. Assad, however, did not go public with his rejection, and the two countries acted in concert in supporting Iran when Iraq attacked across the Shatt al-Arab in September 1980. Voluntary unions are difficult in the best of circumstances. Nasser's attempt to merge Egypt with Syria and Yemen in 1958 did not succeed; Qaddafi's endeavors have had even less success. Although the territorial nation-state is decried as an alien contrivance and a divide-and-rule disease spread by the West, the Arab world appears to prefer political fragmentation to supra-nationism (voluntary association). Furthermore, no single Arab state has the ability to impose its will on the others. Therefore, super-nationalism (coercive association) is also beyond reach.

Syria-U.S.S.R. Treaty of Friendship and Cooperation 227

The Syria-U.S.S.R. Treaty of Friendship and Cooperation was signed in Moscow on October 8, 1980, by Leonid Brezhnev and Hafez al-Assad. The treaty paralleled Soviet pacts with Egypt (May 27, 1971), India (August 9, 1971), Iraq (April 9, 1972), Somalia (July 11, 1974), Angola (October 8, 1976), Mozambique (March 31, 1977), Afghanistan (December 5, 1978), and South Yemen (October 25, 1979). Article 1 of the Syria-U.S.S.R. treaty does not speak about the "unbreakable" friendship between the two countries (the language used in the Egyptian and Iraqi treaties), but it does emphasize long-term association across the whole spectrum of national affairs. Article 2 stresses peace and condemns the arms race. Article 3 commits both countries to the struggle against colonialism and racism, and especially Zionism. Implied in Article 3 is the commitment to support worldwide wars of national liberation. Article 4 mentions Syria's nonalignment, and that Syria recognizes the Soviet Union as a "peace-loving" nation. Article 5 speaks of "regular consultations" between the countries, but the language is vague. Article 6 addresses itself to crisis situations and the need to coordinate positions "to reestablish peace." Article 7 hints at Soviet assistance in the event Assad has difficulty in quelling internal unrest. Article 8 is concerned with economic and technical cooperation. Article 9 discusses the "widening of contacts." Article 10 encourages joint cooperation in the military field. Article 11 prohibits the parties from joining alliances detrimental to the other. Article 12 emphasizes the need to avoid international agreements incompatible with this treaty. Article 13 notes the need for bilateral discussion where conflicting interpretations occur. Article 14 states that the treaty will be in force for 20 years and automatically renewable if neither party objects. Article 15 describes ratification procedures.

Significance

The Syria-U.S.S.R. treaty of 1980 illustrates Syria's former dependence on Moscow and its inability to find satisfaction, let alone security, in its relations with other Arab and Muslim states. On the Soviet side, it displayed Moscow's interest in the Middle East and how readily prepared it was to exploit weakness. Nevertheless, the Syria-U.S.S.R. treaty was less than ironclad. The Soviet Union did not, by the language of the treaty, move to Syria's side in time of crisis. The treaty also did not commit Syria to a version of Soviet socialism. By the same token, the Syrians prevented the Soviets from influencing mass organizations in their country. The treaty did seem to provide the Kremlin with the use of Syrian air and naval facilities, but military assistance to Damascus was not spelled out. The latter was covered in secret agreements. In summary, the Syria-U.S.S.R. treaty was a reaffirmation of Soviet support for Syria in its clash with Israel and the United States. It could be interpreted as having committed Moscow to Syria's defense in the event of hostilities. Israel's invasion of Lebanon and its attack on Syrian forces based in that country tested the significance of the treaty commitments. Syrian forces were overwhelmed by the Israeli advance, and their losses on the ground and in the air were considerable. The Soviet Union dispatched emissaries to Damascus within days of the outbreak of hostilities, and Moscow quickly replenished the weapons lost in battle. Nevertheless, the Syrians did not call for Soviet troops, nor was Moscow inclined to send them. The treaty served to formalize existing relations, but the actions of the states were predicated on perceived objectives, not legal documents. Those perceived objectives underwent further modification in the late 1980s, and by the decade of the 1990s the impact of those modifications was more discernible. Policy shifts inside the Kremlin, especially those prompted by the Gorbachev "reforms," called for a less belligerent Soviet program in the Middle East. Moreover, internal problems led Soviet leaders to reconsider the amount of assistance they could provide countries like Syria. Improved relations with the United States induced the Soviet Union to allow the emigration of Soviet Jews to Israel. In October 1991, Moscow agreed to restore diplomatic relations with Israel. Soviet support for measures against Iraq following the latter's invasion of Kuwait also dramatized a different Soviet relationship with the Middle East states, notably intimacy with the gulf kingdoms. In these changing circumstances, the Syrians also altered their foreign policy. Prime Minister Shamir extended an invitation to Hafez al-Assad to visit Jerusalem, and while the Syrian leader displayed little interest in the "invitation," there were indications that Damascus might consider opening a dialogue with Israel if the Israelis were prepared to return the Golan Heights and open serious negotiations with the Palestinians. Thus, before the U.S.S.R. self-destructed, both Damascus and Moscow demonstrated an increasing interest in diplomatic ventures. Their treaty relationship was more directed at forging agreements than "settling matters on the battlefield."

Tripartite Agreement of 1950 **228**

Following the creation of Israel and the subsequent Arab-Israeli War of 1948–1949, the Middle East was in disarray. The Jordanian Arab Legion had occupied the West Bank of the Jordan River and Egypt had taken control of the Gaza Strip. Israel also added to the territory allocated it in the UN resolution. The survival of the state of Israel and its further expansion both humiliated and frightened the Arab states. Blame for Arab failure to defeat a much smaller enemy was directed at the established governments, and especially those that depended on the British. In an effort to calm Arab fears, stabilize the political condition, and generally promote peaceful relations between Arabs and Israelis, the United States, Great Britain, and France declared their intention to guarantee the territorial integrity and sovereignty of all states in the area. The Arabs were promised assistance against Israeli aggression, and the Israelis were pledged similar help should the Arab states renew hostilities against the new Jewish state.

Significance

The Tripartite Agreement of 1950 was issued at a time when the United States and its Western allies represented the only external powers of importance in the Middle East. Despite war weariness and weakness, the British remained the primary power with a strong physical presence in the region. Moreover, Britain retained forces in Egypt, and the Egyptian monarchy heavily depended on British services and support. Similar conditions existed in the kingdoms of Jordan and Iraq, where the British maintained bases and their military advisors influenced the local armies. By 1956, however, the picture had radically changed. In 1952, the Egyptian monarchy was dissolved and the king exiled. A revolutionary government headed by military officers took control of the government and began to rebuild the armed forces. In 1954, Britain removed its remaining forces from the Suez Canal. In 1955, Egypt signed an arms purchase agreement with the Soviet Union. And in 1956, France and Great Britain attacked Egypt after President Nasser nationalized the Suez Canal and terminated the European-controlled Suez Canal Company. This invasion of Egypt was supported by Israel, which sent troops into the Sinai and ultimately to the eastern bank of the canal. The later actions, despite the U.S. government's condemnation of the invasion, nullified the Tripartite Agreement and its claim to defend the territorial integrity of all the states of the region.

Truman Doctrine 229

The Truman Doctrine emerged from a speech by President Harry S Truman before a joint session of the U.S. Congress on March 12, 1947. President Truman asked the Congress for sufficient authority to deal with events either caused or exacerbated by the Soviet Union. Truman declared that the United States could only be secure in a world free of totalitarian regimes. His allusion was to the Soviet Union and its stated objective of transforming the world into "people's democracies," actually socialist dictatorships. Truman's supposition was that people everywhere wanted the kind of freedom, opportunity, and independence enjoyed in the United States. Only armed minorities, supported or sponsored by the Soviet Union and its associates, could prevent the realization of those objectives. According to Truman, the United States was duty-bound to assist countries struggling to be free. Truman was prompted to commit the United States to protracted foreign involvement because, in areas vital to U.S. interests, Marxist-cum-Soviet forces were gaining influence. World War II had also victimized the victorious. In the aftermath of war, Great Britain was no longer capable of ensuring European preeminence on the Mediterranean littoral or in the Middle East. Britain had played the role of balancer in the region, but with civil war in Greece, and Soviet pressure on Turkey and Iran, that role could no longer be sustained. Fearing a power vacuum that would ultimately be filled by the Soviet Union or affiliated local Marxists, the United States sensed the need to assume a role theretofore played by Great Britain. President Truman had witnessed Soviet efforts to install two socialist republics in northwestern Iran. He was also sensitive to Soviet demands on Turkey that it share control of the vital straits between the Black Sea and Mediterranean. The Soviets also insisted on the return of Turkey's eastern provinces of Kars and Ardahan, which the Bolsheviks had transferred to Turkish sovereignty after World War I. But the situation in Greece was perhaps the most disturbing. Greece was beset by civil war in which forces loyal to the monarchy were pitted against communist guerrillas assisted by Yugoslavia (at that time linked with the Soviet Union) and, to some extent, by Bulgaria and Albania. The Soviets could threaten Iran and Turkey, but the achievement of Moscow's objectives could only come through intervention of the Red Army. That was not likely in the late 1940s because of Soviet concern with postwar rehabilitation. Threats to Iran and Turkey therefore were considered long-range. More immediate was the Greek problem, in which the Soviets were only indirectly involved. In Greece, armed Greek radicals assisted by East European communists were attempting to alter the domestic situation in their favor. The U.S. Congress granted President Truman $400 million for assistance to Greece and Turkey. It also permitted the president to send U.S. military advisors and civilian technicians. The Truman Doctrine was criticized for bypassing the United Nations, but the United States responded that the United Nations could not deal with subversion. The Arab states also opposed the Truman Doctrine. They believed that it perpetuated Western power in the Middle East. Moreover, the United States championed the establishment of the state of Israel and openly supported the Balfour Declaration. The United Nations was debating the Palestine question at the time, and later, in November 1947, it called for partition of the British mandate into Arab and Jewish states. The Arab states saw the Truman Doctrine as reinforcing the UN resolution on partition, and this heightened suspicions about U.S. intentions. Few Arabs in that period were concerned with Soviet or international communism. *See also* RIMLAND (24); EISENHOWER DOCTRINE (208); BAGHDAD PACT (198); CENTRAL TREATY ORGANIZATION (CENTO) (204); TRIPARTITE AGREEMENT 1950 (228); NIXON DOCTRINE (215); CARTER DOCTRINE (203).

Significance
The Truman Doctrine became the centerpiece for U.S. containment of the post–World War II Soviet Union. The United States assumed the role of a global power, and the Soviet Union was judged a primary threat to world peace. With the Truman Doctrine the United States recognized that its days of limited liability were at an end, and it no longer contemplated isolation. At the same time, the Truman Doctrine was an abstract, moral declaration of intention. It addressed itself initially to Greece and Turkey, but in its broader interpretation it meant that the United States was committed to support governments threatened by the Soviet Union from without or by subversive Marxist-Leninist elements within. The United States appeared ready to enter into defensive agreements with states in different stages of development and representative of a variety of lifestyles and differing sociopolitical systems. Although differences were sometimes vast, there was also the implied assumption, sometimes made explicit, that all newly independent states wanted to adopt the free enterprise, capitalist model. The common idiom, through which the United States expected to communicate with the larger world, was economic development. Truman's Four Point Program of economic and technical assistance became the underdeveloped countries' answer to the Marshall Plan. The Truman Doctrine dovetailed with U.S. programs of economic development. "People's capitalism" became the stated U.S. objective, the argument being that a firm economic base allowed for the flowering of political democracy. Political development was hitched to economic achievement. In the context of the Truman Doctrine, the United States plunged into the problems of the

underdeveloped world. American purpose was two-pronged: (1) the containment of international communism and (2) the raising of living standards in the new nations. The seriousness of U.S. efforts cannot be discounted. Nevertheless, Americans suffered from a form of global myopia. The United States expected to see a mirror image of itself in the operations of the underdeveloped societies. Americans ignored historical questions peculiar to those societies. Special psychological and political situations influenced the behavior of the underdeveloped countries, despite changing world conditions or the programs pursued by the United States. The Truman Doctrine, in effect, committed the United States to a world it did not understand, and the consequences were predictable. The United States became the champion of the status quo. It was not in the vanguard of change movements. It also could not adapt to, let alone resolve, local conflicts between racial, religious, ethnic, tribal, or linguistic groups. It did not accept the reality that states gaining their independence after a lengthy period of European imperialism were still inchoate entities, lacking in national consciousness and thus failing to achieve political unity. Nor could Americans adjust to the realization that many new governments were unpopular, that in many instances authority was judged illegitimate and unrepresentative of the masses. This condition caused instability in the underdeveloped states, and no amount of economic assistance could change the picture. Indeed, the more modernization schemes were promoted, the more strained these societies became. The Truman Doctrine committed the United States to world responsibilities, but time would show that much of the world was little interested in U.S. concerns or involvement in their affairs. This did not mean the United States was not a desirable partner under certain conditions. But if the United States intended to work among the new states, its involvement would have to be based on something more than anti-communism.

UN Resolutions: Iraq-Kuwait Conflict 230

The first of 12 Security Council resolutions related to Iraq's August 2, 1990, invasion of Kuwait was approved within hours of the event. The Security Council voted (Resolution 660) 14–0, with Yemen abstaining, to condemn the invasion and to demand the "unconditional and immediate" withdrawal of Iraqi forces. The second (Resolution 661) came on August 6, 1990. It imposed economic sanctions on Iraq and authorized nonmilitary measures to enforce them. The vote was 13–0, with Yemen and Cuba abstaining. On August 9, Resolution 662 was approved. It declared Iraq's annexation of Kuwait to be null and void, and the vote was 15–0. On August 18, Resolution 664 condemned Iraq for holding foreign nationals hostage and demanded their release. This resolution was also approved unanimously. Resolution 665, on August 25, tightened the sanctions by outlawing all trade with Iraq by land, sea, and air. The vote was 13–0, with Yemen and Cuba abstaining. Resolutions 666 and 669 focused on humanitarian aid to the victims of Iraq's aggression. Resolution 667 condemned Iraq for the violence committed against foreign embassies in Kuwait. Resolution 670 was unanimous on the subject of the air embargo; it also permitted detaining Iraqi merchant vessels. In October, the Security Council approved Resolution 674, with Yemen and Cuba abstaining. It held Iraq responsible for the destruction of Kuwaiti property and called for the payment of compensation for damages. On November 28, with Resolution 677, the

Security Council accused Iraq of seeking to alter the demographic composition of Kuwait and by unanimous vote called for an end to the policy. Finally, on November 29, Resolution 678 authorized member-states cooperating with the government of Kuwait "to use all necessary means to uphold and implement" all the resolutions approved since August 2 if Iraq had not fully and unconditionally withdrawn its forces from Kuwait by January 15, 1991.

While the Security Council was concerned with the gulf problem, violence on the Temple Mount in Jerusalem also drew its attention. Resolution 672, passed unanimously, condemned the Israeli use of force against Palestinian demonstrators. Nineteen Arabs were killed in the October 8, 1990, incident. In subsequent resolutions the Security Council "deplored" Israel's refusal to receive a mission of the secretary-general and urged the Israeli government to reconsider its actions. The resolutions directed against Israel sought to link them to a call for an international peace conference on the Israel-Palestinian question, an effort that was repeatedly blocked by the United States. Washington refused to link the Israeli-Palestinian issue with Iraq's invasion of Kuwait, something Saddam Hussain and Iraq had sought to do immediately following Baghdad's conquest of Kuwait. *See also* SANCTIONS (223); IRAQ-KUWAIT: WAR AND CONQUEST (248); TEMPLE MOUNT INCIDENT (184).

Significance

The Security Council actions were unprecedented in the history of the United Nations. The Soviet Union voted affirmatively with the United States, Britain, and France on all 12 resolutions. The People's Republic of China voted in favor of the first 11 but abstained on the use of force in the twelfth. Among the other Security Council members, only Cuba and Yemen opposed the resolutions, but even they abstained on the issue of sanctions. The implementation of Chapter VII of the UN Charter (articles 39–51) was viewed as a positive step in answering aggression collectively rather than unilaterally, although it was noted that the United States had played an instrumental role in gaining the acceptance of the 12 resolutions. Baghdad's efforts to link the crisis in the gulf to Israel's occupation of the West Bank, Gaza, and the Golan Heights, as well as its intrusion into southern Lebanon, were resisted by the United States, but the European powers, especially France, and through it the European Community, pressed Washington to reconsider its position. President Bush continued to fend off this pressure, believing any compromise or linkage would only add to the influence and power of Saddam Hussain in the larger Arab and Muslim world. In January 1991, the president of the UN General Assembly and a delegation visited Israel. The statement issued by the delegation clearly opposed the position taken by both Israel and President Bush. The foreign ministers of the 12 European Community (EC) member-states also met during this period. While asserting the EC's determination to stand with the United States, the foreign ministers also emphasized the need for the United States to show more flexibility in respect to the Security Council resolutions directed against both Iraq and Israel.

UN Security Council Resolution 687 231

Resolution 687 was approved by the UN Security Council on April 3, 1991, by a vote of 12 to 1, with two abstentions, and adopted by the Iraqi parliament on April 6, 1991. The resolution established an official ceasefire in the war between Iraq and the UN coalition. The resolution specified that the ceasefire would take effect from the moment of Iraq's acceptance. The resolution called for the following schedule: (1) sanctions on food imports were lifted and restrictions on imports of civilian goods were eased (emergency civilian goods had been allowed to enter the country earlier); (2) the UN secretary-general was to submit plans for a UN observer force to monitor a buffer zone extending six miles into Iraq and three miles into Kuwait; (3) Iraq was required to supply lists of locations, amounts, and types of its chemical and biological weapons, materials that could be used in nuclear weapons, and ballistic missiles with a range greater than 90 miles; (4) the Security Council was to approve a fund to pay compensation for war damages; the fund would be fed by an unspecified percentage of Iraq's oil revenues, and a commission would administer the fund, taking into account Iraq's needs and its foreign debt; (5) the secretary-general and the International Atomic Energy Agency were to submit plans to the council for a special commission to conduct inspections of Iraq's weapons of mass destruction, and within 45 days after this action, destroy them; (6) the Security Council would lift its ban on Iraqi exports, including oil, if Baghdad handed over its dangerous weapons and nuclear materials for destruction or removal and the council accepted the reparations payment plan; (7) the secretary-general was to submit guidelines to the Security Council for implementation of a new arms embargo against Iraq; (8) the Security Council was to review restrictions on nonmilitary goods imported to Iraq and decide whether to modify them "in light of the policies and practices"; (9) the Security Council would review its ban on some conventional weapons, "taking into account Iraq's compliance with this resolution and general progress toward the control of armaments in the region."

Significance

The Iraqis accepted Security Council Resolution 687 under duress and protest. Claiming the resolution was an assault on the sovereignty of Iraq and a violation of the very UN Charter in whose name it was fostered, Baghdad said it was left with no alternative but to yield. It described the resolution and the Security Council action as "unjust" and a "Zionist conspiracy" aimed at the entire Arab nation, in effect denying the Palestinian quest for self-determination. Beyond Baghdad's rhetoric, however, was the reality that the Iraqi acceptance of the resolution accelerated the withdrawal of U.S. forces from the region and their replacement with a UN observer force. Saddam Hussain remained in power, he would be free to use his forces to crush active resistance to his regime without significant interference, and with the acceptance of the resolution, Baghdad was assured that Baathist and Tikriti control could remain in place. In the months following Operation Desert Storm the UN was made responsible for monitoring Baghdad's compliance with the UN resolutions. UN inspection teams were deployed in Iraq to identify the sites developed in the effort to produce weapons of mass destruction. Despite Iraqi obstructions, including attempts at intimidating or denying access to the teams, the UN pressed its responsibility. When Baghdad opposed the use of helicopter surveillance missions, the United States threatened to renew the air strikes, American forces in Saudi Arabia were reinforced, and naval vessels in the region were placed on high alert. Although the Iraqis yielded to inspection under pressure and more nuclear sites were found, including Iraqi intention to produce hydrogen weapons, the UN Security Council was compelled to pass still another resolution on October 11, 1991, imposing stringent new restrictions on Iraq that were intended to prevent it from building or acquiring nuclear, chemical, or biological weapons. Approved unanimously by the Security Council under Chapter VII of the Charter, it required Iraq to report its military programs for years to come. Iraq was required to provide regular reports and it also had to submit to intrusive inspections to guard against cheating. The Security Council action supported the terms of an agreement entered into in April that would formally end the Gulf War. The character of the UN plan was similar to the restrictions imposed on Germany after World War II. Iraq argued that the restrictions made Iraq a trust territory of the UN and was a throwback to colonial days. The severity of the UN resolution, however, was prompted by the inability to trust Saddam Hussain, who remained at the helm of Iraqi affairs.

Yemen: Merger 232

North and South Yemen peacefully merged into one state on May 22. 1990, and thus was born the new Republic of Yemen. The combined parliaments of the two countries elected Ali Abdullah Saleh president of the new unified Yemen. The actual union of the two Yemens had been approved in November 1989. With 13 million people, the new state became the largest in population in the Arabian Peninsula, and it quickly displayed a larger interest in the affairs of the region. The merger marked the first time in three centuries that Yemen could speak of unity. Sana, the former capital city of North Yemen, was declared the capital of the new state. Aden, the former capital of the southern state, was declared the economic capital. Yemen's new unity was described as a "victory for democracy," but there was no hint as to how the more secular southern region would blend with the more traditional and conservative northern part. Nevertheless, with Saleh's selection as president, the country's vice-president was drawn from the south. Ali Salem al-Baidh, the secretary-general of the south's ruling Socialist Party, was given this honor. The president and vice-president and three other powerful politicians became members of the Ruling Council. Elections were held in 1992. The new government expressed an intention to observe all the treaties entered into by the previous governments. ***See also*** CIVIL WAR: SOUTH YEMEN (241).

Significance

The smooth, virtually unnoticed merger of the two Yemens was in stark contrast to the conquest and forced annexation of Kuwait by Iraq a few months later. Long-time foes and often engaged in vicious conflict, the two Yemens found the political climate conducive to a new beginning. North Yemen, with almost 80 percent of the total population, had stronger ties to the West, whereas South Yemen had been the only chaste Marxist state in the Middle East and was considered an important ally of the U.S.S.R. The changing character of the Soviet Union and the improved relations between East and West no doubt impressed upon the Yemenis the need to transcend their earlier differences. But the drive toward unity was also motivated from within. Ever since the overthrow of the North Yemen imam in the 1960s, the northern state had emphasized a secular course. It was that shift in direction, as well as the diminished character of Marxism in South Yemen, that made the initial plan possible. The two countries also realized that overdependence on external powers was not in their interest. The statesmanship required to bring about the merger, and the compromise that made it possible, could not be ignored. Indeed, Yemen's effort to resolve the Iraq-Kuwait problem without outside interference can be traced to the success experienced in merging their two societies.

Conflict

7

Achille Lauro Incident 233

The *Achille Lauro* was an Italian cruise liner that was seized by four members of the Palestine Liberation Front (PLF), led by Abu Abbas, on October 7, 1985. The PLF was a faction within the PLO, although Yasir Arafat, the leader of the PLO, insisted he knew nothing about the plan to seize the vessel. The *Achille Lauro* had just departed Alexandria when it was commandeered by the hijackers, who demanded that Israel release 50 Palestinian prisoners in return for the safety of the hostages aboard the ship. The vessel anchored at Port Said and Egyptian authorities were given the task of mediating the demands. Yasir Arafat also spoke to the hijackers. During this two-day episode, an elderly American, wheelchair-bound, was murdered and his body dumped overboard. The killing of Leon Klinghoffer was described as a simple act of vengeance. Klinghoffer was also Jewish and the symbolism of his death was intended to dramatize the determination and resolve of the hijackers. Klinghoffer's murder was not disclosed, however, until after the hijackers were promised safe passage out of Egypt by the Egyptian government. Thus, the day following the agreement, an Egyptian plane flew the terrorists out of the country. Their original destination was Tunis, the site of PLO headquarters, but Tunisia refused permission to land. Athens also rejected a request to land there. It was during this odyssey that U.S. F-14 interceptor aircraft located the plane and forced it to land at a NATO base in Sicily. Egypt's president was angered by the U.S. action, calling it an "act of piracy" and claiming the PLO had promised to try the hijackers. Nevertheless, it was Italy that seized them, charged them with murder and kidnapping, and promised a speedy trial. Shortly thereafter, however, Italy released Abu Abbas over the protests of the United States. ***See also*** TERRORISM (108); PALESTINE LIBERATION FRONT (PLF) (163).

Significance

The *Achille Lauro* episode dramatized the character and nature of international terrorism and the length to which terrorists will go in publicizing their cause. The *Achille Lauro* seizure did not move the Palestinian-Israeli conflict from its hardened position. It did not influence the United States to alter its views or its policies in regard to that dispute. It aroused considerable hostility toward the PLO that would be very difficult to offset in the years subsequent to the event. The PLO, on the one side, had painted itself into a corner. Although there was much sympathy for the Palestinian cause, the PLO appeared to damage the Palestinian image. On the other, the PLO struck terror in the minds of people. It disrupted normal activity, and persons affected by these actions were deemed ready to yield to PLO demands. The *Achille Lauro* affair, despite its senselessness, kept the Palestinian problem in public view. On another note, the *Achille Lauro* was an overall embarrassment for Hosni Mubarak, the president of Egypt. Relations with the United States were strained but quickly mended. Elements among the Egyptian population took to the streets in mass demonstration when it was learned the aircraft carrying the hijackers had been forced to land and that the hijackers were in custody. They denounced the United States and called upon Mubarak to sever relations with the United States and to abrogate Egypt's treaty with Israel. The release of Abu Abbas by Italian authorities eased the pressure on Mubarak and the status quo was sustained.

Afghan-U.S.S.R. Conflict (1979–1989) 234

The Soviet Union invaded Afghanistan on December 27, 1979, and commenced a long, tedious campaign to transform the country into a chaste Marxist state dependent on Moscow. The Soviets enlisted what remained of the formal Afghan army in this endeavor. It also established a puppet government in Kabul that it insisted represented the popular aims of the Afghan population. In point of fact, the Afghan people were almost totally opposed to Soviet intervention, and they wanted nothing to do with Marxism. Afghanistan lies in the shadow of the Soviet Union. A southern extension of central Asia, it has long been coveted by Imperial Russia as well as the Bolshevik state. Only the British presence in India prior to 1947 seemed to deny the Russians their quest. Britain made war on Afghanistan twice in the nineteenth century and once in the early part of the twentieth century, to ensure operation of its "Forward Policy," a policy aimed at keeping the Russians from threatening India or the Persian Gulf states. Afghanistan was indifferent to British concerns, and it combatted what it perceived to be English colonialism. When the British withdrew from India after World War II, however, there was no counterforce to Soviet interests in Afghanistan. The Soviet Union entered into arms deals with the Afghans as early as 1954 and 1956. By the 1960s, the Soviet Union was the preeminent foreign power in the country. Afghanistan rejected all overtures by the United States that it join with its neighbors in a collective defense of the region. In fact, Afghanistan considered Pakistan a far greater threat to its interests than the Soviet Union. Afghanistan wanted an outlet to the sea, and the creation of Pakistan in 1947 appeared to deny that objective. Afghanistan also encouraged the Pathans of Pakistan to press for their own independent state of Pakhtunistan, and thus to break their union with Pakistan. Pakistan and Afghanistan military formations skirmished along their mutual frontier in the 1950s and 1960s, and the border was sealed to demonstrate their mutual antagonism. Although sharing common religious traditions, Afghans and Pakistanis could not reconcile their political differences. Pakistan turned to the United States for assistance in 1953–1954 at about the same time the Afghans solicited Soviet aid. Although Pakistan found it possible to move away from its U.S. commitment, the Afghans found that severing ties with the Soviet Union was more difficult. When the Afghan monarchy realized the extent of Soviet penetration, it was too late to correct the situation. The royal house was not destroyed by the Soviets, however. In 1973, a cousin of the king, Mohammad Daud, with the help of radical military figures, terminated the monarchy and declared Afghanistan to be a republic. Daud also drew upon the assistance of the country's intellectuals and especially the Soviet-backed People's Democratic Party of Afghanistan (PDPA). In 1978, Daud was murdered by these same radical military officers, and the government was turned over to the civilian leaders of the PDPA, the equivalent of Afghanistan's communist party. Splits within the PDPA leadership and socialist reforms that aroused the hatred of the tribal population of Afghanistan, particularly the attack on Islam, precipitated clashes within the government and between government forces and the majority tribal population. Defections of Afghan military personnel, assaults on foreign advisors (notably Soviets), and criticism of the regime appeared to threaten the Marxist revolution. The killing of Nur Mohammad Taraki (acceptable to Moscow), head of the Afghan Marxist government, by Hafizullah Amin (unacceptable to Moscow) was a signal to the Soviets that it was time to take control of affairs in Kabul. The Soviet invasion force quickly eliminated Amin and established his nemesis, Babrak Karmal, as the leader of the Afghan government. But Karmal could not win the support of the rebellious tribal folk, who saw their struggle with the Soviets as an act of faith, as well as an attempt to keep Afghanistan free. Although the Soviet Union commanded the Afghan government, it could not thereby obtain the loyalty of the Afghan nation. The result was a protracted guerrilla war pitting approximately 100,000 Soviets and remnants of the Afghan army against a fiercely independent but fragmented tribal people. The Afghan *mujahiddin* fought their enemy according to historical tradition, from hilltops and canyons, in small groups using hit-and-run tactics. They never expected to win a major battle against superior Soviet forces, but it was their intention to make the invaders pay a high price for their adventure. With military assistance supplied by the United States and distributed by Pakistani authorities, the *mujahiddin* proved a formidable foe for the combined Soviet and Kabul forces. The war dragged on much longer than anyone had anticipated, and with each passing year more Soviet troops were killed and equipment destroyed. Moscow accused Pakistan of aiding the resistance and threatened to punish Islamabad if it did not suspend operations in support of the *mujahiddin*. President Mohammad Zia-ul-Haq, who had seized power in 1977, turned a deaf ear to the Kremlin. He became the chief spokesman for the *mujahiddin* cause in Muslim international forums, and his government lobbied UN members, who each year voted overwhelmingly in favor of the Afghan opposition. Annual resolutions of the General Assembly urged the withdrawal of foreign forces from the mountain state. The UN secretary-general appointed Diego Cordovez to act in his behalf, and through these good offices a series of "proximity talks" were held over a six-year period, engaging the Kabul and Islamabad governments. The parties never met in the same room, however, given Islamabad's refusal to recognize the Soviet-installed Kabul government. Mikhail Gorbachev's ascendance to head the Soviet state in 1985 moved matters in the direction of a diplomatic settlement, and the UN effort began to show some gains. In 1986, the Soviets removed Babrak Karmal and placed Najibullah, the security police chief, at the head of the Kabul government. Gorbachev informed the United States that he was prepared to order his troops out of Afghanistan, but he also insisted upon security guarantees for the Najibullah government. Hard bargaining followed, when suddenly Gorbachev announced in February 1988 that he was prepared to enter into a withdrawal agreement. On April 14, 1988, that agreement was formally entered into by Pakistan and Kabul. Pakistan wanted an interim government set up in Kabul before the Soviet troop departure, but under pressure from Washington, it yielded on this demand. The United States and the Soviet Union were made coguarantors of the arrangements agreed to by Pakistan and Afghanistan. Afghanistan's full sovereignty was recognized, but there was no immediate prospect for peace in the country. The *mujahiddin* had not participated in the "proximity talks," nor were they consulted. They were not prepared to put down their arms so long as Najibullah and the Soviet-supported government remained in power in Kabul. The Soviet troops began a phased withdrawal after the April agreement and by February 1989, as Gorbachev had promised, the last regular Red Army soldier crossed back into the Soviet Union. Moscow, however, continued to support the Kabul government, and Soviet advisors remained on station. The United States continued to assist the *mujahiddin* but at a decreasing level. Observers forecast the collapse of the Najibullah government within weeks following the Soviet troop withdrawal. They were proved wrong. A major *mujahiddin* assault was launched against Najibullah's forces in Jalalabad in 1989–1990, but the campaign failed to achieve its objectives. Moreover, the *mujahiddin* suffered very heavy casualties. Indeed, it was not until April 1991 that the *mujahiddin* were able to win a set battle, seizing the border village of Khost. This success, however, did not signal the fall of the Najibullah government in Kabul. Nevertheless, a subsequent agreement by the United States and the Soviet Union to curtail weapons shipments to the belligerants in the continued Afghan fighting appeared to fall hardest on Najibullah. With outside efforts at finding a compromise formula for ending the warfare more intense, Najibullah appeared to be the main obstacle to a settlement. His announcement on March 8, 1992, that he would step aside for an interim government, however, pointed to a formal end of the conflict. His ouster in April brought the complete collapse of his government and tribal forces entered Kabul. ***See also*** COMMUNISM: AFGHANISTAN (117); JIRGAH (88).

Significance

The long-term consequences of the Afghan-Soviet conflict are not yet clear. It was the original Soviet intention to destroy the traditional, primitive, semi-feudal lifestyle of the Afghan people. This drastic procedure was to be a prelude to the metamorphosis of Afghanistan into a chaste Marxist state, wedded to the Soviet Union. Overall, the Soviets perceived themselves as bringing civilization to a backward people while at the same time bolstering their own security. At the conclusion of the Soviet involvement in the war, Afghan's tribal society was still operative, but with significant handicaps. More than a million Afghans were estimated to have died between 1979 and 1989. Several million more were seriously wounded and many incapacitated for life. At least 4 million Afghans remained as refugees in

Pakistan and Iran with no homes or even villages to return to. Informed Soviet scholars have themselves noted that perhaps half of Afghanistan's prewar population had been lost or scattered. Afghanistan's urban and rural life has been damaged extensively. There is nothing resembling an economy and when the Soviet Union self-destructed in 1991, it was still primarily responsible for Najibullah and his administration. The *mujahiddin* coalition, never very firm, has also come apart, however, with Muslim fundamentalists and more nationalistic tribal forces battling for turf and position. Since the death of Pakistan's President Zia in 1988, Pakistani assistance to the *mujahiddin* has not been consistent. And Islamabad is increasingly burdened by the huge Afghan refugee population, which receives less and less world attention. Saudi Arabia and Egypt, two sponsors of the *mujahiddin*, have their own problems and they are less interested in the internal warfare that pits Afghan against Afghan. The war in Afghanistan is not over, and given the low intensity of the conflict, it could contine without direct assistance from outside sources. Pakistan's 1992 decision to cease supplying arms to the *mujahiddin* are Najibullah's decision to step aside projected an end to the formal conflict. After Najibullah's demise, however, Pakistan found it necessary to mediate differences between the victorious Afghan factions, especially those led by Ahmed Shah Masud on the one side and Gulbuddin Hekmatyan on the other. In the interim, Sibghattullah Mojaddedi, another resistance leader, assumed leadership of the Afghan government on April 28, 1992. His tenure was considered a temporary expedient.

Arab Defense Force Proposal 235

After Operation Desert Storm, Egypt, Syria, and the six states of the Gulf Cooperation Council sought to create an Arab Defense Force to insulate newly liberated Kuwait from future Iraqi aggression. In March 1991 an agreement was signed in Damascus between Saudi Arabia, Kuwait, Bahrein, Qatar, Oman, and the United Arab Emirates with Syria and Egypt, that seemed to guarantee the long-term defense of the region. Iran registered strong opposition to any military presence of nongulf Arabs in the area and few Arab states were willing to antagonize Tehran. Nevertheless, the Damascus agreement had called for a 26,000-person force to be stationed in Kuwait, including 3,000 troops from Egypt and a smaller number from Syria. Ten thousand troops were supposed to be assembled from Saudi units, and the remaining 10,000 from the other states combined. ***See also*** COOPERATIVE COUNCIL OF THE GULF STATES (205).

Significance

The Special Arab force for the defense of Kuwait failed to materialize given differences between all the parties. Moreover, Saudi Arabia was suspicious of Syria after it gained influence over Lebanon, and Kuwait saw the Egyptians as only interested in drawing wealth from the region. Little confidence was shown in Egyptian or Syrian forces should there be a new threat from Baghdad. The failure to implement the Damascus agreement on the one side put an end to ideas about pan-Arabism; on the other it meant the United States and other western countries would continue "policing" the region.

Arab-Israeli War, 1948–1949 236

The Arab-Israeli War of 1948–1949 was a consequence of the British decision to abandon their Palestine mandate and permit the new United Nations to decide the fate of the region. On November 29, 1947, the UN

General Assembly, acting on a recommendation of its special committee, approved a resolution by more than the two-thirds required majority to partition Palestine into independent Arab and Jewish states. Jerusalem was to be internationalized. Both the United States and the Soviet Union voted in favor of the resolution. The Arab states, however, were unreconciled to the creation of a Jewish state. On December 17, 1947, the Arab League Council declared that it would not permit the implementation of the UN plan. Arab irregulars began moving toward Palestine from Egypt, Syria, and Lebanon, and many British bases were occupied by Arab forces as the Europeans began their withdrawal. On May 14, 1948, the date established for the final British departure, a People's Council representing the Jewish community (Yishuv) in Palestine met in Tel Aviv and declared the independence of the state of Israel. A provisional government was created, and the new state called for recognition by the nations of the world. On May 15, Arab armies, under the banner of the Arab League, invaded the new Jewish state. Regular armies from Egypt, Transjordan, Iraq, Syria, and Lebanon, as well as contingents from Saudi Arabia, attempted to terminate the state in its infancy. Both the United States, which had recognized Israel de facto, and the Soviet Union, which had recognized it de jure, condemned the Arab action. But the invading armies were not impressed with superpower rhetoric. The Arab armies moved to within 10 miles of Tel Aviv, and the British-commanded Transjordanian Arab Legion overran the West Bank and stormed East Jerusalem. The Iraqi army came within 5 miles of the Mediterranean Sea and almost severed Israel into two parts. The Syrian force moved through the Upper Galilee and attempted to overrun the fortified kibbutz settlements in the region. Israel's small citizen army drew upon supplies seized from British forces. They also obtained needed arms from the East European bloc, especially Czechoslovakia. No less important, training and experience obtained while fighting alongside the Allies in World War II provided a degree of expertise that the Arab armies, despite their numerical strength, could not match. The Israelis either beat back the Arab advance or held firm. In 1949, armistice agreements were signed by Israel with Egypt, Jordan, Lebanon, and Syria. Iraq steadfastly refused to sign any terms that might be interpreted as acceptance of the Israeli state. The armistice was supposed to be a temporary stopgap, and a more permanent peace was envisioned for the foreseeable future. In the aftermath of the 1948–1949 war, however, no Arab state was prepared, or found it possible, to enter into formal negotiations with the state of Israel.

Significance
The Arab-Israeli War of 1948–1949 has had several important consequences:

1. Israel occupied and absorbed considerably more territory than had been allocated under the UN resolution.
2. Transjordan absorbed the West Bank and East Jerusalem, much of the area that had been outlined for the Arab state by the United Nations. Transjordan became the Kingdom of Jordan, given the new territorial realities.
3. Egypt occupied the Gaza Strip along the Mediterranean Sea.
4. The Arab world was humiliated by the defeat to a smaller nation, and it was seized by new turbulence as leaders were sought who could reestablish Arab pride. The military coup that overthrew the monarchy in Egypt in 1952 was one such example. Gamal Abdul

Nasser's rise to power was accelerated by his anti-Israeli posture. On the other side, the king of Jordan, Abdullah, was assassinated in 1951 by Palestinian Arabs because he allegedly came to terms with the Israelis.

5. The Palestinian Arabs who had fled their land and homes in the new Israeli state expecting to return after the Israelis had been defeated were transformed into more or less permanent refugees. Although they desired to return to their ancestral lands, the Israelis could not accept them in the continuing state of belligerency between Israel and its neighbors and because of the space required to settle the influx of Jewish refugees from Europe and the Middle East. Moreover, the vast majority of Palestinians were confined to refugee camps. They were provided with assistance by the United Nations, but never absorbed within the Arab states. Contrasted with the Jews who fled the Arab countries (estimated to be 800,000), the Palestinian Arabs (approximately 1.2 million in 1948) became a symbol of Arab despair on the one side and a dagger pointed at specific Arab states on the other. Guerrilla and terrorist organizations were a predictable outcome of Palestinian statelessness.
6. The United States, Britain, and France agreed to a 1950 Tripartite Pact wherein the three countries pledged to defend the territorial integrity of all the countries of the area. Although it soon proved defunct, the Tripartite Pact and the Truman Doctrine of 1947 focused U.S. national security interests on the Middle East in the immediate post–World War II period.
7. The results of the 1948–1949 war guaranteed a new round of fighting between Arabs and Israelis when the moment appeared propitious. The extended Muslim world verbalized support for the Arab cause, and with the emergence into independence of an increasing number of Muslim states, all of them sensed that Arab, and later Muslim unity could be achieved by collective support for the struggle against Israel. Most Arabs believed that time was on their side.

Arab-Israeli War, 1956 — 237

The Arab-Israeli War of 1956 internationalized a regional conflict and established the pattern for future encounters between the determined adversaries. Israel had consolidated the gains achieved in the 1948–1949 war, established its political system, and devoted particular attention to the ingathering of Jewish refugees from Europe and the Arab countries, as well as Jews from Europe and the United States who opted to live in the Zionist state. The Jewish Law of Return enacted in 1950 accorded free and automatic citizenship to every Jewish immigrant. From 1948 to 1951 the Jewish population of Israel doubled as a result of the arrival of more than 750,000 immigrants. The World Zionist Organization Status Law of 1952 recognized the Jewish Agency as an organ of the Israeli government charged with the development and settlement of the country and the absorption of immigrants. In Arab eyes, Israeli success on the battleground was now compounded by the expansion of the Israeli population and the fear that Israel's unchecked development would make impossible the Palestinian Arabs' ever returning to the lands they had fled in 1948. The Arab states were nonetheless in a poor position from which to launch a direct attack on Israel. Moreover, the annexation of West Bank territories and the transformation of Transjordan into the Kingdom of Jordan in 1950 also negated the idea of statehood for the Palestinians. They received Jordanian identities, but the notion of an independent Arab Palestine was considered moot. Jordan also opted for quasi-neutrality in the struggle, a course followed even after the assassination of King Abdullah in 1951. Frustrated by events, the Palestinians were forced to take the initiative, and after the Egyptian coup of 1952 brought Gamal Abdul Nasser to power, the Palestinian refugees had a formidable base of operations from which to strike at the Israelis. The Egyptians occupied the Gaza Strip during the 1948–1949 war, and it remained under their administration. The Gaza territory was the refuge for more than 200,000 Palestinians, and from this number the Egyptians recruited guerrilla fighters (*fedeyeen*) for hit-and-run attacks inside Israel. These raids were numerous in the period between 1952–1956, and the Israelis were forced to devote considerable resources and attention to the maintenance of national order. Israel thus quickly developed into a highly organized, fully mobilized, garrison state. On the other side, Nasser engaged the Soviet Union in an arms deal in 1955 that promised to bring Egyptian forces to peak levels of sophistication. The U.S. government was disturbed by Nasser's "invitation" to the Soviet Union to meddle in Middle East affairs. And when the United States stopped arms shipments to Egypt and then withdrew its pledge to finance and build the High Dam at Aswan, Nasser turned more convincingly toward Moscow. The Kremlin offered to build the Aswan project, and Nasser was emboldened to nationalize the Suez Canal. The nationalization of the canal angered the British and French. The latter had been forced to relinquish Indochina in 1954, and in 1955 an Algerian liberation movement sought to expel the French from their North African colony. The French were convinced that Egypt was supplying the Algerian insurgents and that Nasser was their principal supporter. The British had extensive interests throughout the Middle East, and Nasser's revolutionary declarations were considered a threat to traditional regimes long dependent on the United Kingdom. The Suez crisis therefore provided the British and French with an opportunity to destroy the Nasser revolution as well as reestablish their preeminence in the area. Britain and France mobilized a joint task force that had as its objective the seizure of the Suez Canal and the surrounding area. Their plans were aborted, however, when threats from the Soviet Union and pressure from Washington and their own publics caused their governments first to restrain and then to withdraw their forces. Israel, however, used the opportunity to strike at Egypt and the *fedeyeen* bases in the Gaza Strip and Sinai Peninsula. Between October 29 and November 5, 1956, Israel swept through the Sinai to the Suez Canal, destroying the *fedeyeen* bases in the process. The Egyptian army also took punishing losses. Although reluctant to leave the canal zone, Israel was imposed upon by the United States, and a United Nations Emergency Force (UNEF) was interposed between the Egyptian and Israeli forces. UNEF was made a buffer in the Sinai, and Egypt was not supposed to return to the Gaza Strip. After the Israeli withdrawal, however, Egyptian administration was again established in Gaza. Israel had also been promised use of the Suez Canal, but this pledge was ignored. Israel had withdrawn to its own frontiers, and it complained about the Suez Canal problem, but the government insisted on the right to navigate the Straits of Tiran and the Gulf of Aqaba (usually referred to as the Gulf of Eilat by the Israelis). The Israeli Knesset declared Israel's right of self-defense and that any attempt to close the Gulf of Aqaba to Israeli shipping would be deemed an act of war. ***See also*** SINAI PENINSULA (26); AQABA, GULF OF (3); TIRAN STRAIT (29); SUEZ CANAL (27); TRIPARTITE AGREEMENT OF 1950 (228).

Significance
The Arab-Israeli War of 1956 had the following consequences:

1. It displayed Israeli resolve to initiate conflict at opportune moments. It also demonstrated Israel's increasing military capability and the skillful deployment of its forces. Military success, however, was not translated into political achievement, as its foes were even more determined to salvage their lost pride as well as reclaim territory.
2. Egypt suffered another humiliating defeat, but Nasser emerged from the conflict with even more established credentials. Nasser was perceived as defending a beleaguered Arab nation against Britain and France, allies of Israel and arch imperialists. Israel's success, therefore, was not the result of superior performance, but rather Egypt's difficulties in warding off the multiple blows of great powers. Britain's and France's retreat was judged a victory for Egypt, the Arab nation, and the emerging Third World. Israel therefore had merely taken advantage of Egypt's distraction closer to home, and a more conclusive contest was still awaited.
3. Despite intentions to maintain the pressure on Israel, Arab unity suffered during the 1956 war. Jordan, sharing the longest frontier with Israel, remained neutral. Lebanon avoided any hint of involvement. Syria was too beset by domestic problems to play a significant role, and Iraq was a member of the Western alliance known as the Baghdad Pact. Nasser realized that the first task of his administration was to strengthen Egypt's military prowess and to proceed along a path aimed at the merger of Arab states. Separate polities meant divided opinion and conflicted policies. Israel's ultimate defeat therefore was predicated on the institutionalization of the concepts "Arab nation" and "Arab unity."
4. The *fedeyeen* attacks on Israel proved to be troublesome, but it was obvious after 1956 that continued use of terrorist tactics would neither defeat Israel nor act as a catalyst for a larger conflict.
5. Despite U.S. condemnation of the joint British-French campaign against Egypt, the United States was perceived as a friend of Israel and an opponent of the Arab revolution. By contrast, the Soviet Union was judged an eager supporter of the Arab cause against Zionism and Western imperialism. The United States and the Soviet Union had replaced the British and the French as the major external powers in the Middle East.

Arab-Israeli War, 1967 (The Six-Day War) 238

The Arab-Israeli War of 1967 was precipitated by Gamal Abdul Nasser's decision to request the UN secretary-general to withdraw the UN Emergency Force (UNEF) from the Sinai. Numerous other events, however, contributed to the outbreak of hostilities. Since the end of the 1956 war, the UNEF had acted as a buffer between Egyptian and Israeli forces. Israel was seen as the immediate beneficiary, especially as Arab summit conferences in Cairo in January 1964 and Alexandria in September 1964 called for intensifying the struggle against the Jewish state. Egypt and other

Arab states were the recipients of Soviet weaponry, and Soviets were actively engaged in training and advising the Egyptian military establishment. From the ashes of the *fedeyeen* movement emerged Al-Fatah, a Palestinian guerrilla organization under the leadership of Yasir Arafat. Al-Fatah became the nucleus for the Palestine Liberation Organization (PLO), an umbrella association for a host of Palestinian terrorist groups. Al-Fatah and the PLO were provided training bases and sanctuaries in a number of Arab states, and the Soviet Union became the chief arms supplier. Using bases in Syria, Jordan, and Lebanon, the PLO struck at Israeli villages and towns and detonated devices in some of the larger cities. Israel had reason to be concerned with other events in the Arab world. In 1958, the pro-Western Iraqi Hashemite dynasty was overthrown in a bloody coup, and radical military elements led by Karim Kassem assumed power. In 1963, Kassem was overthrown, and after a period of instability the Iraqi Baath Party gained power. In 1966, the Syrian Baath also managed a successful coup. Both countries looked to the Soviet Union for assistance. Each proclaimed its determination to liquidate the Israeli state. Syrian artillery on the Golan Heights repeatedly shelled Israeli villages in the Galilee, and Nasser began massing his forces in the Sinai Peninsula following a costly campaign in North Yemen. Thus, when Nasser's demand that the UNEF be withdrawn was granted on May 16, 1967, Israelis had reason to be concerned. On May 22, Nasser ordered the closing of the Straits of Tiran to Israeli ships, and armies of Iraq, Syria, and Jordan began mobilizing along Israel's frontiers. The Israeli president called upon Jordan's King Hussain to pledge neutrality as he had during the 1956 war. Hussain decided to reject this overture. Israel reacted to the crisis by mobilizing its own forces and by forming a government of national unity. On the morning of June 5, 1967, Israel launched lightning attacks against Egyptian airfields, destroying the bulk of the Egyptian air force on the ground. With mastery of the skies thus achieved, Israeli forces again pushed into the Sinai and sped to the Suez Canal. When Jordan's forces opened up all along the Israeli frontier, Israeli troops fought their way into East Jerusalem and the entire West Bank territory, quickly routing the Arab Legion. Israel launched simultaneous attacks on the Golan Heights and eventually forced the Syrians from their fortifications. By June 10 the war was ostensibly over, and the Arab cause had suffered its most devastating defeat since the creation of the Jewish state. ***See also*** SINAI PENINSULA (26); TIRAN STRAIT (29); AQABA, GULF OF (3).

Significance

The Arab-Israeli War of 1967 had the following consequences:

1. Israel occupied the West Bank (Judea and Samaria), the Gaza Strip, and the Sinai Peninsula as well as the Golan Heights. It also unified the city of Jerusalem. By controlling these territories, Israel was strategically positioned to defend its population centers. It neutralized Syrian shelling, placed Israeli forces in close proximity to Egypt's heartland, and appeared to eliminate the Palestinian guerrilla threat from bases in Gaza and the West Bank. But Israel also brought more than a million Palestinian refugees under its administration, a costly and uncertain venture.
2. The Arab debacle in the 1967 war did not end Nasser's rule (he announced his resignation but agreed to remain on when popular sentiment ran in his favor), but his leadership had been

irrevocably diminished. Moreover, the losses suffered by the regular Arab armies gave increasing importance to the PLO. The Palestinian National Covenant of the Palestine Liberation Organization was issued in 1968, and it made it clear that the Palestinians would ultimately achieve what the Arab states were so far incapable of—the liquidation of Israel. Generally reluctant to tackle Israel on the battlefield, the Arab states turned to a form of diplomacy, but at the same time refused to negotiate directly with the Israelis. In November 1967, the UN General Assembly approved Resolution 242, which called for a "just and lasting peace, in which every state in the area can live in security." The resolution also noted the need for "secure and recognized boundaries," but it did not mention a Palestinian Arab right to self-determination. The PLO therefore rejected the resolution. Many Arab states accepted the resolution, especially the part that called upon Israel to withdraw from territories seized in the 1967 war. When Israel refused to relinquish any of the territory, Egypt reopened hostilities without igniting another general war. Between April 1969 and August 1970 approximately 9,000 armed skirmishes occurred between Israeli and Egyptian forces. After blows and counterblows took many lives, and Israeli air raids caused the evacuation of 750,000 inhabitants from cities along the Suez Canal, a new ceasefire was enacted in September 1970. This halt in the fighting had been engineered by the United States, but it only proved to be a temporary respite.

3. The United States recognized the military prowess of Israel. It was no longer judged an underdog in its struggle with the Arab states. Moreover, U.S. defense officials saw in Israel a Western, anticommunist state that it could depend upon should the Soviet Union become more adventurous in the Middle East. Although Soviet weaponry and tactics did not fare well in the 1967 war, the Arab confrontation states were even more dependent on Soviet assistance. The objective for the immediate future therefore was not to encourage the Israelis in all-out hostilities, but to emphasize the illegal Israeli occupation of Arab land. The central theme in the argument suggested that there would be recognition of Israel if the territories were returned and the right of the Palestinian Arabs to a homeland was granted. Israel, however, saw little prospect of a change in Arab attitudes that would promote a genuine settlement. They continued to point to statements from Arafat, Nasser, and others that the Arab cause could only be served when Israel was no more.

Arab-Israeli War, 1973 — 239

The Arab-Israeli War of 1973 is sometimes referred to as the Ramadan War or the Yom Kippur War because it began during a period of religious observance among both Muslims and Jews. The ceasefire arranged by the United States in 1970 held for approximately three years, a period known as "no war, no peace." The year 1970 was also significant in other respects. Nasser died in 1970 and was succeeded by Anwar el-Sadat, a member of the Free Officers involved in the 1952 revolution. Sadat was not the most popular Egyptian figure, but he had served Nasser faithfully and proved to be a good administrator. He was selected because he was judged to be less controversial than some of the other personalities around Nasser. Sadat, however, was called upon to prove himself. And primary attention was given to his handling of the conflict with Israel. Sadat pledged to regain control of Sinai. He also called for recognition of Palestinian rights. Sadat assumed power in the aftermath of the Jordanian army's crackdown on the Palestine Liberation Organization. In fact, Nasser had died in the midst of a futile attempt to reconcile Jordanian-Palestinian and Jordanian-Syrian differences. Jordan's offensive against the PLO reflected King Hussain's concern that the Palestinians plotted his demise and that the PLO had become too influential and too strong a force within his kingdom. The Jordanian-PLO clash caused several thousand casualties and forced the PLO to reestablish its headquarters in Beirut. The bulk of Palestinian guerrillas also took up positions in southern Lebanon, from where they continued their raids against Israeli targets. International terrorism, principally the work of the PLO, also expanded during this period. The seizure of commercial aircraft in flight, attacks on embassies and diplomats, the sending of letter bombs, and the use of a whole range of sophisticated, lethal devices struck fear across the planet. Many of the targets were innocent civilians from lands with little if any involvement in the Arab-Israeli conflict. But terrorism also conveyed a message. It dramatized the plight of the Palestine Arab refugee, and the PLO wanted the world to understand that global tranquility was linked to justice for the Palestinians. It is doubtful, however, that Sadat ordered the Egyptian army to cross the Suez Canal and take on the Israelis because he sympathized with the Palestinians. Sadat was more concerned with demonstrating his leadership qualities, and the best vehicle for such a portrayal was the dramatic canal crossing. Egyptian forces had been detected mobilizing prior to their attack on October 6, 1973, but the Israeli government of Golda Meir decided to ignore intelligence reports. Sadat had made a number of boasts in the three years leading up to this military campaign, and none of these had borne fruit. This time the Egyptian leader was in dead earnest, and the Israelis were caught somewhat by surprise. Egyptian forces swept over the Israeli Bar-Lev Line of defensive fortifications and pressed inland. Israel also found itself under attack from Syria, and the Golan Heights were almost reclaimed by the Syrian drive. The Israelis assumed that the Arabs were intent on making all-out war, but such was not the case. Jordan opted out of the combat, and other Arab states could only send token forces. Sadat was interested in displaying Egyptian power, and his strategy called for limited gains. The Israelis were outnumbered almost 12 to 1 when the fighting began, and retreat was imperative. Nevertheless, with the rapid mobilization of Israeli reserves, a sizable force was assembled and took to the field within days of the initial fighting. Moreover, the United States rushed military supplies to Israel on an emergency basis. Huge C-5A Galaxies brought tons of spare parts and fresh equipment for the Israeli armed forces. The Soviet Union had mustered a similar effort in support of the Egyptians and Syrians. Within a week, however, the tide of battle had turned in favor of the Israelis. The Syrians were beaten back on the Golan Heights; Israel launched a massive counter-offensive against the Egyptians, eventually stormed the Suez Canal, and, for the first time, crossed over into Egypt. The Israeli maneuver cut off the Egyptian Third Army on the Sinai side of the canal. With Israel threatening to destroy the Egyptian force, the Soviet Union hinted that it might send volunteers. President Richard Nixon then ordered U.S. forces on "red alert," a status describing mobilization of all forces, including nuclear contingents. At the same time the U.S. government put pressure on the Israelis not to attack the Egyptian Third Army. The Israelis yielded to U.S. pressure and permitted the Egyptians to obtain water and rations. At the United Nations, Resolution 338 was approved calling for an immediate ceasefire and implementation of Resolution 242 (1967), an explicit demand that the parties find a negotiated settlement. The war ground to a halt, and Henry Kissinger began his shuttle diplomacy, ultimately getting the belligerents to disengage their forces. ***See also*** SINAI PENINSULA (26); GOLAN HEIGHTS (13); RESOLUTION 242 (178); RESOLUTION 338 (179).

Significance
The Arab-Israeli War of 1973 produced the following consequences:

1. Anwar el-Sadat attained new heights of popularity in the immediate aftermath of the conflict. Egyptian forces had also demonstrated more fighting ability than in previous conflicts with Israel. But Sadat used his popular standing to open negotiations with Israel. Each side had displayed courage and a willingness to make great sacrifices, but neither was capable of completely defeating the other. Sadat therefore was receptive to Henry Kissinger and supported the latter's efforts at finding a diplomatic solution. Ultimately, these negotiations prompted Sadat to visit Jerusalem in 1977 and to agree to a peace treaty with Israel in 1979. As he had promised, Sadat regained control of the Sinai for Egypt, a high-water mark in the diplomacy of the Middle East.
2. Syrian leaders did not follow Sadat's lead. Syria became the PLO's major proponent, and the destruction of Israel remained their joint objective. In 1981 Israel annexed the Golan Heights despite outcries in every part of the world.
3. Israeli leadership was shaken by the 1973 war, and Israelis realized their vulnerability for the first time in almost two decades. The Labor coalition that had dominated the government since the state's independence displayed signs of wear. Golda Meir's government (1968–1974) was followed by Yitzhak Rabin's (1974–1977), but Labor could not deal with the deepening malaise. Rabin was also accused of engaging in corrupt practices, and in the 1977 elections, Labor was swept from power. The conservatives, led by Menachem Begin, formed Israel's new government. Begin was identified with militancy and aggressive directness, and Israel moved far to the Right in its programs and especially in its reaction to external events. The Israeli armed forces received even greater emphasis, and strenuous efforts were made to improve firepower, maneuverability, and offensive capability. Although Begin joined with Sadat in declaring an end to Israeli-Egyptian hostility, the conservatives argued the need to deal effectively with Israel's remaining antagonists, especially Syria and the PLO.

Boycott **240**

The Arab states have used the boycott as one of their principal instruments in combatting Israel and its supporters. Established with the formation of the Israeli state, the Arab boycott represented an Arab League decision to ban trade with Israel, or business with companies doing business with Israel. Egypt was the only Arab state to lift the embargo. It did so in 1979 after the signing of the peace treaty with the Israeli state.

Significance
The boycott has been less than effective against the Israeli state and no more successful against the companies doing business with Israel. More an irritant, it has been suggested that it would be lifted in return for Israeli concessions, especially Israel's willingness to cease establishing settlements in the West Bank territory. Israelis have noted that the boycott was imposed 19 years before Israel took control of the West Bank and Gaza Strip, and long before it ever contemplated erecting settlements there. Nevertheless, even the Group of Seven industrialized states, prompted by the United States, took up the offer. The Western leaders noted that lifting the embargo would end Israel's economic isolation from the Arab states. The lifting of the boycott, however, was a minor issue compared to Israel's reluctance to yield "land for peace," and the Israelis had reason to be skeptical given their decision not to return the Golan Heights to Syria. How, for example, would Arab states react to trading with Israel when such land disputes continued to strain Arab-Israeli relations? For Israel, therefore, the Arab trade embargo was of a much lower order of significance.

Civil War: South Yemen 241

A long-running conflict between supporters of South Yemen's former president, Abdel Fatah Ismail, and the secretary-general of the ruling Yemen Socialist Party, Ali Nasser Mohammad, degenerated into a brief civil war in January 1986. In the ensuing struggle, which began as an attempt by the different factions to eliminate each other, 2,000 people were killed, including Ismail. The foreign community, especially that represented by the East bloc, were forced to flee the country. Thousands of Soviets and their dependents were caught up in the fighting and an international effort was launched to gain their freedom. A new government was installed in Aden but efforts had to be made to ward off a continuing threat posed by Ali Nasser Mohammad, who received sanctuary in Sana, in North Yemen. South Yemen insisted upon its neutrality in matters involving the United States and the Soviet Union, and efforts were directed at improving relations with neighboring Oman. Oman's first ambassador to Aden was appointed in November 1987 and trade agreements were entered into in 1988. ***See also*** YEMEN: MERGER (232).

Significance
The civil war in South Yemen proved to be the catalyst for the merger of the two Yemens. Muammar Qaddafi used his good offices to bring the leaders of the two Yemens together in Libya, and despite border skirmishes in 1987, a series of meetings in 1988 focused on reunification plans and cooperative arrangements in the development of petroleum resources.

Friendly Fire 242

The U.S. military concluded that almost 25 percent of American forces killed or wounded in the Persian Gulf war were victims of U.S., or "friendly" fire. Allied fire had accounted for less than 2 percent of U.S. casualties in World War II, the Korean War, and the Vietnam War. The high percentage of losses to friendly fire was attributed to the changing character of warfare and the more sophisticated weapons employed in Operation Desert Storm. Of the 148 Americans killed in combat, 35 died as a consequence of U.S. aircraft assaults or ground fire. Of the 467 wounded in Desert Storm, 78 were wounded by their own forces. ***See also*** OPERATION DESERT STORM (258).

Significance
The greater impersonality of warfare, the increased night-fighting capabilities of modern weaponry, and the speed with which assaults are mounted and carried out were some of the reasons given for the high percentage of "friendly fire" casualties in Operation Desert Storm. The overall lessons learned from Desert Storm revealed that conventional warfare had become more deadly and less time-consuming. Highly mobile forces would be expected to achieve their objectives without resorting to long-term resupply and reinforcement capabilities. In so doing, however, highly active forces were more than likely to cause some damage to their own formations.

Gulf of Sidra Conflict 243

On January 24, 1986, the U.S. Navy began a week-long exercise in and near the Gulf of Sidra in the Mediterranean Sea, not too distant from the Libyan coast. In January, President Ronald Reagan had called Libya "a threat to the national security and foreign policy of the United States." The U.S. president was incensed by what was deemed to be Libyan complicity in terrorist raids at the Rome and Vienna airports in 1985 that had taken a number of innocent lives. Washington led a maneuver to impose economic and political sanctions against Libya, and 1,500 Americans still in Libya were requested to leave. The withdrawal of U.S. citizens working in Libya was not applied to U.S. oil companies, but they, too, ceased operations in June 1986. Libya prompted a meeting of the Islamic Conference and the Arab League, which pledged solidarity with Qaddafi. But this was not until after Qaddafi accused the United States of "aggressive provocation" in the Gulf of Sidra and insisted the gulf was all within Libya's territorial waters and jurisdiction. The Libyan leader boarded a patrol boat in which he said he was prepared personally to confront the U.S. Sixth Fleet. He noted that "a line of death" marked Libya's sovereign extension, and that all of the gulf south of parallel 32.5 was within Libya's national waters. The United States refrained from any action testing Qaddafi's claim during January, but on March 23, a 30-vessel U.S. task force led by 3 aircraft carriers moved into the area. The next day Libyan batteries fired a number of missiles at U.S. ships and planes. Two U.S. aircraft and a naval cruiser retaliated, sinking two Libyan ships and destroying a missile station on March 25. ***See also*** U.S. RAID ON LIBYA (269).

Significance
Qaddafi claimed victory in having defended the Gulf of Sidra. The United States believed it had put Colonel Qaddafi on notice that it considered him a menace to peace in the region and a prime sponsor of worldwide terrorism. The United States had demonstrated its determination to ply the Mediterranean in accordance with established sea law and that it held Qaddafi's claim to virtually the entire Gulf of Sidra to be unacceptable. Nevertheless, the support Qaddafi received from other Arab and Muslim states disturbed Washington's Western allies. Britain, France, and Italy were unconvinced that the Qaddafi declaration on the Gulf of Sidra required the violent response mounted by the United States. The Gulf of Sidra issue remained to be resolved. More immediately, it precipitated moves and countermoves between Qaddafi and Reagan that escalated tension and produced even more violent results.

Halabjah Atrocity **244**

The Halabjah atrocity involved Iraq's use of poison gas against its own citizens during Baghdad's war with Iran. In mid-March 1988, Iranian forces occupied the Kurdish village of Halabjah in northeastern Iraq. Baghdad accused the Kurds of collaborating with Iran in an effort to undermine the Iraqi war effort. Although Halabjah was later evacuated by the Iranians, Saddam Hussain nevertheless ordered an assault on this village, as well as others in the predominantly Kurdish region. Halabjah, however, was singled out for particular punishment. Chemical weapons, notably cyanide, mustard gas, and nerve agents, were dropped on the village, killing an estimated 5,000 of its inhabitants. Although Baghdad denied the use of unconventional weapons of mass destruction, it had also used poison gas against Iranian troops and there was too much physical evidence to weigh against the official denials. Baghdad also refused to allow a UN investigative team to examine the charge. *See also* ETHNIC ATROCITIES (83); KURDISH ENCLAVE PROPOSAL (90).

Significance

The use of poison gas, essentially for the first time since World War I, and against a country's own citizenry, sent shockwaves throughout the world. The United States and the European Parliament (the legislative body of the European Community) both condemned Baghdad's action, but efforts by the U.S. Congress to legislate economic sanctions against Iraq failed. The Reagan administration had some years earlier removed Iraq from the list of terrorist nations and had quietly tilted in favor of Iraq in its war with Iran. Saddam Hussain was permitted to purchase war-making technology from the United States and handsome credits, estimated to range between $4 and $5 billion, had been made available by the Agriculture Department, thus permitting Iraq to become a major purchaser of U.S. farm products. In general terms, Washington believed it could do business with Saddam Hussain, and the fact that he had ordered the use of chemical weapons against his own people was essentially overlooked.

Hama Massacre **245**

The Hama massacre was perpetuated by Syria's Praetorian Guard, the Siraya al-Difai, then led by Rifaat, a brother of Hafez al-Assad. The Assad regime seized power in 1970 and sustained itself through ruthlessness and unyielding coercion. Assad, a representative of the Shiite Alawite sect, ruled over a predominantly Sunni Muslim population. Because of Assad's minority status, he had to ward off assaults on his authority, especially those emanating from Islamic radicals. As leader of the Syrian Baath Party, Assad projected a secularism disturbing to some of the more ardent members of the orthodox religious community. Armed resistance to Assad's rule began in earnest in 1977 with the assassination of Alawi officials. In 1979, 32 Alawi cadets were murdered in Aleppo. Other operations against government installations took a heavier toll of lives. The Baath regime answered these attacks by assaulting Muslim fundamentalists, especially the Muslim Brotherhood. Membership in the Brotherhood was punishable by death. Observers sensed that nothing less than an armed insurrection was underway. On the night of February 3, 1982, Muslim radicals attacked government police headquarters, Baath Party offices, and military barracks. Approximately 250 "atheists" lost their lives in the assault. The purpose of the Muslim Brotherhood's campaign was to fire the passions of the larger Sunni population and to lead them in a revolution against Hafez al-Assad. Assad, however, had an answer for the rebels. Rifaat's Praetorian Guard, assisted by the air force, unleashed a murderous reign of terror on the city of Hama. When the shelling and bombardment subsided, the city lay in total ruin. Thousands had been killed in the counterblow; some estimates run as high as 25,000. The Muslim Brotherhood was not eradicated in the destruction of Hama, but since the massacre there, Muslim radicalism in Syria lost its voice. *See also* BAATH MOVEMENT: ORIGIN IN SYRIA (116); BAATH MOVEMENT: IRAQ (115); MUSLIM BROTHERHOOD (47); ISLAMIC FUNDAMENTALISM (39); HALABJAH ATROCITY (244).

Significance
The Hama massacre illustrates the violence employed in winning and staying in power in countries like Syria. Iraq, also ruled by the more secular Baath, is another case in point. Saddam Hussain, a Sunni Tikriti, rules over a land predominantly Shiite. Saddam's response to the Shiite Al-Dawa Party was little different from the reaction of Hafez al-Assad to the Muslim Brotherhood. In 1977 a Shiite procession between the two holy cities of Najaf and Karbala in Iraq degenerated into an anti–Saddam Hussain demonstration. Saddam's punishment was swift and heavy. After the fall of the shah, however, and the emergence of a Shiite revolutionary order in Iran, the Al-Dawa of Iraq again asserted itself. The Iraqi Baath government was judged illegal with the establishment of the Shiite *wilayat al-faqih* (rule of the jurist) by the Iraqi Shiite leader Imam Baqir al-Sadr. Tariq Aziz, the only Christian in Saddam Hussain's inner circle, was targeted for death by the Al-Dawa, but he escaped with minor injuries. Saddam Hussain's response, however, led to the execution of the religious leader and his sister, the brutal destruction of members of the Al-Dawa, and the mass expulsion to Iran of 35,000 Iraqi Shiites, who were said to be of Iranian descent. These activities in April 1980 were in major part responsible for the war that Iraq launched against Iran in the autumn of that year.

Iraqi-Kurdish Conflict **246**

The Kurds inhabit a region between Turkey, Iran, and Iraq. Throughout the twentieth century the Kurds have demanded the right to establish an independent Kurdistan, but the countries they inhabit have steadfastly refused to grant their claim. In 1961, the Kurdish leader Mustafa Barazani led a rebellion in northern Iraq that was aimed at forcing the Baghdad government to allow Kurdish self-rule or autonomy. Because of the enmity between Tehran and Baghdad, the shah of Iran encouraged the rebellion and supplied these Kurdish forces with significant stores of weapons and other supplies. Iran also offered sanctuary and training facilities for the Kurds in Iranian Kurdistan. Subsequent Baghdad governments refused to yield to the Kurdish demand, and the fighting was protracted and often intense. By the early 1970s Iraq was estimated to have suffered approximately 60,000 casualties and the Kurds many time that number. In 1971, under great pressure, Baghdad agreed to offer the Kurds autonomy within four years. The Kurds rejoiced over their apparent victory, but later realized that the Baathist government was only purchasing time to improve its military capability. In 1972, Iraq signed a treaty of friendship and cooperation with the Soviet Union, and Moscow helped modernize the Iraqi forces. In 1974, the Iraqi army resumed the war against the Kurds. Baghdad sought to gain the removal of Iranian forces that were sent to aid the Kurdish resistance. Baghdad appealed to its compatriots in Algeria, and President Houari Boumedienne proposed a settlement of the Shatt al-Arab boundary, which the shah had long considered in dispute. The ploy succeeded. President Boumedienne's efforts culminated in a treaty that was signed in Algiers in February 1975. The Iran-Iraq Treaty also sealed the fate of the Kurdish resistance. In return for Baghdad's acceptance of Tehran's claim to the mid-channel of the Shatt al-Arab, the shah agreed to terminate his support for the Kurds, including the denial of sanctuary. The leaders of the Kurdish independent movement, however, were promised asylum in Iran. Without Iranian assistance, the Kurds were placed at the mercy of the Iraqi armed forces, and a massive campaign was mounted that finally broke the back of the rebellion. The Iran-Iraq War (1980–1988) prompted Kurdish elements again to assert their claim to self-determination. Hatred for Saddam Hussain drew some Kurds residing in Iraq to support Iran in the conflict. But Iran's capacity to assist the Kurds was questionable. Moreover, there was the matter of the genuineness of Iranian desire to assist a community that spread across the Iraqi frontier into Iran. Iran also had a history of suppressing Kurdish "independence" movements. Nevertheless, Kurds were identified with Iran during the war, and as that war ground to an end, Baghdad decided to punish its "disloyal" countrymen. The use of poison gas in Halabjah in 1988 was intended as a signal to the Kurds that Saddam Hussain had tired of their duplicity and would mete out severe punishment. Approximately 5,000 men, women, and children died in the chemical attack. Even after the ceasefire with Iran, the Iraqi army moved to corner the Kurdish resistance in the extreme northeastern corner of the country. This campaign forced an estimated 60,000 Kurds to flee across the border to Turkey. But the plight of the Kurds in Iraq, as well as in the larger area of Kurdistan, was never so pronounced as in March–April 1991. The Kurds, seizing the opportunity to declare their independent status in the wake of the Iraqi defeat in Operation Desert Storm, and motivated by the words of President George Bush for the Iraqi people to overthrow Saddam Hussain, quickly took control of the Kurdish region of Iraq. In the belief they would be aided by the U.S.-led coalition in consolidating their gains, the Kurds made threatening gestures in the direction of Baghdad. When the United States and its coalition partners declared it was not their intention to interfere in Iraq's internal affairs, however, the picture for the Kurds dimmed considerably. Given U.S. assurances it would not prevent the Iraqi army from retaking the northern territory, Baghdad sent its legions northward. Unprotected, unsupplied, outmanned, and outgunned, the Kurdish resistance was attacked by Iraqi helicopter gunships and heavy artillery, and Kurdish victory soon turned to defeat and rout. The carnage inflicted on the Kurds by the Iraqi forces surpassed anything experienced in the past. As a consequence, and fearful of untold atrocities if they remained in place, virtually the whole Kurdish nation within Iraq took flight, seeking refuge in either Turkey or Iran, or both. Iran allowed the Kurdish refugees to flood across its frontier. Turkey was more circumspect, and although a few thousand Kurds were allowed to pass, the tens of thousands that sought shelter and asylum were held at the border. The Kurds had fled their homes without food or proper clothing, let alone protection from a pursuing army bent on havoc. *See also* SHATT AL-ARAB (25); KURDS (89); BAATH MOVEMENT: IRAQ (115);

HALABJAH ATROCITY (244); ETHNIC ATROCITIES (83); KURDISH ENCLAVE PROPOSAL (90).

Significance
Iraq has not reconciled the claims of its diverse population. The Kurds historically separate themselves from the Arabs and insist on a lifestyle that reflects their traditions and exclusive codes. Unable to wage effective campaigns against either the Turkish Republic or Iran, the Kurds sought self-determination or at least genuine autonomy in Iraq. The Kurds hoped to exploit specific structural and ideological weaknesses within the Baghdad government. But the emergence of Saddam Hussain as the dominant figure among the Baathists proved to be a turning point. Hussain used both carrot and stick in dealing with the Kurdish movement. After the army destroyed Kurdish resistance, the Baghdad government offered greater political autonomy but refused to tolerate anti-state behavior. Following the death of Mustafa Barazani, Kurdish leaders in Iraq generally supported the Baathists. Moreover, the departure of the shah of Iran appeared to open new opportunities for displays of Kurdish nationalism. Iranian Kurds opposed the revolutionary regime of Ayatollah Khomeini, and a movement for Kurdish independence was ignited in Iran and supported by Iraq. But when Iraq attacked Iran in 1980 the Kurds on both sides of the frontier were confused and disorganized. Iranian successes in the Kurdish region of Iraq seemed to tip the balance, and the Kurds again supported the Iranians against the forces of Saddam Hussain. The consequences of this shift proved tragic for the Kurdish community. Saddam Hussain eventually humbled the Iranians. The Iraqi Kurds were punished with a devastating gas attack on some of their villages while their forces were chased into the mountains. The Kurds guessed wrong again when U.S. forces led an assault on Saddam Hussain in the Gulf War of 1990–1991. Led by a son of Mustafa Barazani, the Kurds were overjoyed when Iraq's army was routed in the Kuwaiti theater of operations. But after accepting a temporary ceasefire from the U.S.-led coalition, Saddam Hussain ordered his best troops to destroy the Shiite uprising in the south and the Kurdish play for independence in the north. The Kurds, like the Shiites, had anticipated U.S. assistance in their campaign against Saddam Hussain. But the United States had already declared victory and had begun the withdrawal of its troops. Washington declared it had no interest in engaging in Iraq's internal disputes. Although the United States prevented Saddam Hussain from using fixed-wing aircraft, he was free to use his helicopter gunships. Moreover, the United States refused to supply the Kurds with the necessary armaments. After initial gains, therefore, the Kurds were again in retreat. This time, however, virtually the entire Iraqi Kurdish population feared for their lives, and hundreds of thousands of refugees sought refuge in Iran, where it was granted, and in Turkey, which was far more reluctant to entertain a large influx of Kurds without a guarantee of outside assistance. The Kurds had suffered their most devastating setback in a century of setbacks. Saddam Hussain, however, had weathered his worst storm.

Iraq-Iran War (1980–1988) 247

The historical enmity between Iranians and Iraqis was again dramatized when Baghdad moved its forces across the Shatt al-Arab frontier in September 1980. Iraq and Iran agreed to a treaty in 1975 establishing the navigable channel on the Shatt al-Arab as the official boundary between their two countries. Iraq, however, long had considered the entire waterway as falling within its jurisdiction, and the agreement recognizing Iran's demand was entered into reluctantly and under considerable pressure. The shah's demise in 1979 and the emergence of a revolutionary government in Iran apparently provoked Baghdad to regain control over all the Shatt al-Arab. Iraq also renewed its claim to Iranian Khuzistan, which Baghdad consistently referred to as Arabistan. The Iraqi invasion was in part provoked by the call of Ayatollah Khomeini to his Shiite brethren in Iraq that they should unite with him in ridding the Muslim world of nonbelievers. To Khomeini, the Iraq Baath Party was alien to Islam, and its leader, Saddam Hussain, was described as a corruption of the Muslim faith. A Sunni Muslim, Saddam Hussain was challenged by internal unrest. The majority of Iraq's Muslims were Shiite and they had periodically demonstrated their dissatisfaction with the Baghdad regime. Saddam Hussain was also an ambitious personality. His vision involved leading the Arab world, and Iran's chaotic state in the aftermath of revolution was considered to be Iraq's invitation to greatness. By exploiting Iran's divisive movements, Iraq expected to become the dominant power on the Persian Gulf. Moreover, its Soviet-equipped war machine was judged by some observers to be the best in the Arab states. The Baathist leader had good reason to believe that his armed forces would cut through Iranian ranks and achieve a relatively quick victory. Iraqi troops were initially successful in establishing their presence in Khuzistan (Arabistan), but after seizing the port of Khorramshahr, their advance stalled in the streets of Abadan, Awaz, and other major metropolitan centers. Seeing that the Iranians were still capable of mobilizing reserves, the Iraqis consolidated their gains and appeared to accept a temporary stalemate. On the one hand, the Iraqis believed they could wear down Iranian forces. The revolutionary government had executed a large number of officers, and thousands of troops had deserted their units. On the other hand, the Iraqis expected the Arabs of Khuzistan (the dominant ethnic group in the province) to welcome them as liberators and to join them in common struggle against the Persians. Iraq was also determined to seal its border with Iran and to curtail efforts by the *mullahs,* Iran's religious leaders, to foment unrest among Iraqi Shiites. Efforts by individual Muslim and European leaders as well as representatives from the Muslim Conference and the United Nations to mediate the conflict were fruitless. Iraq publicized its intention to accept a compromise settlement, but Iran insisted that no negotiations were possible until all the Iraqis withdrew from Iranian territory. Apparently able to obtain additional military stores to replenish their forces (it is rumored that Israel and the Soviet Union played a role in funneling supplies to Iran), the Iranians launched a major counter-offensive in March 1982. Using thousands of Pasderan, the ayatollah's Revolutionary Guards, the Iranians drove the Iraqis from their fortified positions. But rather than use regular troops to slow the Iranian advance, Hussain despatched to the front a relatively inexperienced, hastily trained force consisting of non-Iraqis domiciled in the country. The Iranians swept through these units, decimating their ranks and taking thousands of prisoners. Again Saddam Hussain called for a ceasefire, but again the ayatollah rejected the offer. In June, Iraqi troops were forced to give up Khorramshahr and retreat behind their own frontier. The Iranians, however, were encouraged to maintain the pressure and to punish the Iraqis and the

Baathist government for their original act of aggression. Khomeini declared that his Islamic army would not cease their operations until Saddam Hussain was destroyed. Efforts by the Pasderan and the Iranian army to breach regular Iraqi positions, however, were neutralized. The Iraqis took a heavy toll of the Iranian invaders, but there was little indication that the war would taper off. Unconditional surrender continued to be the ayatollah's policy. The tide of war flowed to one side and then the other. The years passed, however, without a decisive battle being fought. Frustrated, Iraq opened an assault on ships moving between Iran and the open sea via the Persian Gulf. In time these attacks, known as the "Tanker Wars," involved vessels in innocent passage from a variety of seaports and a number of countries. Kuwaiti oil tankers were especially vulnerable, and the emir asked for international assistance in countering the actions, especially when Iran followed the Iraqi initiative. The Soviet Union was the first superpower to answer Kuwait's distress signal. But the United States moved into the gulf with the purpose of reflagging a number of Kuwaiti vessels and manning them with U.S. crews. The U.S. naval presence in the gulf also expanded between 1986 and 1988. With a stalemate prevailing on land, the Iran-Iraq War focused on the waters of the gulf. To a degree the war had been internationalized. It was also Washington's decision to "tilt" in favor of Iraq. Iraq was removed from the list of terrorist states, and Baghdad was able to secure assistance and purchases of war materiel from the United States and other Western nations. More significant, the United States used its naval forces to attack Iranian gunboats and destroy Iranian oil rigs in the waterway. But the most important action involved the accidental shooting down of an Iranian passenger airliner on a scheduled flight between Iran and the United Arab Emirates. On July 3, 1988, the U.S. Navy cruiser *Vincennes* fired on the aircraft, destroying it and killing the 290 passengers. Iran tried to get the United Nations to condemn the United States but failed in the effort. Then, on July 18, in a surprise letter to the UN secretary-general, Iran agreed to accept UN Resolution 598, which called for a ceasefire between Iran and Iraq. The next day the Ayatollah Khomeini publicly took responsibility for the action, noting his decision was "more bitter than taking poison." The ceasefire went into effect on August 20, and on August 25 the two sides had their first talks since the war began. Negotiations on formally ending the war were strained and the talks over the Shatt al-Arab proved fruitless until after Iraq's invasion of Kuwait in August 1990. Under pressure from the U.S.-led coalition in Operation Desert Shield, Saddam Hussain surprised the world by agreeing to all the Iranian demands. Iraq removed its forces from territory claimed by Iran, Iran's use of the Shatt al-Arab was acknowledged in the context of the 1975 treaty, and prisoners of war were exchanged. For all intents and purposes, the war between Iran and Iraq was over. ***See also*** OSIRAK (259); ISLAMIC CONFERENCE (211); REFLAGGING: KUWAIT (265); "TANKER WARS" (267); VINCENNES TRAGEDY (270); IRAQ-KUWAIT: WAR AND CONQUEST (248).

Significance

The collapse of the shah's regime ushered in a period of widespread chaos in Iran. The *mullah*-dominated revolutionary government of Ayatollah Khomeini faced insurrection among the minorities of Iran and sometimes aggressive competition from organized political groups, the *mujahiddin*, and, to a lesser extent, the National Front. Moreover, after the Soviet Union's invasion of Afghanistan in December 1979, Saddam Hussain perceived an opportunity not only to reclaim Iraqi irredenta, but also to establish Iraq as the preeminent country in the gulf and throughout the Arab world. Iraqi success in its military campaign in Iranian Khuzistan, rich in petroleum reserves, would not only provide Baghdad with geopolitical advantages, but also could make Iraq an oil-exporting giant comparable to Saudi Arabia. Baghdad's failure to subdue the Iranians, however, caused serious repercussions in Baghdad and in other areas of the Middle East. Israel, for example, destroyed Iraq's nuclear reactor in June 1981. It also assaulted the PLO and Syrians in Lebanon in 1982, meaning that neither Iraq nor Iran could provide assistance for the beleaguered Palestinians. The war also had a profound effect on the Iranian revolution as it helped to dissipate opposition to the Khomeini regime. More over, it gave new importance to the Iranian armed forces. Although internally Iran remained a potential powder keg, the war demonstrated a curious balance between the country's different ethnic, tribal, and ideological groups. In fact, the war allowed the revolutionaries in Iran to consolidate their power. Opposition to their authority was neutralized or eliminated altogether. The smooth transition of political leadership following the death of Ayatollah Khomeini also illustrated the power wielded by the Iranian *mullahs.* Iraq received less than it sought in making war on Iran, but the venture seemed only to whet Saddam Hussain's appetite. His conquest of Kuwait in August 1990 was supposed to give Baghdad control over the gulf and its vast oil reserves. Iran was in no position to prevent the annexation of Kuwait, and Iraq loomed as the supreme player in the region's balance of power. The threat Saddam Hussain posed to Saudi Arabia and the other gulf oil producers, however, could not go unnoticed. And whereas the United States had "tilted" in favor of Iraq in its war with Iran, the United States was not eager to see Baghdad spread its influence beyond its recognized frontiers. Saddam Hussain gambled on international paralysis in the Kuwaiti takeover. Washington, however, was again prepared to shift its policy, not toward favoring Iran, but to prevent Saddam Hussain from weakening the Arabian Peninsula kingdoms and monopolizing the area's petroleum supplies.

Iraq-Kuwait: War and Conquest 248

Iraq invaded Kuwait on August 2, 1990, and promptly subdued the Kuwaiti armed forces, compelling the Kuwaiti emir, Shaykh Jaber al-Sabah, to seek refuge in Saudi Arabia, where he established his government-in-exile. In the meantime, Saddam Hussain, the president and maximum ruler of Iraq, declared Kuwait's annexation and its reestablishment as Iraq's nineteenth province. The Iraqi leader declared Iraq would never return to the status quo ante, that Kuwait had always been a part of Iraq, and that the British had created the emirate with a view to sustaining Arab divisions. Iraq's aggressive move against Kuwait shocked the world community. It also activated the UN Security Council, which in a display of rare unity among its permanent members condemned Baghdad's action and proceeded to pass a number of resolutions demanding the withdrawal of Iraqi forces and the reinstatement of the emir's government. Iraq rejected each resolution, several of which involved economic sanctions. The UN effort was led by the United States, which, sensing a threat to the other gulf kingdoms, began to dispatch forces to the region. A major buildup of U.S. military personnel was begun in Saudi Arabia. President Bush initially said the troops were being sent to Saudi Arabia to prevent possible Iraqi aggression. As the months passed, however, and Saddam Hussain indicated no intention of withdrawing his forces from Kuwait, the U.S. defensive strategy escalated into one calling for offensive capacity. To support the possibility of offensive action against Iraqi forces in Kuwait, the United States sought and obtained a UN resolution permitting the use of force in ousting Iraq from Kuwait after January 15, 1991. The UN involvement gave the U.S. military presence in the gulf international character. Joining U.S. forces were British and French units. The naval armada charged with preventing seaborne cargo from leaving or reaching Iraq was composed of ships from a host of nations. On the ground and also described as part of the international force were troops from Pakistan, Egypt, Syria, and the Gulf Cooperation Council. Although Turkey did not send troops to Saudi Arabia, its forces were mobilized and reinforced along its southern border with Iraq. NATO ordered 42 fighter-bombers to Turkey in January 1991 to bolster Turkish defenses, but the Soviet Union, although supporting the UN resolutions, refused to send any troops to the area. Opposition to the United Nations and the predominantly U.S. force (approximately 325,000 troops by the end of 1990) in the gulf region came from the Palestine Liberation Organization, which supported Baghdad, and from Jordan, Yemen, and the Sudan, which criticized Iraq's invasion of Kuwait but nevertheless sustained good relations with Baghdad. *See also* NINETEENTH PROVINCE (21); UN RESOLUTIONS: IRAQ-KUWAIT CONFLICT (230).

Significance

The Iraqi conquest of Kuwait was aimed at expanding Iraq's control of the world's exportable oil. With Kuwait fields under Iraqi control, Baghdad's oil kingdom rivalled that of the Saudis and gave it management over 22 percent of known worldwide oil reserves. It was also meant to precipitate changes within the Arabian shaykhdoms and kingdoms, especially Saudi Arabia, changes that would ultimately lead to the collapse of the reigning Arab monarchies. The Iraqi Baathists, led by Saddam Hussain al-Tikrit, were perceived pressing for revolutionary alterations in the political geography of the region that would change the balance of power in the Middle East and beyond.

The Bush administration held this view and its military response was geared to reverse the process before it proceeded further. The Israelis seemed to draw a similar conclusion, and although urged to maintain a low profile by Washington, they believed they were the ultimate target of Saddam Hussain. The British were also outspoken on the matter of Iraqi aggression against Kuwait, and they stood with Washington in the effort to pressure Saddam Hussain to withdraw his forces before the January 15, 1991, deadline. Other countries, however, irrespective of their support for the UN resolutions, seemed less eager to press the Iraqis to the point of war. Many countries condemned the aggression. France sent troops, and Japan provided some minor materiel as well as a cash contribution to help pay for the military buildup, but they and a host of others were determined to find a diplomatic solution to the crisis. U.S. public opinion was divided, but those calling for a peaceful settlement were more readily heard. Some prominent members of the U.S. Congress insisted on patience and thought it wise to give the UN-authorized economic sanctions more time to undermine Iraqi resolve. Many self-appointed "mediators" went to Iraq to meet with Saddam Hussain. At first, their efforts were believed instrumental in gaining the release of hundreds of the several thousand foreign "hostages" detained by the Iraqi regime, many of whom were described as "human shields." Iraq, however, released all the foreign hostages when they found the moment propitious, and when more value could be derived from letting them go than by holding them.

An early beneficiary of the confrontation in the gulf was Iran, Iraq's mortal enemy of the 1980s. Iraq released Iranian prisoners of war. Baghdad also returned all the Iranian territory seized during the recent war. As a consequence, and because Iran refused to sanction the presence of U.S. forces in the gulf region, Tehran seemed to offer Iraq solace if not direct support. Most important, Iraq believed it unnecessary to maintain a sizable force on its border with Iran, and those troops were redeployed on the Kuwaiti front where the U.S.-led international force seemed most threatening. Moreover, although the economic blockade had begun to pinch, it had not caused Iraq to reconsider its conquest of Kuwait. And not to be ignored, Iraq was able to trade with Iran on the one side and Jordan on the other, and through these nations with third countries who continued to supply Baghdad with many of the items necessary for its pursuits. At the end of December 1990, for example, the U.S. government informed the German government that approximately 50 German companies continued to do business with Iraq after the August embargo and that some of these transactions involved the development of Iraq's nuclear weapons program.

Israeli-PLO War, 1982 **249**

The Israeli-PLO War of 1982 was Israel's longest since the 1948–1949 Arab-Israeli conflict. On June 6, 1982, Israel moved the bulk of its armor across the Lebanese frontier in a concerted drive to destroy the Palestine Liberation Organization (PLO) based in Lebanon. The spark that ignited the conflagration was the attempted assassination of the Israeli ambassador to Great Britain on June 3. But the campaign was a long time in planning and had been threatened on several previous occasions. Ever since the PLO was forced to flee Jordan in 1970, Lebanon had become its main base of operations against Israel. The PLO had played a major role in the Lebanese Civil War, which erupted in 1975, and although prevented by Syria from crushing the Lebanese Phalange, the guerrillas had seized a number of Lebanon's cities, towns, and villages and had erected an elaborate headquarters in West Beirut. From their positions in the south, the PLO could train their guns and rockets on villages in northern Israel. Terrorist infiltration of Israel by land and sea from these bases was also a constant source of difficulty for the Israelis. The forcible ouster of Lebanese from their homes in the south drove some of them to seek the assistance of the Israelis, and a former officer in the Lebanese army, Major Saad Haddad, worked openly with Israel to create a 600-square-mile (1,550-square-kilometer) southern buffer zone between the PLO forces and the frontier. In 1978, after a series of infiltrations by PLO commandos, and following numerous shelling incidents of Israeli territory by PLO artillery, Israel crossed into southern Lebanon and pushed the PLO back across the Litani River, approximately 18 miles (29 kilometers) from the Israeli border. When Israeli forces were withdrawn, several thousand UN peacekeeping troops were posted in the area, but the PLO reinfiltrated the region and again took up positions menacingly close to Israel. Repeated Israeli counterstrikes, particularly in the form of air attacks, failed to neutralize the PLO. In 1980–1981, Syria began an elaborate emplacement of ground-to-air missile batteries in Lebanon's Bekaa Valley. This weapons system was described as a counter to future Israeli air strikes and thus provided added protection to the PLO in southern Lebanon. The Israeli government spoke of an escalation in the level of terror as a consequence of the Syrian action, and when it threatened to destroy the Soviet-built installations, Washington, fearing a larger conflict, sent Philip Habib to the region to negotiate a reduction in tension. As a result of Habib's mission, Israel received pledges of a ceasefire from its adversaries, and the Israelis agreed to leave the missile base intact. But few promises are kept in the Middle East, and this series of understandings was no different. Repeated violations of the ceasefire precipitated the full-scale Israeli invasion of Lebanon that began in June 1982. Initially, the Israeli advance was described as limited; its stated objective was the removal of PLO contingents in a 25- to 30-mile (40- to 48-kilometer) zone in southern Lebanon. The Israelis swept past the UN peacekeeping force and attacked the PLO coastal cities of Tyre and Sidon, as well as the inland fortifications at Beaufort Castle, Nabatiyah, and Hesbeya. Given their superiority in arms and men, the Israelis quickly overran these bases, but instead of pausing, they continued their strike north through Damur and Khalde, to Beirut itself. Other Israeli columns pushed through Lebanon's central region, eventually flanking the Bekaa Valley on the one side and cutting the Beirut to Damascus Highway on the other. The latter Israeli contingents moved into East Beirut, controlled by the Christian Phalange, and were greeted as liberators by many of the inhabitants. Israel had cautioned Syria to stay out of the fighting, despite the garrisoning of Syrian forces in the country. When Syrian aircraft challenged the Israelis, a number of air battles were fought, with the Syrians coming out on the losing end each time. As the war dragged on Syria came to play less and less of a role, although several thousand of its troops fought alongside the PLO in West Beirut and many thousands more were garrisoned in the Bekaa Valley and in northern Lebanon. Although other Arab countries repeatedly condemned the Israeli action, none joined the struggle. Iran dispatched several hundred volunteers to Syria early in the war, but the Iran-Iraq War continued to drain precious reserves, and the Ayatollah Khomeini was constrained to keep his troops at home. From the middle of June through the summer months, the war settled into a quasi-military, quasi-political standoff. The mainline forces of the PLO, estimated at between 6,000 and 12,000 men, were secreted in a maze of underground tunnels and gun emplacements in West Beirut. The Israelis completely ringed the area, controlling the sea as well as the land approaches to and from West Beirut. Overhead, the Israeli Air Force was unopposed. The Israelis declared that their objective was the "expulsion" of the PLO from Beirut and Lebanon to other countries. If the PLO refused to leave West Beirut, however, the Israelis were prepared to force them out. Philip Habib was again pressed into service by the Reagan administration and asked to find a diplomatic solution to the crisis. The U.S. purpose was to gain the removal of all foreign forces from Lebanon—PLO, Syrian, and Israeli—and to permit the Lebanese to reconstitute their government and rehabilitate their state after almost seven years of unending tragedy. The U.S. diplomatic initiative promised to limit the hostilities; it also provided the PLO with an opportunity to dramatize its cause. As a consequence, the conflict was protracted, not quickly terminated. The Israelis argued that the PLO was using the negotiations to prolong its stay in Lebanon, and despite repeated U.S. government pleas that ceasefires be observed, the Israeli high command, led by Defense Minister Ariel Sharon, increased the pressure on the trapped PLO forces. West Beirut was inhabited by several hundred thousand people, and the Israeli shelling and bombing took a heavy toll of life and property. Moreover, no conflict since the Vietnam War was covered so minutely by the media, and especially by the video camera. The plight of the innocent victims of the war was televised throughout the world on a daily basis. With every picture of the maimed and dead, the rubble and decay, Israel lost what little moral support it still retained at the outset of the fighting. In the United States, Israel's only constant supporter, polls revealed a shift away from continuing assistance to Israel. Time and again the media reminded Americans that the Begin government had embarrassed President Reagan and had undermined U.S. relations with Arab and other Muslim nations. There were also increasing signs of anti-Semitism in Europe as hatred for Israel developed into attacks on European Jewry. Israel's political and diplomatic loss was judged a PLO victory. Thus, despite the hopelessness of its military position in West Beirut and its forced withdrawal in August 1982, the PLO had grown, not diminished, in stature. *See also* PALESTINE LIBERATION ORGANIZATION (PLO) (137); REAGAN PROGRAM ON PALESTINE (177); WEST BEIRUT MASSACRE (187).

Significance

The Israeli-PLO War of 1982 reveals the following consequences:

1. It was fought on two fronts, military and political/diplomatic. Israel won the military engagement. The PLO was the clear victor in the political/diplomatic contest. Israel purchased short-term security, but it was placed under greater pressure to satisfy the Palestinian demand for a national home.
2. Israeli-U.S. relations were severely strained by the conflict, and the U.S. government felt justified in emphasizing its ties to the Arab world while reducing its commitment to Israel.
3. The Soviet Union used the conflict to expand its recruitment of young Marxists in the Middle East who were even more opposed to the traditional regimes because of their seeming inaction in the Lebanon crisis.
4. Although the PLO was beaten in Lebanon, it was far from finished. Indeed, the PLO claimed a major victory, having held off the Israelis longer than the formal Arab armies in the 1956, 1967, and 1973 wars. Moreover, the PLO was in a position to increase the level of international terrorism. It had also gained considerable respect in circles that until then had ignored its existence. The PLO was now able to deal directly with many governments. While the PLO could not overcome the superior military capability of the Israelis, it was in a formidable position to make life difficult for relatively unstable Arab regimes. The United States had a genuine interest in satisfying the demand for a separate Palestine state, especially if it meant lifting the pressure on those Arab countries important to Washington. President Reagan's September 1 proposal for the establishment of a self-governing Palestine entity in association with Jordan was aimed at placing greater pressure on Israel. When Lebanese president-elect Bashir Gemayel was assassinated on September 14, the Israelis moved their armored columns into West

Beirut. On September 17, 1982, the UN Security Council unanimously voted to condemn the Israeli maneuver and to order Israeli forces out of the former PLO stronghold. The departure of PLO units had left the Palestinians, especially those in the refugee camps, without protection. Although Israel justified its occupation of West Beirut on grounds of preventing more intense sectarian strife, it also used the opportunity to destroy Lebanese Muslim resistance units like the Murabitun. Assisting the Israelis in their action were Phalange militias such as that under the leadership of Major Saad Haddad. On September 18 word quickly spread around the world that Palestinian refugees residing in the camps had been taken from their homes by Phalange troops and summarily executed. Although the Israelis admitted having given the Christian militias the opportunity to penetrate the camps, they insisted that their mission was strictly military and that they were supposed to eliminate remaining pockets of PLO resistance. The revelation that noncombatants had been slaughtered, including women and children, sent waves of indignation throughout the world. The destruction of the U.S. embassy in Beirut by terrorists associated with the PLO, and the heavy loss of life, by contrast, caused little public outcry. Despite efforts to pacify the country, Lebanon remained divided, occupied by a variety of armies, and subject to uncontrolled violence.

Lebanese Civil War (1975–1976) 250

The Lebanese Civil War began on April 13, 1975, when violence erupted in Beirut between members of the Christian-Maronite Lebanese Phalange and commandos of the Palestine Liberation Organization. In the next 18 months Lebanon, and especially Beirut, was torn apart. The conflict was not simply that of Lebanese versus non-Lebanese. The complicated demography that is Lebanon produced numerous contests of strength, the lines of which were seldom definable. Lebanon's citizens were not formed into a coherent community, despite the post–World War II success of its economy. When France withdrew from the country, it left behind a political structure that seemed to program the Lebanese for internecine struggle. An indication of the depth of disagreement within Lebanese society surfaced in 1958, when the president of Lebanon, Camille Chamoun, called upon the United States to intervene in his country's affairs to save his government and maintain the delicate balance of forces in the country. President Eisenhower responded affirmatively to the request, and U.S. Marines landed on the shores of Beirut to calm an unstable situation. Conflicts between competing powerful Christian families, between the Maronite Phalange and the Druze community, between the Phalange and the Muslim Lebanese, or between ideologically conservative and radical forces were daily occurrences.

The intervention of the PLO into this highly volatile situation brought all of these rivalries to a head. The PLO had been forced from Jordan in 1970. In desperation, and with Syrian assistance, their headquarters was reestablished in Beirut, and Lebanon became the PLO's chief training ground, its principal supply depot, and a most advantageous geomilitary position from which to strike at Israel. The PLO could not satisfy its needs, however, until it had neutralized the Phalange and, in so doing, the Lebanese government. Thus, the PLO became the catalyst for a new round of fighting between competing groups. Moreover, by shifting its weight to the Lebanese Muslims, to the leftists, and to the Druze, the PLO more or less guaranteed the success of their venture. The Phalange, however, was not likely to yield its prominent role in Lebanese affairs without a struggle, and the civil war was the direct outcome of this jockeying for position. From the outset of the fighting, the PLO hoped to exploit differences within the Phalange. The powerful Christian Maronite families of Lebanon were historical rivals, and playing one off against the other was one technique employed to neutralize the Phalange. Indeed, the PLO remained in the background until January 1976, when the Maronites laid siege to the Palestinian refugee camps of Tall al-Zatar and Jisr al-Bash. The Palestinians in the camps struck back at the Phalange forces, while another PLO force hit the Maronites from the rear. The regular Lebanese army came to the aid of the Phalange, and the fighting quickly escalated. The intensification of fighting between Maronites and Palestinians precipitated hostilities on all lines where partition between the opposed forces was possible. In the northern sector of the country there was conflict between the Muslims and Palestinians of Tripoli and the Maronites of Zgharta. In the Bekaa sector, the Zahleh front was opened, and Palestinian reinforcements arrived from Syria to join in the siege of the Christian enclave. In the Baalbek region, Shiite Muslim Lebanese and Palestinians surrounded the Maronite villages and destroyed most of them. In Akkar, Sunni tribesmen of al-Funaydiq, supported by Syrian-backed Palestinians of the Saiqa commandos, attacked both Maronite and Greek Orthodox hamlets, laying them waste. Maronites and Palestinians also fought over Damur and finally in the outskirts and then in the heart of Beirut. Soon the entire country was engulfed. Government ceased to operate. The Lebanese army and security force could not maintain law and order, and riotous mobs assaulted government buildings, destroying records and setting the buildings ablaze. Prisons were raided and the detainees were released. In the prevailing anarchy the criminal element added their measure of terror to an already disastrous situation. The Lebanese government of Suleiman Faranjiyya turned to the Syrians for assistance. Former president Chamoun opposed Syrian intervention, however, arguing that Damascus had permitted the Palestinians to invade Lebanon in the first place and therefore Syria was already a party to a conflict it was supposed to mediate. Chamoun insisted that the UN Security Council should be informed of the Palestinian invasion from Syria. In Washington, Paris, and several Arab capitals, verbal approval had already been expressed for Syrian intervention. Chamoun could not even muster support for his position from among the other Maronite leaders. All were convinced that only Syria could rectify an already intolerable situation. The Maronites had suffered severe losses and by January 24, 1976, except for East Beirut and the Maronite sector of Mount Lebanon, which extended from Matn to a little beyond Zgharta and from the coast to Zahleh, the whole country had fallen under Palestinian military occupation and, indirectly, under Syrian control. The Palestinians worked to reestablish law and order, and they undertook to enforce the ceasefire (the thirty-third since the civil war began) on all fronts. Chamoun finally agreed to join the other Maronite Phalangists in accepting formal Syrian intervention. When the Syrians moved into Lebanon in force, they found the Palestinians entrenched in key positions and reluctant to assume subordinate posts. Syria, however, had no intention of permitting the

Palestinians a free hand in Lebanon, and the two sides soon engaged in a bloody encounter that took a heavy toll on both sides. The Syrians wanted to sustain the Phalange. The Palestinians and the Lebanese leftists wanted the Phalange destroyed. The two points of view could not be reconciled, and the result was an epochal clash that shattered the latest ceasefire and raised the intensity of the fighting. Despite heavy losses, the Syrian army eventually brought the PLO under its influence, and Damascus played broker between the Maronites, the other Lebanese communities, and the Palestinians. The civil war began to subside in November 1976, but intermittent fighting continued into the 1980s. In 1977, the dead were estimated to be around 60,000; several hundred thousand had been wounded. The once-thriving state was a jumble of rubble. The Lebanese army had disintegrated. The economy had been destroyed, and the once-important business and financial establishments had transferred their headquarters to more tranquil areas in the Middle East and elsewhere. An Arab peacekeeping force was assembled for duty in the country, but Syria supplied the bulk of its force. After an Israeli raid into southern Lebanon in 1978, the United Nations Interim Force in Lebanon (UNIFIL) was stationed in the south, supposedly to keep the PLO and the Israelis from attacking one another. The war brought tragedy and grief to Lebanon, but the country was not at peace. The Israeli invasion of Lebanon in June 1982 reaffirmed this fact. ***See also*** ISRAELI-PLO WAR, 1982 (249); PHALANGES LIBANAISES (138); MARONITES (92); LEBANESE NATIONAL MOVEMENT (133); CAIRO AGREEMENT, 1969 (200).

Significance

The Lebanese Civil War of 1975–1976 destroyed the only experimental democracy in the Arab Middle East. Although a country full of contradictions as well as religious, ethnic, and ideological rivalries, Lebanon before the civil war could be characterized as a working democracy because it provided a forum for Arabs from every country. It was a place where they could meet and mix freely, where they could exchange ideas as well as services. Often described as the "Switzerland of the Middle East," it permitted unrestricted contacts with the outer world. According to a native of the region: "In the Arab world, Lebanon was the only country where an Arab, wherever he came from, could feel completely at home. Issues of general Arab interest were openly debated in the Lebanese Press, which came to be recognized as the "'parliament' of Arabism." Lebanon, notes the observer, was "a free pan-Arab capital." All this ceased to exist in the aftermath of the bloodshed and destruction of 1975–1976. Lebanon instead became an armed camp, divided between the PLO, the Syrians, and the Phalange. The Phalange was isolated and merely tolerated once Damascus consolidated its hold on the country. The eventual restoration of relations between the PLO and Damascus concentrated all power in Syrian hands. The Lebanese government of Elias Sarkis, approved by the Syrians, was merely a symbol of authority; it was powerless to affect events, and it could not manage the fragmented nation. In essence, Lebanon was transformed into a vast military base from which to launch attacks against Israel. It was the temporary home for the PLO and several hundred thousand Palestinians who endeavored to maintain ties with their brethren in the occupied West Bank and Gaza territories. It also became a training ground and staging area for international terrorists and radical movements determined to change the world by force. The withdrawal, under Israeli military pressure, of PLO and Syrian units from West Beirut in August 1982 appeared to herald the end of the civil war. But a tragic illustration that the conflict had merely subsided, not ended, was the assassination of Bashir Gemayel, the Phalangist president-elect who was to succeed Elias Sarkis, on September 23, 1982. Gemayel's election in August "under the guns of the Israeli army" had been publicly denounced by his Muslim and Druze opposition. Considered an intimate of the Israelis, Gemayel was unacceptable to most non-Christians. His death appeared to shatter what little possibility Lebanon had of bridging its many rivalries. Similarly, Syria's reluctance to accept the agreement entered into by the Lebanese government and Israel in May 1983 illustrated the difficulty of resurrecting a coherent political environment in the strife-torn country.

Lebanon Civil War: The Prolonged Middle Stage, 1983–1991 251

The Amal movement, organized and supported by Syria, represented the most potent force in Beirut following the Israeli withdrawal. Moreover, the civil war in Lebanon centered around the capacity of the Shiite Amal, led by Nabih Berri, and allied with the Druze Progressive Socialist Party, to gain the upper hand over the other factions, especially the Sunni Murabitun which had been weakened by the Israelis earlier. The Murabitun took punishing losses in the streets of Beirut in 1985, but the excesses of the Shiite Amal harmed the Amal's relationship with the Druze. When the Amal attacked the Palestinian camps, supposedly to prevent Yasir Arafat from regaining influence in Beirut, Druze forces permitted elements of the PLO to use their mountain strongpoints to target Amal units. The "war of the camps" took a heavy toll of lives. By 1988 it was estimated that almost 3,000 had died. Some observers said the body count was much higher. The conflict was described as a Shiite-Palestinian conflict, and it represented the most significant combat in and around Beirut following the Israeli penetration of Lebanon in 1982. On January 20, 1988, Syria moved to terminate the conflict. It ordered the Amal and other Shiite elements to withdraw and allow Syrian troops to assume their positions around the camps of Shatila and Burj al-Barajneh. Amal lifted its blockade of other Palestinian encampments in other areas of Lebanon at the same time. Syria indicated by its actions it was ready to consolidate its gains in Lebanon, and it systematically went about the business of eliminating all opposition to its rule. Syria still had to contend with Amal-Hizbollah rivalry but here it was prepared to allow Amal greater latitude. Hizbollah, although Shiite, was a fundamentalist organization supported by Iran. Amal was by contrast secular, an agent of Damascus. Hizbollah nevertheless put up stiff resistance and even defeated Amal in several encounters. Hizbollah came to hold a long section of the Green Line separating Muslim West Beirut from Christian East Beirut. Damascus used its good offices in Tehran to mediate this conflict and with Iran's blessing Syrian forces were able to replace Hizbollah units. Nabih Berri, under Syrian pressure, and as part of the deal worked out with Tehran, agreed to disband his militia in all but southern Lebanon, where Syrian writ did not carry. ***See also*** LEBANON CIVIL WAR: THE CONCLUDING PHASE (252); PLO IN SOUTHERN LEBANON (175); HIZBOLLAH (130).

Significance

Damascus had neutralized some of the principal contenders for power in Lebanon. It now turned its attention to the Christian units and factions that kept the Lebanese civil war in motion. By 1990–1991 Syrian troops eliminated the last Christian obstacle when the forces of Michel Aoun were defeated and the latter's claim to the Lebanese presidency was denied. In April 1991, the last chapter in the Lebanese civil war was about to begin. The 1969 Cairo Agreement, which allowed PLO forces to organize in strength in Lebanon, was virtually rescinded. Palestinians in Lebanon, especially members of the PLO, were authorized to disarm by the Lebanese government of Elias Hrawi. Palestinians, it was argued, would no longer be permitted to stand outside the law. Nabih Berri, who had joined Hrawi's cabinet and had long been a nemesis of the PLO, insisted that what applied to Lebanese also applied to Palestinians. Deriding the PLO for resisting the call to disarm, another minister noted that Palestinian guns had "not liberated one inch of Palestine for the past 16 years." Other officials echoed the same sentiments, noting the new Lebanese government had had enough of war and violence and preferential treatment would not be provided any community, let alone the Palestinians.

Lebanon Civil War: The Concluding Phase 252

In August 1990 the Lebanese parliament adopted the first basic changes in the country's constitution since its independence 47 years earlier. President Elias Hrawi, a Christian, said the changes were an "historic achievement." Prime Minister Selim al-Hoss noted that "a new epoch has begun in Lebanon." The Shiite speaker of the house called the changes the "best tidings." Summing up the elation after years of conflict, Voice of the Homeland, a Muslim radio station, declared "the Second Lebanese Republic has been born." The new order replaced the power-sharing system established by the French in 1943, which favored the Christian community in both executive and legislative positions. Whereas the Christians would continue to hold the presidency, the substance of political power had shifted to the cabinet composed half of Muslims and half of Christians. The Muslim prime minister was now required by law to countersign all decrees issued by the president. Seats in the parliament were to be divided equally between Christians and Muslims, replacing the previous six-to-five distribution in favor of the former. The arrangements had been agreed to in a meeting in Taif, Saudi Arabia, some 10 months earlier, but their implementation had been delayed by the intensity of the civil war that had flared in January 1990. That war had been perpetuated by General Michel Aoun, who regarded himself as head of the Lebanese state. Aoun's claim revolved around the inability to find a successor to Amin Gemayel, whose term expired in 1988. Aoun's fortunes, however, disintegrated following the Iraqi invasion of Kuwait in August 1990 and Baghdad's inability to sustain him. Syrian forces moved against Aoun in force, defeating his troops and taking numerous prisoners. Aoun, however, fled to the French embassy, where he sought and received refuge. Aoun's most loyal troops, estimated to be about 800 men, were disarmed by the Syrians and all were summarily executed. Damascus revealed its intention to remain in Lebanon but it signalled President Hrawi to direct his attention at the warring factions that continued to disturb the peace. Hrawi called for the disarming of the various militias, particularly the PLO, insisting there was no longer any room in Lebanon for "a state within a state." *See also* LEBANONIZATION (253).

Significance

The Syrians used the cover of Iraq's invasion of Kuwait not so much to allow the Lebanon government, installed by Damascus, to implement the Taif reforms, but rather to put Syria's indelible imprint on Lebanon. Damascus decided against annexing Lebanon in light of world reaction to Baghdad's annexation of Kuwait, but with the crushing of Aoun, Damascus established itself as the undisputed master of all of Lebanon with the exception of the Israeli-controlled region south of the Litani River. Syria's all-out campaign against Aoun brought an end to a civil war that had ravaged Lebanon since 1975. Subsequent to the Syrian victory, the warring factions within Beirut agreed to withdraw their armed brigades, and for the first time in 15 years the Lebanese population experienced a period of peace. Syria's decision to join the coalition against Iraq also enabled Damascus to consolidate its gains and to realize a part of its quest for a Greater Syria. Thus, far more was involved in the Lebanese political reforms than the rearrangement of power between Lebanese communities. With Saudi and possibly also U.S. agreement, Syria was the acknowledged keeper of Lebanon's equilibrium. Indeed, President George Bush's visit with Hafez al-Assad in Damascus in November 1990, and Syria's "positive" attitude during Operation Desert Storm in January–February 1991, gave Syria a new image in Middle East affairs.

Lebanonization 253

Lebanonization is the Middle East equivalent of Balkanization. But if Balkanization refers to the disintegration of a larger region, Lebanonization centers attention on the fragmentation of a state. The long civil war in Lebanon was a manifestation of the essential incompatibility of the many separate ethnic and religious groups that comprised the state of Lebanon. In the absence of cultural fusion, political fusion was possible only under pressure. Coercion, not voluntary association, linked one group to another. Dissatisfaction with the arrangement among those not able to enhance their future in an expanding community prompted challenges to authority and demands for more representation. Reluctance on the part of those holding the commanding heights to share power with those not so fortunate produced reactions that were often violent. Lebanon has been referred to as a "mosaic society." In 1975 that "mosaic" shattered into its constituent parts, and the result was a prolonged conflict that destroyed what was otherwise a relatively modern, cosmopolitan country. The term *Lebanonization* is now applied to other Middle East states harboring multi-ethnic and religious elements, which are not capable of developing polities representing mutual self-interest. ***See also*** LEBANESE CIVIL WAR, 1975–1976 (250); LEBANON CIVIL WAR: THE PROLONGED MIDDLE STAGE, 1983–1991 (251); PLO IN SOUTHERN LEBANON (175); PHALANGES LIBANAISES (138).

Significance
Lebanonization was a code word used by Middle East and government analysts in describing the aftermath of Operation Desert Storm. It sought to describe the possible dismemberment of Iraq given the uprisings among the Kurdish and Shiite elements of the population and their possible success in separating themselves from Baghdad's authority. Lebanonization as applied to Iraq generally was judged an unacceptable outcome of the U.S.-led assault on the forces of Saddam Hussain. Despite a stated desire to see the overthrow of Saddam Hussain by the UN-sponsored coalition, the breakup of Iraq was judged too high a price for such an objective. Lebanonization, therefore, has a negative connotation. It not only addresses the dilemma of protracted civil war, but also denies

the integrity of established international entities. In effect, the pejorative interpretation given to Lebanonization would imply that existing states, irrespective of the quality and character of their institutions, are preferable to other political arrangements that may be more representative of the groups within that region. Lebanonization, used in such manner, strikes at the essence of self-determination. If Iraq should not be Lebanonized, should Israel, Morocco, Pakistan, Iran, or Turkey?

Liberty Tragedy 254

The USS *Liberty*, an intelligence-gathering naval vessel, was sailing in international waters off the coast of Sinai when, on June 8, 1967, it was struck without warning by Israeli aircraft. It was the fourth day of the Six-Day War and the U.S. ship had no time to react before the assault was launched. Thirty-four U.S. sailors died and 171 were injured by the attack. The craft was plainly marked and easily identifiable; it was not acting provocatively. Except for light machine guns, the *Liberty* was unarmed, and Israeli aircraft made pass after pass against the vessel, sustaining the attack for approximately one and a half hours. Indeed, Israel had made a series of close-in daylight observation flights before the attack. Following the air assault, Israeli torpedo boats attacked at close range, blasting a hole 40 feet long in the hull of the ship and leaving it afire, listing, and dead in the water. Israel later claimed the attack was an accident, a case of mistaken identity. ***See also*** STARK INCIDENT (266).

Significance

The attack on the USS *Liberty* remains a mystery. The Israeli apology was accepted, compensation (exactly how much is also unclear) was paid several years after the incident, and the tragedy was ultimately overwhelmed by other news, particularly Israel's remarkable victory against superior Arab forces and the United States' deepening involvement in Indochina. In the former instance, the U.S. Defense Department viewed the Israelis differently after the Six-Day War. Whereas U.S. military assistance to Israel was relatively limited before that conflict, after the engagement it was decided to expand Israel's military prowess. Washington saw Israel as a formidable future ally in a region perceived to be threatened by international communism. Almost 20 years to the day after the *Liberty* tragedy, the U.S. Navy suffered another loss in Middle East waters. The USS *Stark* was struck by an Iraqi Exocet missile, killing 37 American sailors. Here, too, the perpetrator apologized, paid compensation, and the U.S. government accepted the apology. Here, too, the U.S. government chose to side with the country responsible for the tragedy. The United States tilted in favor of Iraq in its war with Iran, and Baghdad was made a recipient of U.S. weapons. Israel had been judged a bulwark against Soviet penetration of the region, and Iraq became Washington's first line of defense against Iranian fundamentalism.

Libyan Intervention in Chad, 1980–1990 255

Libyan armored units invaded northern Chad in November 1980. Chad had been unstable ever since the Frolinat (Front de Liberation Nationale) founded in 1966 by Goukouni Wuedei took over the government. Frolinat was assisted by Muammar Qaddafi, who wanted to bring Chad under Libya's influence. Goukouni was successful in defeating his rivals, and Libya helped make him president of Chad. Opposition to Goukouni was intense, however, and in 1980 the regime was placed under considerable pressure. The Chadian opposition forces were led by Hissene Habre, a former minister of defense who had the support of the French. On April 3, 1980, President Goukouni made a formal appeal to Muammar Qaddafi for military help against Habre. Qaddafi acted in haste, consolidating control over northern Chad's rich uranium fields. Qaddafi also exerted leverage with Chad's large (45 percent) Muslim population. More immediately, the Libyan leader wanted to reduce French influence in northern Africa. France had been instrumental in deposing Emperor Bokassa of the Central African Republic in September 1979. Qaddafi had close ties to Bokassa, and Libya had expected to acquire military bases in the Central African Republic. The Libyan attack on the Tunisian city of Gafsa in January 1980 also brought a swift French response, and Qaddafi concluded that France was an obstacle to his growing influence in the region. Qaddafi talked about creating a Muslim Saharan Republic including Chad, Senegal, Niger, Mali, and Gambia. But with French persuasion, Senegal and Gambia severed relations with Libya. Qaddafi, however, was determined to press his campaign, and unfriendly governments were declared reactionary and counterrevolutionary. Libya's intervention in Chad was aimed at perpetuating a government totally dependent on Qaddafi. In December 1980, Libyan troops occupied the Chad capital of Ndjamena. Facing condemnation from France, Egypt, Sudan, and a host of Black African states, Foreign Minister Abdul al-Salaam Jalud declared that Libya was protecting a "friendly" government. Libya's detractors were unimpressed with this argument. Egypt cited Libya's intention to absorb Chad and to transform the region into a forward staging area against Sudan and other African states. The capture of the Chad capital by Libyan units flanked the Sudan and put Qaddafi in position to exploit unrest in Sudan's impoverished Darfur province, where 2 million Sudanese of Chadian origin resided. The Sudan Kordofan region, somewhat more distant, was also threatened by the Libyan action. Kordofan was the stronghold of the pro-Mahdi Ansars, the principal opposition to the Numayri regime in Khartoum. Qaddafi agents infiltrated the region in the 1970s and had enlisted support for a conspiracy to overthrow the Numayri government. Numayri did not fear a Libyan invasion from Chad, but he was concerned that Qaddafi would attempt to exploit his country's internal divisions and discontent. Qaddafi's decision to withdraw his troops from Ndjamena in 1981 was followed by another from the Organization of African Unity, which sent 3,500 troops (Nigerian, Senegalese, and Zairian) to help reconcile differences between Goukouni and Habre. Developments in Chad in the summer of 1982 did not favor Qaddafi. In June, Habre's forces entered Ndjamena and forced Goukouni to flee. Habre's assumption of power in Chad was welcomed by Libya's African opponents, Morocco, Senegal, Gambia, the Ivory Coast, Niger, Togo, and Zaire. They recognized the new regime and along with France promised assistance. A meeting of the Organization of African Unity (OAU) was scheduled for November 1982 in Tripoli, Libya, with Qaddafi as chairman. Habre's supporters in the organization insisted that he be permitted to represent Chad at the conference. When Qaddafi registered his opposition to the move, the meeting failed to materialize. Qaddafi's response was defiant. His troops in northern Chad's Aozou Strip were reinforced, and rumors circulated that Goukouni was secreted in the Chadian settlement of Bardai, protected by Libyan arms, and waiting an opportunity to reclaim his lost authority in Ndjamena.

Habre's forces, however, overwhelmed Goukouni's, and the OAU contingent was withdrawn in June 1982. France and the United States quickly recognized the Habre government. The Chadian civil war, however, continued to fester in the mid-1980s without either side winning a clear victory against the other. Nevertheless, the Habre government was able to cling to power with the help of France and members of the Organization of African Unity. In 1987, however, government forces opened an offensive that caught the Libyan-supported opposition off guard. The result was a stunning victory for Habre's forces and a willingness on the part of the opposition, as well as Libya, to accept a ceasefire. In 1988 Qaddafi attempted to shore up his defenses by mobilizing his forces along the Aozou Strip. Frequent skirmishes with the Chadian army followed with neither side achieving an advantage. The overthrow of Numayri in the Sudan, however, had brought a government to Khartoum that was more favorable to Muammar Qaddafi, and with that turn of events the ongoing conflict between Libya and Chad assumed new dimensions. A three-year lull in the fighting was broken when, under cover of the Iraqi conquest of Kuwait, the Libyans assisted Chadian General Idris Deby in overthrowing Habre and forcing him to flee the country in November 1990. Even France was taken by surprise, as a government seemingly favorable to Muammar Qaddafi was formed in Ndjamena. *See also* GREEN BOOK (85); MAHDI (43).

Significance
The Libyan intervention in Chad was a calculated move in a larger plan to spread the seeds of revolution throughout the Third World. Libya had been the recipient of a vast array of weapons from the Soviet Union. Ever since May 1975, when Aleksei Kosygin visited Libya, the country engaged in stockpiling Soviet weapons far beyond Libya's capacity to use them. Qaddafi publicly declared Libya's intention to act as a storage area for weapons that could be drawn upon by Muslim states in their struggle with Israel. Qaddafi, however, appeared interested in objectives that extended beyond the resolution of the Israeli question. The Libyan leader believed that destiny had called him to unite the Muslim world and to direct it in massive revolutionary endeavor. The occupation of Chad therefore was an essential step in the pursuit of a far larger goal. The swiftness of the coup against Habre in 1990 was made possible by Qaddafi and General Omar Hassan Ahmed al-Bashir, who had assumed power in the Sudan. Deby's Patriotic Salvation Movement had received sanctuary and was trained in Libya, but Libya was not the immediate beneficiary of the transfer of power. Qaddafi appeared ready to launch a new effort at spreading his influence in Africa. The Libyan leader, for example, angered the government of Niger when he supported the rebellious Taureg nomads on the border between Libya and Niger. More significant, Qaddafi wanted exclusive control over the Aozou Strip, and if there was a problem for him in Deby's seizure of the Chad's government, it was the Chadian's insistence on holding on to the northern territory. Deby insisted the Aozou Strip must remain in Chad if his nation of 5 million impoverished souls was to have any chance of improving its condition.

Oman War, 1957–1959, 1965–1975 256

The Oman War has passed through two phases. The first phase involved the Al bu Said dynasty and its efforts, with British assistance, to integrate the territories known as Muscat and

Oman into the modern state of Oman. Under the rule of Sultan Said ibn Taymur (1932–1970), Oman remained a backward, isolated territory along the southern shore of the Arabian Peninsula. Trade was minimal. Entry to and emigration from Oman was restricted. Health services were nonexistent. Industries were totally lacking. The sultan's absolute power, however, was bolstered by treaties with Great Britain, and British Indian forces formed the backbone of the sultan's power. The British began assembling a small Omani army in 1920, and law and order was maintained through World War II. In 1957, however, a nationalist rebellion erupted against the sultan's efforts to bring the hinterland under his authority. British forces were again pressed into service, and after considerable effort the revolutionaries were defeated in 1959. Sultan Taymur's rule became even more tyrannical in the 1960s, and popular dissatisfaction spread and deepened. The second phase of the insurrection developed in the mountains of southern Dhofar, in the western part of the country, in 1965. In 1968 Britain announced its decision to withdraw its forces east of Suez. At about the same time, in neighboring South Yemen (independent in 1967), a Marxist regime supported the disgruntled elements in Oman. Dhofar shared a border with South Yemen, and the Marxist government had little difficulty funneling supplies and equipment to the insurgents. Late in 1969, the sultan's forces were routed by a radicalized army called the People's Front for the Liberation of the Occupied Arabian Gulf. Britain was pressured to continue officering the sultan's forces. The Royal Air Force also maintained bases at Salalah in Dhofar and another on the Omani island of Masirah. Nonetheless, the British were convinced that this latest uprising could only be quelled if the sultan were removed and the Omani government implemented needed reforms. Thus, in July 1970 the old sultan was deposed by his son Qabus, and for the first time attention was given to providing society with social services. Qabus also opened his kingdom to foreign investment. The Dhofar insurgency, however, remained out of control. In 1971 the Popular Front for the Liberation of the Arabian Gulf became the Popular Front for the Liberation of Oman and the Arabian Gulf (PFLOAG). The PFLOAG, with South Yemeni and Chinese communist help, spread its message of revolution throughout the Arabian Peninsula. Massive strikes and demonstrations were inspired in Kuwait and Bahrein by the PFLOAG. The PFLOAG also directed its criticism at the Saudi government and enlisted recruits in its struggle with the ruling family. Concerned with these developments, especially the stranglehold the PFLOAG could exert on the Strait of Hormuz, the U.S. government urged the shah of Iran to send army and air force units to Dhofar. Between 1973 and 1975, the Iranians mounted a major offensive, ultimately forcing the insurgents to give up their conquered territories and to retreat across the border into South Yemen.

Significance

Remote, backward Oman remains strategically positioned astride the Persian Gulf and the vital Strait of Hormuz. Its frontage on the Indian Ocean places it in near proximity to the Horn of Africa. It also shared an important border with the Marxist, Soviet-backed, Cuban-supported state of South Yemen. It was vital to the defense of Saudi Arabia. The British heavily influenced Oman in the nineteenth and first half of the twentieth centuries in order to safeguard colonial India and assist in maintaining their preeminence in the gulf. The Omani wars of 1957–1959 and 1965–1975 at first glance might be judged exclusively internal affairs. In point of fact, however, they are related to the country's past and current entanglement with the Great Powers. The British assisted the Al bu Said dynasty to extend its rule over a region theretofore divided between different rulers and coveted by neighboring states. The Europeans opted for the Al bu Said, because their fraternal and cooperative relationship spanned two centuries. Thus when the United States assumed major responsibility for stabilizing the gulf region, the Americans inherited the role until then played by the British. The United States, with Iran's armed forces, reduced the leftist threat represented in the Popular Front for the Liberation of Oman and the Arabian Gulf. South Yemen's plans for expansion were thwarted. Moreover, in order to strengthen Western military capability in the area, Oman granted the United States the use of the bases that were operated by the British, especially those previously in Dhofar and on the island of Masirah. The collapse of the shah's government in 1979 and the subsequent withdrawal of Iranian troops by the Khomeini regime left the United States without a proper proxy. The direct involvement of the United States, only by degree different from that of the British earlier, further exposed the Al bu Said sultan to criticism from Arab radicals and nationalists. However, Oman's security improved in 1990 with the merger of the two Yemens and the declaration by the new government to resolve its outstanding differences with Oman peacefully.

Operation Desert Shield 257

The U.S. response to the Iraqi invasion, conquest, and annexation of Kuwait in August 1990. Fearing Iraqi aggression against Saudi Arabia, President Bush ordered the immediate dispatch of U.S. military forces to the gulf states, the vast majority directed to Saudi Arabia. The operation was in fact the actualization of the Carter Doctrine and the Rapid Deployment Force (RDF) envisaged by it. The RDF in the 1980s had matured into the Central Command (CENTCOM) with its headquarters at McDill Air Force Base in Florida. General H. Norman Schwarzkopf was given command of CENTCOM, and it thus became his task to coordinate the program that placed approximately 525,000 army, marine, navy, and air force personnel in the region by February 1991. Operation Desert Shield became Operation Desert Storm after January 15, 1991, the deadline set by the UN Security Council for the voluntary withdrawal of Iraqi forces from Kuwait. ***See also*** OPERATION DESERT STORM (258).

Significance
Operation Desert Shield was the U.S. answer to Saddam Hussain's aggressive intentions in the region. Although many Americans questioned the reasons for the dispatch of so large a number of U.S. forces, and were even more critical of President Bush's readiness to use it in seeking to retrieve the sovereignty of Kuwait, the deployment was generally believed to be a huge logistical success. Not since World War II had the United States moved so vast a fighting force so far from home in so limited a time frame. Moreover, while some questioned the need to go to war at all, and others insisted on exclusively defensive actions, Operation Desert Shield indicated the seriousness with which the Bush administration approached the possibility of all-out war. No one in high position could estimate the cost of the operation, especially if war became inevitable, but the initial dollar cost for the first four months of Operation Desert Shield was pegged at $30 billion. To help pay for the exercise,

Kuwait, Saudi Arabia, and other gulf states were requested by the United States to help pay the bill. The Japanese were also asked to pay a portion of the cost given their heavy dependence on gulf oil.

Operation Desert Storm 258

Operation Desert Storm is the designation given to the launching of offensive measures against Iraq on January 16, 1991 (January 17 in Saudi Arabia), by the coalition forces led by the United States. Operation Desert Storm replaced Operation Desert Shield, the latter representing the defensive policy assumed in the wake of the Iraqi invasion of Kuwait on August 2, 1990. In announcing Operation Desert Storm, the U.S. administration declared its purpose was the liberation of Kuwait from Iraqi control. Operation Desert Storm was described as a UN effort aimed at gaining Baghdad's adherence to the 12 UN Security Council resolutions that Iraq had ignored while declaring Kuwait its nineteenth province. Twenty-eight countries were members of the coalition but not all participated in the offensive actions undertaken in Desert Storm. The principal and overwhelming force was supplied by the United States, with more than half a million troops from all the services. Great Britain provided the next-largest contingent, followed by France, Saudi Arabia, and Kuwait. Troops from the United Arab Emirates, as well as Qatar elements (notably Pakistanis under contract to the Qatar government) and, later, Egyptian and Syrian soldiers, also saw some combat. The Desert Storm campaign lasted 43 days, all but the last four and a half consisting of a relentless air assault on Iraqi military targets within Iraq and Kuwait. Air raids initially struck at Iraqi command and control centers, nuclear, chemical, and biological warfare assets, and at the Iraqi air force. As the air war escalated, targets were Iraqi lines of communication and transportation, electric power stations, oil-refining capacity, and general infrastructure. Considerable resources were also devoted to the destruction of Iraqi missile capabilities, especially the Scud missiles that were being fired from both fixed and mobile launchers at Saudi Arabia and Israel. Although Israel was not a member of the coalition, and not a belligerent in the war, Baghdad's repeated Scud attacks on Tel Aviv were made with the objective of drawing Jerusalem into the war. Israeli restraint, prompted by the U.S. decision to deploy Patriot anti-missile batteries, manned by U.S. troops, in Israel, negated Iraq's attempt to transform the UN-inspired coalition's aim of punishing Iraqi aggression against Kuwait into a U.S.-backed Arab-Israeli war. Hence, despite repeated blows against its citizens, Israel did not retaliate. After 38 days of bombing from the air, the later weeks of the air campaign having been devoted to pounding Iraqi troops and their fortifications in southern Iraq and especially in Kuwait, Iraqi will as well as capacity to resist a swift and heavy land attack declined markedly. Although the Iraqi threat to use poison gas was a source of concern in CENTCOM headquarters in Riyadh, an ambitious and lightning strike by coalition forces was launched on February 23, the thirty-ninth day of the campaign. Coalition forces pierced Iraqi defenses on the Saudi-Kuwait frontier as a large airborne and armor thrust made an end run far to the west, quickly penetrating southern Iraq and striking to the Euphrates River. The Iraqi forces disintegrated in front of the assault and tens of thousands of prisoners were taken in the first hours of the campaign. Where resistance was encountered, particularly from the Republican Guard in southern Iraq, air power was brought into play and the will of the Iraqi forces crumbled. The strategy employed by General Schwarzkopf and carried forward by his American and foreign commanders proved decisive after 100 hours of land warfare. President George Bush declared Kuwait liberated on February 27, and on March 3, 1991, General Schwarzkopf met with two Iraqi lieutenant generals who were authorized by Baghdad to arrange for a formal cessation of hostilities. The meeting was conducted within Iraq at an airfield believed occupied by the coalition forces. The Iraqis accepted all the demands of UN Security Council Resolution 687 approved on March 2, having earlier accepted the 12 resolutions passed during the crisis. ***See also*** OPERATION DESERT SHIELD (257); UN RESOLUTIONS: IRAQ-KUWAIT CONFLICT (230); GORBACHEV PEACE INITIATIVE (210); KURDISH ENCLAVE PROPOSAL (90).

Significance

Operation Desert Storm was described as the most one-sided major conflict in the twentieth century. Iraq, vaunted before the attack as possessing the world's fourth-largest military establishment, had its army cut in half (42 divisions had been destroyed or made ineffective), had lost the bulk of its armor and artillery (an estimated 4,000 tanks and more than 2,000 guns), had experienced the neutralization of its air force (approximately 150 Iraqi aircraft fled to Iran early in the campaign and the Iraqi air force never seriously challenged the coalition), had its small navy virtually eliminated, and had suffered damage to all its essential war-making capability, both conventional and nonconventional. Although the coalition bombing sought to avoid civilian targets, collateral damage to civilians and their property was also an outcome of the war. But perhaps the most telling defeat was illustrated in the tens of thousands of Iraqi soldiers who refused to fight and gave themselves up to anyone who would promise them a respite from the battlefield. Although Iraqi casualty figures were only estimated, observers believed the allies held between 60,000 and 150,000 Iraqi POWs and had killed approximately 100,000 in the air and land campaign. On the allied side, it was believed less than 200 had died as a direct consequence of Desert Storm. Another 100 died during the period of Desert Shield, and additional losses were suffered after hostilities stopped due to accidents and land mines. Coalition casualties, however, were far fewer than original projections, which suggested as many as 30,000 might die before the campaign to free Kuwait was over. (A House Armed Services Committee report analyzing the Gulf War was released in April 1992. The report questions the number of Iraqi troops confronting the allied coalition and suggests that 700,000 allied troops faced only 183,000 Iraqis when the ground attack began on February 23, 1991.)

The success of Desert Storm raised a number of political questions. It also appeared to rearrange power relationships in the region and beyond. Iraq was no longer judged an immediate military threat to the area. Iraq's political system and future was a large question as Shiite opposition to the Baathist Baghdad regime broke out in the south in and near Basra and Kurdish nationalists asserted themselves in the north. Saudi Arabian influence increased but questions emerged surrounding the character of Saudi rule. Kuwait's oilfields were torched by the fleeing Iraqis, the small country had been savagely ravaged, and armed groups proved difficult to tranquilize. The outcome of the war raised questions about changes in the Kuwaiti political system, including a reduced role for the monarchy. Jordan, which had sided with Iraq in the conflict, attempted reconciliation with its gulf Arab neighbors, but Kuwait and Saudi Arabia proved indifferent to King Hussain's pleadings. The Palestine Liberation Organization, especially its leader, Yasir Arafat, also identified with Iraq, and Palestinians in Kuwait had collaborated with the Iraqis. Thus, the PLO and the Palestinians, like the Jordanians, suffered significant setbacks, especially in their ongoing struggle with Israel. A new Palestinian leadership seemed the only way to re-engage the Saudis and Kuwaitis. New leadership was essential if the United States was expected to press Jerusalem for a settlement to the Palestinian question. Israel displayed no interest in yielding the Occupied Territories given the uncertain conditions at the conclusion of hostilities. Jerusalem's forbearance during repeated Iraqi Scud attacks had prevented the breakup of the coalition, and Israel anticipated something positive in return. Thus Washington tried to interest Saudi Arabia in terminating its state of war with Israel, and the Israelis displayed interest in a plan that included peace treaties with its Arab neighbors. Iran came out of Operation Desert Storm a major winner. Prior to the beginning of hostilities Baghdad made peace with Tehran, returning Iranian territory and prisoners of war. During the war, Iraq secreted a portion of its air force on Iranian soil. On the one side, Iran sought to capitalize on the Iraqi defeat, while on the other, it renewed an older call to drive the infidel (the United States) from the Middle East. In the aftermath of hostilities, Iran envisaged opportunities to spread its influence in Iraq as well as Syria and Lebanon. Although Moscow was constrained to criticize the United States for what it described as an excessive use of force, the Soviets did not interfere with Operation Desert Storm. Soviet efforts to influence Iraq to withdraw from Kuwait, and subsequent efforts to pressure the United States to permit Baghdad, and especially Saddam Hussain, to "save face," all failed, however. Saddam Hussain accused the Soviets of betraying the Iraqis, but Moscow's stock in the Muslim world rose as a consequence of its non-belligerent role in Operation Desert Storm.

Osirak 259

Osirak is the name given to the Iraqi nuclear reactor near Baghdad that was being constructed with major assistance provided by France. Although the Iraqis insisted the reactor would be used solely for the production of electric power, the Israelis argued that it was meant to produce nuclear weapons. International opinion was divided on the subject. Moreover, the matter was considered a domestic affair, and despite the voicing of fears by Americans and Europeans as well as Israelis, construction had entered a late stage. On June 7, 1981, without prior warning, Israeli aircraft attacked and destroyed the Osirak reactor. The world was shocked by this first-ever attack by one country on another country's nuclear facility. Condemnation of the Israeli action was swift and from all quarters. The United States temporarily held up the shipment of additional fighter-bombers that had been promised to the Israeli air force. The United Nations and individual governments noted the seriousness of the attack. Iraq's reaction did not produce an immediate counterblow on Israel's reactor at Dimona, in the Israeli Negev Desert, but Baghdad declared that it would rebuild the facility.

Significance

The Israeli attack on the Osirak nuclear reactor may have established an epoch-making precedent. The reactors of all countries are extremely vulnerable to a concerted attack. Should countries determine for themselves which reactors they will accept and which they will not, difficulties concerning the control of nuclear power are compounded. Pakistan, for example, is believed to be close to becoming a nuclear power. Pakistan's former leader, Zulfikar Ali Bhutto, publicly declared his intention to build an "Islamic bomb." His argument emphasized that other countries had nuclear weapons, so why not a Muslim state? It is alleged that the Libyan leader, Muammar Qaddafi, tried to purchase an atomic bomb and failed. He then turned to Pakistan, which had the trained manpower to build a device. Qaddafi is believed to have provided the finances for the enterprise. It is also believed that uranium ore extracted from the rich deposits in northern Chad was seized by Libya and transshipped to Pakistan for its "Islamic bomb" project. Pakistan, it is said, was motivated to develop nuclear weapons by India's detonation of a nuclear device in May 1974. The French were again involved in assisting Pakistan in the construction of its nuclear facilities. Despite heavy pressure brought on Paris from the United States, the French indicated that they could not renege on a contract. Fear that Pakistan would acquire nuclear capability disturbed India. It also raised questions in Moscow as well as Washington. In 1979 rumors circulated that the United States had contingency plans for a future strike against the Pakistani facility. The United States, however, denied that it had any such intention. There were also reports that the Soviet Union or India might be contemplating an attack prior to the completion of the facility and the possible manufacture of the weapon. None of these rumors could be proved. Pakistan, for its part, consistently defended its right to produce nuclear power for peaceful purposes. At the same time, it denied that it had any intention of constructing atomic bombs.

Pan Am 103 **260**

On December 21, 1988, Pan Am 103 blew up over Lockerbie, Scotland, and all 269 persons aboard the aircraft perished. Ahmed Jibril's Popular Front for the Liberation of Palestine-General Command was believed responsible for setting the device that destroyed the plane in flight. Jibril's organization had its headquarters in Syria, and Jibril maintained his residence in Damascus. Jibril had also been an officer in the Syrian army and was long a member of Syria's terrorist apparatus. Syria's President Hafez al-Assad, therefore, had been implicated in the destruction of Pan Am 103. Moreover, clandestine Syrian operations also included the Libyans and the Iranians. It was widely held that Iran contracted with Syria and Libya in order to gain revenge for the shoot down in the Persian Gulf of one of its commercial aircraft by the U.S. naval warship *Vincennes* in the closing days of the Iran-Iraq War. A U.S. government commission organized to investigate the destruction of Pan Am 103 concluded in 1990 that "the U.S. must be ready to view some terrorist attacks as a matter of security or an act of aggression." On November 14, 1991, the United States Justice Department officially announced indictments against two Libyan intelligence officers and accused them of having engineered the bombing. The indictment also released Syria and Iran from culpability and lifted the suspicion from the Jibril group. The Libyan government issued an immediate denial, stating it did not engage in acts of terror and that the American accusation was linked to a planned military assault. Efforts to extradite the Libyans were resisted by Muammar Qaddafi, and on March 31, 1992, the

UN Security Council voted to impose sanctions on the North African state. It is notable that Libyan oil was not among the sanctioned items. ***See also*** TERRORISM (108); VINCENNES TRAGEDY (270); U.S. RAID ON LIBYA (269).

Significance
Terrorism is closely identified with the Middle East. The "deliberate" destruction of Pan Am 103, clearly singled out more for its psychological impact than its practical importance, illustrates the character and extent of terrorism in the contemporary world. It also demonstrates the ambivalence of the governments concerned with controlling or limiting or punishing acts of terrorism. For example, Hafez al-Assad was visited by President Bush during the latter's November 1990 visit to the gulf region. Syria had condemned the Iraqi invasion of Kuwait and was one of the countries supplying troops to the international force gathered in Saudi Arabia. Bush's visit to Syria and his pledge of support for its government, still high on the American list of terrorist states, resembled an earlier action by the Reagan administration, which in 1983 removed Baghdad from the list of terrorist states in an effort to win the support of Iraq against Iran. Moreover, although considerable evidence had been compiled concerning the destruction of Pan Am 103, the Bush administration was reluctant to make it public. The November 1991 indictment against Libyan agents was said to be based on the objective evidence collected at Lockerbie and traced to the manufacturers of the device in Switzerland as well as the Libyan purchasers. The indictment also traced the path of the terrorists who it said used Malta as a transshipment point. Libya's protest was not unexpected, but analysts argued that Qaddafi had ordered the bombing in retaliation for the F-111 raid on his Tripoli headquarters. Others, more skeptical, hinted that the indictment against Libya was made in order to make it easier for Hafez al-Assad to remain within the good graces of the United States. Moreover, Washington hoped to induce Syria to enter into more substantive peace talks with Israel, and Damascus's designation by the U.S. State Department as a terrorist state was said to be one of the obstacles in broadening the discussions begun in Madrid on October 30, 1991.

Pakistan-India War, 1947–1948 261

The Pakistan-India War of 1947–1948 was confined to and fought entirely in the disputed state of Kashmir. Kashmir is approximately 85,000 square miles (220,000 square kilometers) and borders Pakistan on the northeast and India in the north. When the subcontinent was divided to form the independent states of Pakistan and India in August 1947, former princely kingdoms were given the option of either joining one or the other state or remaining independent. The maharaja of Kashmir was a Hindu ruling a predominantly Muslim population. A somewhat similar situation prevailed in Hyderabad, in the central-southern portion of the subcontinent, where a Muslim ruled a Hindu majority. Both rulers opted for independent status. In September 1948, India invaded Hyderabad, deposed the ruler, and absorbed the territory. It justified its action on grounds that the majority Hindu population wished to be included in the new Indian Union. Pakistan pressed a similar argument in claiming Kashmir, but the Indians refused to apply the Hyderabad precedent to the dispute, and it has continued to be a flash point for conflict between the two nations. The British were responsible for extending Hindu rule over all of Kashmir in the nineteenth century, but the Muslim population was totally unreconciled to the arrangement. The state was managed as an orthodox Hindu entity, with all the privileges and benefits devolving upon the maharaja and the two dominant Hindu castes, the Dogras of Jammu and Kashmiri Brahmins in the Vale of Kashmir. Muslim Kashmiris rebelled in the 1920s and 1930s, but the maharaja maintained his preeminence. Kashmir should have gone to Pakistan at independence because of its Muslim majority, but the British did not interfere with the maharaja's rule. Thus, when communal rioting broke out in the Punjab, and quickly spread to Kashmir, Pakistan reiterated its claim. A Muslim revolt in western Kashmir produced Azad (Free) Kashmir, and a provisional government was formed to handle its political affairs. With chaos prevailing throughout the northern and northwestern segment of the subcontinent, the maharaja was hard-pressed to maintain his independent status. Moreover, Pathan tribesmen from the Northwest Frontier Province and its adjacent tribal area invaded Kashmir to avenge the brutalities committed against their co-religionists. Pakistani authorities were unable to prevent the infiltration even if they had wished to do so. When the tribesmen reached the settled areas of Kashmir, they displayed as much interest in obtaining material rewards as they did in establishing a Muslim government. The maharaja fled to Jammu, in the southern part of the state, where he agreed to accede to Indian rule in return for military assistance. Although the governor-general of India, Lord Louis Mountbatten, informed the maharaja that the ultimate decision on Kashmir would be made by its population, that pledge was never honored. India rushed troops into the state and denied Srinagar, the capital, to the Pathans. From Srinagar the Indian army moved into the Vale and forced the tribal people to retreat. Pakistan's governor-general, Mohammad Ali Jinnah, saw British complicity in the Indian operation, especially as Mountbatten, the last viceroy of British India, had been retained by the Indian government to preside over the new nation. Jinnah ordered the general in charge of the Pakistani army, also British, to send his forces into Kashmir to combat the Indians. The British general, however, was controlled by his superiors in Great Britain, and they vetoed the action. Jinnah used the only option open to him at the time. He supported the Azad Kashmir provisional government and dispatched Pakistani army "volunteers" to the northern state. The clash of Indian and Pakistani forces led Prime Minister Jawaharlal Nehru to call for a withdrawal of the invading Pakistanis in return for a plebiscite by the region's inhabitants. Pakistan countered by calling for an Indian army withdrawal and the formation of a coalition government. Nehru rejected this proposal but referred the dispute to the United Nations. India accused Pakistan of aggression, and Pakistan accused India of genocide. Pakistan also refused to recognize Kashmir's accession to India. After the initial fierceness of the fighting, the war became stalemated. India maintained control of the Vale of Kashmir and Jammu, and Pakistan sustained its influence over Azad Kashmir. A ceasefire was finally arranged by the United Nations in December 1948, and on January 1, 1949, the line between the two forces became the official ceasefire line and remained so into the 1990s. *See also* TWO-NATION THEORY (61).

Significance

The Pakistan-India War of 1947–1948 had the following consequences:

1. Kashmir remained a disputed region, despite numerous attempts by the United Nations to resolve the matter. Pakistan insisted on the right to conduct a plebiscite

under UN auspices, and India argued its right in incorporating the state within the Indian Union. The Kashmir dispute proved insoluble, and it became the key to Pakistan-India relations. The deep hatred felt by one country against the other has its roots in the Kashmir dispute, and it is argued that relations between the two neighboring states will never be peaceful and progressive in the absence of a solution satisfactory to both sides.

2. The second Pakistan-India War (1965) was provoked by the Kashmir dispute, further embittering the two countries.
3. India considers Kashmir to be an integral part of the Indian nation. Pakistan continues to believe that the territory's dispensation can only be determined through a vote of its population. The United Nations is technically still seized of the matter, and the organization is still on record as calling for a plebiscite.
4. The Kashmir dispute is another example of the deep sentiment that motivates Muslims. Not all the Muslims of Kashmir wish to join Pakistan. Nor do they necessarily wish to cut themselves free from India. Nevertheless, Pakistanis see Kashmir as an act of faith, and they cannot rest content until Kashmir represents Muslim interests.
5. Interestingly, Pakistan has received little support from Muslim states in its attempt to wrest Kashmir from India. The passion exhibited in the Palestine issue is not duplicated in Kashmir, except in Pakistan itself.

Pakistan-India War, 1965 262

The Pakistan-India War of 1965 was the first large-scale encounter between the two countries after numerous major and minor skirmishes between 1947 and 1964. Ostensibly fought over the disputed Kashmir state, it could not be contained there, and it spilled over to include Indian and Pakistani territory. The Kashmir dispute had been simmering ever since the ceasefire was established through United Nations efforts in January 1949. Although India moved to formally annex the state in the early 1950s, the matter did not reach crisis proportions until the early 1960s. Communal tensions were again on the ascendancy in Kashmir because of India's stern rule and the unpopularity of the local government. In the midst of widespread dissatisfaction, a sacred relic, believed to be a hair from the Prophet Mohammad's beard, was reported stolen from the Hazrat Bal shrine in Srinagar. As a consequence, widespread rioting occurred in the Vale, where the great majority of Muslims resided. The demonstrations were eventually repressed, but not before the episode had inflamed Pakistani opinion. Prime Minister Nehru's attempt to placate the Kashmiri Muslims was largely unsuccessful, and Pakistan repeated its demand that the Kashmiris be given the right of self-determination. Nehru died in May 1964 and was succeeded by Lal Bahadur Shastri. The president of Pakistan, Mohammad Ayub Khan, decided that the time was right for pressing the Indians to release the Kashmiris. Moreover, Pakistan had drawn close to the communist regime in the People's Republic of China. In 1962, China humiliated India in their brief border war. In 1963, Pakistan and China entered into a border agreement that angered India. After Nehru's death, Pakistan appeared to be using its leverage with China to bring pressure on India. Clashes between Indian and Pakistani troops across the Kashmir ceasefire line became more common. Shastri offered to meet with Ayub to sort out their differences, but their meeting in Karachi in October 1964 was fruitless. Moreover, Shastri was also being pressured by Hindu conservatives who rejected any rapprochement with Pakistan and who demanded that Kashmir be permanently included in the Indian Union. Thus, Kashmir was integrated more closely with India in December 1964, and in January 1965 the ruling party in Kashmir was merged with the Indian National Congress. Pakistanis were angered by these developments, and clashes between Indian and Pakistani forces escalated. The UN Military Observer Group in Kashmir recorded almost 400 violations of the ceasefire line in the first few months of 1965. Adding to the tension was still another conflict between the two countries in an area known as Rann of Kutch, an uninhabited marshland, 350 miles (565 kilometers) from Bombay and 250 miles (330 kilometers) from Karachi on the Arabian Sea. In April and May 1965 Indian and Pakistani forces exchanged blows. By most accounts Pakistan fared better in the fighting. A ceasefire was not achieved in the Rann until June, when the two sides agreed to enter into direct negotiations and then allowed the affair to be decided by an impartial court of arbitration. As a result of the Rann incident, Pakistan believed that it had gained military superiority. Attention again turned to the Kashmir problem. Ayub and his associates, especially Foreign Minister Zulfikar Ali Bhutto, had made the Kashmir dispute a campaign issue. At one point during the campaign, Bhutto promised the nation that Ayub's success at the polls would mean swift action on Kashmir. Following the elections, therefore, Ayub had to deal firmly with India's action of integrating Kashmir with the Indian Union. Ayub's response was to send Pakistan-trained guerrillas into the Indian-held Kashmir with the hope their presence might precipitate a popular uprising. In the absence of Nehru, India's leadership was thought to be feeble and ineffectual. The time was judged propitious to reignite the smoldering dispute. India, however, was not lacking in resolve. As a counter to the Pakistani action, India sent several thousand troops across the ceasefire line in an effort to cut off the passes through which the infiltrators had come. Ayub's response to this Indian countermove was to unleash his regular formations. On September 1, 1965, a Pakistani armored column struck into Indian Kashmir, and after its early success, moved toward a vital road link. India, fearing that its forces would be cut off in Kashmir, decided to expand the war. Indian forces struck against Pakistan directly, assaulting the country at a number of points along the border with West Pakistan, especially in the Punjab. The Indian air force also attacked installations in West as well as East Pakistan, almost a thousand miles away. India claimed that its attack was necessary because Pakistan was planning a strike against India. Pakistan cried foul, but the war intensified and spread. Indian troops made a better showing in this contest than in the earlier skirmish in the Rann of Kutch, but neither side wanted a long, drawn-out campaign. In the course of the conflict China sent India an ultimatum, declaring its willingness to side with Pakistan. The United States had earlier indicated its neutrality by embargoing arms to both sides. The Soviet Union quietly supported India. With their military supplies rapidly diminishing, and before a decisive battle could be fought, India accepted a UN resolution for a ceasefire on September 20. Pakistan issued its acceptance on September 22. The war ended without any change in the status quo. ***See also*** PAKISTAN-INDIA WAR, 1947–1948 (261).

Significance
The consequences of the Pakistan-India War of 1965 were as follows:

1. India was more determined that ever to retain Kashmir. Enmity between India and Pakistan reached new levels of intensity, and the two neighbors became implacable foes.
2. The Soviet Union became a major actor in the affairs of the area. Its offer of good offices was accepted by Shastri and Ayub, and they met in the Soviet city of Tashkent in January 1966. When they failed to work out an agreement, the Soviets drafted one that the two leaders were reluctant to sign, but finally did. Shastri's sudden death in Tashkent that night brought Indira Gandhi to power in New Delhi. She was even more determined to ignore Pakistani protestations over Kashmir. Mrs. Gandhi emphasized using Moscow to balance off Pakistan's friendship with Beijing.
3. The embargo of U.S. military assistance convinced Pakistan that it could not depend on the United States, and it began to explore other sources of aid, ultimately identifying specific Middle East countries, particularly Iran. Although Pakistan remained a member of the Central Treaty Organization and the Southeast Asia Treaty Organization, it was disinclined to follow U.S. leads in challenging Soviet policy.
4. Ayub Khan was forced from power in 1969. His fall started with the popular disfavor aroused by his acceptance of the UN resolution calling for a ceasefire. His acceptance of the Tashkent Agreement was also judged a sellout, and the political opposition exploited the public outcry to mount a political campaign aimed at unseating him.

Pakistan-India War, 1971 263

The Pakistan-India War of 1971 began as a civil war in East Pakistan. The civil war was internationalized by India when it invaded East Pakistan, defeated the Pakistan army, and prompted the creation of the sovereign state of Bangladesh from the Pakistani province. The demand by the Bengalis of Pakistan for just treatment by their leaders in West Pakistan was as old as Pakistan itself. The Bengalis played a major role in the formation and independence of Pakistan. They also represented more than half the population of Pakistan. Nevertheless, given their relatively greater poverty, and their distance from the central nerves of government in West Pakistan (East Pakistan was separated from West Pakistan by approximately 1,000 miles, or 1,600 kilometers, of Indian territory), the Bengalis of East Pakistan were judged, and they also considered themselves, second-class citizens. Political, military, and economic power was concentrated in West Pakistan, and there was demonstrated reluctance to give the Bengalis their "fair share." Pakistan passed from one crisis to another, and two constitutions were promulgated and abandoned before the country experienced its first nationwide election. The election results of 1970, however, revealed that an East Pakistan political party, the Awami League of Mujibur Rahman, had won a majority of seats in the new parliament, although all the league seats were from East Pakistan. The runner-up party, the Pakistan People's Party of Zulfikar Ali Bhutto, won a majority of the seats in the Punjab and Sind, the most populous provinces of West Pakistan. General Yahya Khan, Ayub Khan's successor, had promised a return to civilian rule, and the election was the path chosen to fulfill that pledge. The election results, however, were somewhat unexpected. Yahya was reluctant to allow Mujib to form a government. Bhutto was absolutely opposed. A breakdown in negotiations between the principals produced an impasse, which led to the Awami League's promoting direct action against Pakistan's central authorities. Matters quickly deteriorated. After numerous street demonstrations and the loss of considerable life in East Pakistan, on March 25, 1971, the army was ordered to arrest the Awami League leaders and destroy the party. As a result of these actions, civil war broke out in East Pakistan. Bengali members of the Pakistan army defected, and with other Bengali dissidents, they formed the Mukti Bahini, or Bengali Liberation Army. Supported by India, which also provided refuge for millions of Bengali refugees, the Mukti Bahini fought the Pakistan army to a standstill, until India intervened on December 3, 1971. It was impossible to resupply the Pakistan garrison in East Pakistan once India entered the war. Overflights were forbidden, and rail and road traffic was unheard of between the two wings. The trip by sea from Karachi to the East Pakistan port of Chittagong was approximately 3,000 miles (4,800 kilometers) and would take several weeks if the vessels were not intercepted by Indian naval forces. Pakistani troops in East Pakistan were in a hopeless situation, and rather than protract a losing cause, the garrison surrendered to the Indian invasion force on December 17, 1971. Approximately 90,000 members of the Pakistani armed forces were made prisoners of war. Bangladesh was proclaimed an independent sovereign state, and India immediately recognized its new government. India had also been active on the western front. West Pakistan was attacked by land, sea, and air following a Pakistani armored thrust into the Indian state of Rajasthan and air strikes against Indian airfields. The port of Karachi was bombed, oil installations and ammunition depots were blown up, and ships were sunk in and near the harbor. Pakistan also faced a determined Indian army that advanced against Sind and Punjab provinces. Other elements attacked the Pakistanis stationed in Kashmir. Losses on both sides were heavy. After an initial victory over Indian forces in Kashmir, Pakistan's losses in armor stabilized the front, and further advances were checked. An Indian counter-offensive on December 5–6, 1971, pushed the Pakistanis back, and Kashmir remained firmly in Indian hands. In the Punjab, repeated Pakistani efforts failed to break through Indian defenses. Given Indian air superiority, the large number of casualties, and the inability to replenish their weapons, Pakistan was forced to recognize its increasing weakness vis-à-vis the better equipped, more numerous Indian army. Moreover, India had the support of the Soviet Union. A treaty of friendship and cooperation signed in July 1971 between New Delhi and Moscow guaranteed India a steady flow of weapons. The United States had embargoed arms shipments to Pakistan in 1965, and it had not been lifted. Furthermore, Pakistan received a bad press in the United States. Atrocities allegedly perpetrated by the Pakistani army against the inhabitants of East Pakistan caused revulsion in and outside U.S. governmental circles. Congress was especially predisposed toward India. The Nixon administration, however, sought to befriend Pakistan, and the nuclear carrier *Enterprise* was sent into the Bay of Bengal, ostensibly to evacuate Americans from the war zone. In actual fact, it was meant to intimidate India. Although the United States received some credit for helping to preserve a rump Pakistan (the United States did nothing to prevent the dismemberment of the country and the independence of Bangladesh), it did not provide

Pakistan with tangible assistance. Pakistan was soundly beaten by India. China, unlike 1965, did not even appear threatening to New Delhi. When Pakistan capitulated to superior Indian forces, the country lost more than half its population and approximately one-sixth of its territory. *See also* PAKISTAN-INDIA WAR, 1947–1948 (261); PAKISTAN-INDIA WAR, 1965 (262).

Significance

The consequences of the Pakistan-India War of 1971 were as follows:

1. Pakistan lost East Pakistan. Bangladesh represented the first country created as a result of civil war since the end of World War II. India played the decisive role in creating Bangladesh, and its action was perceived as proof positive that New Delhi's historical intention and its long-range policy was the destruction of Pakistan. India's collaboration with the Soviet Union was viewed as reinforcing Indian ambition in the subcontinent.
2. Given the array of superior power against it, Pakistan looked more closely at its options and attempted to draw more closely to the Middle Eastern states. Relations with Iran were always judged important. They were now considered critical. Moreover, Pakistan attempted to cultivate relations with the Arab states, especially the oil-producing nations. In return for Pakistani manpower, technical know-how, and military assistance, Pakistan sought to obtain large sums of money with which to refurbish its armed forces. Solidarity with the Muslim world was also judged insurance against further Indian encroachment in light of India's desire to have good relations with these same countries.
3. The surrender of the Pakistani armed forces brought a temporary end to military rule in Pakistan, and the first civilian government since 1958 was established by Zulfikar Ali Bhutto. Bhutto's Pakistan People's Party enthusiastically attempted to resurrect Pakistan, to restore the nation's lost confidence, and to provide it with a new political system based upon notions of Islamic socialism.
4. India emerged from the 1971 war as the preeminent power in the region. The long-term Pakistani quest for equality with India ended. Indian's detonation of a nuclear device in May 1974 reinforced the conception of India as a great nuclear power. Indira Gandhi's administration, and her personal rule, was enhanced by the military victory. Prime Minister Gandhi had become so powerful that to neutralize her opposition she was prepared to impose a state of emergency in 1975 and virtually suspend the Indian constitution.
5. The United States had less leverage in the region following the 1971 war. The Soviet Union had considerably improved its position. China had lost much of the influence it had acquired in the 1960s, but it was still an important consideration in both India and Pakistan.

Polisario Front 264

Polisario is an acronym for Popular Front for the Liberation of Saguia El Hamra and Rio de Oro. The Polisario seeks to establish an independent state in what was formerly the Spanish Sahara. Even before Spain relinquished control over the Spanish Sahara, Morocco, which adjoins it, had anticipated absorbing it. Morocco's claim to the region was opposed most vehemently by Algeria, which in turn, was supported by Libya. Morocco had resolved a seven-year border dispute with Algeria in 1970, and the eruption of this conflict threatened an even more violent clash between the opposed forces. Nor could they keep the struggle limited to North Africa. The Polisario were provided with sanctuary as well as bases and supplies in Algeria. In the later half of the 1970s they challenged Moroccan claims on a broad battlefield. Moroccans, up to then at odds with their government and their monarch, King Hassan II, joined in common cause against those who would deny their country's claim. But despite a major effort the fighting could be neither quelled nor contained. The Arab Steadfastness Front, comprising Algeria, Libya, Syria, the People's Democratic Republic of Yemen, and the Palestine Liberation Organization, put its support behind the Polisario. The knowledge that King Hassan had sent troops to Syria and Egypt during the 1973 war against Israel apparently had no effect. Morocco also did not fare well in the Organization of African Unity (OAU). Led by Algeria and Libya, the radical African bloc in the OAU, with special assistance from Ethiopia, Angola, and Mozambique, all of them Marxist states, succeeded in getting the Polisario demand on the agenda. Moreover, 26 of the 50 members of the OAU had been induced by promises of cheap oil and other assistance to admit the Polisario (more formally, the Saharawi Arab Democratic Republic) to membership in the organization. Morocco reminded the OAU membership that Polisario had neither sovereignty nor control of territory. The Moroccan delegation threatened to walk out of the OAU if its position was rejected. Egypt, Sudan, Tunisia, and several African states indicated that they would also leave the organization if Polisario membership was pressed to a vote. Given the impasse, a decision was taken to postpone the issue. The OAU failed to assemble for a scheduled meeting in 1982, ostensibly because divisions over recognition of Polisario could not be bridged. Moreover, Muammar Qaddafi was to chair the meeting, and many African states opposed his leadership. Qaddafi again failed to have the Polisario officially seated at the 1983 meeting of the OAU, convened in Ethiopia. Nevertheless, the Polisario continued its aggressive actions. Morocco called upon and received American military assistance, while Libya stepped up its support for the Front. In addition the Soviet Union and Cuba aided Polisario, and the struggle over the former Spanish Sahara took on the character of an ideological contest. Without either side yielding in the protracted conflict, after 13 years of skirmishing in the barren western Sahara, the UN secretary-general tried his hand at mediating the dispute. In August 1988, Perez de Cuellar submitted his plan to the representatives of Morocco and the Polisario Front. To the surprise of everybody, the plan was accepted on August 30. It called for a ceasefire, a troop withdrawal, deployment of UN peacekeeping forces, and a referendum for the residents of the territory. The timing of the plan, however, has yet to be worked out. King Hassan refused direct talks with Polisario, and Rabat said it would only deal through the office of the secretary-general. Declaring they had been betrayed, the Polisario renewed the fighting with heavy casualties reported on both sides. The secretary-general appointed Uruguayan lawyer Hector Gros to be his special representative and to restart the negotiations, but his efforts were stymied by the intransigence of the parties. Proof that the war in the Western Sahara had not ended came with the announcement in August 1991 that a two-year lull in the fighting had been broken by armed clashes and Moroccan air force raids against Polisario positions at Tifariti, ten miles from the Mauritanian border. Rabat reported its forces were engaged in "clean-up" operations in a "no-man's land" region in anticipation of a UN ceasefire plan scheduled for September. The plan called for the holding of a referendum in 1992, but neither side proved willing to accept the full consequences of the balloting. ***See also*** SALAFISM (55); ALAWITE DYNASTY (64).

Significance

The Polisario has been described as freedom fighters seeking self-determination and fundamentally opposed to Moroccan rule. As with so many other political movements in the Middle East, violence is seen as the only means to a solution. The former Spanish Sahara is a vast desert wasteland, sparsely populated, and not particularly endowed with natural resources other than phosphate. Morocco claims it on historical grounds, and its interest is more associated with national pride than with vital need. On the other hand, Algeria has never been friendly toward Morocco, and the two countries have clashed over jurisdictional rights in areas never well charted. In this instance, there are strong ideological differences between the two countries, and there is no mistaking the more radical makeup of the Polisario and its greater affinity with Algeria. Libya has virtually no interest in the region except its distaste for the Moroccan monarchy and its contention that a Moroccan defeat in the Sahara territory would ultimately topple the regime of King Hassan. Libya therefore views the Polisario as an arm of the revolutionary movement that will sweep aside the remaining monarchies in the Arab world. To this end, Libya enlisted the support of the Soviet Union and Cuba. The fact that the United States moved to King Hassan's side in the conflict confirmed Libya's observations that the Moroccan maneuver was simply a disguised imperialist plot aimed at sustaining reactionary regimes. U.S. support for King Hassan was also said to be the chief reason for the failure of the UN secretary-general's efforts at mediation. Morocco, it was argued, was seeking more time to consolidate its hold on the territory. In the meantime, a third alternative was suggested to the two outstanding ones, i.e., union with Morocco or independence. The third arrangement, emanating from the United Nations, called for an autonomous Saharan region federated with Morocco.

Reflagging: Kuwait **265**

The symbolic transfer of vessels engaged in international commerce from one sovereignty to another without the original owner's giving up possession of its ships. The Iran-Iraq War was protracted by the intransigence as well as determination of the belligerants to secure a victory over the other. Although Iraq initiated the conflict, it was the first country to seek a ceasefire and an end to the hostilities. The Iranians, however, the wounded party in the exercise, refused to yield to the entreaties for peace from Baghdad. Iraq, to increase the pressure on Iran, and seeking to involve the major powers in the struggle, launched an attack on ships drawing oil from the gulf region. Iraq's stated purpose in initiating the "Tanker Wars" was to deny Iran the opportunity to export its oil from the gulf. But Baghdad not only targeted Iranian vessels; it also attacked oil tankers from a variety of nations that were drawing petroleum from the gulf states. Kuwait's ships were especially vulnerable to both Iraqi and Iranian actions, and in an effort to protect them, they called upon the major powers to help in policing the gulf. The U.S.S.R. answered the Kuwaiti call first, and Soviet naval craft began escorting Kuwaiti ships from the region. Washington could not stand by and see the Kremlin maneuver itself into an area deemed critical to U.S. interests. At Kuwait's request, the United States reflagged 11 Kuwaiti tankers, manning and servicing them with U.S. crews. The United States deployed 36 warships in the gulf to facilitate the movement of international commerce. The Soviets had no more than six ships there at any one time. ***See also*** "TANKER WARS" (267); STARK INCIDENT (266); VINCENNES TRAGEDY (270).

Significance
Washington agreed to the changeover and immediately became involved in a shooting war with Iran. Although Iraq had started the "Tanker Wars," Kuwait supported Iraq in its war with Iran and Washington found itself more deeply committed to Iraq. Washington had in fact identified with Iraq in 1983 when it removed Baghdad from its list of states supporting international terrorism. With these restrictions removed, the United States provided Iraq with food and manufactured commodities it could not obtain elsewhere. Washington's actions were driven by its perceived problems with the Iranian revolution, which it judged to be menacing to the peace of the Middle East. Thus, even when an Iraqi aircraft struck the U.S. frigate *Stark* with Exocet missiles and caused a heavy loss of American lives, the United States refused to find fault with Baghdad. The *Stark* affair was judged to be an unavoidable accident. But when Iranian gunboats and planes targeted Iraqi vessels or those of nations friendly to Iraq, the United States felt compelled to take direct action. On several occasions U.S. naval and air forces in the gulf attacked Iranian oil installations and naval craft. The final blow came in 1987 when a U.S. warship destroyed an Iranian civilian airliner that it believed was engaged in a hostile act. The heavy loss of Iranian life aboard the aircraft had a telling effect inside Iran. Tehran saw the U.S. "tilt" toward Iraq as placing it in a no-win situation, and after several Iranian assaults were neutralized by Iraqi defenses, Iran, in 1988, accepted terms for a ceasefire. Kuwaiti ships remained under U.S. flag for a period thereafter. When it was clear that the war would not be restarted, all the vessels were returned to their original owners. The most significant aspect of the reflagging was Washington's belief it could do business with Baghdad.

Stark Incident **266**

On May 17, 1987, an Iraqi warplane fired Exocet missiles at the USS *Stark*, a frigate plying the waters of the Persian Gulf. The ship took direct hits and was severely damaged. Thirty-seven members of the crew were killed in the surprise attack. The American public and members of the Congress were outraged by the assault on the vessel, but the Reagan administration quickly sought to neutralize the anger. Saddam Hussain apologized for the incident, claiming it was an accident, and President Reagan quickly accepted the explanation, declaring Iran "was the real villain in the piece." Baghdad promised to pay compensation for the damage done to the ship and to the families of the victims. ***See also*** REFLAGGING: KUWAIT (265); "TANKER WARS" (267).

Significance
The *Stark* incident triggered a U.S. decision to increase its presence in the Persian Gulf. The reflagging of Kuwaiti oil tankers began in July, and U.S. naval power was directed at Iran, which was held responsible for protracting the war. Iraq, the country

that launched the attack on the *Stark*, received by contrast considerably more assistance, and notably had obtained an "ally," the United States, in its war with Iran.

"Tanker Wars" 267

Iraq initiated attacks against ships moving into and from the Persian Gulf that were deemed to be engaged in commercial operations with Iran. This assault on ships in "innocent passage" was known during the Iran-Iraq War as the "Tanker Wars." Iraq lost the capacity to use the gulf at the outset of the war, but Iran remained free to sell its petroleum and take on supplies at its several ports up and down the waterway. Baghdad's strategy was aimed at cutting off Iran's commercial activity and hence its money supply needed to fight the war. By striking at neutral vessels, Baghdad hoped to deny Iran its outlet to the trading world, and in so doing to force it to a peace settlement. Iran, however, fought back, attacking vessels from countries that had sided with Iraq in the war. Kuwait was a prime example; hence the decision by the U.S. government to reflag Kuwaiti tankers, and to send a flotilla of U.S. warships into the gulf to protect international shipping. In retaliation for Iraq's assault on Iranian oil tankers and other ships carrying supplies to Iran, Tehran began stopping and searching foreign vessels to determine if they were carrying war materiel for the Iraqi armed forces. In January 1986, for example, the U.S. freighter *President Taylor* was boarded and searched by Iranian personnel. Washington's reaction was initially mild, but it was obvious from later developments that President Reagan had reserved a more defiant response. In the meantime, Iran blocked the Strait of Hormuz and detained a number of ships, including two Soviet freighters. After Iraq struck at Iran's oil facility on Khark Island, Tehran began shuttling oil to makeshift loading stations on Sirri Island and other locations further down the gulf. Iran also attacked vessels using the strait, and a Panamanian tanker was hit and set ablaze. By August 1986, there had been 95 confirmed hits against vessels in international waters. Since the beginning of the Tanker Wars, approximately 50 seamen had been killed and many others wounded. ***See also*** REFLAGGING: KUWAIT (265); VINCENNES TRAGEDY (270); STARK INCIDENT (266).

Significance

The Tanker Wars continued into 1988. The reflagging of Kuwaiti vessels by the United States, however, had reduced the frequency of the attacks. Iran was in no position to counter the naval power arrayed in the gulf by the United States. Mine-laying operations were all that was left to Tehran, and even this tactic proved a minor nuisance to the U.S. navy. The U.S. presence in the gulf worked to the advantage of the Iraqis, who were able to regain control of the mouth of the Shatt al-Arab. U.S. naval craft also destroyed Iranian oil rigs at the northern end of the gulf, supposedly in retaliation for damage done to a U.S. frigate. Facing a humiliating defeat due to U.S. intervention (the Iraqis were allowed to increase their military strength during this period), Tehran lashed out with a series of attacks on its "Great Satan," striking futilely at U.S. naval and commercial shipping targets. The United States answered this salvo with one of their own, using aircraft and naval vessels to destroy six Iranian naval vessels, virtually all that was left of the Iranian naval fleet. This event was followed by the destruction of an Iranian passenger airliner, with the loss of 290 passengers and crew, by a U.S. cruiser. The Tanker Wars ended with Iran's declaration a few days later that it accepted the UN terms for a ceasefire between itself and Iraq.

Turkey-Greece-Cyprus War, 1974 **268**

The Turkey-Greece-Cyprus War of 1974 was precipitated by clashes between the Greek Cypriot majority and the Turkish minority on the island. As with other Middle East conflicts, the problem had deep roots. The Ottoman Turks had seized the island from the Venetians in the sixteenth century and relinquished it to the British in 1878. During this extended period Turks had settled on a Cyprus predominantly domiciled by Greeks. The Greek and Turkish communities lived side by side in relative tranquility until the 1950s, when Greek nationalism, reinforced by Greek Orthodox religious fervor, disturbed the tenuous balance. This was also a period in which Greek nationalists were attempting to force the British from Cyprus and unify it with Greece, a program known as enosis. Cypriot Turks opposed the political integration of the island with Greece, and they refused to participate in what Greeks viewed as a national liberation movement. Turkish passivity, even friendliness toward the British, aroused the passions of the Greeks against the Turks. Moreover, Turks and Greeks were historical enemies, and in the aftermath of World War I each had brutalized the other. This underlying bitterness fueled the hostility between the groups on Cyprus. Turks were outnumbered by Greeks by approximately 5 to 1, and with Greece supporting the Greek Cypriots, Turkey was determined to aid its Cypriot Turkish brethren. Moreover, Cyprus was only 40 miles (64 kilometers) off the southeastern coast of Turkey. It was several hundred miles from Greece. Logistically, Turkey was in a good position to assist the beleaguered Turks. Cyprus achieved its independence from Great Britain in 1960. Enosis with Greece was rejected in favor of an independent state, but the Greek majority looked upon the Turkish minority as traitors to the cause. The first head of the Cypriot state was a Greek Orthodox cleric, Archbishop Makarios. His leadership did little to quiet Turkish fears for their safety. The Turks on the island insisted on a form of partition and the right to be governed by their own leaders, but this, too, only intensified the controversy. Both Greece and Turkey threatened direct intervention in 1964. Indeed, the Greek government dispatched armed "volunteers" to Cyprus, and the Turkish community faced increasing pressure. Efforts by the Turkish prime minister to negotiate a settlement were fruitless, and the Turkish air force attacked Greek Cypriot installations in retaliation for atrocities committed against the Turkish inhabitants. Makarios countered by blockading the Turkish portion of the island, and as tension rose higher the United Nations intervened. The U.S. government also brought pressure on Turkey. President Lyndon B. Johnson was informed that the Turks were contemplating an invasion. Johnson cautioned Ankara against such a maneuver, because of the likelihood of Soviet assistance for the Greek Cypriots. Nevertheless, the United States was perceived in Turkey as supporting the Greek position. President Johnson, it was said, had ordered the U.S. Mediterranean fleet to interpose itself between Turkey and Cyprus to prevent a possible Turkish invasion of the island. The Turks were supremely angered by the ambiguous but apparently pro-Greek U.S. position. Although Turkey remained a member of the North Atlantic Treaty Organization, the Turkish government used the Cyprus incident to improve its relations with the Soviet Union. Turkish radicalism received considerable encouragement during this period. The Cyprus issue festered until July 1974 when ultra-conservative Greek Cypriots removed Makarios in a military coup. Greece was ruled by a military junta, and the coup was believed to be the work of the Greek military establishment. Turkey was again aroused and, to prevent a new Greek claim for enosis, the decision was taken to invade Cyprus. UN peacekeeping forces could not stop the Turkish drive. Nor could they quell communal warfare between the island's Greeks and Turks, who proceeded to brutalize each other. As a consequence of the fighting, Cyprus was effectively partitioned. Greeks were forced to flee the Turkish-held sector, and Turks were forced to withdraw from the Greek-dominant region. When the fighting finally subsided, Turkey controlled 40 percent of the island, the Greeks the remainder. Property theretofore owned by the Greeks was transferred to the Turks, and no Greek was permitted to return to his land or home. The identical situation prevailed on the Greek side of the island. Although the Greek junta was replaced by a civilian government in Athens, events had gone too far to produce a compromise formula. U.S.-Turkish relations suffered when the United States embargoed arms to Turkey, and Ankara ordered a number of U.S. bases in the country closed. Arms shipments were not resumed until after the fall of the shah of Iran and the loss of U.S. bases in that country. U.S. ties to Turkey and vice versa were demonstrated in the Gulf War in 1990–1991. Turkey joined the U.S.-led coalition within days of Washington's decision to confront Saddam Hussain's aggression in Iraq. Turkey played a significant role in holding Iraqi forces in northern Iraq while the offensive against the Iraqi army was focused on the southern portion of the country. Turkey also permitted U.S. aircraft to use Turkish air bases for forays against Iraq. The Turkish government was often criticized by its own public for this outward display of support for the United States. Moreover, Turkey had extensive ties with Iraq, and in trade alone, Turkey paid a high price for its commitment to the United States and the UN resolutions condemning Baghdad's aggression in Kuwait. Nevertheless, the U.S.-Turkey relationship was solidified during the crisis, and the fact that Ankara continued to maintain a presence on the island of Cyprus no longer appeared significant. Attempts at reunifying Cyprus have been made, the most serious effort by the UN secretary-general. In the absence of a specific date for the withdrawal of the Turkish armed forces from the island, Perez de Cuellar hoped to arrange an agreement that would permit Greek Cypriots the right to move, live, and work anywhere they choose. But this request was not accepted by the Turks. Interestingly, the Turkish Cypriot economy improved in the late 1980s with a growth rate said to be 6.5 percent. Moreover, Ankara pledged increasing aid to Turkish Cyprus. President George Bush visited Athens in July 1991 and there pledged his assistance in ending the Cyprus conflict. Addressing the partition of the island by Turkish forces, he noted his inability to "accept the status quo." Bush spoke of a compromise formula that could be acceptable to the Greeks, Turks, and Cypriots, but just three days before his visit assaults had been made by Greek terrorists on the Turkish chargé d'affaires and two other Turkish officials stationed in Athens. The American president nevertheless said his country was prepared to act as a catalyst in resolving the Cyprus dilemma. Twenty-nine thousand Turkish troops remained in Cyprus and 40 percent of the island was under Turkish administration. The UN continued to monitor the tense boundary between the Turkish and Greek portions, the so-called "Green Line."

Significance

The Turkey-Greece-Cyprus conflict of 1974 was ignited by the Greek military when it gave support to the conservative faction that overthrew the Makarios government. Turkey was obliged to act in behalf of the approximately 125,000 Turks living in Cyprus. The Turkish invasion brought a harsh but workable solution to the ethnic and religious struggle that plagued the island. The northern portion of Cyprus was transformed into an exclusive Turkish region. The southern area was made almost totally Greek. Turkish troops remained in Cyprus, and the Turkish sector became something akin to an overseas territory of the Turkish republic. Even Makarios's return to power did not alter the situation, but his death in 1977 made reconciliation even more unlikely. The Cyprus issue had a somewhat tranquilizing effect on Greece, as the country moved more to the socialist Left and to a less belligerent posture. Turkey, however, underwent radicalization of Right and Left. Turkish nationalism was provoked to new limits. The Turkish left also expanded and became more violent. Extremism degenerated into acts of terror as rightist and leftist factions assaulted one another. Thousands were victimized by the terrorists, and the Turkish Republic faced anarchical conditions as one coalition government followed another. Although the United Nations maintained peacekeeping forces on Cyprus, the international organization could not resolve Turkish-Greek differences. President Bush's entry into the Cyprus controversy follows other American efforts at mediation. George Ball, Cyrus Vance, and Clark Clifford have all tried to find a solution for the warring communities. Despite these efforts, the declaration in 1983 by the Turkish Cypriots that they identify with the Turkish Republic of Northern Cyprus stands. Notably, only Turkey recognized this unilateral declaration of independence.

U.S. Raid on Libya 269

In the aftermath of the Gulf of Sidra conflict, the United States and Libya exchanged angry verbal gestures. But there were also more expressive representations of differences between Washington and Tripoli. Four Americans died when a bomb exploded aboard a TWA airliner flying between Rome and Athens on April 2, 1986, only days following the Sidra clash. Although Qaddafi denied knowledge or responsibility, the United States believed he had masterminded the bombing in retaliation for the losses suffered in march at the hands of the U.S. Sixth Fleet. Three days later, on April 5, a German discotheque in West Berlin was bombed, killing an American serviceman and a German woman, while wounding more than 200, 60 of them Americans. Another American died later of his wounds. The Reagan administration singled out Muammar Qaddafi as the person responsible for the tragedy. U.S. authorities let it be known that secret messages had been intercepted between East Berlin and Libya implicating Qaddafi. West Germany expelled two Libyan diplomats following the incident. Chancellor Helmut Kohl publicly cited Libyan involvement, but cautioned the Reagan administration not to take military action. The Italians called a European Community emergency session to deal with the crisis, while insisting the United States needed more accurate evidence before tying the action to Libya. The European Community nations, in an effort to head off another military confrontation between the United States and Libya, called for a reduction in the number of Libyan diplomats in their respective countries, but urged a peaceful solution. The United States insisted that the EC members close Libyan embassies altogether and impose an economic boycott on Tripoli, but this the Europeans were not prepared to do. On April 15, 1986, 18 U.S. F-111 fighter-bombers, based in Britain, struck targets in and around the Libyan capital. A barracks, believed to be Colonel Qaddafi's headquarters and home, was the prime target. A port facility believed to be used by terrorist organizations was also hit. Training facilities for terrorists and the city's major airport were also struck. The F-111 attack was combined with carrier-based aircraft strikes on military airfields and barracks in Benghazi. Not all the bombs hit their intended targets. Some fell on residential areas of Tripoli. Libya reported the death of Qaddafi's 15-month-old daughter. It also said two of Qaddafi's sons had been wounded. The government said a total of 37 people had been killed and 93 wounded in the combined air assault. One F-111 was lost to anti-aircraft fire. ***See also*** GULF OF SIDRA CONFLICT (243).

Significance
Global reaction to the U.S. raid on Libya was critical and angry. It was revealed that the continental European allies of the United States had prevented overflights of their territory, necessitating the F-111s taking a circuitous, longer, and more dangerous course to their targets. France, Italy, and Greece were especially outspoken in their condemnation. The Soviet Union cancelled a projected meeting with the U.S. secretary of state. Britain, the only country to support the U.S. action, came in for criticism as well, and Prime Minister Margaret Thatcher was criticized by members of her government and press. The Muslim nations were most disturbed by what they judged was the callousness of the U.S. attack. Already disturbed by the Gulf of Sidra incident earlier, they now had even more reason to support Muammar Qaddafi. Libyans in Europe were especially suspect and in the weeks that followed several hundred, especially students, were ushered out of the country. Repeated U.S. calls for economic sanctions against Libya, however, were rejected. Nevertheless, the economic summit of the seven most industrialized states meeting in Tokyo in May did go on record identifying Libya as the major source of terrorism in the world. The United States believed it possible that dissident Libyan officers would use the opportunity to overthrow Qaddafi, but that proved to be wishful thinking. Qaddafi emerged from the raid stronger, not weaker, and better equipped to deal with critics within his administration. Qaddafi consolidated his increased international popularity, toned down his support for terrorist organizations, and began to emphasize the development of unconventional weapons, especially chemical agents.

Vincennes Tragedy **270**

On July 3, 1988, the USS *Vincennes*, a cruiser operating in the Persian Gulf in support of Washington's open sealanes policy, mistakenly shot down an Iranian passenger airliner. All 290 passengers and crew died in the incident. The U.S. Navy was operating in force in the gulf as a consequence of the Reagan administration's reflagging policy. The purpose of the reflagging was twofold: it protected Kuwaiti vessels in particular and international shipping in general. The overall objective was to keep gulf oil flowing from the region in the midst of what had been described as a "Tanker War." The United States also had tilted in favor of Iraq in its long war with Iran, and Washington had become embroiled in military strikes against Iranian gunboats and oil installations. Shortly before the *Vincennes* destroyed the Iranian airliner, two U.S. warships had skirmished with several Iranian gunboats, sinking two and damaging a third. Minutes later the *Vincennes* picked up a signal of an incoming aircraft. Believing it was an Iranian F-14 attack bomber, it fired its defensive missiles, destroying the plane. Iran condemned the act as a calculated act of terrorism, but failed to gain support at the United Nations or other international forums. Ayatollah Khomeini called for "war" against the United States, but Hojitolislam Rafsanjani, speaker of the Iranian parliament and military commander-in-chief, urged calm and restraint. The war had gone badly for Iran, and this tragic incident apparently convinced the ayatollah's eventual successors that it was time to accept the UN-arranged ceasefire. Khomeini declared his acceptance of UN Resolution 598 on July 19, and an official ceasefire between Iran and Iraq went into effect on August 20. ***See also*** REFLAGGING: KUWAIT (265); IRAQ-IRAN WAR, 1980–1988 (247).

Significance

The destruction of the Iranian airliner, on a scheduled flight from Iran's port of Bandar Abbas to the UAE's Dubai, apparently was the final act in Iran's long, desperate effort to win the war against Saddam Hussain of Iraq. U.S. support for Iraq, and Iran's relative isolation, forced the Iranian leadership to terminate their war effort. Iraq emerged as the victor, although its conquest was minimal considering the Baath's original objectives. Saddam Hussain, however, had other plans. Emboldened by his relative success, and especially by his diplomacy, which had drawn not only the Soviet Union, but also France and the United States to his side, he was determined to press his advantages in the region. With Iran militarily neutralized, Saddam turned his attention to the oil-producing states of the Arabian Peninsula, especially to the bordering state of Kuwait, which Iraq had earlier tried and failed to absorb. The *Vincennes* incident ended one Persian Gulf war and very likely was prelude to the next one.

Yemeni Civil War, 1962–1970 271

The Yemeni Civil War of 1962 was provoked by the overthrow of the absolute monarchy of the Imam Mohammad al Badr, the last of a long line of quasi-religious rulers whose descent is traced to the Prophet Mohammad. The imamate, as the monarchy was known, avoided the currents of modern life until the post–World War II period when Yemen joined both the Arab League and the United Nations. Arab nationalism, however, was perceived as a threat to the imamate, and efforts were made to sustain the isolation of Yemeni society. Yemen even went to the extent of seeking union with Egypt in 1958 to neutralize radical threats to its traditional way of life. The confederation collapsed in 1961 because of fundamental differences between the revolutionary leadership of Egypt's Gamal Abdul Nasser and the traditional role of the imam. President Nasser then opened a campaign to destroy the imamate, and the death of Imam Ahmad in September 1962 gave him his opportunity. A small group of Yemeni army officers loyal to Nasser staged a military coup. Imam Badr, the new ruler, fled to the mountains with devoted supporters and pledged to struggle against the renegades until his rule was reestablished. Nasser accepted responsibility for the coup and sent Egyptian forces to reinforce the Yemeni revolutionary command. Nasser's objective was the transformation of Yemen into a republic wedded to the purposes of Arab nationalism. Religion, he argued, had no place in politics, and the imam's archaic, often brutal rule was antithetical to the needs of the Arab people. The forces loyal to the imam, however, were more numerous and more dedicated than Nasser realized. Egypt was therefore required to make an ever larger commitment of forces and resources to the Yemeni Civil War. Moreover, the imam had the support of the Saudi Arabians, who perceived the coup as an indirect attack on their traditional rule. Thus Egypt found itself in conflict with Saudi Arabia as well as the forces of the imam. Egyptian aircraft struck at Saudi supply points near the Yemeni border, and Riyadh seriously entertained the need to eliminate Nasser before his brand of Arab nationalism proved disastrous to their position. The imam's forces also displayed aggressiveness in the field, and the fighting was protracted, costly, and without conclusion. Egypt was forced to tie down mainline forces in substantial numbers in Yemen, and its weak economy was further strained by the action. After five years Cairo appeared to have had enough. Nasser turned his attention toward Israel and withdrew his forces. The civil war in Yemen continued in sporadic fashion with the departure of the Egyptians. In August 1967, following the Arab-Israeli Six-Day War in June, Nasser met with King Faisal of Saudi Arabia and pledged an end to their involvement in the Yemen civil war. The Sallal regime in Sana was angered by the Egyptian-Saudi decision. It also opposed the formation of a commission comprising Iraq, Morocco, and Sudan, which was charged with drawing up a peace plan for Yemen. In November 1967, the Egyptian-backed Sallal regime collapsed. The imam's forces displayed their power by seizing the northern, eastern, and central areas of the country. Under increasing pressure, the Yemen military took control of the government in December 1967. With assistance provided by the Soviet Union, the nationalists were able to stem the royalist advance. But the three-nation peace commission had failed in its mission, and the war intensified. Neither side, however, was capable of overwhelming the other. Imam Badr gave up his leadership to a six-man Imamate Council, but it, too, was unsuccessful in defeating the revolutionaries in Sana. Saudi aid ceased in March 1969, further exposing the royalists to nationalist counterattacks. Saudi Arabia now saw that its purpose would be served by bringing the disputants together. The Saudis helped form a national assembly representing Yemen's different religious and ideological groups. With this development, some of the key officers in the royalist army defected to the nationalists. In March 1970, King Faisal and the Yemeni prime minister signed an agreement reconciling royalists and nationalists. A new government was envisaged involving both parties, but not members of the former ruling family. Finally, in April 1970, a ceasefire went into effect and the Sana government agreed to include royalist leaders in exile in the new government. The long, costly civil war was officially over.

Significance

The Yemeni Civil War of 1962–1970 symbolized the clash of old and new interests. Nasser was determined to bring an end to all forms of traditional rule in the Arab world. It was his contention that Arab unity was impossible so long as the old monarchies maintained sway over their respective societies. Yemen appeared to be an easier military problem than those elsewhere in the Arab world, but Nasser's miscalculation is portrayed in the escalation of the fighting and the substantial cost to Egypt. Some observers argue that Egypt would have fared better in the 1967 war with Israel had the country's armed forces not lost so heavily in Yemen. Military morale was in fact at low ebb when the Israelis made their lightning strike at Egypt's military installations. The protracted war in Yemen also provided the Soviet Union with an entrée to the southernmost territory of the Arabian Peninsula. The struggle against British rule in the Aden protectorate was intensified by the civil war to the north. Moreover, the Aden insurgents were heavily influenced by radical philosophies, and the Soviets readily made weapons available to these forces. When Aden and the surrounding territory gained its freedom in 1967, the new government of South Yemen had already developed Marxist characteristics and was dependent on Moscow. The Yemenis of the south therefore were eager to support the nationalists in the north against the royalist forces. The southerners also saw the chance to unify the two Yemens under their leadership. Although Saudi action in promoting reconciliation between the parties in North Yemen nullified this quest, it remained an active possibility. In 1979, merger of the Yemens was again urged. Under Saudi influence, however, Sana rejected the overture. A brief border war erupted in 1979 between the two Yemens, and Saudi Arabia considered direct military intervention to oppose the more aggressive, Soviet-backed South Yemen military machine. Iraq negotiated a settlement, and the two governments again entertained the possibility of their unification. This objective became a reality in 1990, when the two Yemens put aside their differences and merged to form a single state.

Index

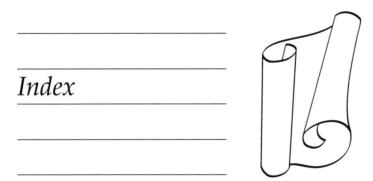

In this index, a reference in **bold** type indicates the entry number where a particular term is defined within the text. Numbers in roman type refer to entries the reader may wish to consult for further information.

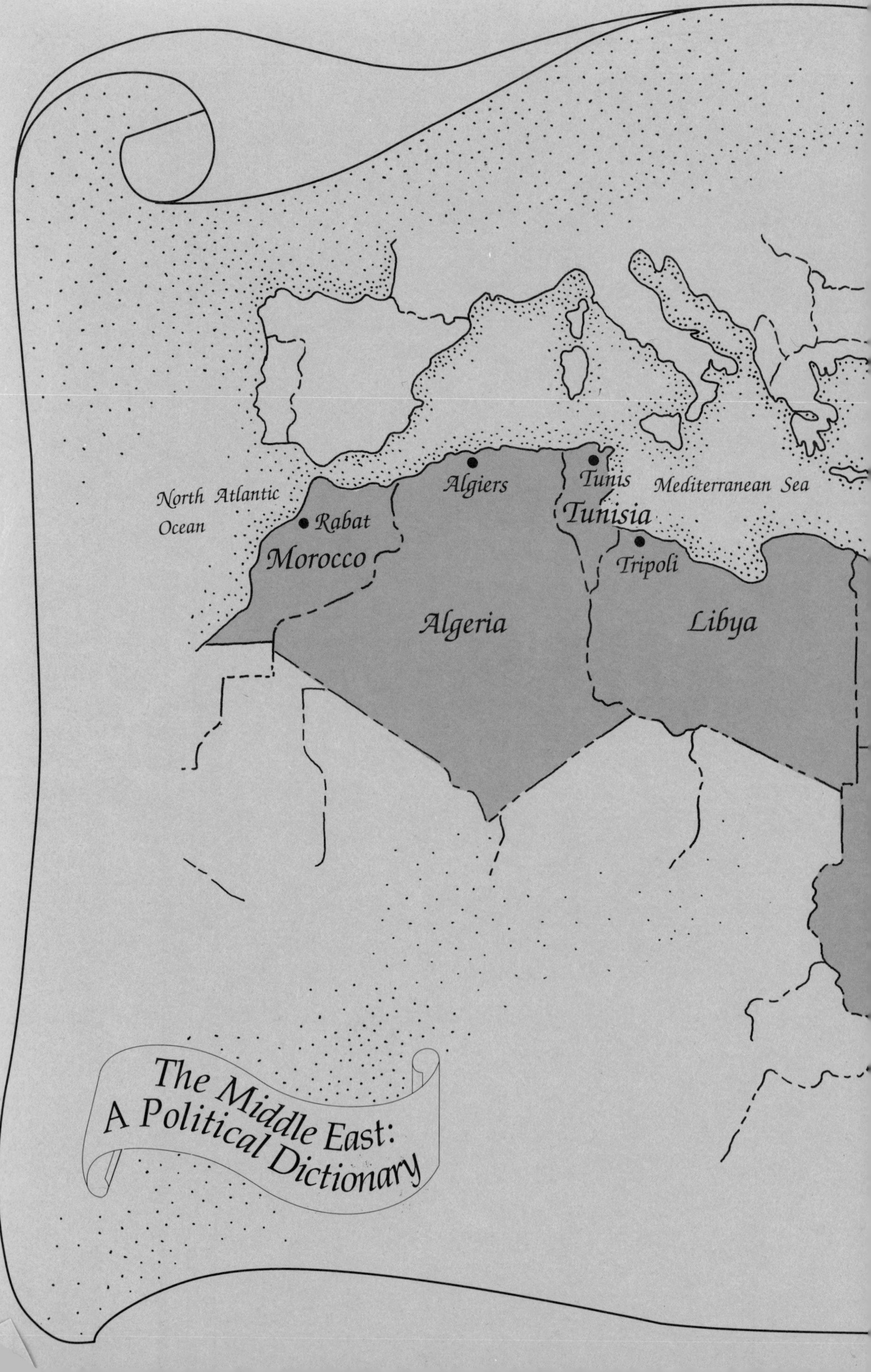
North Atlantic
Ocean
Rabat
Morocco
Algiers
Algeria
Tunis
Tunisia
Tripoli
Libya
Mediterranean Sea
The Middle East:
A Political Dictionary